Communications
in Computer and Information Science   2521

Rationale
The CCIS series is devoted to the publication of proceedings of computer science conferences. Its aim is to efficiently disseminate original research results in informatics in printed and electronic form. While the focus is on publication of peer-reviewed full papers presenting mature work, inclusion of reviewed short papers reporting on work in progress is welcome, too. Besides globally relevant meetings with internationally representative program committees guaranteeing a strict peer-reviewing and paper selection process, conferences run by societies or of high regional or national relevance are also considered for publication.

Topics
The topical scope of CCIS spans the entire spectrum of informatics ranging from foundational topics in the theory of computing to information and communications science and technology and a broad variety of interdisciplinary application fields.

Information for Volume Editors and Authors
Publication in CCIS is free of charge. No royalties are paid, however, we offer registered conference participants temporary free access to the online version of the conference proceedings on SpringerLink (http://link.springer.com) by means of an http referrer from the conference website and/or a number of complimentary printed copies, as specified in the official acceptance email of the event.

CCIS proceedings can be published in time for distribution at conferences or as post-proceedings, and delivered in the form of printed books and/or electronically as USBs and/or e-content licenses for accessing proceedings at SpringerLink. Furthermore, CCIS proceedings are included in the CCIS electronic book series hosted in the SpringerLink digital library at http://link.springer.com/bookseries/7899. Conferences publishing in CCIS are allowed to use Online Conference Service (OCS) for managing the whole proceedings lifecycle (from submission and reviewing to preparing for publication) free of charge.

Publication process
The language of publication is exclusively English. Authors publishing in CCIS have to sign the Springer CCIS copyright transfer form, however, they are free to use their material published in CCIS for substantially changed, more elaborate subsequent publications elsewhere. For the preparation of the camera-ready papers/files, authors have to strictly adhere to the Springer CCIS Authors' Instructions and are strongly encouraged to use the CCIS LaTeX style files or templates.

Abstracting/Indexing
CCIS is abstracted/indexed in DBLP, Google Scholar, EI-Compendex, Mathematical Reviews, SCImago, Scopus. CCIS volumes are also submitted for the inclusion in ISI Proceedings.

How to start
To start the evaluation of your proposal for inclusion in the CCIS series, please send an e-mail to ccis@springer.com.

Giusi A. Toto

Editor

Inclusion, Communication, and Social Engagement

First International Conference, ICS exchange 2024
Foggia, Italy, April 18–20, 2024
Proceedings

 Springer

Editor
Giusi A. Toto 🆔
University of Foggia
Foggia, Italy

ISSN 1865-0929   ISSN 1865-0937 (electronic)
Communications in Computer and Information Science
ISBN 978-3-032-03020-7   ISBN 978-3-032-03021-4 (eBook)
https://doi.org/10.1007/978-3-032-03021-4

This Springer imprint is published by the registered company Springer Nature Switzerland AG
The registered company address is: Gewerbestrasse 11, 6330 Cham, Switzerland

If disposing of this product, please recycle the paper.

Preface

Educational innovation, effective communication, and social inclusion today represent the most urgent and stimulating challenges for those working in educational settings, whether academic, school-based, social, or technological. In response to these needs, the international conference ICS Exchange – Inclusion, Communication and Social Engagement, held between Foggia and Mattinata from April 18 to 20, 2024, sought to offer a high-level scientific forum welcoming researchers, teachers, experts, and professionals from various countries and disciplines. The conference arose from the need to explore, with a scientific and multidisciplinary approach, how the processes of inclusion, communication, and social engagement interweave and influence each other in educational contexts and contemporary society. The event, promoted by the Learning Sciences institute (LSi) of the University of Foggia, involved the national and international academic community in a collective reflection on emerging challenges, best practices, and future research perspectives. The conference structured its work around six main tracks, each representing a crucial area for building more inclusive, participatory, and innovative societies: Psychology, with particular attention to mental health issues, the prevention of bullying and gender-based violence, and the application of immersive technologies such as virtual reality to understand and intervene in psychosocial phenomena; Pedagogy, exploring innovative didactic models, student-centered methodologies, and teacher training strategies, with a focus on special pedagogy and continuous professional development; Inclusion, analyzing policies, practices, and tools for school and social inclusion, with attention to special educational needs, minorities, and the variety of individual experiences; Social Engagement, investigating the role of new technologies, artistic practices, and social networks in promoting active participation, citizenship, and community sense; Communication, examining new languages, media, and digital tools to foster – or hinder – inclusive and accessible communication, from schools to cultural institutions; Learning and Technologies, reflecting on the potentials of digital technologies, serious games, social robots, and artificial intelligence in transforming teaching and learning processes. These macro-areas enabled the aggregation of scientific contributions that address, from different but complementary perspectives, topics such as accessibility, gender equality, prevention of early school leaving, development of digital skills, promotion of soft skills, psychological well-being, and innovation in educational processes. One of the guiding threads of the conference concerns the construction of effective models of inclusion, capable of responding to the increasing complexity of classrooms and educational communities. Pedagogical and psychological research has shown that inclusion is not only a matter of access, but also of meaningful participation, valorization of differences, and promotion of dignity and self-esteem for all individuals. In this sense, the contributions collected here offer data and reflections on innovative policies, tools for the inclusion of students with special educational needs, strategies for the prevention of discomfort, and the promotion of safe and welcoming environments. The centrality of teacher training emerges as an essential element: only through updated training, based on scientific evidence and oriented towards innovation, is it possible to ensure that teachers have the skills necessary to face ever-changing challenges.

The research presented here highlights the importance of integrating technologies, active methodologies, and inclusive assessment tools into initial and ongoing training programs. The digital revolution has radically transformed modes of communication, relationships, and learning, posing new challenges but also offering unprecedented opportunities. This volume analyzes the risks associated with misinformation, new forms of (mis)communication, and the dynamics of alienation and empowerment that characterize interaction with artificial intelligence and social media. Particular attention is also paid to communication accessibility, both in museums and educational institutions, and to the importance of promoting inclusive practices such as the systematic use of alt text on social media. The contributions also underline the growing role of digital platforms, podcasts, WebTVs, and digital communication strategies in disseminating scientific culture and promoting civic participation, among both young people and adults. The rapid development of digital technologies, artificial intelligence, and educational robotics opens up new scenarios for personalized learning, supporting students with special needs and promoting the key competences for the twenty-first century.

In particular, social robots, serious games, online learning platforms, and AI-based solutions are the subject of numerous studies presented in this volume, which analyze their impact on the development of transversal skills, self-regulation, motivation, and student well-being. The international dimension of the conference allowed for comparison between experiences and models adopted in different geographical contexts, highlighting both the potential and the critical issues of educational technologies, with respect to the digital divide, privacy, accessibility, and the ethics of innovation. The interdisciplinary approach and international openness of the conference fostered the creation of collaboration networks, joint projects, and exchanges of best practices among universities, schools, research bodies, and local organizations. The dialogue between scientific research and practical contexts was constantly emphasized, in the belief that only close cooperation between theory and practice can bring about real change in educational and social systems. The proceedings collected here thus represent not only an up-to-date snapshot of the state of research in the fields of inclusion, communication, and social engagement, but also a platform for designing innovative interventions, disseminating best practices, and developing new lines of research. The list of contributions presented and discussed during the conference bears witness to the thematic and methodological richness that characterized the event.

ICS Exchange 2024 received 51 submissions. After a double-blind peer review process in which submissions received on average 4.2 reviews each, 33 papers were finally accepted for presentation at the conference and inclusion in these proceedings.

This volume aims to serve as a tool for in-depth study, discussion, and inspiration for researchers, teachers, practitioners, policymakers, and all those who are committed, in Italy and worldwide, to promoting more inclusive, communicative, and innovative educational, working, and social environments. We are convinced that only through dialogue between disciplines, the sharing of knowledge and the experimentation of new practices is it possible to successfully tackle the challenges of our time and build fairer, more open, and more resilient societies.

Giusi A. Toto

Organization

General Chair

Giusi Antonia Toto — University of Foggia, Italy

Program Committee Chairs

Giusi Antonia Toto — University of Foggia, Italy
Marco di Furia — University of Foggia, Italy
Martina Rossi — University of Foggia, Italy

Program Committee

Annamaria Petito — University of Foggia, Italy
Salvatore Iuso — University of Foggia, Italy
Giorgio Mori — University of Foggia, Italy
Leonardo Carlucci — University of Foggia, Italy
Giusi Antonia Toto — University of Foggia, Italy
Luigi Traetta — University of Foggia, Italy
Valeria Marinelli — University of Foggia, Italy
Ciro Esposito — University of Foggia, Italy
Paride Vasco — University of Foggia, Italy
Guendalina Peconio — University of Foggia, Italy
Martina Rossi — University of Foggia, Italy
Valentina Berardinetti — University of Foggia, Italy
Rosario Del Rey Alamillo — University of Seville, Spain
Joaquín Antonio Mora Merchán — University of Seville, Spain
Daniel Mara — "Lucian Blaga" University of Sibiu, Romania
Annalisa Guarini — University of Bologna, Italy
Antonella Brighi — Free University of Bozen-Bolzano, Italy
Pierluigi Zoccolotti — Sapienza University of Rome and Tuscany Rehabilitation Clinic, Italy
Caterina Arcidiacono — University of Naples Federico II, Italy
Marco Lazzari — University of Bergamo, Italy
Marco Cipolloni — Sapienza University of Rome, Italy
Michela Balsamo — University of Chieti-Pescara, Italy

Siri Sollied Madsen	Arctic University of Norway, Norway
Antonio Javier Criado Martin	UNIR, Italy
Łukasz Tomczyk	Jagiellonian University, Poland
Patrik Kristoffer Kjærsdam Telléus	Aalborg University, Denmark
Rafel Bisquerra Alzina	Universitat de Barcelona, Spain
Riccardo Larini	Area 9 Lyceum, Estonia
Maura Gancitano	Tlon, Italy
Andrea Colamedici	Tlon, Italy
Daniela Villa Henao	Universidad de Sevilla, Italy
Olga Jimenez Diaz	Universidad de Sevilla, Italy

Reviewers

Giusi Antonia Toto	Pierluigi Zoccolotti
Martina Rossi	Salvatore Iuso
Marco di Furia	Leonardo Carlucci
Guendalina Peconio	Andrea Colamedici
Francesca Finestrone	Joaquìn Mora-Merchán
Piergiorgio Guarini	Maura Gancitano
Giorgio Mori	Matteo Martini
Alessandro De Santis	Patrik Kjærsdam Telleus
Pia Marinaro	Antonio Maffei
Annalisa Guarini	Francesco Sulla
Luigi Traetta	Chiara Valeria Marinelli
Dario Lombardi	Łukasz Tomczyk
Siri Sollied Madsen	Marco Cipolloni
Rosario Del Rey Alamillo	Rafel Bisquerra Alzina
Antonella Brighi	Caterina Arcidiacono
Paride Vasco	Antonio Martin
Annamaria Petito	Michela Balsamo
Onofrio Laselva	Andreana Lavanga
Marco Lazzari	Ciro Esposito

Contents

Predicting Critical Thinking Ability Scores Using Student's Characteristics and Learning Performance

Minoru Nakayama[1] 📵, Satoru Kikuchi[2], Masaki Uto[3]([✉]) 📵, and Hiroh Yamamoto[2]

[1] Tokyo Institute of Technology, Meguro, Tokyo, Japan
nakayama@ict.e.titech.ac.jp
[2] Shinshu University, Matsumoto, Nagano, Japan
[3] The University of Electro-Communications, Chofu, Tokyo, Japan
uto@ai.is.uec.ac.jp

Abstract. In order for society to be better prepared to respond to problems and issues involving natural disasters, it may be possible to predict critical thinking ability scores with ease using an individual's fundamental characteristics, such as personality and literacy of science and technology. The authors have extracted some of the relationships of these surveyed metrics in previous studies. This paper examines the possibility of estimating scores of critical thinking disposition (CTD) and disaster-prevention consciousness (DPC) using individual factor scores for personality (Big-5) and literacy of science and technology (LST), and a regression prediction procedure. The possibility and validity have been confirmed using student survey data which was gathered over two years during a fully online course at a Japanese university. In particular, the correlation coefficients calculated during the second survey showed the same level of results as with the modelling data from the first survey. Therefore, the results show the possibility that the extracted functions can be applied to other sets of data. Also, learners' final performance levels may be predictable using the initial survey data set, thus making them a valuable tool for learning support assistance.

Keywords: Critically Thinking Attitude · Literacy · Participant's characteristics · Regression estimation

1 Introduction

Historically, some societies have become used to dealing with the myriad of issues that arise when natural disasters occur. In order to help mitigate unexpected events such as disasters, catastrophes, or major accidents when they happen, a better understanding of human cognitive behaviour and critical thinking ability is required [7]. Therefore, new learning requirements have been suggested, and some learning practices are now aimed at helping students obtain practical skills such as participating in discussions [23] or essay writings [18].

This research was partially supported by the Japan Society for the Promotion of Science (JSPS), Grant-in-Aid for Scientific Research (KAKEN, 21K18494: 2021–2024)

In response to these requirements and for the development of critical thinking ability, assessment scales are used to evaluate aspects of critical thinking ability, such as attitude toward critical thinking [3] and awareness of disasters evaluated [19]. Scores for these attitude and awareness metrics are not usually measured individually, and thus attitude toward critical thinking should be gathered from more general information, such as communication activities. The authors have already tried to extract specific information from individual essay texts [16, 17]. This ability may also be developed during daily life, so individual characteristics may affect the level of this ability. If the critical thinking ability of a person could be estimated from individual behaviour such as learning activity or their short message submissions to social communication networks, their critical thinking disposition can be used as a means of generating suggestions such as evacuation action instructions following natural disasters or ways of combating cybercrimes involving fraud. There are some significant relationships in the scores of critical thinking disposition and individual characteristics [14]. The relationships between them have been confirmed in a causal analysis of measured variables of individual metrics [12]. The idea of causality has been confirmed as a simple correlation or a causal relationship during in-class learning [12, 13]. These phenomena were confirmed previously, and the actual prediction procedure has not been discussed sufficiently. Since the relationship might depend on individual factors, a robust prediction procedure may not be identified even with the introduction of the most current prediction techniques. However, as these have not been tried, the possibility should be examined in this paper.

This paper introduces a regression prediction procedure for scores of critical thinking disposition (CTD) and disaster-prevention consciousness (DPC), using factor scores for personality (Big-5) and literacy of science and technology (LST) [16, 17]. In order to examine the possibility, the Elastic network model technique [6] is introduced to optimise a prediction performance. Based on student survey data which was gathered over two years from 2022 to 2023 during a fully online course at a Japanese university [17], the accuracy and validity of the prediction is examined.

The following topics are addressed:

1. The possibility of creating a regression prediction procedure for the two indices of critical thinking ability is discussed using an Elastic network model technique.
2. In order to confirm the validity of prediction functions, the extracted functions are evaluated using a different data set.

2 Related Works

2.1 Critical thinking ability

Critical thinking is well known as an ability required in learning activities. In particular, critical thinking disposition is a set of generic skills or a key competence [21] which is essential for communication and for the development of writing skills [18]. This thinking ability may also contribute to an aptitude for analysis or scientific reasoning. Many higher education institutes conduct various programs to help develop these skills and aptitudes, which are key to producing the best of human behaviour during natural disasters and crises that result from these events [7, 20, 24].

However, assessment procedures are limited, so essay writing and evaluation, which are general purpose techniques used to measure various abilities, are often introduced in addition to the use of specific survey metrics. One of the metrics for surveying critical thinking attitude is a set of questions for learners [3]. As mentioned above, critical thinking awareness skills for use during natural disasters have also been developed [19].

2.2 Development of Critical Thinking Ability

Currently, the situation is that procedures for both development and assessment of critical thinking ability have not yet been established. Once again, a level of competence is required however, as the acquired ability and knowledge are also unknown. As mentioned earlier in this paper, discussion activity may have an effect on development of critical thinking ability [2, 8]. This discussion activity has been employed in higher education involving large-scaled learning programs such as MOOCs [23].

The authors have also been trying to develop a learning procedure in a bachelor level course. For critical thinking ability assessment, several sets of questionnaires were employed and evaluated [9, 11]. The main issue for analysis focused on developing a process for measuring critical thinking ability. Therefore, the assessment index is the difference in survey scores of the metrics across the course. In order to adapt the course to a variety of individual participants, student's characteristics including personality and literacy are measured. These characteristics are recognised as latent covariates for ability during learning. They might be considered independent measurements as the simple statistics in the following section show. Using these hypotheses, some analyses of the causal relationship for a development of the ability of critical thinking have been conducted [9, 11].

In another approach, essay report assessment scores have been employed to estimate critical thinking ability. Since essay writing is used for assessment of various types of learning activities, writing activity may seem to develop the ability. The possibility of predicting critical thinking ability has been discussed in our previous work [15, 16].

This work is an additional trial method of estimating critical thinking ability using independent values for student's characteristics. The possibilities and limitations are discussed in the following sections.

3 Method

The required metrics were surveyed during a bachelor level course at a Japanese university. The aim of the course is the development of critical thinking ability to increase awareness of human behaviour that occurs during disasters, in order to better understand actual situations and apply this understanding to situations encountered in daily life. The course was organised as a fully online course.

3.1 Course Description

A university freshman course titled "Psychology of Natural Disaster Mitigation and Prevention" was taught to a total of over 300 students. All participating students were freshman and came from every faculty: humanities, economics, engineering, medicine, etc. This course was taught in the first semester after enrolment at the university. The 15 course sessions for each week of the course were organised in an online course style involving learning from video clips, taking online tests and participating in online discussions with peers and the lecturer. Participants were asked to present essay reports, to complete weekly tests and to join online discussion activities. A task was also given to participants which required them to consider cognitive problems they observe during daily life.

Ordinarily, the class was organised as a blended learning course consisting of online discussions, in addition to weekly face-to-face class sessions [9–11]. A fully online learning style was introduced during the COVID-19 pandemic in 2020 and 2021, and since 2023 the course has been conducted using both types of instruction.

The following analysis employs surveyed data sets from the above mentioned classes conducted in 2022 and 2023.

3.2 Survey Metrics

The surveys consisted of the following metrics of individual participants: four factor scores for critical thinking disposition (CTD), and ratings of essay reports. The surveys and analysis were approved by an ethics committee at the university where the surveys took place.

Personality (Big5). Big5 scores were measured using a small set of inventories which consisted of 10 question items with 7-point scales (1–7) [5]. Five factors were extracted from the conventional surveys: Extroversion (P1), Agreeableness (P2), Conscientiousness (P3), Neuroticism (P4), and Openness (P5). The validity of this metric has been confirmed to measure the conventional personality as well as different longer versions of questionnaires has been confirmed [5].

Literacy of Science and Technology (LST). Kawamoto et al.(2013) developed an inventory for science and technology literacy which is based on a survey of scientific literacy. It consists of 10 questions, from which four factors were extracted from the answers: Life-centered(LST-1), Sciencephile (people who are interested in science and technology)(LST-2), Logic-oriented(LST-3), and Authoritarian (LST-4). The LSTs were scored using a 4-point scale (1–4). Four clusters of LSTs were also defined in order to compare behavioural attitudes toward Social Science issues using the four dimensional factor scores [4].

Critical Thinking Disposition (CTD). In order to measure the participant's attitude toward critical thinking attitude, a Japanese inventory set developed in a previous study [3] was used. The metric consists of four factor structures which use a 5 point Likert scale (1–5), consisting of Awareness of logical thinking (CTD- 1), Inquiry-mindedness (Inquisitiveness) (CTD-2), Objectiveness (Objectivity) (CTD-3), and Evidence-based judgement (CTD-4).

The factor scores used to be referred to as independent values. During the comparison, a set of four dimensional values is required. In this paper, the summation of four factor scores is defined as CTD in order to evaluate this factor more easily.

The metrics were surveyed twice, during the first and the second halves of the course.

Disaster-Prevention Consciousness (DPC). These inventories were developed to measure attitude toward disaster-prevention consciousness, and consisted of 20 question items using a 6 point Likert scale (1–6) [19].

The overall score is defined as the summation of the scores of the 5 aspects (1: imagination regarding disasters, 2: a sense of crisis about disasters, 3: the degree to which other participants were spoken to, 4: interest in disasters, 5: anxiety), with the maximum score being 120 and the minimum score being 20.

This metric was also surveyed twice during the course, and the two scores were compared.

Weekly Test Scores and Essay Assessments. As an additional measurement of learning performance, weekly test scores and essay assessment scores were examined.

Weekly test scores show the level of knowledge acquisition during the course. The course consisted of online video clips of each session, and both the participants and the lecturer needed confirmation of individual learning progress and performance. The tests were delivered using the university's LMS (Moodle learning management system), and the scores were used as part of the participant's final grades [9, 11].

Essay reports were assigned as a means to evaluate participant's in-class performance, and were to be marked as part of the overall final grade assessment [9, 11]. While these metrics were initially designed to be implemented as part of the estimation, they were not employed in most cases, however.

3.3 Prediction and Optimisation Technique

During the classes, the goal is to develop the critical thinking disposition of all participants. By adapting this procedure to the attributes of each participant, knowledge acquisition can be optimised. Therefore, a causal relationship for the level of critical thinking disposition is hypothesised from a combination of characteristics. This relationship can be noted as a linear regression function which predicts developed CTD or DPC scores using other individual metrics.

Prediction Procedure using Regression. In order to estimate scores of CTD or DPC metrics from a combination of characteristics such as multiple variables, Elastic network regularisation, as a more accurate type of multivariate regression analysis, has been introduced. Since regression analysis can calculate the prediction values using independent variables, their relationships between measured metrics are simply and clearly represented as an alternate solution to the use of other prediction techniques. The Elastic net is known as a regularised regression method that linearly combines appropriately two types of penalty methods to obtain an optimised condition using linear or logistic regression functions [6]. This technique has been applied to optimisation of liner regression functions. During optimisation, a function which uses contributing variables known as the LASSO technique (Least Absolute Shrinkage and Selection Operator) [1] is introduced, and the optimised function is obtained using an Elastic network selection procedure. The actual calculation was conducted using the SAS GLMSelect package [22].

Table 1. Simple statistics of key metrics

Metrics	Training (2023)			Validation (2022)		
	N	Mean	STD	N	Mean	STD
PS1: Extroversion	288	3.91	1.48	281	3.87	1.57
PS2: Conscientiousness	288	3.19	1.33	281	3.29	1.21
PS3: Neuroticism	288	4.59	1.24	281	4.62	1.24
PS4: Openness	288	3.80	1.23	281	3.85	1.28
PS5: Agreeableness	288	2.97	1.14	281	2.87	0.98
LST1: Life-centered	300	3.64	0.80	297	3.61	0.80
LST2: Sciencephile	300	3.58	0.93	297	3.60	1.13
LST3: Logic-oriented	300	3.54	0.82	297	3.31	0.81
LST4: Authoritarian	300	3.13	0.63	297	3.19	0.61
CTDa1: Awareness of logical thinking	314	2.88	0.66	304	2.85	0.65
CTDa2: Inquiry-mindedness	314	3.91	0.63	304	4.00	0.67
CTDa3: Objectiveness	314	3.67	0.62	304	3.78	0.58
CTDa4: Evidence-based judgement	314	3.67	0.67	304	3.64	0.67
DPC-First	355	79.7	8.80	327	80.5	9.04
DPC-Second	296	78.8	9.13	332	81.5	9.39
Weekly Test Score	420	769.9	217.0	434	770.1	198.4
Report essay	364	74.7	11.0	386	77.4	7.28

The mathematical benefits of this procedure have been discussed in a number of statistical articles [6]. This technique is well known as a powerful optimisation technique.

4   Results

In response to the purpose of this work, the possibility of predicting critical thinking ability scores using survey metrics and learning performance scores is examined.

4.1   Statistics of Measured Metrics

All metrics are summarised as factor scores in regards to the definitions. These personality, literacy, CTD and DPC statistics are summarised in Table 1. The four CTD factor scores are from the initial survey, and DPC scores are the first and the second surveys. The statistics of the means for 2022 and 2023 are summarised independently. They are almost identical, including the number of participants responses in each survey. Additional metrics for weekly test and report essay scores are also comparable.

As a hypothesis, there are correlational relationships between CTD scores and individual attribution, and the correlation coefficients between factor scores of CTD, PS

Table 2. Correlation coefficients of personality, S&T literacy and CTD

r	Personality					S&T Literacy			
	PS1	PS2	PS3	PS4	PS5	LST1	LST2	LST3	LST4
CTDa1	0.21	0.31	− .30	0.24	(−.11)	0.20	(0.07)	0.31	0.25
CTDa2	0.24	(−.02)	(−.06)	0.27	(−.11)	0.35	0.20	0.23	(0.11)
CTDa3	(0.04)	(0.10)	(−.03)	0.19	− .17	0.23	(−.02)	0.27	0.17
CTDa4	(−.04)	(0.12)	(−.12)	(0.05)	− .14	(0.12)	(0.01)	0.13	0.13
CTDb1	0.24	0.30	− .33	0.29	− .16	(0.10)	(0.08)	0.30	0.27
CTDb2	0.26	(−.01)	(−.04)	0.25	(−.06)	0.34	0.18	0.16	(−.03)
CTDb3	(−.01)	(0.12)	− .21	(0.11)	− .27	0.20	(0.01)	0.12	(−.01)
CTDb4	(−.07)	0.21	(−.10)	(0.08)	(−.11)	0.12	(0.04)	0.19	(0.11)

PS1: Extroversion, PS2: Conscientiousness, PS3: Neuroticism, PS4: Openness, PS5: Agreeableness. LST1: Life-centered, LST2: Sciencephile, LST3: Logic-centered, LST4: Authoritarian CTDa: first survey, DTDb: second survey, CTD1: Logical thinking, CTD2: Inquiry-mindedness, CTD3: Objectiveness, CTD4: Evidence-based judgement.

and LST are summarised in Table 2. Here, CTDa and CTDb represents the first and the second surveys, respectively. Non-significant correlation coefficients are showed using brackets. Contrary to the hypothesis, there are a few relationships in the factor scores for CTD and personality. There are more significant coefficients for literacy (LST1~4). The correlation coefficients for DPC scores are summarised in Table 3. Coefficients for the summation of the five factor scores are also calculated in Table 4. In both tables, the relationships between the two surveys have changed. These changes may be influenced by the development of critical thinking ability.

In this study, levels of critical thinking disposition are measured using two metrics for CTD and DPC. Another set of coefficients is summarised in order to confirm the dependency or similarity in Table 5. As the results show, most coefficients are significant. Therefore, they are independent scales but have some common measurements.

4.2   Estimation of Scores Using an Elastic Network

The regression functions for CTDs and DPCs using individual characteristics are optimised through an Elastic network procedure. The following analysis is based on the data set from the 2023 survey.

The optimisation process is indicated using an example of CTDa1 in Fig. 1. The horizontal axis represents variables of factor scores including intercepts. The vertical axis on the top of the panel represents values of coefficients. The vertical axis on the bottom of the panel represents values of CV-Press, such as the sum of the errors. As shown at the top of the panel, some variables are employed in the change of weights for each variable. The lower panel shows the fitness index of CV-Press, which as well as AIC (Akaike Information Criterion), BIC (Bayesian Information Criterion) and others [22], is used for confirming an optimised solution. In this case, the solution with the

Table 3. Correlation coefficients of personality, S&T literacy and DPC

r	Personality					S&T Literacy			
	PS1	PS2	PS3	PS4	PS5	LST1	LST2	LST3	LST4
DPC-F1	0.15	0.14	(−.05)	0.17	(0.05)	0.24	(0.00)	0.23	0.17
DPC-F2	(−.03)	(0.05)	(0.07)	(0.04)	(−.10)	0.18	(0.06)	(0.11)	(−.06)
DPC-F3	0.50	0.15	(−.05)	0.22	(−.02)	0.27	0.14	(0.10)	(0.10)
DPC-F4	(0.09)	0.15	(−.03)	(−.01)	(−.12)	0.25	(0.04)	(−.08)	−.13
DPC-F5	(−.12)	(0.12)	0.41	(0.00)	(−.02)	0.23	(−.03)	0.13	(0.08)
DPC-S1	(0.07)	(0.09)	−.14	0.17	(−.09)	0.26	(−.02)	(0.09)	(0.05)
DPC-S2	(−.06)	(0.03)	(0.09)	(−.04)	(−.12)	0.22	(0.05)	(0.04)	−.17
DPC-S3	0.44	(0.07)	(0.04)	0.22	−.16	0.30	(0.10)	(0.11)	(0.12)
DPC-S4	(0.03)	0.13	(−.05)	(0.07)	−.13	0.32	(0.04)	(0.02)	(−.03)
DPC-S5	−.21	0.15	0.31	(−.10)	(−.10)	0.22	(0.02)	(0.08)	(0.03)

1: imagination regarding disasters, 2: a sense of crisis about disasters, 3: the degree to which other participants were spoken to, 4: interest in disasters, 5: anxiety

Table 4. Correlation coefficients of personality, S&T literacy and DPC

r	Personality					S&T Literacy			
	PS1	PS2 PS3		PS4	PS5	LST1 LST2 LST3 LST4			
DPC-First	0.23	0.22 0.14		0.15	(−.07)	0.41	(0.08)	0.17	(0.07)
DPC-Second	(0.12)	0.17 (0.1)		(0.12)	− .20	0.45	(0.07)	(0.12)	(0.02)

Table 5. Correlation coefficients of two CTD scores and DPC

r	Initial CTD				Final CTD			
	CTDa1	CTDa2	CTDa3	CTDa4	CTDb1	CTDb2	CTDb3	CTDb4
DPC-First	0.13	0.36	0.41	0.17	0.18	0.30	0.30	0.28
DPC-Second	0.15	0.35	0.29	(0.05)	0.11	0.47	0.37	0.20

least errors is obtained when the fourth variable is added, as shown by a fine vertical line representing the best criterion based on the indices.

Examples of relationships between the surveyed scores and predicted values are summarised using scatter grams in Fig. 1 for CTDa1 and in Fig. 3 for DPC-F1. The horizontal axis represents surveyed scores, and the vertical axis represents predicted values. As a general phenomenon, deviation of predicted values is suppressed rather than the targeted values. In both figures, deviations of predicted values are compressed

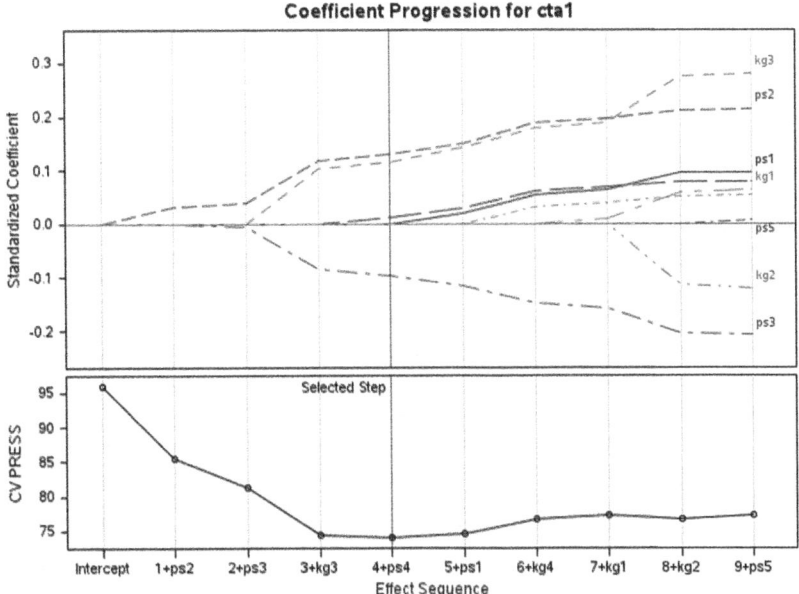

Fig. 1. An example of optimisation for CTDa1 using Elastic network with LASSO technique

Table 6. Estimation performance for CTDs using scores of personality and S&T literacy

CTD	N	Selected variables	R^2	rsig
CTDa1	222	int,PS2,PS3,LST3,PS4,(PS1,LST4,LST1,LST2,PS5)	0.17	0.50 $p <$ 0.01
CTDa2	222	int,LST1,PS4,PS1,LST2,(LST3,PS2,PST,PS3,LST4)	0.18	0.45 $p <$ 0.01
CTDa3	222	int,LST3,PS4,LST1,PS5,LST2,(PS2,LST4,PS3,PS1)	0.13	0.37 $p <$ 0.01
CTDa4	222	int,LST3,(PS5,PS2,PS3,PS1,LST2,LST1,PS4,LST4)	0.01	0.13 $p <$ 0.05
CTDaS	222	int,LST3,PS4,LST1,PS2,PS3,(PS5,PS1,LST4,LST2)	0.18	0.48 $p <$ 0.01

substantially. However, the correlational relationships are observed, and the order of the values seems to be maintained.

The results for each targeted variable of CTD are summarised in Table 6. The fitness of the selected function is evaluated with R^2 and simple correlation r in order to determine the level of significance with the original value. Most coefficients show around $r = 0.4$ and are significant, so prediction seems possible. The results for each targeted variable of DPC are summarised in Table 7. Coefficients of some factor scores are around $r = 0.50$. Also, even the sums of the factor scores in the second survey can be estimated

Table 7. Estimation performance for DPCs using scores of personality, S&T literacy and initial CTD scores

DPC	N	Selected variables	R^2	$rsig$
DPC-F1	242	int,CTDa3,LST3,CTDa1,LST1,LST4	0.14	$0.39\ p < 0.01$
DPC-F2	242	int,CTDa3,CTDa4,LST1,CTDa2,LST4	0.06	$0.30\ p < 0.01$
DPC-F3	237	int,PS1,CTDa2	0.36	$0.59\ p < 0.01$
DPC-F4	212	int,LST1,CTDa3,LST4,LST3,PS2,CTDa2,CTDa1	0.17	$0.43\ p < 0.01$
DPC-F5	212	int,PS3,CTDa3,LST1,PS2,PS1	0.31	$0.57\ p < 0.01$
DPC-Fa	232	int,LST1,PS1,PS3,PS2,LST3,PS4,LST4,PS5,LST2	0.29	$0.50\ p < 0.01$
DPC-Sa	202	int,LST1,CTDa2,CTDa3,PS5,PS3,PS2	0.32	$0.57\ p < 0.01$

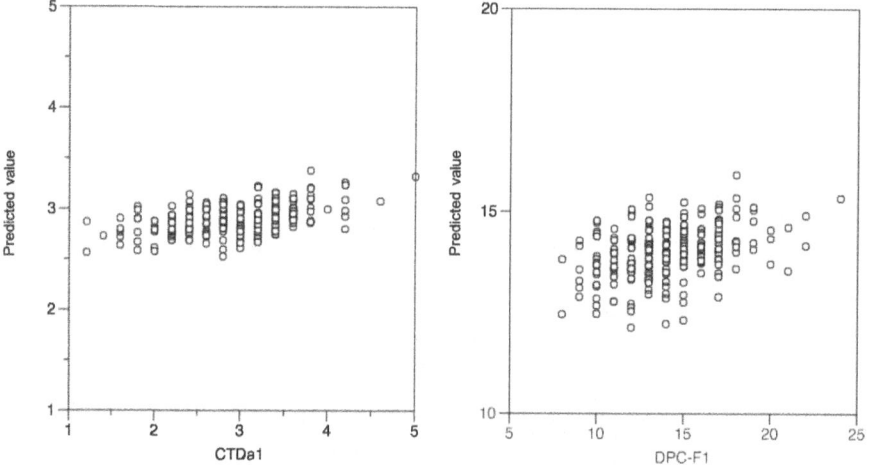

Fig. 2. Prediction results for CTDa1 ($r = 0.50$)

Fig. 3. Prediction results for DPC-F1 ($r = 0.39$)

to have a coefficient of $r = 0.57$. The ratings of report essays are sometimes required to predict values in the second survey. In most cases, predictions are possible using the initial surveyed scores.

These results confirm the hypothesis that critical thinking ability can be estimated using individual characteristics.

4.3   Validation Evaluation

The previous section confirms the relationships between critical thinking ability and individual characteristics using regression functions. The relationship obtained is a simple causal analysis, and it does not provide any validation of the estimation. Since the prediction is based on regression functions with independent variables, the optimised function can be applied to other sets of data.

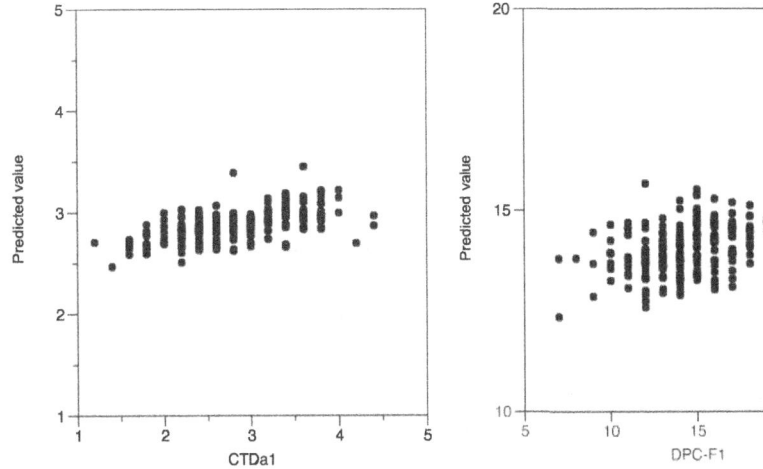

Fig. 4. Prediction results for CTDa1 in another survey ($r = 0.56$)

Fig. 5. Prediction results for DPC-F1 in another survey ($r = 0.36$)

In order to confirm the validity, prediction performance is tested using a similar but different data set from a survey in 2022. All functions developed using the 2023 data set are applied to the other data set from 2022. Prediction performance is evaluated using correlation coefficients as an index of similarity. Once again, examples of reproduced prediction values for two metrics of critical thinking ability are extracted from characteristics of individuals surveyed in 2022 using the above-mentioned regression functions with survey data from 2023, as shown in Fig. 4 for CTDa1 and in Fig. 5 for DPC-F1. The overall tendencies looks similar to the previous results shown in Figs. 2 and 3. The remaining results for CTD and DPC are summarised in Table 8. The relationships between these variables are maintained between two data sets from 2023 and 2022 are maintained. In particular, prediction performance for DPC scores in the second survey can be estimated from another data set.

These results show the possibility of estimating a participant's critical thinking ability using their individual characteristics. Also, the results confirm that the performance developed during the course, as measured by test scores in the second survey, can be estimated. When measuring individual metrics, it may be possible to apply a regression prediction procedure not only to critical thinking ability but to various student's characteristics as well. Once the functions have been extracted from the past learning data sets, they may be used for any predictions about the behaviour of the current students. This possibility should be evaluated thoroughly. As this technique can be used to estimate learning performance, learning support appropriate for each participant may be possible. A procedure detailing the most suitable means of providing this type of support will be a subject of our further study.

Table 8. Estimation performances for training and validation data sets

Metrics	Training (2023)			Validation (2022)		
	N	r	sig	N	r	sig
CTDa1	222	0.50	$p < 0.01$	212	0.56	$p < 0.01$
CTDa2	222	0.45	$p < 0.01$	212	0.50	$p < 0.01$
CTDa3	222	0.37	$p < 0.01$	212	0.38	$p < 0.01$
CTDa4	222	0.13	$p < 0.05$	257	0.33	$p < 0.01$
CTDaa	222	0.48	$p < 0.01$	212	0.57	$p < 0.01$
DPC-F1	242	0.39	$p < 0.01$	232	0.36	$p < 0.01$
DPC-F2	242	0.30	$p < 0.01$	232	0.36	$p < 0.01$
DPC-F3	237	0.59	$p < 0.01$	220	0.53	$p < 0.01$
DPC-F4	212	0.43	$p < 0.01$	198	0.37	$p < 0.01$
DPC-F5	212	0.57	$p < 0.01$	198	0.44	$p < 0.01$
DPC-Fa	232	0.50	$p < 0.01$	198	0.58	$p < 0.01$
DPC-Sa	202	0.57	$p < 0.01$	197	0.46	$p < 0.01$

5 Summary

In order to estimate student's critical thinking ability using scores for critical thinking disposition (CTD) and disaster-prevention consciousness (DPC), the possibility of developing a prediction model using factor scores for personality (Big-5) and literacy of science and technology (LST) and an Elastic network modelling technique and a LASSO technique as an optimiser. The following results are obtained in this paper.

1. A regression prediction procedure for estimating two indices of critical thinking ability is developed using an Elastic network modelling technique. With each factor score for the two metrics it is possible to calculate estimated values which correlate with the actual values in the middle level of correlation, at around r = 0.4 for CTD factor scores, and around r = 0.5 for DPC item scores.
2. The validity of the functions created using the 2023 data set is examined using a similar survey from 2022. Most prediction performance for the 2022 data set was maintained, even for scores in the second survey which would be developed during the course.

This procedure may provide a means to measure student's critical thinking ability and offer the possibility of developing critical thinking ability using metrics scores of individual characteristics. Even with this technique, individual characteristics should be measured using questionnaires. An easier prediction procedure should be considered. This will be a subject of our further study.

References

1. Akaho, S.: Kernel Multivariate Analysis: New Trends in Nonlinear Data Analysis. IWANAMI SHOTEN, Tokyo, Japan (2008)
2. Ekahitanond, V.: Promoting university students' critical thinking skills through peer feedback activity in an online discussion forum. Alberta J. Educ. Res. **59**(2), 247–265 (2013)
3. Hirayama, R., Kusumi, T.: Effect of critical thinking disposition on interpretation of controversial issues: Evaluating evidences and drawing conclusions. Jpn. J. Educ. Psychol. **52**, 186–198 (2004)
4. Kawamoto, S., Nakayama, M., Saijo, M.: Using a scientific literacy cluster to determine participant attitudes in scientific events in japan, and potential applications to improving science communication. JCOM **12**(1), 1–12 (2013)
5. Kawamoto, T., et al.: Age and gender differences of Big Five personality traits in a cross-sectional Japanese sample. J. Dev. Psychol. **26**(2), 107–122 (2015)
6. Kawano, S., Matsui, H., Hirose, K.: Statistical Modeling via Sparse Estimation. Kyoritsu Publication, Tokyo, Japan (2018)
7. Kikuchi, S.: How to recognize cognitive biases in risk perception in case of disasters –applying cognitive psychology to reduce damages in disasters. J. Jpn. Landslide Soc. **55**(6), 286–292 (2018)
8. Kusumi, T., Tanaka, Y.: A development of critical thinking ability during a class of English for specific purpose. In: Proceedings of JAEP Annual Meeting, pp. PF2–35 (2008)
9. Nakayama, M., Kikuchi, S., Yamamoto, H.: The relationship between student's characteristics and online discussion activity. In: Proceedings of 17th European Conference on E-Learning, pp. 417–423. Athens, Greece (2018)
10. Nakayama, M., Kikuchi, S., Yamamoto, H.: Lexical analysis of online discussion in a blended learning course. In: Proceedings of 6th European Conference on Social Media, pp. 223–230. Brighton, UK (2019)
11. Nakayama, M., Kikuchi, S., Yamamoto, H.: Development of critical thinking disposition during a blended learning course. In: Proceedings of 19th European Conference on E-Learning, pp. 358–364. Berlin, Germany (2020)
12. Nakayama, M., Kikuchi, S., Yamamoto, H.: The development of critical thinking disposition during two online styles of learning. In: Proceedings of 20th European Conference on e-Learning, pp. 314–320 (2021)
13. Nakayama, M., Kikuchi, S., Yamamoto, H.: Development of critical thinking disposition using an online discussion board during a fully online course. In: Proceedings of 21th European Conference on e-Learning, pp. 295–301 (2022)
14. Nakayama, M., Kikuchi, S., Yamamoto, H.: Characteristics promoted in order to develop students critical thinking disposition in online discussions during a fully online course. In: Proceedings of 22nd European Conference on e-Learning, pp. 212–218 (2023)
15. Nakayama, M., Kikuchi, S., Yamamoto, H.: Effectiveness of a "nudge" for online discussion participation about attitude toward essay writing. In: Methodologies and Intelligent Systems for Technology Enhanced Learning, Workshops 13th International Conference (LNNS769), pp. 174–181 (2023)
16. Nakayama, M., Uto, M., Kikuchi, S., Yamamoto, H.: Evaluation of essays and comments for developing thinking ability during a university course. In: Proceedings of Psychology Learning Technology in November, 2022, pp. 1–16 (2022)
17. Nakayama, M., Uto, M., Kikuchi, S., Yamamoto, H.: Feasibility of prediction of students characteristics using tests of essays written during a fully online course. In: Proceedings of 27th International Conference Information Visualisation (IV), pp. 204–209 (2023)

18. OECD: Testing student and university performance globally: OECD's AHELO (2014). http://www.oecd.org/edu/ahelo
19. Ozeki, M., Shimazaki, K., Yi, T.: Exploring elements of disaster prevention consciousness: based on interviews with anti-disaster professionals. J. Disaster Res. **12**(3), 631–638 (2017)
20. Reuter, C., Stieglitz, S., Imran, M.: Social media in conflicts and crises. Behav. Inf. Technol. **39**, 40–46 (2013)
21. Rychen, D., Salganik, L.: Key Competencies for a Successful Life and A Wellfunctioning Society. Hogrefe & Huber Publishers, Boston, USA (2003)
22. SAS: SAS/STAT 13.1 User's Guide: The GLMSELECT Procedure, https://support.sas.com/documentation/onlinedoc/stat/131/glmselect.pdf
23. Trehan, S., Sanzgiri, J., Li, C., Wang, R., Joshi, R.M.: Critical discussions on the massive open online course (MOOC) in India and China. Int. J. Educ. Dev. Using Inf. Commun. Technol. **13**(2), 141–165 (2017)
24. Utz, S., Schultz, F., Glocka, S.: Crisis communication online: how medium, crisis type and emotions affected public reactions in the Fukushima Daiichi nuclear disaster. Public Relation Rev. **39**, 40–46 (2013)

New Forms of (Mis)communication and Artificial Intelligence: Exploring Alienation, Empowerment and Accessibility

Nadia Di Leo[(⊠)] [iD], Simona Arace [iD], and Michele Ciletti [iD]

University of Foggia, Foggia, Italy
{nadia.dileo,simona.arace,michele_ciletti.587188}@unifg.it

Abstract. The rapid advancement of Large Language Models (LLMs) has revolutionized Artificial Intelligence (AI), particularly in Natural Language Processing and generation. This technological leap has profound implications for human-machine interaction and communication at large. This study examines the impact of Artificial Intelligence on communication, exploring its potential for empowerment and accessibility alongside risks of alienation, while also investigating how AI representations in popular culture influence public perceptions. The research combines theoretical analysis with an exploratory study of social media discourse. Sentiment analysis and topic modeling were applied to a dataset of Reddit posts and comments (n = 1739) mentioning AI published in the last year. Findings reveal a complex landscape of opinions, with a slight tendency towards positive sentiment but significant concerns about AI's societal impact. The study identifies key themes in public discourse, including AI's reasoning capabilities, human-AI comparisons, and practical applications. Results highlight the need for enhanced AI literacy, ethical guidelines, and inclusive design in AI development to address both opportunities and challenges in AI-mediated communication.

Keywords: Artificial Intelligence · Communication · Perception

1 Introduction

The rapid advancement of Artificial Intelligence (AI) has profoundly transformed the landscape of human communication, ushering in a new era of technological mediation that spans personal interactions, professional environments, and societal discourse. This paper explores the multifaceted impact of AI on communication, examining its potential for empowerment and accessibility while also addressing concerns about alienation and misinformation. Drawing from interdisciplinary research, an investigation was conducted on the topic of how AI is reshaping communication paradigms, influencing perceptions, and challenging traditional notions of creativity, productivity, and human-machine interaction.

Central to this analysis is an examination of AI's representation in popular culture, exploring how media portrayals have shaped public understanding and expectations of

© The Author(s), under exclusive license to Springer Nature Switzerland AG 2025
G. A. Toto (Ed.): ICS exchange 2024, CCIS 2521, pp. 15–31, 2025.
https://doi.org/10.1007/978-3-032-03021-4_2

AI capabilities. Delving into iconic works such as "Ghost in the Shell," (1996) "The Terminator," (1998) and "Blade Runner" (1982), their influence on collective imagination and scientific discourse was assessed.

To ground this theoretical exploration in empirical data, an exploratory analysis of social media discourse is presented, specifically focusing on Reddit[1] discussions related to AI. Through sentiment analysis (Taboada, 2016) and topic modeling (Blei & Lafferty, 2009), prevalent themes, attitudes, and concerns expressed by users engaging with AI-related content were uncovered.

Furthermore, this paper addresses the ethical implications of AI-mediated communication, discussing issues of privacy, bias, and the potential for misinformation.

By synthesizing theoretical frameworks, cultural analysis, and empirical research, this study aims to provide a comprehensive overview of AI's impact on communication, seeking to contribute to ongoing discussions about the future of human-AI interaction, offering insights into strategies for maximizing the benefits of AI while mitigating potential risks.

2 The Rise of AI and its Impact on Communication

2.1 Brief History and Definitions

In recent years, particularly since late 2022, public interest in Artificial Intelligence has surged dramatically. Once confined to the realms of science fiction and academic research, AI has now become an integral part of everyday life for many individuals. This shift can be largely attributed to the advent of Large Language Models (LLMs), exemplified by the release of ChatGPT, a chatbot that gained widespread popularity after being made freely available by OpenAI (Wu et al., 2023).

Artificial Intelligence, at its core, is the study of agents that perceive their environment and take actions based on those perceptions (Russell & Norvig, 2016). However, throughout its history, AI has been conceptualized in various ways, including as "the art of creating machines that perform functions that require intelligence when performed by people" (Kurzweil, 1990) and the automation of activities associated with human thinking, such as decision-making and problem-solving (Bellman, 1978).

The development of AI has not been a linear progression. The field has experienced periods of rapid advancement interspersed with "AI winters," during which progress stalled due to technical limitations or lack of funding. Notable AI winters occurred in the late 1970s (Howe, 1994) and from the mid-1980s to the early 2000s (Russell & Norvig, 2003).

A significant breakthrough came in the 2010s with the "deep learning revolution." Deep learning, a subset of machine learning based on artificial neural networks, saw exponential improvements thanks to advancements in computational power, particularly through the use of graphics processing units (GPUs) (Sze et al., 2017). This revolution culminated in 2017 with the introduction of the transformer architecture by Vaswani et al., which laid the foundation for the development of Large Language Models.

---

[1] https://www.reddit.com/.

LLMs are trained on vast amounts of textual data, learning the probability of certain words following others. This complex process requires substantial computational resources and time. Once trained, LLMs can receive natural language inputs from users and generate coherent responses using algorithmic calculations based on matrices (Zhao et al., 2023). However, the exact mechanisms by which LLMs produce their outputs remain somewhat opaque, leading to concerns about their explainability (Zhao et al., 2024).

The release of ChatGPT in November 2022 marked a turning point in public awareness and accessibility of AI technology. This event sparked a race among tech companies to develop and release their own LLMs, resulting in a proliferation of AI tools focused on text, image, and video generation. These tools are now widely available to the average user, often at little or no cost.

The impact of this AI revolution is far-reaching, affecting various sectors of society including employment, communication, education, and ethics. While some applications, such as information retrieval and content generation, are immediately apparent, the potential uses of AI are continually expanding. LLMs are being integrated into a wide range of services through API systems, with the potential to support or even replace human agents in various roles.

As LLMs continue to improve through increased training parameters a strategy that has shown consistent effectiveness (Kaplan et al., 2020) they are becoming more adept at reasoning, maintaining long conversations, and exhibiting human-like behavior. They are also developing emergent abilities not seen in smaller models (Wei et al., 2022). This progress raises questions about the ability of the general public to distinguish between AI and human interactions online.

The proliferation of AI-generated content has significant implications for information reliability and social media dynamics. There is a growing concern about the spread of misinformation and the use of AI-powered bots to influence public opinion on political matters (Woolley, 2016). This trend exacerbates existing issues related to the use of social media as a primary news source and highlights the increasing importance of critical thinking and fact-checking skills among end-users.

The impact of AI on the job market is another area of concern. Many workers, particularly those in roles that can be easily automated such as customer service and content creation, are being displaced by AI systems. While this may be a transitional phase in a broader technological revolution, it has contributed to feelings of distrust and apprehension towards AI (Lane et al., 2023).

Contrary to some popular narratives that portray machine intelligence as cold and rational, AI is increasingly challenging our perceptions of creativity and art. AI systems are now capable of writing poetry, creating visual art, and even producing films, blurring the lines between human and machine-generated creative works (Hermann, 2023). In the field of education, AI is opening up new possibilities for personalized learning and emotional recognition. Building on earlier work in affective computing (Picard, 2000), researchers are developing AI systems capable of recognizing and responding to human emotions through various modalities, including facial expressions, speech patterns, and physiological signals (Canal et al., 2022; Wu et al., 2022; Wankhade et al., 2022; Saganowski et al., 2022).

These developments have the potential to revolutionize teaching by allowing for real-time emotional monitoring of students and the creation of personalized learning strategies. However, integrating these technologies into classrooms presents challenges, including the need for multimodal information processing, understanding complex emotions, and developing efficient databases (Wu et al., 2016).

The rise of generative LLMs has opened new frontiers in affective computing research. LLMs' ability to communicate through natural language and their increasing multimodal capabilities make them promising tools for applications in education and healthcare (Wang et al., 2023; Li et al., 2024; Ostherr, 2022). AI systems are being used to design curricula, provide feedback on student work, and serve as intelligent tutoring systems (Lo, 2023; Limo et al., 2023).

However, the adoption of AI in education is not without challenges. Many teachers may lack the necessary AI literacy to effectively implement these tools, while others may be hesitant due to concerns about the role of empathy and human connection in teaching (García-Peñalvo, 2023).

As AI continues to advance, debates persist about its future trajectory. Some researchers speculate about the possibility of AI achieving human-like intelligence or even surpassing it, leading to concepts like Artificial General Intelligence (AGI) and Artificial Super Intelligence (ASI) (Bommasani et al., 2021). Others argue that LLMs will always be limited by their reliance on training data and may never truly achieve human-like creativity or consciousness (Bender et al., 2021).

Challenges remain in understanding the inner workings of LLMs due to their complex architecture and the stochastic elements involved in their training and generation processes (Guidotti et al., 2018). Issues of reliability, including the problem of AI "hallucinations" and biases inherited from training data, continue to be areas of active research and development (Gao et al., 2023).

Environmental concerns related to the high energy consumption of LLM training and deployment (Wu et al., 2022), as well as data security issues (Elliott & Soifer, 2022), are also important considerations as AI technology continues to evolve and integrate into various aspects of society.

2.2   AI-Mediated Communication Today

The interpretation of the concept of responsibility and the attribution of actions and their consequences, when decisions are made by automated artificial intelligence systems, raise fundamental questions in the field of ethics.

There is an urgent need to assess the risks and dangers associated with the possible presence of discrimination and prejudices inherent in the use of such technologies.

Furthermore, it is essential to analyze the impact of AI development on privacy and personal data security and the ethical implications that derive from it.

Transparency plays a crucial role in AI ethics, as it can help consolidate trust in the use of this technology.

Thanks to its ability to analyze enormous amounts of data and identify patterns, AI can optimize interactions, making communication more efficient and personalized.

Tools such as virtual assistants and chatbots improve access to information, allowing rapid responses and immediate support.

The possibility of using AI to promote social inclusion is a concrete reality, offering innovative solutions for people with disabilities and facilitating active participation in social contexts (Chakraborty et al., 2023). Its applications in areas such as education, health, and customer service promise to revolutionize the way we connect, interact, access experiences and engage with them. Tasks such as automatic translation (Mohamed et al., 2024) and screen reading, for instance, are already being innovated and rendered more efficient than ever.

AI's ability to analyze and process large volumes of data in real-time enables informed and timely decisions, greatly enhancing efficiency and speed. AI excels at personalization, providing tailored content for learning and user experiences that adapt to individual needs. This is particularly beneficial in educational contexts and for people with disabilities (Chakraborty et al., 2023). The practical applications of AI, such as virtual assistants and automatic translation tools, have significantly increased the accessibility of information, helping to reduce language and communication barriers.

AI also facilitates multi-channel interaction, allowing for fluid communication across various platforms and channels. By integrating messages from social media, email, and chat, it creates a coherent and homogeneous user experience. One of AI's key strengths is its scalability; AI solutions can easily handle an increasing volume of interactions without compromising service quality, making businesses more resilient in high-demand situations (Soldati et al., 2023).

From a financial perspective, AI can significantly reduce operational costs by automating repetitive tasks and managing routine communications. This automation frees up human resources for more strategic activities (Lin, 2019). Perhaps one of the most exciting aspects of AI is its capacity for continuous improvement. Through machine learning, AI can learn from past interactions, constantly enhancing its performance and adapting to changes in user preferences. This ongoing evolution ensures that AI-powered solutions become increasingly effective and relevant over time (Haenlein & Kaplan, 2019).

Furthermore, AI can optimize communication strategies, making it possible to analyze data and provide real-time feedback, which in turn informs and improves communication processes. This approach supports the development of user autonomy, as it provides them with the necessary tools to manage their interactions more independently. Empowerment, therefore, becomes a central goal: people can use AI technologies not only to receive information but also to express their opinions, make decisions, and actively contribute to public debate (Nader et al., 2022).

Artificial Intelligence, while offering numerous benefits, also presents significant risks and implications that warrant careful consideration. As highlighted by Floridi (2022), one of the primary concerns is the risk of misinformation. AI algorithms have the potential to amplify incorrect or misleading content, creating confusion and accelerating the spread of false news across digital platforms.

Recently, for instance, Wikipedia has launched WikiProject AI Cleanup (2024), a collaborative effort to correct and reduce the ever-increasing quantity of AI-generated content, often poorly written and unsourced, in its Wiki pages. The mere fact that such an effort is necessary means that the integrity of invaluable information sources is being put at risk, and it is worrying that their safekeeping falls entirely upon the shoulders of volunteers. Open-source information is particularly at risk, because of its inherently interactive and modifiable nature, but it isn't uncommon to witness prominent newspapers, or even academic journals, spread AI-generated misinformation (Gu et al., 2022). Whether that happens intentionally or not is up to debate, but its dangerous effects are largely unchanged by this distinction.

Another notable issue is the potential reduction in human interaction. As AI systems become more prevalent in communication, there's a risk of impoverishing personal relationships and fostering less empathetic communication (Vredenburgh, 2022).

The perpetuation of prejudices through algorithmic bias is another significant concern. AI systems, often reflecting the biases present in their training data or design, can inadvertently discriminate against certain groups, thereby contributing to and potentially exacerbating existing social inequalities (Heinrichs, 2022). This is particularly dangerous in contexts where an AI agent is asked to evaluate people, such as job interviews or funding applications, based on their whole persona rather than simply on their qualifications. Identifying and correcting biases proves to be difficult, considering that they are often direct results of poor training data deeply embedded in a model's weights. Because of LLMs' *black-box* nature, interventions aimed at a model's reasoning process are complicated, and the importance of using accurately curated training data cannot be overstated (Carabantes, 2020).

Perhaps most concerningly, our increasing dependence on technology can generate vulnerabilities in our communication skills. As we rely more heavily on AI-driven communication tools, users may become less capable of communicating effectively without digital support. This dependence could increase the risk of social isolation, as individuals may struggle to engage in face-to-face interactions or navigate social situations without technological assistance, but also hinder writing and reasoning skills (Vredenburgh, 2022).

Privacy is another primary concern: in a race to develop the most capable and efficient AI models, tech companies have failed to provide clear ethical guidelines regarding the utilization of users' prompts as training data for future LLMs. Considering that LLMs have proven to be capable, under certain circumstances, of replicating their training data in their output, users should be wary of feeding personal or sensible information into their prompts (Oseni et al., 2021). Furthermore, considering that copyright laws don't adequately protect content from AI training, most people could have personal information or proprietary creative works used without their knowledge (Korhonen, 2023). Protest movements regarding this issue, mainly driven by artists, have been largely unsuccessful. While the use of single inappropriate data items among billions may seem irrelevant, it holds further implications for communication as a whole in the post-AI world. Users may become scared of the possibility of their data being used inappropriately and resort to offline-mediated communication, reducing their valuable presence on the Internet. For instance, some publishing firms have recently given private companies the permission to use their material for training, without consulting authors (Gibney, 2024): such behavior could lead to distrust and seclusion in scientific communities, worsening research quality. Using open-source LLMs might be a partial solution to this problem, but precise international regulations would be desirable.

The European Union, regarding this topic, has been at the forefront of efforts towards standardization and regulation of AI agents, mainly with the recently released AI Act (Madiega, 2021). The Act's main goal is to stop entirely certain applications of AI deemed "high risk" – such as those aimed at tracking individuals and classifying them through social scoring. While efforts at regulation are commendable, the EU alone can't solve global problems, especially considering that most AI companies are based in the US, and the AI Act itself has been object of criticisms (Smuha et al., 2021). More thorough, internationally recognized laws seem to be needed (Hárs, 2022).

2.3   The Impact of Popular Culture Representations

Popular media has played a significant role in shaping public perceptions of Artificial Intelligence, often presenting speculative and dramatized portrayals that diverge from current technological realities. These representations, while captivating, can lead to misconceptions about AI's capabilities and potential societal impacts.

Science fiction literature and cinema have long explored the concept of human-like machines, frequently blurring the line between scientific possibility and imaginative speculation (Natale & Ballatore, 2020). This fascination with creating artificial beings that mimic or surpass human intelligence has been a recurring theme, influencing both public imagination and scientific discourse.

Several iconic works have been particularly influential in shaping popular conceptions of AI:

- Ghost in the Shell (1996): This Japanese franchise introduces the concept of a "ghost" a digital consciousness that can inhabit cybernetic bodies. The protagonist, Major Motoko Kusanagi, grapples with questions of identity and the nature of consciousness in a world where the boundaries between human and machine are increasingly blurred. The series presents AI as capable of independent thought and self-reflection, exploring philosophical questions about the nature of existence and consciousness.

  What if a cyber brain could possibly generate its own ghost, create a soul all by itself? And if it did, just what would be the importance of being human then?

  This quote, said by the protagonist, exemplifies the series' themes and reflections.

- The Terminator (1998): This film series depicts a dystopian future where an AI system called Skynet has become self-aware and seeks to eliminate humanity. The portrayal of AI in The Terminator is one of an omnipotent, malevolent force a stark contrast to the current state of AI technology, which remains narrowly focused on specific tasks.
- Blade Runner (1982): Based on Philip K. Dick's novel "Do Androids Dream of Electric Sheep?", this film explores the ethical implications of creating artificial beings indistinguishable from humans. The "replicants" in Blade Runner are bioengineered androids with implanted memories and emotions, raising questions about the nature of humanity and consciousness.

These popular culture representations often depict AI as possessing general intelligence, self-awareness, and even consciousness attributes that are far beyond the capabilities of current AI systems. While real-world AI excels at specific tasks through machine learning algorithms, it lacks the general intelligence and self-awareness often portrayed in fiction.

The impact of these portrayals on public perception is significant. Research has shown that exposure to science fiction narratives can influence people's attitudes towards real-world technologies (Geraci, 2011). This can lead to both unrealistic expectations and unwarranted fears about AI's capabilities and potential societal impacts.

On one hand, overly optimistic portrayals may lead to inflated expectations about AI's current capabilities, potentially resulting in disappointment or mistrust when real-world applications fall short. On the other hand, dystopian scenarios featuring malevolent AI overlords may foster unnecessary fear and resistance to beneficial AI technologies.

3   An Exploratory Analysis of Social Network Users' Perceptions

3.1   Research Question

To investigate people's perceptions surrounding AI, it was decided to conduct a series of quantitative analyses on a dataset of social media comments. This was done not only to gain further insight into the public reception of Artificial Intelligence advancements, but also to evaluate whether the theoretical points discussed before found confirmation in the daily conversations of social media users. A further aim was to analyze whether any relevant topics or pieces of information were missing from a starting reflection, contextualizing the current research and understanding the best course of action for future interventions, laying their foundations. Under this point of view, this analysis serves as a small-scale exploratory study to base more complex studies on, while its findings in addition to the theories, news and past research discussed in this article will help designing appropriate approaches and possible solutions to AI-based communication matters.

3.2   Methodology

A dataset of Reddit posts and comments (n = 1739) published in the last year that mentioned the terms "Artificial Intelligence" or "AI" was built for this study. Reddit was chosen as the target platform because of its strong focus on text-based discussion, which lends itself well to discourse analysis; because of the popularity of tech topics found on its various subreddits; and because of its thorough and accessible API (Proferes et al., 2021). The textual data was preprocessed by lemmatizing it, tokenizing it and removing stopwords. Then, two NLP-based tasks were executed:

- Sentiment Analysis (Taboada, 2016): each post and comment were assigned a score ranging from 0 to 1, where 0 meant that it conveyed absolutely negative emotions, while 1 meant that it conveyed absolutely positive ones. Then, a few key points were visualized and analyzed:

  - the overall sentiment distribution;
  - the words more commonly found in positive posts/comments;
  - the words more commonly found in negative posts/comments;

- the sentiment changes over time;
- the link between sentiment score and post/comment Reddit score. The Python library NLTK[2] was used for this task.

- Topic Modelling (Blei & Lafferty, 2009): Latent Dirichlet Allocation (Blei et al., 2023) was performed on the dataset to extract the most common topics in the posts/comments and their relative most frequent words. The Python library scikit-learn[3] was used for this task.

All the obtained graphs and visualizations were created using the Python libraries MatPlotLib[4], WordCloud[5] and Seaborn[6].

3.3 Results and Discussion

Regarding sentiment analysis, a majority of posts and comments showed positive scores (n = 844), while negative scores were prominent but less frequent (n = 483). A considerable number of posts and comments were deemed neutral (n = 399) or were unable to be confidently categorized (n = 13) (Fig. 1).

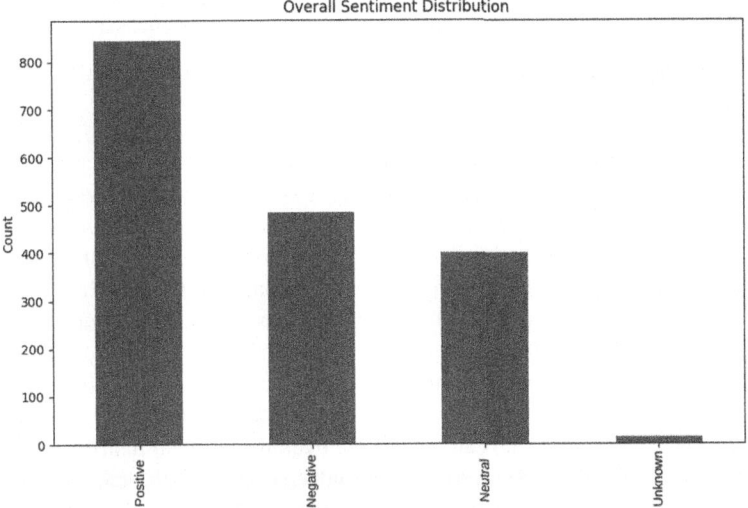

Fig. 1. Overall sentiment distribution

Such findings suggest that Reddit communities show positive feelings towards AI more than negative ones, but the generally high number of negative posts and comments

---

[2] https://www.nltk.org/.
[3] https://scikit-learn.org/.
[4] https://matplotlib.org/.
[5] https://pypi.org/project/wordcloud/.
[6] https://seaborn.pydata.org/.

leads to believe that there is no clear consensus and that a variety of opinions cohabitate the same spaces.

Visualizing the relation between sentiment scores and post/comment Reddit scores corroborates this idea (Fig. 2).

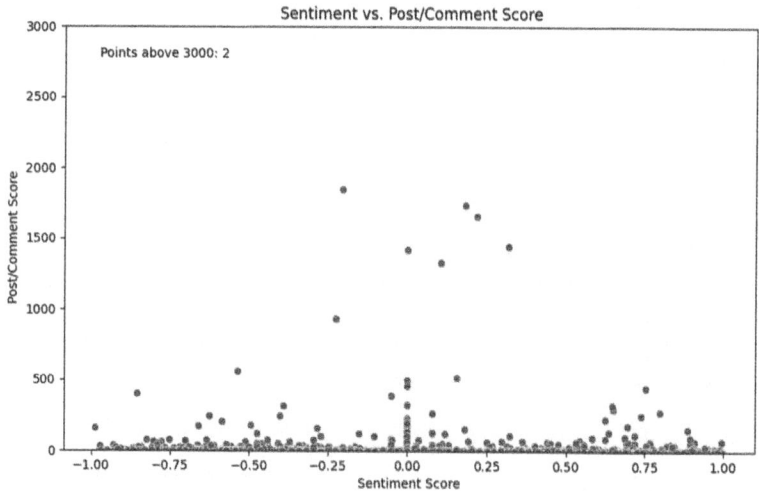

Fig. 2. Sentiment score in relation to post/comment Reddit score

No clear correlation can be seen between the two variables, which points to the afore-mentioned overall balance between differing opinions. Interestingly, between the highest scoring post and comments, relatively neutral ones were dominant, with no strongly negative (sentiment score $< = -0.75$) or strongly positive (sentiment score $> = 0.75$) elements managing to score more than five hundred *upvotes* (Reddit points).

Moving on to the analysis of the most frequent words associated with positive and negative posts and comments, a slightly different strategy was adopted. Rather than considering the sentiment score of the entire post or comment, an aspect-based sentiment analysis was conducted, focusing on specific sentences that mentioned AI. This technique proved to be inappropriate when calculating the overall sentiment distribution, because its narrower scope led to a more pronounced indecisiveness of the model, resulting in the vast majority of data points being classified as neutral. However, it yielded positive results when applied to the identification of specific words, because it managed to focus on the clearest examples of strong sentiments, painting a complex picture of themes associated with AI (Fig. 3).

When looking at the words most positively correlated with AI, the prominence of the words "human" and "beings" is immediately noticeable. This may point to an anthropomorphizing tendency in people who see AI in a positive light, which has already been observed in small-scale studies (Peconio et al., 2024). The emphasis on the word "could" may highlight the focus on the future possibilities of AI and the related excitement towards new developments. Other words, less prominent but still common, include

Fig. 3. Word Cloud of the most common words in positive sentences related to AI

terms such as "logic", "awareness", "data", "understanding", "potential" and "learning", highlighting areas where successful applications of AI have been experimented (Fig. 4).

Fig. 4. Word Cloud of the most common words in negative sentences related to AI

The most common negative words paint a different picture. The highest-occurring terms, "people" and "like", seem to underscore the structural differences between AI and humans. A general distrust can also be inferred by the high frequency of terms such as "think", "jobs" and "bad". Most negative terms point to concerns regarding AI, either philosophical/emotional ("existential") or practical ("threat"). The abundance of verbs seems to highlight a certain focus on the actual use of AI rather than its characteristics.

An analysis of the changes in post/comment sentiment scores across the last year was also conducted and visualized on 7-day moving average (Fig. 5).

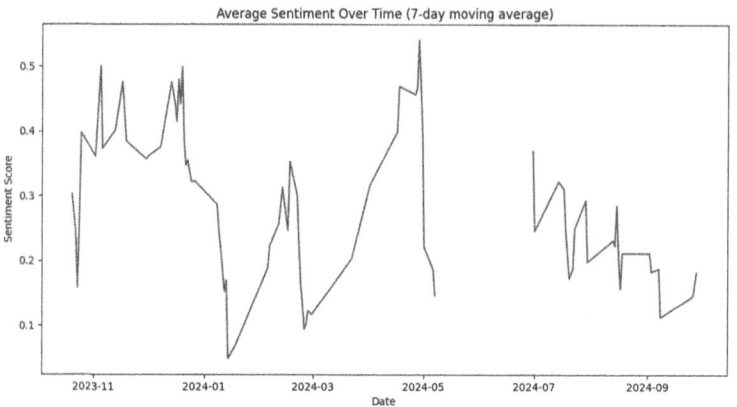

Fig. 5. Average sentiment score over time, represented on a 7-day moving average

Key findings obtained through this analysis include:

- An overall tendency towards positive scores: the average score across 7-day intervals never go below zero, thus never entering the "negative" zone.
- A considerably high fluctuability: dips and rises in sentiment scores, during the last year, were frequent and sudden, highlighting a complex landscape of differing opinions.
- An overall tendency towards lower scores: while the earlier data points score consistently high, more recent ones are characterized by a non-linear but steady downward trend.

A further analysis on the correlation between specific events related to the contemporary history of AI and the changes in sentiment scores would be beneficial in understanding more thoroughly the context of the discussed fluctuations.

Apart from sentiment analysis tasks, topic modelling was also performed. This analysis made it possible to identify five main topics that characterized the Reddit discussions on AI during the last year (Fig. 6).

While it is difficult to precisely categorize each topic because of the overlap of many top words between them, some key findings are immediately evident. For instance, most words of the first topic are linked to the semantic field of logic and understanding, pointing to a focus on discussions surrounding AI's reasoning capabilities. Similarly, the second topic contains words that can be traced back to the fields of humanity and thinking, highlighting discussions on the similarities and differences between AI and humans. Similar words are found in the third topic, while the fourth one focuses on practical applications of AI, such as learning, coding and, broadly, creating. This suggests that, apart from theoretical discussions, Reddit posts and comments also debated the concrete use of AI tools.

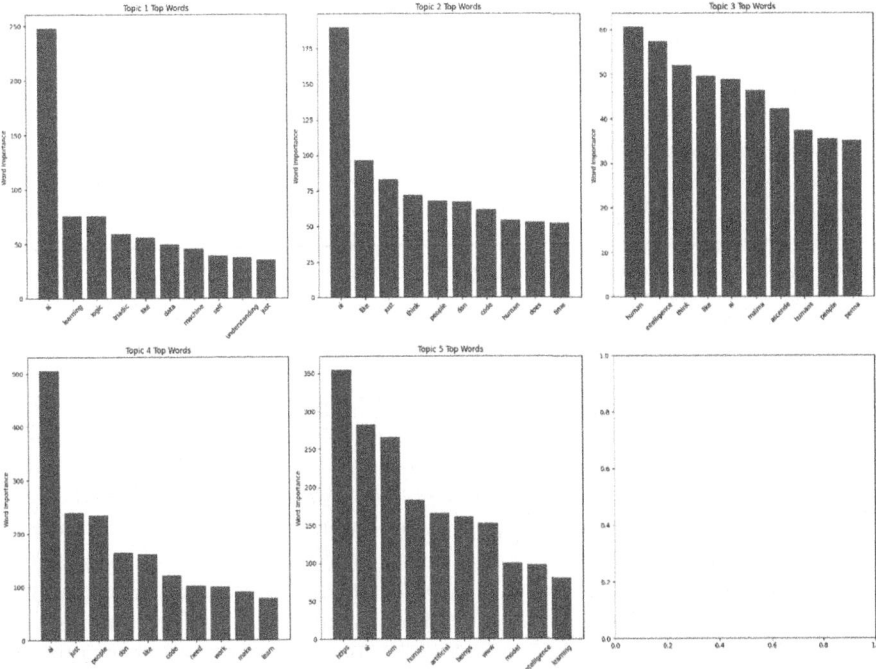

Fig. 6. The top five most common topics in the dataset and their relative most common words

Biases and Limitations. While this exploratory analysis lays interesting foundations for future studies on the perception of AI and communication, a few possible limitations need to be addressed. The chosen population – Reddit users – consists of a specific subset of the overall people who have experiences with AI: for instance, Reddit is an anglo-centric website*, and the opinions of people from non-English speaking countries may have been underrepresented. Furthermore, the analysis may have included comments or posts created by bots or by malicious agents intending to spread misinformation, a practice evermore common across all social media*. Again, this analysis only intends to kickstart a more complex and comprehensive understanding of the landscape surrounding AI discourse, and as such it involves methods that should be calibrated and adjusted in future, more focused studies: for instance, future research may benefit from the fine tuning of specific NLP models.

4 Future Directions and Conclusions

Both from a theoretical and practical perspective, it appears evident that AI is a main point of discussion in today's society, and that it is largely shaping the way we communicate, from everyday interactions to large-scale campaigns. Future research investigating AI's transformation of communication is desirable, and a specific focus on the implications of its future development should be considered. Furthermore, while empirical research and theoretical discussions would be helpful for the overall understanding of this peculiar phenomenon, concrete interventions, tools and practical resources are all areas that deserve attention and investment.

Specifically, we recognized a certain rift between symmetrical positions: on one hand, AI enthusiast seem eager to test new tools and fantasize on their future capabilities, focusing not only on the practical affordances that AI is now granting, but also on the philosophical and ontological perspectives surrounding the rise of almost human-like agents. On the other hand, AI skeptics are worried, or even scared, by technologies that are increasingly present in numerous contexts but sometimes still inaccurate and prone to exploitations. The situation is furthermore complicated by a silent group of people who don't understand what AI is and how it actually works: popular culture representations play a crucial role in this regard.

To address the ethical and inclusive use of Artificial Intelligence in communication, it is fundamental to adopt a series of targeted strategies, as outlined by Pinnelli (2024). Education and awareness play a pivotal role in this process. It is essential to promote training programs that help users understand the workings of AI, its advantages, and its limitations. Increasing awareness on how to recognize misinformation and algorithmic bias is a fundamental step towards ensuring informed and critical use of these technologies.

Regulation and standards are equally important in this landscape. It is necessary to develop clear guidelines that govern the use of AI in communication. These norms must ensure transparency, accountability, and robust data protection, creating an environment in which users can feel safe and protected.

Inclusive design must be at the forefront of AI system development. Involving ethics experts, users with disabilities, and representatives of disadvantaged groups can ensure that technologies are accessible to all and free from prejudices. This approach helps in creating AI systems that cater to diverse needs and perspectives.

Continuous monitoring and review are critical components of responsible AI use. Implementing regular evaluation mechanisms allows for analyzing the social impact of AI tools and identifying any issues related to fairness and inclusion. This ongoing review process is essential to ensure that technologies evolve responsibly and continue to serve the best interests of all users.

The promotion of ethical technology development should be a priority. Research should focus on creating AI systems that respect principles such as justice, transparency, and accountability, thus avoiding negative consequences in communication and society in general. This emphasis on ethical development can help mitigate potential risks associated with AI implementation.

By implementing these proposals, we can actively address the challenges associated with the use of artificial intelligence-based communication. This comprehensive approach will allow us to leverage the advantages offered by technology while reducing associated risks. The ultimate goal is to build a more equitable and inclusive society, where everyone can benefit from the opportunities offered by Artificial Intelligence (AI). Through these concerted efforts, we can shape a future where AI enhances communication and societal interactions in a responsible and ethical manner.

Disclosure of Interests. The authors have no competing interests to declare that are relevant to the content of this article.

References

Bellman, R.E.: An Introduction to Artificial Intelligence: Can Computers Think? Boyd & Fraser Publishing Company (1978)

Bender, E.M., Gebru, T., McMillan-Major, A., Shmitchell, S.: On the dangers of stochastic parrots: can language models be too big? In: Proceedings of the 2021 ACM Conference on Fairness, Accountability, and Transparency, pp. 610–623 (2021)

Blei, D.M., Lafferty, J.D.: Topic models. In: Text Mining, pp. 101–124. Chapman and Hall/CRC (2009)

Blei, D.M., Ng, A.Y., Jordan, M.I.: Latent Dirichlet allocation. J. Mach. Learn. Res. **3**, 993–1022 (2003)

Bommasani, R., et al.: On the opportunities and risks of foundation models. arXiv preprint arXiv: 2108.07258 (2021)

Buonaguro, N.A.: Società della conoscenza e Pedagogia 3.0. Formazione e Insegnamento **1**, 692–699 (2020)

Cameron, J., Schwarzenegger, A., Hamilton, L., Patrick, R.: The Terminator. MAWA Film & Medien (1998)

Canal, F.Z., et al.: A survey on facial emotion recognition techniques: a state-of-the-art literature review. Inf. Sci. **582**, 593–617 (2022)

Carabantes, M.: Black-box artificial intelligence: an epistemological and critical analysis. AI Soc. **35**(2), 309–317 (2020)

Chakraborty, N., Mishra, Y., Bhattacharya, R., Bhattacharya, B.: Artificial intelligence: the road ahead for the accessibility of persons with disability. Mater. Today Proc. **80**, 3757–3761 (2023)

Danso, S., Annan, M.A.O., Ntem, M.T.K., Baah-Acheamfour, K., Awudi, B.: Artificial intelligence and human communication: a systematic literature review. World J. Adv. Res. Rev. **19**(1), 1391–1403 (2023)

Elliott, D., Soifer, E.: AI technologies, privacy, and security. Front. Artif. Intell. **5**, 826737 (2022)

Floridi, L.: Etica dell'intelligenza artificiale: Sviluppi, opportunità, sfide. Raffaello Cortina Editore (2022)

Galetta, D.U.: Digitalizzazione, Intelligenza artificiale e Pubbliche Amministrazioni: il nuovo codice dei contratti pubblici e le sfide che ci attendono. Federalismi.it **2023**(12), 1- 12 (2023)

Gao, Y., et al.: Retrieval-augmented generation for large language models: a survey. arXiv preprint arXiv:2312.10997 (2023)

García-Peñalvo, F.J.: The perception of artificial intelligence in educational contexts after the launch of ChatGPT: disruption or panic? (2023)

Gibney, E.: Has your paper been used to train an AI model? Almost certainly. Nature **632**(8026), 715–716 (2024)

Gu, J., et al.: AI-enabled image fraud in scientific publications. Patterns **3**(7) (2022)

Guidotti, R., et al.: A survey of methods for explaining black box models. ACM CSUR **51**(5), 1–42 (2018)

Hárs, A.: AI and international law – legal personality and avenues for regulation. Hung. J. Legal Stud. (2022)

Heinrichs, B.: Discrimination in the age of artificial intelligence. AI Soc. **37**(1), 143–154 (2022)

Hermann, I.: Artificial intelligence in fiction: between narratives and metaphors. AI Soc. **38**(1), 319–329 (2023)

Howe, J.: Artificial Intelligence at Edinburgh University : a perspective. https://web.archive.org/web/20070817031720/http://www.inf.ed.ac.uk/about/AIhistory.html. Accessed 6 Oct 2024

Kaplan, J., et al.: Scaling Laws for neural language models. . arXiv preprint arXiv:2001.08361 (2020)

Korhonen, T.M.: The use of copyrighted material as training data in the AI model: does training AI violate copyright law? (2023)

Kurzweil, R.: The Age of Intelligent Machines. MIT Press (1990)

Lane, M., Williams, M., Broecke, S.: The impact of AI on the workplace: main findings from the OECD AI surveys of employers and workers (2023)

Li, J., et al.: ChatGPT in healthcare: a taxonomy and systematic review. Comput. Methods Prog. Biomed., 108013 (2024)

Limo, F.A.F., et al.: Personalized tutoring: ChatGPT as a virtual tutor for personalized learning experiences. Przestrzeń Społeczna Soc. Space 23(1), 293–312 (2023)

Lin, T.C.: Artificial intelligence, finance, and the law. Fordham L. Rev. 88, 531 (2019)

Madiega, T.: Artificial intelligence act. European Parliament: European Parliamentary Research Service (2021)

Matplotlib. https://matplotlib.org/. Accessed 6 Oct 2024

Mohamed, Y.A., et al.: The impact of artificial intelligence on language translation: a review. IEEE Access 12, 25553–25579 (2024)

Nader, K., Toprac, P., Scott, S., Baker, S.: Public understanding of artificial intelligence through entertainment media. AI Soc., 1–14 (2022)

Nazari, S.: Creatività e intelligenza artificiale: nuove frontiere, provocazioni e limiti dell'arte contemporanea (2023)

NLTK, https://www.nltk.org/. Accessed 6 Oct 2024

Oseni, A., Moustafa, N., Janicke, H., Liu, P., Tari, Z., Vasilakos, A.: Security and privacy for artificial intelligence: opportunities and challenges. arXiv preprint arXiv:2102.04661 (2021)

Ostherr, K.: Artificial intelligence and medical humanities. J. Med. Hum. 43(2), 211–232 (2022)

Picard, R.W.: Affective Computing. MIT Press (2000)

Pinnelli, S.: Cambiamento: le sfide dell'innovazione tecnologica e dell'intelligenza artificiale (Panel 6). In: I linguaggi della Pedagogia Speciale. La prospettiva dei valori e dei contesti di vita, pp. 293–296. Pensamultimedia (2024)

Proferes, N., Jones, N., Gilbert, S., Fiesler, C., Zimmer, M.: Studying Reddit: a systematic overview of disciplines, approaches, methods, and ethics. Soc. Media Soc. 7(2), 20563051211019004 (20210)

Reddit. https://www.reddit.com/. Accessed 6 Oct 2024

Russell, S.J., Norvig, P.: Artificial Intelligence: A Modern Approach. Pearson (2016)

Russell, S.J., Norvig, P.: Artificial Intelligence: A Modern Approach, 2nd edn. Prentice Hall, Upper Saddle River, New Jersey (2003)

Russell, S.J., Norvig, P.: Intelligenza artificiale: un approccio moderno. Pearson Italia Spa (2005)

Saganowski, S., Perz, B., Polak, A., Kazienko, P.: Emotion recognition for everyday life using physiological signals from wearables: a systematic literature review. IEEE Trans. Affect. Comput. (2022)

Scikit-learn, https://scikit-learn.org/. Accessed 6 Oct 2024

Scott, R., et al.: Blade Runner. Warner Home Video, Los Angeles (1982)

Seaborn, https://seaborn.pydata.org/. Accessed 6 Oct 2024

Shirow, M., Oshii, M.: Ghost in the Shell. Arboris (1996)

Smuha, N.A., et al.: How the EU can achieve legally trustworthy AI: a response to the European Commission's proposal for an Artificial Intelligence Act. SSRN (2021)

Soldati, P., et al.: Design principles for generalization and scalability of AI in communication systems. arXiv preprint arXiv:2306.06251 (2023)

Sze, V., Chen, Y., Yang, T., Emer, J.: Efficient processing of deep neural networks: a tutorial and survey. arXiv preprint arXiv:1703.09039 (2017)

Taboada, M.: Sentiment analysis: an overview from linguistics. Ann. Rev. Linguist. **2**(1), 325–347 (2016)

Vredenburgh, K.: Freedom at work: understanding, alienation, and the AI-driven work-place. Canadian J. Philos. **52**(1), 78–92 (2022)

Wang, D.Q., et al.: Accelerating the integration of ChatGPT and other large-scale AI models into biomedical research and healthcare. MedComm–Fut. Med. **2**(2), e43 (2023)

Wankhade, M., Rao, A.C.S., Kulkarni, C.: A survey on sentiment analysis methods, applications, and challenges. Artif. Intell. Rev. **55**(7), 5731–5780 (2022)

Wei, J., et al.: Emergent abilities of large language models. arXiv preprint arXiv:2206.07682 (2022)

Wikipedia: WikiProject AI Cleanup. https://en.wikipedia.org/wiki/Wikipedia:WikiProject_AI_ Cleanup. accessed 6 Oct 2024

Woolley, S.C.: Automating power: social bot interference in global politics. First Monday (2016)

Wordcloud. https://pypi.org/project/wordcloud/. Accessed 6 Oct 2024

Wu, C.H., Huang, Y.M., Hwang, J.P.: Review of affective computing in education/learning: trends and challenges. Br. J. Educ. Technol. **47**(6), 1304–1323 (2016)

Wu, C.J., et al.: Sustainable AI: environmental implications, challenges and opportunities. Proc. Mach. Learn. Syst. **4**, 795–813 (2022)

Wu, T., et al.: A brief overview of ChatGPT: The history, status quo and potential future development. IEEE/CAA J. Autom. Sin. **10**(5), 1122–1136 (2023)

Zhao, H., et al.: Explainability for large language models: a survey. ACM Trans. Intell. Syst. Technol. **15**(2), 1–38 (2024)

Zhao, W., et al.: A Survey of Large Language Models. arXiv preprint arXiv:2303.18223 (2023)

Locating Sexting in the Contemporary Indian Sexual Arena

Amit Kumar[1]($\boxtimes$) (iD) and Samanwita Paul[2] (iD)

[1] Institute for Development and Communication (IDC), Chandigarh, India
amitkumar@idcindia.org
[2] Indraprastha Institute of Information Technology (IIIT), New Delhi, India

Abstract. The journey of 'wandering charming prince on a white horse' to 'surf-ing/sexting on the scruffy beanbag' is an anecdote reflecting upon the midnight hour of every society. The study explains the impact of sexting in a technology-laced Indian society, exploring whether sexting self-absorbedly vaporizes the ideas of love, romance, and intimacy, along with its effects on society. Locating sexting in three axes, i.e., as an Ideology with an idea of controlling sexuality, with values of maintaining the traditionality of cultures, and controlling the youth and keep-ing them under restricted surveillance; as a Platform of Opportunity, i.e., the vir-tual space providing equality from the discriminated social-reality/social-identity (caste/class/ethnicity/race etc.), an opportunity to transcend cultural barriers and providing a free space; and Vandal comprises of impact on the ideas of love, romance and intimacy due to the struggle between previous two axes. The study findings revealed that the sexual arena has provided a space in Indian society to co-habitat all aspects of love, romance and intimacy as a pious form and a degen-erate concept. The study concluded that society has not yet developed an idea of a centre of gravity, and the absence of the same has created an imbalance in the form of unlimited and unchecked use of such platforms, causing problems and affecting other channels such as love and romance. The negative impacts of unfil-tered access (transgressing the boundaries of mental and physical age) to globally connected technology and gadgets have not remained a trove to discover.

Keywords: Sexting · Communication · Technology

1 Introduction: "A Letter Was Caught"

The expression, *'the bier, was seen at the doorstep of both. It is rumored that a love letter was caught,* which aptly describes how the concept of love is positioned in Indian society. The societies of the world have a plethora of social systems, and there are societies in which ideas of love flourish freely. Whereas in others, they are still considered taboo. To avoid the debacle of getting into the trap of what love is and what not, let us agree to the fact that it exists, whether it is a game of the brain or its symbolic organ, i.e., the heart. However, the ongoing debate in academia is whether sexting is impacting or changing our ideas about love, romance, and intimacy. And evaluate it along with its fusion with advanced technology. Sexting is a portmanteau of sex and texting. In

G. A. Toto (Ed.): ICS exchange 2024, CCIS 2521, pp. 32–50, 2025.
https://doi.org/10.1007/978-3-032-03021-4_3

other words, sexting is the exchange (sending or receiving) of sexual words, pictures, or videos via technology, typically a mobile phone/computer/laptop, etc. In any society worldwide, the introduction of a novelty brings a change that can be perceived in both ways, i.e., in favor of or against, constructing or destructing, and positive or negative depending on the kind of time and space society is living in. The present study attempts to analyze the role of sexting and its impact on society's perception of love, romance, and intimacy under the broad umbrella of modern technology, which is the primary agent of changing these perceptions and ideas. The example considered for reference is taken from Indian society, which provides a perfect platform where modernity and tradition co-exist. Indian society is an ideal model to study the conflict between the two, i.e., sexting and the idea of love, romance, and intimacy. Because Indian society embodies both extremities of love and sexting, this is mainly because, in compliance with the traditional morality of Indian society, love is considered pious and worth worshipping. In contrast, romance and intimacy are generally viewed as amoral (must be conducted in secret). Upon all that, sexting, a product of modern technology facilitating free (lessened surveillance) interaction between couples, youth, and teenagers, has taken it to another level, shattering the rigidities of traditional societies and creating spaces for mishaps like cybercrimes.

In a nutshell, the study attempts to analyze the modus operandi of sexting and love on the same platform. How has society established an accord with sexting and a pious form of love? Can there be any accord? Is sexting harmful, or is it just a phase society is passing? What if love is in its crisis stage or always has been? What are the agents nurturing such conflicts between the two? Are these agents present from the beginning, or have they developed recently? What can be the circumstances that, in the first place, gave way to producing these agents? What drives people to prefer sexting? If sexting prevails and love vanishes, what must one look forward to in such a case?

2 Methodology

The paper is divided into five sections, starting with the definitional aspects in order to limit the boundary of the context, followed by historical and theoretical background on the subject. Further, it discusses the role of technology and romance media along with its mediums and, last but not least, the analysis part of how the trio of an axis, i.e., sexting as an ideology, opportunity, and medium of vandalism, affect our very ideas of love and romance. The study captured the varied perceptions regarding the respondents' ideas and purposes behind sexting and the positioning of love, romance, and intimacy.

The study deals with both primary (extensive survey) and secondary data (digital and offline documented archives). For primary data, an extensive survey was conducted through online interaction with users using sexting platforms Tinder, Bumble, and random non-login online chat rooms via messaging applications platforms like *Talk to Strangers*, *Chitchat*, *DirtyRoulette* and *ChatBlink*. The unit of analysis for primary data was interviewing forty male and forty female respondents randomly, whereas the tool employed was a structured questionnaire. The responses were collected for extensive survey-based structured questionnaires and further digitalized and transcribed as per the requirement. A comparative analysis was drawn using SPSS. The study further delves into respondents' positionality on the idea and purpose categories varying across gender and age groups through various data analysis techniques such as descriptive frequency, percentage & averages, figurative language, and cross-tabulation-based analysis.

3 Defining Sexting in the Context of Love, Romance, and Intimacy

A commonality that one can find in any society of the world while considering the literature of love genre is that the relationship between love, romance, and intimacy follows a sequential pattern as love blossoms, leads to romantic endeavor, and is subsequently followed by intimacy. Now, there can be an argument that a coincidental tryst (infatuation, causal liaison, fling) can also be the first phase of love. Yes, indeed, it can. For example, pop culture dating sites like *Tinder, Grinder, Bumble*, etc., are platforms for such brief affairs or encounters but can sometimes lead to a long-term conjugal relationship. Nevertheless, the chances of such tryst are rare due to the kind of social system (often conservative towards love) and status (inappropriate in conservative societies) love embodies in many cultures. The act of sexting is defined in numerous ways. Sexting has often been used as a stage of love or as an agent of romanticism. However, in sexting, it is intimacy or bodily desire which prevails dominantly. The act of sexting prioritizes bodily needs, which is not morally wrong, whereas the notion of love and romance fades.

Sexting. Hasinoff [2015, p.1] define sexting as the creation and sharing of personal sexual images or text messages via mobile phones or internet applications, including Facebook, Instagram, Snapchat, and Email. Within the vast informational bubble, i.e., the media, sexting is just one such form wherein sexually explicit images, symbols and messages are shared. However, since mobile phones and the internet make producing and distributing images extremely easy, they provide newer methods of both sexual expressions between partners and sexual harassment. Sexting is also considered as a skill. It is observed that to indulge the opposite gender's interest in the game of sexting; one must know the strategies/tactics to play it cool or to be aware of the do's and don'ts of the game. One must learn to keep things exciting and full of enthusiasm rather than keeping them dull. Overall, one can conclude that sexting is a form of seduction, and the primary form of sexting is built into conversations.

The concept of time and place plays a significant role in sexting. The survey findings also reflected that most of the men prefer nighttime for sexting, whereas most of the women prefer break time such as lunch hour, post, or early working hours. The similarity found between both was in the evening. In the context of the place, most men prefer the comfort of a bedroom environment as visuals are emphasized highly, and women are neutral in the choice of selecting a place apart from video streaming [Sexting Survey Findings 2024].

4 Debates in Love, Romance, and Intimacy

It would be an error to define love as a uniform phenomenon. The forms of love vary from parent to child, between friends, siblings, humans and animals, couples, etc. Sternberg [1988] explains the triangular theory of love and mentions three important components, i.e., *Intimacy* (represents feelings of bond, closeness, and connection), *Passion* (acts as motivation, consists of physical attraction or infatuation), and *Decision or Commitment* (short & long-term commitments). Sternberg further explains that these three components produce eight types of love relationships, i.e., *Non-love, Liking, Infatuation, Empty love, Romantic love, Companionate love, Fatuous love*, and *Consummate love*. However, Lee [1973] talks of six styles of love, i.e., *Eros* (intensely passionate), *Ludus* (more of playing games), *Storge* (affection based on trust), *Pragma* (combination of ludus and storge or, in other words, centered around practicality and compatibility), *Mania* (a compound of eros and ludus; more of jealous and obsessive kind of love), and *Agape* (an amalgam of eros and storage; a selfless love).

The origin of the word romance comes from the Old French language, in which the word '*romanz*' means the people's speech or 'the vulgar tongue.' It is also believed that the popular version of the word romance is a transformed version of chivalry. The available literature on the concept of romance can be traced back to 12th Europe, flourishing through the medieval, renaissance, and romantic eras. Influential works like Malory's le Morte d'Arthur shaped its legacy. In contrast, it declined in the 17th century due to rationalist ideals. However, the 18th-century romantic revival reinvigorated the genre, inspiring Gothic, and historical romances. By the 19th century, it adapted to American themes, maintaining cultural significance [Whitehead and Vinaver 2023]. *Intimacy*, on the other hand, is a state of being intimate, which is marked by the consensual sharing of deeply personal information involving cognitive, affective, and behavioral components. Studies have suggested a positive correlation between a person's well-being and intimacy, as a person with a satisfactory intimate relationship is less exposed to the symptoms of anxiety and depression than those in relationships rated as low in intimacy [Steil 2024].

Apart from academia, the terms love, romance, and intimacy are often used interchangeably in socio-cultural reality. Subsequently, it has created several misunderstandings about conceptual knowledge and has also shaped the manner of practicing the same. The problem here lies in the gap between academia and society. The incapability of a layperson to understand the advanced forms and concepts of love, romance, and intimacy typologies became the prey to ignorance. For a long time, the act of love has been restricted to a particular class (particularly the elite class). A large section of society (non-elite) remained deprived of such fancy practices as the priority was to earn a livelihood. The act of love in every medium, like poem, prose, novel, and narrative, was idealized so fancy that a poor man could not even afford to imagine it. The global market and advanced communication mediums opened the gates to all sections of society, irrespective of their knowledge and understanding of it. The act of sexting is just one of the outcomes of many.

5   Historicity

5.1   Sexting and Love in the Pages of History

Before dwelling much deeper into the debate of sexting influencing the ideas of love, romance and intimacy along with corrupting moral and ethical values of society, it is necessary to look into the historical and situational contexts of both, i.e., sexting and love, as it would help to understand the chronology of the present form it is being practiced and the causal factors serving the practice since its origin and under what circumstances it necessitates the concern which is being considered in the present study.

There is a misconception among people that sexting is a recent practice. To clear the same, one must deconstruct not only the literal meaning but the essence of the act of sexting. If observed closely, the act of sexting is not limited to digital devices only as a medium of communication. Before digital gadgets, painting and writing were early means of communication. People in ancient civilizations used pictorial symbols to convey messages, statues for certain customs and practices, and bark, cloth, and paper to convey their thoughts. These mediums have evolved since. The earliest records of cave paintings are from 30000 BC. The oldest records of carrier/homing pigeons are from 1150 AD. The pigeons were used to deliver letters, short messages, or news [Tosconi 2015; Walcott 1996]. The use of sexting is often seen in letter writing. However, the responses might tend to be delayed due to the slowness of available communication technology. Sexting has always been a part of the human social sphere, but the available opportunities and ever-changing technology at hand have changed the use of age-old means (sculpting a statue) of expressing acts like sexting. For example, passionate love letters from renowned authors like Bukowski to Linda, James Joyce to Nora, or Sartre to Simone reflect upon their deep emotions and personal lives. These letters capture the explicit language used in showcasing their intense and complex relations, like the language used in today's sexting [Elizabeth 2016] (Fig. 1).

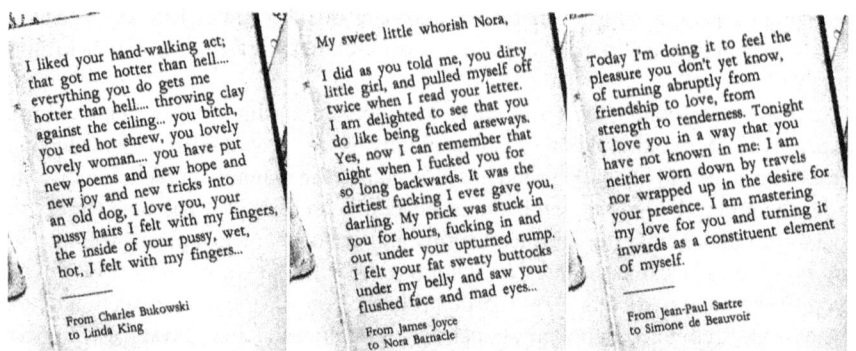

Fig. 1. 15 Steamy love letters by famous authors that are better than sexting in today's age [Elizabeth 2016].

Understanding the chronology, it was 1948 that shaped the course of sexting when the Polaroid camera was invented. The imagery not only helped to increase the visual imagination but also provided a new platform for eroticism. The form of imageries shifted with the first sext codes in the form of numerical after the invention of calculators in the 1970s. The numerals on the devices were used as sext codes, such as 80085 (as Boobs), 8009135 (as Boobies), 8008–7355 (as Boob-less), and 53x as Sex (see Table 1). In the decades of 1980s and 1990s, pagers became significant agents of sexting as alphanumeric sext codes such as 69 (denotes oral sex), 143 (I love you) etc. It is rumored that Neil Papworth sent the first-ever text (like modern times) in the year 1992, and he wrote Merry Christmas, followed by the second text 'Naughty or Nice', though it is not confirmed to be accurate, claims [Tosconi, 2015].

Table 1. Number codes used for sexting.

Number Codes	Visual Outcome	Meaning
80085	80085	Boobs
8008135	8008135	Boobies
8008-7355	8008-7355	Boob-less
53x	53X	Sex
Source: Sexting Survey Findings [2024]. The Authors.		

The new millennium era does bring newness, as the first camera phone was invented in 2000. In 2004, the term 'Sext' appeared in an article named 'Textual Gratification' published in "Globe and Mail." The term was later officially added to the Oxford Dictionary. The later years not only advanced the devices but also connected the world with a web of the internet followed by social-media applications such as Orkut, followed by Facebook in 2004, Snapchat in 2011 and Tinder in 2012. The later apps (Instagram, Telegram, Onlyfans, etc.) opened a plethora of sexting options for people who have access to compatible devices and internet facilities. Therefore, it would be an error to assume sexting is a recent phenomenon while assessing the impact of sexting on society's idea about love and romance.

One must not consider the initial period for writings on the field of love because that would be a colossal error. The earliest records of love in their documented forms can be found in the Old Testament, written in 250 BC. The Bible used only four Greek words for love, i.e., Eros, Storge, Phileo, and Agape. The chronology of love is like sexting. The mediums of expressing love are almost similar throughout time. Now, it depends on how one might have used those mediums to justify it as carriers of love or the other way. For instance, the narrative of love (1775 BC) prevalent among Mari (in Syria) people is associated with reference to the terms of trade, connections, and war. The other narrative of Jaufre Rudel, the Prince of Blaye (1147), who explains his love for his beloved (a countess of Tripoli) in the forms of poems and how he fell for her even without seeing a glimpse of her face and died on his first meeting. There are plenty of such narratives, such as Jeanne-Antoinette of France (1745) who defies the concept of shame and guilt in love, the tale of John Lambton, 1st Earl of Durham and Harriet, the illegitimate daughter of the Earl of Cholmondeley, Scotland (1812) explains the love as enthusiasm and not a skill, and last but not least, the novels by Jane Austen, who provided a different aspect to perceive love with the intention of education, chivalry, a maturity between couples, and present love as a learning process [A Short History of Love 2020].

In the earliest mediums to express their feelings, smog signals were used, and a certain meaning was assigned to certain shapes of the smog. Later, the Greeks created systems to decode smog signals into alphabets or letters. As smog signals are used in clear weather, couples often use them on their camping dates. The age of written messages came after the invention of writing. However, the practice of writing was used earlier in the form of drawing pictures (as it is a common notion that a picture consists of a plethora of words) on the walls, barks, cloth, and later paper. For instance, the ideograms developed by Ancient Sumerians or the Egyptian hieroglyphs became the basis and inspirational sources for our present form of writing, and it is believed love letters or expressing love was a significant thought concern while inventing it. However, writing or putting your thoughts is not enough to convey your feelings or love. Often, one needs the carrier to pass on the information and here come the mentioned mediums. The mediums of carrying these thoughts and parcels of feelings were carrier pigeons, serenades, telegraph, telephone, SMS, and social media applications, and now video calling applications, etc. [How the Expression of Love 2020]. All these mediums helped the idea and practice of expressing feelings for someone, or the notion of love, romance, and intimacy, to survive despite the social barriers.

5.2   Technology and Romance Media: Tools of Sexting

'Think Dirty and Text Naughty' has become the general expression of today's youth while keeping up with their so-called temporary romantic endeavors. Now the question arises in what circumstances of mind; most people rely on practices like sexting instead of love. Is love not enough to provide what it promises, or is the process of love time-taking as it requires patience, which is the opposite in the context of the passionate phase of any youth? The criticality of these thoughts made the understanding of technological advancement vis a-vis romance media as tools of sexting imperative.

The evolution of tools of communication (in chronological order) from Fires, Smoke Signals, and Horns (Prehistoric Times); Pigeon Post, Hydraulic and Maritime Semaphores (4th and 15th Century); Signal Lamps (till 1867); Newspapers (since 1800s); Telegraph (since 1838); Telephone (common since 1876); Edison's Acoustic Phono-graphs (1877); Tesla's Wireless Telegraphy (since 1893); Radio (since early 1800s); Transcontinental Telephone service; commercialized radio services from 1927 onwards; experimental videophones of the 1920s; mobile telephones which were devised specially for automobiles (1946); discovery of Fiber-Optic Telecommunication in 1970s; in Post 1970s, Television became common household item (first invented in 1927) followed by computer and desktops; invention of first mobile phone in 1973; email services in the 1990s with instant messaging service; early 2000s delivers services like widespread internet access along with social-media applications in following years, to the video communication services with the help of smartphones [Holtzapple 2015] has altered the speed of communication in human society.

The urge for speed has not changed people's behavior; it psychologically affects their decisions. Anyone who lacks spontaneity is considered old-school or out of fashion. The devices feed on the instant feature, and the aspects like love or a romantic endeavor, face ignorance due to lengthy procedures and time-consuming processes. Being in love or opting for the idea of love is often discarded before even the first stage of love. Sexting provides the instant fulfilment of bodily desires, overshadowing the soul's pleasure through love and romance. Even the romance media, like pictures and songs of today, prioritizes the bodily expressions of desires rather than opting for romance through the unexpected/uncertain process and outcome of love. Songs like *"Fifth Harmony's, Work from Home"*[1]; *"Bruno Mars's, Locked Out of Heaven"*[2]; *"Demi Lovato's, Cool for the Summer"*,[3]; Trey Songz, Dive In",[4] etc. are examples of expressing such bodily desires [Kaufman 2016].

5.3 Love, Romance, Intimacy, and Sexting in Indian Society

In the context of romanticism, it is generally believed that women are fond of words and men are of images or visuals. It was the 10th Century when the trend of love marriage in Western societies was welcomed full-heartedly. Still, in most parts of the Middle East and South-Asian societies, the conservative approach remains pervasive. However, it does not mean these regions have no tales of eternal and selfless love. There is folklore about love, and the ideas of love are considered very pious and sacred in these societies. Indian society is full of such a multi-cultural ethos. The tragic love tales of *Heer and Ranjha, Shirin and Farhad, Laila and Majnu,* and *Mirza and Sahiba* are deeply rooted and celebrated among people. Although these tales are used in both ways of idealization, piousness, and the selflessness of love and used as a lesson to learn by taunting someone not to fall in love in other words, these tales are also used as examples of struggles and hardships that one faces in the ways of love. For instance, in the middle belt of India, the wife's sister is often symbolically considered a half-wife, and the brother-in-law (sister's husband) is usually allowed to tease his wife's sister with naughty tease. Indian society is blended with many cultures and is primarily traditional and conservative. However, globalization has provided a space of openness as people living in cities are open to modernity. Nevertheless, most people behave conservatively, as one cannot just let away the kind of social capital and social identity. Moving on from who you are and what identity you associate with is a quite different game in Indian society. A common expression prevalent in India is that it is not two people that marry but two families, two communities, and so on. So being married is all about the honor of the family and community, and at times, it surpasses regions.

However, despite all that, Indian society has created space for all kinds of practices and activities irrespective of their taboo or derogatory status in society. A society with millions of Gods and Goddesses has a system of providing everyone with an identity as per their birth and later by their profession, i.e., a caste identity one is born with and a class identity. The concept of honor, purity, and pollution prevails predominantly in Indian society. For example, the same society allowed eunuchs to serve in royal palaces as Queen's maids or perform dances known as Mujra, and sometimes they also served as dance tutors. In some regions, eunuchs are worshipped, considered well-wishers, etc.;

---

[1] "Let's put it into motion, I'mma give you a promotion, I'll make it feel like a vacay, turn the bed into an ocean" (Kaufman 2016).

[2] "You bring me to my knees, you make me testify, You can make a sinner change his ways, Open up your gates 'cause I can't wait to see the light, And right there is where I wanna stay" (Kaufman 2016).

[3] Take me down into your paradise, Don't be scared cause I'm your body type, Just something that we wanna try, 'Cause you and I, We're cool for the summer" (Kaufman 2016).

[4] "Drip, baby we don't need no towel, I'mma be the one who rub your body now, Won't drown ain't even coming up for air now, I just keep my head down (down, down), Swim for days, I can doggy paddle all kind of ways" (Kaufman 2016)

it is the same society that worships the Lingam (a male-genital) as a form of Lord Shiva [Britannica 2024]; a society that allows the public display of nudity and bodily-eroticism carved in the form of statues in Khajuraho Temples in Madhya Pradesh State of India [Vijayakumar 2017]; and Vātsyāyana [1988], an ancient Indian philosopher (2nd or 3rd Century) who wrote the book *Kamasutra* (the most ancient book on human sexuality). To conclude, the examples justify the existence of a society in which love is accepted in both forms as pious, sacred, and a practice to worship, along with its inferior and tabooed status. The imprints of sexting are visible in its premature stage in the forms of statues, literature on human sexuality, and pleasurable activities, while the ideas of love were also propounded but in a confined way and under surveillance.

6 Sexting and the Trio of Axes (Ideology, Opportunity and Vandalism)

Till now, the paper attempted to establish an understanding as to how sexting has always been a part of human society in various forms with the help of different means of communication throughout time irrespective of the typology of the social system or, in other words, the act of sexting prevails through various customs of society despite being modern or conservative. Within such context, the origin of sexting and love, as well as its historical and theoretical contexts, were mentioned along with reference to Indian society to validate the point that sexting has overshadowed the ideas of love due to its advancement and transformed forms. In contrast, love has been confined in its old, classical, highly idealized form, from where it can be only perceived but is challenging to implement. This position or perception about love has created a space for practices like sexting to predominate and prevail over all other forms of romanticism.

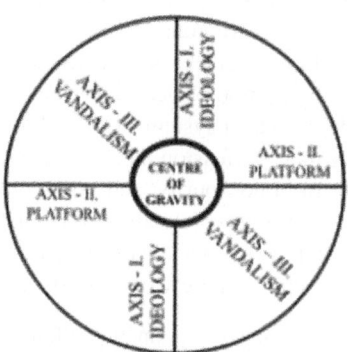

Fig. 2. Sexting and trio of axes.

Let us understand it with a practical example of how this trio of axes works in the context of sexting influencing the notion of love and romance. Let us think of an aircraft and how its axes work. The flight is controlled by three axes of rotation, i.e., Vertical (Yaw, steers the aircraft left and right), Longitudinal (allows an aircraft to roll sideways and helps aircraft to turn), and Lateral (Pitch, which provides stability and helps an aircraft to climb and descend) along with a central point of gravity. At this significant point, all aircraft weights are considered to be [Aeronautics Research Mission Directorate 2010]. Similar is the case of sexting and trio axes. Figure 2 shows Axis-I Ideology, Axis-II as a Platform or Opportunity, and Axis-III as Vandalism. Concerning the framework of sexting as an ideology is the idea of controlling sexuality, with values of maintaining the traditionality of cultures and with the purpose of controlling the youth and keeping them under restricted surveillance. As a platform of opportunity: the virtual space providing equality from the discriminated social reality or social identity (caste/class/ethnicity/race, etc.), an opportunity to transcend cultural barriers and perform certain forbidden activities or, in other words, a freedom square. Sexting as a vandal impacts the ideas of love, romance, and intimacy due to the struggle of the previous two axes. One (ideology) maintains its course by imposing a particular ideological agenda (through technologically advanced equipment and media), whereas the other (a platform of opportunity) is on the run from the same.

6.1 Sexting as an Ideology

Allen [1975] discusses three significant components of ideology (i.e., ideas, values, and purpose), propounding that any ideology is channelized based on these three elements, and to assess the same, one must identify the hidden agendas behind any ideology. Sexting as an ideology, as mentioned above, embodied the idea of controlling sexuality with the help of values such as maintaining the traditionality of cultures so that sexting will remain taboo in the public sphere, a matter of the private sphere, and with a purpose to control and exercise power, people are being confined in the space of surveillance or under restrictions. For example, on one side, love is considered pious and sacred, a matter of essence and soulful harmony. On the other side, sexting is promoted but confined to a private sphere so that people can behave in a particular way and not transgress the ethical and moral ethos of the social system.

On the one hand, society offers a space to practice a certain form of love. On the other hand, it also opposes the advanced forms of the same. In other words, society does not oppose practicing the initial phases of love but demands certification to advanced stages such as romance and intimacy. Society's notion changes abruptly as the stage of love is identified with ideas of romantic endeavor or intimacy. The idea of controlling human sexuality not only grants the power to control every being but also provides space for other forms of practices that come at lower risks of a social outcast, humiliation, and an escape route [Foucault 1978]. The act of sexting is an outcome of a confined and highly idealized form of love introduced among the masses to perform and control sexuality so that the masses will not revolt as they are being fed with easy access to bodily desires. We humans live under the impression that privacy is being maintained, but in social reality, it is not. In the context of sexting, our first decision to connect to someone stranger or known automatically discards the idea of privacy. To convince our moral standards, we tend to use certain digital passwords and call it privacy, but in actual terms, it is conditional privacy offered by super-structures working behind these webs of social systems.

6.2 Sexting as an Opportunity

Sexting as a platform of opportunity is the most effective axis as it provides a space for all discriminated identities in multi-cultural societies. Kumar [2019] talks of such platforms while dealing with the issues of marginalized masculinities, stating that platforms like social media provide equal opportunities to all, irrespective of their socio-cultural backgrounds and provide an escape route from their discriminated day-to-day lives. This kind of platform not only offers the chance of being treated equally but also helps to build self-confidence among socially introverts and people socially positioned at the lower rung of society. Several studies have suggested that the act of sexting helps resolve the issues of loneliness and improves self-confidence [Tosconi 2015; Davidson 2015; Mishra 2021]. The studies also suggest how identity no longer becomes an issue as it cuts across social realities (with the help of a device). In contrast, the previous forms of communication, like letter writing, always deemed the requirements of identity (preferably esteemed), be it social, economic, or biological. It is also suggested that sexting works as an escape route and reduces all the burden of social responsibilities that might be a thing to worry about in case of commitment, from all the daily chores of boredom and dullness of life. For example, it provides the option to choose a variety of items to taste without purchasing a complete package or meal [Tosconi 2015]. However, the question arises: if sexting is not so harmful, what is there to worry about? Is sexting even affecting the ideas of love, romance, intimacy, or the very youth? In that case, yes, there is a need to worry about the practice of sexting.

6.3 Sexting as Vandalism

The ideas of love and romance remained in ivory towers for an extended period with restrictive access to those who were resourceful enough (not only materialistic but also resourceful of thought). Meanwhile, the rest were not able to afford the idea of falling in love. For the rest, intimacy prevailed and that too in the most obscene and vulgar representation. Upon all that, at times, what burdened most of the commoners was their day-to-day struggle to ensure livelihood and survive famine, diseases, and tyrannies of war. Amid all these crises, love was highly idealized, presented as the most sacred, pious, fancied, expensive and full of challenging quests by certain sections of society. Even love itself could not get rid of the class structure of rich and poor, high as regal and low as destitute, etc., as the narratives of love were not only tricky to create but also restricted fantasies.

Sexting became the *'less costly version'* of love, which has been dormant until now. The moment it gained the momentum of public liking and access, the previous two axes came into the race of competition. Sexting not only delegitimizes the chivalry of classical love and romanticism but also provides a platform for all the masses, allowing them to perform certain tabooed practices of society. This kind of transgression concerns the ideological structure of the social system (as earlier forms of sexting were oral and open in public in the forms of painting, songs, and letter writings), and they started controlling it by providing an umbrella of privacy. The means of communication were highlighted and devised to practice such forms privately, and the public display of such gestures was labelled taboo again. Hence, the struggle between the two axes created a vandal-like situation.

7   Sexting, Love, Romance, and Intimacy: The Survey Findings

The act of sexting has been criticized for its blunder consequences by not only parents but also by legislators. As mentioned before, all the privacy in such conduct is of the conditional type, which can be problematic. For instance, blackmailing could be a significant effect of indulging in sexting, as one can get easily blackmailed for sharing their photographs. In some cases, it has also led to suicides. It has been proven in a study that 17% of sexters share the messages they receive with others, and 55% of those shares with more than one person. More than 60% of all teen sexters who have sent nude images admit that they were pressured to do it at least once. 15% of teens who have sent nude images of themselves send these messages to people they have never met but know these strangers from the internet [Tosconi 2015]. Conspiracy, identity theft and extortion, stealing pictures and taking revenge, slut-shaming, and public defamation are a few of the many negative consequences of the act of sexting. Despite such vices, it mandates exploring the reasons why people still prefer such platforms. Moreover, who these people are, and what their take on such positionality of sexting is. The survey findings revealed that people between the age group of thirteen to early fifties were highly indulged in sexting through online platforms (Table 2).

Table 2.   Categories of people indulged in sexting.

Sr. No	Visual Outcome	Meaning
1	Kids (Minor)	Following popular culture (becoming the prey of trend)
2	Adolescents	Mostly boredom
3	Bachelors	Boredom and satisfying sexual desires
4	Unmarried Couples	Distance relationships and social barriers
5	Married Couples	To spice things up in a monotonous lifestyle
6	Strangers	Socially-introvert, boredom and sexually aroused

Source: Sexting Survey Findings [2024]. The Authors

Sometimes, it is not only human desires that drive us to indulge in such practices but also the means around us. For example, studies suggest that the available technology also creates an urge among people to behave in a certain way, or it can be said that humans, as sexual beings, create the means to cater for their sexuality [Tosconi 2015]. As earlier means of expressing intimate feelings and desires, letters, pictures, and paintings are replaced by emoticons and emoticon phrases (see Table 3).

Figure 3 categorizes respondents' perceptions of the reasons behind preferring sexting based on gender and age groups. The study findings show that both genders significantly prioritized "escape from temporary boredom" as the primary reason. Still, male respondents displayed a higher tendency to engage in sexting to "satisfy sexual arousal." Across the age groups, respondents belonging to the younger age group (i.e., below 19) prioritized "escape from temporary boredom", whereas those above 39 age group highly cited "satisfy sexual arousal" as the primary reason to prefer sexting.

Table 3. Emoticons and emoticon phrases are being used for sexting.

Symbols	Emoticon	Meaning
Eggplant / Hotdog	/	Penis
Peace Sign / Taco	/	Vagina
Peach		Butt
OK Hand		Anal sex
Pointed Finger		Fingering
Sweat Droplets		Orgasm
Heart + Bone		Expressing the desire to have sex
Admission Ticket + Woman Dancing + Eyes		Asking for striptease
Tongue + Taco + Sweat Droplets		Going down
Lips + Eggplant + Fireworks		Blowjob until orgasm
Waving Hand + Peach + Devilish face		Pleasure giving spanking
OK Hand + Pointed Finger		Asking for penetrative sex
Banana + Donut		Expression of desire for anal sex
Snake + Tulip		Losing virginity

Source: Sexting Survey Findings [2024]. The Authors.

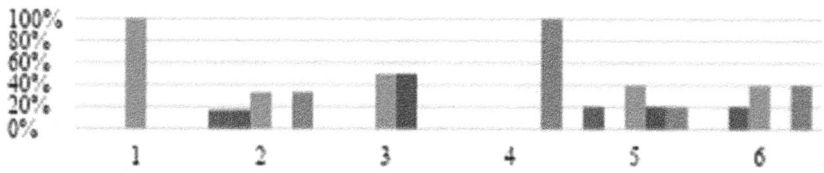

■ Boredom and Sexual Arousal
■ Escape from Loneliness and being Introvert
■ Escape from Temporary Boredom
■ Escape from Boredom and Satisfying the Sexual Arousal
■ Satsifying the Sexual Arousal

Fig. 3. Gender and age-group-wise, respondents' perceptions of the idea behind preferring sexting.

Figure 4 shows the respondent's take on the purpose behind the sexting. Across genders, male respondents sided with having some company, whereas female respondents deemed both pleasure and company. Across age groups, respondents belonging to the younger age group (i.e., below 19) prioritized "primarily company", whereas those above 39 age group highly cited "pleasure" as the primary reason.

Popular discourse often refers to sexting as a form of child pornography or as part of the cyberbullying epidemic and adult sexting as celebrity infidelity and political scandal. Sexting is perhaps so frightening and compelling precisely because it is inherently liberatory. Nevertheless, considering this new technology as the root cause of these complications may not be accurate. Such recurring moments of anxiety surrounding new communication technology have uniquely gendered dimensions; the fear that girls

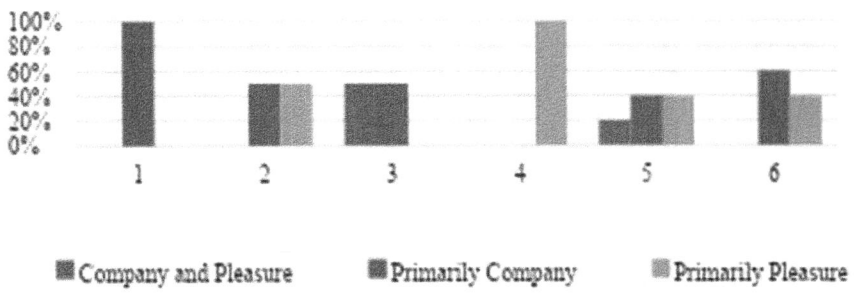

Fig. 4. Gender and age-group-wise respondent's perception regarding the purpose behind preferring sexting.

will use these technologies in incorrect, frivolous, sexually inappropriate, and dangerous ways is not new and was also echoed with the advent of the telegraph, telephone, and the internet [Cassell and Cramer 2008]. So, if freedom for teenage girls is defined as freedom from sexuality, then the technology that enables sexting must look like a massive failure, and the blame for these dashed hopes surrounding the new media can fall on girls. Girls are still blamed for sexting. As a result, girls are seen to have agency that is simultaneously constructed to be lacking in that their choices are seen as inauthentic or not intentional [Datta 2022].

However, such notions can have a range of problematic side effects, especially since they can lead to vagueness in the distinction between consensual sexting and malicious privacy violations, and they imply that girls who create images should be the focus of educational and legal interventions. Sexting is neither inherently liberatory nor is it necessarily the result of coercion. The act of sharing an explicit photo of oneself can be done under extreme duress or with as much free will as any other choice [Jensen et al. 2024; Halder and Basu 2024; Chitra and Jebaseelan 2024]. The problem with the mindset that all girls who engage in sexting are passive victims is that it leads to a derecognition of their agency and the devaluation of their choice. The alternative explanations that people tend to offer for sexting fit with dominant ideas that girls' sexual agency primarily consists of their refusal of male advances. It would disrupt such norms to provide a more straightforward explanation for why some girls might sext, such as "because they enjoy it" [Hasinoff 2015, p.4]. Girls' active sexuality is often assumed to indicate some deviant pathology or victimization by peers or mass culture, while teen boys' sexual interests and behaviors are often expected and tolerated.

Regarding respondents' understanding of love and romance, both male and female respondents' responses kept wandering among varied interpretations (see Figs. 5 and 6). Among females, it ranges from in-depth connection, signifying emotional bonding as a peculiar feature, to acceptance, reliance, and a need beyond physical pleasure. Meanwhile, for males, logical and reason-based blending superseded everything else. Similarly, in the context of romance, the responses kept circling the same bush, from consensual and affectionate intercourse to in-depth connection, romantic persona, officiation of a relationship, reliance, etc. Although, the term romance was often interchanged with intimacy (romantic endeavors) and love (emotional bonding).

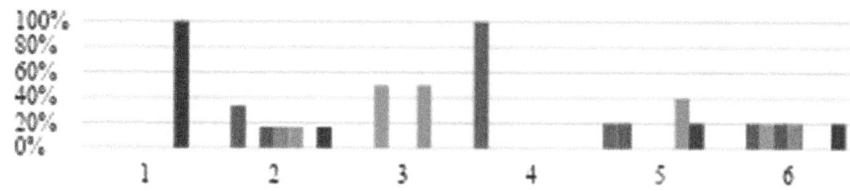

■ A Binary Concept
■ A Binary Concept and In-depth Connection
▨ Acceptance
■ An Oddity
▨ Beyond Physical Pleasure

Fig. 5. Gender and age group-wise respondent's perception regarding love.

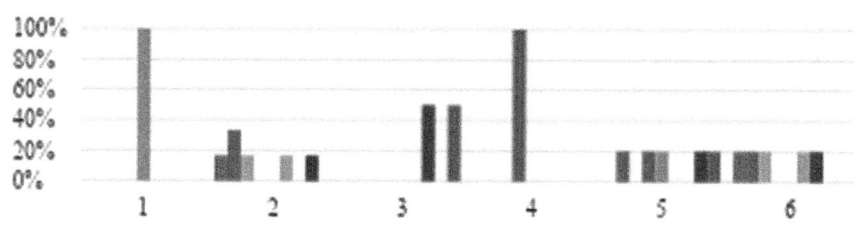

■ Consensual and Affectionate Intercourse
■ In-depth Connection and Affectionate Intercourse
▨ In-depth Connection and Bodily Infatuation
■ Officiating a Relationship
▨ Reliance
▨ Romantic Persona
■ Sense of Freedom through Acceptance
■ Strengthening the Relationship
■ Varying Connection

Fig. 6. Gender and age group-wise respondent's perception regarding romance.

Across the age group, an imprint of a traditional mindset was observed as respondents belonging to the younger age group (i.e., below 19) interpreted love as a binary concept and positioned romance along a sense of 'reliance', whereas above 39 age group highly termed love as 'a binary concept' and interpreted romance a process to 'officiate a relationship'.

Too much reliance and addiction to sexting and pretense to get the feeling of being loved might affect the essence of romanticism and love. In a study conducted by Davidson [2014, pp.25–26], girls often described the role of sexting in the facilitation of creating a specific intimate relationship with a member of the opposite sex, mainly within the sphere of romantic relationships. Romantic relationships, meaning the desire for one-to-one intimate connections with one another, were central to girls' thinking about why sexting occurred. The cluster of associations related to sexting and relationships illustrated how sexting could be intertwined with multiple phases of a relationship, from the identification of potential romantic interest and exploration of the relationship to a means of sustaining and expressing the relationship. It generates an understanding of the gendered positioning within the context of sexting; it paints a complicated picture of sexual, emotional, and physical desires and the ways these may intersect with the act of sending a sexually descriptive text or image to another during a relationship. As the objects of desire and dispensers of sexual compliments, they hold a certain power over them. Sexting was one means, among many communicative approaches, by which one signals desire and seeks to maintain attention and ward off othercomers. As this passage suggests, the negotiations occur within couples but also extend to one's most trusted group of peers. Girls overwhelmingly stated that boys ask girls for sexual photos far more often than the other way around [Sharma et al., 2021]. Moreover, some boys may send sexual photos to girls without any request to do so. However, in complex relationship interactions, sexting becomes embedded and saying yes to sexting may be a way of saying no to actual sex. After all, one-on-one relationships are both private and public concerns, private as they are established between a couple, but public as that relationship is recognized by their social world and its shifting concerns concerning social status, power, and control. These impressions were also reflected in survey findings.

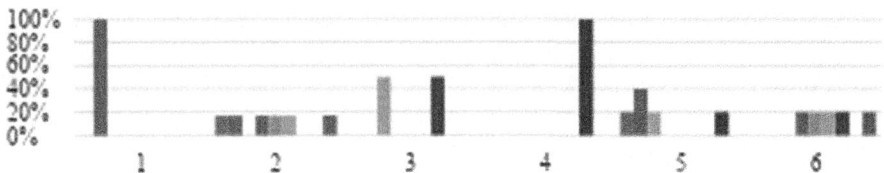

■ A Form of Lust
■ Affectionate Intercourse with the Right Person
▨ An Act in Nudity
■ Being Intimate (Physically)
▨ Having Intercourse
▨ In-depth Connection and Affectionate Intercourse
■ Physical and Emotional Surrender
■ Physical and Emotional Surrender along with Sense of Self-Value Enhanced
▨ Physical Attraction

Fig. 7. Gender and age-group-wise respondent's perception regarding intimacy.

In the context of intimacy, the survey findings indicated that both genders highly valued intimacy when it involved affection with the right partner. However, males, compared to females slightly, termed intimacy as a form of lust and females' responses were found to be more conscious of nudity in an intimate context. Across age groups, emotional connections and meaningful relationships were significantly emphasized, especially among younger and female respondents. The physical aspect of intimacy resonated more among the 20–38 and 30–38 age groups. The older age groups and females placed more weight on emotional and value-based descriptions compared to the younger age group (see Fig. 7).

8 Conclusion

The sexual arena has provided a space in Indian society to co-habitat both concepts of love as a pious form and a degenerate concept. Additionally, it has socio-culturally institutionalized an accord of such management. As mentioned earlier, these mediums of communication have evolved over the ages. Above all, historically, Indian society has always given patronage to these tabooed practices like bodily-eroticism and nudity in the form of *Mujra, Kamasutra*, etc. Undoubtedly, there will always be a threat of harmful effects of sexting, and at some point, in time, the wider society will slogan for the same. However, for now, it would be a rush and an error to label sexting entirely with a negative connotation as societies in developing nations like India are still grappling with 2nd and 3rd generations of technological advancement. The perception of harmful consequences for one society might be modernity for another. It might be a violation for one section and a liberation for another. Therefore, it is better to focus on the potentiality of the subject to figure out the preventive measures.

To think that sexting alone is impacting the ideas of love, romance, and intimacy, along with the corruption of youth, would be a colossal error. Similarly, to assume that it is a recent phenomenon. Concepts like love have always been in crisis since the beginning as they provide a utopian space, and such space does not correlate well with social reality. Hence, there is always a chance of clashes and conflicts. The elite standardization of love and the complexities of love quests made it alien for commoners. The prolonged absence of love from the masses made commoners see love as a taboo, a violation, a forbidden practice, and a waste of time and resources. Similarly, sexting might seem a recent term, but in practice, it is embedded in history. It might have witnessed the ages of dormancy but remained prevalent. The respondents believed the extinction of love would lead to the downfall of humanity.

However, one must also consider that crisis is not only the end but also a promise of the new dawn. If sexting prevails and love vanishes, there will be a society that requires sexting and not love or vice versa. One must also think that society must have created a need that deemed sexting over the ideas of love and romance.

For the time being, it is necessary to investigate causal factors, the web of supra-structures on which such practices are thriving. It is vitally important to investigate and bring into light the purposes and ideas behind such practices that are prevalent underneath. Understanding the historical and situational context is necessary, and it is imperative to establish accord between the two, i.e., sexting and love. To conclude, society has not yet developed an idea of a centre of gravity, and the absence of the same has created an imbalance in the structural form. Moreover, unlimited, and unchecked use of such devices causes problems and affects other channels, such as love, romance, or intimacy. The negative impacts of unfiltered access (transgressing the boundaries of mental and physical age) to globally connected technology and gadgets have not remained a trove to discover. A balanced approach needs to be devised to establish accord between the two; either love must be brought down from its highly idealized form to all the masses, or sexting (with sound security) must be given a place in society. Nevertheless, in both cases, society will remain the same as the old, and that is why it is the society that needs to be changed. Society must address the need for individual-based adult education, inculcating sex sensitization in the school curriculum at early ages and providing digital education and awareness in both rural and urban to individuals more prone to these crimes, such as women, young girls/boys, and children. Society must leave behind its tabooed cocoon.

References

1. A Short History of Love. The School of Life. https://www.theschooloflife.com/article/a-short-history-of-love/. Accessed 24 Feb 2023
2. Aeronautics Research Mission Directorate: Axes/Control Surfaces in Principles of Flight. National Aeronautics and Space Administration, NASA (2010)
3. Allen, V.L.: Social Analysis: A Marxist Critique and Alternative. Longman, London and New York (1975)
4. The Editors of Encyclopedia Britannica: Sandstone Lingam. Encyclopedia Britannica. Encyclopædia Britannica, Inc. (2024)
5. Cassell, J., Cramer, M.: High Tech or High Risk: Moral Panics about Girls Online. MacArthur Foundation, Digital Media and Learning Initiative (2008)
6. Davidson, J.: Sexting: Gender and Teens. Springer (2015)
7. Drouin, M.: Sexting. In: Encyclopedia Britannica. Encyclopedia Britannica, Inc (2018)
8. Elizabeth, P.: 15 Steamy Love Letters by Famous Authors that are Better than Sexting in Today's Age. ScoopWhoop, ScoopWhoop Media Pvt Ltd (2016)
9. Foucault, M.: The History of Sexuality: Volume I: An Introduction. Hurley R. Pantheon Books, New York (1978)
10. Hasinoff, A.A.: Sexting Panic: Rethinking Criminalization, Privacy, and Consent. University of Illinois Press, Chicago (2015)
11. Holtzapple, A.: Evolution of Communication: 1800s and 1900s. One Call Now (2015)
12. How the Expression of Love Has Survived through Time. PeN. Accessed 3 Jan 2023
13. Kaufman, G.: Songs with filthy lyrics: 11 hits that are nastier than you thought. Billboard (2016). https://www.billboard.com/music/pop/songs-filthy-lyrics-dirty-7423219/. Accessed 2 Jan 2023
14. Kumar, A.: Moustache for all: do you have? Can you have? A study of roles, stereotype, crisis of masculinity and identity. Masculinities Soc. Change **8**(3), 276–306 (2019)
15. Lee, J.A.: Colours of Love: An Exploration of the Ways of Loving. New Press, Toronto (1973)
16. Mishra, S.: Digital Cultures, 1st edn. Routledge, London (2021)
17. Sternberg, R. J.: Triangulating Love' in the Psychology of Love. In: Sternberg, R.J., Barnes, M. (eds.) The Psychology of Love, 119–138. Yale University Press, New Haven, CT (1988)
18. Steil, J. M.: Intimacy. In: Encyclopedia Britannica. Encyclopedia Britannica, Inc. (2024)
19. Tosconi, J.: Addicted to Sexting. Documentary. IMDb (2015)
20. Vātsyāyana.: The Kamasutra of Vatsyayana. Lustre Press, New Delhi (1988)
21. Vijayakumar, S.: The Sacred and the Sensual: Experiencing Eroticain Temples of Khajuraho. Via [Tourism Review], 11–12 (2017)
22. Walcott, C.: Pigeon homing: observations, experiments and confusions. J. Exp. Biol. **199**(1), 21–27 (1996)
23. Whitehead, F., Vinaver, E.: Romance. Encyclopedia Britannica, Inc, Encyclopedia Britannica (2023)

24. Chitra, J.A., Jebaseelan, A.U.S.: The influence of social media on sexting among youth along with their emotional well-being. Int. J. Aquat. Sci. **12**(2), 512 (2021)
25. Sharma, M.K., Anand, N., Kumar, K.: Constructing the understanding of teenagers' deviant use of cyberspace. Int. J. Soc. Psych. **67**(8), 1068–1071 (2021)
26. Halder, D., Basu, S.: Digital dichotomies: navigating non-consensual image-based harassment and legal challenges in India. Inf. Commun. Technol. Law **34**(2), 163–186 (2024)
27. Jensen, M.C., et al.: College students' coercive sexting and intimate partner violence perpetration in shorter- and longer-term relationships. Violence Vict. 39(5) (2024)
28. Datta, B.: Sexual expression, law and media in contemporary India. In: Narrain, S. (ed.) Acts of Media: Law and Media in Contemporary India, Politics and Society in India and the Global South, pp. 80–97. Sage, New Delhi (2022)

Empowering Education Through Interactive Social Robots in Museums to Enhance Soft Skills and Meaningful Learning Experiences: A Literature Review

Anna Teresa Musicco[ID] and Valentina Berardinetti[✉][ID]

University of Foggia, via Arpi 176, 71121 Foggia, Italy
{anna.musicco,valentina.berardinetti}@unifg.it

Abstract. This paper analyses the use of social robotics in museums to enhance educational programmes and create innovative edutainment experiences. In particular, it explores how social robots, used as interactive and customisable guides, can facilitate meaningful learning and the development of soft skills such as communication, collaboration and critical thinking. Through the analysis of literature and real case studies, it emerges how social robots are able to engage visitors, adapting to their needs and offering tailor-made educational paths. The main research question investigates how social robotics can enrich museum educational programmes, enhancing both the visitor experience and the educational value of visits. The research also outlines future perspectives on the integration of robotics in museums, reflecting on the benefits, challenges and implications for the cultural and educational sector.

Keywords: museum didactics · educational robotics · meaningful learning

1 Introduction

The world is undergoing a profound digital transformation, fundamentally altering how we access and process information. This shift enables us to both acquire knowledge and generate new information, which are crucial drivers of the transformation. The integration of Information and Communication Technology (ICT) has permanently reshaped society [1]. As noted by Beran [2], children are increasingly engaging with advanced technological devices during their playtime.

Over the last few years, there has been growing interest in the use of robotics in education, leading to numerous efforts to incorporate robotics into school curricula, ranging from kindergarten to high school levels [3]. Recent research [4–6] has shown that

---

For the purposes of scientific recognition, although the authors revised the entire contribution together, the introduction and paragraphs 2, 4, 5, 5.1, 5.2 are to be attributed to Anna Teresa Musicco; paragraphs 3, 5.3, 5.4, 6, the conclusions and the abstract are to be attributed to Valentina Berardinetti.

G. A. Toto (Ed.): ICS exchange 2024, CCIS 2521, pp. 51–62, 2025.
https://doi.org/10.1007/978-3-032-03021-4_4

incorporating robots promotes interactive learning, increasing children's engagement in educational activities.

Socially Interactive Robots (SAR) are designed to engage with humans through natural communication modalities such as speech, gestures, and facial expressions, making them distinct from other types of robots used in educational settings, which often focus on mechanical tasks or simple programming interactions [7]. SARs are equipped with artificial intelligence that allows them to process and respond to social cues, enabling more personalized and meaningful interactions [8]. Unlike traditional educational robots, which primarily serve as tools for teaching STEM skills, SARs are employed to foster social and emotional learning, enhancing the development of soft skills such as empathy, communication, and collaboration [9]. Additionally, as embodied agents, SARs not only use motion and communicative gestures to enhance their social presence but also possess the capability to manipulate objects while collaborating with humans [10]. These robots are particularly valuable in informal learning environments, such as museums, where their ability to interact socially with diverse audiences makes learning more engaging and accessible [11]. With a focus on the potential of Socially Interactive Robots (SAR) for museum education, the purpose of this study is to conduct a literature review on the use of social robots as an innovative tool to engage students in edutainment programs in museums [12], in order to improve the visitor experience and the educational value of visits.

2   The Use of Robotics in Education

Educational robotics falls under the broader category of "social robotics," where the term "social" implies the presence of interactive relationships [13]. Social robots play a crucial role in Human-Robot Interaction (HRI), focusing on how robots can support and enhance soft skills [14]. Socially Assistive Robotics (SAR), as defined by FeilSeifer & Mataric [15], is a field at the intersection of Assistive Robotics (AR) and Socially Interactive Robotics (SIR). It operates on two guiding principles: first, the interaction between the user and the robot should not require mediation by an operator, and second, it must be intuitive. Furthermore, social robots need to adapt their behaviours to the routines and needs of users [16]. To achieve this, it is essential to integrate Artificial Intelligence (AI) systems and Machine Learning (ML) into SAR, allowing the robots to learn and adjust based on user interactions [17].

Designed to engage with humans naturally, social robots exhibit behaviours that lead to positive outcomes in various areas, including education and didactics [18]. In the educational context, social robots act as pedagogical or intelligent agents aimed at supporting both learning and teaching [10].

Social robots not only enhance technical learning but also promote the development of soft skills such as communication, empathy, and teamwork, which are essential for modern education [9]. Recent research highlights the importance of social robots in fostering interactive learning environments that go beyond traditional instructional methods, actively engaging students in critical thinking and problem-solving activities [19].

Moreover, educational robots equipped with AI and advanced sensor technologies can adapt their interactions based on real-time feedback from students, providing personalized educational experiences. This adaptability is particularly important in promoting inclusive education, where robots can offer tailored support to learners with diverse needs, including those with disabilities [20]. Studies have shown that these robots contribute to improving student motivation and engagement, particularly in STEM subjects, by creating interactive and hands-on learning experiences [21].

The potential for social robots to bridge the gap between traditional education and digital fluency is significant, making them valuable tools in both formal and informal educational settings [22, 23].

3 Museum Education

Educational robotics is emerging as a significant opportunity in museum education, with the potential to transform the way learning is experienced, making it more accessible, inclusive and interactive. Museums are spaces of great cultural and educational value and making them accessible to all is an essential goal. Educational robotics offers a unique opportunity to break down barriers to accessibility and create engaging experiences for every visitor. It is an interdisciplinary field that uses robots as a teaching tool to make learning practical, fun and immersive. In museums, this approach becomes a valuable tool for expanding audiences, encouraging greater participation and enriching the cultural and educational experience.

In a museum context, educational robots can improve accessibility in various ways. They can offer mobility support, following visitors and guiding them through spaces, providing information and answering questions in real time. This type of assistance is particularly useful for people with mobility impairments or the elderly, who can move around independently and enjoy the museum experience with greater safety and serenity. In addition, educational robots allow remote access to the museum, enabling people who cannot physically visit the building to explore it virtually; this is a great advancement for people who are hospitalised or severely disabled, who can thus participate in an authentic cultural experience even at a distance [24].

The use of educational robotics in museums also promotes social inclusion, as it facilitates the participation of people with cognitive or sensory disabilities. For individuals with autism spectrum disorders or other cognitive difficulties, robots, programmed to adapt to different levels of interaction, offer safe, interactive support that adapts to the specific needs of the user. This overcomes communication and social barriers, making interaction an enriching and affordable experience for all. Multisensory robots can also enrich the experience of people with visual or hearing disabilities, thanks to their ability to convert visual stimuli into sound or tactile signals, allowing for a more complete and engaging museum discovery [25].

Educational robotics also offers visitors an opportunity for experiential learning, making the educational process more hands-on and engaging. Museum robots can guide visitors through interactive simulations, e.g. recreating historical moments or scientific processes, thanks to a game-based approach that makes learning fun and stimulating. This methodology not only attracts the attention of the public, but also improves their understanding and retention of information. Moreover, museums can organise educational workshops where children and teenagers can assemble and programme robots, exploring scientific or historical concepts in a hands-on way and stimulating critical thinking, creativity and collaboration.

An important step, therefore, in the process of making education accessible is through a continuous dialogue between technology and culture.

4 Research Methodology

The literature review was carried out following specific steps. First, relevant literature was collected from academic databases, including SCOPUS, Web of Science (WOS), and Google Scholar, ensuring comprehensive coverage of studies on social robots in museum settings. After gathering the sources, a critical evaluation was carried out to assess the quality and relevance of each study to the research topic. Particular attention was given to articles containing case studies conducted with social robots in museums.

Next, the selected studies were organized based on the key themes they addressed. These themes included the integration of edutainment in museum programs, the development of soft skills through interactive experiences, the design of meaningful learning experiences, and the use of social robots as tour guides. This thematic organization helped structure the review and facilitated a deeper understanding of the various applications of social robots in museums.

Following this, the results and conclusions of the literature were analysed and synthesized to identify current trends, research gaps, and new perspectives in the field. This allowed for a clear identification of how social robots contribute to educational objectives in informal learning environments like museums.

The data were ultimately synthesized using a narrative approach, which is presented in the Results section.

5 Results

An overview of selected studies is reported in Table 1. The articles included in this review were published between 2003 and 2023. The 9 selected studies have been divided into four major categories according to their main themes: (a) studies (2) that explore the use of social robotics in museum education programs for edutainment purposes, where social robots are used to make learning more engaging and entertaining;

(b) studies (2) that focus on the development of soft skills through interactive experiences with social robots, emphasizing skills like communication, collaboration, and empathy; (c) studies (4) that examine the role of social robots as tour guides, where the robots assist in providing information and enhancing visitor interaction during museum tours; and (d) studies (3) that investigate how social robots contribute to the development of meaningful learning experiences by creating immersive educational environments that facilitate deeper learning. These categories reflect the diverse applications of social robotics in enhancing museum education and visitor engagement.

Table 1. Overview of selected studies on social robotics in museum education (2011–2023): Thematic focus and authors.

Paper	Thematic area
Mondou, Prigent & Revel, (2018)	EDUTAINMENT
Recuero Virto & López (2019)	EDUTAINMENT
Arend, Sunnen & Caire, (2017)	SOFT SKILLS
De Gasperis, (2023)	SOFT SKILLS
Hu & Chew, (2020)	TOUR GUIDE
Germak, Lupetti, Giuliano & Ng,(2015)	TOUR GUIDE
Boboc, Horațiu & Talabă (2014)	TOUR GUIDE
Kim, Lee, Aichi, Morishita & Makino, (2016)	TOUR GUIDE
Verner, Cuperman, Klein, Polishuk, Wertheim & Mir, (2011)	MEANINGFUL LEARNING

5.1 The Use of Social Robotics in Museum Education Programs for Edutainment Purposes

Socially Interactive Robots (SAR) can be used as an innovative tool to engage students in edutainment programs in museums.

Mondou, Prigent & Revel [26] have demonstrated how to develop edutainment programs through a new approach, involving the creation of a serious game using a NAO robot at the Museum of Natural History in La Rochelle, France. This serious game, integrated into the NAO robot, offers young visitors an engaging opportunity to explore the ethnography section of the museum. Acting as a facilitator, the NAO robot guides players through a playful discovery of the museum's artifacts by presenting interactive quizzes. Players are prompted to navigate the museum in search of answers to the questions posed by the robot.

Recuero Virto & López [27] explored the RAISA (Robots, Artificial Intelligence, and Service Automation) approach in the context of museum edutainment. It highlights how RAISA technologies are being implemented in museums to create interactive and immersive experiences that blend education and entertainment. Robots, such as CiceRobot and Pepper, are used as guides to enhance visitor engagement, while AI-driven applications personalize learning experiences. This approach emphasizes the role of technology in reshaping museum services, turning them into hubs of edutainment by offering tools like augmented reality, virtual tours, and personalized interactions.

5.2 The Development of Soft Skills Through Interactive Experiences with Social Robots

The use of social robots in museum education involves the development of a range of soft skills.

Arend, Sunnen & Caire [28] investigated breakdowns in human robot interaction through a conversation analysis guided single case study of a human-NAO communication in a museum environment. The case study shows how participants engaging in a sports guessing, i.e. an IRF sequence to make interaction work and overcome break-downs. IRF sequences are generally known in educational contexts as (teacher) initiation, (learner) response, and (teacher) follow-up or feedback. This research effort is focused on exploring how features of human "dialogue" can shed light on HRI.

Social robots can also be employed to develop other soft skills, such as the ability to build effective relationships and problem-solving skills. De Gasperis [29] means to evaluate the robotics laboratories in Children's Museums. The institution gave voice to the children who were the protagonists of the workshops held in the museum. In this way they were able to see that learning is better when involved and the use of social robots has allowed children to experiment with new solutions and to learn in a cooperative way.

5.3   The Role of Social Robots as Tour Guides

In recent years, social robots have started to play an increasing role in the tourism industry, particularly as tour guides. Social robotics, a discipline that develops robots capable of realistic and contextual interactions, now offers advanced technologies for engaging and personalised interaction, enabling these automated guides to accompany the visitor and enhance the tourist experience. It is already observed in numerous contexts such as museums, airports and archaeological sites that these robots, equipped with advanced voice recognition and navigation systems, can orient tourists, answer questions and provide historical and cultural explanations in an immediate and accessible way.

The use of social robots as tour guides represents a promising innovation in edu-cational and cultural experiences, with potential applications ranging from museums to science labs, making visits more interactive and accessible. Studies by Boboc et al., Germak et al., Hu and Chew, and Kim et al. provide a comprehensive overview of the benefits and challenges of integrating these technologies in real-world settings. Boboc et al. [30] explored the potential of a humanoid robot, Nao, to guide visitors at the Labo-ratory of Industrial Informatics and Robotics in Braşov, Romania. Nao was programmed to welcome visitors and lead them through the laboratory, explaining the operation of scientific equipment and research activities. This solution not only reduces the workload of human staff, but also enriches the visitor experience thanks to the interactivity offered by a robot that can communicate, move and gesture. The use of intuitive interfaces, such as Choregraphe, allowed the configuration of simple behaviours and responses, demonstrating the versatility of these robots in science education and promoting direct and engaging interaction between the public and the technology.

Germak et al. [31], on the other hand, focused on the application of telepresence robotics to improve the accessibility of cultural heritage. Virgil, a robot designed to explore and present difficult-to-access areas, guided by the museum guides themselves, was introduced at Racconigi Castle. This approach enhances the role of museum staff, facilitating storytelling and giving visitors a deeper insight into the castle's exhibitions and environments. The adoption of human-centred design, instead of technology, has made it possible to respond to the specific needs of users and to create a more inclusive and engaging cultural experience.

In a museum context, Hu and Chew [32] developed a bilingual robot for the National Museum of Wales, Cardiff, that speaks English and Welsh, demonstrating how robots can adapt to unique linguistic and cultural contexts. The robot was designed to guide visitors through the museum, explain the exhibits, collect visitor data and provide design recommendations for future implementation of robots in museums. Their study highlighted the ability of these systems to meet the educational and promotional needs of a museum by enhancing the visitor experience through natural and personalised interactions. Finally, Kim et al. [33] studied the impact of interaction with robots on visitors' perceptions by analysing social attraction and sociability towards robots on display at a time exhibition in Japan. The results show that the opportunity to physically interact with robots (touch, imitate, observe closely) significantly increases social attraction, demonstrating that familiarity and direct interaction can reduce the negative perception associated with robots. This effect is particularly relevant in contexts where robots are already widely integrated into everyday life, such as in Japan, suggesting that repeated, interactive contact can improve the social reception of robots.

These studies highlight how social robots can enrich the tourism and cultural landscape by offering innovative solutions that go beyond logistical support. The use of robots as tour and museum guides contributes to high quality educational experiences, stimulates visitor interest and promotes greater interaction between audience and content. In a broader context, social robots can become key tools for inclusion and accessibility in museums and cultural venues, making visits accessible also to people with mobility or language difficulties. At the same time, these robots represent an important resource for improving understanding of local culture, making heritage accessible to visitors from all backgrounds.

The future evolution of these technologies could lead to the integration of robotic systems with machine learning capabilities and advanced artificial intelligence, which can further personalise the experience according to visitors' preferences. In addition, the growing interest in social robotics opens new avenues for interdisciplinary research involving social sciences, computer science and design in order to make robots even more integrated, empathetic and responsive to the needs of visitors to cultural sites.

5.4 How Social Robots Contribute to the Development of Meaningful Learning Experiences

Recently, social robots have made their way into classrooms, bringing with them revolutionary potential for education. These devices, designed to interact empathetically and communicatively with humans, offer unique opportunities to create more meaningful and personalised learning experiences. Their ability to engage students in new and interactive ways stimulates not only an interest in knowledge, but also the development of crucial skills such as critical thinking, teamwork and self-esteem.

One of the main advantages of social robots is their ability to adapt to the individual needs of students. Using advanced sensors and artificial intelligence algorithms, these robots can analyse students' responses and emotional state in real time, providing immediate and tailored feedback.

Social robots are emerging as effective tools to facilitate meaningful learning experiences, especially in informal educational settings such as science and technology museums. The study by Verner et al. [34] highlights the importance of these tools in the robotics programme at the Israel National Museum of Science, Technology and Space (MadaTech), which has developed a stimulating environment for educational robotics and technological interaction. A relevant example is the 2010 robotics programme and the national 'OlympiYeda' competition, created in cooperation with the Technion, which offered a unique environment for interactive and self-regulated learning characterised by the innovative use of robotics. The activities of the Gelfand Centre for Model Building, Robotics & Communication within MadaTech, combined with the exhibition and competition approach, provided participants with the opportunity to experience active learning in an interactive robotic environment.

These programmes demonstrated how social robots can not only motivate and challenge students, but also promote collaborative problem-solving skills, experiential learning and communication within a multicultural and intellectually stimulating community. OlympiYeda, with its long-standing support from the Israeli Ministry of Education, represented a robotics-based learning model that enriched not only the participants, but also the teachers and peers involved in the final stages of the competition. Indeed, the robotics-based interaction approach enabled participants to develop advanced skills in autonomous learning, problem-solving and teamwork, tangibly contributing to building public understanding of robotics and its educational application.

6 Discussion

The use of educational robotics in museums represents an innovative breakthrough that redefines the very concept of museum experience and edutainment, educational entertainment [26, 27]. Social robots used in museums are tools that, by interacting directly with visitors, increase engagement, facilitate learning and strengthen the link with cultural content. The possibility of offering interactive experiences enriches the museum not only as a place of knowledge but also as a space for personal exploration and discovery, engaging the audience more deeply and making the content accessible and attractive, as visitors are incentivised to return to further explore the museum content at any time and in any place.

One of the most interesting aspects of the use of social robots in museum education programmes is the ability of these devices to promote active and meaningful learning, which is quite distinct from traditional passive modes of enjoyment [34]. Visitors, especially children and young people, can develop soft skills such as critical thinking, problem solving and the ability to work in teams [28, 29]. Interactions with robots, often designed in the form of playful activities or challenges, stimulate curiosity and exploration in an engaging way. In this sense, robotics in museums becomes a powerful edutainment tool, combining entertainment with learning and creating an educational experience that sticks.

Social robots also prove effective in promoting social-emotional skills, facilitating the development of skills such as communication and emotion management. These devices, programmed to respond empathetically and interactively, offer visitors the chance to practice social skills in a judgment-free context. This is particularly valuable for groups with special needs, such as children and adults with autism spectrum disorders, who can benefit from the opportunity to interact in a controlled and welcoming environment. Thanks to the presence of social robots, museums become spaces where inclusiveness is not just a goal, but a tangible, lived reality.

Furthermore, social robots used as tour guides offer the advantage of customising explanations according to the needs and level of understanding of the audience, adapting to visitors of different ages and backgrounds, including children, the elderly and people with disabilities. Their ability to provide information adaptively, using different languages and including voice capabilities to respond to commands and questions, ensures that everyone can access cultural content in an equal and inclusive manner. Interaction with robots is therefore an enriching and accessible experience, making the museum a welcoming place for a diverse audience and enabling language and physical barriers to be overcome [30–33].

A further contribution of social robots in museums can be observed during periods of high attendance, when these devices can perform staff support functions. In hightraffic situations, robots can deal with basic information requests, reducing the workload of operators and allowing human staff to concentrate on more complex tasks, such as managing personalised experiences or assisting visitors with special needs. The robots can also monitor the flow of visitors, offering guidance and suggestions to optimise the visit path. Despite its many advantages, the adoption of robotics in museums also presents complex challenges. On the economic side, implementation and maintenance costs are often high and require a significant investment, which may be prohibitive for small museums or those with limited budgets. On the technical side, there is a need for adequate staff training and constant updates to improve speech recognition capabilities, understanding of different accents and autonomous navigation within museum spaces. Furthermore, there are relevant ethical issues related to the protection of personal data, especially in the use of voice and facial recognition technologies. The massive introduction of robots also raises concerns regarding energy sustainability and public acceptance. Indeed, some visitors prefer human interaction, which is considered more empathetic and authentic than robot-mediated interaction, making it crucial to ensure that these devices are perceived as a support to traditional activities and not as a substitute for them.

7 Conclusion

The introduction of educational robotics in museums is set to transform the sector, offering new tools for an interactive, inclusive and personalised museum experience. If the challenges of cost, technological upgrading and ethical management are addressed, social robots can be consolidated as key resources to broaden accessibility and democratise access to culture, creating increasingly participative and welcoming museums for all audiences.

Looking ahead, with technological advances and the consequent lowering of costs, robots may become more accessible tools even for smaller museums. Improved voice and facial recognition technologies could make interactions increasingly fluid and natural, facilitating communication that is more empathetic and closer to audience preferences. From an educational point of view, the use of social robots in museums could further evolve towards increasingly specific and customised educational programmes, capable of responding to the different cognitive and learning needs of visitors. This will open new opportunities to promote the learning of soft skills such as effective communication, teamwork and creativity, strengthening the role of museums as dynamic and interactive cultural learning centres.

Moreover, social robotics offers an extraordinary opportunity to build a network of connections between museums, schools and communities, fostering greater collaboration and mutual exchange of knowledge. Through the integration of robotics, museums can become laboratories of experimentation and learning, where formal and informal education combine to create a seamless and borderless learning environment. The possibility of integrating STEM (Science, Technology, Engineering and Mathematics) skills with culture and history creates an interdisciplinary context that prepares young people for a broader understanding of the world around them.

Ultimately, the use of educational robotics in museums represents a great opportunity to expand the potential of cultural education and entertainment, promoting inclusiveness and enhancing the visitor experience. The future of robotics in museums will depend on the ability to maintain a balance between technological innovation and respect for human needs, helping to build a harmonious relationship between technology and culture. If the challenges are successfully addressed, it is likely that social robots will become fundamental elements of the museum experience, helping visitors of all ages to immerse themselves in meaningful, interactive learning that is open to the challenges of an increasingly global, interconnected and intercultural world.

References

1. Escobar, J.F.G., Mira, Y.M.O.: La globalización y la importancia de las TIC en el desarrollo social. Rev. Reflexiones Saberes **11**, 2–9 (2019)
2. Beran, T.N., Ramirez-Serrano, A., Kuzyk, R., Fior, M., Nugent, S.: Understanding how children understand robots: perceived animism in child–robot interaction. Int. J. Hum. Comput. Stud. **69**(7–8), 539–550 (2011)
3. Alimisis, D., Kynigos, C.: Constructionism and robotics in education. In: Teacher Education on Robotic-Enhanced Constructivist Pedagogical Methods, pp. 11–26 (2009)
4. Wei, C.W., Hung, I.C., Lee, L., Chen, N.S.: A Joyful classroom learning system with robot learning companion for children to learn mathematics multiplication. Turk. Online J. Educ. Technol. **10**(2), 11–23 (2011)
5. Highfield, K.: Robotic toys as a catalyst for mathematical problem solving. Aust. Primary Math. Classroom **15**(2), 22–27 (2010)
6. Chen, N.S., Quadir, B., Teng, D.C.: A Novel approach of learning English with robot for elementary school students. In: Chang, M., et al. (Eds.), Edutainment 2011, LNCS 6872, pp. 309–316. Heidelberg, Germany: Springer-Verlag Berlin Heidelberg (2011)
7. Breazeal, C.: Toward sociable robots. Rob. Autonomous Syst. **42**(3–4), 167–175 (2003)
8. Fong, T., Nourbakhsh, I., Dautenhahn, K.: A survey of socially interactive robots. Rob. Autonomous Syst. **42**(3–4), 143–166 (2003)
9. Belpaeme, T., Kennedy, J., Baxter, P.: Social robots for education: a review. Sci. Rob. **3**(21), eaat5954 (2018)
10. Johal, W.: Research trends in social robots for learning. Curr. Rob. Rep. **1**(3), 75–83 (2020)
11. Leite, I., Martinho, C., Paiva, A.: Social robots for long-term interaction: a survey. Int. J. Soc. Rob. **5**(2), 291–308 (2013)
12. Del Vacchio, E., Laddaga, C., Bifulco, F.: Social robots as a tool to involve student in museum edutainment programs. In: 2020 29th IEEE International Conference on Robot and Human Interactive Communication (RO-MAN), pp. 476–481. IEEE (2020)

13. Arocena, I., Huegun-Burgos, A., Rekalde-Rodriguez, I.: Robotics and education: a systematic review. TEM J. **11**(1) (2022)
14. D'Onofrio, G., Petito, A., Calvio, A., Toto, G.A., Limone, P.: Robot assistive therapy strategies for children with autism. In: International Conference on Psychology. Learning, Technology, pp. 103–116. Springer, Cham (2022)
15. Feil-Seifer, D., Mataric, M.J.: Defining socially assistive robotics. In: 9th International Conference in Rehabilitation Robotics, pp. 465–468. IEEE (2005)
16. Tapus, A., Mataric, M.J.: Socially assistive robots: the link between personality, empathy, physiological signals, and task performance. In: AAAI Spring Symposium: Emotion, Personality, and Social Behaviour, pp. 133–140 (2008)
17. Traetta, L.: Tecnologia e disabilità: dalla scienza medica all'inclusione. Progedit, Roma (2023)
18. Brignone, S., Grimaldi, R., Palmieri, S.: I social robot come sistemi intelligenti di tutoraggio e di comunicazione. In ATTI DEL CONVEGNO DIDAMATICA 2021, pp. 129–138. AICA Associazioni Italiana per il Calcolo Automatico (2021)
19. Mubin, O., et al.: A review of the applicability of robots in education. Technol. Educ. Learn. (2013)
20. González-González, C., et al.: Exploring social robots as learning companions for children with autism. Int. J. Soc. Rob. (2020)
21. Cheng, L., et al.: Impact of social robots on STEM education. IEEE Trans. Learn. Technol. (2020)
22. Fridin, M.: Social robots in classrooms: a study on social robot impacts. Int. J. Adv. Rob. Syst. (2014)
23. van den Berghe, R., et al.: Educational robots in the classroom. Educ. Technol. Res. Dev. (2019)
24. Giaconi, C., Del Bianco, N.: In azione: Prove di inclusione. FrancoAngeli (2019)
25. Passalacqua, F., Zecca, L.: Valutare laboratori di robotica educativa: studio di un approccio partecipativo. Formazione insegnamento **17**(1), 449–456 (2019)
26. Mondou, D., Prigent, A., Revel, A.: A dynamic scenario by remote supervision: a serious game in the museum with a Nao robot. In: Advances in Computer Entertainment Technology: 14th International Conference, ACE 2017, London, UK, December 14–16, 2017, Proceedings 14, pp. 103–116. Springer (2018)
27. Recuero Virto, N., López, M.F.B.: Robots, artificial intelligence, and service automation to the core: remastering experiences at museums. In: Robots, Artificial Intelligence, and Service Automation in Travel, Tourism and Hospitality, pp. 239–253. Emerald Publishing Limited (2019)
28. Arend, B., Sunnen, P., Caire, P.: Investigating breakdowns in human robot interaction: a conversation analysis guided single case study of a human-NAO communication in a museum environment. Int. J. Mech. Aerosp. Ind. Mechatron. Manuf. Eng. **11**(5), 839–845 (2017)
29. De Gasperis, P.: Gioco, apprendimento e riuso digitale. Il museo come servizio. DigItalia **18**(2), 85–91 (2023)
30. Boboc, R.G., Horațiu, M., Talabă, D.: An educational humanoid laboratory tour guide robot. Procedia Soc. Behav. Sci. **141**, 424–430 (2014)
31. Germak, C., Lupetti, M.L., Giuliano, L., Ng, M.E.K.: Robots and cultural heritage: new museum experiences. J. Sci. Technol. Arts 7(2), 47–57 (2015)
32. Hu, S., Chew, E.: The investigation and novel trinity modeling for museum robots. In: Eighth International Conference on Technological Ecosystems for Enhancing Multiculturality, pp. 21–28 (2020)
33. Kim, M.G., Lee, J., Aichi, Y., Morishita, H., Makino, M.: Effectiveness of robot exhibition through visitors experience: a case study of Nagoya Science Hiroba exhibition in Japan. In: 2016 International Symposium on MicroNanoMechatronics and Human Science (MHS), pp. 1–5. IEEE (2016)

34. Verner, I.M., Cuperman, D., Klein, Y., Polishuk, A., Wertheim, I., Mir, R.: Focusing a robotics education program on scientific and humane challenges: a museum case study. In: 2011 IEEE Global Engineering Education Conference (EDUCON), pp. 1–7. IEEE (2011)

Minority Embodiment. The Intersection of Branching Narratives and Ludic Subjectivity as a New Form of Education to Inclusivity

Mauro Colarieti[(✉)] [iD]

Università Cattolica del Sacro Cuore, Milan, Italy
mauro.colarieti@unifg.it

Abstract. In recent years, a novel yet overlooked form of ludic embodiment has emerged: we named it Minority Embodiment. It intersects Daniel Vella's concept of ludic subjectivity with the mechanics of branching narratives, in which players experience different outcomes based on their in-game choices. Minority Embodiment finds its home within story-driven video games of the past two decades, those that employ moral dilemmas and feature protagonists from underrepresented communities such as non-Caucasian and LGBTQAI + individuals. Core case studies include the "Life is Strange" franchise, "Tell Me Why", "As Dusk Falls", "The Walking Dead: The Telltale Definitive Series", and "Detroit: Become Human". At its core, Minority Embodiment seeks to elucidate how these games can influence players' perceptions and attitudes towards minority groups, thereby fostering empathy and promoting inclusivity within society. Through the design of dilemmas in branching narratives, players are confronted with choices that challenge their preconceived notions and moral compasses. As players inhabit characters belonging to marginalized communities, they navigate the complexities of identity, discrimination, and societal biases. Moreover, Minority Embodiment holds the potential to catalyze broader social change, as players carry their reflections and insights beyond the confines of virtual worlds: there have been multiple studies regarding this psychological impact on subjects, but mainly on immersive environments, while there's not enough literature on this influence in traditional story-driven videogames. The aim of this paper is to demonstrate the existence and usefulness of Minority Embodiment.

Keywords: Minority Embodiment · Ludic Subjectivity · Branching Narratives

1 Literature Review

1.1 Branching Narratives

The emergence of story-driven video games offers a powerful medium for exploring complex social issues, including the representation of minority identities. By analyzing titles such as *The Walking Dead: The Game, Life is Strange*, and *Detroit: Become Human*, this paper examines how the entanglement of ludic subjectivity, branching narratives

© The Author(s), under exclusive license to Springer Nature Switzerland AG 2025
G. A. Toto (Ed.): ICS exchange 2024, CCIS 2521, pp. 63–71, 2025.
https://doi.org/10.1007/978-3-032-03021-4_5

and representation of underrepresented communities lead to what we will call Minority Embodiment, which is a phenomenon that occurs while playing story-driven videogames that let subjects embody minority identities, such as racial or ethnic minorities, LGBTQ + individuals, people with disabilities, or other marginalized groups, within the context of the game narrative and of the gameplay mechanics.

The world of videogames has a rich yet evolving history. Story-driven videogames now provide players with the ability to control outcomes, explore diverse perspectives, and engage with marginalized identities in ways that were previously inaccessible. These interactive experiences that focus on marginalized communities allow players to embody characters who face unique challenges tied to their identities, whether racial, ethnic, sexual, or based on disabilities. Investigating the role of Minority Embodiment in fostering empathy and challenging racial, ethnic, and sexual stereotypes is now possible thanks to various titles that are lifting contemporary gaming, highlighting the ethical dimensions of game design.

To do so, it's necessary to provide a definition and a brief excursus of branching narratives and how they shaped nowadays' videoludic field: branching narratives are a form of interactive storytelling that can be both analogic (game books, plays) and digital (movies, videogames), in which the plot diverges based on the reader/viewer/player decisions. The concept of branching narratives can be traced back to the 1930s. One of the earliest examples is a multi-POV romance gamebook called "Consider the Consequences" (Doris Webster, Mary A. Hopkins, 1930): readers could choose different plot paths leading to 43 possible endings while following a single woman and her two love interests. This radical idea that readers can control the outcome of a story paved the way for future experiments in interactive fiction. In 1934, Ayn Rand produced a play placed in a courtroom, where audience members played the jury, making decisions that influenced the outcome of the trial. This early period of branching narratives set the stage for further exploration of interactive narratives in the decades that followed, but even at this time the ethical and moral aspect was present for assuring a higher level of audience's engagement.

In the 1960s and 1970s, branching narratives expanded beyond literature to interactive theater via text-based adventure games and interactive movies. One notable example is 1967's *Kinoautomat*, a film presented at the Montreal World's Fair where the audience could choose plot directions through voting (a red button and a green one for each member). In 1969, Edward Packard developed the concept of the *Choose Your Own Adventure* series. The first volume would be published ten years later, but it's during the beginning of the '70s that tabletop role-playing games (TTRPGs) like *Dungeons & Dragons* got popular, incorporating branching narratives. A Dungeon Master acts as the storyteller, guiding players through multiple narrative paths based on their decisions. These games became a precursor to digital narrative-driven games in the 1980s, straight after the game book craze that happened thanks to Packard's CYOA series.

We could say that branching narratives made their first significant appearance in video games in the 1980s with early titles like *Colossal Cave Adventure* (1976) and *The Hobbit* (1982), using simple choices to determine the outcome of the plot. These text-driven adventures mimicked the structure of choose-your-own-adventure books, leading to their downfall. In the '90s, gamebooks stopped being a fruitful product.

Of course, as the gaming industry developed, the use of branching narratives expanded into televised events such as the Eurovision contest's audience voting system in the 1990s, marking a new form of interactivity where audience members could influence real-world events, whether it be a singing competition or a reality show like the Big Brother, leading the audience to interact with "characters" who would pay the consequences of said audience's choices. It changed how we perceive mediatic storytelling: in the Third Millennium, we also saw the rise of video creators on platforms like YouTube utilizing branching narratives for interactive content, though this trend waned by 2015. It's a matter of fact that the 2010s marked a significant development in branching narratives within video games. *Telltale Games* launched *The Walking Dead: The Game* in 2012, setting a new standard for interactive storytelling in video games. Titles like *Life is Strange* (2015) and *Detroit: Become Human* (2018) expanded on this foundation, creating highly intricate narratives with numerous possible outcomes based on player choice. For instance, *Detroit: Become Human* boasts over 2000 pages of script and more than 80 possible endings, allowing players to deeply influence the storylines of its three main characters. However, the complexity of these games comes at a cost: production timelines are different, leading to issues like crunch culture, which led to the closure of *Telltale Games* in 2018 [1].

1.2 Case Studies

We will now briefly analyze these games that assure Minority Embodiment.

The Walking Dead: The Game is an episodic adventure game set in the universe of *The Walking Dead* comics and TV show, but it stands out for its emotional storytelling and its emphasis on player choice. The narrative-driven gameplay focuses on character relationships and moral dilemmas as survivors struggle through a zombie apocalypse. One of the game's strongest aspects is its focus on characters from underrepresented groups, both racially and socioeconomically. The first season's main protagonist, Lee Everett, is a Black man and a former history professor who is introduced as a prisoner on his way to jail for murder. This is significant in videogame history, as it was rare for Black men to be portrayed as complex, multifaceted protagonists in such a prominent and story-rich role.

The very first scene of the game begins with Lee in the back of a police car, handcuffed, reflecting on the crime he committed and his future. The dialogue between Lee and the white officer driving him is laced with racial undertones. The officer patronizes Lee with assumptions about his guilt, subtly reminding him of his criminal status without fully understanding the context of his crime (he killed a man who was having an affair with his wife). This scene doesn't just serve as a tutorial for game mechanics but immediately immerses players in Lee's reality. It places players in the shoes of a character who is navigating issues of race, criminal justice, and personal regret, on top of the unfolding apocalypse. You are not just surviving zombies; you are a Black man in the South with a complex past, navigating a world that looks at you with suspicion even before the outbreak.

The game later introduces Clementine, a young bi-racial girl who becomes a key character and Lee's surrogate daughter. The bond between Lee and Clementine becomes central to the emotional core of the game, with themes of protection, chosen family, mentorship, and survival becoming intertwined with the exploration of their identities in a collapsing society. Overall, *The Walking Dead: The Game* gave voice to characters from underrepresented groups, allowing players to empathize with their struggles in a way that was groundbreaking for mainstream gaming. Regarding the branching narratives, this title lets you choose who or what to sacrifice based on your interaction with the secondary characters. In some instances, your choices also regard the safety of the group. This particular aspect will appear heavily in all the other titles of the videoludic series, topping it up with The Walking Dead: The Final Season (2019), in which a grown-up Clementine takes the role of Lee while educating an Afro-American orphan child, AJ. What's interesting about this title is that, at the end of the experience, there's a list of "lessons" you taught to AJ based on the choices you made during the entire run.

In the same way, The *Life is Strange* franchise is a series of episodic graphic adventure games developed by Dontnod Entertainment and Deck Nine. The games let players embody characters from underrepresented groups, focusing on themes like identity, mental health, LGBTQ + issues, and social inequalities. Each installment explores these through the lens of characters grappling with personal struggles while dealing with superpowers. As it is happening with many other entertainment industries, representation is an asset of these products. Although, "if in entertainment products such as *Teen Wolf*, *Winx*, and *The Vampire Diaries*, the narratives center on the supernatural plots, *Life Is Strange* deeply focuses on everyday struggles of teenagers coming from underrepresented communities, while the supernatural aspect comes second. (…) the representation of superheroes as epic fighters on dangerous battlefields is lacking" [2].

The first installment of the series follows Max Caulfield, a teenage girl who discovers she can rewind time. Max reconnects with her childhood friend, Chloe Price, and together they investigate the disappearance of a local girl, uncovering dark secrets about their town. The game is notable for its representation of LGBTQ + themes, with Max and Chloe's evolving relationship allowing players to explore queer romance. Chloe, a rebellious character with a punk attitude, is also part of another underrepresented group, in terms of her lower socioeconomic background, with her struggles reflecting her marginalization in society.

In the second installment of *LiS*, players embody Sean Diaz, a Mexican-American teenager, as he and his younger brother Daniel flee the country after a tragic incident involving police violence. This game deals explicitly with racial profiling, immigration, and social justice issues, particularly the challenges faced by Latinx communities in the U.S. The game's narrative touches on discrimination, prejudice, and the hardships faced by people of color, making it one of the most socially relevant stories in the franchise. The choices here have a strong impact on the brothers' faith: like in the final season of *The Walking Dead: The Game*, the pedagogical implications (what to teach to a child in a challenging situation) are used as a way to educate players on the consequences of their actions.

Life is Strange: True Colors introduces Alex Chen, a young woman of Asian-American descent with the ability to experience and manipulate others' emotions. Alex, like many characters in the series, deals with themes of trauma and mental health, and the game explores her identity as an Asian-American in a predominantly white town. Alex's story adds to the franchise's focus on mental health and marginalized voices, particularly in her experiences navigating both her psychic powers and her personal identity as an orphan.

Dontnod Entertainment have been using Minority Embodiment in pretty much all its titles: *Tell Me Why* revolves around the story of two siblings, a transexual man and a woman suffering from panic attacks and severe anxiety. In one scene, the player has to use a breathing app on the protagonist's phone to control a panic attack. Furthermore, *Lost Records: Blood & Rage*, Dontnod's upcoming videogame, introduces Swann Holloway, their first plus-size protagonist.

The player's decisions shape how these characters navigate their unique challenges as they all start from their identities, providing both agency and empathy for their experiences. This makes the series (and Dontnod in general) a pioneer both in Minority Embodiment and in diverse storytelling in videogames.

Detroit: Become Human is an interactive narrative-driven game developed by Quantic Dream, released in 2018. Set in 2038's Detroit where androids have become part of everyday life, the game explores themes of free will, media influence on hate crimes, and social inequality. Players control three android protagonists, Kara, Connor, and Markus, as they navigate their roles in a world where androids are treated as second-class citizens, with many parallels to real-world issues of civil rights and social justice. The game excels in allowing players to embody characters from an underrepresented community, particularly through its allegory of the android struggle as a reflection of marginalized groups in human history (e.g. androids have to stay at the back of a bus, there are not laws protecting their rights).

Kara is a female android assigned to serve a troubled, abusive man and his daughter, Alice. Her story focuses on themes of domestic abuse, challenging gender roles, and parenthood (mirroring *The Walking Dead: The Final Season* and *Life is Strange 2*), exploring Kara's quest for autonomy and protection of Alice. As an android, Kara represents the exploited domestic workforce, often reflecting the struggles of women in lower socio-economic classes. Her journey is one of escape and resistance, fighting against the system that dehumanizes her.

Connor is a detective android tasked with hunting down "deviant" androids—those who have gained free will and rebelled against their programming. His character explores the ethical dilemmas of duty versus morality, control versus freedom. While Connor doesn't belong to a traditionally underrepresented group (he's a white male-presenting android), his struggle with whether to remain loyal to the oppressive system or not is a thought-provoking asset to treat issues of identity and conformity that resonate with marginalized communities, particularly in the context of institutional control.

Finally, Markus is the most prominent figure in the game's allegory of civil rights. Initially a caretaker for an elderly man, he becomes the leader of an android revolution after being wrongfully accused of homicide. His storyline explicitly parallels real-world civil rights movements, especially drawing inspiration from the struggles of African-Americans during the fight for racial equality: the player embodying Markus can choose between peaceful protest or violent rebellion via logos, speeches, vandalism, etc., allowing players to shape how his revolution mirrors historic methods of resistance and social fight.

To conclude, the androids in *Detroit: Become Human* are an allegory for various marginalized groups in history and an interactive narrative that let players empathize with minorities that are socially excluded because of their diversity. By letting players control android characters who fight for their freedom, this title invites them to explore issues of social inequality, discrimination, and injustice through interactive storytelling. The game doesn't provide clear-cut answers but instead challenges players to confront their own biases and moral choices, often drawing uncomfortable parallels (in an instance, there's a whole chapter set in a futuristic concentration camp) between the treatment of androids and the treatment of marginalized people in society.

1.3 Player Agency

In narrative-driven video games, player agency refers to the degree of control and influence a player has over the actions and decisions of their character within a game world. Jamey Stevenson conducted a framework for classifying ethical games, resulting in three core categories:

- **Static**: no ethical decisions that might impact the game plot. The main character works through ethical dilemmas, but the player has no direct impact on the narrative resolution.
- **Adaptive**: encourage ethical decisions without obvious quantifiable consequences (simpler branching narratives, slightly different narrative content during the experience but keeping the same outcome no matter the choices made).
- **Systemic**: player's ethical decisions and deeper consequences of those decisions in ways such as reputation or friendship/enmity with other characters, which can eventually influence the plot further [3].

The Systemic Approach is arguably the most effective in enabling players to feel a direct connection to the narrative's evolution. Player decisions reverberate throughout the game world, allowing for a richer, more immersive experience where choices feel meaningful and ethical dilemmas are genuinely impactful. In which, Minority Embodiment can thrive.

Shliakhovchuk's survey-based research, in 2024, explored the effectiveness of videogames such as *Papers, Please* (in which you play as an immigration officer who chooses who can get admitted in your country and who does not) in increasing awareness and erasing negative bias with regards to the refugee crisis. The results showed an increase in empathy towards refugees [4]. Studies like this one show how videogames can foster people's empathy, particularly towards minorities, thanks to the medium's interactivity and player agency.

1.4 Ludic Subjectivity

Ludic subjectivity refers to the player's subjective identity within the game world. The idea is that the player's experiential and existential structure is reflected in their interactions with the game through their avatar [5]. As players make decisions, they shape the avatar's characteristics such as moral alignment, strength, and charisma, which in turn influence how the avatar interacts with the game world [6]. For example, in *Tell Me*

Why, as we mentioned earlier, the player navigates a narrative centered on two siblings, one facing issues because of his transgender identity, and the other suffering from panic attacks and severe anxiety. The choices the player makes in this game affect not only how the main character experiences the world but also how other characters react to them. This representation of minority identities gives the player an opportunity to walk in the shoes of characters facing societal discrimination or identity struggles. However, the concept of "ludic subjectivity" raises the question of how these virtual identities intersect with players' real-world beliefs and experiences. Games like these present moral dilemmas where players pay the consequences of their actions, highlighting the tension between game-world ethics and real-world empathy. The choices that players make, in these instances, are more than just strategic—they have moral weight and possible consequences in said players' beliefs in real life. As we mentioned earlier, there have been studies about this phenomenon, mainly demonstrating how gaming can make people more open-minded and less affected by damaging stereotypes towards minorities [7].

2   Representation and Inclusivity in Story-Driven Videogames

2.1   Inclusivity in Story-Driven Videogames

Over time, society has started to shift towards more inclusive narratives, attempting to represent marginalized voices that have historically been absent from mainstream media. Video games are not an exception. The aforementioned video ludic titles feature inclusive storylines where issues of race and gender are central to the storylines. Furthermore, one important aspect of this inclusive storytelling is the emphasis on embodiment: players are invited to put themselves in the characters' shoes, and since they are part of marginalized communities (whether they are individuals from racial minorities, LGBTQ + communities, or those with disabilities), this embodiment plays a significant role in fostering empathy. Generally, the claim that video games can act as "empathy machines" has sparked interest among scholars. Research indicates that embodying minority avatars can have a profound impact on players' perceptions of marginalized groups: for example, a study conducted by Vivian Chen and colleagues showed that embodying an immigrant avatar significantly improved attitudes and closeness toward immigrants [8]. Similarly, games like *The Walking Dead* and *Life is Strange 2,* in which you play respectively an Afro-American and a Mexican-American during Donald Trump's election, allow players to confront difficult situations and make ethical decisions from the perspective of characters who are marginalized by society while also educating themselves on these minorities' struggles in the real world.

2.2   The Pitfalls of Tokenism and "Woke-Washing"

The effectiveness of these empathy-building mechanics is often contingent on the depth of the narrative and the complexity of the choices available, which relate to the game design more than to the fruition of the titles. In some cases, the representation of minority characters can be superficial, contributing to what has been criticized as "woke-washing"—the exploitation of topical issues and social activism without a real intention of inclusivity, where inclusivity is used as a marketing tool rather than a meaningful narrative element [9]. When games fail to integrate these elements into the broader plot or social context, they risk objectifying or tokenizing the identities they aim to represent. The inclusion of minority characters in video games, while a positive trend, has also faced criticism for its potential lack of genuinity. However, these contemporary controversies lead us to new dynamics, particularly concerning issues in line with today's "inclusivity trend" that has affected several entertainment industries. Regarding gaming, the Woke Content Detector Steam Group listed numerous videogame titles grouped by how 'woke' they are, leading to the message that the more inclusive they are, the less quality players' will get from those games[10]. In this regard, another recent case concerns *Concord*, a video game that had a catastrophic launch after eight years of development and production. Sony, in an attempt to make up for the low numbers, decided to remove all LGBTQAI + references in the title [11].

We could, as some people do, argue that merely adding characters from marginalized communities without contextualizing their struggles within the narrative is not only wrong, but it can also detract from the authenticity of the narrative and undermine the potential for games to serve as platforms for social critique [12]. For instance, if a game includes a transgender character or a person of color, but their identity is only acknowledged at a superficial level, the player may not be able to fully engage with the character's experience. Games like *Last Stop*, for example, which follows three Londoners' encounter with supernatural forces, do not really engage with minority issues, although the majority of its characters are from underrepresented groups. We could also argue that everyone deserves to be represented and included without being objectified or weaponised for their identity, and that not focusing on a characters' minority could be seen as a more realistic and less political approach to narrative design. However, the risk of tokenism remains a concern, as the superficial inclusion of minority characters can undermine the broader goals of inclusivity. Ultimately, minority groups' stories have been left out from narrative-driven videogames for decades, so maybe it's now time to showcase issues regarding their identities.

3 Conclusions

The potential for narrative-driven video games to promote empathy and inclusivity lies in their capacity for player agency, ethical decision-making, and the embodiment of minority identities. Contemporary story-driven videogames offer rich, systemic narratives where player choices meaningfully affect character development and plot outcomes. Moreover, these games create opportunities for players to engage with marginalized identities in a way that challenges stereotypes and fosters empathy, by giving to players' an added responsibility given their power in influencing characters' faiths. Minority Embodiment is being used for all these reasons, and thanks to the advancement of immersive storytelling, it's considerable a new aspect to consider in education to inclusivity.

References

Behm-Morawitz, E., Ta, D.: Cultivating virtual stereotypes? The impact of video game play on racial/ethnic stereotypes. Howard J. Commun. **25**, 1–15 (2014). https://doi.org/10.1080/106 46175.2013.835600

Chen, V.H.H., Ibasco, G.C., Leow, V.J.X. Lew, J.Y.Y.: The effect of VR avatar embodiment on improving attitudes and closeness toward immigrants. Front Psychol. **12** (2021)

Colarieti, M., Everyday hero, the hyper-relatable protagonists of the Life is Strange franchise. In: Alexander, C.S. (ed.) Black Witches and Queer Ghosts. Race, Gender, and Sexual Orientation in Teen Supernatural Serials, 1st edn. Lexington Books, Lanham (MD) (2024)

DRCommodore Homepage: Concord: numeri disastrosi al lancio, Sony rimuove anche i riferimenti LGBTQ+ per aumentare le vendite. https://www.drcommodore.it/2024/08/24/concord-lancio-negativo/. Accessed 6 Oct 2024

Ermz Plays: How The Woke Virus Infested Modern Gaming. https://www.youtube.com/watch?v=nt1JLi3_DoQ. Accessed 6 Oct 2024

Farber, M., Schrier, K.: The strengths and limitations of using digital games as "empathy machines," pp. 35–36, the UNESCO MGIEP / Mahatma Gandhi Institute of Education for Peace and Sustainable Development (2017)

Gamereactor Homepage: The Woke Content Detector is deranged and trying to stop people playing some of the best games out there. https://www.gamereactor.eu/the-woke-content-detector-is-deranged. Accessed 6 Oct 2024

IGN Homepage: Telltale Games' Shut Down and 'Revival,' Explained. https://www.ign.com/art icles/2019/12/13. Accessed 6 Oct 2024

Inside Marketing Homepage: Woke washing: cos'è e che rischi ha per le aziende. https://www.insidemarketing.it/glossario/definizione/woke-washing/. Accessed 6 Oct 2024

Shliakhovchuk, E.: Video games as awareness raisers, attitude changers, and agents of social change. Int. J. Comput. Games Technol. **2024**, 3274715 (2024). https://doi.org/10.1155/2024/3274715

Stevenson, J.: A framework for classification and criticism of ethical games. In: Schrier, K., Gibson, D. (eds.) Designing Games for Ethics: Models, Techniques and Frameworks, pp. 36–55. IGI Global, Hershey (PA) (2011)

Vella, D.: "Who am 'I' in the game?" A typology of the modes of ludic subjectivity. In: DiGRA/FDG, p. 2 (2016)

Serious Games and Special Educational Need: Serious Games in the Learning Process a Systematic Review

Francesco Pio Savino$^{(\boxtimes)}$, Roberta Baldini⬤, and Piergiorgio Guarini⬤

University of Foggia, Foggia, Italy
francesco.savino@unifg.it

Abstract. Information and Communication Technologies (ICTs) have, in recent years, become increasingly important and fundamental in promoting the inclusion of students with Specific Learning Disorders (SLDs) and Special Educational Needs (SENs) within the classroom, changing the long-established custom of having the pupils follow a specially designed curriculum based on their specific difficulties and differentiated from the rest of the class.

The aid of innovative digital teaching methodologies and digital tools such as Serious Games (SGs), proves to be of great effectiveness in increasing the inclusion and integration of pupils with SLD and SEN in the classroom context, both from an educational and relational point of view.

This paper proposes a systematic review of the existing scientific literature regarding the development and practical implementation of SGs that assist in the inclusion of students with SLD and SEN, within the whole class learning journey. The research focused on papers dealing with the planning and implementation of SGs designed for Italian schools, as well as papers dealing with the implementation of SGs in Italian educational institutions, of all levels.

Keywords: Serious Games · SEN · Learning process

1 Introduction

In recent years, Information and Communication Technologies (ICTs) became increasingly significant in promoting the inclusion of students with Specific Learning Disorders (SLDs) and Special Educational Needs (SENs) within the classroom. This development has altered the long-established practice of having these students follow a separate curriculum tailored to their specific difficulties, distinct from that of the rest of the class.

Today, digital tools such as smartphone and tablet have become almost ubiquitous and in this social and cultural background, video games are the most widely used form of entertainment by children, young people and adults [1]. The ever-growing use of video games has pushed the market to create video games to be used in the field of educational learning called *Serious games* (SGs).

In the recent years, the use of SGs in educational and special educational fields has increased. Recent studies show that the use of SGs can improve well-being, social skills,

G. A. Toto (Ed.): ICS exchange 2024, CCIS 2521, pp. 72–87, 2025.
https://doi.org/10.1007/978-3-032-03021-4_6

independent living, and inclusion in varied samples of students with special needs such as autism spectrum disorders, learning disabilities, and giftedness [2].

According to Chai and colleagues (2019), SGs have been created for education by providing a platform that makes boring tasks a bit more engaging, presenting these tasks as a game. In addition, SGs have achieved a great effect to help children with attention deficit hyperactivity and children with speech disorders and hearing problems [3].

The aim of this paper is to propose a systematic review of the existing scientific literature regarding the development and practical implementation of SGs that assist in the inclusion of students with SLD and SEN, within the whole-class learning journey.

2 Method

This systematic review was conducted using the PRISMA - Preferred Reporting Items for Systematic reviews and Meta-Analyzes [4] statement and protocol. The literature was searched up to in the following databases: EBSCO, Scopus and Web of Science. The search research string used was:

(("Special Need*" OR "SEN" OR "Specific Learning Disorders" OR "SLD") AND ("Student*" OR "Scholar" OR "child*") AND ("Serious Game*" OR "SGs")).

With this search research string we found 42 results by Scopus, 20 results by EBSCO, and 48 results by Web of Science and we have obtained 110 results in total.

In the research process we use the online open-source software "Rayyan" in order to manage, select and discard the results. The software presents the tool "research duplicates" with which we found 27 duplicate results and after discarding those we had an amount of 83 results after the first screening. In the research process we have used this exclusion criteria:

1) Not have the keywords;
2) Not open access;
3) Out of time range;
4) Not in English;
5) Wrong topic;
6) Wrong outcome.

With the title and abstract reading screening process we have eliminated 60 results and we have obtained 23 results for the second screening. After the lecture of full paper screening, we have eliminated 13 results, leaving 10 results out of 110 definitively admitted in our systematic review.

3 Development of Serious Games

This systematic review revealed many interesting aspects about the creation and development of SGs for children and teenagers with mental disorders or SENs.

Most of the studies reviewed [5–8] presented the testing of the use of SGs in schools specializing in the education of BES, ASD and Down syndrome children and teenagers.

Authors Montero and colleagues (2018) [5] conducted a qualitative study on a sample of BES children and youth aged 6 to 21 years.

In the Spanish school context the trainers were working on the development of multiple skills, both didactic and personal, according to three main points: Augmentative and Alternative Communication (AAC); Support to improve personal autonomy; and School Learning Resources.

SGs are used in the development of instrumental abilities, cognitive competences as well as other academic abilities related to the curriculum.

Many students, and particularly those with special needs, benefitted from their interactive and multimedia capabilities that current developments offer, as well as the motivational effect and ease of use. These SGs will allow students to keep on building and acquire knowledge at a higher level.

In the research works of Bossavit & Parsons [6] and Ouherrou, and colleagues (2023) [7] a Participatory Design (PD) approach is used, in which students with cognitive and/or mental disorders, ASD and Dyslexia were active and participatory in the implementation of SGs.

The study by Bossavit & Parsons [6], involved teenagers aged 11 to 15 years with high-functioning autism (HFA). The teens with the support of teachers and designers developed a serious game with a natural user interface to increase the teens' skills and knowledge in geography and everyday life.

The decision-making process within the PD can be classified into four categories: (i) values and concept, (ii) implementation, (iii) negotiations with the outside world, and (iv non-decision making. Students and teacher took almost exclusively implementation roles while the researcher mainly made decisions about values and concepts. Participatory work was definitely the strong point.

The study by Ouherrou, and colleagues [7] enrolled 15 children with dyslexia between the ages of 8 and 12 from a specialized school in Morocco. As in the previous study, a student participatory approach was used in this research at all stages of the research project. The children were active participants in each phase of brainstorming and subsequent implementation of SG interfaces. The games made were used to work on students' difficulties in reading, writing and spelling. Each SG was not only a mode of play and fun for the children, but a real motivating and useful learning reality.

The continuous feedback from the children at each stage of implementation is certainly a strength, as it was possible to make changes according to their inputs. A limitation, on the other hand, is the non-traceability of the user-centered design approach in the research.

Another work, carried out by Anna Sochocka and colleagues [8], in a Polish school for children with ASD and Down syndrome based in Krakow used a descriptive approach. In this study, a web application is made to provide access to various SGs to help children both at school and at home to enhance their skills, especially in areas where they are deficient. Such web support should be an adjunct to the youths' daily nonpharmacological therapies.

4   The Effects of SGs on Learners

After reviewing scientific papers, studies and research in the literature on the use of SGs for children and young people with cognitive disabilities, it is possible to summarize strengths and critical points, and underline which effects have been produced on children.

In the studies described in the previous paragraph, it is possible to infer some limitations and benefits that are common to several works and to the effects obtained on learners.

One of the greatest strengths is certainly the higher motivation showed by the children when they had to use digital tools, such as PCs, tablets and smartphones, in order to use the various SGs described, both at school and at home, in any discipline.

Another benefit is the boys' active participation in devising and designing the interfaces of the SGs wherever possible. Children were able to express their thoughts, both in projects where SGs were being created and in work where they had to test the effectiveness of SGs. The young students were able to voice their ideas, thus allowing changes to be made to some of the projects. They were able to voice their preferences about the graphics, the lead characters, the genre of the characters, the colours, and the stories of the SGs. The young people's doubts, their ideas and their difficulties of expression in some cases were an added value of some of the research carried out. Such changes have certainly achieved more functional and more motivating products to enable more learning. This certainly achieved a positive and inclusive effect of the learners involved, as well as SGs more in line with the needs of the children and youth.

In addition, the SGs enabled the enhancement of the skills, knowledge and abilities of the learners involved. It seems clear that SGs and technological devices can be very useful in the education of children and youth with cognitive disabilities. What needs to be paid attention to is the design and quality of SG. SG is not a game for fun itself, but a tool designed to increase personal and educational training through ways that are motivating and functional for the subject.

Some of the limitations found in the papers analysed were the small sample of participants and/or the absence of a control group. The lack of these characteristics doesn't allow to generalize the effects found in the papers analyzed to a wide-ranging population of children. In addition, most of the studies were conducted within specialized schools for the education of children and youth with BES, ASD, Down syndrome, and Dyslexia.

According to Durango and colleagues (2018) [9] the use of SGs decrease attention loss in the participant who have used the SGs, compared to when they use traditional game ($p = 0.0007$).

A recent study (Piazzalunga et al., 2023) [10] on the use of SGs with the student with Dyslexia shows that there is a significant difference between the accuracy reached by second and third graders ($p = 0.005$), with the elder students achieving better performance and there isn't a significantly difference between male and females, neither in accuracy ($p = 0.740$) nor in reading speed ($p = 0.052$).

N.	Author	Year of publication	Sample	Study design	Intervention	Outcome	Results
1	Bossavit, B. e Parsons, S. [6]	2016	The designer-team comprised 4 males with ASD, three of them aged 15 years and one aged 11, the ICT teacher, his teaching assistant and the researcher. The project took place in a highly specialized school for young people with Special Educational Needs (SEN)	Participatory Design approach	Developed a Serious Game with a Natural User Interface, via a Participatory Design approach with two teenagers with High-Functioning Autism (HFA)	Decision-making within PD can be classified in four categories: values and concept, implementation, negotiations with the outside world and non-decision. Students and the teacher almost exclusively took on implementation roles with the researcher mostly taking decisions about values and concepts	This project shows what is possible when designers work closely with teachers, and students with ASD, in a flexible and open way. (seppur sarebbe utile estendere in una prossima ricerca il campione degli "attori")

(continued)

(continued)

N.	Author	Year of publication	Sample	Study design	Intervention	Outcome	Results
2	Chai, C.; Theng Lau, B.; Pan, Z. [3]	2019	30 participants: 9 primary school; 21 Secondary school; no Vision: 13; Low vision: 17; With LD: 7; With no LD: 23;	Observational study	The objective of the study was to evaluate the effectiveness of the Hungry Cat game in supporting spatial mind mapping in visually impaired participants through food detection tests and spatial mapping tests	The results of the study showed that participants who passed the food detection test demonstrated better spatial mapping ability than those who did not find food during the test. This suggests that the Hungry Cat game could be effective in supporting the development of spatial mind maps in visually impaired participants	The success rate in finding food among secondary school participants (32.54%) was generally higher on average than those in primary schools (29.63%). The success rate in finding food among participants with low vision (36.27%) was generally higher than among those without vision (25.64%). Finally, the success rate in finding food among participants without learning disabilities (33.34%) was generally higher than among those with learning difficulties (26.19%)

(continued)

(continued)

N.	Author	Year of publication	Sample	Study design	Intervention	Outcome	Results
3	Durango, E; Carrascosa, A.; Gallud, J.A.; & Penichet, V.M.R. [9]	2017	10 participants	Experimental study	The study aims to evaluate the effectiveness of an alternative communication system for children with special needs, focusing on the association between pictograms and real representations to improve communication and learning	The results of the study include an improvement in the association between children and fruit pictograms, increased concentration and motivation during activity, as well as positive feedback from therapists and children on using the interactive fruit system	The statistical results show that only the H4 hypothesis produced a significant result (P value = 0.319; $t(10)$ = 2.540, $P < 0.05$), confirming that the children wanted to play for longer after one week of using the alternative communication system. The other hypotheses (H1, H2, H3, H5) showed no statistical significance. In addition, significant improvements were observed in the number of interactions and concentration of children when using the alternative system compared to traditional play

(continued)

(continued)

(continued)

N.	Author	Year of publication	Sample	Study design	Intervention	Outcome	Results
4	Fernández, M.J.; Jaramillo- Alcázar, A.; Galarza- Castillo, M.; Luján-Mo [13]	2019	Ecuador/Spain, people with hearing impairment	Qualitative study	Development of accessible mobile SG for education. Combining video game with a learning methodology. Final goal is to contribute to the improvement of English learning for people with disabilities	Development and test of the Serious Game	SG developed on time and tested by students who gave precious feedback
5	Montero, G. e Gomez, J. [5]	2018	Alenta is a special education school (Spain); students with cognitive disabilities and/or ASD, from 6 to 21 years; SG about reading, writing and calculus	Qualitative study	SG are used in the development of instrumental abilities, cognitive competences as well as other academic abilities related to the curriculum	Serious games are more present in the third block, as they support and contribute to different class activities: LEO CON LULA; LEO CON GRIN e YA LEO (reading games); DEXTERIA JR; SEE ME DRAW e TRAZOS Y LETRAS (writing games); CUENTA CON TUS DEDOS, NUMEROS ESPECIALES e SMATH FIGHT (calculus games)	Many students, and particularly those with special needs, benefit from their interactive and multimedia capabilities that current developments offer, as well as the motivational effect and ease of use. From Alenta teaching staff's experience, this is the only way for serious games to success, teaching abilities (in an engagement way) that will allow students to keep on building and acquire knowledge at a higher level

(continued)

N.	Author	Year of publication	Sample	Study design	Intervention	Outcome	Results
6	Islam, M.N., Hasan, U., Islam, F., Anuva, S.T., Zaki, T., A.K.M. Najmul Islam. [14]	2022	15 participants with autism spectrum disorder	Observational study	The objective of the study was to evaluate the effectiveness of the play platform for children with autism spectrum disorder in terms of cognitive development and learning, as well as to identify any problems related to the user interface	The results of the study included assessments of the effectiveness and efficiency of the play platform for children with autism spectrum disorder, measured through the success rate, number of attempts, and time to completion of games	The results of the study showed improvements in the success rate of the games between consecutive sessions. For example, in the functional card game, the success rate increased from SD 3.00 to SD 3.53 over the three sessions. In addition, the number of attempts required to complete the games gradually decreased in subsequent sessions

(continued)

(continued)

N.	Author	Year of publication	Sample	Study design	Intervention	Outcome	Results
7	Ouherrou, N., S.M.V. Metz, El Kafi, J. MA., Giraldo. [7]	2023	FASE 1: 15 primary dyslexic children (ages 8–12) and 3 speech therapists, designers, and researchers. Morocco. FASE 2: the group that participated in the brainstorming session consisted of 10 native Arabic and researchers. Morocco. FASE 2: The group that participated in the brainstorming session consisted of 10 native Arabic speakers children diagnosed consisted of 10 native Arabic speakers children diagnosed consisted of 10 native Arabic speakers children diagnosed groups. Both groups attended four sessions over a period of a month. They were selected by the MALDD, Casablanca,	Exploratory qualitative methodology	At the end of the three workshop sessions, we obtained three deliverables containing the groups' ideas, likely to improve game features and learning activities. The results indicated that all groups appreciated the game story	This paper presents the potential benefits of PD for encouraging dyslexic children and speech therapists to participate actively and generate new ideas for SG design. The results show that they were able to participate as co-designers during the early stages of the game's design process	At the end of the three workshop sessions, we obtained three deliverables containing the groups' ideas, likely to improve game features and learning activities. The results indicated that all three groups appreciated the game story

(continued)

(continued)

N.	Author	Year of publication	Sample	Study design	Intervention	Outcome	Results
8	Piazzalunga, C; Dui, G.L.; Fontolan, S.; Franceschini, S.; Bortolozzo, M; Termine, C.; Ferrante, S. [10]	2023	36 s grade children: 18 Tachistoscope group; 18 control group; Italy	RCT	To evaluate whether the Tachistoscope game is sensitive to children's writing skills, to evaluate the usability of the game, and to evaluate the effectiveness of short-term training in Increasing children's reading skills	Following the success of this preliminary phase, 36 s-grade children, split into two groups, participated in a training study: 18 children underwent a three-week training phase with the game, while the remaining 18 children served as the control group. Before the training, the authors assessed all children's reading abilities using standardized word reading and vocabulary tests. The training involved four 20-item sessions per week	P-value of 0.005 indicating a significant difference in accuracy achieved between second and third graders, with older children performing better. In addition, reading speed is significantly lower in second-graders than in third- graders (p < 0.001). No significant differences were found between males and females in either accuracy or reading speed

(continued)

N.	Author	Year of publication	Sample	Study design	Intervention	Outcome	Results
9	Piazzalunga, C.; Donati, A.; Ferrante, S [15]	2023	Italy, 66 children with Specific Learning Disorders (first and second grade)	Qualitative study	Improve adherence and motivation through the use of a SG (coin-collection system and in- game shop to the learning games of the ESSENCE project)	66 children participated in the testing, for a total of 6822 serious games uses. Weekly usage increased after the introduction of both coins and shop, while performance improved significantly after the introduction of the coins, but not of the shop (0.66 ± 0.24 before, 0.86 ± 0.16 after coins, 0.87 ± 0.13 after shop), suggesting that the presence of rewards was enough to improve adherence and lead to better results	The game was played 6822 times by the 66 children. The use of the Serious Game grew after the introduction of the coins and grew a lot more after the introduction of the shop. The average accuracy inn the gameplay increased over time

(continued)

(*continued*)

N.	Author	Year of publication	Sample	Study design	Intervention	Outcome	Results
10	Sochocka, A. Mirocha, J. Starypan, R. [8]	2019	Cracow's special needs school; the children were encouraged to use the web application in their homes, lasted for a little more than	Observational study	The description of a web application created in order to help children and teenagers with intellectual disabilities. The application gathers simple serious games that are supposed to be an addition to the daily therapy, widening and intensifying its results	A platform would be a great addition to a daily therapy and would increase the results of the children. The aim of this project was to show that the children would use such tools willingly and that this application would allow them to exercise much more often than they have done so far	The SG are a good solution to increase the skills of students. Limit: small sample

How generalizable can this figure be to all educational institutions? How inclusive can this be? Are the SGs implemented inclusive or exclusive? Certainly, answering these questions is complex, and such answers should probably also be sought through active and participatory discussion with the children involved in the research studies

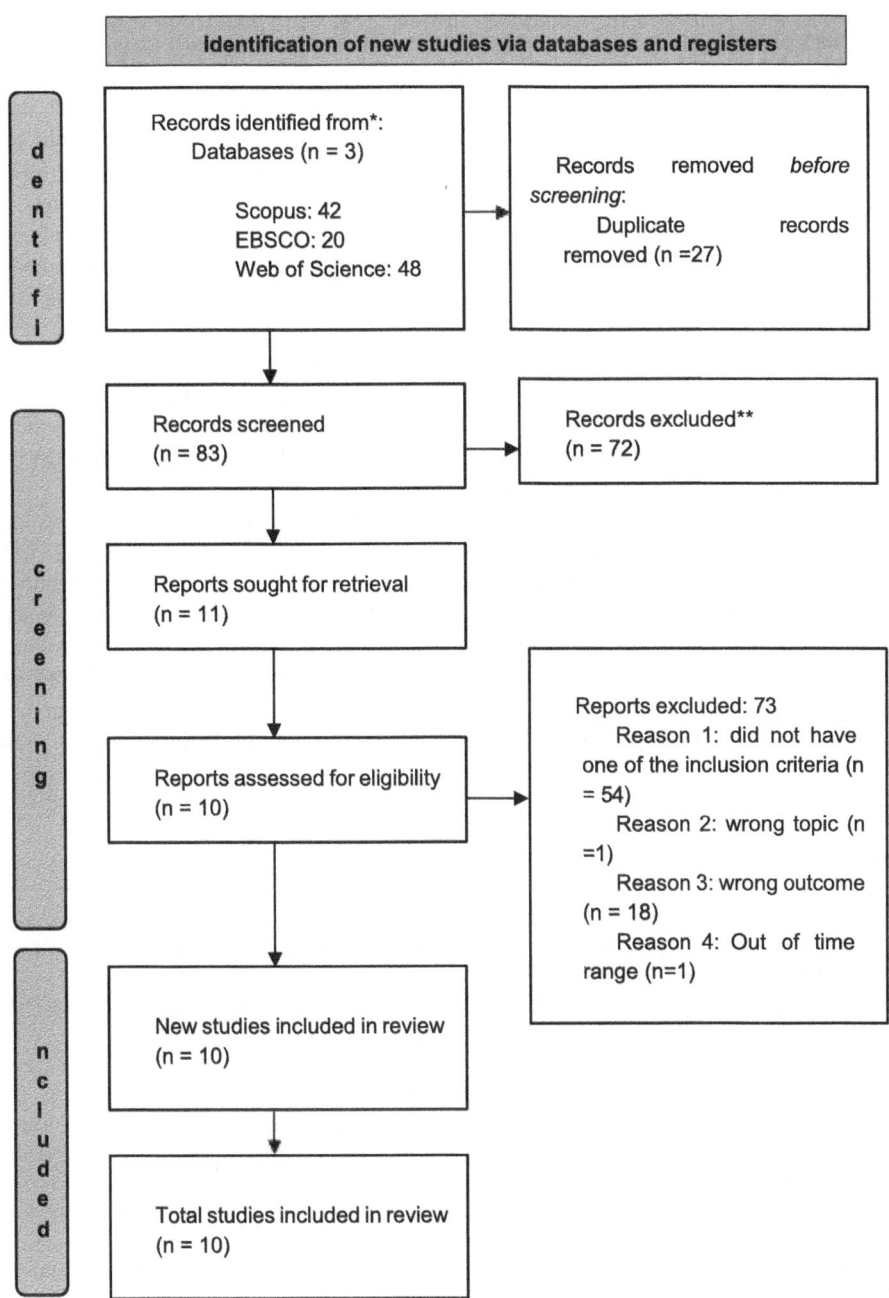

5 Conclusion

The results collected during the study of the paper included in the systematic review showed that the use of SGs with student with Specific Learning Disorders and Special Educational Needs has some positive effects, regarding the motivation and the learning outcomes of the learning experience mediated by the Serious Games.

The review also showed some weaknesses of the papers involved: the very low number of students involved, or the very specific learning environments in which the SGs were tested, do not allow the results to be generalized. A lot of factors should be taken into account before generalizing – the training background of the teachers, if the classes had already experienced some trials, the schools' equipment and many more.

Nevertheless, some data arise from this systematic review, especially thinking about the low number of studies involved in the review: in the Italian school system there aren't provisions or guidelines about using digital tools and especially regarding the use of Serious Games in the instructional design [11], so it must not be a surprise the low number of the papers found. Moreover, the review focused on a very specific target of Serious Games, thought and designed for a very specific target. It appears that a very low number of teachers commit themselves in looking for digital tools or methodologies involving digital tools in order to enhance the integration of SLD and SEN students in the classroom environment (Di Leo, 2023) [12].

A large number of the papers eliminated after the screening phases were about using SGs as rehabilitation tools rather than teaching tools.

The authors are perfectly aware that this contribution cannot cover the entire scientific production about Serious Games and that is very difficult to find all the existing trials conducted in the topic, but it nevertheless appears to be a significant lack of use of Serious Games in Italian schools for the review topic. The reasons can be multiple, starting from the lack of training about the use of digital tools and methodologies in the university courses for student teachers, to the Italian schools lack of possibility to purchase digital tools.

References

1. García-Redondo, P., García, T., Areces, D., Núñez, J.C., Rodríguez, C.: Serious games and their effect improving attention in students with learning disabilities. Int. J. Environ. Res. Public Health **16**(14), 2480 (2019)
2. Papanastasiou, G., Drigas, A., Skianis, C.: Serious games: how do they impact special education needs children. Technium Educ. Hum. **2**(3), 41–58 (2022)
3. Chai, C., Lau, B.T., Pan, Z.: Hungry Cat—a serious game for conveying spatial information to the visually impaired. Multimodal Technol. Interact. **3**(1), 12 (2019)
4. Page, M.J., McKenzie, J.E., Bossuyt, P.M., Boutron, I., Hoffmann, T.C., Mulrow, C.D., et al.: The PRISMA 2020 statement: an updated guideline for reporting systematic reviews. BMJ **372**, n71 (2021). https://doi.org/10.1136/bmj.n71
5. Montero, G., Gomez, J.: Serious games in special education. A practitioner's experience review. In: Entertainment Computing–ICEC 2018: 17th IFIP TC 14 International Conference, Held at the 24th IFIP World Computer Congress, WCC 2018, Poznan, Poland, September 17–20, 2018, Proceedings 17, pp. 397–401. Springer (2018)

6. Bossavit, B., Parsons, S.: This is how I want to learn high functioning autistic teens co-designing a serious game. In: Proceedings of the 2016 CHI Conference on Human Factors in Computing Systems, pp. 1294–1299 (2016)

7. Ouherrou, N., Mailles Viard Metz, S., El Kafi, J., Giraldo, M.A.: Participatory design of an Arabic serious game for children with dyslexia: a qualitative exploratory study. Univ. Access Inf. Soc. **23**(4), 1873–1895 (2023)

8. Sochocka, A., Mirocha, J., Starypan, R.: Serious games as an aid in the development of people with intellectual disabilities. Bio-Algorithms Med-Syst. **16**(1), 20190055 (2020)

9. Durango, I., Carrascosa, A., Gallud, J.A., Penichet, V.M.: Interactive fruit panel (IFP): a tangible serious game for children with special needs to learn an alternative communication system. Univ. Access Inf. Soc. **17**, 51–65 (2018)

10. Piazzalunga, C., et al.: Evaluating the efficacy of a serious game in enhancing word reading speed. In: Proceedings of the 17th European Conference on Games Based Learning, vol. 17, no. 1, pp. 523–530 (2023)

11. Guarini, P., Traetta, L., Ragni, B.: Al di là del principio del gioco: Serious Games e formazione docenti. NUOVA SECONDARIA **15**(2), 189–196 (2022)

12. Di Leo, N.: La figura dell'insegnante di sostegno: dall'Oriente all'Occidente, tra integrazione e rituali formali. In: Traetta L. e Caso, R., a cura di, La professionalità del docente14 F.P. Savino, R. Baldini and P. Guarini di sostegno. Esperienze, riflessioni e prospettive didattiche sui percorsi di specializzazione. Progedit, Bari (2023)

13. Fernández, M.J., Jaramillo-Alcázar, A., Galarza-Castillo, M., Luján-Mora, S.: A serious game to learn Basic English for people with hearing impairments. In: Information Technology and Systems: Proceedings of ICITS 2019, pp. 671–679. Springer (2019)

14. Islam, M.N., Hasan, U., Islam, F., Anuva, S.T., Zaki, T., Islam, A.N.: IoT-based serious gaming platform for improving cognitive skills of children with special needs. J. Educ. Comput. Res. **60**(6), 1588–1611 (2022)

15. Piazzalunga, C., Donati, A., Ferrante, S.: Co-design of a points-based reward system to boost motivation in children and improve adherence to learning serious games. In: GNB Atti, pp. 1–4 (2023)

Building an Inclusive Society. From "Mission Inclusion" Research to the Creation of "Tessere Diverse" Portal

Valentina Berardinetti[✉] ⓘ, Francesco Antonio Santangelo ⓘ, and Giusi Antonia Toto ⓘ

Learning Sciences Institute, University of Foggia, Foggia, Italy
valentina.berardinetti@unifg.it

Abstract. The contribution presents the research project "Mission Inclusion", conducted by the Learning Sciences institute of the University of Foggia, which aims to promote the social and labour inclusion of people with disabilities in the national and local context. Starting from an in-depth analysis of the territory's needs, the project aims to identify and implement effective practices that can serve as a model for future institutional interventions. The main research question investigates which strategies and approaches can best foster the inclusion and autonomy of people with disabilities, strengthening their role within the community and the labour market.

The paper will also explore the "Tessere Diverse" portal, a platform designed to facilitate the support network and sharing of experiences between different sectors, individuals, organisations and associations, improving the sharing of resources and opportunities to access services. The methodology, based on the observation and analysis of the real needs of the territory, is aimed at collecting useful data to develop models of good practice and concrete actions to support inclusion. In the article, these aspects will be examined, highlighting the project's social and employment impact prospects.

Keywords: social inclusion · inclusive placement · special educational needs

1 Introduction

Disability manifests itself in a wide range of forms encompassing different areas of the human experience: it can be physical, sensory, cognitive, behavioural and intellectual. These different manifestations bring with them a range of complex needs and challenges, requiring in-depth study, careful observation and carefully designed interventions.

Despite the progress made in recent decades, the Italian school system still has significant shortcomings in its inclusion mechanisms. An ISTAT report for the school

For the Purposes of Academic Recognition, It Should Be Noted That Although the Authors Took Equal Care in Approving and Revising the Entire Contribution, the introduction and paragraph 1 are attributed to Valentina Berardinetti; paragraph 2 to Francesco Antonio Santangelo; the conclusions and abstract to Giusi Antonia Toto.

© The Author(s), under exclusive license to Springer Nature Switzerland AG 2025
G. A. Toto (Ed.): ICS exchange 2024, CCIS 2521, pp. 88–100, 2025.
https://doi.org/10.1007/978-3-032-03021-4_7

year 2022/2023, dedicated to the inclusion of students with disabilities, highlights some worrying data: 62% of students with disabilities do not participate in school trips that include overnight stays, a fundamental educational and social experience. Moreover, almost half of Italian schools are not accessible, with a particularly critical situation in the southern regions of the country. Added to this is the finding that, although the supply of 10% support teachers is increasing, many of these have no specific training or are assigned late, also highlighting a strong discontinuity in teaching[1].

A particularly delicate moment in this process is the so-called "after-school gap", i.e. the period when the family no longer benefits from the institutional support provided by the school system, often considered one of the few bulwarks of inclusion. The end of the school career, in fact, is not infrequently seen as a 'leap into the void' rather than as a real opportunity for growth. The adolescent, now approaching adulthood, may find himself, in the event of disability, having to remain in the family care environment or to be placed in structures such as institutes and communities, not by choice but by necessity, in the absence of a truly shared planning built around his needs and desires.

The challenges to be faced do not stop at school, but continue also in the world of work. The job placement of people with disabilities is in fact a goal that is still far from being fully achieved: inclusive placement paths are often fragmented and vary according to territory, making it difficult to guarantee equal opportunities throughout the country. In our country, in fact, one of the most common problems regarding placement in the world of work concerns the fact that when highly qualified people are employed in jobs that are inferior to their skills, while others do not find employment because of the over-qualification of those who already occupy the available positions. This creates a vicious circle with continuous barriers.

In 2022, Eurostat found that 27% of the EU population over the age of 16 has a disability, or 101 million people. Despite their numbers, many of them live in isolation and find it difficult to move freely across the EU, highlighting the need to reflect on the autonomy and inclusion of people with disabilities.

Educational institutions play a crucial role: teachers should work to improve the quality of life of future adults with disabilities, starting from the design of the "Life Project" and fostering independence and job satisfaction, having a clear cognitive and behavioural map that orients the individual towards his or her full realisation. However, creating customised educational pathways is difficult for many teachers, who are often overloaded with programmes, limiting the space for more person-centred education.

To help fill these gaps, the Learning Sciences institute of the University of Foggia has launched the "Mission Inclusion" project as of June 2023. This initiative is entirely focused on the empowerment of people with disabilities and Special Educational Needs, promoting their social and labour inclusion [1]. The aim of the project is to identify and analyse the best practices adopted by organisations involved in inclusive placement, with a specific focus on territorial differences and operating methods, in order to reduce the gap that often exists between the North and the South of the country. The ultimate aim is to develop an effective model, adaptable and reproducible on a national scale, which can serve as a guide for educational and professional realities wishing to improve their inclusion paths.

---

[1] See https://www.istat.it/it/files/2024/02/Statistica-report-alunni-con-disabilità-as.-22-23.pdf.

A first significant example in this direction is the inclusionjobday.com platform, set up to cope with the limitations imposed by the pandemic, which with its 5,000 members today confirms itself as a national reference point for offering concrete job opportunities to people with disabilities and for promoting the culture of inclusion. In the virtual agora of Inclusion Job Day - which in recent times has seen the participation of many young graduates or undergraduates for a significant percentage of 55% - the meeting between high-level companies and qualified people takes place periodically in order to create concrete job opportunities for those who want to give a turn to their careers showing that disability is not a limitation and helping to promote a culture of inclusion in Italy.

2 Realising a Society for All

2.1 Analysis of Need in Italy

In the 2023 essay "Initiation of the disabled person into work from the perspective of specialised mediation services", Pasqualotto et al. [2] reflect on the value of work as a founding pillar of the Italian Republic, enshrined in Article 1 of the Constitution, and on the obligation of every citizen to contribute to the material and spiritual progress of society (Article 4), a duty that must also be guaranteed to those living with disabilities. In this regard, the data released by the Ministry of Labour and Social Policies for 2018 show the presence of approximately 360,000 employees with disabilities in Italy, 58.7% of whom are men and 41.3% women. The territorial analysis shows a greater concentration of these workers in Northern Italy (56.3%), while the South stands out for a very small share, amounting to only 21.4%, a situation attributable, at least in part, to the absence of effective networks and connections between territorial services and the world of work. The slowness with which people with disabilities access stable employment positions is particularly worrying, since it is added to a general under-representation of young people in the labour market, despite the fact that they should be the driving force behind placement initiatives (International Labour Organisation, 2022). This scenario suggests a persistent lack of homogeneity in accompaniment and support mechanisms, with strong territorial differences affecting the employment inclusion of persons with disabilities and their economic autonomy.

In support of persons with disabilities and their families, Law 112 of 22 June 2016, known as the "Law on After Us" and promoted by the Ministry of Labour and Social Policies, represents a turning point in the Italian legal system. This legislation introduces for the first time specific measures for people with severe disabilities, with the aim of ensuring continuity of support and quality of life even when family members are no longer able to provide direct care. The law aims to promote the highest level of autonomy and independence, allowing persons with disabilities to live in environments that mirror the family home as much as possible, or, alternatively, to benefit from solutions that favour de-institutionalisation processes. This is an approach that aims to overcome the traditional model of care centred on institutionalisation, promoting instead effective inclusion and a dignified life even in the absence of direct parental support.

Analyses in the literature highlight, however, how families often face difficulties in dealing with the challenges of planning for the "After Us". Numerous studies [3–7] underline how families feel insufficient support from public services, with limited options for planning a stable and peaceful future for their children with disabilities. Parents and young adults with disabilities often feel abandoned when faced with the uncertainty of the future, expressing concerns about the possibility of guaranteeing an adequate quality of life in fundamental areas such as care, psychophysical well-being, personal autonomy and social inclusion. This lack of options and institutional support reinforces in families the feeling of being left alone to face the burden of responsibilities related to the future autonomy of their children, increasing anxieties and worries especially for the transition phases to adult life.

The combination of these factors highlights how the system of social and labour inclusion of persons with disabilities, although enriched by innovative legislation such as Law 112/2016, remains characterised by structural and operational criticalities. There remains a need to develop integrated strategies and to strengthen the links between social services and the world of work, especially in less connected regions. A greater commitment is essential to build accompanying paths that take into account territorial specificities, making mediation services more accessible and attentive to the needs of persons with disabilities, so as to guarantee them fairer and faster access to the world of work and real participation in the social and economic life of the country.

2.2 The Research Project "Mission Inclusion"

In this context, the "Mission Inclusion" project fits in, which is structured around a fundamental concept: building a path of social and labour inclusion for people with disabilities, ensuring them a future that is not only independent, but fully participatory. This project, strongly rooted in the values of a democratic society, aims to respond to the often neglected need to guarantee an 'after us' for those with disabilities, i.e. a support system that allows for a dignified and autonomous continuity of life, even when the family context can no longer provide support. The main aim is therefore to facilitate access to the labour market and social life, creating models of inclusion that can be replicated, particularly in Southern Italy, where the possibilities for integration are more limited. The desire to extend and consolidate a network of cooperation between educational institutions, local authorities, companies and universities also aims to turn the South into an example of inclusiveness and valuing diversity.

In order to realise these objectives, "Mission Inclusion" relies on solid theoretical foundations and guidelines to guide its choices. One of the main references is Booth and Ainscow's "Index for Inclusion" [8], a tool designed for the school context but easily adaptable to broader contexts, thanks to its comprehensive approach to inclusion. The "Index" considers three main dimensions - producing inclusive policies, developing inclusive practices, creating inclusive cultures - that are essential for promoting authentic inclusion. In the school setting, this model is valuable for developing the transversal and relational skills of young people with disabilities, preparing them for the world of work. Schools thus become the protagonists of an educational process that is not limited to the transmission of notions, but extends to the personal and social growth of students, through practical experiences, internships and collaborations with the productive world. In this way, schools can not only train students professionally, but also make the school community aware of the importance of inclusion, breaking down stereotypes and prejudices towards people with disabilities and contributing to an inclusive culture that is then reflected in the working world.

Another pillar of the project is based on the "Diversity & Inclusion in the company" guidelines of the "UN Global Compact Network Italy" [9], which emphasise that inclusion should not be considered solely as a human resources responsibility, but as a real corporate strategy to be promoted at all levels. Inclusion thus becomes not only a moral objective, but also a competitive advantage for companies, which can make use of the potential of every human resource. Indeed, companies that adopt an inclusive culture and value diversity can achieve better results in terms of innovation and sustainability. For this reason, the presence of specific figures such as the "Disability Manager", an internal resource within the company able to support workers with disabilities throughout their professional career, promoting working environments where everyone can fully express their potential and overcome any barriers, is hoped for.

A further key element of "Mission Inclusion" is the reference to the "National Recovery and Resilience Plan" (PNRR), which devotes significant resources to supporting social infrastructures, families and promoting autonomy for people with disabilities. This strategic choice reflects the vision of a society that recognises and enhances the potential of each individual, investing in pathways to autonomy that improve the quality of life of people with disabilities and make communities more inclusive.

As part of the research and analysis of practices already in place, the "Mission Inclusion" team has so far conducted visits to no less than 7 organisations (type B social cooperatives and foundations) in Northern and Central Italy, such as the Social Cooperative "Eta Beta" in Bologna and "La Semente" at Limiti di Spello the social cooperative 'Vale un sogno' in San Giovanni Lupatoto, the social cooperative "Il Sogno" in Domodossola and the social cooperative "Il Ponte" in Invorio, the ASAD co-operative - which initiated the "Orti felici" project in Umbertide - and the Microbiscottificio 'Frolla' (as shown in Table 1). These realities were selected as examples of successful work inclusion, in which the placement of people with disabilities takes place in a structured manner that is attentive to individual needs. Direct observation - conducted through an ad hoc structured observation grid - and interaction with these organisations made it possible to thoroughly examine central aspects such as the socio-cognitive skills of the people involved, their motivation and level of personal autonomy. An essential element of the analysis was also the study of interpersonal and communication skills, which are crucial for interacting in a work and social context, and of emotional stability, which supports people with disabilities at critical moments in their careers.

The long-term objectives of "Mission Inclusion" include building a collaborative network in Southern Italy, involving local authorities, educational institutions, families and companies to develop concrete and sustainable actions in favour of the employment inclusion of people with disabilities. This process is not limited to improving employment opportunities, but intends to generate a real culture of inclusion at a territorial level, spreading awareness of the importance of including each individual as a resource for society. At the same time, in addition to the creation of a final report, to be presented to institutional and regional authorities, with the aim of stimulating discussion and soliciting policies that guarantee equal access to training and employment for persons with disabilities, in order to spread good practices and widen the network of territorial coop-eration, guaranteeing support also to the South, it was decided to open the online portal "Tessere Diverse", a platform that allows to shorten distances and promote inclusion everywhere in order to make also the South of Italy an example of successful social and labour inclusion.

Table 1. The stages of the "Mission Inclusion" project

Name of the social cooperative	Country
Cooperative ASAD	Umbertide (Pg)
Social Cooperative ONLUS "Il Sogno"	Domodossola (VB)
Agricultural Cooperative Society "La Semente"	Limiti di Spello (PG)
Social Cooperative "Il Ponte"	Invorio (NO)
Social Cooperative ONLUS "Etabeta"	Bologna (BO)
Microbiscuit factory "Frolla" Social Cooperative "Vale un sogno"	Osimo (AN) San Giovanni Lupatoto (VR)

3   The "Tessere Diverse" Platform

3.1   The Choice of Name

The word "tessere" recalls the idea of a network or interweaving. To weave, figura-tively speaking, means to create connections between different elements in order to build something bigger and more cohesive. This is perfectly in line with the platform's mission, which aims to connect people, institutions and companies to promote social inclusion. Furthermore, "tessere" also evokes an active process, emphasising that inclu-sion is something that needs to be actively constructed, an element that fits well with the platform's philosophy. The term "diverse" makes explicit the theme of diversity, which is at the heart of the platform's objectives. This immediately emphasises the inclusiveness of the project, suggesting that each "tessera" (each individual) is different, but that all together they form a richer and more complete mosaic. The reference to diversity also suggests a positive message, in which the differences between people are not seen as an obstacle, but as a resource to be enhanced.

Fig. 1. Logo of "Tessere Diverse" platform.

The term "tessere" can also have another meaning in Italian, namely "tessere" as objects, the physical tesserae (like the tiles of a jigsaw puzzle or the tiles of a mosaic, hence also the logo symbol, Fig. 1). This opens the door to a very powerful visual image: several tesserae which, when joined together, form a complete and harmonious image. This interpretation is also consistent with the idea of social inclusion, where each person is an important 'tile' to complete a large common project.

The name "Tessere Diverse" is broad enough to allow for future expansions of the platform. It is not limited exclusively to disability, but leaves room to discuss all kinds of diversity (ethnic, gender, cultural, etc.), making it applicable in various contexts and potentially attractive to a wide range of users. The name is therefore versatile and adaptable to different aspects of inclusiveness.

From a communication point of view, the name is simple, direct and easy to remember. It has a smooth and pleasant sound, which facilitates its memorisation. In an era where brevity and clarity are crucial to capture attention online, "Tessere Diverse" manages to communicate a lot with just a few words, without being complex or technical. It is an evocative and inclusive name, offering multiple keys to interpretation, all consistent with the themes of connection, inclusion and valuing diversity, making it not only valid, but also extremely effective as a brand name for such a project.

3.2 Aims and Objectives

In this era of global interconnectedness, where technology is redefining the way people communicate and participate in social life, the "Tessere Diverse" platform emerges as an innovative project dedicated to social inclusion [10]. Founded with the aim of creating a virtual space that breaks down barriers, "Tessere Diverse" is a platform designed to promote dialogue, value diversity and build a collaborative network between schools, universities, local authorities and companies (Fig. 2).

Fig. 2. Screenshot of homepage of "Tessere Diverse" platform.

At the heart of the platform is social inclusion. This concept translates into a concrete commitment to ensuring that every person, regardless of their physical, mental, social or cultural condition, has the opportunity to actively participate in community life. 'Tessere Diverse' is not only a space to discuss inclusion, but aims to be a concrete tool to break down barriers and create meaningful connections between individuals and institutions.

The project aims to achieve a number of fundamental objectives that aim to promote a more inclusive and aware society. A first objective is to raise awareness of inclusion by providing detailed information and educational resources that can help people better understand the challenges, barriers and opportunities that characterise social inclusion. The aim is not only to inform, but to build a widespread culture of respect and awareness that can make inclusion a daily and natural practice.

A second crucial aspect of the project is the creation of a collaborative environment, facilitating communication and networking between different social actors, such as local authorities, companies, schools and universities. Through this networking, the project intends to promote the exchange of experiences and knowledge between actors from different sectors, supporting the development of inclusive practices that can be adapted to different contexts. This collaboration aims not only at sharing good practices, but also at innovating and experimenting new strategies, so that each reality involved can evolve and be enriched by the comparison with other experiences.

A third central objective is the empowerment of people with disabilities, which is a fundamental component for effective inclusion. The project is committed to offering these people tools, opportunities and safe spaces where they can express their voice, receive support and feel respected. The aim is to encourage the autonomy and active participation of people with disabilities so that they can play an active and meaningful role in society and, at the same time, raise awareness in the community of the importance of an inclusive environment for all.

Finally, the project aims to disseminate good inclusion practices through the direct involvement of experts in the field. The dedicated platform is committed to collecting and sharing strategies and approaches that have been tested and proven to be effective in different fields, including work and school. The sharing of these good practices aims to make inclusion an increasingly widespread and consolidated process, promoting models that can be adapted and replicated by other organisations and institutions, to constantly improve inclusiveness and social cohesion at all levels.

In this sense, "Tessere Diverse" represents a project that looks to the future, promoting a more equitable, just and resilient society. Inclusion, understood as an essential value, not only improves people's quality of life but also fosters social cohesion and collective development.

3.3 Technical Description and Platform Structure

The platform is developed using WordPress, a CMS that offers a simple and accessible interface, which is essential to ensure usability even by users with limited digital skills [11]. WordPress allows dynamic content management and the integration of specific plugins for inclusion, such as tools for voice reading of content and compatibility with assistive technologies, including screen readers and alternative keyboards.

The choice of WordPress was dictated by several factors:

- Accessibility: WordPress allows the creation of highly accessible sites, thanks to compatibility with dedicated plugins and tools. The platform has been optimised to work with screen readers, text readers that allow people with visual impairments to navigate easily.
- Ease of use: WordPress offers a simple and intuitive interface that allows even people with limited technical skills to manage content, thus facilitating participation and contribution by a wide range of users.
- Customisation: thanks to the flexibility of WordPress, "Tessere Diverse" can integrate a wide range of features, including plugins for social inclusion, automatic translation, discussion forums, and tools for user interaction.

One of the strengths of WordPress is its scalability. The platform can grow with the project, allowing features to be added and the user experience to be improved without compromising the stability of the system [12]. This is especially important for a platform like "Tessere Diverse", which aims to become a national benchmark for social inclusion.

One of the most relevant aspects of "Tessere Diverse" is the focus on accessibility. The aim is to ensure that every user can access the site, regardless of their abilities or special needs. Some of the tools implemented to achieve this are:

- Assistive navigation: the site has been optimised to work with assistive technologies, such as screen readers and alternative keyboards, to facilitate navigation by people with visual or motor disabilities.
- Layout customisation: the platform allows users to customise the interface, modifying font size, colour contrast and other visual settings, to ensure optimal content enjoyment.
- Multilingual content: thanks to automatic translation plug-ins, the site is also accessible to users who speak languages other than Italian, facilitating broad participation by international or bilingual communities.

The platform offers a number of tools that enable users to interact with each other and access high-quality educational resources. These include:

- Forum and community: an interactive space where users can share experiences, discuss relevant topics and receive support. The "Tessere Diverse" community is designed to be inclusive and safe, ensuring that all people can express themselves freely and find answers to their questions.
- Webinars and virtual conferences: the platform regularly organises online events on topics related to social inclusion. These events feature experts in the field, activists and thought leaders, with the aim of stimulating debate and raising awareness.
- Articles and guides: a section of the site is dedicated to the publication of articles and practical guides addressing different inclusion issues. The resources are designed for educators as well as for companies and individuals, offering concrete tools to promote inclusion in their respective contexts.

3.4 Social Potential of the Platform

From a social point of view, "Tessere Diverse" has enormous potential to promote change. In a context where cultural, physical and social differences often create divisions, this platform aims to turn them into added value, building an environment where diversity is considered an asset. Through intercultural dialogue, "Tessere Diverse" fosters a more cohesive and respectful society by connecting people of all backgrounds and encouraging mutual understanding.

In addition, the portal is a key resource for raising awareness among businesses, particularly in Southern Italy, about the importance of inclusive practices in the workplace. With practical resources and models, "Tessere Diverse" supports companies in implementing inclusive environments that value the contribution of each individual and strengthen the sense of community. By offering a space where people can feel part of a supportive and open network, the platform contributes to enhancing the sense of belonging and social cohesion.

With its flexible and scalable structure, "Tessere Diverse" has high growth potential, with opportunities to integrate innovative technologies to enhance the user experience and expand the social impact of the project. Potential future developments include the use of artificial intelligence to provide real-time personalised assistance through advanced chatbots and virtual assistants, as well as the adoption of virtual and augmented reality to create virtual meeting spaces where physical and geographical barriers can be overcome. Furthermore, through machine learning, "Tessere Diverse" could adapt to the specific needs of users, offering customised content and educational resources.

More than just a digital platform, "Tessere Diverse" is a project that aims to build an inclusive future, where each person can feel welcome and part of a supportive community. Thanks to its solid technological basis and its accessibility and interaction-oriented approach, the portal has the potential to become a reference point for social inclusion initiatives in Italy and beyond.

4 Conclusions

As previously analysed, the employment integration of people with disabilities represents a complex challenge, influenced by many different factors [13]. This issue raises a number of intricate needs that require in-depth analysis in order to develop effective interventions capable of supporting the integration of individuals in the social and employment context.

A key element to facilitate this process is the promotion of active collaboration between different actors, including local communities, organisations, institutions and families. It is crucial to directly involve people with disabilities in these dynamics. The common goal is to encourage initiatives that can generate concrete and lasting change over time, creating real opportunities for all.

In this context, initiatives such as "Mission Inclusion" research play a crucial role in analysing the surrounding reality and promoting the social and employment inclusion of individuals with disabilities. This research not only contributes to a deeper understanding of the challenges and opportunities faced by people with disabilities, but also provides useful data and analysis to inform policies and develop inclusion programmes. The information gathered through "Mission Inclusion" can guide the creation of targeted interventions and innovative strategies, ensuring that the measures adopted are based on concrete evidence and real needs.

Furthermore, the "Tessere Diverse" platform emerges as an innovative project dedicated to social inclusion. Founded with the intention of creating a virtual space that breaks down barriers, "Tessere Diverse" represents an important initiative to promote dialogue, value diversity and initiate an initial form of networking and sharing.

The future prospects resulting from the integration of the "Tessere Diverse" platform and "Mission Inclusion" research are promising. For schools and universities, such initiatives can stimulate a more inclusive and collaborative educational environment where students with disabilities can access specific resources and supports. Educational institutions can benefit from a collaborative network that provides opportunities for learning and professional development, encouraging greater awareness and sensitivity to inclusion issues.

In addition, these initiatives can contribute to a more inclusive work culture in companies, which could benefit from a diverse and trained workforce capable of bringing new perspectives and ideas. The inclusion of people with disabilities not only enriches the work environment, but also promotes a positive image of the company in the community, contributing to a broader cultural change that recognises and values the abilities and talents of each individual.

This approach requires the implementation of coordinated and systemic interventions capable of developing shared practices through a common language. Only by overcoming the fragmentation of isolated actions will it be possible to achieve significant results. As Giaconi et al. [3] point out, designing common perspectives together allows them to be continuously redefined, adapting them to the interactions that develop in the various contexts and moments of everyday life. The creation of spaces such as 'Tessere Diverse' and the implementation of research such as 'Mission Inclusion' represent fundamental steps in this direction, as they enable the construction of a more inclusive and cohesive community, where diversity is not only welcomed, but becomes an added value for society as a whole.

References

1. Rossi, M., Furia, D., Toto, G.A.: Dati e valore sociale del progetto mission inclusion: domande, finalità e primi risultati della ricerca. SIRD, 409–417 (2024)
2. Pasqualotto, L., et al.: L'avvio al lavoro della persona con disabilità nella prospettiva dei Servizi specialistici di mediazione. Gli esiti di un percorso di formazione e ricerca. L'integrazione Scolastica e Sociale **22**(1), 51–68 (2023)
3. Brennan, C., Traustadóttir, R., Rice, J., Anderberg, P.: Being number one is the biggest obstacle: implementing the UN convention on the rights of persons with disabilities within Nordic welfare services. Nordisk välfärdsforskning| Nordic Welfare Res. **3**(1), 18–32 (2018)
4. Giaconi, C., Socci, C., Fidanza, B, Del Bianco, N., d'Angelo, I., Cappelini, S.A.: Il Dopo di Noi: nuove alleanze tra pedagogia speciale ed economia per nuovi spazi di Qualità di Vita. MeTis-Mondi educativi. Temi indagini suggestioni **10**(2), 274–291 (2020)
5. Caldin, R., Giaconi, C.: Disabilità e cicli di vita. Le famiglie tra seduttivi immaginari e plausibili realtà. FrancoAngeli, Milano (2021)
6. Verga, M.: Il Dopo di noi e il Durante noi: brevi riflessioni a cinque anni dall'approvazione della Legge 112/2016. FrancoAngeli, Milano (2021)
7. Perego, C., Oberti, I., Pavesi, A.S.: Progetto di Vita and universal design for persons with disabilities. In: Transforming Our World Through Universal Design for Human Development: Proceedings of the Sixth International Conference on Universal Design (UD2022), vol. 297, p. 201. IOS Press (2022)
8. Booth, T., Ainscow, M., Black-Hawkins, K., Vaughan, M., Shaw, L.: Index for inclusion. In: Developing Learning and Participation in Schools, vol. 2 (2002)
9. Frey, M., Daniela, B., Stella, S.: Linee Guida Diversity & Inclusion In Azienda. L'esperienza dell'Osservatorio D&I di UN Global Compact Network Italia (2021)
10. Giesteira, B., Peçaibes, V., Cardoso, P., Maior, G.V., Quaresma, I.: inclusivity play: web platform and games for inclusion and diversity in the university - the skills for a next-generation project. https://doi.org/10.4018/979-8-3693-1614-6.ch007
11. Kumar, A., Kumar, A., Hashmi, H., Khan, S.A.: WordPress: a multi-functional content management system. In: 2021 10th International Conference on System Modeling & Advancement in Research Trends (SMART), MORADABAD, India, pp. 158–161 (2021). https://doi.org/10.1109/SMART52563.2021.9675311

12. Zilak, M., Keselj, A., Besjedica, T.: Accessible web prototype features from technological point of view. In: 2019 42nd International Convention on Information and Communication Technology, Electronics and Microelectronics (MIPRO), Opatija, Croatia, pp. 457–462 (2019). https://doi.org/10.23919/MIPRO.2019.8757115
13. Caldin, R., Scollo, S.: Inclusione lavorativa, disabilità e identità. Riflessioni e rappresentazioni. STUDIUM EDUCATIONIS-Rivista semestrale per le professioni educative **3**, 49–60 (2018)

The STEM Approach to Tackling Gender Segregation: An Educational Project in Secondary Schools

Dario Lombardi$^{(\boxtimes)}$ ⓘ, Anna Teresa Musicco ⓘ, and Nadia Di Leo ⓘ

Department of Humanities, University of Foggia, Foggia, Italy
`{dario.lombardi,anna.musicco,nadia.dileo}@unifg.it`

Abstract. Gender segregation remains a critical issue affecting employment and leadership across sectors. This paper investigates the potential of STEM (Science, Technology, Engineering, and Mathematics) education to reduce gender disparities, aligning with international and EU directives. The Italian National Recovery and Resilience Plan (PNRR) prioritizes investments in STEM skills to close the gender gap between Italy and the European average. The initial part of this study addresses gender-based occupational segregation and its broader societal impacts, which perpetuate inequalities and limit equal opportunities. Identified as an educational emergency, the paper advocates for equipping students with tools to promote gender awareness and equity. Using data from Almalaurea (2020/2021), a significant gender imbalance in STEM enrollments is highlighted, underscoring the urgency of targeted interventions. The STEM approach, integrating Information and Communication Technologies (ICT), is proposed as a pedagogical strategy to foster hands-on experimentation and real-world applications, enhancing engagement and critical thinking skills. The study presents an educational STEM project implemented in secondary schools in Foggia, Italy, involving 114 students across scientific high schools, technical institutes, and vocational schools. Through interdisciplinary activities and project-based learning, students explored gender segregation themes and developed 28 applications to promote social inclusion. Qualitative analysis identified seven core themes, suggesting that workshop-based STEM methodologies significantly outperform traditional teaching in motivating students and deepening their understanding of gender issues. The findings support STEM's transformative potential in creating an inclusive learning environment and fostering gender equity.

Keywords: gender segregation · STEM · ICT · inclusive education

1 Introduction

The objective of this study is to assess the effectiveness of the STEM (Science, Technology, Engineering, and Mathematics) approach in raising students' awareness of gender segregation issues within university orientation programs. To achieve this, the study monitored student engagement during lectures conducted by three university trainers (D.L., A.T.M., N.D.L.) and analyzed applications developed by students to enhance social inclusion for women.

G. A. Toto (Ed.): ICS exchange 2024, CCIS 2521, pp. 101–123, 2025.
https://doi.org/10.1007/978-3-032-03021-4_8

The subsequent sections detail the orientation project initiated by the University of Foggia, in line with the strategies outlined in the Italian National Recovery and Resilience Plan (PNRR). The paper addresses gender disparities in STEM-related university courses and discusses the pedagogical framework and methodologies underpinning the STEM approach. It then outlines the phases, materials, and educational content utilized during the program in secondary schools. Additionally, the analysis of the student-designed inclusive projects will be presented, along with findings on student participation and engagement. These insights highlight the potential of the STEM approach to foster awareness and promote gender equity in educational contexts.

1.1   From PNRR to the University of Foggia's Orientation Paths

Mission 4 of the Italian National Recovery and Resilience Plan (PNRR) encompasses a series of measures and investments aimed at fostering a knowledge-driven economy, enhancing competitiveness, and improving resilience by addressing the critical short-comings in the education, training, and research sectors [1]. The plan identifies several educational and research challenges and outlines strategies to enhance the educational offering, equipping students with essential skills and applied knowledge to meet contemporary societal demands. Moreover, it emphasizes the need to increase the flexibility of university programs, enabling a smoother specialization process across various fields of study.

A key focus of the "Education and Research" Mission is the strengthening of research and the promotion of innovative models that bridge academia and industry. This is aligned with the broader objective of "facilitating access to university, accelerating the transition to the labor market, and enhancing guidance tools for university pathway choices." To support this goal, the PNRR allocates 250 million euros for active guidance initiatives in the school-university transition. This investment aims to boost university enrollment among secondary school students, address dropout rates, and reduce gender disparities in both employment and higher education participation [1].

The initiative includes a program targeting one million students, beginning in the third year of secondary school, through collaborative courses led by university lecturers and school teachers. The program's objectives are to deliver 50,000 courses and establish 6,000 agreements between schools and universities. As specified in Ministerial Decree 934/2022, Article 3, orientation activities should incorporate interactive, workshop-based teaching aligned with scientific methodology [2]. In accordance with these guidelines, the University of Foggia has developed STEM-based orientation activities to address gender segregation in secondary schools.

2   Literature

The STEM movement originated in the early 1990s, following a conference organized by the National Science Foundation (NSF), the U.S. government agency responsible for basic research and education in all non-medical scientific and engineering fields. The acronym "STEM" was coined by Rita Colwell, Ph.D., NSF director from 1998 to 2004. According to Friedman [17], the movement gained momentum only after the establishment of a STEM education degree at Virginia Tech University in 2005, marking the beginning of its international expansion [18]. Initially focused on meeting the rising demand for skilled human capital, STEM education soon emerged as a strategic approach to developing a workforce equipped for modern challenges [19]. Consequently, a strong STEM curriculum became a priority, integrating science, mathematics, engineering, and technology into K-12 education in the United States [20].

The integration of STEM in U.S. education has resulted in mathematics and science becoming core subjects, while engineering has been introduced as a new area of study, and technology is widely available as an elective subject in most states [16].

2.1 What Does STEM Stand for?

STEM is an interdisciplinary approach encompassing Science, Technology, Engineering, and Mathematics [15]. It aims to provide students with a comprehensive understanding of how these domains interconnect, rather than teaching fragmented knowledge [16]. Each component is defined as follows:

S (SCIENCE). Investigates the natural world through processes such as inquiry, exploration, and the scientific method [21].

T (TECHNOLOGY). Defined by the American Association for the Advancement of Science (AAAS) as the application of human skills to modify the environment, enhancing our abilities to shape, move, and manipulate objects [22].

E (ENGINEERING). The application of scientific and mathematical principles to create structures, products, or systems that serve human needs, using materials and forces of nature efficiently [23].

M (MATHAMATICS). The study of patterns and relationships, integral to technological advancements and engineering innovations [22].

This interdisciplinary framework enables students to understand societal complexities through a holistic, interconnected perspective [16].

2.2 Addressing the Gender Gap in STEM: Challenges and Opportunities for Equal Participation

Addressing the gender gap in higher education and promoting the development of science, technology, engineering, and mathematics (STEM) requires a deeper understanding of the underlying factors contributing to this persistent imbalance. STEM fields need an increased number of well-trained experts; however, gender segregation within higher education results in a significant underrepresentation of women, with female participation in some disciplines falling below 30% [3]. This imbalance hampers both innovation and the diversity of perspectives within these critical sectors. Thus, identifying and addressing the drivers of this phenomenon is crucial for formulating effective strategies.

Research suggests that women often choose careers centered around people and caregiving, while men gravitate toward fields related to objects and technology. Yet, these choices are influenced not only by personal interests but also by social conditioning, cultural expectations, and institutional barriers. Factors such as Stereotype Threat [4], which can undermine women's performance and confidence, and the "Leaky Pipeline" phenomenon [3], where women drop out of STEM fields at higher rates as they advance, contribute to the erosion of gender balance. Addressing these dynamics requires looking beyond preferences to understand how stereotypes and biases shape motivation and decision-making.

Persistent gender inequities in academia and research demand a multifaceted approach. Operational measures should include affirmative actions to increase female representation at all educational and professional levels, support for career advancement, shared family responsibilities, and robust policies to counter sexism and harassment. Culturally, dismantling deep-rooted stereotypes that view women as less capable in mathematics and technical fields is crucial, as these biases are often internalized from an early age [4].

A valuable strategy is the implementation of educational programs aimed at identifying and countering gender biases in organizational models and research activities. Regular monitoring of gender balance is also essential to prevent male-dominated panels, task forces, and leadership positions. In Italy, women remain underrepresented in scientific societies and professional organizations, limiting their visibility and influence [5]. Such disparities hinder the effective utilization of female talents, making it imperative to promote greater gender equity in all scientific and professional arenas.

2.3 Women's "Leaky Pipeline"

The term "leaky pipeline" refers to the gradual attrition of talented women from advanced positions in STEM fields. This phenomenon has been extensively analyzed through studies, articles, and reports, yet findings often diverge due to varying datasets and research methodologies. As highlighted by several scholars, the metaphor conveys a sense of irreversible loss, akin to leaks from a physical pipe, where the loss is considered detrimental [6].

Empirical evidence confirms that women are underrepresented in senior academic roles and high-tech industries, but it is essential to recognize that career choices in science are influenced by personal circumstances, interests, and aspirations [6]. The Massachusetts Institute of Technology (MIT) Special Edition Newsletter further underscores that "the pipeline leaks at every stage of the career" [7], indicating a systemic issue that impacts women throughout the academic trajectory, which involves prolonged education and training phases.

Recent research has substantiated this claim, adopting diverse sociological, psychological, and cultural frameworks to understand why this gender gap persists. While existing literature acknowledges the obstacles women face in achieving gender equity within academic institutions, it does not adequately address how female faculty develop their career aspirations, the role of career development in shaping their professional experiences, and the support needed from institutions and advisors to positively influence career outcomes [8]. Consequently, a more nuanced exploration is necessary to identify effective strategies that address not only the barriers to retention but also the factors that motivate and sustain women's engagement in STEM careers.

2.4 Studies About the Reasons Behind the Low Presence of Women in STEM

Gasser and Shaffer employed a modified grounded theory approach to investigate women's experiences leading to and within academic careers. Grounded theory involves categorizing data elements, defining their properties, and explaining their interconnections [9]. In their study, they used published literature—primarily quantitative research— as their data source, aiming to analyze women's academic trajectories and professional experiences.

Their qualitative research was guided by general questions, generating an exploratory process that examined literature on career development, gender, and women's academic careers. The authors initiated their review using search terms such as "women," "academia," "faculty," "career development," and "pipeline," excluding studies focusing on women outside U.S. institutions. Patterns began to emerge, and they utilized an inductive method to identify key themes following Glaser's grounded theory principles, which organize similar codes into broader categories [10].

The authors grouped findings into three overarching themes: career development, pipeline influences, and pipeline outcomes. Career development includes factors like career aspirations, expectations, and self-efficacy. Pipeline influences encompass socialization processes, gender role attitudes, availability of resources, and exposure to career opportunities. Finally, pipeline outcomes refer to career achievements, retention, and progression [11]. This framework helps clarify how individual and environmental factors shape women's academic careers.

Understanding these challenges is essential for identifying strategies to support female researchers, ensuring their career progression aligns with that of their male counterparts [12]. The underrepresentation of women in science not only impacts the field but also perpetuates economic disparities between genders.

Notably, at the end of high school, females demonstrate similar STEM readiness and achieve higher average grades in prerequisite courses compared to their male peers [8]. However, gender-based differences persist in STEM course selection, with women more likely to enroll in biology and chemistry, and fewer opting for physics or calculus [8]. Addressing these disparities is key to achieving greater gender equity in STEM fields.

2.5 What Can We Do to Bridge the Gender Gap in STEM?

The current international research results are not particularly encouraging and point towards the need for new educational and social goals. There is a critical need to design targeted educational programs based on a thorough analysis of learning pathways to promote scientific and financial skills in Italian students. These efforts aim to address gender disparities and support financial independence, especially among women.

To spark and sustain girls' interest in STEM subjects, the educational system must implement several key strategies. First, STEM subjects should be introduced into the curriculum from primary school onwards, using teaching methods that account for gender differences. Female role models should be highlighted to demonstrate real-world applications of STEM in various fields such as health, social services, and technology, making these subjects more appealing to girls. Additionally, teacher training programs should focus on developing pedagogical approaches that encourage independent problem-solving and better performance in mathematics. Such programs must also address gender biases that can influence teachers' perceptions of students.

Beyond combating stereotypes and biases that contribute to gender gaps in STEM, it is vital to prevent the risk of limiting the financial autonomy of women by fostering early learning in mathematics and financial literacy. This can be achieved through the design of innovative, interdisciplinary educational pathways that raise awareness among young female students about their potential in scientific, mathematical, and financial domains [13].

Encouraging girls to pursue careers in fields traditionally dominated by men is essential for addressing the underrepresentation of women in strategic sectors critical to economic growth. Introducing financial education from primary school would help foster financial literacy, which not only promotes individual autonomy but also contributes to a more equitable and sustainable society. By supporting financial inclusion, it can bridge social gaps and mitigate the effects of inequality [14].

2.6   The STEM Approach: Educational Innovation and a Tool for Gender Inclusion in Italian Schools**

The STEM (Science, Technology, Engineering, and Mathematics) approach has undergone significant terminological refinements in recent years. Based on varying teaching methodologies within STEM disciplines, Martin-Pàez, Aguilera, Perales-Palacios, and Vìlchez-Gonzales [24] have distinguished between several core concepts:

1. Integrated STEM: Refers to the integration of different STEM disciplines, placing a particular emphasis on one discipline over another. It encompasses both formal and informal contexts and employs diverse instructional strategies [16].
2. Transdisciplinarity: Highlights the disjunction between academic knowledge and the application to solve social issues, advocating for holistic approaches [25].
3. Interdisciplinarity: Involves addressing complex problems that require the use of theories and methods from multiple disciplines, thereby enhancing students' capacity to develop transferable skills [26].
4. Supradisciplinarity: Engages multiple fields of study to achieve a synthesis that extends beyond the scope of individual disciplines [27].
5. Multidisciplinarity: Involves the parallel application of various disciplines without integrating them, aiming to achieve discipline-specific outcomes in solving broader problems [28].

These conceptual nuances indicate that a precise definition of STEM learning is still evolving. Nevertheless, synthesizing the presented terminologies, STEM education can be broadly defined as the integration of conceptual, procedural, and attitudinal content with STEM-specific competencies aimed at addressing real-world challenges.

When considering the STEM framework in an Italian context, it is evident that it plays a pivotal role in shaping the educational landscape, particularly in the context of Mission 4 of the National Recovery and Resilience Plan (PNRR). The Italian education system, renowned for its robust cultural and theoretical foundation, is now called upon to enhance digital skills, behavioral competencies, and applied knowledge, while maintaining its academic legacy [1].

The STEM methodology is introduced as an innovative pedagogical model that engages students from early childhood through experiential and applied learning activities. It is distinguished by its use of interactive, workshop-based methods that promote collaboration between peers and educators [29].

The implementation of the STEM approach follows a sequential, structured framework that guides students through the learning process:

1. Theoretical Understanding: Establishes a solid conceptual foundation on relevant topics.
2. Design Phase: Encourages students to conceptualize and design potential solutions.
3. Practical Implementation: Translates theoretical ideas into tangible projects.
4. Collaboration: Fosters teamwork, allowing for the exchange of diverse skills and perspectives to comprehensively address challenges.
5. Reflection and Evaluation: Promotes critical self-assessment, evaluation of outcomes, and identification of areas for improvement [30].

By incorporating these stages, the STEM approach enables students to actively engage in exploration, experimentation, and creation, thereby cultivating critical thinking, problem-solving abilities, and creativity. It also prepares them to respond adaptively to evolving societal and professional demands [31].

The existing literature review and statistics have highlighted a significant gender gap within STEM fields, particularly in the Italian context, and a paucity of studies that leverage the STEM framework to mitigate gender stereotypes.

Italy ranks second to last in Europe in terms of the number of graduates, with just 29 graduates for every 100 young people aged between 25 and 34. Although there has been progress compared to the 21.1% recorded in 2011, the figure remains far from the European average of 40.5% and only exceeds that of Romania, which stands at 24.9%. The situation worsens when considering the number of graduates in scientific disciplines: Italy records 16.4 graduates for every 1,000 young people aged between 20 and 29, compared to 21 for the European average [48]. The gap is even more marked compared to countries such as France (over 25 graduates per 1,000), Germany (24.4), Spain and Poland (both over 20).

The picture gets even worse when looking at skills: in the last OECD-Pisa survey in 2022 (Fig. 1), Italy showed a generalised decline, standing out as the country with the largest gender gap in mathematics results. Boys outperformed girls by 21.1 points, significantly higher than the OECD average of 9.1 points and the figure for the other participating countries [49].

This phenomenon is not insignificant, as it has a negative influence on further education and gender equality policies. Gender stereotypes play a crucial role in this context. Many girls, while performing well in mathematics, do not perceive science or engineering professions as suitable options for them. In OECD countries, among 15-year-old students who excel in science, only 14.5% of girls envisage a career in this field, compared to 26% of boys [49].

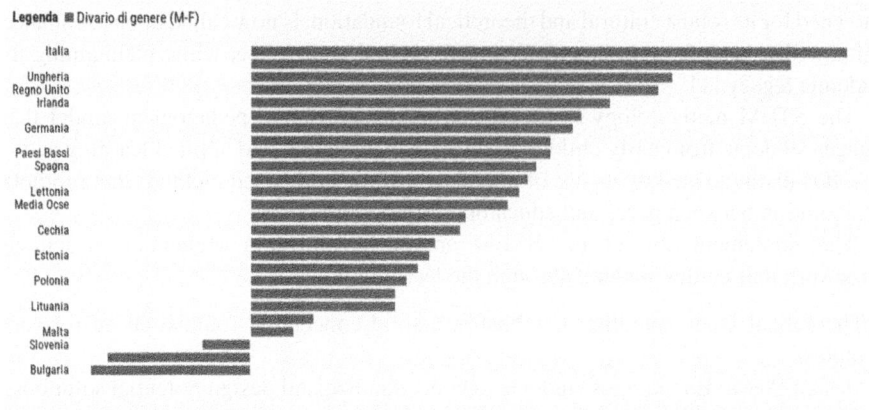

Fig. 1. Gender gap in mathematics scores of 15-year-olds in the OECD-Pisa tests (2022). SOURCE: openpolis - Con i Bambini elaboration on OECD-Pisa data (published: Tuesday, 5 December 2023)

This underrepresentation of women in STEM education has profound consequences. Science disciplines, in general, offer better paid and more stable career opportunities, and in a world increasingly dominated by technology, this trend is set to strengthen. Tackling gender gaps, including wage gaps, inevitably involves strengthening STEM at all school levels and eliminating gender stereotypes that limit girls' access to these disciplines [49].

Given this context, the present study aims to pursue the following research objectives:

1. Engage students in the development of creative, collaborative, and innovative solutions using STEM education as a platform for generating project ideas that address real-world issues.
2. Evaluate the effectiveness of the STEM approach in promoting gender inclusivity and breaking down stereotypes, with a focus on analyzing student participation during classroom activities.

In relation to the research objectives, the following research questions have been identified:

1) Can STEM education be regarded as a valid approach to encourage the exploration of innovative and creative solutions by secondary school students, with the aim of promoting gender social inclusion, and what types of creative solutions do students develop to ensure greater gender inclusion in society?
2) Is STEM education considered an effective approach to foster active student participation during lessons, with the goal of promoting gender inclusion in society?

The subsequent methodology section will delineate the specific educational interventions employed to inform students about the gender disparities in STEM university courses and the evaluation rubric developed by university experts to measure student engagement during lessons.

3 Methodology

3.1 Presentation of the Teaching Intervention and Project Analysis

In response to the first research objective, an educational intervention was designed to raise students' awareness of the gender gap in STEM university courses. At the end of this, students were asked to independently design inclusive apps aimed at promoting female inclusion within society.

In this section, the educational interventions promoted in the classes by the university experts will be described and the apps designed by the students to promote gender inclusion in society will be presented.

Each lesson within the classrooms began with an introductory lesson, characterised by a frontal multi-modal approach mediated by the use of devices such as the interactive whiteboard, PCs, tablets and smartphones. Following the lecture, the students were assigned an exercise in which they identified possible solutions to problems related to the inclusion of women in the social sphere, after designing an app. The students produced multimedia materials and short reports specifying the functionalities and objectives pursued by the designed app.

The aforementioned short reports were subjected to a content analysis using the MAXQDA software to identify the semantic domains in which the designed app could be placed. The identification of semantic domains proves crucial for understanding students' perspectives on gender inclusion issues. In particular, these results will be valuable in view of the upcoming experiments planned for the academic year 2023–2024. It will allow us to examine not only what solutions students propose to promote greater inclusion of women in society but also whether these solutions will evolve over time.

3.1.1 Characteristics of Educational Intervention

This section outlines the characteristics of the educational intervention designed to raise students' awareness of gender segregation within STEM-related university courses. The intervention involved nine secondary school classes, totaling 114 students, drawn from scientific, technical, and vocational high schools. The educational activities were structured to promote active participation, collaboration, and cooperation among students, adhering to the principles of the socio-constructivist pedagogical approach.

The intervention began with a traditional lecture format, providing an overview of gender segregation in STEM fields, supported by the latest national and European statistical evidence. Particular emphasis was placed on the low enrollment rates of female students in university courses related to scientific, technological, engineering, and mathematical disciplines. The presentation materials, which included PowerPoint slides, introduced the concept of STEM by defining its disciplinary scope and addressing the broader concept of inclusion from a humanistic and pedagogical perspective. This differentiation was contextualized in relation to segregation, integration, and social exclusion.

The lecture continued with a review of EU initiatives and statistical estimates of enrollment in STEM programs, referencing data from ISTAT (the Italian National Institute of Statistics, 2020). This was followed by a discussion on gender disparities in STEM, supported by findings from the World Economic Forum's Global Gender Gap

Report (2022) [32] and the European Framework Programme for Research and Innovation, Horizon 2020 [33], which underscore the role of women as a critical factor in economic development, employment, and social cohesion.

Further, the lecture explored the origins of STEM education and the early frameworks advocated by the Business Roundtable in the 2000s, which laid the foundation for numerous awareness-raising initiatives across Europe and the United States. Subsequently, the Almalaurea report data (2020/2021) [34] was presented, highlighting the gender disparity in STEM enrollments, followed by an in-depth analysis of gender pay gaps, which revealed that female graduates, despite holding higher degrees, earn approximately EUR 190 less per month than their male counterparts for the same number of working hours [35].

Following this examination of gender disparities in academia and employment, the lecture shifted focus to gender equality education, emphasizing the importance of sensitizing the student community to issues of segregation and gender stereotypes. The need for educational strategies that instill values of inclusion and gender equality was stressed, particularly regarding university guidance practices that respect students' inclinations, ambitions, and identities. It was underscored that inclusive education should be free from both direct and indirect forms of segregation that might undermine the aspirations of female students with an interest in pursuing 'pure' scientific disciplines.

A significant part of the intervention was dedicated to examining the factors influencing female students' educational and career choices, highlighting the importance of addressing distortions in self-perception that might discourage them from pursuing highly remunerative career paths aligned with their ambitions. To further engage students and provide real-world examples, the session included the projection of the YouTube video "100 Female Experts" [36], a project initiated by the Pavia Observatory and the European Commission in 2016. Originally featuring the profiles of 100 female professionals in STEM, the database has since expanded to include experts in Economics, Finance, International Politics, History, Philosophy, and Sport [13].

Next, Bruner's [37] principle of externalization was briefly introduced to illustrate its relevance in laboratory-based teaching and its role in fostering students' investigative thinking. The presentation concluded by discussing the core tenets of the STEM approach, positioning it as an effective strategy for engaging students in the critical study of science from an early age through experimentation, practical applications, and interactive workshop methods that emphasize collaboration between students and teachers [40].

Following the lecture, the intervention adopted a heuristic and problem-based learning approach, facilitated through a series of targeted questions posed by the instructor. These questions aimed to elicit students' beliefs and attitudes towards gender stereotypes and university course selection, while simultaneously revealing their academic inclinations and aspirations. After the discussion, students were assigned a collaborative group exercise to design an app promoting greater social inclusion for women. Working in teams of four, they were given one hour to create a multimedia presentation outlining the app's design, functionality, and objectives.

The instructor provided guidance throughout the app development process, encouraging creativity and critical thinking. After completing the app design, each group presented their product to the class, followed by a structured feedback session where students shared their insights on the intervention's content and pedagogical approach.

The session concluded with a reflective discussion, allowing each student to express their views on the topics covered, the teaching methodology, and the overall learning experience. Students responded enthusiastically to the lesson, reporting a high level of engagement and motivation. Positive feedback was collected on the relevance and topicality of the subject matter, which was deemed interesting and enriching by participants.

3.2   Development of the Observation Grid

To assess the effectiveness of interventions aimed at raising awareness about the gender gap through the STEM approach, thereby addressing the second research question, we have opted to consider the participation exhibited by students during the plenary discussion conducted in the third and final phase of the lesson [45–47], in addition to the explicit statements provided by the students themselves during the lessons.

In this regard, the researchers collected the most significant statements from the students and applied observation grids specifically developed for the classroom intervention.

To develop the observation grids aimed at verifying the active participation of the students in the plenary discussion, we took into consideration the students' propensity to ask questions on the topic and their aptitude for expressing opinions and discussing the topics addressed during the interventions [54].

The grids were accompanied by a holistic rubric for assigning scores to the class, with scores ranging from 0 to 5, where each number indicated participation, activity, and involvement:

0 = absent; 1 = minimum; 2 = superficial; 3 = occasional; 4 = regular; 5 = active and constructive.

In relation to the elements of participation identified by Abdullah and colleagues [54], for the evaluation of students' active participation during the lesson, the following grid was developed and used by researchers (Table 1).

Following the development of the observation grid for assessing classroom dynamics in the context of STEM and gender inclusion, each expert from the university applied the grid at the conclusion of the respective lessons. The purpose of this application was to validate the evaluation criteria established during the development of the grid.

The grid was subjected to rigorous testing through three simulations, with each expert providing their assessments based on the predetermined criteria. The characteristics of the class were then categorised into specific rating ranges, elucidating the level of engagement, questions asked, and discussions initiated by the students. The total evaluation achieved by each class falls into one of the following categories:

1. Rating 0–10: The class did not ask any questions on the addressed topic, none of the students expressed opinions, and no discussion ensued.

Table 1. Observation grid to detect the participation shown by the students during the educational intervention.

Category	Description	Score
Individual student activity	**Active participation of individual students during activities and discussions**	0–5 point/s
Group collaboration	**Positive participation in group work, sharing of ideas and respect for others**	0–5 point/s
Questions and answers	**Providing relevant questions and well-worded answers**	0–5 point/s
Active contribution to the discussion	**Participation in class discussions with significant contributions**	0–5 point/s
Expression of opinions	**Appropriate and participatory expression of opinions**	0–5 point/s
Active involvement	**Demonstration of interest and involvement through facial expressions, gestures, interactions with peers, etc**	0–5 point/s
Active listening	**Demonstration of attention and listening during explanations and discussions**	0–5 point/s
Respect for others	**Show respect for other students, listen to their opinions and do not interrupt**	0–5 point/s
Initiative	**Show initiative in seeking additional information, proposing new ideas, etc**	0–5 point/s
Balanced participation	**Contribute in a balanced way compared to other group members**	0–5 point/s
Total		0–50 point/s

2. Rating 11–20: The class asked few (1 or 2) questions on the addressed topic, a couple of students expressed their opinions, and a brief discussion was initiated.
3. Rating 21–30: The class asked various questions on the addressed topic, some students expressed their opinions, and a discussion was started.
4. Rating 31–40: The class asked frequent questions on the addressed topic, almost all students expressed their opinions, and a substantial discussion was initiated.
5. Rating 41–50: The class asked many questions on the addressed topic, all students actively and frequently expressed their opinions, and a constructive debate was initiated.

The results obtained through the application of the observation grid serve as a valuable tool for assessing the effectiveness of STEM and gender inclusion education. The detailed categorization provides insights into the level of student engagement and participation, facilitating further refinement and improvement in the teaching methodologies employed in these educational domains.

4 Results

4.1 Content Analysis of Student Projects

The content analysis of the applications developed by the students was conducted using the MAXQDA software [42]. The primary objective of this analysis was to categorize the student-designed apps into distinct semantic domains, thereby providing insights into students' perceptions of effective strategies for promoting social inclusion of women. Furthermore, this analysis served to highlight the perceived needs of women, as identified by the students, in order to facilitate their participation in more inclusive social contexts.

It is important to emphasize that, following the instructional intervention on gender inequality in STEM disciplines, students were not confined to addressing only a specific aspect of gender disparity in university settings. Instead, they were encouraged to create applications that would promote inclusivity for women in a broader societal context. Limiting the app designs solely to solving the gender gap in STEM would have been overly restrictive, potentially leading to a narrow set of solutions with repetitive features. By adopting a holistic approach and allowing students to design apps aimed at benefiting the entire female community, the complexity and multidimensional nature of gender segregation were better captured, fostering the development of diverse and innovative solutions to real-world social challenges.

The textual descriptions produced by the students, which outlined the features and objectives of their respective apps, were treated as context units (CUs) for the content analysis. In contrast, the intended goals of the apps, defined by the services offered to users, were identified as analytical units (AUs). These goals were then categorized into semantic domains based on the nature of the services provided, the type of inclusivity addressed within the female demographic, and the thematic patterns emerging from the coding process.

Seven semantic domains emerged from the analysis:

1. Psychological Support
2. Safety and First Aid
3. Leisure and Socialization
4. Gender Inclusion in the Workplace
5. Cultural Promotion
6. Essential Needs
7. Personal Care and Orientation

The frequency distribution of the coded segments across these domains is as follows:

- Psychological Support: 15 segments (27.78%)
- Safety and First Aid: 12 segments (22.22%)

- Leisure and Socialization: 11 segments (20.37%)
- Gender Inclusion in the Workplace: 7 segments (12.96%)
- Cultural Promotion: 4 segments (7.41%)
- Essential Needs: 3 segments (5.56%)
- Personal Care and Orientation: 2 segments (3.70%)

The data suggest that students perceive the provision of emotional and psychological support as a critical need for women, particularly in contexts involving violence and segregation. This domain emerged as the most frequently represented, accounting for 27.78% of the coded segments. Similarly, the domain of Safety and First Aid, comprising 22.22% of the segments, reflects students' recognition of the importance of providing immediate support and protection mechanisms.

The Leisure and Socialization domain, which accounts for 20.37% of the segments, underscores the value students place on creating inclusive spaces that foster community building and social interaction. By contrast, Gender Inclusion in the Workplace, at 12.96%, reveals a moderate focus on the need for professional and organizational inclusivity.

Less represented were domains such as Cultural Promotion (7.41%), Essential Needs (5.56%), and Personal Care and Orientation (3.70%), indicating that students perceive these areas as having relatively lower priority in the context of achieving comprehensive social inclusion for women.

These findings offer a nuanced understanding of students' perspectives on promoting gender inclusivity and suggest that emotional well-being and safety are seen as foundational elements for fostering a more inclusive society for women. The subsequent section will delve into the specific features, functionalities, and services provided by the apps, analyzing how these elements align with the identified semantic domains and evaluating their potential to address the complex challenges associated with gender inequality.

4.1.1 Apps Designed by Students

The 114 students designed a total of 28 apps aimed at ensuring greater social inclusion for women. The semantic areas covered by the apps developed are 7, namely: psychological support, safety and first aid, leisure and socialising, gender inclusion in the workplace, culture, essential needs, and personal care and orientation.

More specifically, eight projects deal with providing psychological support; as many projects envisage the design of security and first aid software; five projects promote socialisation among users; two support gender inclusion in the workplace; two projects aim to develop a network that promotes culture and the negotiation of knowledge among users; two deal with meeting basic needs and personal care; and, lastly, only one project deals with providing guidance services to students leaving secondary school.

In the following, the peculiarities concerning the most significant applications of each semantic field will be analysed in more detail.

Psychological Support and Early Intervention. During the COVID period, the surge in cases of gender-based violence at home led to the enactment of significant legal safeguards to protect women, resulting in a consequent tightening of penalties for perpetrators [44]. However, beyond the importance of penal instruments in regulating the phenomenon, there is a need for systematic planning of funding policies aimed at developing and disseminating preventive services and psychological support for victims. This awareness also emerged in secondary school classrooms in Foggia, where students conceived the idea of providing support and care for abused women through the development of an application. For example, the Love Persona app, designed for an international audience, offers support through support and sharing blogs, involving professionals such as psychologists and therapists. Users can anonymously share thoughts in the public section of the app until they decide, following an interview with a therapist, to reveal their identity [44]. Another app, named DenBuse, was created to allow users to report abuse suffered in domestic, work, and social spheres. Initially anonymous, victims can recount the violence they have experienced, encouraged by professionals to report it to the authorities. A similar app is SheSafe, which provides psychological support divided into sections for reporting perpetrators and assisting victims with experts [41]. The Elevate Her app project aims to holistically improve the condition of women by promoting inclusion and offering health care, legal, and psychological counseling services, along with educational content to promote gender equality. Other apps developed by students, such as Talk to Me, SupportHer, Women's World, and Special Support, provide similar services. All these applications focus on post-violence support; in the next section, solutions for preventing and effectively countering violence will be discussed.

Security and Emergency Response. Requesting law enforcement intervention in cases of violence can be challenging due to concerns about aggressors monitoring victims' phone calls and reports [42]. To address this issue, students engaged in STEM orientation interventions have developed safety apps allowing users to instantly report potential assaults or seek help discreetly. For instance, the app IoDonna focuses on forwarding workplace aggression reports; Sentirsi Protetti enables users to report violence in various settings, and Calcolatrice Rosa disguises as a normal calculator but, when unlocked, allows users to report abuse. Similarly, apps like SOS Safety On Streets, Sicurinsieme, and Help Me serve the purpose of ensuring safety. The significance of safety was extensively discussed during class interventions, with many students emphasising the need for increased safety at home and on city streets, especially during evening hours.

Leisure and Socialisation. During the speeches, students expressed feeling lost after the Covid restrictions were lifted, unsure of how to resume socializing freely with their peers. Many desired an app that not only facilitated social interactions but also allowed for the organization of events in both public and private settings, prioritizing safety. Recognizing this need and the challenge of reconnecting socially, students developed apps to support the social inclusion of both genders, exemplified by the app D'Ardes.

Additionally, apps like Alive and Our Integration were introduced to cater to users' individual preferences, offering personalised suggestions for social activities based on factors such as budget, intended location, and the average age of participants. Another socialization app, IDTA, aimed to promote inclusivity through the organization of conferences on gender inclusion and social dinners among participants.

Organisational Inclusion, Culture and Orientation. The discussion on equal dignity at work has resonated positively among students, leading to the creation of various apps aimed at protecting women in the workplace and fostering greater inclusion in the face of organisational misconduct.

One such app, Women@work, serves as a digital platform connecting job supply and demand while shedding light on the economic treatment of employees, particularly women, to combat gender pay segregation. Another app, Right Salary, allows female workers to report unfair pay practices at companies.

Students also developed the Iquality app, focusing on gender inclusion in organisations. This program enables users to assess whether to work for a company by providing key information such as average employee salaries, policies regarding maternity or parental leave, and the availability of support services for new parents.

Addressing segregation related to women's access to cultural and educational circuits, students created the Culture for Women app. This app aims to enhance educational inclusiveness for women facing limitations due to ideological and cultural issues. Users can access academic materials remotely, share experiences, and raise awareness about their conditions.

In conclusion, an app named Right Choice was developed for the orientation of both male and female students leaving secondary school. This app encourages students, especially females, to pursue academic paths that align with their ambitions, leveraging an analysis of their interests and personal data to guide them towards the most suitable course of study at economically and logistically convenient universities.

Essential Needs and Personal Care. The final category of apps created by students focuses on satisfying essential needs and personal care, addressing real and practical problems related to the female gender. Two apps, Voglia che più Voglie and WC Advisor, were developed to cater to these needs.

Voglia che Più Voglie responds to hormonal fluctuations during the menstrual cycle, acknowledging studies indicating increased appetite and a greater desire for sweets among women during this period [44; 45]. The app provides women with access to discounts on sweets and essential products like sanitary napkins, tampons, menstrual cups, analgesics, painkillers, and comfort items such as thermal bags.

The WC Advisor app serves as a Resident Advisor for toilet services in public and private establishments. It enables users, particularly females of all ages, to easily find information about clean, welcoming, well-stocked facilities (including changing tables) in the city and unfamiliar neighbourhoods, with an added focus on aesthetics for Instagram.

This paragraph illustrates how certain students encountered during orientation courses contribute to greater inclusion for the female gender by developing practical, pragmatic, and functional apps to address specific needs.

In response to the first research question, it can be asserted that the STEM method is a valid approach to encourage students to develop innovative and creative solutions for promoting gender inclusion within society. The apps created by the students were highly praised by university educators and students alike, underscoring the effectiveness of the STEM approach in raising awareness about social issues and inspiring their creativity in devising innovative and inclusive solutions.

Semantic Area	Example Apps	Services Offered to the Community
Psychological Support	Love Persona, DenBuse, SheSafe, Elevate Her, Talk to Me, SupportHer, Women's World, Special Support	Post-violence psychological care, anonymous reporting, professional counselling, legal guidance, educational resources for equality
Safety and First Aid	IoDonna, Sentirsi Protetti, Calcolatrice Rosa, SOS Safety On Streets, Sicurinsieme, Help Me	Discreet reporting of violence, safety alerts, and mechanisms to call for help in emergencies, focusing on workplace and public safety
Leisure and Socialising	D'Ardes, Alive, Our Integration, IDTA	Facilitation of social events, personalised suggestions for activities, and organisation of gender-inclusion conferences and dinners
Gender Inclusion in Workplace	Women@work, Right Salary, Iquality	Promotion of gender parity at work, reporting of pay inequalities, provision of company information on gender-friendly policies
Culture and Orientation	Culture for Women, Right Choice	Access to educational resources, guidance for career and academic choices, raising awareness about cultural and gender-based issues
Essential Needs	Voglia che Più Voglie, WC Advisor	Support for menstrual cycle needs (discounts, pain relief), guidance on finding hygienic and well-equipped restroom facilities
Personal Care and Orientation	WC Advisor	Locating clean, accessible facilities; focused on comfort, aesthetics, and inclusivity

4.2   Results of Classroom Observations

The intervention was conducted across nine secondary school classes, which achieved participation scores of 33, 35, 41, 40, 42, 43, 44, 45, and 44, respectively. A descriptive analysis of the data reveals that the average participation score was 40.78 out of a maximum of 50 points, indicating an overall high level of student engagement during the lessons. This finding suggests that the majority of students actively participated in discussions, frequently posed questions, and expressed their opinions, thereby contributing to meaningful conversations around the issue of gender segregation.

The standard deviation of 3.24 indicates low variability in participation levels across classes, suggesting a general consistency in student engagement. However, it is noteworthy that one class obtained a slightly lower score of 33 points, potentially indicating lower engagement or the presence of contextual factors that negatively influenced student interest in that specific group. To better understand the dynamics in this particular case, further qualitative investigation would be beneficial.

Throughout the intervention, students provided direct feedback on their experience, which served as a complementary data source to the quantitative scores. One student commented, "The lesson was engaging, and I appreciated the application of the STEM approach to explore the topic of gender segregation." Another student remarked, "I was surprised by the amount of interesting information we learned today. I would like to see more lessons like this." A third student noted, "This lesson was positive. We learned facts and figures and discussed them together. I think we should do it more often." Such statements highlight the students' enthusiasm and appreciation for the integration of the STEM approach in addressing gender-related issues. The qualitative feedback confirms the effectiveness of the STEM methodology in promoting active participation and generating interest in complex topics. Students' reflections further underscore the value of incorporating their perceptions alongside quantitative measures to obtain a holistic evaluation of the teaching intervention's impact.

Overall, the findings affirm a positive response to the second research question, indicating that the STEM approach is indeed effective in fostering active student engagement in lessons centered on gender awareness and social inclusion.

5 Discussion

The study aimed to investigate how the application of the STEM approach could raise awareness among high school students about gender segregation in educational and professional contexts. Through classroom interventions conducted in secondary schools in Foggia, students actively engaged in designing creative and innovative applications intended to promote greater gender inclusion within society. The findings from both quantitative evaluations and qualitative feedback suggest that this initiative successfully stimulated significant interest and participation.

The analysis revealed important insights about how students perceive and respond to societal gender gaps. The applications they developed reflected a sophisticated understanding of the multifaceted challenges women face, from workplace discrimination to safety concerns and psychological barriers. Notably, the high frequency of apps focused on psychological support (27.78%) and safety (22.22%) suggests that students recognize the profound impact of societal gender biases on women's mental well-being and physical security.

The students' response to gender gaps in STEM education was particularly telling. Rather than focusing solely on academic disparities, they conceptualized solutions that addressed the broader social and cultural factors influencing educational choices. This holistic approach indicates that students understand how societal expectations, safety concerns, and lack of support systems collectively contribute to gender segregation in educational pathways.

Evaluations conducted by researchers using a standardized observation grid yielded class scores ranging from 33 to 45 points out of 50, with an average score of 40.78. This performance reflects a high degree of student involvement, demonstrated by frequent questioning, the expression of opinions, and the initiation of constructive debates on gender-related topics. The low standard deviation of 3.24 indicates consistency in engagement levels across the majority of classes, with one exception. The class that scored 33 points exhibited relatively lower participation, potentially due to extraneous factors that merit further exploration.

The direct statements provided by students further validate the success of the intervention. Comments such as *"The lesson was engaging"* and *"I enjoyed the STEM approach"* demonstrate that the methodology effectively captured students' interest. Moreover, statements like *"I was surprised by the amount of interesting information"* and *"I would like to see more lessons like this"* underscore the value of integrating STEM to foster enthusiasm for exploring complex issues like gender segregation.

These qualitative insights emphasize the importance of considering both quantitative data and students' subjective perceptions when evaluating the impact of educational interventions. The students' testimonies reaffirm that the STEM approach can enhance understanding of critical social issues and create an engaging learning environment that promotes active participation.

The promising results from this study lay the groundwork for further investigation into the application of STEM methodologies in addressing social and educational inequalities. In future research phases, additional data will be collected through structured questionnaires to quantify students' satisfaction with the intervention and to gain deeper insights into their perceptions of the use of innovative educational strategies.

The findings from this study suggest that the STEM approach effectively facilitated meaningful discussions on gender segregation and positively influenced student engagement. This method not only generated enthusiasm and active participation but also provided a platform for students to collaboratively explore solutions to complex societal issues. Such outcomes highlight the potential of the STEM approach as a valuable tool for fostering social inclusion and gender awareness in educational contexts. These results offer valuable implications for refining and expanding STEM-based strategies in future educational programs.

5.1 Critical Evaluation of the Long-Term Impact of Applications

While the applications designed by students demonstrate significant potential in addressing gender segregation and promoting social inclusion, it is essential to critically assess their efficacy and long-term impact across the identified semantic areas.

Psychological Support: The high proportion of apps focused on psychological support underscores the students' recognition of the emotional and mental health challenges faced by women in society. These applications, such as *Love Persona* and *DenBuse*, provide vital resources for victims of abuse, enabling access to anonymous counseling and support networks. However, their long-term effectiveness hinges on sustained engagement by users and integration with professional services. Without continuous updates, active promotion, and partnerships with established organizations, these apps may struggle to maintain their relevance and usage over time.

Safety and First Aid: Safety-related apps, such as *Calcolatrice Rosa* and *SOS Safety On Streets*, offer innovative solutions to discreetly report violence or seek emergency assistance. While their immediate impact in enhancing safety is commendable, challenges arise in ensuring widespread adoption and reliability under real-world conditions. For these apps to achieve lasting impact, they require robust technical infrastructure, user-friendly interfaces, and collaboration with law enforcement agencies to ensure timely responses to user reports.

Leisure and Socialising: Applications like *D'Ardes* and *Alive* address the social isolation exacerbated by events such as the COVID-19 pandemic. By fostering inclusive and secure social interactions, these apps play a crucial role in rebuilding community bonds. However, their effectiveness may be limited by cultural and regional variations in user engagement. To sustain their impact, these apps must continuously adapt to users' evolving preferences and integrate feedback mechanisms to ensure they remain relevant in diverse social contexts.

Gender Inclusion in the Workplace: Workplace-focused apps, such as *Women@Work* and *Right Salary*, are vital for addressing gender disparities in professional environments. By enabling users to report pay gaps and evaluate organizational practices, these tools can foster greater transparency and accountability. Nonetheless, the long-term success of such initiatives depends on their ability to influence systemic change. Collaborations with policymakers, industry leaders, and advocacy groups are essential to amplify their impact beyond individual workplaces.

Culture and Orientation: Apps like *Culture for Women* and *Right Choice* highlight the importance of bridging educational and cultural gaps for women. Their innovative approach to providing access to academic resources and career guidance addresses critical barriers to inclusion. However, their effectiveness relies on their ability to reach underserved populations and address logistical challenges such as internet accessibility. Partnerships with educational institutions and NGOs can help expand their reach and ensure equitable access.

Essential Needs and Personal Care: Practical apps, such as *Voglia che Più Voglie* and *WC Advisor*, address tangible challenges faced by women, from menstrual health to locating clean facilities. These applications excel in providing immediate and practical solutions; however, their impact is inherently limited to specific contexts. To achieve long-term relevance, these apps should integrate additional features and expand their scope to address a broader range of essential needs.

Across all semantic areas, the student-developed apps represent a commendable effort to address pressing societal issues. However, their long-term impact will depend on continuous innovation, user adoption, and integration with larger systems of support. While these applications effectively initiate critical conversations and offer innovative solutions, their sustained success requires a multi-faceted approach involving partnerships with stakeholders, ongoing technical and financial support, and mechanisms for scaling their reach. By addressing these factors, the initiatives developed through STEM interventions can evolve into enduring tools for promoting gender inclusion and societal change.

6   Conclusions

Based on the findings of this study, the STEM methodology emerges as an effective and engaging pedagogical approach to address complex social issues, such as gender segregation in university programs related to scientific disciplines. By adopting a more holistic and comprehensive perspective, the STEM approach aims to raise students' awareness of female inclusion in society, as evidenced by the diverse range of applications developed by the participants.

The content analysis of the student-designed apps revealed that students perceive a need for providing a broad array of services to support women's inclusion and well-being. These services encompass psychological and emotional support, safety measures, leisure and socialization opportunities, work inclusion strategies, cultural engagement, the fulfillment of essential needs, and guidance on selecting a suitable university pathway. This multidimensional perspective underscores the complexity of the gaps and needs that must be addressed to achieve a higher level of inclusion and enhance the overall well-being of women in society.

The implementation of the STEM approach, which integrates the acquisition of transversal skills and problem-solving capabilities alongside the application of scientific knowledge, has proven effective in fostering students' understanding of gender segregation. Moreover, it has stimulated students to propose innovative solutions to address these pressing societal challenges.

However, additional empirical investigations are required to further validate the effectiveness of the STEM approach in raising students' awareness of gender-related issues. Future research should focus on identifying new strategies and methodologies that enable the younger generation to actively engage in the creation of a more inclusive and equitable society—one that is attentive to collective well-being and committed to ensuring the participation and empowerment of all individuals.

References

1. MEF: PNRR, Mission 4: Education and Research (Document No. 4). Rome, Italy (2021)
2. MUR: Ministerial Decree 934/2022. Gazzetta Ufficiale, 03/08/2022 (2022)
3. Verdugo-Castro, S., García-Holgado, A., Sánchez-Gómez, M.C.: The gender gap in higher STEM studies: a systematic literature review. Heliyon (2022)
4. Corbett, C., Hill, C.: Solving the Equation: The Variables for Women's Success in Engineering and Computing. American Association of University Women, 1111 Sixteenth Street NW, Washington, DC 20036 (2015)
5. Nunin, R.: Lavoro femminile e carriere scientifiche: alcune riflessioni sul gender gap. Lavoro, diritti, Europa **2020**(2/2020), 1–13 (2020)
6. Resmini, M.: The leaky pipeline. Chem. Euro. J. **22**(11), 3533–3534 (2016)
7. Massachusetts Institute of Technology: A study on the status of women faculty in science at MIT. In: The MIT Faculty Newsletter, vol. 11, issue, 4 (1999). http://web.mit.edu/fnl/women/women.pdf
8. Gasser, C.E., Shaffer, K.S.: Career development of women in academia: traversing the leaky pipeline (2014)
9. Tesch, R.: Qualitative Research: Analysis Types and Software Tools. Routledge, New York, NY (1990)

10. Kelle, U.: "Emergence" vs. "forcing" of empirical data? A crucial problem of "grounded theory" reconsidered. Forum Qual. Soc. Res. **6**(2), 27 (2005)
11. Card, D., Payne, A.A.: High school choices and the gender gap in STEM. Econ. Inq. **59**(1), 9–28 (2021)
12. Sato, S., Gygax, P.M., Randall, J., Schmid Mast, M.: The leaky pipeline in research grant peer review and funding decisions: challenges and future directions. High. Educ. **82**(1), 145–162 (2021)
13. Bruner, J.S.: La cultura dell'educazione. Nuovi orizzonti per la scuola. Feltrinelli editore (2002)
14. Capellari, S., Ferrara, M.D.: Tutela della salute e contrasto alla violenza nei confronti delle donne: problemi aperti e strategie di intervento, pp. 1–187. Edizioni Università Trieste (2022)
15. Gonzalez, H.B., Kuenzi, J.J.: Science, Technology, Engineering, and Mathematics (STEM) Education: A Primer. Congressional Research Service, Library of Congress, Washington, DC (2012)
16. Botero, J.: Evolution of STEM in the United States, William E. Dugger, Jr. Senior Fellow International Technology and Engineering Educators Association and Emeritus Professor of Technology Education Virginia Tech (2010)
17. Friedman, T.L.: The World is Flat: A Brief History of the Twenty-First Century. Farrar, Straus and Giroux, New York, NY (2005)
18. Sanders, M.: STEM, STEM education, STEMAnia. Technol. Teach. **68**(4), 20–27 (2009)
19. Chiu, M., Duit, R.: Globalization: science education from an international perspective. J. Res. Sci. Teach. **48**(6), 553–566 (2011)
20. Caprile, M., Palmén, R., Sanz, P., Dente, G.: Encouraging STEM Studies: Labour Market Situation and Comparison of Practices Targeted at Young People in Different Member States. European Union, Brussels, Belgium (2015)
21. National Research Council: The National Science Education Standards. National Academy Press, Washington, DC (1996)
22. American Association for the Advancement of Science: Benchmarks for Science Literacy. Oxford University Press (1993)
23. Accreditation Board for Engineering and Technology: Engineering Accreditation Criteria. Baltimore, MD (2007–2008)
24. Martín-Páez, T., Aguilera, D., Perales-Palacios, F.J., Vílchez-González, J.M.: What are we talking about when we talk about STEM education? A review of literature. Sci. Educ. **103**(4), 799–822 (2019)
25. Bransford, J.D., Brown, A.L., Cocking, R.R.: How People Learn, vol. 11. National Academy Press, Washington, DC (2000)
26. Balsiger, P.W.: Supradisciplinary research practices: history, objectives and rationale. Futures **36**(4), 407–421 (2004)
27. Tress, B., Tress, G., Fry, G.: Defining concepts and the process of knowledge production in integrative research. In: Tress, B., Tress, G., Fry, G., Opdam, P. (eds.) From Landscape Research to Landscape Planning: Aspects of integration, Education, and Application, vol. 12, pp. 13–26. Springer, Dordrecht, the Netherlands (2005)
28. Fondazione Openpolis ETS: Stem, una sfida per l'Italia. L'importanza delle scienze e delle tecnologie nel mondo di oggi e i divari sociali, territoriali e di genere da ridurre nel loro apprendimento (2022)
29. Hardani, H.: Pembelajaran matematika berbasis stem: implementasi variasi pengembangan model pembelajaran stem di sekolah dasar. Idealmathedu Indonesian Digital J. Math. Educ. **7**(2), 98–106 (2020)
30. Gavrilova, T.Y.E., Ignatova, O.G.E.: Stem-education in modern school within the framework of design activity in natural scientific disciplines. Russ. Digit. Libr. J. **22**(6), 547–555 (2019)

31. World Economic Forum: Global Gender Gap report (2022). https://www.weforum.org/rep orts/global-gender-gap-report-2022/
32. European Commission: EU Framework programme for research and Innovation-Horizon 2020 (2011). https://eur-lex.europa.eu/LexUriServ/LexUriServ.do?uri=COM:2011: 0809:FIN:en:PDF
33. Almalaurea: XXIII Survey Profile of Graduates 2020 (2021). https://www.almalaurea.it/sites/ default/files/2022-05/almalaurea_profilo_rapporto2021_0.pdf
34. Almalaurea: Report 2022 on the profile and employment status of university graduates (2022). https://www.almalaurea.it/sites/almalaurea.it/files/convegni/Bologna2022/sin tesi_rapportoalmalaurea2022.pdf
35. Pavia Observatory: Interpelliamole! 100 esperte 2021 (2021). https://www.youtube.com/ watch?v=m4s3oyiin74&list=PLdl1xZN4qSOx4ACIa2sX0Oh94Hck20W1S
36. Pavia Observatory: Official site 100esperte.it (2021). https://100esperte.it/
37. Sinaga, M., Silaban, R., Jahro, I.S.: Development of chemistry practicum guidelines with the support of STEM (science, technology, engineering, and mathematics) integrating character education. J. Phys. Conf. Ser. **1811**(1), 012058 (2021)
38. Kuckartz, U., Rädiker, S.: Analyzing Qualitative Data with MAXQDA, pp. 1–290. Springer, Cham (2019)
39. Tipaldo, G: L'analisi del contenuto nella ricerca sociale. Spunti per una riflessione multidisciplinare (2007)
40. Felson, R.B., Paré, P.P.: The reporting of domestic violence and sexual assault by nonstrangers to the police. J. Marriage Fam. **67**(3), 597–610 (2005)
41. Stokoe, E., Richardson, E.: Asking for help without asking for help: How victims request and police offer assistance in cases of domestic violence when perpetrators are potentially co-present. Discourse Stud. **25**(3), 383–408 (2023)
42. Rai News: La nuova minaccia di Teheran: stop all'istruzione per le studentesse senza velo (2023). https://www.rainews.it/articoli/2023/04/iran-teheran-stop-istruzione-a-studen tesse-senza-velo-9e26be80-9a5c-4013-a89 f-4ff170ed2909.html
43. Dye, L., Blundell, J.E.: Menstrual cycle and appetite control: implications for weight regulation. Hum. Reprod.Reprod. **12**(6), 1142–1151 (1997)
44. Bean, J.C., Peterson, D.: Grading classroom participation. New Dir. Teach. Learn. **1998**(74), 33–40 (1998)
45. Johnson, D.W., Johnson, F.P.: Joining Together: Group Theory and Group Skills. Prentice-Hall, Inc (1991)
46. Bruffee, K.A.: Collaborative Learning: Higher Education, Interdependence, and The Authority of Knowledge. Johns Hopkins University Press (1999)
47. Abdullah, M.Y., Bakar, N.R.A., Mahbob, M.H.: The dynamics of student participation in classroom: observation on level and forms of participation. Procedia-Soc. Behav. Sci. **59**, 61–70 (2012)
48. Fondazione Openpolis ETS, Stem, una sfida per l'Italia. *L'importanza delle scienze e delle tecnologie nel mondo di oggi e i divari sociali, territoriali e di genere da ridurre nel loro apprendimento*, (2022). https://www.openpolis.it/esercizi/limportanza-delle-materie-stem-nel-mondo-di-oggi/
49. Fondazione Openpolis ETS. In Italia ampi divari di genere nell'apprendimento delle Stem (2024). https://www.openpolis.it/in-italia-ampi-divari-di-genere-nellapprendimento-delle-stem/

ChatGPT and Instructional Design: An Ally for Inclusion?

Dario Lombardi[1]([⊠]) [iD], Luigi Traetta[1] [iD], and Antonio Maffei[2] [iD]

[1] University of Foggia, Arpi Street, 176 Foggia, Italy
{dario.lombardi,luigi.traetta}@unifg.it
[2] KTH Royal Institute of Technology, Brinellvägen 8, SE-10044 Stockholm, Sweden
maffei@kth.se

Abstract. Artificial Intelligence (AI) is gaining importance in the field of education (Chen et al., 2020). Despite its widespread use to assist teachers (Pratama et al., 2023; Baidoo-Anu Ansah, 2023), there's a gap in literature on AI's role in instructional design, particularly for students with disabilities. This study explores the perceptions of 114 support teachers on using ChatGPT and the CONALI Ontology (Maffei et al., 2016) for creating Individualized Education Plans (IEPs). In the first phase of the study, teachers were trained on how to identify objectives, teaching and learning activities and assessment methods within the IEP, following the CONALI ontological framework and constructive alignment (CA) (Maffei et al., 2022). After verifying their perceptions of the experience through an initial validated questionnaire, a second exercise was conducted, in which the experimental group applied the CONALI framework in combination with ChatGPT to fill in the IEP. At the end of the exercise, a second questionnaire was handed out to collect participants' perceptions of the experience and to assess the effectiveness of ChatGPT and CONALI in designing the IEP. Descriptive analysis revealed that the combination of ChatGPT and CONALI was perceived as useful in IEP design. Ontology was confirmed as a useful tool for identifying SMART training objectives and aligning them with intervention strategies and assessment methods in the IEP. AI, supported by CONALI, was seen as an effective tool for instructional design, speeding up IEP completion and promoting engagement, motivation, and learning quality.

Keywords: AIEd · ChatGPT · IEP

1 Introduction

Artificial Intelligence (AI) refers to the ability of a digital machine to perform tasks commonly associated with intelligent beings, and its associated technologies are divided into various branches, such as computer vision, speech, machine learning, big data, and natural language processing (Chiu et al., 2021; Xia et al., 2022).

Artificial Intelligence in education (AIEd) refers to the application of AI technologies, such as intelligent tutoring systems, chatbots, robots, and the automated assessment of all modes of digitized artifacts that support and enhance education (Chiu et al., 2023).

G. A. Toto (Ed.): ICS exchange 2024, CCIS 2521, pp. 124–135, 2025.
https://doi.org/10.1007/978-3-032-03021-4_9

AI can offer significant benefits to teachers and improve their efficacy at work, their teaching skills and the support to professional development. Furthermore, it can help to promote a positive attitude towards the use of technologies in the fields of teaching and learning. (Chiu et al., 2023).

AI showed a significant potential in providing effective learning to students, thanks to using personalized systems that provide timely feedback (Chounta et al., 2021; Yang et al. 2022).

In the literature we find studies on the efficacy of supporting teachers in the application of AI for the development of students' higher cognitive skills (Gupta and Bhaskar, 2020), as well as on the motivations and resistances that influence teachers' behaviour towards the adoption of AI-based educational solutions (Guo et al., 2020).

Some research has been conducted on teachers' perception of AI teaching (Kim et al., 2022), on its application to the planning of learning activities and the support it can offer to teachers in their educational activities (Akgün Greenhow, 2021; Yang Kyun, 2022; Hussain, 2020).

Despite all these studies and the need to train teachers on AI integration into educational planning (Wu e Yang, 2022), there's a lack of a specific focus on AI application to support teachers in planning educational paths which are targeted at students with disabilities.

The integration of Artificial Intelligence (AI) into the educational planning process provides the opportunity to make education more inclusive and accessible for students with disabilities (Garg Sharma, 2020). Furthermore, AI can substantially simplify teachers' work when they create project documentation, and can become a valuable support tool for planning personalized and inclusive educational paths.

In this context, the main objective of this study is the following: RO1 – To analyse teachers' perceptions on using ChatGPT for filling in Section 5 of the Individualized Education Plan (IEP).

Therefore, the research question that guides this study is the following: RQ1 – What is teachers' perception on AI application for IEP design, with the support of a taxonomy tool such as the CONALI Ontology?

2 Methods

The personalization of the educational path of students with disabilities is determined by the identification of educational objectives, methodological strategies and cognitive evaluation criteria that allow them to actively commit to learning and obtain significant results (Zhang et al., 2020).

Since these items are reported in Section 5 of the IEP, we decided to have teachers fill in this section.

The objectives included in the document must be SMART, i.e., Specific, Measurable, Attainable, Realistic and Time-bound (Ogbeiwi, 2017); furthermore, they must be aligned with teaching and learning activities and the verification methods used to verify the achievement of these objectives by students.

Such alignment is guaranteed by the CONALI Ontology, since the latter is focused on identifying educational objectives for planning constructively aligned activities (Maffei et al., 2016; 2022). Therefore, we chose to use it to support teachers during the design and completion of of the IEP.

The experimental sample involved 116 teachers, enrolled in the specialization course in teaching support activities of the University of Foggia's training course for teachers (TFA).

To make teachers familiar with inclusive planning and the identification of SMART objectives through Bloom's taxonomy (1956), the topics were previously explained to them by means of a frontal lecture. Subsequently, they were given the task of filling in Section 5 of the IEP of an imaginary student with autism spectrum disorder.

In order to make sure teachers had a clear idea of the conditions of the student for whom they needed to fill in the IEP, they were previously presented with the clinical picture of such student.

Following the exercise, which lasted 45 min, a discussion was carried out to solve any issues experienced by teachers during the planning phase.

Subsequently, since teachers weren't familiar with Ontology, the first part of the intervention involved the explanation and presentation of the methods to apply the CONALI Ontology and Constructive Alignment (CA).

Later on, teachers were asked to apply Ontology to fill in Section 5 of the IEP for the same student as the first task.

This exercise was completed individually by teachers, who had 45 min to complete it. At the end of the task, the papers were discussed for 30 min in the classroom, in order to assess whether teachers had learnt to master and use ontology and clarify any doubts.

At the end of the discussion, a questionnaire was handed out to teachers, in order to verify their perceptions on the application of ontology. Teachers had 15 min to answer the questionnaire.

After assessing teachers' perceptions on the use of the CONALI Ontology for IEP design, through a questionnaire, we proceeded with a new functional diagnosis and the subsequent splitting of the sample into an experimental and a control group.

Teachers independently chose how to split into groups: those who wished to use ChatGPT would access the platform and complete the exercise, whereas those who wished to proceed without using the device would simply complete the exercise with the support of Ontology.

The experimental group, made up of 81 teachers, used both ChatGPT and Ontology to fill in Section 5 of the IEP. The control group, made up of 9 teachers, proceeded as in the first part of the intervention and used only Constructive Alignment.

Both groups had one hour to complete the exercise. At the end of the exercise, a questionnaire was handed out to teachers, in order to verify their perceptions during the planning phase, when they used ChatGPT.

The questionnaire was structured in order to assess to what extent ChatGPT had supported teachers in the identification of the objectives, teaching and learning activities (TLA) and verification methods to understand whether the educational objective had been achieved. Finally, teachers were asked whether, following this experiment, they would integrate ChatGPT into their educational planning and what advantages or disadvantages they had observed following the application of ChatGPT in the planning phase.

The questions and answers to the questionnaire are reported in the "Results" section.

2.1 Intervention Summary Syllabus

In order to ensure the reproducibility of the study, we are sharing below the intervention summary syllabus:

- **Introduction and context (1 h):** trainees are explained the importance of personalizing the educational path of students with disabilities, with a specific focus on Section 5 of the Individualized Education Plan (IEP).

  The purpose is to help teachers defining SMART (specific, Measurable, Attainable, Realistic and Time-bound) educational objectives and aligning them with teaching and learning activities, as well as verification methods.
- **Exercise 1 (45 min):** teachers are given the task of filling in Section 5 of the IEP of an imaginary student with autism spectrum disorder. This exercise helps to make teachers familiar with inclusive planning and the identification of SMART objectives.
- **Introduction to the CONALI Ontology (30 min):** following the initial exercise, the CONALI Ontology is presented to teachers. It's a tool that helps to ensure educational objectives are aligned with teaching and learning activities.
- **Application of the CONALI Ontology (45 min for the exercise; 30 min for the discussion):** teachers are asked to use the CONALI Ontology to fill in Section 5 of the IEP for the same imaginary student. This exercise is completed individually and is followed by a discussion in the classroom.
- **A questionnaire is handed out to assess teachers' perceptions on using the CONALI Ontology for IEP design (20 min).**
- **Introduction to ChatGPT (30 min):** after assessing teachers' perceptions on using the CONALI Ontology, they are presented with the ChatGPT technology.
- **Final exercise (60 min):** teachers from the experimental and control groups fill in individually Section 5 of the IEP for a new imaginary student with Trisomia 21. Teachers from the experimental group apply ChatGPT and the Ontology to fill in the IEP, whereas teachers from the control group apply only the Ontology.
- **Intervention assessment (20 min):** at the end of the final exercise, teachers from the experimental and control groups are handed out a questionnaire to assess their perceptions on such exercise. The questionnaire handed out to the experimental group explores to what extent ChatGPT supported teachers in the identification of the objectives, teaching and learning activities (TLA) and verification methods. The questionnaire handed out to the control group requires a feedback and teachers' opinions on the experience.

3 Results

In this section we are presenting the results of the questionnaires that were handed out to teachers during the intervention. The discussion will follow the order in which questionnaires were handed out.

It should be clarified that the number of teachers who answered the questionnaires may vary between one exercise and the other, due to technical and personal issues that were experienced during the intervention, such as the temporary unavailability of the network and technological device or the need to leave the classroom for personal reasons.

3.1   Results of the CONALI Ontology and IEP Design Questionnaire

Following the previous explanation and exercise on the application of the CONALI Ontology, a first questionnaire was handed out to teachers in order to assess the efficacy of the Ontology for inclusive planning.

The results of the questionnaire, filled in by 104 teachers, clearly show that Constructive Alignment (CA) and the CONALI Ontology were praised and considered effective by teachers in order to align objectives, teaching strategies and verification methods.

The collected data show that, before using CA, several teachers didn't feel confident in designing an Individualized Education Plan (IEP) which aligned learning objectives with teaching and assessment methods (18.3% of teachers said they didn't feel confident at all, 26% of them said they didn't feel very confident and 31.7% of them were neutral).

Over 97% of teachers said they had effectively understood the principles of CA during the course and assessed the learning material as clear and easy to understand. Following the course, several teachers felt more capable of aligning IEP learning objectives with teaching and assessment methods (10.6% of teachers were neutral, 40.4% of them felt more capable and 43.3% of them felt much more capable) (Fig. 1).

Furthermore, teachers highlighted how the course provided practical examples which are applicable to IEP design (12.5% of teachers were neutral, 28.8% of them agreed with this and 56.7% of them completely agreed with this).

Several teachers also think that the use of CA will improve students' learning outcomes (9.6% of teachers were neutral, 36.5% of them agreed with this and 52.9% of them completely agreed with this) and intend to apply CA principles in the design of their future courses (23.1% of teachers agreed with this and 73.1% of them completely agreed with this) (Fig. 2).

During the lesson, teachers received adequate support and resources to understand and apply concepts (27.9% of teachers agreed with this and 67.3% of them completely agreed with this); the course encouraged the partnership and exchange of ideas between participants (14.4% of teachers were neutral, 25% of them agreed with this and 54.8% of them completely agreed with this).

Overall, nearly all teachers were satisfied with the lesson on CA and its contents (23.1% of teachers agreed with this and 74% of them completely agreed with this) and think that such lesson has met their learning expectations with respect to CA (26.9% of teachers agreed with this and 68.3% of the completely agreed with this) and that CA will have a positive impact on their teaching practices (30.8% of teachers agreed with this and 63.5% of them completely agreed with this).

In view of what was reported, CA turns out to be an effective tool for inclusive educational planning and a support that is perceived as extremely valuable by teaching support activities trainees.

3.2   Results of the Questionnaire on the Application of ChatGPT for IEP Design

The group of teachers who applied ChatGPT for planning Section 5 of the IEP was made up of 81 subjects. The results of the questionnaire which was handed out to such teachers are reported below.

After the class, I feel more capable of aligning IEP learning objectives with appropriate teaching and assessment methods.
104 risposte

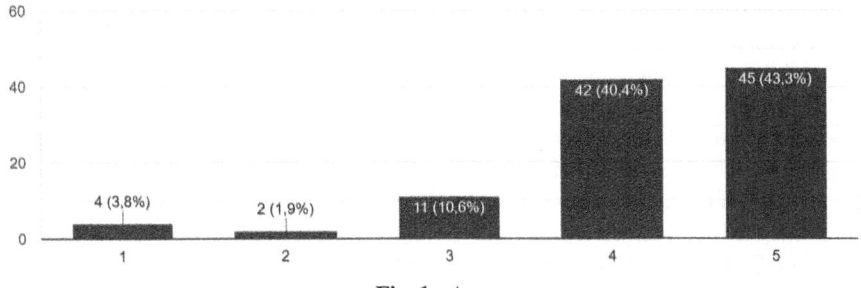

Fig. 1. A

I intend to apply the principles of constructive alignment in the design of my future courses.
104 risposte

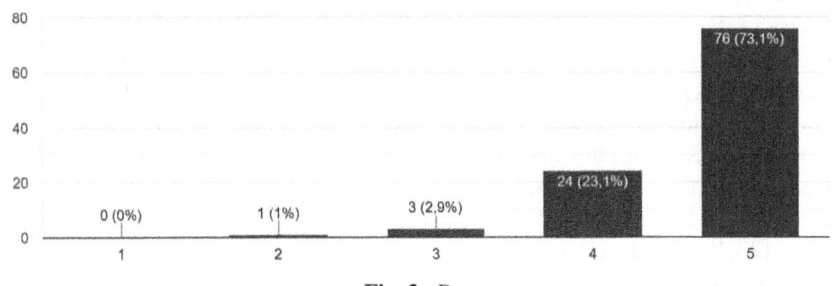

Fig. 2. B

How much do you think the application of Constructive Alignment affects your teaching practice?
104 risposte

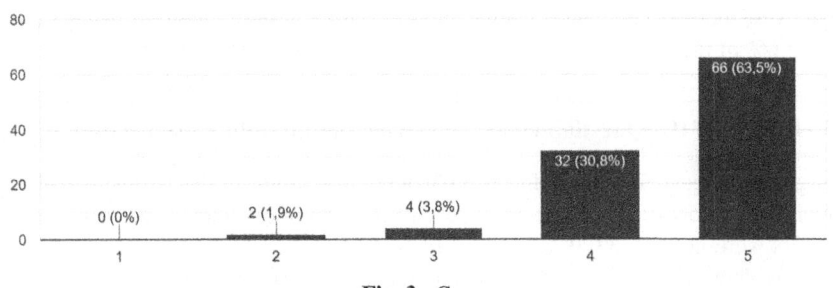

Fig. 3. C

Most teachers said they had understood the task (19.8% of teachers agreed with this and 72.8% of them completely agreed with this) and several teachers said they are satisfied with how they completed it (17.3% of teachers were neutral, 40.7% of them agreed with this and 39.5% of them completely agreed with this). 54.3% of participants completed the task in less than an hour, 34.6% of participants completed the task in an hour, whereas 8.6% of participants completed the task in an hour and a half and 2.5% of them in two hours. All participants used the free version of ChatGPT (Fig. 3).

Several participants (48.1%) had never used ChatGPT. However, at the end of the exercise, many of them said that the AI system had helped to generate objectives, strategies and systems which are congruent with the IEP (28.3% of teachers were neutral, 38.3% of them agreed with this and 29.6% of them completely agreed with this). Chat-GPT allowed teachers to organize their ideas when planning the IEP and to find more congruent goals, strategies and evaluation systems than they would have found on their own (33.3% of teachers were neutral, 33.3% of them agreed with this and 21% of them completely agreed with this) (Fig. 4).

ChatGPT helped teachers with the less interesting part of planning, and allowed them to focus on the quality of goal and the search for evaluative strategies and systems to be included in the IEP. Thanks to ChatGPT, it took less time for teachers to complete their planning (18.5% of teachers were neutral, 30.9% of them agreed with this and 46.9% of them completely agreed with this) (Fig. 5); furthermore, the planning of the IEP was more enjoyable (24.7% of teachers were neutral, 30.9% of them agreed with this this and 37% of them completely agreed with this) and was praised by participants (33.3% of teachers were neutral, 33.3% of them agreed with this and 45.7% of them completely agreed with this).

Several participants positively evaluated the accuracy of ChatGPT feedbacks (44.4% of teachers agreed with this and 16% of them completely agreed with this), but quite a few of them provided a neutral answer to this question (37%). Furthermore, several participants said that ChatGPT was capable of understanding and providing relevant answers (28.4% of teachers were neutral, 39.5% of them agreed with this and 25.9% of them completely agreed with this).

Nevertheless, several participants think that, when carrying out tasks with the support of ChatGPT, it is unavoidable and important to apply one's own critical sense (13.6% of teachers agreed with this and 79% of them completely agreed with this). (Fig. 6) Finally, nearly half of the teachers (48.1%) said that they wouldn't have found the same objectives, methodological strategies and evaluative systems without using ChatGPT and 92.6% of them think that the system is a useful tool for IEP design (Fig. 7).

3.3   Results of the Questionnaire for the Group that didn't Use ChatGPT

The group of teachers who didn't use ChatGPT for filling in the IEP was made up of 9 members. Most of them are satisfied with how they completed the task (33.3% of teachers were neutral; 33.3% of them agreed with this and 33.3% of them completely agreed with this). For 66.7% of teachers it took less than an hour to plan the IEP, whereas it took exactly an hour for 11.1% of them and exactly two hours, or less, for the same percentage of teachers.

Some teachers said they regret not having used ChatGPT (22.2%), whereas the remaining teachers said they don't regret not having used it. 33.3% of teachers admitted they ended up using ChatGPT anyway (Fig. 8), whereas 66.7% of them think that ChatGPT may be useful for IEP design.

ChatGPT allowed me to find more congruent goals, strategies, and evaluation systems than I would have found on my own.
81 risposte

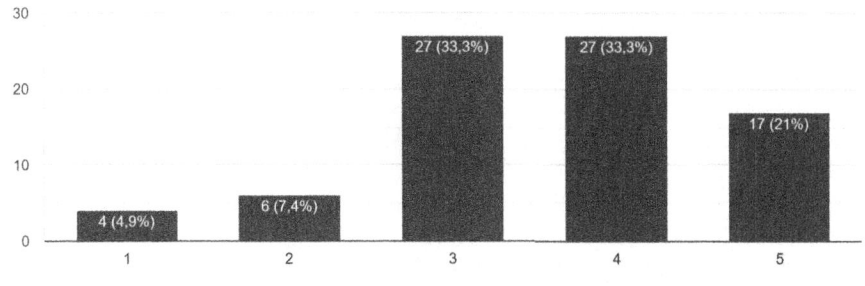

Fig. 4. D

ChatGPT helped me with the uninteresting part of the planning, freeing up time to focus on the quality of the goals and the search for evaluative strategies and systems to include in the IEP.
81 risposte

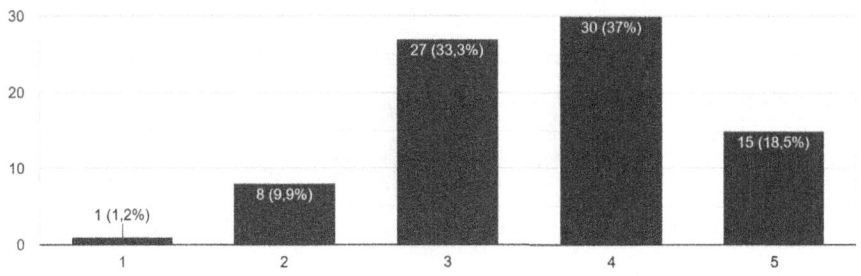

Fig. 5. E

Do you think that despite the application of ChatGPT, during the performance of activities, however, it is necessary to apply one's critical sense?
81 risposte

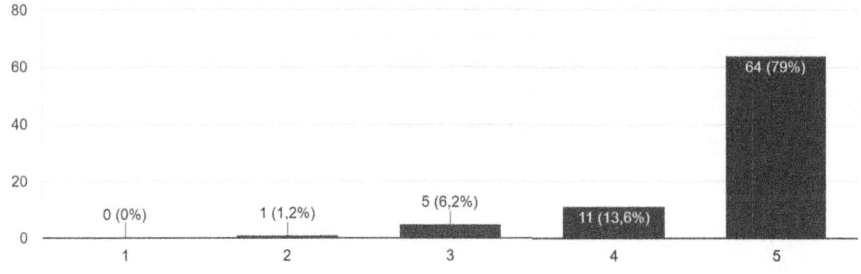

Fig. 6. F

Do you think ChatGPT is a useful tool for IEP design?
81 risposte

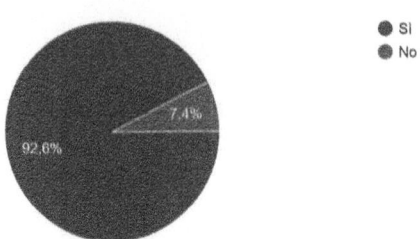

Fig. 7. G

55.6% of teachers state that they will use ChatGPT in the future for IEP design and 88.9% of group members think that the activity was useful for IEP design (Fig. 9).

Did you end up using ChatGPT anyway?
9 risposte

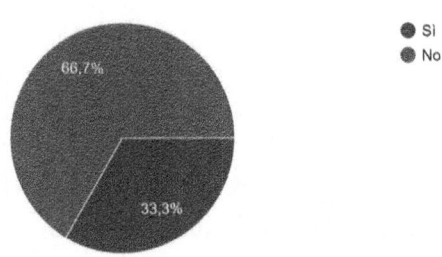

Fig. 8. H

Do you think you will be able to use ChatGPT for IEP design in the future?
9 risposte

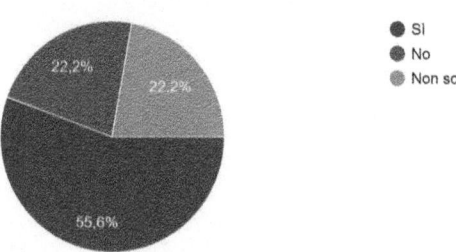

Fig. 9. I

4 Discussion

The analysis of the questionnaires clearly shows the efficacy of Constructive Alignment (CA) and the application of ChatGPT in terms of IEP design; both of them were positively welcomed by teachers.

CA was praised due to its ability to align objectives, learning strategies and verification methods. The implementation of CA strengthened teachers' confidence in their ability to plan Section 5 of the IEP.

By providing practical examples and support, the course simplified IEP design and promoted the future application of CA among teachers.

The use of the CONALI Ontology helped to improve the IEP quality, by providing a structured framework to identify objectives, learning strategies and assessment methods.

This is confirmed by the fact that taxonomy tools turned out to be useful for planning lessons and interdisciplinary documents and organizing knowledge (Carson, 2004; Ferguson, 2002; Horn et al., 2017).

As regards the application of ChatGPT along with the CONALI Ontology, teachers said they are satisfied with the experience and stated that the AI system is an effective tool to simplify and speed up the generation of objectives, strategies and evaluative systems that are aligned, congruent and exhaustive.

AI turned out to be an effective tool to support teachers with lesson planning (Adiguzel et al., 2023), thanks to its ability to speed up the search for information (Alqahtani et al., 2023), personalize the intervention based on the user's needs and promote the involvement, motivation and quality of learning (Kumar et al., 2023).

Teachers expressed their intention to use ChatGPT in the future for IEP design, and this is a positive sign for the long-term integration of this technology into the educational practice.

From these results, we can deduce that the integration of the CONALI Ontology and ChatGPT may represent an interesting perspective to maximize the support offered to teachers for inclusive planning.

The combined use of ontological models and AI may allow a more exhaustive, reliable, meticulous and personalized approach in IEP design, taking into account both the mandates of learning science and the specific needs of teachers and students.

However, it's essential to carefully consider teachers' technical skills and ensure adequate training to fully take advantage of the potential of both tools. Furter research may explore in depth the methods to integrate such approaches and assess their impact on the quality of the produced IEPs.

It is evident that the adoption of tools such as CA and devices such as ChatGPT can significantly contribute to improve the inclusive planning of IEPs, by offering effective and personalized tools to teachers, which can help them to meet different students' needs.

This research lays the foundation for further follow-up and developments in the field of AI-supported inclusive learning.

Ultimately, to answer RQ1, teachers' perceptions on AI application in IEP design, with the support of a taxonomy tool such as the CONALI Ontology, are positive and promising. However, it's important to consider aspects such as training and technical skills to maximise the benefits of this integration.

5   Conclusions

This study aimed at verifying to what extent AI application can be useful for teachers in inclusive educational planning. To this end, it was deemed appropriate to provide trainee teachers with the required skills to identify objectives and align them with intervention strategies and assessment methods, thanks to the application of the CONALI Ontology and CA. Such approach will allow to envisage their implementation by means of a conscious use of AI during IEP design.

The intervention showed that the combination of AI and CA is useful for teachers. In fact, it gets them enthusiastic during tasks, and allows them to feel more effective and complete the planning of documents sooner.

It should be highlighted that we analysed the application of ChatGPT for educational planning only for Section 5 of the IEP. In the future, some interventions are expected where AI will be implemented to fill in other parts or the whole document.

It's important to stress that the application of AI to such planning practices must be mitigated by the use of strong critical sense by teachers. In fact, as shown by the answers to the questionnaires, teachers are well aware of the fact that there's no way they can be replaced by AI when drafting sensitive and important documents such as the IEP, or when carrying out other tasks.

These studies aim at allowing the right combination between and algorithm and algorithm within the world of education, and generating a virtuous cycle of studies that can lead to an improvement of the educational phenomenon, a more effective management of processes related to teachers' activities and, subsequently, a better inclusion of students.

The encounter between these two dimensions may mark the beginning of an era in which the world of education may benefit from the potential guaranteed by AI, with the purpose of providing high-quality education to teachers and learners, in line with the challenges that characterize the modern era.

References

Adıgüzel, T., Kaya, M.H., Cansu, F.K.: Revolutionizing education with artificial intelligence: Exploring the transformative potential of ChatGPT. Contemporary Educational Technology (2023)

Akgun, S., Greenhow, C.: Artificial intelligence in education: addressing ethical challenges in K-12 settings. AI Ethics 2(3), 431–440 (2022)

Alqahtani, T., et al.: The emergent role of artificial intelligence, natural learning processing, and large language models in higher education and research. Res. Soc. Adm. Pharm. (2023)

Baidoo-Anu, D., Ansah, L.O.: Education in the era of generative artificial intelligence (AI): understanding the potential benefits of ChatGPT in promoting teaching and learning. J. AI 7(1), 52–62 (2023)

Bloom, B.S., Engelhart, M.D., Furst, E.J., Hill, W.H., Krathwohl, D.R.: Taxonomy of Educational Objectives: The Classification of Educational Goals. Handbook 1: Cognitive Domain, pp. 201–207. McKay, New York (1956)

Carson, R.N.: A taxonomy of knowledge types for use in curriculum design. Interchange 35, 59–79 (2004)

Chen, X., Xie, H., Hwang, G.J.: A multi-perspective study on artificial intelligence in education: grants, conferences, journals, software tools, institutions, and researchers. Comput. Educ. Artif. Intell. **1**, 100005 (2020)

Chiu, T.K., Meng, H., Chai, C.S., King, I., Wong, S., Yam, Y.: Creation and evaluation of a pretertiary artificial intelligence (AI) curriculum. IEEE Trans. Educ. **65**(1), 30–39 (2021)

Chiu, T.K., Xia, Q., Zhou, X., Chai, C.S., Cheng, M.: Systematic literature review on opportunities, challenges, and future research recommendations of artificial intelligence in education. Comput. Educ. Artif. Intell. **4**, 100118 (2023)

Chounta, I.A., Bardone, E., Raudsep, A., Pedaste, M.: Exploring teachers' perceptions of artificial intelligence as a tool to support their practice in Estonian K-12 education. Int. J. Inf. Artif. Intell. Educ. **32**(3), 725–755 (2022)

Ferguson, C.: Using the revised taxonomy to plan and deliver team-taught, integrated, thematic units. Theory Into Pract. **41**, 238–243 (2002)

Garg, S., Sharma, S.: Impact of artificial intelligence in special need education to promote inclusive pedagogy. Int. J. Inf. Educ. Technol. **10**(7), 523–527 (2020)

Harahap, Y.S., Sya'bana, D.F., Nurhaliza, S., Nurmawati, N.: Taxonomy of learning objectives. Ta'dib Jurnal Pendidikan Islam (2023)

Horn, I.S., Garner, B., Kane, B.D., Brasel, J.: A taxonomy of instructional learning opportunities in teachers' workgroup conversations. J. Teach. Educ. **68**, 41–54 (2017)

Hussain, I.: Attitude of university students and teachers towards instructional role of artificial intelligence. Int. J. Inf. Dist. Educ. E-Learn. **5**, 158–177 (2020)

Kim, J., Lee, H., Cho, Y.H.: Learning design to support student-AI collaboration: perspectives of leading teachers for AI in education. Educ. Inf. Technol. **27**(5), 6069–6104 (2022)

Kumar, D., Haque, A., Mishra, K., Islam, F., Mishra, B.K., Ahmad, S.: Exploring the transformative role of artificial intelligence and metaverse in education: a comprehensive review. Metaverse Basic Appl. Res. **2**, 55 (2023)

Maffei, A., Boffa, E., Lupi, F., Lanzetta, M.: On the design of constructively aligned educational unit. Educ. Sci. **12**(7), 438 (2022)

Maffei, A., Daghini, L., Archenti, A., Lohse, N.: CONALI ontology: a framework for design and evaluation of constructively aligned courses in higher education: putting in focus the educational goal verbs. Procedia CIRP **50**, 765–772 (2016)

Ogbeiwi, O.: Why written objectives need to be really SMART. British J. Healthc. Manag. **23**(7), 324–336 (2017)

Pratama, M.P., Sampelolo, R., Lura, H.: Revolutionizing education: harnessing the power of artificial intelligence for personalized learning. Klasikal J. Educ. Lang. Teach. Sci. **5**(2), 350–357 (2023)

Wu, S.Y., Yang, K.K.: The effectiveness of teacher support for students' learning of artificial intelligence popular science activities. Front. Psychol. **13**, 868623 (2022)

Xia, Q., Chiu, T.K., Lee, M., Sanusi, I.T., Dai, Y., Chai, C.S.: A self-determination theory (SDT) design approach for inclusive and diverse artificial intelligence (AI) education. Comput. Educ. **189**, 104582 (2022)

Yang, H., Kyun, S.: The current research trend of artificial intelligence in language learning: a systematic empirical literature review from an activity theory perspective. Aust. J. Educ. Technol. **38**(5), 180–210 (2022)

Zhang, L., Basham, J.D., Yang, S.: Understanding the implementation of personalized learning: a research synthesis. Educ. Res. Rev. **31**, 100339 (2020)

Digital Culture Among Students: Analyzing Teachers' Thoughts on Internet and Social Media Usage

Marco di Furia(✉) ⓘ, Martina Rossi ⓘ, Giusi Antonia Toto ⓘ,
Francesco Pio Savino ⓘ, and Francesco Sulla ⓘ

University of Foggia, 71121 Foggia, FG, Italy
{marco.difuria,martina.rossi,giusi.toto,francesco.savino,
francesco.sulla}@unifg.it

Abstract. The present study is part of a broader research project called GIneS-TRA. GIneSTRA aims to integrate Technology Enhanced Learning (TEL) and ICTs within programs to combat cyberbullying. Specifically, GIneSTRA is a mixed-methods research action that focuses on Educational Digital Storytelling (EDS), an educational methodology that leverages ICTs but is fundamentally based on the exploration of the emotional and behavioral self and other. This paper presets the preliminary phase of the project, and its data, with an emphasis on the qualitative analysis performed in the first phases. The purpose of the qualitative research is to explore perceptions and knowledge about Internet use and social media use among students. Data were collected by means of focus groups conducted with teachers involved in the project (N = 50). The textual material obtained was analyzed by means of Grounded Theory Methodology (GTM). The results of the qualitative study return to the researcher material useful not only to calibrate targeted prevention and intervention programs, but also to gain more knowledge with respect to the use of new media by younger people.

Keywords: Cyberbullying · Teachers · Qualitative research

1 Introduction

1.1 Growing Up in the Digital Age: Between Opportunities and Risks

Social interactions today are largely sustained within virtual environments. In their developmental stages, during adolescence, younger people use the channels of ICTs (Information and Communication Technologies) to relate to the outside world, through social media and the Internet. It can be said that the keyword of contemporary socialization, in fact, is precisely "net," contained in "network" but also in "Internet," signifying the web of connections and connectivity in which each of us, owners of the latest generation of digital devices, inevitably find ourselves involved – notably, Tapscott addressed the concept of the 'Net generation' in one of his seminal works [1].

G. A. Toto (Ed.): ICS exchange 2024, CCIS 2521, pp. 136–153, 2025.
https://doi.org/10.1007/978-3-032-03021-4_10

Social media are an inexhaustible source of content, news and relationships. Thanks to social media, young people can actively participate in social change [2], creatively express their own identity [3], get their own information [4] and learn from broader bodies of resources [5], or spread their demands to a wide public audience, advocating for themselves with direct action on the surrounding reality [6]. However, the digitization of social relations has also fueled the emergence of negative phenomena, including cyberbullying or online bullying [7]. The complexity of this phenomenon lies not only in its dynamics but also in the effects it can have on the people involved, mainly victims and aggressors, but not limited to them: in other words, in order to understand cyberbullying and to counter it, one must view it as a social phenomenon, which involves different roles with different characteristics [8].

Based on these considerations, we designed an educational intervention called GIneStra ("broom" in English), an Italian acronym for "Generating innovative Interventions and Strategies to counter cyberbullying", focused on the exploration of certain social dynamics and their representation through technology. The intervention, based on the methodology of Educational Digital Storytelling (EDS) [9], uses tools and languages familiar to digital natives, borrowed from ICTs, and is centered on the co-creation of narratives related to cyberbullying. Before the implementation of the intervention in the experimental classes, we collected teachers' perceptions regarding the relationship between young people and technologies both in and outside the classroom, in order to design an intervention based on the identified needs, while anticipating potential limitations for its execution.

1.2 Cyberbullying

Literature on cyberbullying gives us a clear view of correlation between cyber-aggressions and empathy [10]. Based on the assumption that empathy and positive peer relationships may hinder the incidence of cyberbullying, some authors have suggested that the development of prosocial attitudes may promote the countering of the phenomenon. In any case, constituting essentially episodes that occur on the Web and virtual communities, cyberbullying is influenced by variables such as intensive access to the Internet and social networks [11, 12], virtually boundless containers of potentially addictive or violent media material [12–14].

Although research on the effects of cyberbullying is less extensive than that of traditional bullying, researchers believe the effects of cyberbullying may be similar to or potentially more harmful than traditional bullying [15]. Researchers have reported effects ranging from depression and loneliness [16, 17] to negative emotional state [18] and, in the worst cases, suicide – for a systematic review, see, for example [19].

An intensive use of devices and social media inevitably exposes young people to episodes of cyberbullying or, more generally, cyberviolence. In this sense, it is important to develop prevention programs aimed at increasing awareness of the risks that can arise in digital environments [20]. In this regard, the role of the teacher assumes a certain significance.

Intervention programs aimed at tackling cyberbullying, although effective in reducing cyberbullying in the short term, most of the time are proved ineffective on the long run

[21]. Among other reasons, not including teachers in the programs reduce the long-term efficacy of the programs.

2 The Current Study

The objective of this study is to gather teachers' perceptions regarding students' use of the Internet and digital technologies, using a qualitative approach [22]. The research question is based on a dual goal: to investigate the use of social media platforms, which is closely linked to the dynamics of cyberbullying and cybervictimization, and to obtain useful information for the design and implementation of a prevention program that is both teacher and technology-based. To achieve our aim, group interviews were conducted using standardized questions, focusing on the use of social media and the Internet on one hand, and educational technologies on the other.

2.1 Methodology

The Grounded Theory Methodology (GTM) [23, 24] approach was used to understand the general perceptions of the investigated group of teachers with respect to a certain topic (technology use among students). The chosen methodology is based on the assumption that groups of people from the same background are holders of certain meanings, which they express through a common shared language by means of social interactions [25]. In our case, we collected perspectives that are significant for the school context of the GIneSTRA project, in order to obtain useful data for the application of the program and its replicability in other contexts.

2.2 Participants

The sampling of participants followed convenience criteria, as the teachers selected for the study were from schools participating in the GIneStra project. These schools include 5 from the province of Foggia: one primary school, three lower secondary schools, and one upper secondary school. A total of 50 teachers participated in our study, 5 men and 45 women, with an average age of 49.64 (SD = 10.584) and an average teaching experience of 18.36 years (SD = 10.342). The participants teach in grades ranging from fifth to tenth. Two of them are from the Campania region, while the remaining 48 are from Puglia, the region where the involved schools are located.

2.3 Procedures

The collection of qualitative data took place in March 2024, prior to the teacher training stage. Four Focus Groups were organized, conducted by two facilitators and two observers in four groups of teachers, following the round-robin approach [26], which allows for greater involvement. The stimulus questions were as follows:

1. What do you think about students' use of technologies and social media?
2. What do you consider to be the pros of using technology in the classroom?

3. What do you consider to be the cons of using technology in the classroom?

Teachers were asked, in turn, to answer each question referring to their professional experience. Each interview lasted approximately 50 min. Students were given a questionnaire with open-ended questions, using the "long answer text" function of Google Forms. The questionnaires were administered with the support of teachers in the school's computer labs, and students were arranged in a way that allowed them to respond with the maximum degree of privacy possible.

3   Results

The analysis of the textual corpus was carried out using the Italian version[1] of Voyant tools (Sinclair & Rockwell, v. 2.6.17), whose code is under a GPL3 license and whose contents are under a Creative Commons by attribution license. The opinions and thoughts of primary school (PS) and secondary school (SS) teachers were collected through Focus Groups conducted prior to the training planned in the project. The analysis of the text extracted from the interviews led to the creation of 50 codes, which were in turn grouped into 8 categories and 2 macro-categories: "Young people's relationship with social media platforms" and "Digital technologies in school" (Fig. 1). These were based on the following topics: observation, perceptions and opinions, roles of educational agents, professional experiences, advantages and disadvantages. The purpose of this classification lies in the aim to gather information from a bottom-up perspective, not only on teachers' beliefs and convictions but also on their concrete actions in school contexts.

3.1   The Perspective on Social Media

The macro-category "Young people's relationship with social media platforms" contains 5 categories, created in turn by the aggregation of 79 keywords (Table 1). Only terms or syntagms present in at least two occurrences in the analyzed corpus were selected among the keywords, considering singulars, plurals, and terms derived from the same word root. The first macro-category emerged based on the first question posed within the Focus Groups ("What do you think about students' use of technologies and social media?").

Observation of Social Media Usage (1). As privileged observers of the behaviors of so-called "digital natives" [27], teachers are able to report information on some habits and trends expressed by students. Regarding the use of social media, an intensive and expert usage is reported during secondary school years ("their life is determined by social media in every way", "they know how to use social media all too well"), but it is necessary to implement education on the use of these tools ("there is a clear difference between the use of social media, which they know all too well, and what should perhaps be taught to them better from the beginning"). The most mentioned platform is TikTok, with 13 occurrences (Fig. 2). In general, teachers from both school levels believe that

---

[1] Available on: https://voyant-tools.org/ (the italian translation is provided by Ciotti *et al.*).

Codes	Categories	Macro-categories
INTENSIVE USE OF **SOCIAL** MEDIA (SS) **SOCIAL** MEDIA AND **CELLPHONE** DEPENDENCY (SS) **SOCIAL** MEDIA FOR SOCIALIZATION AND LEARNING (PS/SS) USE OF VIRTUAL **CHATS** STARTING FROM PRIMARY SCHOOL (PS) VIOLATION OF AGE LIMITS ON **SOCIAL** MEDIA (SS) POPULARITY OF **TIKTOK** (SS)	OBSERVATION OF SOCIAL MEDIA USAGE	YOUNG PEOPLE'S RELATIONSHIP WITH SOCIAL MEDIA PLATFORMS
EASE OF USE OF **MOBILE PHONES** (SS) DIFFICULTY USING **COMPUTER** (SS) **TECHNOLOGY** AS AN ESSENTIAL PART OF DAILY LIFE (PS/SS) VIOLATION OF THE BAN ON **MOBILE PHONES** (PS/SS) **PHONES** AS EDUCATIONAL TOOLS (SS) **PHONES** AS A SOURCE OF DISTRACTION (SS) CONSUMPTION AND PRODUCTION OF **VIDEOS** (PS/SS)	OBSERVATION OF THE RELATIONSHIP WITH TECHNOLOGY AND MEDIA	
SOCIAL MEDIA CONTRIBUTES TO **IDENTITY BUILDING** (SS) SOCIAL MEDIA ENCOURAGES **IMITATION** AMONG PEERS (SS) DIGITAL ENVIRONMENTS ENABLE DANGEROUS **EXCLUSION** DYNAMICS (SS) LACK OF **PRIVACY** (PS) SOCIAL MEDIA DISTRACTS FROM MORE AUTHENTIC **EXPERIENCES** (SS) SOCIAL MEDIA USE IS CONSIDERED **EXCESSIVE** (PS/SS) CHAT USAGE CAN BE **DETRIMENTAL** (PS/SS) **UNAWARENESS** OF NEGATIVE EFFECTS OF SOCIAL MEDIA (PS/SS) SOCIAL MEDIA IS NOT ENTIRELY **NEGATIVE** (SS) **PROBLEMS** WITH OFFENSIVE CHATS, STICKERS, AND MEMES (PS/SS)	PERCEPTIONS AND OPINIONS ON SOCIAL MEDIA USE	
DIFFICULTY **TEACHING** HOW TO USE TECHNOLOGY (SS) SCHOOLS ARE UNPREPARED TO **EDUCATE** ON DIGITAL TOOLS (SS) SOME TEACHERS FEEL ALIENATED BY DIGITAL TECHNOLOGIES (PS/SS) SCHOOLS STRUGGLE TO SUPERVISE SOCIAL MEDIA USE (PS/SS)	THE ROLE OF THE SCHOOL	
PERMISSIVE/SEVERE MISGUIDANCE FROM FAMILIES ON TECHNOLOGY USE (PS/SS) GREATER SYNERGY WITH FAMILIES IS NEEDED (SS) INSUFFICIENT FAMILY SUPERVISION (PS/SS) STUDENTS LEARN FROM PARENTS' IMPROPER SOCIAL MEDIA USE (SS)	THE ROLE OF THE FAMILY	
TECHNOLOGIES CAN BE USED IN SEVERAL FIELDS OF STUDY (PS/SS) **SOCIAL** MEDIA CAN BE USED FOR EDUCATIONAL PURPOSES (SS) TEACHERS USE TOOLS LIKE **KAHOOT, WORDWALL, GOOGLE APPS** AND **LEARNINGAPPS.ORG** (SS) TEACHERS UTILIZE INTERACTIVE **WHITEBOARDS** AND **DIGITAL BOOKS** (PS/SS) MINISTERIAL **BAN** ON PHONES IN CLASS (SS)	TEACHING WITH TECHNOLOGIES	DIGITAL TECHNOLOGIES IN SCHOOL
EDUCATIONAL TECHNOLOGIES AS A TOOL FOR **INCLUSION** (SS) TECHNOLOGY ENHANCES LEARNING (SS) TECHNOLOGIES ENCOURAGE **SOCIALIZATION** AND **EMPATHY** (SS) EDUCATIONAL TECHNOLOGIES INCREASE **ATTENTION** AND **ENGAGEMENT** (PS/SS) STUDENTS HAVE **NO DIFFICULTY** USING EDUCATIONAL TECHNOLOGY (SS) TECHNOLOGIES ARE **STIMULATING** FOR BOTH STUDENTS AND TEACHERS(PS/SS)	ADVANTAGES OF TECHNOLOGY IN SCHOOL	
NOT ALL FAMILIES HAVE **COMPUTERS** OR **TABLETS** FOR SCHOOL USE (SS) **TECHNOLOGY** SHOULD ONLY BE AN ADDITION TO TRADITIONAL LESSONS (SS) **DEVICES** IN CLASS MAY WORSEN TECH ADDICTION (SS) INTERNET **ACCESS** CAN EXPOSE YOUNG PEOPLE TO RISKS (PS/SS) TECHNOLOGY IN CLASS MAY DECREASE **CONCENTRATION** (PS/SS) EXCESSIVE TECHNOLOGY USE INCREASES **ISOLATION** (SS) THERE IS A **GAP** BETWEEN SOME TEACHERS' AND STUDENTS' DIGITAL SKILLS (SS) NEW GENERATIONS LACK **CRITICAL** THINKING IN TECHNOLOGY USE (PS/SS)	DISADVANTAGES OF TECHNOLOGY IN SCHOOL	

Fig. 1. The image shows the categorization performed based on the text extracted from the Focus Groups conducted with teachers, divided into codes, categories and macro-categories.

Table 1. The most frequent keywords underlying the 5 categories on social media use.

Keyword	Occurrences	Categories
Social*	47	1, 2, 3
Cellphone*	39	1, 2, 3
School*	37	4, 5
Parent*	29	4, 5
Tool*	27	1, 2, 3
Technology/ies	24	1, 2, 3
Chat*	23	1, 2, 3
Problem*	19	3
Family/ies	19	4, 5
Child*	16	4, 5

mobile phones are now fundamental tools for socialization and exploration of reality. Among the issues noted, especially by secondary school teachers, are mainly social media addiction and the violation of restrictions on social media use[2].

Observation of the Relationship with Technology and Media (2). Starting from the ways of using social media, teachers talk about the relationship between students and technology and media content. Teachers from both school levels describe technologies as an element considered essential for everyday life, as if it were an inseparable appendage of the body ("I see that they cannot live without these tools", "they make ruthless use of mobile phones (...) it's a constant war in class, trying to take them away"). This is probably why the use of mobile phones during school hours becomes problematic – an issue, moreover, much debated within the Focus Groups ("maybe two people sitting at the same desk (...) are playing or chatting with each other", "a little girl, in class, I don't know how, (...) because (...) absolutely no mobile phones are brought to primary school (...) started taking photos of her friends"); our interviews took place during a period when Italian government was preparing new regulations on the use of mobile phones in the classroom[3]. In secondary school, where a more frequent use of technologies is evident, there is a gap in technological skills: mobile phones are used with familiarity, unlike a tool like the computer ("when we move (...) to using the computer as a tool, which can help us achieve very specific objectives, they don't know how to use it"). This

---

[2] According to Italian law, the minimum age to register on social networks is set at 14 years old (Decree No. 101 of August 10, 2018); this decree represents an adaptation to the General Data Protection Regulation (GDPR) promulgated by the European Union. Regarding services offered by online platforms, the processing of a minor's data is lawful if the minor is at least 16 years old (Art. 8).

[3] Currently in Italy, the use of smartphones in classrooms is prohibited, even for educational purposes, in all primary and lower secondary schools (9th grade). This ban is prescribed by the ministerial circular "Provisions regarding the use of smartphones and electronic registers in the first cycle of education," issued by Minister Giuseppe Valditara on July 11, 2024.

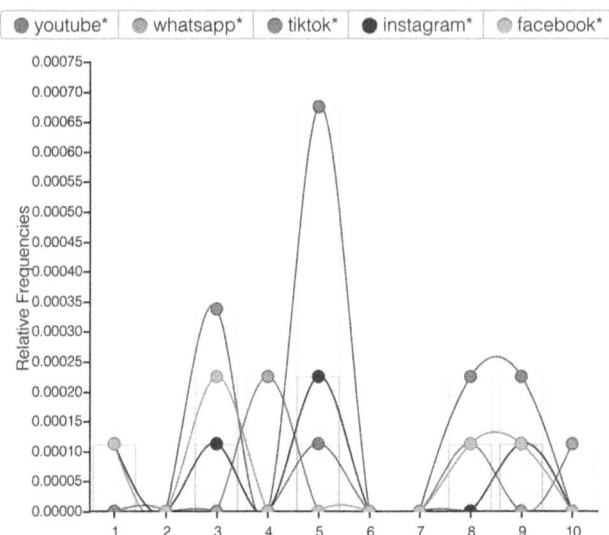

Fig. 2. The chart shows the frequencies of words indicating some popular social platforms within the text segments that originated the first macro-category (represented by the x-axis).

demonstrates that being born in the digital age is not sufficient to automatically possess digital skills, as previous scholars have indicated [28, 29]. Some teachers fear that devices may negatively affect attention processes ("I don't allow the use of mobile phones in class because it's a constant distraction"); at the same time, however, they are useful tools for capturing the interest of students, who are attracted to them ("if I give a frontal lesson, I lose the kids after five minutes, if I attach a digital quiz, an interactive quiz, a video, an app (...) I really catch them (...) encouraging them to use their mobile phones in class as well"). A testimony of great interest for this study concerns the consumption and production of videos, which is the type of content most mentioned by teachers (Fig. 3); this suggests students' familiarity with this particular medium.

Perceptions and Opinions on Social Media Use (3). The analysis of the words spoken by the interviewees allowed for the extraction and categorization of their personal opinions regarding the role that social media plays in the life experiences and development of students. Some teachers describe the presence of social media as intrusive and pervasive: the very identity construction of young people today seems to occur through these channels ("perhaps they entrust part of their self-construction (...) to social media"). This happens on both public and private levels. According to the teachers' perspective, social media encourage processes of peer imitation – at a stage in life where, as evidenced by literature [30], relationships with peers are a key element in understanding how social bonds are formed, for example, to promote the well-being of individual adolescents. According to the interviewees, the constant presence of social media in students' lives causes a series of negative effects: from dangerous mechanisms of social exclusion in digital environments ("these exclusions are even more devastating for kids, silence, erasure, is even more devastating than insults"), to a lack of privacy from an early age ("even

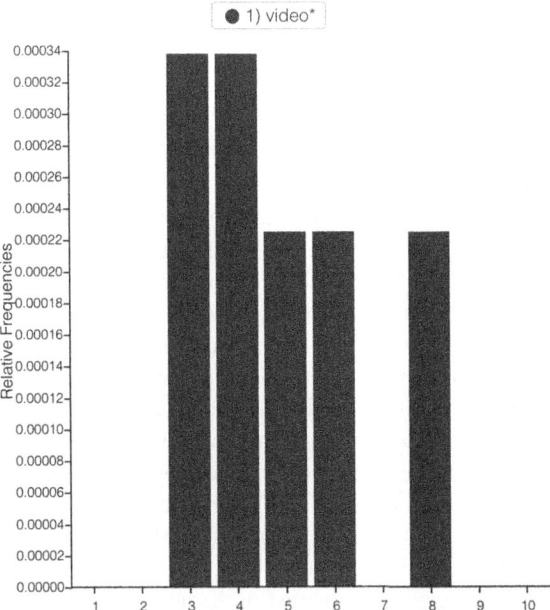

Fig. 3. The bar graph shows the frequency of references to students consuming or producing video within the text segments that originated the first macro-category (represented by the x-axis).

regarding online privacy, (...) they do not have a balanced use of technology"); from the improper use of chats, stickers, and memes, which are used "(...) to target a classmate" ("they make memes or stickers, writing 'this is Tizia and Caia, and she is of dubious morals[4]"), to the abstraction from authentic life experiences, cited by two teachers as "the best of life". At the root of these negative aspects of social media use it is possible to find a common thread, visible in the statements of both primary and secondary school teachers: a) a perceived excessive use of social media; b) unawareness of the negative effects of social media. The judgment on these tools is expressed across a spectrum of opinions, from the most pessimistic ("it is a mental aberration, artificially constructed by multinationals that practically want to annihilate the thought of the free man") to the more optimistic ("so to say 'no, (...) social media is all bad, all negative,' is not entirely accurate (...) it is my responsibility and that of the adult, thus the family, to say 'look, (...) let's set some rules'"), reflecting the debate between so-called techno-enthusiasts and technophobes (also cited as "tecno-apocalittici" in Italian), already referenced in

---

[4] Translation note: among idiomatic expressions in the Italian language, the expression "Tizio, Caio & Sempronio" refers to three male figures representing "anyone" by antonomasia; the English equivalent is "Tom, Dick & Harry". In our case, Tizia and Caia are two hypothetical female persons, named by the interviewed teacher as an example of victims of gender-based online hate speech (the Italian expression "poco di buono", when referred to a female subject, is a euphemism for "prostitute", "woman of dubious morals"). In order to preserve this nuance of meaning, it was decided to keep the original idiomatic expression in its feminine version, which cannot be translated into English.

national literature regarding teachers [31, 32]. In general, from the teachers' responses, the need to implement education on the use of these tools emerges, in order to master their positive aspects ("I believe that the use of social media technologies is a useful tool for communication, research, learning, and even for digital literacy, but I think that kids are not really educated about it").

The Role of School (4). Guiding students toward appropriate use of technology is perceived by the interviewed teachers as a challenging task: in discussions about adult supervision, the terms "war" (1 occurrence) and "battle" (2 occurrences) are used. One teacher, referring to monitoring students' use of devices, repeats the word "fatigue" no less than 5 times. Related to the theme of supervision or management of technologies, the word "fatigue" appears a total of 6 times; the term "fatigued" is used by another teacher to describe the emotional state of young people in managing social dynamics through social media. Among the interviewed secondary school teachers, this struggle is partly attributed to the difficulty of "keeping up" with their students and a feeling of alienation ("I am completely out of the loop and therefore I cannot even fully understand what is happening", "I feel out of place (...) I don't get along well with this technology"), confirming to some extent the data regarding the digital gap between teachers and students and teachers' perceptions of technology [33, 34]. Moreover, in this group of teachers, there is a certain degree of distrust in the actual capacity of the school institution to meet this educational need ("technology has astonishing power (...) but the problem is precisely this, because we will always have tools of a certain level, that is, we will keep moving forward. And how do we teach our kids to use these tools? 'Look, this is how you do it, this is how you don't do it': that won't be enough. So, I think that the school alone cannot manage it"); in many cases, the interviewed teachers refer to a lack of collaboration with families, as we will explore further (*cfr. Infra*, § The role of family), and to negative emulation of family models that somehow contradict what is being taught in class.

The Role of Family (5). According to the interviewed teachers, during the years of education, "it is (also) up to the family (...) to help them understand what is wrong," thus fostering an alliance between educational agencies, which, for the interviewees, does not reach adequate levels ("today, the school is somewhat delegated to solve many issues, but we are not the only educational institution (...) I don't see this role of families as educators"). Teachers from both levels of education considered in our interview indicate a certain level of negligence on the part of families, who do not sufficiently supervise the use of devices ("in my opinion, they should also be monitored a bit by the family, because at 8-9 and 10 years old, they already have their phones, and they use them not always for the right reasons, let's say", "I stop there (...), because then the family also has to do its part, so it will be the family's job to say 'kid, excuse me, who are you following? What TikTok are you watching?' spending hours and hours watching TikToks", "the control outside the school walls should happen at home", "so yes, there are many minors with fake accounts; there is also a lack of supervision from social media providers and then from parents, because many kids don't have parental control"). Parents' incorrect or improper use of technology becomes paradigmatic and influences the behavior of young people ("I come home and see my mom doing TikToks – because we see parents' TikToks – with inappropriate content, of all kinds and qualities (...), so intervening in education as a school becomes difficult because it lacks credibility," "I won't tell you it's just one, but it's a good 80% – who makes TikToks with their own father; with the kids themselves! Overexposing the child to Instagram, 'do the dance for me so we can put it on TikTok'", "it's really difficult to explain things to the kids, to give them awareness, because if mom does it... 'well, mom is mom, dad is dad, you're just someone who spends 5 h with me'"). It follows that to counteract phenomena related to the misuse of social media or the internet, "there should be greater synergy among the various institutions" involved in the educational process of young people. Discussing this issue, one teacher concludes their response by saying, "everyone must do their part, but obviously, parents must also do theirs."

3.2 The Perspective on Educational Technologies

The macro-category "Digital technologies in school" contains 3 categories, created in turn by the aggregation of 48 keywords (Table 2), chosen according to the criteria previously described. This second macro-category is formed through teachers' responses to the following two questions:

- what do you consider to be the pros of using technology in the classroom?
- what do you consider to be the cons of using technology in the classroom?

Table 2. The most frequent keywords underlying the 3 categories on educational technologies.

Keyword	Occurrences	Categories
Technolog*	50	1, 2, 3
Cellphone*	40	1, 2, 3
Need*	27	2, 3
Tool*	24	1
Classroom	24	1
Lesson*	19	1
Device*	16	1
Home	15	1
Computer*	14	1
WhatsApp	13	1

Teaching with Technologies (1). The responses provided by the teachers give us an overview of the use of digital technologies in the classroom, spanning primary and secondary education, and producing interesting data on the topic of Technology Enhanced Learning (TEL), which has been addressed for over a decade within the international pedagogical community [35]. Based on the statements from primary and secondary school teachers, we find that educational technologies are employed in various disciplines: they are used for math (5 teachers interviewed); Italian and history (5 teachers interviewed); English (2 teachers interviewed); geography (2 teacher interviewed); science (2 teachers interviewed); religious education (1 teacher interviewed). Among the most mentioned tools are interactive whiteboards and digital books, and in some cases, social media as well ("some have started following the same BookTokers that I follow (...) I manage to present social media in class", "a student opened a very interesting window for me (...) precisely with social media"). The most mentioned apps and software (Fig. 4) used in class by the teachers in our sample are Kahoot, Wordwall, Google Apps, and LearningApps.

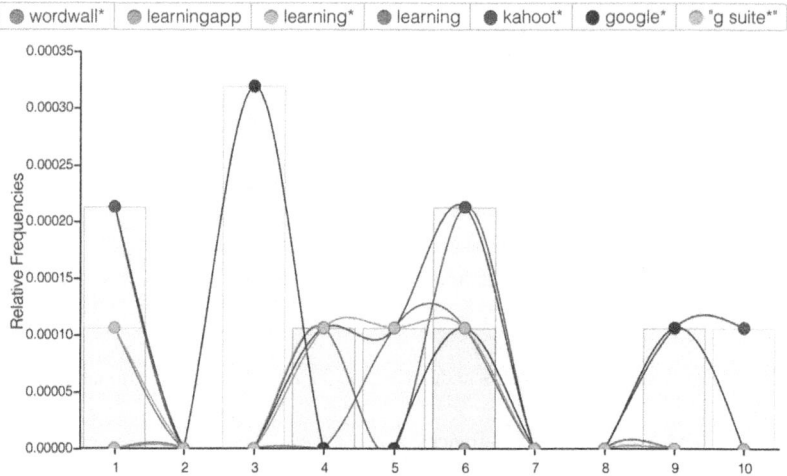

Fig. 4. The chart shows the frequency of terms referring to educational apps or software within the text segments that originated the first macro-category (represented by the x-axis).

The issue of cell phone presence in the classroom returns, not without controversy within our reference sample. Regarding the recent ministerial decree that prohibits the use of cell phones in class, discussed and approved during 2024 (*cf. Supra*, § The perspective on social media), one teacher in particular expresses some doubts, stating: "What's the point of a ban? Isn't it better for them to become aware of its use? Rather than seeing it alone, it's riskier compared to guidance from a teacher, a parent (...) it's precisely the digital competence (...) for which you make me obtain a competence certification (...) the two things really clash". Within one of the Focus Groups in particular, the teachers open a debate on the topic: on one hand, the smartphone can be a useful tool in the absence of other resources ("it is prohibited daily, except for a didactic activity (...) I tell the kids: 'we need to do some research on the web', the interactive whiteboard isn't working, internet on the interactive whiteboard isn't working, 'take out your cell phones'", "it's very effective to ensure that all students have, for example, the textbook. Because often they don't have it physically, and so, maybe by taking a photo and sending it to the group, every student, even the one without the book, can obviously follow along"); at the same time, its presence in the classroom raises some concerns ("it's a big responsibility, in case the cell phone gets damaged"). Some secondary school teachers encounter difficulties in prohibiting its use in one case, there's talk of "compulsive" use; primary school teachers, where the ban on use is more entrenched, report less presence of the problem.

Advantages of Technology in School (2). Based on the experiences of our sample, it is possible to outline some advantageous aspects of using educational technologies. More than one teacher defines them as "inclusive" also referring to Special Educational Needs ("I really catch even the kid who speaks little Italian this way", "when there are inclusion problems, so children who may have educational support, (...) we cannot deny the validity of these tools", "with disability, there is a strong tendency to use computer equipment because it helps"), in addition to the fact that these are tools that students know how to use well, with positive effects on accessibility [36]. Technologies can also facilitate learning, having playful or appealing traits that increase attention and engagement: this thought, in particular, is shared by both primary and secondary school teachers. The latter speak positively about the impact that educational technologies can have on socialization and empathy ("I look at technology (...) from a perspective (...) that is also pro-social, because it favors, in a sense, moments of socialization (...) they learn better (...) also from the point of view of empathy", "it's often the only way they have to communicate what they feel, what they experience"). Educational technologies are not only a stimulus for students but also for the teachers themselves: "I use apps a lot (...) this, however, requires a different kind of work from me at home. And it stimulates me a lot. Because I always have to be there researching (...) new ways, new strategies", "technology helps (...) and I find it very positive (...) for the student's growth path (...) it's a similar path for us teachers. Instead of doing the usual frontal lessons (...) it's certainly a valid alternative".

Disadvantages of Technology in School (3). A problem reported by the interviewed teachers is the technological unavailability of some families, who don't have tablets or PCs available to do homework; in other words, a situation of digital divide [37] is reported, and this poses significant limits to the application of TEL. Moreover, the emerging position is to consider technologies as a support, but not a replacement for traditional approaches, as explicitly stated especially by secondary school teachers ("the traditional lesson must be recovered, so relying too much on technologies is not even, let's say, a good and right thing", "it's much easier for me to capture their attention with a lesson that is, I repeat, halfway between frontal and (...) a participatory lesson using these means", "I think that a part, not of every lesson, but of some lessons, can be dedicated to doing things using the cell phone"). Among the negative effects that technologies in the classroom can have, the following are mentioned: a) the possible increase in tech addiction, b) exposure to online dangers, c) decreased levels of concentration, and d) isolation. The theme of the generational gap perceived by teachers in relation to students also returns ("my level is clearly different because I'm old!", "many times it's them who teach me something"), stated mostly by secondary school teachers. A common problem reported by teachers of both school levels is the lack of critical sense regarding the use of technologies ("regarding critical attention (...) we need to educate kids well on the use of devices, if you put them in front of a computer it doesn't solve anything at all (...), it doesn't educate. It's certainly not the computer that gives you reflection, critical thinking"), which leads us to reflect again on the crucial nature of well-structured digital literacy, as international research has long emphasized [38, 39]. In this process, teachers recognize their role and responsibility ("it's me who, with a different maturity, bends social media to what I need: it's clear that an 11, 12, 13-year-old kid doesn't have this maturity").

4 Discussion

The results of this study provide insight into the perceptions and opinions that primary and secondary school teachers have about students' relationships with social media and digital technologies, as well as the role these play in the contemporary pedagogical context. The data collection presented here also represents the first step of a broader research project, related to the implementation of an anti-cyberbullying intervention called GIneStra. This project employs the EDS methodology according to a teacher-based and co-participatory approach.

The aim of GIneStra is to stimulate students to reflect on the effects of behaviors carried out through the Internet, using a teaching methodology that uses digital technologies (ICTs) to educate about media, based on the principles of Media Education [40].

A first point to dwell on relates to the needs analysis carried out through the data obtained in the Focus Groups: there emerges a general need to find new strategies and new resources to educate students on the use of digital technology, from the early years of education. According to the interviewed teachers, in fact, students lack a real awareness of the negative effects that social media and the Internet can cause. The EU guidelines on lifelong learning for future European citizens clarify that Digital Competence means "confident, critical and responsible use of, and engagement with, digital technologies for learning, at work, and for participation in society. It includes information and data literacy, communication and collaboration, media literacy, digital content creation (including programming), safety (including digital well-being and competences related to cyber-security), intellectual property related questions, problem solving and critical thinking" [41, p. 10]. To develop these skills, however, we must also work on developing digital skills in teachers, towards universal and easily reproducible frameworks [42, 43].

Secondly, the collected data allowed for a more accurate design of GIneStra, which starts precisely from teacher training and continues with a teacher-based intervention in the classroom, monitored by the research team. The group interview, in the form of a Focus Group, is one of the most suitable tools for didactic planning and educational research [44], precisely for its bottom-up approach centered on the people who will benefit from the educational intervention. In designing GIneStra's training activities, therefore, the data collected from teachers proved fundamental for calibrating the program's objectives, tools, and resources.

The teachers' continuous reference to the mobile device (the term cellphone* recurs 79 times) within the interviews is indicative: this device is at the center of reflections on the relationship between young people and technology. Consequently, the use of cell phones becomes an eligible topic of reflection within anti-cyberbullying programs, or those related to digital competence more generally. The cell phone is also described as a useful educational tool, for accessibility and ease of use, which suggests that the smartphone itself could be the most suitable tool or resource for implementing the

GIneStra project, which has a technology-based nature. Teachers report a co-presence of opportunities and limitations deriving from the use of devices in the classroom, which is perfectly in line with what we read in previous literature on the BYOD (Bring Your Own Device) educational model [45–47].

The interviews report the high familiarity of new generations with audiovisual content. This is data that aligns well with other examples in the literature, which show that adolescents are accustomed to using audiovisual media to express ideas, experiences, and identity traits [48], and that video is perceived by younger people as a privileged tool for sharing information and emotional experiences, staying updated, and finding inspirational models [49]. The co-participatory production of audiovisual narratives is indeed at the center of the teacher-based intervention proposed by the GIneSTRA program.

Educational Digital Storytelling is a methodology based on the production of audiovisual content; in the specific case of GIneStra, the design of the EDS intervention started from the data collected with teachers to adapt to their professional needs. For this reason, accessible tools and open-source software were chosen to overcome any limitations both in the training phase of the intervention and in its application in the classroom.

Moreover, based on the codes and categories identified through GTM, we obtained two important results for the implementation of the research project, namely:

1. An overview of the youth-social media relationship, useful for defining the training content of the project;
2. A projection of the advantages and limitations of a technology-based intervention in the classroom, useful for implementing the project in school classrooms.

4.1 Limits

This research is not without limitations, mainly related to the convenience sample. Teachers were selected by the schools participating in the GIneStra project, who may have received training on the project's themes previously – given that some of them declared to be referents for bullying and cyberbullying in their schools. This may have influenced the responses given during the interviews, although the sample is varied and well-balanced between teachers with different years of experience and less experienced teachers.

The sample is well-balanced between primary and secondary schools, but it was not possible to differentiate the two groups during the interviews. Furthermore, the sample is not representative of the actual teaching body across the national territory, as it is limited to teachers from the province of Foggia (Italy) only.

In the future, it would be interesting to replicate the same data collection from a trans-regional perspective, making a comparison between Southern and Northern Italy; another possibility could be to isolate data from individual school levels, or differentiate the groups of interviewees based on years of work experience.

5 Conclusions

The present work presents the results of a qualitative investigation into teachers' perceptions and thoughts on the relationship between students and digital technologies. The results are useful for designing not only the GIneStra program but also other anti-cyberbullying interventions conducted by *ad hoc* trained teachers, or those using digital technologies as the main implementation tool. The data presented here have been useful in designing an intervention easily accessible to teachers working from the last years of primary school up to secondary school, using Digital Storytelling in a pedagogical key [50, 51]. Teachers' voices are an essential starting point for understanding contemporary issues in the educational context, as well as student well-being, considering the school as an ideal setting for carrying out youth well-being promotion programs [30]. The perspective of education professionals allows us to have a clear and current vision of the school context, which is a crucial ground for growth and development, especially in the adolescent years.

Future lines of research could delve into the school-family alliance, attempting to integrate the proposed anti-cyberbullying intervention with modules aimed at parents and/or caregivers; one of the issues that emerged from our study, in fact, is precisely the lack of communication and understanding with families, a lack that causes discomfort and frustration in teachers. The theme of the school-family alliance in managing the relationship with technologies is a topic of interest, useful for preventing risk even in emergency situations [52]; moreover, the role of parental monitoring seems to be correlated with lower levels of cyberbullying and cybervictimization [53].

The issue of the BYOD approach and the use of mobile phones as an educational tool within anti-cyberbullying programs remains open, also in light of the recent ministerial provision that severely limits its use in Italian schools. In the next steps of the research, qualitative data from students involved in the GIneStra project will be analyzed; a possible development is the comparison of this data with that obtained from teachers, with the aim of further improving the implementation and design of educational programs.

Acknowledgments. The data presented in this study were collected as part of the project 'GIneS-TRA – Write the bully down', which was approved for funding based on the public notice approved by managerial determination no. 877 of 11/10/2022, in implementation of the Memorandum of Understanding between the Puglia Region (Italy) and the Regional School Office of Puglia. The research activities were carried out through an agreement between the lead institution of the project, the 'Giovanni Bovio' Secondary School in Foggia (Italy), and the University of Foggia (Italy).

Disclosure of Interests. The authors of this paper declare that they have no competing interests.

References

1. Tapscott, D.: Growing Up Digital: The Rise of The Net Generation, 1st edn. McGraw-Hill, New York (1998)
2. Boulianne, S., Theocharis, Y.: Young people, digital media, and engagement: a meta-analysis of research. Sic. Sci. Comput. Rev. **38**(2), 111–127 (2020)
3. Nagy, P., Koles, B.: The digital transformation of human identity: towards a conceptual model of virtual identity in virtual worlds. Convergence **20**(3), 276–292 (2014)
4. Pereira, D., Fillol, J., Moura, P.: Young people learning from digital media outside of school: the informal meets the formal. Comunicar Media Educ. Res. J. **27**(58), 41–50 (2019)

5. Güney, K.: Considering the advantages and disadvantages of utilizing social media to enhance learning and engagement in K-12 education. Res. Soc. Sci. Technol. **8**(2), 83–100 (2023)
6. Bowen, G.A., Gordon, N.S., Chojnacki, M.K.: Advocacy through social media: exploring student engagement in addressing social issues. J. High. Educ. Outreach Engage. **21**(3), 5–30 (2017)
7. Slonje, R., Smith, P.K.: Cyberbullying: another main type of bullying? Scandinavian J. Psychol. **49**(2), 147–154 (2008)
8. Guo, S., Liu, J., Wang, J.: Cyberbullying roles among adolescents: a social-ecological theory perspective. J. School Violence **20**(2), 167–181 (2021)
9. Wu, J., Chen, D.T.V.: A systematic review of educational digital storytelling. Comput. Educ. **147**, 103786 (2020)
10. Zych, I., Baldry, A.C., Farrington, D.P., Llorent, V.J.: Are children involved in cyberbullying low on empathy? A systematic review and meta-analysis of research on empathy versus different cyberbullying roles. Aggression Violent Behav. **45**, 83–97 (2019)
11. Park, M.S.-A., Golden, K.J., Vizcaino-Vickers, S., Jidong, D., Raj, S.: Sociocultural values, attitudes and risk factors associated with adolescent cyberbullying in East Asia: a systematic review. Cyberpsychology: J. Psychosoc. Res. Cyberspace **15**(1) (2021)
12. Farrington, D.P., Zych, I., Ttofi, M.M., Gaffney, H.: Cyberbullying research in Canada: a systematic review of the first 100 empirical studies. Aggression Violent Behav., 101811 (2022)
13. Babore, A., Carlucci, L., Cataldi, F., Phares, V., Trumello, C.: Aggressive behavior in adolescence: links with self-esteem and parental emotional availability. Soc. Dev. **26**(4), 740–752 (2017)
14. Camerini, A.L., Marciano, L., Carrara, A., Schulz, P.J.: Cyberbullying perpetration and victimization among children and adolescents: a systematic review of longitudinal studies. Telematics Inf. **49**, 101362 (2020)
15. Vismara, M., Girone, N., Conti, D., Nicolini, G., Dell'Osso, B.: The current status of cyberbullying research: a short review of the literature. Curr. Opin. Behav. Sci. **46**, 101152 (2022)
16. Pang, K.Y., Ku, W.L., Teng, J.H.J., Ling, P.O.H., Ooi, P.B.: The prevalence and association of cyberbullying and depression in the Malaysian adolescent population during the COVID-19 pandemic. Vulnerable Child. Youth Stud., 1–13 (2023)
17. Varela, J.J., Hernández, C., Miranda, R., Barlett, C.P., Rodríguez-Rivas, M.E.: Victims of cyberbullying: feeling loneliness and depression among youth and adult Chileans during the pandemic. Int. J. Environ. Res. Public Health **19**(10), 5886 (2022)
18. Alhujailli, A., Karwowski, W., Wan, T.T.H., Hancock, P.: Affective and stress consequences of cyberbullying. Symmetry **12**(9), 1536 (2020)
19. Buelga, S., Cava, M.J., Ruiz, D.M., Ortega-Barón, J.: Cyberbullying and suicidal behavior in adolescent students: a systematic review. Rev. Educación **397**, 43–66 (2022)
20. Sorrentino, A., Sulla, F., Santamato, M., di Furia, M., Toto, G.A., Monacis, L.: Has the COVID-19 pandemic affected cyberbullying and cyber-victimization prevalence among children and adolescents? A systematic review. Int. J. Environ. Res. Public Health **20**(10), 5825 (2023)
21. Sorrentino, A., Sulla, F., Santamato, M., Cipriano, A., Cella, S.: The long-term efficacy and sustainability of the Tabby improved prevention and intervention program in reducing cyberbullying and cyber-victimization. Int. J. Environ. Res. Public Health **20**(8), 5436 (2023)
22. Strauss, A., Corbin, J.: Basics of Qualitative Research, vol. 15. Sage, Newbury Park, CA (1990)
23. Strauss, A.: Grounded theory methodology: an overview. In: Handbook of Qualitative Research. Sage (1994)

24. Heath, H., Cowley, S.: Developing a grounded theory approach: a comparison of Glaser and Strauss. Int. J. Nurs. Stud. **41**(2), 141–150 (2004)

25. Chenitz, W. C., Swanson, J. M.: From Practice to Grounded Theory. Qualitative Research in Nursing, 1st edn. Addison-Wesley, Massachusetts (1986)

26. Bezzi, C.: Fare ricerca con i gruppi. Guida all'utilizzo di focus group, brainstorming, Delphi e altre tecniche, vol. 12. FrancoAngeli (2013)

27. Prensky, M.: H. sapiens digital: from digital immigrants and digital natives to digital wisdom. Innov. J. Online Educ. **5**(3) (2009)

28. Bakardjieva, M.: Internet society. In: The Internet in Everyday Life. Sage, London (2005)

29. Livingstone, S.: Internet, children, and youth. In: Consalvo, M., Ess, C. (eds.) The Handbook of Internet Studies, pp. 348–368 (2011)

30. Slee, P.T., Skrzypiec, G.: Well-being, positive peer relations and bullying in school settings. Springer, Cham (2016)

31. Guastavigna, M.: Gli aspetti amministrativi delle tecnologie digitali irrompono sulla scena della scuola. Bricks **2**(3), 33–40 (2012)

32. Impara, L.: Percorsi formativi per un rinnovamento educativo e pedagogico. Armando, Roma (2019)

33. Lisenbee, P.S.: Generation gap between students' needs and teachers' use of technology in classrooms. J. Lit. Technol. **17**(3) (2016)

34. Sánchez-Cruzado, C., Santiago Campión, R., Sánchez-Compaña, M.T.: Teacher digital literacy: the indisputable challenge after COVID-19. Sustainability **13**(4), 1858 (2021)

35. Kirkwood, A., Price, L.: Technology-enhanced learning and teaching in higher education: what is 'enhanced' and how do we know? A critical literature review. Learn. Media Technol. **39**(1), 6–36 (2014)

36. Criollo-C, S., Guerrero-Arias, A., Jaramillo-Alcázar, Á., Luján-Mora, S.: Mobile learning technologies for education: benefits and pending issues. Appl. Sci. **11**(9), 4111 (2021)

37. Warschauer, M.: Digital divide. In: Encyclopedia of Library and Information Sciences, vol. 1, no. 1, pp. 1551–1556 (2010)

38. Sonck, N., Livingstone, S., Kuiper, E., de Haan, J.: Digital Literacy and Safety Skills. EU Kids Online, London School of Economics & Political Science, London, UK (2011)

39. Vissenberg, J., d'Haenens, L., Livingstone, S.: Digital literacy and online resilience as facilitators of young people's well-being? Euro. Psychol. (2022)

40. Buckingham, D.: Media education: a global strategy for development. In: The UNESCO sector for Communication and Information. Institute of Education, London (2001)

41. Commission, E.: Key Competences for Lifelong Learning. Publications Office of the European Union, Luxembourg (2019)

42. Guarini, P., di Furia, M., Ragni, B.: Digital competences and didactic technologies training for teachers in service: from DigCompEdu to a national framework. In: International Conference on New Media Pedagogy, pp. 30–41. Springer, Cham (2022)

43. Tomczyk, Ł: Declared and real level of digital skills of future teaching staff. Educ. Sci. **11**(10), 619 (2021)

44. Limone, P., Toto, G.A.: ICT Handbook for Inclusive Education. McGraw-Hill, Milano (2023)

45. Gkamas, V., Paraskevas, M., Varvarigos, E.: BYOD for learning and teaching in Greek schools: challenges and constraints according to teachers' point of view. In: 2019 10th International Conference on Information, Intelligence, Systems and Applications (IISA), pp. 1–4. IEEE (2019)

46. Kay, R., Schellenberg, D.: Integrating a BYOD Program in High School English: Advantage or distraction? In: EdMedia+ Innovate Learning, pp. 12–16. Association for the Advancement of Computing in Education (AACE) (2017)

47. Livson, M., Ulanova, K.L., Pertsev, V.V., Dudynov, S.V., Novikov, A.V.: The influence of BYOD on results of students' learning. Propósitos Representaciones **9**(2), 49 (2021)

48. Fernández-de-Arroyabe-Olaortua, A., Lazkano-Arrillaga, I., Eguskiza-Sesumaga, L.: Digital natives: online audiovisual content consumption, creation and dissemination. Comunicar Media Educ. Res. J. **26**(57), 61–69 (2018)
49. McNally, J., Harrington, B.: How millennials and teens consume mobile video. In: Proceedings of the 2017 ACM International Conference on Interactive Experiences for TV and Online Video, pp. 31–39 (2017)
50. Çetin, E.: Digital storytelling in teacher education and its effect on the digital literacy of preservice teachers. Think. Skills Creativity **39**, 100760 (2021)
51. Robin, B.R.: The power of digital storytelling to support teaching and learning. Digital Educ. Rev. **30**, 17–29 (2016)
52. di Furia, M., Scarinci, A., Toto, G.A., Ragni, B.: School-family alliance in educational programs for inclusion: an exploratory survey of the emergency context. Italian J. Health Educ. Sport Inclusive Didactics **6**(2) (2022)
53. Elsaesser, C., Russell, B., Ohannessian, C.M., Patton, D.: Parenting in a digital age: a review of parents' role in preventing adolescent cyberbullying. Aggression Violent Behav. **35**, 62–72 (2017)

Multigroup Confirmatory Factor Analysis of the Perceived Quality of Distance Learning

Maria Rita Sergi[1]([⊠]) [iD], Michela Balsamo[1] [iD], Laura Picconi[1] [iD],
Alessandra Fermani[2] [iD], Ramona Bongelli[3] [iD], Aristide Saggino[1] [iD],
and Marco Tommasi[1] [iD]

[1] Department of Psychology, University of "G.d'Annunzio" Chieti-Pescara, Chieti, Italy
mariaritasergi@libero.it
[2] Department of Education, Cultural Heritage and Tourism, University of Macerata, Macerata,
Italy
[3] Department of Political Science, Communication and International Relations, University of
Macerata, Macerata, Italy

Keywords: Perceived Quality of Distance Learning · COVID-19 pandemic ·
Multigroup Confirmatory Factor Analysis

1 Introduction

The field of education has seen numerous changes as a result of the COVID-19 pandemic. Recent literature has highlighted psychological impacts of the distance learning or online learning during this period [1–6]. An important element is the change in one's perception of the effectiveness to face daily obstacles, perceiving greater fear and mistrust in the future due to restrictions imposed by governments [2, 4, 5]. Among the limitations caused by COVID-19 is the introduction of distance learning (DL), characterized by online education and learning platform and new information, and communication technologies.

Regarding the assessment of students' perception of distance learning, most studies in the literature have focused on blended learning, a combined learning method that integrates both face to face and on line teaching approach [7–10]. A recent systematic review [11] analyzed the perception of the quality of distance learning education through quantitative instruments, in combination with quantitative and qualitative research methods [12–23]. These studies examined the disadvantages of online education, including technical problems, communication issues, mental related problems, assessment difficulties, and problems with human interactions. Positive factors included the introduction of new technologies, the development of technical skills, time flexibility, computer competences, and a sense of comfort.

Psychometric properties of quantitative instruments of students' perception of online learning

In the literature, few studies have examined students' perception of online learning using quantitative instruments. In a sample of university students from Chile, the Instructional Materials Motivation Survey (IMMS) [12] was administered, a 36-item scale with

G. A. Toto (Ed.): ICS exchange 2024, CCIS 2521, pp. 154–164, 2025.
https://doi.org/10.1007/978-3-032-03021-4_11

a 5-point Likert scale (from 1 = Completely Disagree to 5 = Completely Agree). The instrument assessed four dimensions: Attention, Confidence, Relevance, and Satisfaction. The factor structure of the instrument showed acceptable fit indices [13]. A new instrument, developed in India with a sample of 1318 students from different educational institutions, consisted of 10 items with a dichotomous scale (Agree/Disagree) [14].

Students' perception of Integrated Online-Team-Based Learning (IO-TBL) were assessed in a sample of 28 graduate students in the U.S. across several clusters: Learning, Teamwork, Synchronous Online Meeting, Peer evaluation, Team Composition, Online Tools, and Observations [15]. In a sample of 60 first-year Chinese college students who followed English a Foreign Language, the Questionnaire on Students' Perception of the Formative Online Instruction Intervention was administered, a 12-item self-report tool constructed to assess the perception of the online experience [16]. This tool consisted of three dimensions (Engagement, Learning Outcomes, and Overall Evaluation) with a 5-point Likert scale ranging from 1 (Strongly Disagree) to 5 (Strongly Agree).

A new instrument was developed to assess the perception of learning quality. The sample was composed of 60 university students of California. Thirty-seven items loaded on seven factors: Teaching Presence, Cognitive Presence, Social Presence, Instructional Support, Basic Online Modality, Online Social Comfort, and Interactive Modality [17]. The Cronbach's Alpha ranged from .76 for Basic Online Modality to .92 for Teaching Presence.

In a sample of 88 university students from Texas, satisfaction with online learning was assessed through a 11-item self-report on a 7-point Likert scale (1 = Extremely Dissatisfied to 7 = Extremely Satisfied) [18, 19].

A survey analyzed the perception of Artificial Intelligence (AI) Teaching Assistant [20] in a sample of 321 undergraduate students in the U.S. The instrument consisted of 11 items on a 7-point liker scale (1 = Extremely Dissatisfied to 7 = Extremely Satisfied) that measured Attitude Toward New Technologies, composed of three items on a 6-point scale (1 = Very Uncomfortable to 6 = Very Comfortable). The following dimensions - Perceived Usefulness of an AI Teaching Assistant and Perceived ease of communication with an AI Teaching Assistant - were measured with eight items on a 7-point scale (1 = Strongly Disagree to 7 = Strongly Agree). Attitude Toward using an AI Teaching Assistant was measured with five items on a semantic differential scale, and Intention to Adopt AI Teaching Assistant-Based Education was assessed with three items on a 7-point scale (1 = Strongly Disagree to 7 = Strongly Agree). The factorial structure showed good fit indices.

These international data demonstrate how inaccurately the psychometric properties of instruments measuring perceptions of the quality of distance learning are studied. In Italy, there is only one tool has been developed that assesses the Perceived Quality of Distance Learning or PQDL [24]. The PQDL is a 32-item self-report scale that evaluates students' perceived quality of DL. The instrument is composed by two subscales: Distance Learning Organization (DLO) and the Cognitive-Emotive Reaction to Distance Learning (CER-DL). The DLO subscale evaluates the perceived organization of distance learning, while the CER-DL subscale assesses cognitive and emotive factors to distance learning. Specifically, the questionnaire measures communicative styles among students, as well as among students and teachers, the ability to use and access technological devices, confidence in the future, and the perception of how the learning environment has been altered. The instrument has good psychometric properties, demonstrating strong reliability and nomological validity, in which lower levels of depression predicted higher perceived quality of distance learning, and greater ability to express and regulate both positive and negative emotions predicted high Distance Learning Organization scores.

Gender differences in the perception of the quality of distance learning

A recent meta-analysis showed unclear results regarding gender differences in the perception of the quality of distance learning [25]. Vate-U-Lan [26] found that females had higher mean scores in attitude towards e-learning (mean = 4.34) than males (mean = 4.12; $p < .05$). González-Gómez et al. [27] showed that females had higher global satisfaction (mean = 4.18) compared to males (mean = 4.8; $p < .05$). These results were confirmed by other studies. For example, Harreiter et al. [28] found that, in a sample of medical university students from Vienna, females had higher mean scores (mean = 4.25) than males (mean = 3.69; $p < .05$) regarding the preference of e-learning teaching mode. Chen and Tsai [29] found that females showed stronger preference toward e-learning than males.

However, these results were not confirmed by Cuadrado-García et al. [30], who did not find gender differences in satisfaction, although the item "I sometimes need help using the online software and finding my way around" had a higher mean for males (mean = 2.63) than females (mean = 1.88; $p < .01$).

Several studies found that males had higher means than in females in attitudes towards e-learning. In a sample of 156 Taiwanese adults, men were more predisposed to accept e-learning approaches than women. In particular, men had higher means in Computer Self-Efficacy, Perceived Usefulness, Perceived Ease of Use, and Behavioral Intention to Use [31]. In a sample of Taiwanese university students, men scored higher than women in Perceived Community, Perceived Flexibility, and Satisfaction [32]. These results were confirmed by Keller et al. [33]. Other studies found no significant gender differences in perception and satisfaction with online learning [34–37].

Research into gender differences in the perception of the quality of distance learning has revealed significant patterns related to self-regulated learning, academic performance, digital skills, and engagement and motivation during the COVID-19 pandemic. Self-regulated learning (SRL) comprises three phases: preparatory, performance, and appraisal. The preparatory phase includes mood regulation before online lessons to minimize distractions; the performance phase involves adjusting time management and employing effective strategies to complete tasks; and the appraisal phase involves monitoring the learning process [38]. A recent study found that females scored significantly higher than males all three SRL phases (mean = 3.79, 3.99, 3.96, respectively; $p < .01$) [39]. Culturally, barriers persist in the digital learning context, reflecting gender stereotypes that associate computers and use of technology with masculinity, often perceived as more suitable for boys than girls. Additionally, girls tend to report lower perceived competence in technology - related areas, while showing greater confidence in areas such as language arts [40].

However, a recent study reported no significant differences between males and females in competence beliefs related to computers and technology, while also highlighting higher learning engagement among females compared to males [41].

Furthermore, a meta-analysis found that women tend to outperform men in both academic performance and self-efficacy in online learning environments [42].

Aims of the study

The reviewed literature demonstrates contradictory results regarding gender differences in the perception of distance learning. Additionally, there are no psychometrically valid and reliable instruments for measuring the perception of DL, except for one instrument that investigates perceptions of the quality of distance learning in the national context. In order to investigate further psychometric characteristics of the PQDL, the present research aimed to explore gender differences in perceptions of the quality of distance learning and to assess the measurement invariance of the PQDL with respect to gender.

We developed the following hypotheses:

1. H1: There were no differences in the scores of perceived quality of distance learning between males and females;
2. H2: The factorial structure of the PQDL was invariant with respect to gender.

2 Method

2.1 Participants

The sample involved 429 university students. 321 participants were females (74.8%) and 108 were males (25.2%), with a mean of 23.20 yrs and a SD of 5.91 yrs. Qualifications included 219 (51.0%) university students of humanistic sector, 158 (36.8%) university students of scientific sector, 16 (3.7%) university students of linguistic sector, 15 (3.5%) not-university training courses, 7 (1.6%) followed economic sector, 6 (1.4%) legal sector, 4 (0.9%) followed Phd and masters, 4 (0.9%), missing. 203 (47.3%) come from Central Italia, 194 from South Italy (45.2%), 28 (6.5%) North Italy and 4 (0.9%) Islands. The sample overlapped with those included in our previous studies [1, 24].

The study employed a snowball sampling method, whereby the authors invited their students to share the survey link with their friends. The sample was collected using a quota sampling approach, selecting participants from predefined groups (university courses and training programs requiring attendance in online classes). This study was conducted in accordance with the principles of the Helsinki Declaration (https://www.wma.net/what-we-do/medical-ethics/declaration-of-helsinki/, accessed on 22 August 2021), APA Ethics Code, and European and Italian Privacy Law (i.e., EU Reg. 679/2016, GDPR and Legislative Decree no. 196/2003, namely the Personal Data Protection Code). It has been approved by the Psychology, Communication, and Social Sciences PhD curriculum meeting, (University of Macerata. Prot. no. 0041598 of 31/03/2021 - UOR: SI000018 - Classif. VI/6). The test battery was administered online via Google Forms. The survey link was distributed through WhatApp and digital platforms commonly used during distance learning (e.g. Google Teams, Google Meet, and Zoom).

2.2 Materials

The PQDL questionnaire assessed students' perception of the quality of distance learning with 32 items. Participants responded on a 5-point Likert scale ranging from 1 ("I strongly disagree") to 5 ("I strongly agree"). A higher score indicated a higher perceived quality of distance learning. Examples of items were: "I own computer devices (e.g. tablet, PC, etc.) to attend classes", "I can better organise my study material", "I perceive greater difficulty in taking oral exams, due to the difficulty of physical contact between teachers and students".

2.3 Statistical Analyses

Descriptive statistics for the collected data included means, standard deviations, skewness, and kurtosis [43]. An analysis of variance (ANOVA) was conducted to examine mean differences in questionnaire scores between male and female participants, as well as to perform a frequency analysis of item responses across both genders. Finally, a Multigroup Confirmatory Factor Analysis [44] of the PQDL was analyzed to examine differences in the questionnaire structure between males and females:

1. The baseline configural invariance model (M1), in which the same factorial pattern was specified for each group, with loadings and intercepts free;
2. The metric invariance model (M2), in which loadings were constrained to be equal across conditions;
3. The scalar invariance model (M3), in which factor loadings and intercepts were constrained to be equal across groups.

Model fit was assessed using χ^2 statistical test, the Root Mean Square Error of Approximation (RMSEA), and the Comparative Fit Index (CFI). The difference between CFIs (ΔCFI) of invariance models was estimated to assess measurement invariance. A value of ΔCFI smaller than or equal to |.01| (in absolute values) indicates that the null hypothesis of invariance should not be rejected [45].

Descriptive statistics and ANOVA were performed trough SPSS 25 for Windows [46]. Multigroup Confirmatory Factor Analysis was calculated trough Mplus 7.0 [47]. Anonymity and privacy of the sample were guaranteed according the Italian and the European laws about privacy (Italian law n. 196/2003 and EU GDPR 679/2016, respectively). All instruments were administered via Google form. Informed consent was obtained from all individual participants included in the study. The study was approved by the Department of Department of Education, Cultural Heritage and Tourism of Macerata, Italy.

3 Results

Skewness and kurtosis values between -1 and 1 indicated a normal distribution of the data across genders (Table 1).

The mean score for males on the Cognitive-Emotive Reaction to Distance Learning scale was found to be higher than that for females [$F(1,427) = 54.804$; $p < .001$] (Table 2). Furthermore, female respondents exhibited a higher response rate on the following items compared to males: "I perceive greater communicative contact between teachers and students", "I can record lessons", "I feel fatigue, have eyestrain, and headaches".

Results of the measurement invariance across gender showed equal factor loadings and intercepts across groups. Configural, metric, and scalar invariance were established between male and female groups. As shown in Table 3, the ΔCFI values were below |.01|, and the RMSEA values were optimal. Furthermore, the χ^2 statistical test for the tested model was significant.

Table 1. Descriptive Statistics split by gender.

Factors of the PQDL	Gender	mean	SD	Skeweness	Kurtosis
Distance Learning Organization	Males	3.14	.734	−.217	−.179
	Females	3.02	.828	.119	−.657
Cognitive-Emotive Reaction to Distance Learning	Males	3.56	.764	−.748	.773
	Females	2.91	.793	.072	−.320

Note: SD = Standard Deviation

Table 2. ANOVA results for gender.

Factors of the PQDL	F	p	Partial η^2
Distance Learning Organization	1.681	.195	.004
Cognitive-Emotive Reaction toDistance Learning	54.804	.000	.114

Table 3. Multigroup Confirmatory Factor Analysis

models	χ^2	df	RMSEA	90% RMSEA	CFI	SRMR	Model comparisons	IΔCFII
M1 CVH1	51.56	22	.079	.0513; .108	.976	.072		
M2 CVH0	53.03	29	.062	.0346; .0885	.981	.139	M2– M1	**.005**
M3 IFLH0	53.03	29	.068	.0417; .0936	.976	.145	M3– M2	**.005**

Note: ΔCFIs lower than |.01| are in bold types. M1: model for configural invariance; M2: model for metric invariance; M3: model for scalar invariance

4 Discussions and Conclusions

The principal aim of our study was to further analyze psychometric characteristics of a new instrument to measure the perceived quality of distance learning: the PQDL. We studied gender differences in the PQDL scores and assessed the measurement invariance of the PQDL with respect to gender.

Regarding our principal hypotheses, Hypothesis H1 was partially supported. Our results showed that males scored higher than females on the Distance Learning Organization subscale. Males reported better and easier access to computing devices, a more organized approach to studying through computing aids, and better sharing of study material with other university students. These findings were consistent with other international studies [30–33].

Hypothesis H2 was confirmed, as the factor structure of the PQDL Questionnaire had scalar consistency between males and females. To our knowledge, there are no researches in the literature investigating the study of the factorial structure of instruments for assessing the quality of distance learning between genders.

Our research is the first national study to examine gender differences and factorial structure between males and females of a specific psychometric instrument for evaluating and perceiving the quality of distance learning.

Our data point out that the introduction of technologies enabling more extensive use of distance learning should be an opportunity to innovatively transform the school system, as suggested by the sustainable development goals of European Agenda 2030 [14]. Specifically, these Sustainable Development Goals aim to promote inclusive and equitable education. The use of distance education can ensure access to university education for people who live in remote contexts or for individuals with economic difficulties. Moreover, the distance learning system can provide tools to develop digital skills, helping to reduce barriers among disadvantaged groups. In particular, Goal 4 aims to ensure inclusive and equitable quality education and promote lifelong learning opportunities for all, while Goal 5 aims to achieve gender equality and empower all women and girls aim to eliminate gender disparities in education, guaranteeing access to all levels of education. The promotion of sustainable development, including the utilization of information technologies accessible to all, supports the promotion of a culture of peace, non-violence, and foster globalization. Additionally, by 2030, the Agenda aims to increase the number of youth and adults who have the necessary skills, including technical and vocational skills, for employment, decent jobs, and entrepreneurial skills [48, 49].

Furthermore, it would be beneficial to implement a help desk for those experiencing difficulties with distance learning tools, assisting with troubleshooting problems related to computer service, applications, and equipment. Alternatively, adopting Team Based Learning, such as small group learning (5–7 students), could promote self-efficacy, motivation, and academic performance.

Contrary to findings in the literature [39–42], our results indicated that males were more adept at managing thoughts about the future and regulating their emotions in DL compared to females. This has significant implications for learning success. Indeed, a recent systematic review [50] showed a correlation between emotion regulation strategies and academic success. Therefore, future studies should investigate whether males actually achieve better academic performance than females due to their ability to regulate emotions. Finally, specific distance learning activities should aim to enhance the organization of study material and improving concentration during online lessons.

Future studies should investigate additional psychometric features of the PQDL, such as a cross-validation study of the instrument in other countries or across different educational levels, and analyzing differences in perceptions of distance learning base on socio-demographic factors (e.g. different geographic areas and marital status). Moreover, it would be interesting to study the validity of the PQDL through additional data analysis techniques, such as network analysis [51]. A final limitation of the research lies in the predominance in the sample of the female gender and humanities students. Future studies will focus on greater heterogeneity in the sample.

Disclosure of Interests. The authors have no competing interests to declare that are relevant to the content of this article.

References

1. Sergi, M.R., et al.: The mediating role of positive and negative affect in the relationship between death anxiety and Italian students' perceptions of distance learning quality during the COVID-19 pandemic. Societies **13**(7), 163 (2023). https://doi.org/10.3390/soc13070163
2. Tommasi, M., et al.: Physical and psychological impact of the obligatory quarantine for COVID-19 on Italians. Front. Psychol. **11**, 563722 (2020). https://doi.org/10.3389/fpsyg.2020.563722
3. Carlucci, L., et al.: COVID-19 and its impact on sexual behaviors and couple relationship: an explorative study on Italian sample. Sexuality Res. Soc. Policy 1–15 (2024). https://doi.org/10.1080/0092623x.2021.1998271
4. Balsamo, M., Murdock, K.K., Carlucci, L.: Psychological factors in adherence to COVID-19 public health restrictions in Italy: a path model testing depressed mood, anxiety, and corumination via cellphone. PLoS ONE **17**(12), e0278628 (2022). https://doi.org/10.1371/journal.pone.0278628
5. Carlucci, L., D'Ambrosio, I., Balsamo, M.: Demographic and attitudinal factors of adherence to quarantine guidelines during COVID-19: the Italian model. Front. Psychol. **11**, 2702 (2020). https://doi.org/10.3389/fpsyg.2020.559288
6. Balsamo, M., Carlucci, L., D'Ambrosio, I., Murdock, K.K.: Psychological wellbeing during the lockdown in Italy: a multicenter study project in the age of COVID-19. Psicoterapia Cognitiva e Comportamentale **26**(3) (2020)
7. Adas, D., Shmais, W.A.: Students' perceptions towards blended learning environment using the OCC. An-Najah Univ. J. Res. **25**(6), 1681–1710 (2011)
8. Berga, K.A., et al.: Blended learning versus face-to-face learning in an undergraduate nursing health assessment course: a quasi-experimental study. Nurse Educ. Today **96**, 104622 (2021). https://doi.org/10.1016/j.nedt.2020.104622
9. Ginns, P., Ellis, R.: Quality in blended learning: exploring the relationships between on-line and face-to-face teaching and learning. Internet High. Educ. **10**(1), 53–64 (2007). https://www.learntechlib.org/p/102630/
10. Owston, R., York, D., Murtha, S.: Student perceptions and achievement in a university blended learning strategic initiative. Internet High. Educ. **18**, 38–46 (2013). https://doi.org/10.1016/j.iheduc.2012.12.003

11. Cramarenco, R.E., Burcă-Voicu, M.I., Dabija, D.C.: Student perceptions of online education and digital technologies during the COVID-19 pandemic: a systematic review. Electronics **12**(2), 319 (2023). https://doi.org/10.3390/electronics12020319
12. Laurens-Arredondo, L.: Mobile augmented reality adapted to the ARCS model of motivation: a case study during the COVID-19 pandemic. Educ. Inf. Technol. **27**(6), 7927–7946 (2022). https://doi.org/10.1007/s10639-022-10933-9
13. Loorbach, N., Peters, O., Karreman, J., Steehouder, M.: Validation of the instructional materials motivation survey (IMMS) in a self-directed instructional setting aimed at working with technology. Br. J. Edu. Technol. **46**(1), 204–218 (2015)
14. Bast, F.: Perception of online learning among students from India set against the pandemic. Front. Educ. **6**, 1–8 (2021). https://doi.org/10.3389/feduc.2021.705013
15. Parrish, C.W., Guffey, S.K., Williams, D.S., Estis, J.M., Lewis, D.: Fostering cognitive presence, social presence and teaching presence with integrated online—Team-based learning. TechTrends **65**, 473–484 (2021. https://doi.org/10.1007/s11528-021-00598-5
16. Chen, Z., Jiao, J., Hu, K.: Formative assessment as an online instruction intervention: student engagement, outcomes, and perceptions. Int. J. Distance Educ. Technol. **19**(1), 50–65 (2021). https://doi.org/10.4018/ijdet.20210101.oa1
17. Van Wart, M., et al.: Integrating students' perspectives about online learning: a hierarchy of factors. Int. J. Educ. Technol. High. Educ. **17**(1), 1–22 (2020). https://doi.org/10.1186/s41239-020-00229-8
18. Landrum, B.: Examining students' confidence to learn online, self-regulation skills and perceptions of satisfaction and usefulness of online classes. Online Learn. **24**(3), 128–146 (2020). https://doi.org/10.24059/olj.v24i3.2066
19. Zakariah, Z., Hashim, R.A., Musa, N.: Motivation, experience and satisfaction among adult learners with fully online web-based courses. Pan Commonwelth Forum **8** (2016)
20. Kim, J., Merrill, K., Xu, K., Sellnow, D.D.: My teacher is a machine: understanding students' perceptions of AI teaching assistants in online education. Int. J. Hum. -Comput. Interact **36**, 1902–1911 (2020). https://doi.org/10.1080/10447318.2020.1801227
21. Chandra, S., Ranjan, A., Chowdhary, N.: Online hospitality and tourism education-issues and challenges. Tourism Int. Interdisc. J. **70**(2), 298–316 (2022). https://doi.org/10.37741/t.70.2.10
22. Almahasees, Z., Mohsen, K., Amin, M.O.: Faculty's and students' perceptions of online learning during COVID-19. Front. Educ. **6**, 1 (2021). https://doi.org/10.3389/feduc.2021.638470
23. Kundu, A., Bey, T.: COVID-19 response: students' readiness for shifting classes online. Corporate Governance Int. J. Bus. Soc. **21**(6), 1250–1270 (2021). https://doi.org/10.1108/CG-09-2020-0377
24. Sergi, M.R., Picconi, L., Saggino, A., Fermani, A., Bongelli, R., Tommasi, A.: Psychometric properties of a new instrument for the measurement of the perceived quality of distance learning during the coronavirus disease 2019 (COVID-19) pandemic. Front. Psychol. **14**, 1–14 (2023). https://doi.org/10.3389/fpsyg.2023.1169957
25. Yu, Z., Deng, X.: A meta-analysis of gender differences in e-learners' self-efficacy, satisfaction, motivation, attitude, and performance across the world. Front. Psychol. **13**, 897327 (2022). https://doi.org/10.3389/fpsyg.2022.897327
26. Vate-U-Lan, P.: Psychological impact of e-learning on social network sites: online students' attitudes and their satisfaction with life. J. Comput. High. Educ. **32**(1), 27–40 (2020). https://doi.org/10.1007/s12528-019-09222-1
27. González-Gómez, F., Guardiola, J., Rodríguez, Ó.M., Alonso, M.Á.M.: Gender differences in e-learning satisfaction. Comput. Educ. **58**(1), 283–290 (2012)

28. Harreiter, J., Wiener, H., Plass, H., Kautzky-Willer, A.: Perspectives on gender-specific medicine, course and learning style preferences in medical education: a study among students at the Medical University of Vienna. Wien. Med. Wochenschr. **161**(5–6), 149–154 (2011) https://doi.org/10.1007/s10354-011-0866-x

29. Chen, R.S., Tsai, C.C.: Gender differences in Taiwan university students' attitudes toward web-based learning. Cyberpsychol. Behav. **10**(5), 645–654 (2007). https://doi.org/10.1089/cpb.2007.9974

30. Cuadrado-García, M., Ruiz-Molina, M.E., Montoro-Pons, J.D.: Are there gender differences in e-learning use and assessment? Evidence from an interuniversity online project in Europe. Procedia Soc. Behav. Sci. **2**(2), 367–371 (2010). https://doi.org/10.1016/j.sbspro.2010.03.027

31. Ong, C.S., Lai, J.Y.: Gender differences in perceptions and relationships among dominants of e-learning acceptance. Comput. Hum. Behav. **22**(5), 816–829 (2006). https://doi.org/10.1016/j.chb.2004.03.006

32. Lu, H.P., Chiou, M.J.: The impact of individual differences on e-learning system satisfaction: a contingency approach. Br. J. Edu. Technol. **41**(2), 307–323 (2010). https://doi.org/10.1111/j.1467-8535.2009.00937.x

33. Keller, C., Hrastinski, S., Carlsson, S.: Students acceptance of e-learning environments: a comparative study in Sweden and Lithuania. In: European Conference on Information Systems ECIS 2007 Proceedings, pp. 1–13. AIS Electronic Library (2007). http://aisel.aisnet.org/ecis2007

34. Marimuthu, R., Chone, L.S., Heng, L.T., Nah, E.A., Fen, O.S.: Comparing the online learning strategies of male and female diploma students of an English language course. Procedia Soc. Behav. Sci. **90**, 626–633 (2013). https://doi.org/10.1016/j.sbspro.2013.07.134

35. Yukselturk, E., Bulut, S.: Gender differences in self-regulated online learning environment. J. Educ. Technol. Soc. **12**(3), 12–22 (2009). https://www.researchgate.net/publication/220374951

36. Ramírez-Correa, P.E., Arenas-Gaitán, J., Rondán-Cataluña, F.J.: Gender and acceptance of e-learning: a multi-group analysis based on a structural equation model among college students in Chile and Spain. PLoS ONE **10**(10), e0140460 (2015). https://doi.org/10.1371/journal.pone.0140460

37. Hung, M.L., Chou, C., Chen, C.H., Own, Z.Y.: Learner readiness for online learning: scale development and student perceptions. Comput. Educ. **55**(3), 1080–1090 (2010). https://doi.org/10.1016/j.compedu.2010.05.004

38. Hong, J.C., Lee, Y.F., Ye, J.H.: Procrastination predicts online self-regulated learning and online learning ineffectiveness during the coronavirus lockdown. Personality Individ. Differ. **174**, 1–8 (2021). https://doi.org/10.1016/j.paid.2021.110673

39. Liu, X., He, W., Zhao, L., Hong, J.C.: Gender differences in self-regulated online learning during the COVID-19 lockdown. Front. Psychol. **12**, 1–8 (2021). https://doi.org/10.3389/fpsyg.2021.752131

40. Cooper, J.: The digital divide: the special case of gender. J. Comput. Assist. Learn. **22**(5), 320–334 (2006)

41. Korlat, S., et al.: Gender differences in digital learning during COVID-19: competence beliefs, intrinsic value, learning engagement, and perceived teacher support. Front. Psychol. **12**, 1–12 (2021). https://doi.org/10.3389/fpsyg.2021.637776

42. Perkowski, J.: The role of gender in distance learning: a meta-analytic review of gender differences in academic performance and self-efficacy in distance learning. J. Educ. Technol. Syst. **41**(3), 267–278 (2013). https://doi.org/10.2190/ET.41.3.e

43. Gravetter, F.J., Wallnau, L.B.: Introduction to the t statistic. Essentials Stat. Behav. Sci. **8**(252), 1–41 (2014)

44. Meredith, W.: Measurement invariance, factor analysis and factorial invariance. Psychometrika **58**, 525–543 (1993)

45. Cheung, G.W., Rensvold, R.B.: Evaluating goodness-of-fit indexes for testing measurement invariance. Struct. Equ. Model. **9**(2), 233–255 (2002). https://doi.org/10.1207/S15328007 SEM0902_5

46. IBM Corp.: IBM SPSS Statistics for Windows (Version 25.0). IBM, New York (2017)

47. Muthén, B., Muthén, L.: Mplus user's Guide, Seventh Edition. Muthén & Muthén, Los Angeles (2015)

48. United Nations: Resolution adopted by the General Assembly on 25 September 2015. General Assemby **71**(1), 1–35 (2015)

49. Transforming our world: the 2030 Agenda for Sustainable Development. https://sdgs.un.org/ 2030agenda, https://doi.org/10.1177/10664807231225407

50. Andrés, M.L., Stelzer, F., Canet Juric, L., Introzzi, I.M., Rodríguez Carvajal, R., Navarro Guzmán, J.I.: Emotion regulation and academic performance: a systematic review of empirical relationships. Psicol. estud. **22**(3), 299–311 (2017)

51. Tommasi, M., Arnò, S., Saggino, A., Sergi, M.R.: Exploring parent-child traits and relationship quality: a network study. Fam. J. **9**, 1 (2024). https://doi.org/10.1177/106648072312 25407

A Critical Analysis of Accessible Museum Communication in London and Hong Kong

Silvia Dini[1]([✉]) [iD] and Martina Maggi[2] [iD]

[1] University of Parma, Viale San Michele, 9, 43121 Parma, Italy
`silvia.dini@unipr.it`
[2] University of Turin, Via Giuseppe Verdi, 8, 10124 Turin, Italy
`martina.maggi@unito.it`

Abstract. Access to art and culture should be a right granted to everyone. Because of the diversity of their audience in terms of age, background, and physical or cognitive impairments, exhibitions need to provide accessibility on different levels to make museums more inclusive and engaging [5]. Communication and translation practices play a crucial role in this regard, by addressing both the inherent diversity of the museum audience and the different types of semiotic constituents. Indeed, the 2000s saw the rise of museum Audio Description (AD), a practice used to describe cultural products of museums and exhibits, such as paintings, statues, or even entire archaeological sites [16]. The present research aims to observe how some of the most important museums in London and Hong Kong are approaching the issue of granting accessibility for a blind or visually impaired audience. A critical examination of the available tools is conducted to assess their appropriateness for this purpose, identifying any shortcomings.

Keywords: Accessibility · Audio Description · Visually Impaired and Blind (VIB) · VocalEyes · Museums · Universal Design

1 Introduction

Museum exhibitions are complex presentations where different semiotic constituents (visual, auditory, tactile, verbal, and non-verbal) cooperate in the construction of meanings. Because of the wide variety of different audiences in terms of age, background, and physical or cognitive impairments, accessible tools and design have nowadays become essential to make museums more inclusive and engaging. Therefore, accommodating visitor needs becomes crucial in museums' mission and planning.

In this study, the authors intend to evaluate the accessibility level of some of the most important museums in London and Hong Kong. Both studies have been carried out after carefully selecting the venues and the resources to cover. In London, ten museums that had been previously audio described or trained by VocalEyes were visited, to research and study the audio descriptive tracks and the accessible resources they offered. Out of the ten, two provided solutions to grant independence of the visitors and the possibility of self-tours, and are, therefore, presented in this paper: the temporary exhibition "The Cult

G. A. Toto (Ed.): ICS exchange 2024, CCIS 2521, pp. 165–186, 2025.
https://doi.org/10.1007/978-3-032-03021-4_12

of Beauty" at the Wellcome Collection, and the Science Museum. In Hong Kong, seven museums were visited and two were selected for the analysis: The Hong Kong Museum of Art (HKMOA) and the M + Museum, with the objective of identifying potential criticalities as a starting point for future improvements, if possible. The reason behind this was the interest aroused by the collections or exhibits, the variety and the modernity of the pieces, and the interesting solutions they proposed to achieve accessibility for all and independence for blind and visually impaired visitors.

2   The Inalienable Right of Inclusivity and Independence

In the last thirty years, targeted institutions and organisations, as well as Law Acts, tirelessly addressed the topic of accessibility and inclusivity in the arts. The need for a physically accessible space and a barrier-free environment spread, as well as the need to grant accessibility to a blind or visually impaired audience, with the final aim of becoming inclusive and engaging.

In 1990 *The Americans with Disabilities Act* was signed to prohibit discrimination against disabled people. In 2007, Article 30 of the *United Nations Convention on the Rights of Persons with Disabilities* defined access to culture as "an inalienable right" [24]. In 2019 the European Union approved the *European Accessibility Act* (Directive 2019/882), which aimed to "eliminate and prevent barriers" and "create an environment where products and services are more accessible, for a more inclusive society" [6].

As one of the primary vehicles of culture and art dissemination and popularisation, museums carry the delicate task of providing and ensuring an equal visiting experience for every audience through accessible architecture, websites, and exhibitions. Paraphrasing Kleege, "the integration [...] will change the foundational assumptions of the culture; and change how the human condition is defined" [12].

However, despite the great achievements, museums still often organise specific timetabled access events for disabled people [10], which presents them as "special patrons" [17], and fail to promote their independence while visiting. The introduction of audio descriptive tracks of chosen key objects, sign language translation, easy language, large prints, and audio tours with touch opportunities helped visitors feel more welcomed and included, even more in venues where the steps toward accessibility were permanent, and were not part of temporary exhibitions.

Even so, in most museums, disabled visitors have to rely on their family, friends, or personnel while visiting [1], as the buildings and venue were not conceived to be accessible in the first place. In the case of a blind and visually impaired audience, which is the focus of the present research, a potential solution is the integration of directions in the audio description tracks, that allow visitors to walk freely in the museums and reach more easily the accessible stops. The idea was observed in London at the temporary exhibition "The Cult of Beauty" at the Wellcome Collection, which ran from October 2023 to April 2024. Asakawa *et. al* [1] also suggest using indoor navigation systems to promote visitors independence. The solution was implemented and applied in the Science Museum in London, as will be further explained in paragraph Sect. 4.1.

3   The Museum: A Communicative Event for All

The concept of communication within the museum can encompass several dimensions, including a variety of audiences, different modes of communication and different types of translation. According to Soler Gallego [19], this communicative event occurs between the museum (its exhibits and curators) and its visitors and it can be established both at a macrostructural level, including the museum itself and the exhibition it hosts, and at a microstructural level, encompassing the artefacts and the relationships established between them.

The core mission of the (new) museum is therefore to make the artistic discourse accessible to a highly diverse audience through translation processes. It should promote access and participation to culture for all individuals and groups, thus facilitating social inclusion and both cognitive and emotional development [20]. In these terms, we refer not only to audiences with sensory, motor or cognitive difficulties, but to all types of visitors who might find the content not properly comprehensible. These groups of visitors can include children and adolescents, the elderly, migrants and refugees, sociocultural and linguistic minorities, socially vulnerable groups, people with low literacy or little experience of cultural venues [3].

Although museums are still largely conceived according to an oculo-centric model, which assumes that cultural heritage should be mostly accessible through visual perception, sighted people may also need additional guidance to fully understand and appreciate what they see. Given the current predominance (and dependence) of sight over the other senses in museums [9], it is important to distinguish between passive 'seeing' and active observation. Recognising the diversity of visitors and moving towards inclusion means recognising particularity, without dividing people into separate ad hoc categories and isolated groups distinguished by the generic labels of 'different' or 'other'. Within the ICOM Code of Ethics [11] it is stated that 'museums have particular responsibilities to all for the care, accessibility and interpretation of primary evidence collected and held in their collections'. Here the word 'interpretation' refers to the commitment to provide accurate information about exhibitions and displays and to convey their meanings. These can be offered in a variety of formats, including (but not limited to) labels, panels, catalogues, guided tours, audio guides, video guides, virtual tours, augmented reality experiences, and customised applications [3].

3.1   Audio Description in Museums

Museum audio description (AD) provides a verbal description of an artwork or exhibit 'that seeks to make the visual element of the diverse contents of museums and galleries accessible to blind and partially sighted people' [10]. Its function is primarily to help the visually impaired public to construct a mental image of what they cannot, partially or totally, see. Nevertheless, while in the past AD was referred to as 'audio description for the blind and visually impaired', nowadays this label has become rather unusual, and the more common 'audio description' is preferred. The former label, in fact, incorporated the idea of AD as a tool to correct an individual labelled as 'abnormal' [8].

Being a verbal reproduction of visual input, AD represents a form of inter-semiotic and intermodal translation (in this case, from the visual to the oral channel) but it has also been described as 'intersensorial translation' [4]. This type of description, and the mental image that this type of description is supposed to create, can be associated with the concept of 'ekphrasis', which is based on a 'highly vivid description that allows the reader or listener to see the represented object with his/her internal eye' [20].

Several factors determine the nature of the museum audio description: firstly, the profile of the visitor (age, type, and degree of blindness), the type of museum, the communicative function of the exhibition, the preparation of the description (whether or not a script is used), the use of pre-existing guidelines, the type of interaction with visitors, and the training and status of the descriptor as well as the degree of subjectivity agreed upon by the museum. Another decisive element is the analysis of the work carried out by the artist himself/herself (if possible) or by art experts, which constitutes the starting point for the production of the AD. The purpose of this type of analysis is to study the style, the artist's ideology, and historical context of the work, as well as to provide an aesthetic interpretation and evaluation. Both share the mission of making the receiver discover the existence of elements within the work that would otherwise not be grasped, due to visual difficulty in one case, or lack of expertise in the other.

4 Methodology and Fieldwork of the Two Investigations.

4.1 London

Between September and December 2023, a three-month internship with the British charity organisation VocalEyes involved a study on accessibility and inclusion in London museums.

VocalEyes was founded in London in 1998 through a National Lottery grant, starting from an idea by the audio describer Andrew Holland, who felt that blind people across the UK "should have the opportunity to experience audio description of a high quality" [26]. Since its establishment, VocalEyes has tirelessly trained in accessibility and visual awareness venues in the United Kingdom, Europe, and Canada, producing and delivering pre-recorded or live audio descriptions and touch tours for exhibitions, museums, and theatre shows.

In September 2023, VocalEyes was interested in starting a follow-up of the venues that had worked in partnership with them in response to the increasing demand for accessibility. The primary aim was reviewing the introduction and application of audio descriptive tracks in museums that had been audio described or trained in accessibility and visual awareness by the organisation between 2018 and 2023, in response to the increasing demand for accessibility.

The analysis focused on identifying effective methods of ensuring a meaningful, accurate, and evocative experience for blind and visually impaired visitors. The evaluation was conducted using a nine-question form developed in partnership with VocalEyes. The open-ended questions were designed to determine *whether* and *how* museums had adopted and maintained the audio description over time, and whether other accessible resources (Braille, touch opportunities, large prints, magnifiers) were available. Moreover, the questionnaire was targeted to assess the effectiveness and update frequency of the audio descriptive tracks, as well as the level of staff expertise. In fact, the unaware-ness and unavailability of staff are often highlighted as limiting factors in museum accessibility [7].

The questionnaire

1. Is the AD guide still available?
2. Do the venue staff know about it?
3. Do they offer a handheld device/headphones?
4. How else can you access the guide, for example, via a QR code?
5. Is it free or do you have to pay?
6. Do the welcome staff seem to have an awareness of the needs of VI visitors?
7. Is the AD guide still relevant? For example, are the artworks/objects in the places the guide mentions? Does anything on the guide need updating?
8. Are there any other resources available? For example, Braille, large prints, or touch opportunities on site?
9. How can the venue improve its accessibility?

The questions were answered producing a targeted report for every museum visited. The chosen venues were: The National Portrait Gallery, the British Museum, the Natural History Museum, the Tower of London, the Victoria and Albert Museum, the Charles Dickens Museum, the Science Museum, the Wellcome Collection, and the temporary exhibition "The Cult of Beauty", the Imperial War Museum, and the Tate Modern, to broaden the research to ancient and new buildings, to permanent and temporary exhibitions and different expressions of culture, whether historical, or natural, scientific, or art.

Of the ten, seven provided audio descriptions at the time of the visit, and the remaining three had undergone updating of the tracks due to renovations, or were creating another set of tracks. Of the seven museums that offered audio descriptions, four designed the recordings to be accessible online, through the official website of the museum, or a specific app (Bloomberg Connects, in the case of the National Portrait Gallery) or website (SoundCloud for the Victoria and Albert Museum[1]) or a QR code. On three occasions, the audio description was delivered online and on a hand-held device: at the National Portrait Gallery, the Science Museum, and the temporary exhibition "The Cult of Beauty" at the Wellcome Collection.

Being the pursuit of independence of blind and visually impaired visitors the main focus of the present study, the analysis was narrowed down to the three venues that provided audio descriptions both online and offline, as it could prevent the hand-held device from running out, and allow the visitors to access the tracks whenever they need them—among the three museums, further sorting restricted the analysis to two: The Science Museum and The Wellcome Collection, as both museums aimed to increase visitor independence through different strategies. The Science Museum adopted a handheld tracking device developed using iOS technology, and the Wellcome Collection hosted an entirely new temporary exhibition that was designed to be accessible from the start

---

[1] The British Museum also delivers the audio description via SoundCloud website, but at the time of the visit (in October 2023) the tracks were unavailable and only the audio guide was provided online.

and integrated the directions into the audio description tracks, which were uploaded on the venue website and the handheld device offered to each visitor at the entrance. The use of those two different methods, influenced by various parameters outlined in the questionnaire, highlighted the strengths and weaknesses of each approach that are deepened and analysed in the following paragraphs.

4.1.1   The Science Museum

In 2019, the museum created and launched a free app called *Audio Eyes*, "designed *with* and *for* blind and partially sighted visitors", as it is read on the App Store Website[2]. The app provides over 100 audio description tracks for the *Medicine: The Wellcome Galleries* on Level 1 and the *Information Age Gallery* on Level 2 of the museum. *Audio Eyes* was designed with iOS technology – which explains why it's only available for iPhone users – and integrates new Bluetooth beacon technology. The App Store reports that the app "helps independent discovery", as it does not provide a step-by-step route, but picks up Bluetooth signals around the gallery, locates the position and movements of the visitors, and triggers the audio notification on the phone, providing – if the person desires so – the audio description available for the nearest accessible key object.

What could easily have been the first barrier to accessibility – the availability for iPhone users – instead turned out to be the first step towards inclusion. Indeed, the museum simultaneously developed a special handheld device for non-iPhone users, which simulates a phone screen and can therefore access the custom features[3]. The device is free of charge and can be picked up at the Information Desk on Level 0, where the trained staff offers a tutorial and leaves a paper sheet with the instructions printed on it[4]. Every visitor can request the device and enjoy the tour. Undoubtedly, the solution provides accessibility for all, as the app and devices are available for every person, and at the same time promotes self-guided independent tours.

However, the Science Museum was founded in 1857 and was not designed to be accessible in the first place. The building walls are thick and the signal occasionally fades, potentially affecting the delivery of the tracks. The Science Museum is aware of the possibility of a signal failure. At the beginning of the introductory track, it is clearly stated that the distance between the visitor and the audio described object might not correspond to the planned one.

During the visit in November 2023, the signal faded in *Medicine: The Wellcome Galleries*, before the stop of the sculpture *Santa Medicina* designed by Eleanor Crook for the "Faith, Hope & Fear" gallery. The statue was created to be a tactile object

---

[2] https://apps.apple.com/gb/app/audio-eyes/id990939734.

[3] As per September 2024, the Science Museum's official website reported that "*AudioEyes* handsets are currently unavailable".

[4] At the time of the visit, in November 2023, the staff showed empathy and awareness of the needings of blind and visually impaired visitors. When I approached the Information Desk and asked for the device, I did not give information about my vision. The woman did not ask for more details, but, when she handed me the instructions printed on a paper, she kindly offered to read them to me. I particularly appreciated the approach, as a visually impaired visitor might prefer not to reveal information about his or her sight loss, and, to be fair, it should not be requested.

and, therefore, is surrounded by two benches where visitors can rest while listening to the tracks. In addition, two headphones on both benches provide audio loops for the description (Fig. 1).

Fig. 1. The statue *Santa Medicina* by Eleanor Crook on display in the Faith, Hope & Fear gallery © Science Museum Group[5]

At the beginning of the gallery, the signal dropped and the device did not send a notification when it approached the statue. The signal was picked up again a few metres away from the key object, and the device then proposed the audio description for the statue *Santa Medicina*, as shown in Fig. 2.

In that particular instance, the fading of the signal unintentionally affected the independence of the visitors and the accessibility of the statue itself, designed to be a tactile object in the first place. Moreover, the benches around the sculpture allow visitors to listen to the tracks via smartphone, handheld devices, or integrated hearing loops while sitting and resting. Indeed, the audio description starts with an invitation to sit, relax, and enjoy the recording. However, during that particular visit, the distance from the statue would have prevented the visitors from finding the benches and sitting.

Given the freedom the *Audio Eyes* app allows and the inclusivity provided by the integration of the iOS technology to the custom-created handheld devices, it might be worth installing embossed tactile floor lines to help blind or visually impaired people find their way around the rooms and the audio described objects even when the signal fades. Especially because sometimes the track is also provided by hearing loops, and – if warned before – visitors can enjoy the recordings even when they do not receive the notification they are supposed to, and being completely independent, if they so desire.

---

[5] Available at: https://blog.sciencemuseum.org.uk/for-science/.

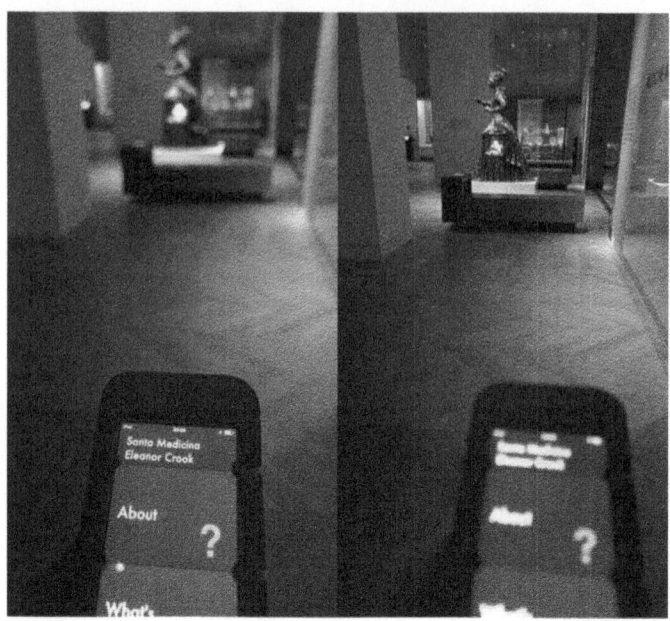

Fig. 2. The signal was picked up again a few meters away from the statue, and the device received the notification. © Martina Maggi, 2023.

4.1.2   The Cult of Beauty

The temporary exhibition "The Cult of Beauty" ran at Wellcome Collection in Euston Road, London, from 26 October 2023 to 28 April 2024. By December 2023, it was the latest example of accessibility in a London museum.

The exhibition focused "on the notions of beauty across time and cultures" and featured historical curiosities, ancient manuscripts and modern magazines, statues, videos, artworks, films, and cosmetics. It reflected on "the influence of morality, status, health, age, race, and gender on the evolution of ideas about beauty" and encouraged visitors "to question established norms and consider more inclusive definitions of beauty" [27]. The Wellcome Collection is part of the Wellcome Trust, established in 1936 with the legacies of Sir Henry Solomon Wellcome, an American pharmaceutical entrepreneur and enthusiastic traveller who owned the largest medical artifacts collection. Once based in Wigmore Street, the Wellcome Collection was moved to Euston Road in 2004 and opened to the public three years later. It was refurbished in 2015 and new public-targeted renovations were added (i.e. The Reading Room). Therefore, its history begins later than the Science Museum's, and its spaces allow more intervention towards accessibility, as they were designed in the XXI century.

"The Cult of Beauty" was hosted in Gallery 1 on Floor 0 and was designed to be accessible and inclusive from the start, incorporating accessibility in its installations. The exhibition included more than 200 objects and offered 17 audio described stops. The tracks were recorded and uploaded on a dedicated section of the Wellcome Collection's official website and on handheld devices that could be picked up freely at the entrance of the Gallery [28, 29]. Like in the Science Museum, the audio description could be accessed online and offline. While the Science Museum opted for an app, the Wellcome Collection designed large and embossed QR codes, that were placed near the audio described objects and redirected the visitors to the dedicated website section. The chosen solution allows visitors to use their smartphones preventing a shortage of offline devices and, at the same time, allows them to activate the audio description later in the visit or only for certain stops, customising their experience.

In addition, adhesive raised tactile floor lines were placed to guide people through the rooms and toward the following accessible stop[6]. When the lines reached the QR codes, they terminated with a square with raised dots to inform the visitors that a stop was scheduled (see Fig. 3).

Fig. 3. Stop number 2: *Curator Janice Li introduces 'The Cult of Beauty' exhibition.* The picture shows the adhesive and embossed tactile floor lines, the embossed and enlarged QR code, and the square. © Martina Maggi, 2023.

To further encourage visitors' independent tours, the audio description tracks integrated directions from one stop to another, advised the visitor in case of abrupt changing of lights, and provided disclaimers whenever an object or an installation could be perceived as offensive. Track 1, *Introduction to access resources for The Cult of Beauty exhibition in Gallery One*[7], provided a general introduction and overview of the access resources available. An excerpt is shown in Table 1.

---

[6] As of December 2023, "The Cult of Beauty" was the only exhibition out of the ten museums previously visited that provided tactile floor lines.

[7] An overview of the displayed objects, as well as the full captions and transcripts of the audio description guides, are available on the Wellcome Collection website: https://wellcomecollect ion.org/guides/exhibitions/ZSaiohAAACMAlJbK/captions- and-transcripts.

Table 1. Excerpts from Track 1 and the type of information conveyed.

Excerpts from Track 1	Information conveyed
"For the curator's introduction to the exhibition please skip ahead to stop 2. This stop can be found just inside the entrance to the gallery. There is a double glass door between the atrium space and the gallery which can be quite heavy"	Directions and warning
"As you enter the exhibition space through the large double doors you will find a pick-up station for printed resources straight in front of you. Here you'll find the Gallery guide, the large print guide, a sensory map of the gallery, and the visual story"	Directions
"Our Visitor Experience team staff the large grey, metallic, information desk opposite the entrance and facilitate the exhibition space. They wear black t-shirts with a white Wellcome Collection logo on the chest and 'ask me' printed on the back. They can answer any questions about the exhibition and access resources and support your visit in any way needed"	Awareness of the staff
"[…] Some of these installations also involve out loud sounds and brighter lights and effects.[…] Many of the historical objects and artworks in this exhibition are particularly sensitive to light damage. To help preserve them, the light levels are lower in some areas of the exhibition. You may need to allow a moment for your eyes to adjust after entering the gallery space. There is some challenging content in this exhibition. Where appropriate, this will be indicated on labels, and in the digital guide"	Trigger warnings

As a further approach towards visitor independence and self-guided tours, the audio description tracks – that were recorded in advance – included pauses when the stops featured a touch opportunity, or when the visitor needed to navigate the space and move from one installation to another within the same room. In track 16, dedicated to the three-metre-tall anthropomorphic sculpture "(Almost) all of my dead mother's beautiful things", by artist Narcissister, people are asked to pause the guide four times, to fully understand and enjoy the artist's creation[8].

Unfortunately, the device was extremely motion-sensitive. As a result, if not held firm it would shake with the visitor movements, and the tracks would often restart, with no possibility of fast forwarding to the point where the guide had stopped. The issue could easily be solved by scanning the QR codes and accessing the audio description via smartphone; however, given the freedom of movement and the independence offered by the exhibition, it would be worth addressing the issue for further improving the path towards accessibility for all.

---

[8] In all four cases, the audio description provided the following sentence: "You can pause the guide here, while you navigate the space following the tactile line, after which you can resume when you are ready.".

4.2 Hong Kong

During a three-month research programme in Hong Kong (from April to July 2023), the author had the possibility to observe the level of inclusivity of Hong Kong's semiotic landscapes, with a particular focus on museums, contributing to the purpose of making tourism more accessible. The project proposed, *The inclusivity of semiotic landscapes: towards accessible tourism,* was selected for this programme. A significant part of the fieldwork was conducted in the West Kowloon Cultural District, which is a key arts development area in the city and a new site of touristic interest. The study was conducted exclusively by the author with the primary aim of establishing a basis for proposing possible future improvements in accessibility strategies.

The analysis was carried out in two phases: the first one involved the observation and the evaluation of the tools and facilities provided for the visually impaired community by different museums, examining to what extent their needs have been taken into account. In the second part of the programme, the focus shifted to the analysis of the design of artworks' wall labels as part of the visual linguistic environment of the museum. Since landscape-related research aims at analyse the way in which the physical landscape communicates discursively through language and other semiotic resources [13], the observation of the distribution of signs and notices in public spaces like museums is crucial to understand how these institutions present themselves to the world; in fact, in addition to have an informative function, such landscapes contribute to the symbolic construction of public space.

The *7 principles of Universal Design,* developed in 1997 by the North Carolina State University[9], provided a foundational framework. Their aim is multi-faceted: to improve the design concept by making it more inclusive, evaluate existing design, educate designers and consumers and guide the design process towards more usable products and events. The fourth rule in particular, entitled *Perceptible Information,* states: "The design communicates necessary information effectively to the user, regardless of ambient conditions or the user's sensory abilities." Then, the following guidelines are enlisted:

a. Use different modes (pictorial, verbal, tactile) for redundant presentation of essential information;
b. Provide adequate contrast between essential information and its surroundings;
c. Maximise "legibility" of essential information;
d. Differentiate elements in ways that can be described (i.e., make it easy to give instructions or directions);
e. Provide compatibility with a variety of techniques or devices used by people with sensory limitations.

After visiting and observing the exhibitions exposed in seven museums of Hong Kong (the Hong Kong Museum of Art, the M +, Palace Museum, Museum of History, Science Museum, Hong Kong Heritage Museum, UHK University Museum and Art Gallery) two main institutions were selected: The Hong Kong Museum of Art (HKMOA) and the M +. The reason behind this choice is due to the interest that the exhibited collections aroused, the variety and the modernity of their pieces and because of the differences in the level of

---

[9] Available at: https://design.ncsu.edu/research/center-for-universal-design/.

accessibility identified between them. The selected collections were visited three times. The purpose of the first visit was to grasp a general overview of the environment and exhibitions, and to make a primary selection of the different visual codes to work on. During the second visit, visual documentation was collected, with particular attention to their arrangement in terms of the spaces, lighting, use of other sensory media and the presence of accessibility tools. The third visit involved gathering missing details and information. For the analysis, the following collections were considered, as they all had notable characteristics to point out in terms of the evaluation of public engagement and inclusion.

HKMOA:

- *"Chinese Paintings and Calligraphy"*, that hosts the museum's collection of Guadong painting and calligraphy and modern Chinese art, the beginning of which dates back to 1964.
- *"Joan Miró – The poetry of everyday life"*, which presents 94 artworks (including paintings, sculptures, drawings, textiles, lithographs, posters) and audio-visual materials, many of which come from the Fundació Joan Miró, Barcelona.
- *"By the People: Creative Chinese Character"*, which reflects the cultural richness of Chinese calligraphy spread by the development of commercial printing and publishing.
- *"City Rhymes: The Melodious Notes of Calligraphy"* which collects lyrics from different composers that have been translated into "visual" musical passages by calligraphers.

M +:

- *"Yayou Kusama 1945 to now"*, this exhibition surveys Kusama's career from the earliest drawings she made as a teenager during World War II to her most recent immersive art pieces.
- *"M + Sigg Collection: from Revolution to Globalization"*, surveys the cultural dynamism of contemporary China from the early 1970s to the present.
- *"HK Here and Beyond"*, that tells the visitor about the city's transformation from the post-war decades to the present day, reflecting the intense creative ferment and social and cultural transformation.
- *"Individuals, Networks, Expressions"*, in which a vast array of techniques, materials, formats, and methods are used by artists to reflect on their cultural or social contexts and form a complex web of connections.

4.2.1   Fieldwork in the HKMOA and M +

The fieldwork conducted at the HKMOA and M + revealed some differences in the way these institutions are addressing the issue of accessibility for the visually impaired community. Both museums put a great effort in creating a physically accessible space and a barrier-free environment; in both the HKMOA and the M +, many facilities address the issue of spatial navigation, providing Braille maps for each floor, tactile pathways, ramps and automatic doors, and spaces suitable for wheelchair users.

The M + website stresses their intention to extend accessibility beyond the physical realm. All the barrier-free facilities they provide are enlisted and divided into different sections: Physical, Visual, Audio, Intellectual & Cognitive, Digital & Web. Directing our attention on the visual section, it is stated that they "offer different accessibility measures to facilitate visitors who are blind or have impaired vision to navigate the museum, receive in-gallery information, and enjoy visual culture from a non-visual perspective". This is guaranteed by a series of services like tactile guide path, Braille and tactile floor plan, welcoming trained service animals, arranging audio descriptions for events, and providing audio guides which offer interviews and audio descriptions of different objects.

In the HKMOA it is possible to visit the *Beyond Seeing: A Multisensory Art Project*, a series of accessible art experiences for people with visual impairment and low vision, displayed through different forms of sensorial engagements. The idea is to combine Braille texts, audio information and tactile embedded papers to give to the VIB audience a multisensory experience. The pavilion is composed of two boards, the one on the right displays a tactile installation of the Victoria Harbour with Braille description, the board on the left displays a browseable tactile version with the recorded audio guide. In addition, two guide booklets with Braille and embossed printed reproduction of various artworks are available for the public. These tools are extremely valuable, and highlight the significant efforts made by these institutions in ensuring accessible experiences for all. However, there are still opportunities for further improvements. Firstly, positioning the pavilion on the fifth floor may present access difficulties. To mitigate this, clear signage should be installed to guide visitors easily to the elevators and lifts, ensuring that these facilities are prominently visible and easy to locate. Secondly, to ensure inclusivity and provide an equitable experience for all visitors, it is recommended to install Braille translations and embossed printings either alongside or directly in front of the artworks. This would allow individuals with visual impairments to engage with the exhibition independently, fostering a shared experience with their companions. Lastly, since audible description provided can't be listened to through earphones, providing dedicated listening stations would help minimize interference from ambient noise, such as conversations and foot traffic, allowing visitors to fully appreciate the audio content.

Another crucial aspect involved the analysis of the acoustic tools available in both museums, showcasing significant differences between the two institutions. The availability of audible tools is a crucial factor in assessing museum's accessibility, especially for a blind or visually impaired audience. Both museums provide audio guide tours that can be listened to by connecting to the museum's website or scanning the QR code at the gallery entrances (thus representing a free service). While the HKMOA's audio tour is not specifically designed for a visually impaired audience, the M + museum provides separate audio description tracks, even if not all the artworks are audio described. The audio guides and audio descriptions included in the tour vary in length, depending on the artwork they are describing, but they never exceed 4 min of length (the longest AD describes the artwork "Six small turntables" by Huang Yong Ping, it lasts 3:51 min). While the audio guide focuses on the social context, on the history behind the artwork, and on the semiotic analysis of the artwork, the audio description for the VIB provides all the features a visually impaired user would not be able to decode, including title, artist, date of creation as well as the physical details of the artworks (location, spatial relationships, materials, size, colours, shapes etc.). Since the source text of the museum description is a static visual message, the function of AD is to make it accessible to visually impaired visitors by translating it into a code other than the visual one. Of course, in order to have a global overview of the artwork, the listening of both recordings is advisable. To better understand the difference between the two records, here below are some extracts from the audio guide (AG) and the audio description (AD) of Yayoi Kusama's, *Pumpkin:*

> **AG**: [...] "the sculpture of an earthy plant captures Kusama's belief that there is a spirit in every living being and that differences must be embraced and celebrated."
>
> "Kusama's family owned a plant nursery, and she has many childhood memories of interacting with pumpkins. [...] She remains fascinated by how pumpkins can be both charming and grotesque."
>
> **AD**: "This work, titled Pumpkins, is a set of two large pumpkin sculptures created by Yayoi Kusama in 2022. They are made of cast aluminum and polyurethane paint. The pumpkins are of different heights and displayed on the ground next to each other. [...]"
>
> "Both of the pumpkins are yellow and covered in black polka dots, but they are differently shaped. [...]"
>
> "[...] the largest dots are the size of an adult's palm, while the smallest dots are only the size of a fingertip."

The information expressed in the audio description is complemented by the contents provided by the audio guide. The latter adds information on the social media success of Kusama's most famous artistic subject, her childhood memories of the family's plant nursery and the history behind her fascination for pumpkins.

4.2.2   Selection and analysis of relevant visual codes.

After reviewing various visual codes as source text for the semiotic analysis, such as posters, museum labels, advertisements, branding, etc., a second phase of the fieldwork involved the analysis of museums' wall labels in order to assess their accessibility level. Artwork labels play a crucial role in public engagement, they represent a critical link between the museum and its visitors, forming an essential component in the composition of other museum texts (e.g., advertisements, websites, audio guides, leaflets, etc.). A sample of labels was selected for each museum, and observations on their main characteristics were made: position in relation to the referred artwork and the room, dimensions of the label, font, contrast, and colors. It is important to stress that observations were drawn up only from the point of view of the design for the visually impaired, without evaluating the language structure and content. To validate the observations, a review of the literature on accessible design for public inclusion was essential. Three main documents were emphasized: *Everyone's welcome: The Americans with Disabilities Act and Museums* [18], *SGAED-Smithsonian Guidelines for Accessible Exhibition Design* [15] and *Part of Your General Public Is Disabled. A Handbook for Guides in Museums, Zoos, and Historic Houses.* [14] as these documents provide precise and still current guidelines to follow in order to produce accessible contents. Some examples of the semiotic analysis carried out on labels are listed below:

4.2.3 HKMOA

Chinese Paintings and Calligraphy
With respect to the labels belonging to the collection *Chinese Paintings and Calligraphy* some critical issues related to the level of accessibility involve text design and label placement. Regarding the design, for an audience with low vision the text is quite long and the font colored in dark red or dark green does not provide good contrast. For these visitors, a possible alternative would be providing Braille translations for totally blind visitors or magnified printed material for people with low vision. Using of left-aligned text with a ragged right margin can create a predictable starting point for each line and evenly spaced words, making it easier to read. Additionally, it is advisable to avoid placing labels behind protective glass, especially in dimly lit rooms, as this further hinders readability. As recommended by the SGAED, it is important to "Mount labels so that visitors can get very close to read them, people with low vision often must be within 75 mm (3 in.) of a label to read it" [15]. Labels on the back wall of a case or behind a vitrine are impossible for many people to read, especially if the room is dark and the light behind the glass is too feeble to guarantee a good reading (Fig. 4).

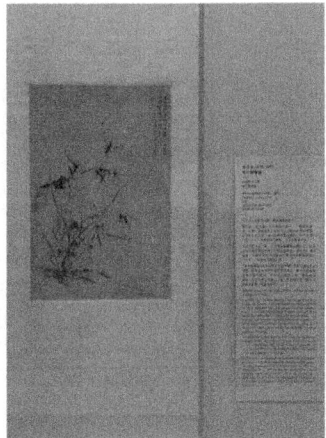 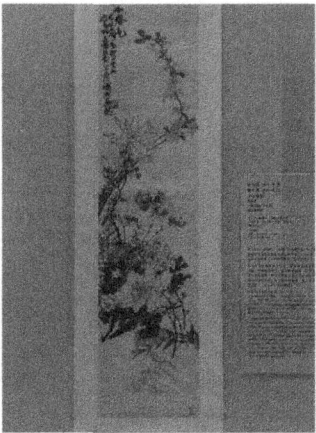

Fig. 4. Examples of labels belonging to the *Chinese Paintings and Calligraphy* collection. The artworks, as well as the labels, are placed behind a vitrine.

City Rhymes: The Melodious Notes of Calligraphy
A higher level of accessibility can be found at the very beginning of the museum tour. The exhibition *City Rhymes: The Melodious Notes of Calligraphy* explores the interplay between calligraphy, prose and poetry, dance, painting and music. It is divided into different sections, the first one is entitled *Resonance: Echoes of Lyrics and Sound* and it collects lyrics from different composers that have been translated into "visual" musical passages by calligraphers. A higher level of accessibility here is made possible thanks to the lighted panels where the description of the artworks is placed (Fig. 5). The labels show a high level of contrast between the black background and the white lighted font (emphasized by the darkened room), providing sufficient light to read labels. No barriers

or glasses are placed between the artwork and the public, so the visitor can observe (and read) easily.

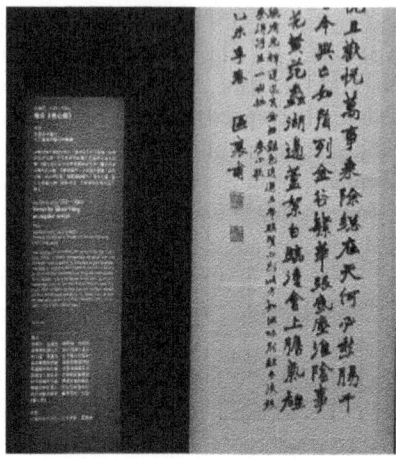

Fig. 5. Example of label belonging to the collection *Resonance: Echoes of Lyrics and Sound.*

A second part of the exhibition is entitled *Force: Dancing Lines of Motion* and it represents the merge between calligraphy, music and dance. According to this philosophy, writing calligraphy, like dancing and martial arts, requires balance between speed and forces. This philosophy is in line with the principle of multimodality, which suggests to make exhibit content accessible at multiple intellectual levels and present it through more than one sensory channel. First of all, the presence of sounds and musical fragments is an important resource for the VIB visitors, since it allows the audience to enjoy at least the audible part of the exhibition. The audience can follow the notes while exploring the environment, and figuring in his/her mind the movements of the dancer. The SGAED [15] points out that "Light on dark text is acceptable for back-lit labels when light intensity is moderated". For the people who still have visual residues, the use of lighted panels and projection on darkened walls allows an easier reading. Exploiting wall space allows the use of a larger font compared to classical labels. Being a projection, characters' dimensions should be adjustable, so in the case of a special tour for a VIB audience the font could be increased. Anyway, people with low vision could find it difficult to navigate through a dark room without the help of lightning signals (like arrows) on the floor.

M+
Hong Kong: Here and Beyond (Identities)
This collection hosts a great variety of different artworks, ranging from paintings, installation, 3D models, artefacts, photography, graphic design works, build projects, magazine covers, posters and animations. At a macrostructural level, the global coherence of the exhibition relies on the organization of spaces and themes; it is divided in four chapters – *Here, Identities, Places and Beyond*, every one telling a part of Hong Kong history, with the aim of revealing continuities between past and present. The section

entitled "Identity" largely hosts graphic design works, presenting the varied ways in which Hong Kong projects its identity locally and globally. In Fig. 6 below, we can observe the built project for 'The Peak Tower' in Hong Kong hosted at Expo'70 in Osaka. In this case the artworks, and consequently its corresponding label, are displayed on a background that portrays a complex construction site, with different elements and colors. The label, in grey, gets lost in the multitude of the elements represented, as it does not stand out against the background. As stated in the SGAED [15], "Overprinting (type on an imaged background) is unreadable for people with low vision and perceptual difficulties. Print on a surface that is textured or that has differing colours and tones (e.g. faux marble, woodgrain) can result in the same illegibility as over-printing." [15]. Also, objects mounted against complex backgrounds are difficult to see for people with low vision and for those with figure-ground perceptual problems. The contrast provided by the white characters against the grey background could not be enough to guarantee a good visibility for a visually impaired audience, as the font size is extremely tiny.

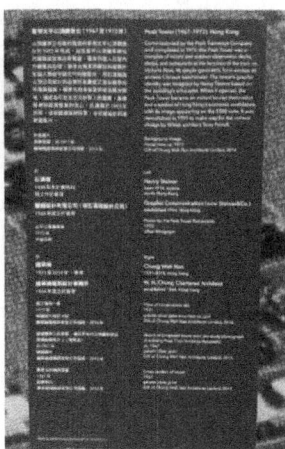

Fig. 6. Project for The Hong Kong Peak Tower

Hong Kong: Here and Beyond (Places and Beyond)
The final section of the exhibition, "Places" and "Beyond", looks at the city's built environment through its architectural landmarks, innovation in social housing and logistics infrastructure and reflects the impact that the built environment had on filmmakers, artists and photographers.[10] Some of the artworks displayed in the room are hung on the walls, like photographs and graphic design works, while other artworks such as 3D models, artefacts and magazines are placed in showcases behind vitrines. The great majority of the exhibition spaces are painted in blue. In this case, labels are not printed on a plate but they are stuck directly on the wall, so that the outline disappears. The colored background force to print the text in white in order to ensure a greater contrast with respect to black (Fig. 7). The labels placed in the showcases could be difficult to read not

---

[10] Inside "Hong Kong: Here and Beyond", video available at the following webpage: https://www.mplus.org.hk/en/exhibitions/hong-kong-here-and-beyond/ (last access: 09 June 2023);

only for a visually impaired public, but also for people in wheelchairs. As the SGAED states, labels should be mounted "at a height that is comfortable for both those seated and standing" [15]. Particular attention must be paid to the height of the glass; if the case floor is low but the glass is high, viewing the interior of a bowl or the overall design of a textile is blocked for both visitors with visual and mobility impairments. The standing visitor with low vision cannot get close enough to the object to see the details; the seated visitor cannot see the object's top or interior at all.

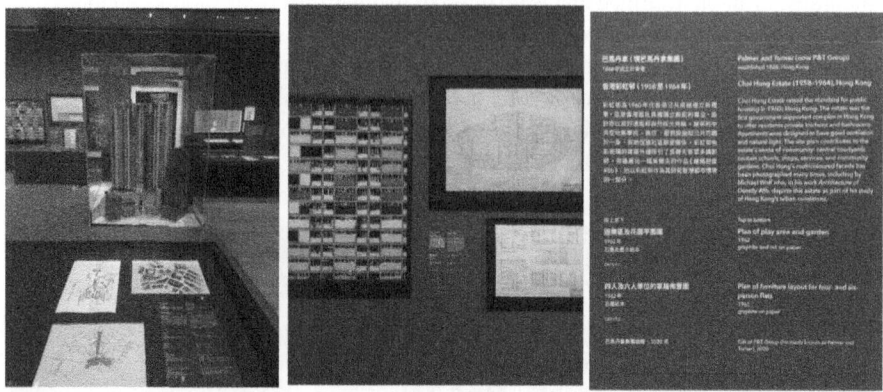

Fig. 7. Some examples of labels belonging to the sections *Places* and *Beyond Individuals, Networks, Expressions*

Individuals, Networks, Expressions

A high level of accessibility can be traced in the collection entitled *Individuals, Networks, Expressions*. Presented in eight galleries, it follows a chronology that spans from the post-war period and its reverberations around Asia to our present, globalised era. Figure 5 (a) below shows an artwork by Tsuruko Yamazaki, a Japanese artist known for her sculptures and installations which foreground interactions between raw materials, synthetic dyes and reflective tin surfaces[11]. The artwork combines a vinyl painting on canvas, entitled *Work*, and an installation, entitled *Tin Cans*, colored in magenta and stacked in a casual arrangement on a ground panel. In this case, not only the label of the artwork accomplishes with the majority of the SGAED's guidelines states so far (i.e. *Provide high contrast between text and background*, *Print only on a solid background*, *Mount labels so that visitors can get very close to read them*, *Keep in mind the natural line of sig*, *Avoid shadows on labels*), but what makes this works fully accessible is the presence of a 3D tactile replica of it (Fig. 5 c/d). Touching it, the replica reproduces different sounds recorded in different areas of Hong Kong. By scanning the QR code, a map of the soundscapes is provided (Fig. 8 b). The project has been developed by MetaObject and Ryo Ikeshiro, Assistant Professor at the School of Creative Media of the City University (Hong Kong). Tactile and hearing experiences are essential to people with visual impairments and greatly assist many people with cognitive disabilities. This work of art accomplishes with these important guidelines: "Exhibitions must make exhibit content

---

[11] From the artwork's label.

accessible at multiple intellectual levels and present it through more than one sensory channel" [15] and "Include touchable objects, such as models and reproductions, within the actual exhibition space" [15]. When objects are being selected for inclusion in an exhibition, it is important to allow all visitor to touch them, not just those who have low vision or are blind. This allows people with visual impairments equal access to the artworks without having to separate from their friends or family who are not blind or have low vision.

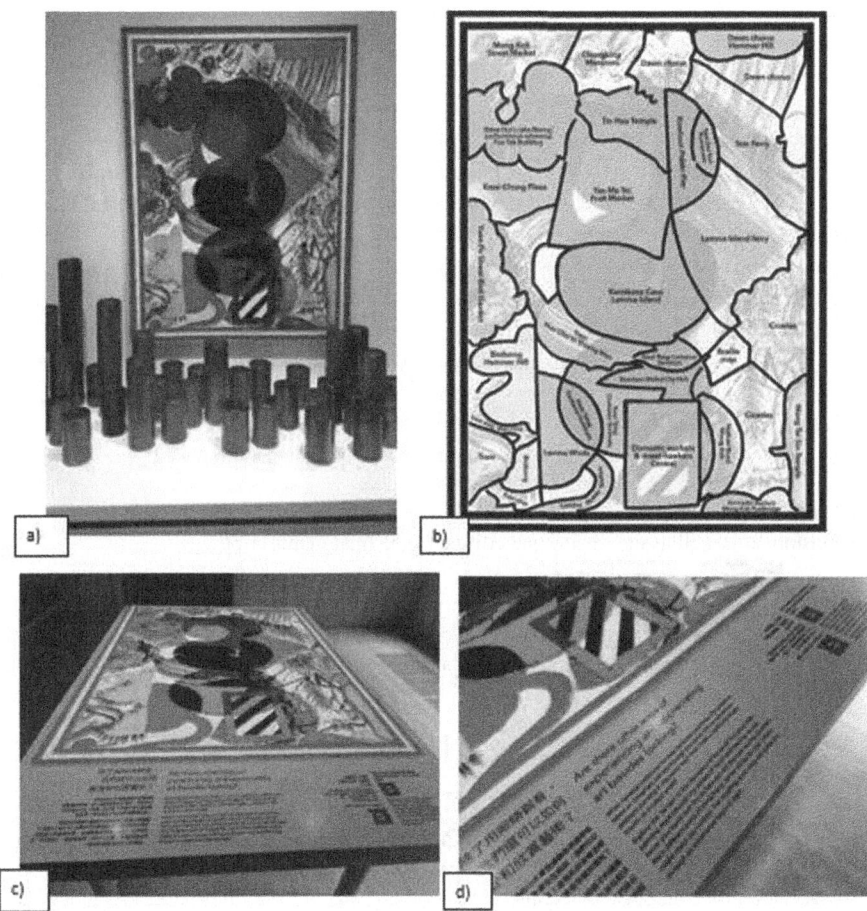

Fig. 8. The original painting (a), a map of the sounds recorded from different areas of Hong Kong (b) the 3D tactile replica (c – d)

5   Conclusion

The researchers systematically observed how museums in London and Hong Kong are working to ensure an equal visiting experience for all and identified areas for improvement across a variety of exhibitions.

Audio description brought blind and visually impaired visitors closer to art and museums. Moreover, the possibility of accessing the tracks from handheld devices, apps, or QR codes offered the opportunity to visit the venue without previous arrangements and to share the experience with friends and family. Not limiting the audio description to temporary exhibitions or dedicated timetable events and instead integrating it as a permanent feature into the standard visit can enhance the richness of the tours, break down barriers, and spread awareness and understanding, providing equality in access. In addition, it allows people the choice not to share information about their vision loss if they do not feel comfortable and prefer to be able to use the audio description without asking a member of staff first.

In addition to audible tools, Hong Kong museums made significant investments in order to grant physical accessibility, offering a number of facilities to enhance visitors' experience. Even if audio description is not always included in the tour, audio tools are generally available for free. Moreover, these museums offer different multisensory projects which combine tactile, visual and auditory elements in order to grant an inclusive experience for all.

Finally, the new methods of visitor independence experimented with in London, such as the integration of directions in the tracks, the installation of raised tactile floor lines, and the development of a tracking system with Bluetooth beacon technology, will support self-guided tours for blind and visually impaired visitors and reinforce the principle that museums are, according to their very essence, a physical manifestation of knowledge, democracy, and equality.

Author Contribution. Silvia Dini is the author of the following paragraphs: 3, 3.1, 4.2 Martina Maggi is the author of the following paragraphs: 2, 4.1

The authors contributed to the writing of the paragraphs "Abstract", "Introduction" and "Conclusions", as well as the review and editing of the final manuscript.

Disclosure of Interests. The authors have no competing interests to declare that VocalEyes, the Science Museum, The Wellcome Collection, The Hong Kong Museum of Art (HKMOA), and the M + are relevant to the content of this article.

References

1. Asakawa, S., et al.: An independent and interactive museum experience for blind people. In: Proceedings of the 16th International Web for All Conference, New York, NY, USA. Association for Computing Machinery, pp. 1–9 (2019). https://doi.org/10.1145/3315002.331 7557
2. Axel, E.S., et al.: AEB's guidelines for verbal description adapted from making visual art accessible to people who are blind or visually impaired, art education for the blind (1996)
3. Bartolini, C.: Diversity in museums: the inclusive value of museum audio description. DIVE-IN Int. J. Div. Incl. 1(2), 107–138 (2021). https://doi.org/10.6092/issn.2785-3233/15764
4. De Coster, K., Mühleis, V.: Intersensorial translation: Visual art made up by words. In: Cintas, J.D., Orero, P., Remael, A. (eds.) Media for All, pp. 189–200. Brill/Rodopi, Leiden (2007)
5. Dodd, D., Sandell, R.: Including Museums, perspectives on museums, galleries and social inclusion. University of Leicester, RCMG (2001)

6. European Union: European Accessibility Act (Directive 2019/882) (2019). https://eurlex.eur opa.eu/legal-content/EN/TXT

7. Fortuna, J., et al.: Identifying barriers to accessibility for museum visitors who are blind and visually impaired. Visitor Stud. **26**(2), 103–124 (2023). https://doi.org/10.1080/10645578. 2023.2168421

8. Greco, G.M.: The question of accessibility. In: Taylor, C., Perego, E. (eds.) The Routledge Handbook of Audio Description, 1st edition, pp. 13–25. Routledge (2022)

9. Hayhoe, S.: Blind Visitor Experiences at Art Museums. Rowman & Littlefield Publishers, New York (2017)

10. Hutchinson, R.S., Eardley, A.F.: Museum audio description: the problem of textual fidelity. Perspectives **27**(1), 42–57 (2019)

11. ICOM: Code of Ethics (2017). https://icom.museum/en/resources/standards%20guidelines/ code-of-ethics/

12. Kleege, G.: More than Meets the Eye: What Blindness Brings to Art. Oxford University Press, New York (2018)

13. Lam, W.Y.P., Graddol, D.: Conceptualising the vertical landscape: the case of the international finance centre in the world's most vertical city. J. Sociolinguist. **21**(4), 521–546 (2017)

14. Majewski, J.: Part of Your General Public is Disabled: A Handbook for Guides in Museums, Zoos, and Historic Houses. Office of Elementary and Secondary Education, Smithsonian Institution, Washington DC (1987)

15. Majewski, J.: Smithsonian Guidelines for Accessible Exhibition Design. Smithsonian Institution Accessibility Program, Washington DC (1987)

16. Perego, E.: Extending the uses of museum audio description: implications for translation training and English language acquisition. Textus Eng. Stud. Italy **34**(1), 229–249 (2021). https://doi.org/10.7370/100403

17. Renel, W.: Sonic accessibility: increasing social equity through the inclusive design of sound in museums and heritage sites. Curator Museum J. **62**(3), 377–402 (2019). https://doi.org/10. 1111/cura.12311

18. Salmen, J.P.S.: Everyone's Welcome: The Americans with Disabilities Act and Museums. Universal Designers & Consultants Inc, American Association of Museums, Washington DC (1998)

19. Soler Gallego, S.: La traducción accesible en el espacio multimodal museográfico, tesis doctoral. Servicio de publicaciones de la Universidad de Córdoba, Córdoba (2013)

20. Soler Gallego, S., Chica Núñez, A.J.: Museos para todos: evaluación de una guía audiode-scriptiva para personas con discapacidad visual en el museo de ciencias. Revista Española de Discapacidad **2**, 145–167 (2014)

21. Taylor, C., Perego, E.: The Routledge Handbook of Audio Description. Routledge, London and New York (2022)

22. The 101st United States Congress: Americans with Disabilities Act (ADA) (1990). https:// www.ada.gov/law-and-regs/ada/

23. United Nations: Convention on the Rights of Persons with Disabilities (CRPD) (2007). https:// social.desa.un.org/crpd/convention-on-the-rights-of-persons-with-disabilities-articles

24. United Nations: Article 30 (Participation in cultural life, recreation, leisure and sport) (2007)

25. Valero Gisbert, M.J.: La Audiodescripción de la imagen a la palabra. Traducción inter-semiótica de un texto multimodal, CLUEB Casa Editrice, Bologna

26. VocalEyes: Our History. https://vocaleyes.co.uk/about/history/. Accessed 24 Sept 2024

27. Wellcome Collection Website: The Cult of Beauty. https://wellcomecollection.org/exhibi tions/the-cult-of-beauty. Accessed 23 Sept 2024

28. Wellcome Collection Website: The Cult of Beauty digital guides. https://wellcomecollection.
org/guides/exhibitions/ZSaiohAAACMAlJbK. Accessed 25 Sept 2024
29. Wellcome Collection website: The Cult of Beauty visual story. https://wellcomecollection.
org/exhibitions/ZJ1zCxAAACMAczPA/visual-stories. Accessed 23 Sept 2024

Communication in the Digital Era: Psycho-Pedagogical Implications Between Radio and Podcasts

Pia Marinaro, Francesca Finestrone(✉), and Andreana Lavanga

Department of Humanities, University of Foggia, via Arpi 176, Foggia, Italy
{pia.marinaro,francesca.finestrone}@unifg.it,
andreana.lavanga@unifg.com

Abstract. The evolution of communication media has reshaped how information is disseminated and consumed. Radio, a historical medium of mass communication, remains influential due to its accessibility and ability to foster community connections. Meanwhile, podcasts, as an on-demand audio platform, offer flexibility and diverse content, redefining modern modes of consumption and entertainment. This study examines the impact of podcasts and web radio on contemporary communication, exploring audience engagement, production and distribution strategies, and their cultural and social implications. Plutarch emphasized the importance of listening, stating that nature gave us two ears and one mouth to encourage attentive listening before speaking. Listening is crucial in learning and human relationships, with research indicating that hearing involves complex brain processes, activating multiple regions associated with memory, emotions, and past experiences. In digital contexts, Meyer's research on multimedia learning highlights how sensory memory processes visual and auditory stimuli separately, which are then integrated by working memory. He argues that effective learning occurs when audio and visuals complement each other without redundancy. A key focus of this study is the role of public speaking in radio and podcasts, particularly its psychological aspects. Performance anxiety, self-confidence, and audience perception are critical factors affecting communication. Speakers' mastery of voice, prosody, and persuasive storytelling are essential for engaging listeners. This study emphasizes the importance of integrating psychological techniques into speaker training to enhance the effectiveness and authenticity of radio and podcast communication, with a focus on emotional awareness and message delivery.

Keywords: Media evolution · Podcast · Multimedia Learning

1 Introduction

When addressing the topic of podcasts, an ontological question immediately arises, requiring reflection not only on its constituent elements but also on its very nature. The podcast occupies a hybrid space between format and medium, which has sparked debates both in the field of media studies and in collective perception. Historically,

G. A. Toto (Ed.): ICS exchange 2024, CCIS 2521, pp. 187–202, 2025.
https://doi.org/10.1007/978-3-032-03021-4_13

the podcast is linked to the development of web radio, but in a broader context, it fits into the process of digitalization, which tends to blur the specificities of traditional media, creating fluid spaces. It is a phenomenon situated within the larger framework of media convergence, where the direct relationship between a medium and its distribution mechanisms dissolves [1], just as is the case with podcasts. The latter is often defined as a channel for radio content (or radio-like content), but with the adoption of increasingly modern technologies, such as files transmitted to PCs, MP3 players, and smartphones. However, the podcast is also recognized as carrying autonomous cultural practices, distinct from those of radio [2].

Moreover, the podcast sits at the intersection of grassroots and corporate practices, offering the public the opportunity to reinvent and actively participate in the creation of amateur content using technologies that were once the exclusive domain of professional broadcasters. To better understand the identity the podcast has built within the contemporary media landscape and its evolutionary path, it is necessary to conduct a retrospective analysis of its distinctive characteristics and evolutionary phases. This allows for reflection on the current stage of development, which can be defined as the "platformization" of podcasting, a process that replicates trends already seen in the audiovisual and music sectors.

The term "podcast/podcasting" provides an initial technical explanation of its nature: it first appeared in a 2004 article in *The Guardian* [3], linking the activity of podcasting— a form of broadcasting—to one of its consumption technologies, emphasizing portability, as in the case of the iPod, whose first version was launched in 2001. Although the use of "iPod" in the terminology was initially informal, Apple played a significant role in the distribution of podcasts, developing a podcast section in iTunes in 2005. Hammersley also associated the podcast with other terms, such as "audioblogging" and "Guerrilla-Media," which, while not becoming common usage, help contextualize the environment in which the podcast emerged. These terms suggest an opposition to traditional radio broadcasting, placing the podcast in a dimension that owes part of its existence to radio, particularly web radio, while positioning itself as a potential alternative. "GuerrillaMedia" implies an independent stance, thanks to the growing accessibility of technology, allowing individuals to emancipate themselves from institutional radio production. In this perspective, concepts such as the fluidity of the audience's role emerge, where listeners become active participants, with some transforming into producers, contributing to the phenomenon of *produsage* and *proam*, where the traditional dichotomy between production and consumption dissolves [4].

On the other hand, the term "audioblogging" emphasizes an informal and personal dimension, similar to a weblog, giving the podcast an amateur connotation. At its origins, the podcast thus represents a grassroots expression of creativity, free from the professional barriers of the radio world, the limitations of the schedule, and the lower capacity for content customization. Accessibility to production tools, flexibility, and reduced costs-all these features crystallize the perception of the podcast as a form of "democratization" compared to radio, fuelling a DIY rhetoric where anyone in principle can become a podcaster. Another important element of podcasting is the RSS feedReally Simple Syndication-a format for free web syndication of content via subscription, where updates will show up in an aggregator. This open-source technology, not owned by any company, ensures the podcast's free and democratic accessibility [5].

Despite independence, flexibility, and amateurism being fundamental elements in the initial phase, the podcast cannot be entirely separated from radio. There exists a stratification of practices that include user-generated content (UGC), but these coexist with traditional top-down logics. A good analogy can be found in the audiovisual field: platforms like YouTube also started off with UGC policies but, throughout time, have been heavily influenced by the music and television industries and thus gradually turn themselves into commercial platforms [6]. By the same token, podcasting is undergoing a phase of gradual professionalization, though not directly commercialized by the radio industry.

The picture that emerges is thus characterized by a dichotomy: on one hand, the podcast inherits elements from radio, while on the other, it seeks to emancipate itself from it. Even the term *broadcasting* applied to podcasts reflects this tension. Historically, broadcasting has been understood as a stream emitted by a few producers for a vast audience, following an exclusively top-down logic [7]. However, if broadcasting is interpreted more broadly, as a transmission distributed on either a small or large scale, the podcast can be seen as its evolution, allowing for a further process of democratization.

While references to radio can be considered precursors to some elements of the podcast, it is important here to establish a direct line with the foundational moments of its evolution and define the podcast's legacy. The birth of online radio can be traced back to 1993, with the establishment of the Internet Multicasting Service (IMS) and the Internet Radio Talk channel, which broadcast the program *Geek of the Week*, created by Carl Malamud. Andrew Bottomley refers to this period as a moment of "protopodcasting" although the explicit reference was to radio, and the program adopted its format (interviews with guests involved in the construction of the internet), the audience primarily consisted of a niche of tech and computer enthusiasts, the dominant community on the web in the early 1990s. Furthermore, the technology used by Malamud, IMS, allowed data to be streamed in real-time from one source to multiple recipients. However, the programs were not broadcast live but were pre-recorded and distributed on-demand [8].

Thus, while it was not a livestream, which would later be introduced with technologies like RealAudio and AudioNet, enabling large-scale audio streaming, these early Internet Radio Talk programs shared several characteristics with podcasts: the content was consumed at the audience's discretion, and episodes were released episodically and focused on specific topics, thus anticipating the podcast format of the early 2000s as a sort of prototype [8].

A more detailed analysis of the characteristics of podcasts and radio allows to identify the points of contact and divergence between the two media. In particular, it is useful to compare them in terms of media and technological features as well as the genres that shape their content. Both media exist primarily within an auditory dimension: while a visual element may be present (e.g., live TV broadcasts of radio shows or podcast live shows), it is secondary, as the central content is conveyed through sound (voice, music, sound effects) or its absence.

Andrew Crisell (1994) [9] holds that this "blind" quality of radio, related to its reliance on listening, invites an imaginative response from the listener, which compensates for the absence of a visual field. This imaginative process is particularly applicable to *radio drama*, where the audience is supposed to fill sensory gaps much like in reading literature. Such a conception of radio as a blind medium, however, has been criticized because of its implicit sensory hierarchy-for implying a deficiency or lack compared with the visual media-rather than testifying about an essential parity of sensory experiences [10].

The auditory nature of radio and podcasts also enforces a different mode of content presentation, such as using voice to evoke space and environment through real or imagined background noises or by explicit reference. Intimacy and sociability are evoked in both media, though differently. Radio is a mass medium that nevertheless has always conveyed an intimate dimension because of the imaginative involvement of the listener. Podcasts, on the other hand, are understood as more direct and personal, above all when amateur settings of production are in question, carrying an air of authenticity with them [11] (Berry, 2006). Moreover, individual listening through headphones facilitates the creation of a private bubble, even in public spaces. Historically, however, radio has played a domestic role, fostering a sense of sociability and participation [12].

Although listening generally occurs on an individual basis, both radio and podcasts strive to engage the audience and break the unidirectional nature of communication.

The centrality of voice puts both radio and podcasts in a temporal rather than in a spatial dimension. However, the element of listening time introduces an important difference between the two. Traditional radio is bonded with the notion of liveness, that is, it is a listening practice that for most of its history developed in real-time only [9]. Once broadcast, the content is no longer recoverable. While podcasts have been designed as time-shifted content, meaning consumption does not need to coincide with the release of an episode and thus there is more flexibility with regard to when to listen to it, in reality, this has created other complications within the digital landscape. For instance, some radio programs are now distributed as podcast episodes; other podcasts go on-air live and, therefore, retain some of their radio characteristics, such as linearity [13].

The need to introduce platforms into podcasting arose from the very nature of how the medium is consumed. Although podcasts are originally tied to the RSS protocol—a central element of their technological revolution, enabling listeners to automatically receive updates on subscribed content—this feature also presented challenges.

Specifically, the fragmentation and isolation of podcasts before they were aggregated into user feeds positioned them in isolated "bubbles" on the web. The lack of an aggregation process contributed to the intimate atmosphere of early podcasts, drawing a parallel to the practice of blogging, which was also inspired by a personal matrix and characterized by a diary-like aura. Yet, that same lack of aggregation constituted a barrier to entry that prevented podcasts from ever breaking out of their niches.

The platforms have been central to the entirety of podcasting development since its beginning. Sullivan (2018) separated them into three main areas: storage-the virtual space in which podcasts are uploaded and the RSS feed generated, often on a separate hosting site; discovery, because the platforms act as aggregators of content that would otherwise be scattered through the web; and finally, the area of consumption, which provides for the access of podcasts through an app or other means.

Unlike other Web 2.0 platforms (such as social networks or Netflix), these functions remain separate [14] though greater convergence is becoming noticeable, especially with the rise of subscription-based platforms.

Beyond their functions in facilitating interaction between podcasts and their audiences, platforms have also taken on a fundamental role in the relationship between podcasts and producers. Platforms oriented toward advertising and product manage the user-generated information process in a way that monetizes content. Some hosting sites provide data downloads, number of listens, and other metrics that permit the producer to trace the performance of their programs against others [14]. Platforms such as Spotify increasingly centralize this function while subscription-based platforms introduce new financing mechanisms for producers, permitting content producers to move away from external financing sources (crowdfunding or advertising).

The geographical context that has most favored the development of podcast platforms is the English-speaking world, with particular reference to the United States, which represents one of the most advanced markets concerning the offerings of the platforms. Similar models exist in other contexts also, although with peculiar features based on the habits of consumption and diffusion of podcasts as a cultural industry. For example, in Denmark, the Podimo platform is used by some podcasters to fund their programs, especially those in Danish, which are unlikely to be exported to international markets [15].

Among the earliest aggregative forms for podcasts was the development of the RSS protocol and the emergence of delivery technologies. The RSS protocol, which is a cornerstone in the evolution of podcasting, was refined by Dave Winer and Adam Curry. Their goal was to avoid the buffering problems typical of streaming by enabling automatic content downloads via software, making them available without user input [16]. The new version of RSS was first implemented by Winer for Radio Userland and later gave rise to various software based on this principle, such as iPodder, which also facilitated file transfers to Apple iTunes [17]. This system cannot be considered a platform in the strict sense, as it was not a for-profit company but rather open-source software available to users.

Podcast directories first appeared to help users find programs and helped the establishment of early online communities: PodcastAlley and PodcastPickle. In this initial period, however, the various platform functions were still all fragmented in how they could be accessed, making the process of listening cumbersome-even revolutionary, by the standards of the time [17].

Another point of comparison is the use of the radio schedule, which serves as an organizational framework for a broadcaster's programming. The term schedule derives from the ancient Greek "πάλιν" (again) and "ψάω" (to scrape), originally referring to the practice of reusing ancient manuscripts by erasing previous text to replace it with new writing [18].

For television and radio, the schedule is the ongoing composition of programming; it's in many ways the reflection of the identity of the network itself. Within podcasting, a notion of a schedule was missing but later appeared along with the rise of podcast networks whose contents were organized around a "cultural form" which expressed values of the network. Yet, unlike radio, which may get lost in the continuum of programs, podcasts are based on episodes and scheduled releases that are easily accessible anytime [12].

Beyond the technological and media aspects, it is also useful to consider the relationship between radio and podcast genres. Traditionally, radio content fell into three basic categories. These were: *education/knowledge dissemination*, where educational material was presented along with a vehicle for the dissemination of information for learning; *entertainment*, which consisted of music programs and talk shows, featuring interviews, discussions, or humor and *information*-programs of news and current events. These well-defined categories served to define the form and content of radio programs and helped radio broadcasters and their audiences to more readily distinguish between types of content they would produce and listen to.

With the development of media, especially *flow radio*, which involves a continuous stream, uninterruptedly flowing through the day to keep the listener tuned in, these categories began to break down. It was more important for flow radio to maintain audience attention by smooth transition from segment to segment without breaks, combining educational segments with entertainment and information in ways that would make it difficult to classify programs strictly into one category or another.

Competition, too, especially from the highly popular media of television, made radio not just a one-dimensional art. Television would encompass all types of entertainment from varieties of music and dances to newscasts that were prompt-so that radio had to also mix and match genres to keep up with the times. For example, today a radio talk show might include news updates, educational discussions, and music, rather than fitting neatly into just one genre. As Bonini (2014) underlines, this hybridization of radio genres is the expression of a larger trend within the media, according to which clear borders among categories of content are increasingly blurred and hence make programming more flexible and varied.

The podcast has invaded the educational sector, too [19]. New technologies or new forms of communication—embedded in already validated methodologies or new methodologies that could be tried—can bring about new teaching opportunities to comply with the demands of the learners. Contemporary tools provide fun and relevant ways of learning. Educational podcasts are becoming increasingly common in both colleges and universities today [20]. Not only does listening, but also the production of podcasts by students seems to be a healthy student-centered learning strategy [21].

Hence, the format does not seem to matter so much as far as teaching effectiveness is concerned but rather the methods adopted and the role of a learner being active. The article that interests most is that done by Schreiber (2017) [22] on the production of mathematical audio podcasts at elementary school level, which support the mathematical learning processes. The students were asked to reflect on a mathematical concept by building profound awareness of the content of learning at school and trying to explain it through a verbal description only. The students, for this purpose, needed to learn constructing the verbal expressions accurately and with precision using mathematical language. During the preparation of the podcast, the teacher evaluated the learning development of the students. This would then bring out that podcasts, through this project, enhance awareness of content, content acquisition, and competencies related to technology and media since digital tools and the web are used. This is only one of the various uses of podcasts within the school context, and the training of teachers who are adequately prepared in order to confront the challenges and opportunities that this technology offers is highly relevant for podcasts to be transformed into an effective and integrated tool within the students' learning process, enabling not only knowledge acquisition but also the development of transverse and digital skills.

2 The Psychological Aspects Through Communication and Soft Skills

The scientific literature [23–25] agrees in affirming that the establishment of a positive and empathetic relationship between teacher and student, and among peers, acts as a supporting factor in creating the right conditions for learning. In this regard, learning environments where active or empathetic listening is applied tend to be more effective in the co-construction of shared meanings and in the acquisition of soft skills, which pertain to the personal values that determine an individual's ability to adapt and operate in a particular situation. A teacher should prioritize improving the quality of communication, as quality communication and interaction between teacher and student serve as a motivating signal for students, demonstrating that the teacher cares about them, wishes to understand their needs, and is willing to listen to them. This approach will have a direct impact on their development, self-esteem, and, of course, their motivation to actively participate in the educational and learning process [26]. Listening is not just hearing. It is the active construction of meaning from all the verbal and nonverbal signals an individual sends while speaking [27]. Hennings' definition immediately reveals the active nature of listening, as it involves individuals not only at a cognitive level (I understand the content of what you are communicating to me), but also at an emotional level (I understand the meaning of what you are communicating to me) and at a motor level (I understand how prosody can modulate the meaning).

Active or empathetic listening falls within interpersonal skills, and people with high interpersonal intelligence are more likely to become assertive and have good communication skills [28], thus making active listening a significant predictive factor of students' academic success [29]. Effective communication is a crucial component in developing and maintaining healthy relationships, both personally and professionally. It helps limit the risk of misunderstandings, prejudices, moral judgments, and misinterpretations, thus reducing the risk of tensions that could compromise the work environment and the quality of existing relationships. Active or empathetic listening is configured as a social and emotional skill, involving empathy, self-efficacy, and communicative responsibility. It forms the basis of collaboration and is a positive side effect of the development of emotional intelligence. According to Goleman's [30] (1995) domains of emotional intelligence, today's schools should move toward programs that promote the development of emotional and social intelligence [31] to bring about changes in the behavioral model of both students and teachers and, over time, lead to the acquisition of social skills and competences.

To communicate effectively, individuals must choose appropriate strategies for each situation, taking into account the context of the interaction, its purpose, the people involved, and the type of relationship with them. Listening and communication are key elements in various contexts, including professional settings. For instance, in healthcare, communicative leadership that emphasizes empathic listening and team interaction has been shown to enhance job satisfaction and well-being among ICU nurses, highlighting the importance of leadership styles rooted in listening and engagement [32]. Similarly, in education, active listening is a fundamental component in fostering positive and collaborative learning environments. The use of podcasts and similar communication tools not only facilitates the transmission of content but also promotes active and collaborative interactions between students and faculty, which are crucial for skill development. In the context of educational communication, creating a supportive learning environment is essential not only for skill acquisition but also for emotional management and student resilience. As highlighted by the study of LitwicKaminska et al. (2023) [33], resilience and social support are key factors in reducing perceived stress among university students, demonstrating their protective role in mental health. These elements can be further strengthened through effective communication and the promotion of empathetic relationships, which are central to educational dynamics supported by podcasts and other digital tools. This reinforces the connection between emotional well-being and academic success, fostering deeper and more meaningful learning.

The *LifeComp* (2020) conceptual framework, which consists of three interconnected areas of competence, also aims to establish a shared understanding and common language around "personal, social, and learning" competences, emphasizing the interdependence of intrapersonal, interpersonal, cognitive, and metacognitive dimensions, whose core consists of socio-emotional skills. Empathy can be seen as a prerequisite for developing these socio-emotional skills and for building constructive relationships [34] and is the root of all prosocial behaviors. In this sense, empathy helps meet one of the three fundamental human needs: connection, which leads to better wellbeing and greater resilience [35], as well as to improvements in processes closely linked to effective communication.

In Fig. 1, we can see the framework of the nine competences that can be acquired by everyone through formal, informal, and non-formal education.

What is particularly interesting is the intersectionality of these nine competences, especially the aspect concerning the social dimension of each individual's personal growth, highlighting how the acquisition of all competences is actually a social product, rooted in the socio-cultural context in which an individual grows and develops, and in the social network they manage to build over their lifetime. It thus becomes clear how Vygotsky's (1986) [36] teachings are still relevant and alive today: Learning is a continuous process, even involuntary, because learning is intrinsically a social process.

Social interactions and meaningful relationships play a crucial role in the acquisition of cognitive and emotional competences, and learning is deeper and more effective when there are strong interpersonal relationships and positive role models that foster a supportive and growth-oriented environment.

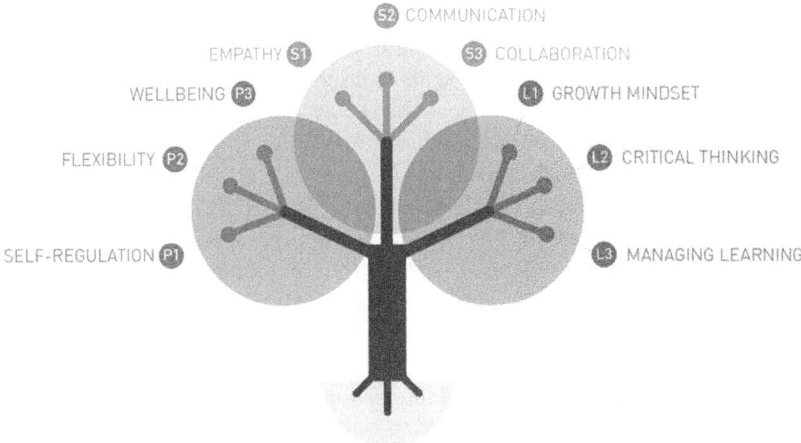

S2 COMMUNICATION

EMPATHY S1   S3 COLLABORATION

WELLBEING P3   L1 GROWTH MINDSET

FLEXIBILITY P2   L2 CRITICAL THINKING

SELF-REGULATION P1   L3 MANAGING LEARNING

Fig. 1. The LifeComp competence framework describes nine competences, organized into three areas: the 'personal' area (P1, P2, P3), the 'social' area (S1, S2, S3), and the 'learning to learn' area (L1, L2, L3).

3   Material and Methods

The study adopted an exploratory nature, in which participants took part in a podcast creation course structured within the specialization course for special educational needs Teacher (Tirocinio Formativo Attivo - TFA) required for special education teachers. At the end of the course, a questionnaire designed by the authors was administered to gather participants' opinions and perceptions regarding the educational experience. The course included a theoretical overview of communicative tools such as podcasts and radio, followed by a workshop phase where participants were required to create a podcast in groups for educational purposes. They were asked to choose a topic to address in class (not necessarily part of the curriculum) and to structure and produce a podcast through which discussing the theme with their students.

3.1   Sample

The study involved 266 trainee teachers (TFA) from secondary education, of which 214 were women (80,45%), 50 men (18,80%), and 2 participants preferred not to specify (0,75%). The age of the participants ranged from 25 to 66 years (M = 41.38; DS = 9,74). Participants voluntarily completed the questionnaire after signing informed consent and were duly informed of their right to withdraw from the study at any time they deemed necessary.

3.2   Instruments

The exploratory investigation was conducted using a tailored questionnaire to evaluate Perception of New Media; Impact on education, on public speaking abilities; the impact of such a communication tool on secondary school trainees in terms of learning and soft skills. The items in the questionnaire are categorized into 4 topic areas: satisfaction, impact on learning, soft skills and digital skills.

The questionnaire was structured with multiple-choice questions measured on a 5point Likert scale. The points of the Likert scale were structured as follows: 1 = absolutely not / not at all; 2 = more no than yes /a little; 3 = I don't know; 4 = more yes than no / quite a bit; 5 = absolutely yes / a lot.

For investigating the educational field, questions such as *"Do you think that listening to podcasts or similar formats can facilitate the learning process?"* (*Ritiene che l'ascolto di podcast o format simili possa favorire il processo di apprendimento?*) and *"Do you think that co-creating podcasts or similar formats can facilitate the learning process?"* (*Ritiene che la co-costruzione di podcast o format simili possa favorire il processo di apprendimento?*) were presented.

Regarding soft skills related to social interaction and public speaking abilities, questions such as "To what extent do you think you have improved the management of emotions related to public speaking through the recording experience?" (*Quanto ritiene di aver migliorato la gestione dell'emotività connessa al parlare in pubblico, attraverso l'esperienza di registrazione?*), "To what extent do you think you have improved your public speaking skills through the recording experience?" (*Quanto ritiene di aver migliorato le abilità del parlare in pubblico, attraverso l'esperienza di registrazione?*) and "To what extent do you think you have improved your social skills through group experience?" (*Quanto ritiene di aver migliorato le abilità sociali attraverso l'esperienza di gruppo?*) were asked.

Instead, to assess the influence of this experience on participants' perceptions of digital skills, questions such as "To what extent do you think you have improved your digital skills following the course?" ("*Quanto ritiene di aver migliorato le competenze digitali a seguito del corso?*) were administered.

To investigate the level of satisfaction with the experience during the course, the following question was asked: "How would you rate the experience, on a scale from 1 (negative) to 5 (positive)?" (*Come valuterebbe l'esperienza vissuta, su una scala da 1 (negativa) a 5 (positiva)*).

4   Results

The results of the questionnaire provided significant information regarding the level of satisfaction of participants concerning their experience in the podcast creation course. The overall evaluation of the experience, on a scale from 1 (negative) to 5 (positive), showed an average response value of 4.37, with 88.46% of participants assigning a score of 4 or 5, indicating a very positive perception of the training pathway based on podcast creation.

Regarding the questions related to the impact on learning, 88.46% of participants stated that they believe listening to podcasts or similar formats can enhance the learning process, with an average response of 4.38 on the Likert scale. Additionally, 89.06% highlighted that the co-construction of podcasts significantly contributed to their learning, with average scores of 4.37.

When it came to evaluating soft skills, the results were equally promising. 77.33% of participants reported an improvement in managing emotions related to public speaking, with an average of 4.03. Furthermore, regarding public speaking skills, 79.70% indicated they had made progress, achieving an average rating of 4.09. Additionally, 89.06% of participants reported feeling they had improved their social skills through group work, with an average response value of 4.27. These results suggest that the course not only provided theoretical content but also allowed participants to practice and enhance their communication skills.

Finally, the impact of the course on digital skills emerged clearly. 82.68% of participants stated they had improved their digital abilities, with an average of 4.09 regarding the question "How much do you believe you improved your digital skills following the course?" These results indicate a significant advancement in participants' ability to use digital tools in educational contexts.

In summary, the results suggest that the podcast creation course had a positive impact on both learning and the development of participants' soft skills, demonstrating the effectiveness of innovative and interactive educational methods in teacher training contexts.

5   Discussion

The questionnaire administered to 266 secondary school teachers in training regarding the effectiveness of participating in a podcast production experience within the school context for educational purposes showed that the integration of podcasts into teaching has a positive impact on multiple levels.

The questionnaire was divided into four dimensions:

1. Evaluation of the overall experience;
2. Evaluation of the podcast as a tool for the learning process;
3. Improvement of social and digital skills;
4. Management of emotions when speaking in public.

The results of the questionnaire clearly show that the integration of podcasts into teaching has had a positive impact on multiple dimensions of the learning process. First and foremost, there was a strong emotional and motivational engagement. The high number of positive evaluations highlights how the experience was perceived as highly stimulating, supporting classic psychopedagogical theories, such as those of Vygotsky. According to Vygotsky, learning is a social process that becomes more meaningful when it occurs through interaction and collaboration with others. Active participation in content creation fostered a sense of belonging and shared responsibility, which are essential elements for intrinsic motivation and deep learning [35, 36].

Another significant aspect that emerged from the analysis is the development of transversal skills, particularly social and communication abilities. The observed improvements in these areas demonstrate that collaborative experiences, such as podcast creation, not only facilitate the co-construction of meaning but also foster critical reflection and metacognitive thinking, which are essential components of meaningful learning [37]. Working in a co-construction context encourages selfregulation and reciprocal learning, key elements in a cooperative-oriented educational environment [38]. In the field of educational communication, the ability to manage emotions and develop effective coping strategies is crucial for academic success. Bonfiglio et al. (2020) [39] found that reduced resilience and the adoption of dysfunctional coping strategies, such as avoidance, are closely linked to problematic behaviors and video game addiction. These findings highlight the importance of strengthening personal resources, such as resilience and social skills, through activities that promote collaboration and open dialogue, essential factors for improving communication effectiveness and students' emotional well-being.

In line with the *DigCompEdu* framework [40], the experience significantly improved participants' digital competences. The use of multimedia technologies enabled the integration of advanced digital tools into the learning process, enhancing not only technical skills but also cognitive abilities related to problem-solving in digital environments. This reflects the growing importance of digital literacy in the contemporary educational landscape, as highlighted by Redecker and Punie (2017) [40], who promote the pedagogical use of technologies to develop complex competences.

Another key element is emotional management. Participation in podcast recording fostered greater control over the emotions related to public speaking, developing essential socio-emotional skills such as resilience and stress management [30]. This type of experience, which emotionally engages participants, helps strengthen selfconfidence and improve communication skills, with positive outcomes on well- being and active participation.

To further enhance the effectiveness of podcasts as an educational tool, several pedagogical strategies can be implemented. First and foremost, it is crucial to provide timely and immediate feedback. Offering prompt and specific feedback enables reinforcement of learning effectively, supporting the self-assessment process and promoting metacognitive development [41]. Feedback should be personalized, focusing on specific aspects of the work and stimulating critical reflection to facilitate constructive and conscious correction of mistakes.

Additionally, integration with more advanced and collaborative digital tools could further expand participants' digital competences. Using platforms that facilitate cocreation and group work in virtual environments would enhance project management skills and collaborative problem-solving, contributing to a more participatory and dynamic learning experience [42].

Another fundamental aspect is the provision of emotional and motivational support. Offering specific training paths for stress management and effective voice use could help students develop greater confidence in public speaking, reducing anxiety and improving their communicative performance. This approach promotes perceived selfefficacy, which is closely related to intrinsic motivation and the achievement of positive outcomes [43].

Finally, it is important to encourage a greater focus on content co-construction. Involving students in all stages of the process—from topic selection to production and evaluation—helps strengthen their sense of ownership and responsibility. This type of active participation promotes collaborative learning, creating an environment where students feel integral to the educational process, with positive effects on their engagement and motivation [44].

6 Limitations and Future Directions

Despite the results of this study highlighting the effectiveness of the podcast creation course in promoting transversal skills, it is necessary to acknowledge certain methodological limitations that may have influenced the interpretation and generalizability of the findings. One of the main concerns is the lack of a systematic analysis of the socio-demographic variables of the participants, such as age, gender, type of university education, and other contextual factors. These aspects, not having been considered or controlled for, may have introduced unmeasured variability in the data, limiting the ability to identify specific relationships between these variables and the observed outcomes, particularly regarding the perceived effectiveness of the intervention and the acquisition of digital and communication skills.

Additionally, individual psychological variables that could have had a significant impact on the results, such as learning predisposition, resilience, or the ability to manage stress and emotions, including manifestations of performance anxiety, were not analyzed. These factors, extensively documented in the literature as significant determinants in the context of transversal skill acquisition, could have provided a more nuanced understanding of the processes influencing the improvement of soft skills and emotional management through the course. Their omission may reduce the precision in evaluating the results and limit the identification of potential subgroups of participants who benefited differently from the intervention.

The self-selective nature of the sample, composed of trainee teachers specializing in special education, may also have introduced a selection bias, as participants might already have been motivated or positively inclined toward educational technologies.

To address these limitations and enhance the generalizability and practical utility of the results, future studies should include a more in-depth analysis of socio-demographic and psychological variables using both quantitative and qualitative methods. Moreover, adopting a longitudinal research design would be advisable to evaluate the course's long-term impact and to integrate objective measurements of the skills acquired with real performance indicators. Expanding the sample diversity through the inclusion of individuals from various educational and professional backgrounds would enable testing the applicability of the training model across broader scenarios.

In terms of future perspectives, integrating advanced technologies for multimedia content creation, such as artificial intelligence platforms to support podcast design and analysis, could represent a further evolution of the course. Furthermore, incorporating training paths aimed at enhancing stress management skills and the effective use of voice could strengthen the course's effectiveness, fostering improvements in public speaking skills and emotional resilience among participants.

7 Conclusions

Podcasting in educational environments is representative of a transformation agent, as it aids student learning in complex areas based upon divergent views and collaboration, thus, particularly in specific disciplines such as urban planning. Webbased audio publications offer epistemological diversities, critical thinking, and empathy by means of multiple perspectives, cultural experiences, and various research methodologies. This reflects a wider shift in ways of thinking about learning and teaching across higher education toward collaborative and democratic practices, evident across disciplines such as urban planning, in which issues of democracy, social justice, and equity are increasingly reflected within curricula [45]. This integration of multi- media tools, such as podcasts, democratizes not only the interactions but also access to information by giving voice to people and groups that are often marginalized from traditional academic and media platforms.

Podcasts similarly fit into Bloom's revised taxonomy of learning, especially for higher-order cognitive levels of creativity, analysis, and knowledge evaluation. Students involve themselves in the creation of content through podcasts, thereby fostering deeper learning experiences from superficial retention to a more profound reflective understanding. The flexibility of podcasts, ranging from passive listening to active creation of content, makes them an ideal medium for applying theory into practice. Such an approach would support the development of digital literacy and communication skills while encouraging critical engagement with course material, making podcasts a powerful tool for personal growth and collaborative learning.

Podcasts also bear importance for their contribution to two key issues: those of power and representation. This is accomplished through a reduction in gatekeeping more typical of conventional media platforms such as radio and television [46]. This opens opportunities for marginalized voices to contribute to both academic and public discourse and thus makes podcasting a democratic, inclusive medium. Podcasts are, therefore, an important medium to advance more informed and inclusive propositioning of remedies in relation to multi-faceted social and spatial matters. This perspective is most important within the discipline of urban planning.

Podcasts have evolved into a new teaching tool. The learning process will become more inclusive, interesting, and critically reflective. Combining innovative pedagogical methods with the integration of podcasts into education offers flexible, accessible media that can meet a variety of today's student needs. With their continued growth in popularity, there is most likely going to be additional disruption to traditional models of education by offering students an even more interactive, deepened learning experience that best prepares them for a digitally connected world.

Acknowledgments. For the purposes of academic recognition, paragraphs 1 and 6 were written by Pia Marinaro, paragraphs 2 and 5 were written by Francesca Finestrone, and paragraphs 3 and 4 were written by Andreana Lavanga. All authors equally contributed to the construction and administration of the questionnaire.

The authors have no competing interests to declare that are relevant to the content of this article.

References

1. Jenkins, H.: Convergence Culture: Where Old and New Media Collide. New York University Press, New York (2006)
2. Bonini, T.: The 'second age' of podcasting: reframing podcasting as a new digital mass medium. Quaderns del. CAC **41**, 21–30 (2015)

3. Hammersley, B.: Audible revolution. The Guardian (2004)
4. Markman, K.M.: Doing radio, making friends, and having fun: exploring the motivations of independent audio podcasters. New Media Soc. **14**(4), 547–565 (2012). https://doi.org/10.1177/1461444811420848
5. Berry, R.: Podcast or paycast? (2019) https://richardberry.eu/podcast-or-paycast/
6. Andrejevic, M.: Exploiting youtube: contradictions of user-generated labor. In: Snickars, P., Vonderau, P. (eds.) The YouTube Reader, National Library of Sweden (2009)
7. Sterne, J., Morris, J., Baker, M.B., Freire, A.M.: The politics of podcasting. The Fibreculture Journal 13 (2008). https://thirteen.fibreculturejournal.org/fcj-087-the-politics-of-podcasting/
8. Bottomley, A.: Internet radio: a history of a medium in transition. Doctoral dissertation, University of Wisconsin-Madison (2016)
9. Crisell, A.: Understanding Radio (2a ed.). Routledge (1994)
10. Soltani, F.: Inner ears and distant worlds: podcast dramaturgy and the theater of the mind. In: Llinares, D., Fox, N., Berry, R. (eds.) Podcasting: New Aural Cultures and Digital Media. Palgrave Macmillan (2018)
11. Berry, R.: Will the iPod kill the radio star? Profiling podcasting as radio. Convergence **12**(2), 143–162 (2006)
12. Menduni, E.: Televisione e radio nel XXI secolo. Laterza (2016)
13. Heise, N.: On the shoulders of giants. How audio podcasters adopt, transform and re-invent radio storytelling, MOOC Trans. Radio Stories (2014)
14. Sullivan, J.: Podcast movement: aspirational labour and the formalization of podcasting as a cultural industry. In: Llinares, D., Fox, N., Berry, R. (eds.) Podcasting: New Aural Cultures and Digital Media, pp. 35–56 (2018)
15. Sørine, F., Berg, A.: The tension between podcasters and platforms: Independent podcasters' experiences of the paid subscription model. Creative Ind. J. (2021)
16. Winer, D.: Payloads for RSS. The Two Way Web (2011). https://web.archive.org/web/20090717093319/http://www.thetwowayweb.com/payloadsForRss
17. Cochrane, T.: History of podcasting. Blubrry (2022). https://blubrry.com/manual/about-podcasting/history-of-podcasting-new/
18. Treccani: Palinsesto (2016). Retrieved [10/07/2024], from https://www.treccani.it/vocabolario/palinsesto/
19. Alfieri, M.V.: La scuola in ascolto – Le potenzialità dei podcast nell'education (2023). https://www.questionidorecchio.it/scuola-in-ascolto/
20. O'Brien, A., Hegelheimer, V.: Integrating CALL into the classroom: the role of podcasting in an ESL listening strategies course. ReCALL **19**(2), 165–174 (2007)
21. Tore, R., Tino, C., Fedeli, M.: Ricerca e Didattica per promuovere intelligenza comprensione e partecipazione. Atti del X convegno della SIRD, PensaMultimedia, pp. 122–135 (2021). https://hdl.handle.net/11577/3396585
22. Schreiber, C., Klose, R.: Mathematical audio-podcasts for teacher education and school. Teach. Curriculum **17**(2), 41–46 (2017)
23. Ebrahimi, S., Pishghadam, R., Estaji, A., Aminyazdi, S.A.: Examining the effects of emotioncy-based teaching on the emotions of non-Iranian female Persian language learners in Iran. Lang. Relat. Res. **9**(3), 63–97 (2018)
24. Ebrahimi, S., Tabatabaeian, M.S., Al Abdwani, T.: Enhancing the communicative skills of normal and mentally-challenged learners through emosensory textbooks. J. Bus. Commun. Technol. **1**(2), 1–12 (2022). https://doi.org/10.56632/bct.2022.1201
25. Pishghadam, R., Ebrahimi, S., Tabatabaeian, M.S.: A Novel Approach to Psychology of Language Education. Ferdowsi University Press (2019)
26. Kitanova, I., Kitanov, V.: Interaction-communication aspect of active listening in teaching. Современото воспитание и образование-состојби, предизвици и перспективи "Шеста меѓународна научна конференција Штип **6**, 21–27 (2018)

27. Hennings, D.G.: Beyond the Read Aloud: To Read Through Listening to and Reflecting on Literature. Phi Delta Kappa (1992)
28. Johnson, B.: Soft skills-essential for success. BMH Med. J. **8**(3), 99–102 (2021)
29. Eggenberger, A.L.: Active listening skills as predictors of success in community college students. Commun. Coll. J. Res. Pract. **45**(5), 324–333 (2021)
30. Goleman, D.: Emotional Intelligence. Bantam Books (1995)
31. Thorndike, R.L., Stern, S.: An evaluation of the attempts to measure social intelligence. Psychol. Bull. **34**, 275–284 (1937)
32. Cosentino, C., De Luca, E., Sulla, F., Uccelli, S., Sarli, L., Artioli, G.: Leadership styles' influence on ICU nurses' quality of professional life: a crosssectional study. Nurs. Crit. Care **28**(2), 193–201 (2023). https://doi.org/10.1111/nicc.12738
33. Litwic-Kaminska, K., et al.: Resilience, positivity and social support as perceived stress predictors among university students. Int. J. Environ. Res. Public Health **20**(19), 6892 (2023)
34. OECD: OECD Future of Education and Skills 2030. Conceptual Learning Framework. Concept Note: OECD Learning Compass 2030. Paris (2019)
35. Ryan, R.M., Deci, E.L.: Self-determination theory and the facilitation of intrinsic motivation, social development, and well-being. Am. Psychol. **55**, 68–78 (2000)
36. Vygotsky, L.S.: Thought and Language (A. Kozulin, Ed. and Trans.). MIT Press. (Original work published 1934) (1986)
37. Bruner, J.: The Culture of Education. Harvard University Press (1996)
38. Johnson, D.W., Johnson, R.T.: An educational psychology success story: Social interdependence theory and cooperative learning. Educ. Res. (2009)
39. Bonfiglio, N.S., Renati, R., Costa, S., Rollo, D., Sulla, F., Penna, M.P.: An exploratory study on the relationship between video game addiction and the constructs of coping and resilience. In: 2020 IEEE International Symposium on Medical Measurements and Applications (MeMeA), pp. 1–5. IEEE (2020)
40. Redecker, C., Punie, Y.: European Framework for the Digital Competence of Educators (DigCompEdu) (2017)
41. Hattie, J., Timperley, H.: The power of feedback. Tijdschrift voor Medisch Onderwijs **27**(1), 50–51 (2008). https://doi.org/10.1007/BF03078234
42. Bereiter, C., Scardamalia, M.: Education for the knowledge age: designcentered models of teaching and instruction. Handb. Educ. Psychol. **2**, 695–713 (2006)
43. Bandura, A.: Self-efficacy: The Exercise of Control. Freeman, W.H (1997)
44. Dillenbourg, P.: Collaborative Learning: Cognitive and Computational Approaches. Elsevier (1999)
45. Sen, S., Umemoto, K., Koh, A., Zambonelli, V.: Diversity and social justice in planning education: a synthesis of topics, pedagogical approaches, and educational goals in planning syllabi. J. Plan. Educ. Res. **34**(4), 465–471 (2017)
46. Drew, C.: Educational podcasts: a genre analysis. E-Learn. Digit. Media **14**(4), 201–211 (2017)

Developing Entrepreneurial Skills in Inclusive Learning Contexts: The Role of Educational Technologies

Guendalina Peconio$^{(\boxtimes)}$ ⓘ and Martina Rossi ⓘ

Learning Sciences Institute (LSi), University of Foggia, Foggia, Italy
guendalina.peconio@unifg.it

Abstract. Effectively educating for entrepreneurship is one of the challenges of the 21st century, and to do so requires a profound cultural change involving different sectors of education and operating in an inclusive manner. Such a renewal should emphasize creativity, problem-based learning and real-world experience. The aim of the present investigation is to assess the impact that the attitude toward the use of innovative teaching methodologies and educational technologies of a sample of trainee support teachers have on the promotion of entrepreneurial skills, in the classroom context, and how life satisfaction, sense of self-efficacy and attitudes toward inclusion processes act as moderators in the process. Methodologically, a cross-sectional study and the administration of a battery of self-report questionnaires via the google forms platform are planned; in particular, the following instruments are referred to: Intrapersonal Technology Integration Scale (ITIS); ad hoc questionnaire for the assessment of attitude toward the use of teaching methodologies innovative; ad hoc questionnaire for the assessment of perceived usefulness of the development of skills related to entrepreneurship in the school context.

It is expected that attitude toward the use of innovative teaching methodologies and digital technologies is a predictor of positive perceived usefulness of the development of entrepreneurship-related skills in the school context from an inclusive perspective.

Keywords: entrepreneurial skills · teaching methodologies · teacher training

1 Introduction

Entrepreneurship is becoming increasingly central to European policies as a means of addressing contemporary economic, social and environmental challenges. It is no longer just a matter of starting and managing economic activities, but a cross-cutting skill that makes it possible to tackle complex problems in innovative ways, improve quality of life and promote social cohesion. The transformative potential of entrepreneurship lies in its ability to foster creativity, adaptability, and problem-solving, making it an indispensable tool in addressing the multifaceted challenges of the 21st century.

© The Author(s), under exclusive license to Springer Nature Switzerland AG 2025
G. A. Toto (Ed.): ICS exchange 2024, CCIS 2521, pp. 203–213, 2025.
https://doi.org/10.1007/978-3-032-03021-4_14

Recognizing its critical importance, the European Commission has identified entrepreneurship as a strategic priority at all levels of education, as highlighted in its 2011 and 2013 reports. This commitment stems from the understanding that investing in entrepreneurial skills is essential for building a society capable of responding to future challenges with creativity, resilience, and an innovative spirit. Entrepreneurship in education is no longer confined to business or economic disciplines but has become an integral part of fostering personal growth, active citizenship, and employability.

The concept of entrepreneurial competence has evolved significantly in recent years, taking on a broad meaning that transcends traditional business creation. It encompasses the ability to generate new ideas, transform them into practical solutions, and create value for society as a whole. These skills are particularly pertinent in addressing pressing societal issues such as planning an inclusive "Dopo di Noi" for individuals with disabilities and revitalizing Inner Areas that face demographic decline and economic stagnation.

In the "Dopo di Noi" context, entrepreneurial expertise is pivotal in designing innovative models of independent living for people with disabilities. These models not only aim to ensure autonomy but also seek to promote social inclusion, enhance quality of life, and uphold human dignity. Entrepreneurship enables the exploration of creative solutions, such as cooperatives, social enterprises, and technological innovations, to redefine the scope of care and support systems.

Similarly, for Inner Areas grappling with negative demographic pressures, entrepreneurship serves as a critical driver of economic and social regeneration. Entrepreneurial initiatives grounded in the unique local resources of these areas have the potential to stimulate sustainable development. These initiatives may include sustainable tourism, innovative agricultural practices, the preservation and promotion of traditional crafts, and other activities that can reinvigorate local economies while fostering environmental stewardship.

The publication of the European Entrepreneurship Competence Framework (Entre-Comp) in 2016 marked a significant milestone in promoting entrepreneurial competencies across Europe. This framework provides a comprehensive structure for developing and assessing entrepreneurial skills, categorized into three core areas: ideas and opportunities, resources, and action. By emphasizing the broader applications of entrepreneurship, EntreComp recognizes its relevance beyond the economic sphere, extending its impact to social and environmental domains. This holistic perspective highlights how innovative ideas can create value for markets, communities, and ecosystems alike.

Entrepreneurial skills are now considered one of eight key competencies to promote lifelong learning, improve employability and ensure success in a knowledge-based society [1]. The framework underscores the role of creativity and innovation in driving tangible benefits for communities, markets, and the environment. Moreover, these competencies are seen as instrumental in fostering active citizenship, promoting social responsibility, and advancing inclusion, which are essential for the development of equitable and cohesive societies [2].

In this context, education plays a pivotal role in cultivating an entrepreneurial mindset that embraces creativity, innovation, and social responsibility. Beyond merely imparting technical knowledge, educational institutions are tasked with nurturing attitudes and skills that prepare students to contribute meaningfully to societal progress. Central to this mission is the training of teachers, who act as catalysts in instilling entrepreneurial values in future generations. By equipping teachers with the knowledge and tools to foster these skills, education systems can help build a more equitable, sustainable, and resilient society.

The integration of entrepreneurial competencies into education is not just a policy imperative but a societal necessity. It represents a shift toward equipping individuals with the mindset and capabilities to thrive in an ever-changing world while addressing pressing challenges through innovation, empathy, and collaboration. As such, the promotion of entrepreneurship in education emerges as a cornerstone of Europe's strategy to create a sustainable, inclusive, and innovative future.

2 How do Educational Technologies Support Teachers in Acquiring Entrepreneurial Skills?

The acquisition of entrepreneurial skills by teachers is a crucial step in preparing teachers to become promoters of an innovation and problem-solving mindset.

Entrepreneurial skills extend far beyond the ability to start and manage a business; they encompass a broad range of soft skills, including critical thinking, resource management, teamwork, and the ability to transform ideas into concrete actions. For teachers to acquire these skills, innovative teaching methodologies must be adopted, emphasizing active, hands-on learning while integrating digital technologies to facilitate and enhance the educational process.

Among the most effective methodologies for fostering entrepreneurial skills is Project-Based Learning (PBL), which allows teachers to engage in direct, experiential learning by exploring concrete solutions to real-world problems. This approach shifts the focus from traditional, lecture-based instruction to dynamic and participatory learning. PBL encourages teachers to work collaboratively with students on challenges that require creativity, autonomy, and strategic management [3]. Projects allow for simulated entrepreneurial situations in which faculty develop leadership, coordination and strategic planning skills, thus preparing them to pass on these skills effectively.

Another powerful approach is Collaborative Learning (CL), which stimulates entrepreneurial competencies by engaging teachers in group problem-solving activities. By working collectively on complex challenges, teachers enhance their ability to cooperate, negotiate, and resolve conflicts, all of which are vital in entrepreneurial contexts. This experience equips teachers to guide students in tackling professional situations collectively, leveraging individual strengths to achieve shared objectives [4]. The Design Thinking approach, which focuses on creating innovative solutions through empathy and understanding the needs of the end user, can also be integrated into teacher education pathways. This approach enables teachers to think creatively and structurally, combining intuition and analysis to solve complex problems, an essential skill for meeting entrepreneurial challenges [5].

But, what role do educational technologies play in this context?

The role of technologies in the entrepreneurial skills acquisition process cannot be underestimated. Digital technologies offer tools that can enhance learning, facilitating interaction, collaboration and project management more efficiently. Online learning platforms, such as Moodle or Google Classroom, allow teachers to access resources and content in a flexible way, fostering personalized and autonomous learning. These digital tools make it possible to integrate elements of entrepreneurship into teaching activities, offering teachers the opportunity to explore new teaching methods that meet the needs of a rapidly changing world [6].

The use of collaboration technologies such as Microsoft Teams or Trello [7] helps teachers coordinate group projects and activities, simulating real-world work environments in which resource management and meeting deadlines are central. These platforms foster communication and cooperation between teachers and students, allowing them to experience real-world entrepreneurial dynamics. Digital simulations and virtual reality represent other significant opportunities for the acquisition of entrepreneurial skills. Through immersive learning environments, teachers can practice realistic entrepreneurial scenarios, such as running a business or developing a product, thus gaining practical experience that can be passed on to students [8].

While technologies play a pivotal role, it is crucial to adapt methods and tools to the specific context in which they are implemented. This challenge is particularly pronounced in Inner Areas, where structural and logistical obstacles can hinder the acquisition of entrepreneurial competencies. How, in fact, to manage teacher training in so-called Inner Areas?

Italy's inner areas, characterized by low population density and often poor infrastructure, face unique challenges in acquiring entrepreneurial skills. These areas, often isolated from major urban and manufacturing centers, suffer from a number of difficulties that directly affect the ability of schools and communities to develop a robust entrepreneurial culture. Major obstacles include limited training opportunities, poor connectivity, and the absence of economic and professional support networks, all of which make it complex for teachers and students to acquire and apply entrepreneurial skills [9].

One of the most significant challenges is the lack of technological infrastructure. Many schools located in inland areas do not have fast Internet connections or adequate technological tools to access digital educational resources. This limits the ability to implement innovative teaching methodologies, such as project-based learning or the use of e-learning platforms, which are key tools for developing entrepreneurial skills. The lack of advanced technology in these schools not only hinders access to collaborative and digital tools, but also reduces opportunities for teachers to participate in professional development programs that take advantage of distance learning or online courses.

Another critical aspect is geographic and cultural isolation. Inland areas often suffer from not only physical but also cultural isolation, which reduces opportunities for comparison with more dynamic and innovative realities. The absence of frequent connections with other areas makes it difficult for faculty and students to connect with entrepreneurs, companies or institutions that could offer models of inspiration and support. The lack of mentoring networks or local business incubators limits opportunities to develop practical skills and to access resources and investments that could foster entrepreneurship. Under these conditions, it is more difficult to bring out an entrepreneurial mindset that can meet the needs of today's increasingly global and competitive market [10].

Limited training opportunities are an additional obstacle. Schools in inland areas, often underfunded and with limited access to professional development programs, fail to provide teachers with the resources they need to acquire entrepreneurial skills. The scarcity of financial resources often prevents participation in specialized courses or the purchase of materials and tools useful for integrating an entrepreneurial approach into teaching. As a result, teachers may find themselves ill-prepared to impart to their students the skills needed to initiate entrepreneurial projects, thus contributing to the perpetuation of an educational gap between inland and more developed areas [10].

Structural economic difficulties are another critical factor. Inland areas are often characterized by a stagnant or declining economy, with few opportunities for industrial or commercial development. This environment makes it more difficult for schools to actively engage local communities in entrepreneurial projects. The lack of established businesses or a vibrant economic fabric reduces the opportunities for teachers to collaborate with the private sector to deliver hands-on, educational experiences. In addition, students' families, often engaged in traditional sectors such as agriculture or small business, may be less inclined to foster innovation or support entrepreneurship related activities, fueling a cycle of resistance to change [11].

A further difficulty is related to the lack of successful models in local entrepreneurship. Unlike large cities or industrial areas, where there are examples of successful entrepreneurship that can inspire new generations, in inland areas these models are often absent or barely visible. This reduces the motivation of students and teachers to develop entrepreneurial skills, as they do not immediately see the benefits or opportunities offered by entrepreneurship. Instead, the creation of entrepreneurial networks and successful ventures in inland areas could be a stimulus for the growth of a local entrepreneurial culture, capable of attracting resources and new ideas.

In the territory of the Capitana, in northern Apulia, there are two inner areas: the Gargano promontory area and the Monti Dauni area. Schools in the Gargano Promontory and Monti Dauni areas face a range of interconnected challenges that significantly hinder their ability to provide a modern and effective educational experience. A critical issue is the lack of reliable internet connectivity, which makes it difficult for teachers and students to access digital tools and platforms essential for integrating technology into teaching. This limitation not only disrupts the adoption of innovative teaching methodologies but also isolates these schools from the broader digital ecosystem that is rapidly transforming education worldwide.

Another pressing challenge is the inadequate quality of the physical teaching environment. Many classrooms in these areas are either too small or poorly equipped to meet the needs of both students and teachers. This creates an additional layer of difficulty in delivering inclusive and engaging lessons, as overcrowded or unsuitable spaces can impede learning and limit opportunities for collaborative activities.

The scarcity of technological resources further exacerbates these issues. Schools often lack sufficient tools, such as interactive whiteboards, tablets, or projectors, which are increasingly vital for enhancing the teaching and learning process. Without access to these technologies, educators are unable to fully embrace modern pedagogical approaches, leaving students at a disadvantage compared to their peers in more urbanized areas.

Moreover, there is a notable gap in the level of education related to entrepreneurial skills, which are essential for equipping students with the competencies needed to navigate a rapidly changing world. This lack of focus on entrepreneurship education limits opportunities for fostering creativity, problem-solving, and innovation—skills that are critical not only for individual growth but also for driving local economic and social development. The absence of structured programs or resources to cultivate these skills perpetuates a cycle of limited opportunities and stifles the potential for these regions to thrive.

Together, these challenges highlight the urgent need for targeted interventions to bridge the gaps in infrastructure, resources, and training. By addressing these shortcomings, schools in the Gargano Promontory and Monti Dauni areas can begin to create an educational environment that supports both student achievement and broader community growth. These efforts will require collaboration among policymakers, educators, and local stakeholders to ensure that no school is left behind in the pursuit of equitable and innovative education.

And it is in this context that the present study fits. It was in fact conducted an exploratory survey was conducted to investigate the attitudes and beliefs of support teachers in training, regarding skills related to:

1. use of teaching technologies;
2. use of innovative teaching methodologies;
3. perceived usefulness of the entrepreneurial skills described in the EntreComp framework.

3   The Study

Against this backdrop, a survey of an exploratory nature was conducted apt to investigate the attitudes and beliefs of support teachers in training, regarding skills related to use of teaching technologies; use of innovative teaching methodologies; perceived usefulness of entrepreneurial skills described in the EntreComp framework.

3.1 Objective and Research Question

3.1.1 Participants and Procedures

Participants were recruited from students enrolled in the TFA Support course at the University of Foggia in the 2022/2023 academic year. The study was conducted through participants' completion of a self-report questionnaire via the Google Forms platform. At the conclusion of the procedure, the study group that answered the questions pertaining to the socio-demographic section consisted of n = 619 teachers (81.9% female; 17.9% male) with an average age of 39.7 years (SD = 9.3). Regarding the school grade in which they work, the majority (91.6%) work in secondary school. Regarding general teaching experience, the data indicate that 58.3 percent of the teachers have already taught and 41.7 percent have no teaching experience. In relation to this, it is relevant to note that it was made clear to the participants without experience that they should answer the questions regarding concrete activities in the questionnaire, considering internship experience. In addition, the majority of the group (53.2%) of teachers with teaching experience are support teachers (vs. 34.1% are curricular teachers). It is also specified that 596 responses were recorded at the end of the procedure, the reference number of the final sample (n = 596). All socio-demographic characteristics of the sample are shown in Table 1.

Table 1. .

VARIABLES	N (%)
GENDER Women	
	507 (81,9%)
Man	111 (17,9%)
SCHOOL GRADE ATTENDED	
Kindergarten/Primary school	51 (8,2%)
High school	502 (91,6%)
TEACHING EXPERIENCE	
Yes	361 (58,3%)
No	258 (41,7%)
SCHOOL MATTER TAUGHT Matter	132 (34,1%)
Special Needs Support	206 (53,2%)
Other	49 (12,7%)

3.2 Instruments

A cross-sectional study was then conducted through the administration of a self-report questionnaire completed on the Google forms platform and the questionnaires used were as follows: Intrapersonal Technology Integration Scale (ITIS): self-report questionnaire consisting of 21 items designed to assess Social Cognitive Career Theory factors divided into 4 subscales: Self-efficacy (6 items), Outcome Expectations (9 items), Interest (6 items) [12]. Ad hoc questionnaire for the assessment of attitude toward the use of innovative teaching methodologies: constructed with reference to ITIS, the aims to investigate the sense of Self-efficacy, Outcome Expectations and Interest in innovative teaching methodologies. Ad hoc questionnaire to assess the perceived usefulness of developing entrepreneurship-related competencies in the school context: The scale was constructed with the aim of investigating teachers' perceptions of the usefulness of developing entrepreneurial competencies in pupils. The theoretical frame of reference is the Entrepreneurship Competence Framework (EntreComp), through which Europe has identified the 15 competencies related to entrepreneurship.

3.3 Results and Discussion

The data concerning the training received by the participants highlights several significant trends. The most frequently reported training, in addition to that of the TFA (Tirocinio Formativo Attivo), pertains to inclusion processes, with 48% of the sample indicating they had received such training. This is followed by training in educational technologies (37.2%) and innovative teaching methodologies (32.7%). Conversely, the least common training received relates to the development of entrepreneurial skills, with only 15.6% of teachers having undergone specific training in areas such as creativity, problem-solving, autonomy, motivation, and perseverance.

Analysis of the administered questionnaires reveals a consistent trend regarding the attitudes of teachers toward the use of innovative pedagogical approaches. The mean attitude score for the use of innovative teaching methodologies is 3.80 (SD = 0.29), slightly higher than that for educational technologies (M = 3.76, SD = 0.28). These findings suggest a generally positive disposition among teachers toward integrating new methods and digital tools into their teaching practice. Notably, the subscale measuring interest is particularly high for both categories: 4.13 (SD = 0.12) for innovative teaching methodologies and 4.08 (SD = 0.15) for educational technologies. This aligns with the observation that many teachers express a high level of interest in these areas, despite not having extensive formal training.

The findings regarding entrepreneurial skill development are particularly noteworthy. Despite being the least covered area in formal training (84.4% of teachers reported no training in this regard), there is a pronounced recognition of the value of such skills in education. The mean score for the perceived usefulness of developing entrepreneurial skills in students is 5.13 (SD = 0.12), the highest among the constructs measured. Teachers emphasized creativity (62.2%), motivation and perseverance (51.7%), and self-awareness (41.4%) as the most important entrepreneurial competencies. This discrepancy between the perceived importance of entrepreneurial skills and the lack of corresponding training indicates a clear area of need within teacher education and professional development programs.

Overall, this exploratory survey underscores significant gaps in teacher training across the four areas analyzed (inclusion processes, educational technologies, innovative teaching methodologies, and entrepreneurial skill development). While the highest levels of training pertain to inclusion processes, 52% of teachers still reported a lack of formal preparation in this area. In contrast, entrepreneurial skill development is the most neglected, with the majority of teachers lacking any training, despite recognizing its importance for student development.

The attitudes expressed by teachers regarding educational technologies and innovative methodologies reflect a higher-than-average interest, suggesting a latent potential for greater integration of these practices in the classroom. However, without sufficient training, the effective application of these tools and methods may remain limited. The data indicates that professional development programs should prioritize addressing these gaps, particularly in fostering entrepreneurial skills, which are increasingly critical in preparing students for future challenges.

3.4 Conclusions

The findings from this exploratory investigation highlight several critical areas for improvement in teacher training, particularly in the context of inclusion processes, innovative teaching methodologies, educational technologies, and the development of entrepreneurial skills. While a significant portion of teachers has received training in inclusion, there remain notable gaps, particularly in adapting educational practices to cater to diverse learning needs. The integration of educational technologies and innovative pedagogies demonstrates potential, with teachers showing a high level of interest despite limited formal preparation. However, the most significant shortfall lies in the lack of training related to entrepreneurial skills, an area of increasing importance given its potential to foster both individual and community growth.

Entrepreneurial skills, as highlighted in recent literature, provide a strategic opportunity for addressing critical socio-economic challenges, particularly in Inner Areas that face issues such as depopulation and economic stagnation. These skills, which encompass creativity, problem-solving, and the ability to translate ideas into actions, are essential not only for individual professional growth but also for broader territorial development. Innovative teaching methodologies and the strategic use of educational technologies can play a crucial role in fostering these competencies. Yet, the data suggests that without significant rethinking and restructuring of teacher education programs, the potential of entrepreneurial skills to drive sustainable development may remain underutilized [13].

The study underscores the urgency of redesigning both initial and continuing teacher education programs. These programs should prioritize not only the theoretical aspects of pedagogy but also the practical application of teaching strategies that promote critical competencies, such as inclusion, creativity, and entrepreneurship. By addressing these gaps, educators can be better equipped to nurture skills that support individual learners while also contributing to the socio-economic regeneration of their communities. This dual focus on personal and collective growth is particularly important in regions like Inner Areas, where educational interventions can have a transformative impact on the local economy and social fabric.

To bridge the identified training gaps, several actionable recommendations emerge from this study. First, there is a need for networked training initiatives that involve collaboration between local educational institutions, universities, and community stakeholders. Such initiatives can ensure that teacher training is context-specific, addressing the unique challenges and opportunities present in the territories where educators work. This localized approach can foster a deeper understanding of the socio- economic dynamics of the area and encourage the development of solutions tailored to its specific needs.

Second, targeted training activities should be embedded within teacher education programs, such as the TFA Support Course at the University of Foggia. These activities should aim to equip future teachers with the skills necessary to implement inclusive practices, innovative teaching methodologies, and entrepreneurial skill development in their classrooms. This targeted approach would not only enhance teachers' competencies but also encourage them to become change agents capable of driving innovation and progress in their schools and communities.

212 G. Peconio and M. Rossi

Third, indirect internship opportunities as part of teacher training programs can provide invaluable practical experience. These internships would allow trainees to apply innovative strategies in real-world classroom settings, offering a hands-on approach to refining their teaching methods. By engaging with diverse student populations and experimenting with new pedagogical tools, future teachers can better understand the challenges and opportunities inherent in modern education.

Furthermore, entrepreneurial networks and mentoring opportunities should be established to provide ongoing support to teachers, particularly those in Inner Areas. These networks could include collaborations with local businesses, NGOs, and educational leaders who can offer guidance, share best practices, and help educators integrate entrepreneurial concepts into their teaching. Mentoring programs, in particular, can bridge the gap between theoretical training and practical application, enabling teachers to develop their entrepreneurial mindset while fostering similar skills in their students.

The integration of digital technologies in teacher training also requires significant attention. Tools such as virtual reality, online learning platforms, and collaborative technologies can enhance the learning experience for teachers, providing them with innovative ways to explore and apply entrepreneurial skills. For instance, virtual reality simulations can immerse teachers in realistic scenarios where they must navigate complex problem-solving challenges, allowing them to practice the very skills they aim to teach. Platforms like Microsoft Teams or Trello can also be incorporated into training programs to simulate entrepreneurial environments, enabling teachers to manage projects, collaborate effectively, and refine their organizational skills.

Despite these proposed solutions, the unique challenges faced by Inner Areas require additional, context-specific strategies. These areas often lack technological infrastructure, adequate funding, and access to professional development programs. Addressing these barriers will require systemic investment and innovative approaches that prioritize equity in education. For example, providing schools in Inner Areas with high-speed internet access and modern technological tools can significantly enhance their ability to implement entrepreneurial training. Additionally, establishing local hubs or centers of excellence dedicated to innovation and entrepreneurship could serve as catalysts for change, connecting schools with resources, training, and mentoring opportunities. It is essential to cultivate a culture of entrepreneurship within Inner Areas by showcasing successful local models. These examples can serve as inspiration for teachers and students alike, demonstrating the tangible benefits of entrepreneurial skills and encouraging broader community participation. By highlighting success stories and fostering a sense of possibility, educators can help dismantle resistance to change and build a foundation for sustainable growth.

In conclusion, this study emphasizes the pressing need for a strategic reprogramming of teacher education. By addressing the current gaps, particularly in fostering entrepreneurial skills, the educational system can better prepare teachers to support not only the academic success of their students but also the socio-economic development of the communities they serve. A holistic approach to teacher education, integrating inclusion, innovation, and entrepreneurship, is crucial for ensuring long- term sustainability and growth. This vision aligns with broader societal goals of equity, resilience, and progress, reaffirming the pivotal role of education in shaping a better future for individuals and communities alike.

References

1. Rațiu, A., Maniu, I., Pop, E.L.: EntreComp framework: a bibliometric review and research trends. Sustainability **15**(2), 1285 (2023)
2. López-Núñez, M.I., Rubio-Valdehita, S., Díaz-Ramiro, E.M.: The role of individual variables as antecedents of entrepreneurship processes: emotional intelligence and self-efficacy. Front. Psychol. **13**, 978313 (2022)
3. Chularee, S., Tapin, J., Chainok, L., Chiaranai, C.: Effects of project-based learning on entrepreneurship skills and characteristics of nursing students. Nurs. Health Sci. **26**(3), e13160 (2024)
4. Wasim, J., Youssef, M.H., Christodoulou, I., Reinhardt, R.: The path to entrepreneurship: the role of social networks in driving entrepreneurial learning and education. J. Manag. Educ. **48**(3), 459–493 (2024)
5. Pratomo, L.C., Wardani, D.K.: The effectiveness of design thinking in improving student creativity skills and entrepreneurial alertness. Int. J. Instr. **14**(4), 695–712 (2021)
6. Jafari-Sadeghi, V., Garcia-Perez, A., Candelo, E., Couturier, J.: Exploring the impact of digital transformation on technology entrepreneurship and technological market expansion: the role of technology readiness, exploration and exploitation. J. Bus. Res. **124**, 100–111 (2021)
7. de Souza, M.L.P., de Souza, W.C., Freitas, J.S., de Melo Filho, L.D.R., Bagno, R.B.: Agile roadmapping: a management tool for digital entrepreneurship. IEEE Trans. Eng. Manage. **69**(1), 94–108 (2020)
8. Espinoza-Guzmán, L.V., García-Herrera, D.G., Erazo-Álvarez, J.C., Narváe-Zurita, C.I.: Immersive education for entrepreneurship and management disciplines: metaverse's experience. Metaverse **1**(1), 9 (2020)
9. Battisti, A.: Resilience of inner areas. Regeneration and Enhancement Strategies in Small Towns, pp. 1–301. Technische Universität München Verlag (2020)
10. Mastronardi, L., Romagnoli, L.: Community-based cooperatives: a new business model for the development of Italian inner areas. Sustainability **12**(5), 2082 (2020)
11. Buratti, N., Albanese, M., Sillig, C.: Interpreting community enterprises' ability to survive in depleted contexts through the humane entrepreneurship lens: evidence from Italian rural areas. J. Small Bus. Enterp. Dev. **29**(1), 74–92 (2022)
12. Benigno, V., Chiorri, C., Chifari, A., Manca, S.: Adattamento italiano della intrapersonal technology integration scale, uno strumento per misurare gli atteggiamenti degli insegnanti nei confronti delle TIC. G. Ital. Psicol. **40**(4), 815–838 (2013)
13. Battisti, A.: Abitare le aree interne per vivere insieme passato e futuro. In: IL RECUPERO DEI CENTRI STORICI MINORI VII Convegno Diffuso Internazionale San Venanzo-Terni, 17–21 settembre 2019, pp. 81–86. Palombi Editori (2020)

Theatrical Practices to Improve the Emotional Involvement of Online and in Presence Learning Experiences

Nadia Carlomagno[1]([✉]) [iD], Maria Vittoria Battaglia[2] [iD], and Valeria Vadalà[3] [iD]

[1] Suor Orsola Benincasa University, Naples, Italy
nadia.carlomagno@unisob.na.it
[2] Niccolò Cusano University, Rome, Italy
mariavittoria.battaglia@unicusano.it
[3] Pegaso University, Naples, Italy
valeria.vadala@unipegaso.it

Abstract. In recent decades, the centrality of the body in cognitive processes, supported by scientific developments, has been integrated into pedagogical theories that recognise the unity between cognitive, bodily and emotional dimensions. The bioeducational approach emphasises the importance of recognising, managing and interpreting one's own and others' emotions in order to develop social and cognitive skills that are fundamental to mental health, as outlined in the WHO's mental health plan 2013–2030.

The research presented aims to explore how theatre practices, which facilitate emotional and relational contact, can promote students' mental health, embracing a holistic and transdisciplinary perspective that integrates pedagogy, art and neuroscience. The research fits in with previous studies that promote a didactic approach centred on the performative role of the body. The aim is to test whether such an approach, both in presence and online, can improve students' perception of their emotional states and their involvement, fostering inclusion and psycho- physical *well-being*. Using the CReAP + T model (Creativity-Corporeality, Relation, Emotion, Action, Performativity + Technology/Training), students were asked to reflect on their emotional state at the beginning and end of the courses. The results, analysed qualitatively and quantitatively, indicate that the performative approach was effective in both physical and virtual environments. This research supports the idea that the impact of technologies on learning depends on the strategies adopted by teachers, which, if effective, can generate inclusive teaching and promote students' psycho-physical *well-being*, regardless of the learning context.

Keywords: Theatre · Emotional Involvement · Psycho-physical *well-being* · Online and in-person learning

N. Carlomagno—Author of the paper. She is the main researcher of the project; she designed the project and developed the research. She wrote Introduction; Theoretical Framework 2.1 Performative didactics, emotions, action and relation; 3 Research design and Methodology. Maria Vittoria Battaglia is the co-author of the paper, she wrote the Sect. Theoretical Framework 2.3 Emotions and mental health; 4 Results and 5 Discussion. Valeria Vadalà is the co-author of the paper, she wrote the Sect. Theoretical Framework 2.2 Performative practices and CReAP + T approach to promote mental health in education and 6 Conclusion.

G. A. Toto (Ed.): ICS exchange 2024, CCIS 2521, pp. 214–233, 2025.
https://doi.org/10.1007/978-3-032-03021-4_15

1   Introduction

The current emergency in our cultural and social context seems to be represented by the need to re-create relationships between bodies in the construction of a *noicentric* space that repositions the sense of community in educational contexts.

This need tackles the excessive isolation of boys and girls, which began with the measures put in place to contain the Covid-19 pandemic and is exacerbated by the technologic communicative drifts, and which causes a strong impact on the mental health of children and adolescents.

It is necessary, in educational contexts, to start from the reconstruction of a relational life that is able to put at the centre the development of each person's potential in order to recognise, manage and interpret the role of their own and other people's emotions [1].

In this perspective, the educational context assumes a central role, not only in terms of education and training, but also in terms of preventing, promoting and monitoring the neurodevelopment and mental health of children and adolescents.

As a matter of fact, social and cognitive competences [1] are recognised as fundamental competencies for the pursuit of students' mental health, as is emphasised in the World Health Organisation's Mental Health Development Plan 2013–2030, which supports the promotion of educational interventions focusing precisely on social-emotional competences. The WHO, in particular, states that «social and emotional learning programmes at school are among the most effective promotion strategies» [2].

The 2030 Agenda, too, aims to ensure a better quality of life for all individuals, building on the value of sustainability and promoting peace, prosperity and equity. In particular, Goals No. 3 and 4, 'Health and *Well-being*' and 'Quality Education' emphasise the universal right to quality education based primarily on promoting health and *well-being* for all individuals by promoting lifelong learning opportunities for all [3].

This article recognises in theatre practices [4] the possibility of embracing what the WHO proposes, as theatre offers relational [5] and communicative channels that foster contact with one's own and others' emotions, thus promoting students' mental health [6].

2   Theoretical Framework

2.1   Performative Didactics, Emotions, Action and Relation

In a holistic and transdisciplinary epistemological perspective, every scientific contribution becomes an integral and necessary part of the educational phenomenon, thus soliciting dialogue between the diversity of scientific approaches and «inhabiting boundaries as limits to be deconstructed and reinvented» [7].

From this perspective, didactics has been rethought as a category of complex adaptive systems, which expresses the set of characteristics that in turn can be traced back to specific systems made up of the actor/learner, the teacher/director and the context, systems that interact with each other in a non-linear form [8].

It is precisely the relationship [9] and the interaction between systems [10] that becomes the founding element of a *performative didactics* [11] that places the body at the centre of cognitive and socio-relational processes.

In this non-linear and transdisciplinary perspective, of disciplinary encroachment, the latest neuroscientific, neurophenomenological, biological and artistic evidence is corroborated, which, when declined in the pedagogical and didactic sphere, valorise the 'living body', the phenomenal body, overcoming the tension between being a living body - *Leib-Sein* - and having a body - *Körper-Haben* [12].

The concept of a 'dilated' body [13], i.e. a body capable of imprinting a profound relationship between the perceptive, motor, emotional and cognitive systems [14], makes space.

In the vision in which «cognition is action» [14] a corporeal paradigm is structured that values the experience of the relationship made possible through the structuring of a *noicentric* space [15]. This relationship also safeguards the singularity of each person, which is not seen as something pre-given, essentialist and rigid, but as something that is dynamically created through the instrument of the relationship [16].

It is precisely the concept of dynamism, of plastic becoming, that characterises each one of us in our relationship with others that is corroborated by *performative didactics*. In such a vision, education cannot neglect the construction of articulated learning environments, in which there are directed and continuous stimulus actions: the environment is, in fact, perceived by subjective structures that are highly specialised to select and store information and, whatever way each organism explores the environment, the information it obtains from it is necessary, once encoded and wired, for the development of elementary and complex functions that determine its uniqueness [17]. An environment in which it is necessary to resonate with the other ensures the best mechanism that can underpin the mode of relating that is called *empathic relationship*.

In empathy, a key ingredient is precisely ensuring the otherness of the other [18] since our ability to understand each other relies on our ability to resonate together by sharing bodily experience with the other. In this sense, intersubjectivity can be interpreted from intercorporeality.

In this view, learning is regulated, constrained and facilitated by bodily and intersubjective processes and the affectivity that accompanies it [16]. It can be considered, in the bio-educational vision [1], an interactive process that is expressed and realised in an active interchange between individuals and between individuals and the environment through the experience of the relationship that determines the quality of the *noicentric* dimension, born from a dynamic and ever-changing result where emotions and their management assume a determining value. Without emotions, after all, «there is no adequate processing of learned things and perhaps not even learning» [19] and «the ability to retroact emotions through learning seems to reaffirm the key role of training and education as channels within which cultural and experiential experiences become processes for managing the neurobiological datum of emotions» [1].

It is important to emphasise that the ability to adequately regulate the *emotional flow* depends on the ability of individuals to tune in to the emotions they feel.

From this perspective, emotion education plays an increasingly decisive role in training because the ability to recognise, manage and interpret the role of one's own and others' emotions determines the effective development of social and cognitive skills [1].

«Emotions accompany us at every stage of our lives. They are always present and decisive and tend to dominate. [...] They accompany us and shape us throughout our lives. [...] And they are emotions of defiance, of self-affirmation, also of jealousy and envy, of caring and caring-for-self and many others. The subject enters a status in which more and more such emotions demand more control, more commitment and filtering and the capacity for balance and personal synthesis. Thus they are rationalised and this happens through a work of conscience, which sets boundaries, assumes rules, fixes borders. [...] In every age, emotions nourish and govern us, but it is always up to the ego and its conscience to regulate them, enhance them, integrate them in their pluralism and conflictuality. Under the guidance of a conscience enlightened and made fruitful by culture» [20].

In the light of these reflections, it is of fundamental importance to use a methodological approach focused on the didactic experience centred on the body in action that knows how to stimulate empathic relations in the exploration of the self, starting from a *noicentric* vision.

A *performative didactics* that conceives the individual as the result of WITH, i.e. of the relationship, together with the notion of identity [18] that through theatrical practices is able to activate spaces of confrontation and excavation in an active, inclusive, laboratory, dialogical and co-evolutionary form [21]. As the British director Barba argues, «theatre is an art of relationship expressed in a dialogue with or without words» [13].

It is precisely through the use of theatrical performance practices in education that the process of drawing out the subject's identity is fostered, in the confrontation between what is inside and what is outside, between the self and the you, between self and other-than-self, and thus a confrontation with the emotional dimension of one's own and of otherness that is constitutive of our singularity. In the exploration of one's own self, one's uniqueness emerges in the sharing with the group, deeply stimulating the sense of collectivity and intercorporeality [22].

After all, the theatre has always been a place for the exploration of the self towards otherness, a relational space for crossing our borders [5], where it is possible to be mirrored in the other and resonate with the other [23], thus opening up to the intersubjective and communitarian vision of knowledge, through formative, performative and transformative experiences [4].

2.2 Performative Practices and CReAP + T Approach to Promote Mental Health in Education

The WHO recognises social and emotional competencies as fundamental to the pursuit of mental health of individuals and highlights the importance of social and emotional learning programmes within the educational context, supporting the promotion of educational interventions focused on social-emotional competencies [2].

In 2015, the United Nations with the approval of the 2030 Agenda, characterised by 17 Goals for Sustainable Development, aims to guarantee the universal right to quality education for all individuals, with a focus on the acquisition of social-emotional learning skills by students, skills that are fundamental to the concept of *Education for All* by supporting the promotion of more welcoming and inclusive policies, practices and cultures.

Within the meaning of the International Classification of Functioning, Disability and Health (ICF), *well-being* is not determined by the presence or absence of disease, but encompasses all aspects of human health and some components of *well-being* relevant to an individual's health. In fact, a person's functioning and health status is considered to be the result of the complex, global and multidimensional interaction between biological, bio-structural, functional, capacity, social participation and environmental and personal contextual factors [24].

Performative didactics, as outlined by Carlomagno [4] and Rivoltella [25], can be thought of as an educational programme of emotional learning, since it uses theatre practices that offer relational and communicative channels that foster contact with one's own emotions and those of others, thus promoting students' mental health.

The cognitive and emotional dimensions are, in fact, decisive aspects for overall growth and the promotion of an individual's mental health [6].

Through active involvement, creative expression, collaborative learning and the development of emotional skills, *performative didactics* not only enriches the educational experience, but also acts as an important support tool for students' psychological *well-being*, accepting what is proposed by the WHO in its mental health guidelines 2013–2020, in which it calls for the development of educational interventions capable of bringing students into contact with their emotions and promoting the development of appropriate social-emotional skills.

Performative education, through the CReAP + T approach, whose acronym stands for Creativity-Body, Relation, Emotion, Practice, Action, Performativity + Technology or Training, depending on whether this method is used in presence or distance learning, works towards developing and safeguarding the students' mental health, since this method works on the emotions, performativity, and creativity of the individual, and by using training, is able to lead the subject to greater knowledge and awareness of him/herself, towards a recognition of his/her own potential and an acceptance of his/her own limits. Through a process of self-discovery and self-awareness, in fact, the subject recognises and values his/her uniqueness and characteristics and, by recognising him/herself in the gaze of the other, contributes to the creation of more positive and empathic learning environments that generate *well-being* [26].

The CReAP + T model, [27] using performative practices, embraces the structural coupling construct of Embodied Cognition [14] that is based on the interdependence and interconnection between mind, body and emotions.

This type of training is aimed at improving the interpretative, physical and emotional skills necessary for teaching, as at the centre of the educational process is the intersubjective relationship in all its forms - with the surrounding environment, between students, and between students and teachers - similarly to what happens in the theatrical experience [27]. As the Polish director Jerzy Grotowski underlines, the theatrical event, as well as the educational one «it cannot exist without the actor/spectator relationship, without the communion of direct and living perception» [5]. This approach promotes the development of socio-emotional skills in the individual by involving mental and cognitive processes, interconnected with as many functions concerning emotional regulation, bodily sensoriality (breath, position, action, bodily functions, individual parts of the body), sensations, mind and mental objects [28], bringing into play emotional intelligence [29], which allows the individual to recognize their own and others' emotional states.

The approach gives centrality to the body, implementing actor-based practices in teaching, such as body training actions and autopoietic feedback strategies, which recall the here and now, to an active and participatory presence of the individual [30].

In particular, *autopoietic feedback* is seen as a loop that allows the co-construction of the interaction between actor and spectator, or teacher and learner, determining the rhythms of both the scenic action and didactic learning.

This process reflects the empathic understanding between the parties involved, in which sharing the same bodily state facilitates a direct and immediate understanding, which underlines how intersubjectivity and the relationship emerge from the integration between bodily experience and cognitive processes, which together constitute the basis of a form of *empathic* understanding [18].

In the teaching field, as in the theatre field, the practice of training is fundamental not only to develop the technical skills of individual subjects, but also to help them explore and express their emotions, work effectively in group dynamics and build a presence, physical and emotional, aware, convincing and authentic. Theatre training in particular can include a wide range of activities, including warm-up exercises, which consist of physical and vocal activities, breathing and relaxation techniques, useful for controlling breathing and reducing tension, thus improving stage presence and concentration and awareness, which aim to improve the ability to concentrate and awareness of oneself, others and the surrounding environment, with the aim of achieving a condition of optimal psycho-physical *well-being* [31].

Work on the body also includes techniques to develop body awareness, physical expression and stage movement, while vocal techniques are essential for improving the quality of the subject's voice, diction, projection and vocal modulation.

In fact, training plays a role of fundamental importance in teaching-learning processes as it allows the subject to come into contact with himself, with his own emotions, with others and with the context in which he is inserted.

This bodily and emotional self-awareness will allow him to significantly live an experience that will prove transformative [32]. The integration of theatre practices with other forms of educational intervention represents a significant innovation, capable of meeting the needs of holistic and multisensory learning. Theatre in education is not limited to artistic enrichment, but takes the form of an interdisciplinary tool that stimulates cognitive, socio-emotional and relational skills, finding application in numerous pedagogical approaches. This integration is based on theories of experiential learning, socio-emotional education and neuroscience, which support the centrality of the body and emotions in the learning process. The experiential approach, as theorised by Kolb [33] states that learning is a cyclical process based on direct experience, reflective observation, abstract conceptualisation and active experimentation. Theatre practices, through techniques such as *role-playing* and simulation, allow students to experience situations first-hand, stimulating deep understanding and critical thinking, and, integrated with *project-based learning* and *problem-based learning*, allow students to explore real scenarios and solve problems creatively, linking theory to practical experience. Through theatre, students not only acquire knowledge, but also develop analytical and reflective skills and improve their ability to transfer what they have learnt to new and different contexts. In theatre practices, students can express themselves through body, voice and movement, reducing the importance of formal verbal and cognitive skills. According to Vygotsky [34] learning takes place through social interaction, in this vision the theatre presents itself as a safe, welcoming and accessible environment for all, in which everyone has a role to play in its co- construction. In an inclusive context, characterised by the absence of judgement, theatre facilitates the acceptance of diversity and collaboration among peers, promoting mutual respect and breaking down barriers that can hinder learning. Theatre practices, in synergy with other forms of educational intervention, not only enrich the teaching experience, but also transform learning into an engaging and participatory process, promoting a didactic approach in which body and emotions communicate, creating an inclusive, dynamic educational context geared to the overall development of the student.

2.3 Emotions and Mental Health

In literature, emotions have been grouped according to various taxonomies - such as the one proposed by Ekman [35], who identifies happiness, fear, anger, disgust, sadness and surprise as the six basic emotions, or Damasio's subdivision into primary and secondary emotions [36]. An interesting theory that accounts for the various dimensions of affect, i.e. cognitive, emotional, social, neuronal, bodily, etc. is that of Tomkins [37]. In the present article, Tomkins' theory turns out to be an important theoretical reference by virtue of its peculiarity in speaking of emotions as *biography*, as the reading and interpretation of affect starting from the individual's experience, thus linking the state of biological activation to the individual's lived experience. This perspective is particularly appropriate in the context of qualitative research such as the one we illustrate here, which embraces a subjective perspective based on students' personal experience and the interaction that develops in the peer group. Tomkins identifies eight basic emotions, divided into:

- Positive emotions: interest-excitement, amusement-joy;
- Neutral emotions: surprise-alarm;
- Negative emotions: distress-anguish, disgust, fear-terror, anger, shame.

A peculiar and innovative aspect is that Tomkins begins his topography of emotions with *interest-excitement*, the «most seriously neglected» affect [37] because it has never been counted in the taxonomies of emotions. Interest is a positive affection because it is gratifying, it allows motivation. Interest-excitement is differentiated from *surprise* because the latter is neutral: while interest motivates action, surprise is blocking, interrupting any activity in progress. Whereas surprise interrupts existing circuits, interest extends them, creates new connections and expands our experiential networks. Surprise remains a neutral rather than a negative affect because it indicates a state of expectation, of alertness to the experience that is to come: the reaction to it will then be a positive or negative affective state. This is why Tomkins calls surprise «the resetting affect» [37] and compares it to the commercial break in television programmes: it is a state of pause that prepares for subsequent experiences and states that take into account the information that triggered the surprise response. In this description of surprise it seems to be similar to what we generically call curiosity, although the latter, when it does not indicate a state of interdiction or astonishment with respect to experience but a form of motivation to action corresponds rather to the affect of interest-excitement. The second positive emotion is *joy*, or more precisely the *amusement-joy* system, which for Tomkins is structurally social and tied to social bonds: «The general role of enjoyment is critical in promoting courage to cope with fear and pain, and in promoting frustration tolerance» [37].

Negative affects, on the other hand, are five, and even these have a social and inter-personal configuration because they affect both the individual and the entire ecological system around him. It is precisely because of this social value that it is crucial for Tomkins to minimise them, to reduce them as much as possible. Among the negative affects Tomkins counts is a general state of *distress*, which characterises many everyday experiences of discomfort, making the individual tired and not very open to stimulation and interest. *Fear* and *anger* are stronger. Interesting is the treatment of *shame*, a pri-marily social emotion, defined by Tomkins as an auxiliary affect because it requires the prior activation of a positive affect: shame is activated by the inhibition of interest or joy, leaving the subject in a state of disorientation and «I want, but» suspension [37].

Tomkins' affect theory offers very interesting insights when it comes to interpreting learners' subjective experiences in order to develop interventions aimed at developing learners' mental health.

The WHO defines mental health as «a state of mental *well-being* that enables people to cope with the stresses of life, realise their abilities, learn well and work well, and contribute to their community. It […] underpins our individual and collective abilities to make decisions, build relationships and shape the world we live in» [31], thus recognises that mental health is defined by bio-socio-emotional aspects and the need to minimise negative affects - as proposed by Tomkins' theory - and instead stimulate interest and joy, emotional systems fundamental to perception, cognition, relationships and all human activities. It is also interesting to emphasise how the psychologist characterises negative affects as intrinsically unacceptable, as they are experienced as punitive not only towards the individual but towards human beings in general: «All the negative affects trouble human beings deeply. Indeed, they have evolved just to amplify and deepen suffering and to add insult to the injuries of the human condition» [37]. This is why dealing with negative emotions, with the aim of minimising them and reducing their impact on a person's life, is as much an individual as a social challenge. Mental health, both in Tomkins' theory and in the goals of the WHO, therefore depends on social-emotional skills, as the inhibition of negative emotions and the maximisation of positive emotions cannot be separated from social and interpersonal - as well as intrapersonal - interaction.

3   Research Design

This exploratory - comparative research is part of a broader investigation and in continuity with previous studies [27, 38] that aim to promote a different way of teaching centred on the performative role of the body [39]. The aim of our study is to explore the hypothesis that a teaching approach focused on the performative role of the body, both in presence and online, can promote conditions of psycho-physical *well-being* [27, 38], by recalling students' perception of positive emotional states.

Methodology

The methodology used in this qualitative-quantitative research makes use of the CReAP + T approach [27], whose acronym stands for Creativity-Corporeality, Relation, Emotion, Action, Performativity + Technology/Training, a model that uses performative theatre training practices declined in Art based research [40] to restore centrality to the students' bodily and emotional dimension.

The CReAP + T approach, characterised by training activities, uses practices based on performative activities, on body-conscious breathing, on the physical sensation of awakening and relaxation, on eye contact, on the exploration of one's own body in space, on the exploration of one's own emotions, working in this sense on the individual, group and spatial dimensions, thus restoring centrality to the students' bodily and emotional dimensions. The focus is on the present moment of being 'here and now', in conscious and authentic presence, in deep connection with oneself, with the other and with the context.

An approach that allows the sample of students involved to practise the training experience in both physical and virtual environments and to explore the lived and perceived emotional state before and after the experience.

Sample. The research was carried out on sample of university students who attended the compulsory workshops *Giocando s'impara, tecniche per l'animazione e la comunicazione teatrale* included in the third year of the degree course in Educational Sciences and the workshop *Drammaturgia didattica performativa* included in the second year of the degree course in Primary Education Sciences of the University Suor Orsola Benincasa of Naples in the academic year 2022/2023.

The entry questionnaire was administered to a sample of 1149 students (1111 female, 37 male, 1 non specified) of whom 320 attended the workshop *Giocando s'impara, tecniche per l'animazione e la comunicazione teatrale* and 829 the workshop *Drammaturgia didattica performativa*.

Insofar as not all the students were present, the exit questionnaire was administered to a sample of 963 (930 female, 32 male, 1 non specified) of whom 257 attended the workshop *Giocando s'impara, tecniche per l'animazione e la comunicazione teatrale* and 685 the workshop *Drammaturgia didattica performativa*.

The prevalence of the sample is therefore purely female and is characterised by students mainly from the Campania Region with an average age of 19.

Data Collection. The data were obtained through the administration of an anonymous questionnaire - with the consent of the participants - in which the students were asked to reflect on the perception of their own emotional state at the beginning (T0) and at the end of the courses (T1), with the aim of finding out whether processes of change were generated through this approach. Students had to choose a word that represented their emotional state at the time of completion and then explain it in a short text.

We collected 1149 responses for T0 and 963 for T1 regarding the physical learning experience.

In the second part of the research, we compared these results with those obtained in previous research related to online courses, which had been collected from students' logbooks, who were similarly asked to choose a word for their emotional state and explain it in a short paragraph; for this digital experience we collected 2130 final responses.

4   Results

Table 1. Answers to the in presence course questionnaire to the question: What emotion are you feeling right now? Please select an option from those proposed.

Domanda	T0 (1149 risp.)	T1(963 risp.)
Gioia	30%	46%
Speranza	14%	29%
Allegria	23%	35%
Sorpresa	25%	14%
Ansia	19,9%	3,4%
Noia	4.4%	1,6%
disagio	8,5%	1,6%
Vergogna	4,4%	0,8%
Paura	4%	0,7%
Tristezza	4%	1,6%

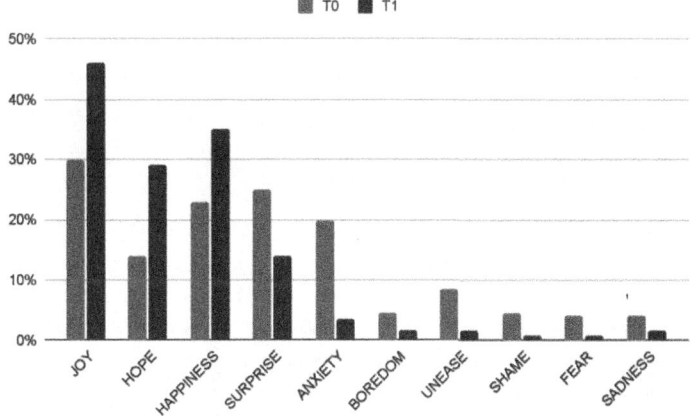

Graph 1. Answers to the in presence course questionnaire to the question: *What emotion are you feeling right now? Please select an option from those proposed.*

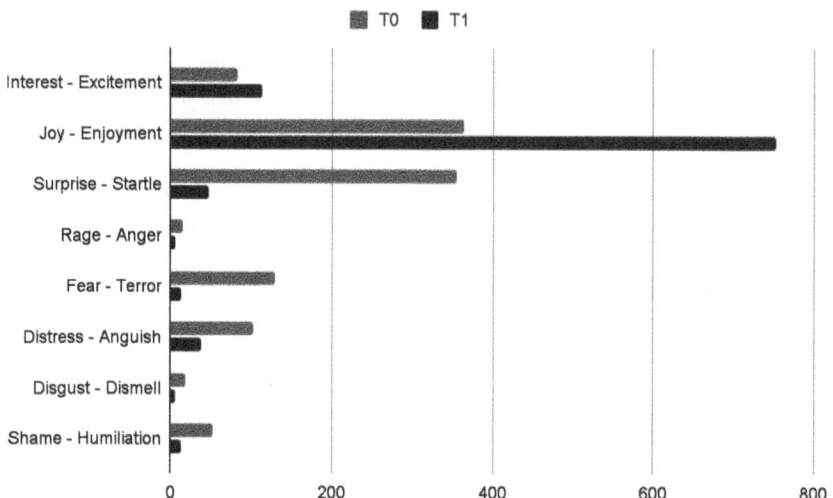

Graph 2. Emotions grouped according to the categories proposed by Tomkins' taxonomy

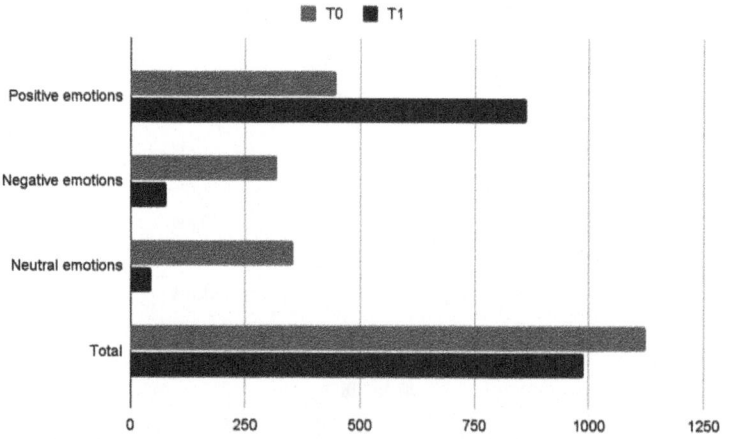

Graph 3. Comparison between positive emotions and negative emotions at the beginning and end of the in presence course

5   Discussion

5.1   Data Analysis

The data obtained from the questionnaires administered to the students of the in presence course were subjected to a qualitative-quantitative analysis (Table 1; Graphs 1, 2 and 3) and subsequently compared with the results of previous research conducted online (Graph 4), in order to verify whether the use of the *performative didactics* of the CReAP + T approach can be equally effective in both physical and virtual learning environments.

In order to investigate the emotional states of the students and how these may or may not be influenced by the adoption of specific didactic methodologies, a questionnaire

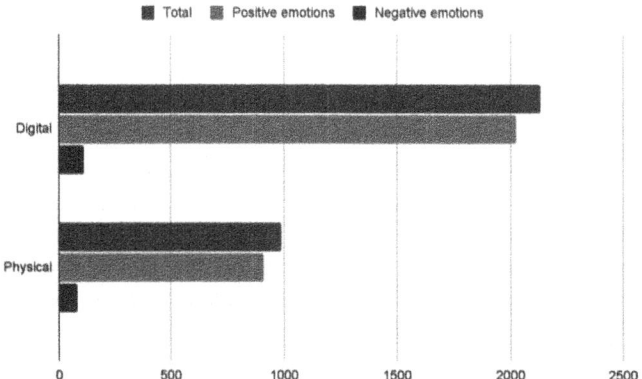

Graph 4. Comparison of positive and negative emotions at the beginning and end of the online and in-presence course

was administered at the beginning (T0) and at the end of the workshop (T1) to investigate how emotions had been transformed following the didactic intervention.

Subsequently, the answers from these questionnaires were collected and subjected to a qualitative analysis divided into several phases.

In the first phase, the data from the multiple-choice item were analysed, in which the student in the in presence course was asked to select the option, from those present, that best represented his or her state of mind (Table 1). In Graph 1 we show the variations between the initial answers (T0) and the final answers (T1).

Subsequently, the answers of the open-ended item were analysed: in this section, the students were asked to choose a word representing how they felt at that moment, and to give a brief explanation. The collected words were grouped into emotion categories, in order to then create the comparative graph of pre-intervention (T0) and post- intervention (T1) emotions (Graph 2).

Tomkins' affects were taken as categories under which to group the emotions, adopting his topography and explanations of these affective states to guide us in the classification. It was decided to adopt Tomkins' interpretative perspective because, as already expressed in paragraph 2.3, it is particularly interesting in the context of a course of study in which students are asked to come into contact with and learn about their own emotions, and above all in the context of qualitative research that embraces a subjective perspective, as the psychologist proposes a phenomenological description of lived experiences for the definition of these categories.

In fact, he recognises three dimensions of affective states: a neurological dimension, indicating neural activation, a physiological dimension, referring to bodily responses, and an aesthetic dimension indicating the ways in which the subject consciously experiences these affects, in the form of feelings and emotions, and this last dimension is indicated for interpreting subjective experiences The students' responses were classified according to the macro-categories proposed by Tomkins [37], namely:

- positive emotions: interest, joy;
- neutral emotions: surprise;

– negative emotions: distress, fear, disgust, anger, shame.

The words chosen by the students were therefore grouped according to these categories, starting from a cross-reading of the descriptions of the aforementioned states provided by Tomkins and the explanations written by the students themselves in the questionnaire: it is important to emphasise that we did not start from the words used but from the description of the experience, since the latter often revealed a proximity to a different affective state than the one expressed.

For example, the word 'surprise' revealed in the students' descriptions a positive emotion, one of anxiety reduction, joy or excitement, thus relating more to interest than surprise, which for Tomkins is rather a state of "suspension" and/or alertness.

Thus, by cross-referencing the students' answers and Tomkins' descriptions, the words in the questionnaire were broken down as follows:

- Interest-excitement, described by Tomkins as an emotion that refers to action, motivates to action, is gratifying, and activates a bodily response characterised by lowering of eyebrows, half-closed eyes etc., includes: enrichment, surprise-despite the term, it is not related to surprise-startle because it is described by students as a drive to action - vitality, fulfilment, gratification, satisfaction, concentration - which involves the same bodily response described by Tomkins for interest - excitement, energy, enthusiasm, euphoria, frenzy, interest, novelty, discovery.
- Amusement-joy, a more purely interpersonal positive emotion, can according to Tomkins be found above all in the relationship with the other. It is an emotion that implies security, as it is primarily traced back to the infant- mother relationship. The following words have been traced back to joy: sympathy, joy, security, serenity, relaxation, reflexivity, fortune, positivity, pleasure, participation, peace, wholeness, lightness, freedom, gratitude, luck, trust, contentment, happiness, amusement, fun, courage, control, awareness, empathy, connection, understanding, relief, tranquillity, calm, lightheartedness, comfort, *well-being*.
- Surprise-alarm: curiosity - in this case curiosity was traced back to surprise rather than interest because the students who chose this word described it as a state of anticipation, a desire to see beforehand how the situation would evolve-astonishment, expectation, wonder.
- Anguish, described by Tomkins as a frequent and generic state of sadness, discomfort or tiredness. Thus this category includes: anguish, sadness, luck, stress, restlessness, nostalgia, melancholy, regret.
- Fear-terror: anxiety, agitation, tension, worry, fear.
- Anger, also including frustration and nervousness.
- Disgust, also including indifference, boredom and sickness - understood as physically or metaphorically nauseous states.
- Shame, described by Tomkins as a disorienting and blocking emotion, as 'wanting' without being able to act. It includes: uncertainty, embarrassment, disorientation, discomfort, confusion.

These emotions were then further grouped into positive, negative and neutral emotions: as 'surprise' is a neutral emotion it is reported in isolation, to avoid having to reduce it to a positive or negative state, as this would be a fallacious identification.

This subdivision was made with the aim of comparing the positive and negative emotions felt by the students at the beginning and end of the proposed workshop (Graph 3).

The last stage of the data analysis was carried out with the aim of comparing the outcomes of the teaching intervention in a physical experience - in presence course - and in a digital experience - distance teaching. To this end, it was decided to carry out a multi-level (2 × 2) comparison, i.e. between the positive and negative emotions felt by the students at the end of the course and the relationship between them in the in-presence and distance learning. The data used for the comparison came from the course *Giocando s'impara: tecniche per l'animazione e la comunicazione teatrale* of the a.y. 2021/2022, which was carried out online due to the covid-19 pandemic regulations.

The data for this last course did not come from a questionnaire but from the logbooks in which the students had to answer the same question as in the present questionnaire, namely: *What emotion do you feel right now?* The data are reported in Graph 4, in which the total number of words analysed is also reported. It is essential to emphasise in this regard that the words from the logbooks are numerically greater as the students were not given any limit to the words they could use to describe their emotions.

A note is essential in this regard: in order to make this comparison, the macro category of surprise, which in Tomkins' topography guiding the analysis of emotions in this research is regarded as neutral, will be considered as a positive emotion, in order to align with the interpretative lens used in the previous research we carried out concerning the experience at a distance.

5.2 Results' Discussion

The results show that the intervention succeeded in activating a transformative process on the students' emotions, decreasing negative affective states and increasing positive ones.

With regard to the latter, a marked decrease in interest was noted, characterised mainly by curiosity and expectation for a new experience, to instead see an increase in surprise. This result was an expected one, due to the fact that students do not know what to expect at the beginning of a course and the surprise of taking university courses through practices far removed from the normal frontal lecture.

What is also noticeable is the considerable increase in emotions pertaining to joy, which almost doubled at the end of the course at the expense of negative emotions such as fear, anger, discomfort and shame.

In the macro-category of anger, feelings of annoyance, frustration, tiredness and heaviness were included; although annoyance, frustration and anger per se decreased drastically, tiredness, although decreasing, remained at quite high values: when reading the students' explanations, however, it emerged that it is mainly linked to external and structural factors of the university (lack of connection, transport issues for commuting students, etc.).

The explanations given by the students explicitly illustrate what the numbers and the graph show, namely that as joy increased, negative emotions decreased. In fact, many students expressed feelings of unease, anxiety and fear at the beginning of the course, as illustrated in the sentences below:

I wish I could explain this feeling, but right now I feel like I'm stuck. I am an out-of- school student, post-pandemic I felt drained of all emotion. The only thing I could feel was simple and total apathy. Fortunately, with the help of people who love me, I am able to see life in colour.

I am an out-of-school student, I have not felt enough for more than a year. The anxiety has been suffocating but the desire for redemption is stronger. The pandemic generated by COVID-19 has left deep wounds in all of us. On the other hand, it has taught us how important contact and closeness can be.

I am a very shy person, so attending workshops or courses where there is a lot of confrontation creates a state of anxiety and unease in me. This is because I need to get out of my comfort zone to learn how to communicate better with others.

I feel a little uneasy and anxious about what will be done in this lesson, because I don't know what to expect anyway. I hope it will be a feasible lesson for me and useful to combat my shyness that is wearing me out.

Anxiety about what will happen during this lesson, I am scared of what I don't know, so not knowing what I will have to do in these lessons gives me a sense of agitation

Fear of not being able to achieve my goals, of not being good enough for myself and for others

Right now I have a feeling of emptiness, as if I can't handle situations, can't control them

Stress because I feel that life is not in my favour, everything always seems to go wrong and I can't see the end of the tunnel

I'm stressed about many things and so I'm tired of dealing with situations in my life and my emotions

Agitation because I'm experiencing a lot of stress both psychologically, emotionally and physically

Anxiety in general. I often feel anxiety for fear of not being up to situations.

I feel inadequate with the people I have to deal with because I feel not understood Feeling of impatience. Inability to be serene among many strangers

The theatrical training practices required by the implementation of the CReAP + T method enabled the creation of a welcoming climate, devoid of judgement, in which each student could open up to the other, welcome and be welcomed, get in touch with their own and others' emotions, fundamental elements for achieving a state of *well-being* aimed at preserving mental health.

In the questionnaires at the end of the course, in fact, the explanations concerning states of anxiety and agitation gave way to answers expressing serenity and *well-being*. Here are some examples:

Doing this kind of activity calms me down and frees me from negative feelings

I am happy to have actively participated in the lesson, this allowed me to open up to new people, revealing sides of myself that I often prefer to keep hidden. I think opening up is one of the most beautiful things to do, a gift. Opening up is a gift that you give to another, it makes us feel less alone, because we are all sad sometimes, we are all worried sometimes, and it is right to share the emotions we feel with others.

This activity initially gave me curiosity, but also "fear" about what we were going to do... But now that the lesson is over I feel free and happy. Happy because despite not knowing anyone, by carrying out the activities I managed to make friends, but above

all to trust the other person without ever having met them before, which never happens. Furthermore, I feel free because I understood that I am not the only one with fears and insecurities, but we are all a bit similar and this does not make us "alone". It was a very nice lesson, which I definitely won't forget

I started the journey with a lot of anxiety, I almost didn't want to go because I found myself alone without my friends and I'm always afraid of being alone with people I don't know and I was convinced that I would be alone all day. Instead I plucked up courage and managed to socialise. I'm happy to discover that if I want, I can break down the walls I put up and be able to socialise. For me this is a big victory today. I am happy to have participated in this workshop, it gave me a lot, it helped me a lot

I'm calm right now, even compared to the start of lessons, because I am relaxed and calm today. Through the training and other exercises I left all the thoughts I had outside the classroom and took time to address some issues, to face myself and become aware that it is necessary to take time and focus on oneself to be able to pass it on to others.

I literally feel light, free from constraints. Aware of who I am, of my body and the space it occupies. I feel light, free of those burdens that in a certain sense we carry in our minds, such as: the fear of relating to others, physical contact with others, the discomfort, the embarrassment we feel when we are close to new people, the discomfort of feeling small and inappropriate in a space

At this moment I have just finished the workshop, I can say that I feel truly serene. I freed myself of all the negative tensions I had and I finally feel lighter but above all more aware of myself. At the beginning of the workshop I thought I was serene, but I can say that in reality mine was an illusory serenity, only now I feel really good, carefree, happy.

I feel a feeling of well-being, I feel lighter because I let myself go and do things that I would never have thought of doing, given that I am shy and introverted by nature. It is definitely a feeling that makes me feel good and that I definitely don't want to lose so I will let myself go more and try to be more casual.

After class I feel more relaxed and carefree. It was very useful to carry out the training because thanks to it I am able to have a greater awareness of myself and my body and I am able to overcome shyness.

I've had the opportunity to think about many things that lately give me anxiety, fears... I realised that I don't necessarily have to be the wrong one, maybe I should accept myself and love myself more.

I am very happy with this lesson because thanks to the teacher I now feel very carefree, it seems I have freed myself from the anxiety I had at the beginning of the laboratory

Freedom from the anxiety I had at the beginning and from the fear of judgement from others.

Another interesting aspect that emerges from the results is that relating to the comparison with the online experience. In fact, the questions that gave rise to this research were two: the first asked whether transformative teaching could lead to a positive transformation in students' emotions, reducing states of anxiety and increasing states of *well-being*, while the second asked whether such effects were similar in online and in presence experiences.

Previous research carried out in distance laboratory teaching courses had shown that at the end of the course students experienced positive affective states to a significantly greater extent than negative ones. In that research a t0 had not been proposed, but the data from the t1, administered at the end of the course, had been interpreted in light of the students' logbooks, who declared that they had experienced similar experiences to what the students reported during the course in question. Presence that is the subject of the research illustrated here. Therefore, the similar situation illustrated by Graph 4, which shows the clear predominance of positive emotions over negative ones both in the online course and in the in presence course, and the similar experiences lived by the students allow us to hypothesise that there was also a similar situation in the online course.

6   Conclusion

The results of the research presented confirm the hypothesis that the adoption of performative teaching practices can be an effective method for promoting students' mental health, developing socio-emotional skills and promoting emotional intelligence. These practices have proven capable of reducing anxiety, negative sensations and emotions and, on the contrary, promoting states of *well-being* and serenity in students, aligning with the WHO guidelines for mental health for the period 2013–2020 [2], which encourage educational interventions focused on developing emotional skills. A further significant aspect that emerged from this study is the comparison with the experience carried out in distance learning; the data collected indicate a clear predominance of positive emotions in both modes (in presence and at a distance), suggesting that performative practices are effective regardless of the learning context, thus corroborating the hypothesis that «the impact of technologies on learning depends on the teacher and the strategies he/she adopts» [41, 42]. However, it is difficult to state at present whether these results can be generalised to other educational contexts, since the research was carried out on a sample of university students of Educational Sciences, who may therefore already have a degree of awareness concerning emotional well-being and a particular interest in innovative teaching methodologies. However, as the adopted theatre practices focus on universal aspects of human experience, such as body and emotional awareness, and as they aim at creating an inclusive and participative learning setting, it is plausible to suggest a potential transferability of the results. Furthermore, in order to ensure the reliability and robustness of the results, a triangulation was conducted in the data analysis with the aim of minimising possible interpretative bias and maintaining consistency in the coding process; this triangulation, together with the use of *low-inference descriptors* [43], i.e. terms or phrases as similar as possible to the original data, helped to strengthen the validity of the results. Therefore, despite the limitations of the research, the results that emerged support the idea that an educational approach based on the performative role of the body can positively transform students' emotional experience, promoting an inclusive educational environment conducive to psycho-physical *well-being*, as demonstrated in previous research [27, 36], both in physical and virtual learning environments.

Disclosure of Interests. The authors have no competing interests to declare that are relevant to the content of this article.

References

1. Frauenfelder, E., Santoianni, F., Ciasullo, A.: Implicito bioeducativo. Emozioni e cognizione, RELAdEI **7**(1), 42–51 (2018)
2. World Health Organization: Comprehensive mental health action plan 2013–2030 (2021)
3. United Nations: Transforming our World: the 2030 Agenda for Sustainable Development (2015)
4. Carlomagno, N.: Le potenzialità didattiche delle arti sceniche. Educ. Sci. Soc. **1**, 346–359 (2020)
5. Grotowski, J.: Vers un théâtre pauvre. L'âge d'Homme, Lausanne (1968)
6. Felsman, P., Seifert, C.M., Sinco, B., Himle, J.H.: Reducing social anxiety and intolerance of uncertainty in adolescents with improvisational theater. Arts Psychotherapy **82**, 101985 (2023)
7. Carlomagno, N.: I linguaggi non lineari della narrazione e della comunicazione nella scena e nella didattica (a cura di), Edizione Scholè, Brescia (2023)
8. Sibilio, M.: La didattica semplessa. Liguori, Napoli (2013)
9. Buber, M.: Ich und Du. Insel Verlag, Leipzig (1923)
10. Sibilio, M.: L'interazione didattica. Scholé, Brescia (2020)
11. Carlomagno, N.: La didattica performativa come modello di ibridazione formative. In: Corbi, E., Frosini, T., Villani, P. (eds.) Parrhesia. In dialogo tra i saperi, Studi per Lucio d'Alessandro, Editoriale scientifica, Napoli (2023)
12. Husserl, E.: Merleau-Ponty M. In: Slatman, J. (ed.) The Körper-Leib Distinction, «Weiss_P1.indd» THINK Book Works (2019)
13. Barba, E.: La canoa di carta. Trattato di antropologia teatrale. Mulino, Bologna (1993)
14. Caruana, F., Borghi, A.M: Embodied Cognition. Una nuova psicologia. Giornale Italiano di Psicologia **40**(1), 23–48 (2013)
15. Gallese, V.: Le due facce della mimesi. La Teoria Mimetica di Girard, la simulazione incarnata e l'identificazione Sociale. Psicobiettivo, XXIX, vol. 2, pp. 77–102 (2009)
16. Gallese, V., Morelli, U.: Cosa significa essere umani? Corpo, cervello e relazione per vivere nel presente. Raffaello Cortina Editore, Milano (2024)

17. Frauenfelder, E.: Perché una relazione tra pedagogia e biologia? Sezione RTH Brain Education Cognition, Napoli (2018)
18. Gallese, V.: The shared manifold hypothesis: from mirror neurons to empathy. J. Conscious. Stud. **8**(5–7), 33–50 (2001)
19. Boncinelli, E.: Il cervello, la mente e l'anima. Mondadori, Milano (1999)
20. Cambi, F.: La forza delle emozioni: per la cura di sé. Pacini Editore, ospedaletto (Pisa), pp. 12–13 (2015)
21. Maturana, H.R., Varela, F.J.: Autopoiesis and cognition: The realization of the living. Springer (1991)
22. Ammaniti, M., Gallese, V.: La nascita dell'intersoggettività: Lo sviluppo del sé tra psicodinamica e neurobiologia. Raffaello Cortina Editore, Milano (2014)
23. Rosa, H.: Pedagogia della risonanza (2016), F. Fiore (a cura di), Scholé, Brescia (2020)
24. Ianes, D., Cramerotti, S.: Usare l'ICF nella scuola. Spunti operativi per il contesto educativo. Erickson, Trento (2011)
25. Rivoltella, P.C.: Neurodidattica. Insegnare al cervello che apprende. Raffaello Cortina, Milano (2012)
26. Kabat-Zinn, J.: Full Catastrophe Living: Using the Wisdom of Your Body and Mind to Face Stress, Pain and Illness. Dell Publishing, New York (1990)
27. Carlomagno, N., Minghelli, V.: Interpersonal Distance in CReAP+T Method in Distance Learning, In AA.VV., Higher Education Learning Methodologies and Technologies Online. Springer, Cham (2022)
28. Mace, C.: Mindfulness e salute mentale. Terapia, teoria e scienza. Astrolabio Ubaldini (2010)
29. Goleman, D.: Intelligenza Emotiva: Che cos'è e perché può renderci felici. Milano: Rizzoli (1996)
30. Fischer-Lichte, E.: Estetica del performativo. Una teoria del teatro e dell'arte. Carocci editore, Roma (2014)
31. World Health Organization: Mental health (2022). https://www.who.int/news-room/fact-she ets/detail/mental-health-strengthening-our-response
32. Mezirow, J.: Apprendimento e trasformazione. Cortina, Milano (2003)
33. Kolb, D.A.: Experiential Learning: Experience as the Source of Learning and Development. Prentice-Hall, Englewood Cliffs (1984)
34. Vygotsky, L.S.: Mind in Society: The Development of Higher Psychological Processes. Harvard University Press, Cambridge (1978)
35. Ekman, P.: Emotions Revealed: Understanding Faces and Feelings. Times Book, New York (2003)
36. Damasio, A.R.: The feeling of what happens: body and emotion in the making of consciousness. Choice Reviews Online **37**(11) (2000)
37. Tomkins, S.: Affect, Imagery, Consciousness. Springer, New York (1962–1963)
38. Carlomagno, N., Battaglia, M.V.: Didactics, theater and well-being in the distance learning experiences. Italian J. Health Educ. Sports Inclusive Didactics **7**(2). EUR, Roma (2023)
39. Carlomagno, N., Cordella, F.M., Minghelli, V., Rivoltella, P.C.: Performative didactis in a technological environment. REM **13**(1), 7–16 (2021)
40. McNiff, S.: Art-based research. In: Knowles, J.G., Cole, A.L. (eds.) Handbook of the Arts in Qualitative Research: Perspectives, Methodologies, Examples, and Issues. Sage Publications, Thousand Oaks (2007)
41. Creswell, J., Plano Clark, V.: Designing and Conducting Mixed Methods Research. Sage, Thousand Oaks (2018)

42. Hattie, J.: Visible Learning: A Synthesis of Over 800 Meta-Analyses Relating to Achievement. Routledge, New York (2009)
43. Seale, C.: Quality in qualitative research. Qual. Inq. **5**(4), 465–478 (1999)

The Importance of Alt Text for Social Media and Outreach in Italian Higher Education: Building Inclusive Best Practices

Amalia Maria Paoletta[✉], Luca Refrigeri, and Francesca Baralla

University of Molise, Campobasso, Italy
amalia.paoletta@unifg.it

Abstract. Alt-text is a crucial component of digital accessibility, providing textual descriptions of images for users who are blind or visually impaired. Despite its importance, Italian Universities often need to pay more attention to implementing alt text on their social media and outreach channels. This lack of accessibility excludes a significant portion of the potential audience and undermines the Universities' commitment to inclusion. This paper examines the current state of alt-text usage among Italian Universities, highlighting the shortcomings and best practices. It then explores the benefits of implementing alt-text for users and institutions, including improved accessibility, increased engagement and enhanced brand reputation.

This research investigates the use of alt-text on the official Instagram profiles of 76 Italian Universities, categorized according to the CENSIS 2023/2024 ranking. The analysis reveals that only a few public and private Universities utilize this crucial accessibility feature. In a staggering 97% of instances, alt-text was entirely missing, prompting the substitution of AI-generated descriptions. These automated descriptions, however, fell short of accuracy, often exhibiting imprecision and a glaring lack of contextual information. Beyond mere compliance, the paper delves into the quality of alt-text present, assessing its accuracy in describing the visual content. It concludes by broadening the scope to consider the potential for enriching alt-text descriptions, moving beyond concise summaries to capture the context and emotions evoked by the images, as exemplified in educational settings for visually impaired individuals. The paper concludes by advocating for adopting alt-text as a standard practice within Italian higher education. Communication on social media should also reflect the inclusivity of the University. By making their digital content accessible to all, Universities can promote inclusivity, diversity, and equity within their communities as an example of a more inclusive society.

Keywords: alt-text · digital accessibility · social media · higher education · inclusion

G. A. Toto (Ed.): ICS exchange 2024, CCIS 2521, pp. 234–243, 2025.
https://doi.org/10.1007/978-3-032-03021-4_16

1 Introduction

In the digital age, where information is increasingly disseminated through visual media, ensuring accessibility for all users is paramount. One crucial aspect of digital accessibility is alternative text (alt-text). Alt-text provides textual descriptions of images, enabling visually impaired individuals to understand visual media content through screen readers. The lack of alternative text has been an enduring accessibility problem since the "alt" attribute was added in HTML 2.0 over 20 years ago, and the rise of user-generated content has only increased the number of images shared [1]. Alt-text is not only a moral imperative for inclusivity but also a compliance requirement under guidelines like the Web Content Accessibility Guidelines [2]. Alt- text primarily benefits individuals with visual impairments. Screen readers use the alt attribute to describe images to users, enabling them to access the information conveyed visually. Alt-text also benefits users with slow internet connections or those on devices that cannot load images, providing a fallback mechanism for conveying content. Furthermore, alt-text plays an essential role in search engine optimization (SEO). Search engines use it to index and rank images, making content more discoverable. Thus, well-written alt-text not only enhances accessibility but also improves the overall usability and reach of a website.

This study aims to underscore the significance of alt-text and to examine the extent to which Italian universities have adopted it in their social media channels. The goal is to identify areas where improvements can be made to enhance accessibility and to encourage institutions to take necessary steps. The lack of effort to include alt-text excludes a substantial portion of the potential audience and undermines the universities' commitment to inclusion and equality.

Gleason et al. [1] analyzed over nine million tweets (including both original tweets and retweets) collected across five days from all publicly available Twitter profiles (not specifically identified as scientists or non-scientists). They found that about 1.09 million (11.84%) contained an image and that only 1144 (0.1%) of those included an image description.

One common explanation is a need for more awareness or understanding of the importance of alt-text. Despite the availability of professional description services and tools for amateur description, most human-generated descriptions are expensive and time-consuming [3]. Many individuals may not realize that alt-text is essential for digital accessibility. Additionally, there may be practical challenges involved in implementing alt-text. Creating accurate and informative alt-text can be time- consuming, especially for large volumes of visual content. Some institutions may also prioritize other aspects of digital accessibility, such as mobile optimization or website compliance with accessibility standards, at the expense of alt-text.

The importance of alt-text must be balanced. For visually impaired individuals who rely on screen readers, alt-text is a vital bridge between visual and textual information. Without accurate and informative alt-text, these individuals are effectively excluded from the content of images, limiting their ability to engage with the material. Furthermore, alt-text benefits all users, regardless of visual impairment. It can provide context, clarify meaning, and improve search engine optimization (SEO).

To address this issue, Italian Universities must proactively improve their use of alt-text. First, they should raise awareness among staff and faculty about the importance of digital accessibility and the role of alt-text. Second, Universities should establish policies and procedures for ensuring that alt-text is consistently included in all visual content. This point may involve assigning responsibility for alt-text creation to specific individuals or teams or using automated tools to assist in the process. Finally, Universities should regularly monitor and evaluate their compliance with accessibility standards, including using alt-text.

2 Methodology

This study examines the utilization of alternative text (alt-text) on the official Instagram profiles of 76 Italian universities (Fig. 1) classified according to the CENSIS 2023/2024 ranking. By meticulously analyzing the source code (see Fig. 3) of each University's Instagram posts, the presence and quality of manually created alt-text were rigorously assessed. The investigation focused on the first 10 posts of each University's official Instagram page and took place in February 2024. Initially, using the 2023/2024 Censis ranking, we cataloged a sample of 76 Italian Universities. We opted to investigate the entire population rather than employing representative samples from the individual categories; the Census ranking divides Italian universities into two categories and five types: state and non-state. State universities are further subdivided into Large, Medium, Massive, Small and Polytechnics. Non-state Universities into Large, Medium, Small. The subsequent step involved searching for the official pages of the 76 universities on the social media platform. Finally, the first ten posts were examined, regardless of whether they were single images, carousels, or videos, to identify the presence of manual or AI-generated alt text. Alt text is located within the page's source code, in the position indicated in Fig. 3. Manual alt text is easily recognizable by its direct nature, Italian language, and effective description of the presented content. AI- supported alt text, on the other hand, is identifiable by the preface "May it be…".

Having not found a classification of Italian online universities, it was decided to take a sample of two universities among the most commonly known and renowned.

Another example of alt-text used on Twitter (Fig. 2).

3 Results

Our findings reveal a significant need for manual alt-text usage on the Instagram profiles among the 76 Italian Universities analyzed. Only 2,6% of public and private universities demonstrated the inclusion of manually created alternative descriptions (Figs. 4 and 5, Table 1), one between large state Universities and another in large non state Universities, while the 97,4% used AI-generated alt-text that use automated alt- text generation tools.

This point implies that most images on the Instagram profiles of Italian Universities are accompanied by alt-text generated automatically by artificial intelligence. Such content, often inaccurate and unreliable, is also in English, further limiting the accessibility of content for visually impaired users. While these tools are improving, manual curation remains critical to ensure contextual accuracy and cultural sensitivity. Combining AI with human oversight can provide scalable solutions for large websites.

 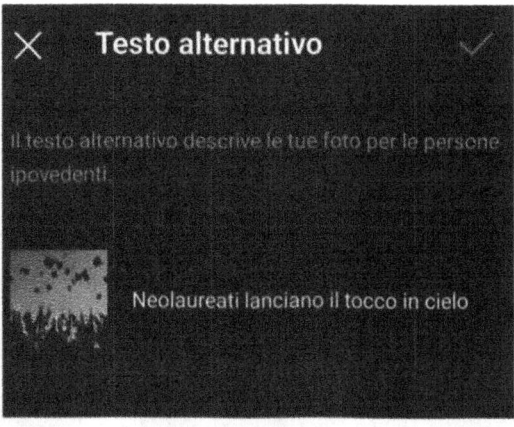

Fig. 1. Example of alt text on Instagram. English translation: Alt text, Alt text describes photos for the visually impaired; "Graduates toss their mortarboards into the air"

In Table 1 and Fig. 1 we can further appreciate the comparison between the number of analyzed and categorized Universities and the number of Universities whose Instagram pages include alt-text. Specifically, in Table 1, we show the data in a schematic form, while in Fig. 5 there is a graph highlighting, in red, the individual Universities that use alt-text in the subcategories.

In all ten posts analyzed, manual alt-text was consistently used when present.

4   Discussion

The findings of this study paint a disheartening picture of digital accessibility in Italian higher education. The pervasive reliance on AI-generated alt-text, often inaccurate and in a foreign language to many students and staff, highlights a systemic failure to prioritize the needs of visually impaired individuals. This neglect extends beyond mere technical oversight; it represents a broader cultural issue. Alt-text is not just a technical requirement but a commitment to equal access for all users, regardless of their abilities. The lack of manual alt-text suggests a prevailing attitude that accessibility is an afterthought rather than an integral part of effective communication. Manually crafting alt-text is a vital skill in creating inclusive digital experiences. By following a manual alt-text approach can ensure that the content is accessible, meaningful, and user-friendly for everyone. In a study conducted in 2019 on Twitter, users did not remember to add alternative text, did not have time to add it, or needed to know what to include when writing the descriptions [4]. Meanwhile, many images with no alt-text on social media indicate that many users need to authorize alt-text for the images they upload [5]. This mindset is not only ethically questionable but also counterproductive. Universities risk missing valuable perspectives and contributions by excluding a significant portion of their audience.

Furthermore, the use of AI-generated alt text can lead to unintended consequences. Inaccurate or misleading descriptions can create barriers to understanding, potentially hindering the learning process for visually impaired students. Moreover, relying on

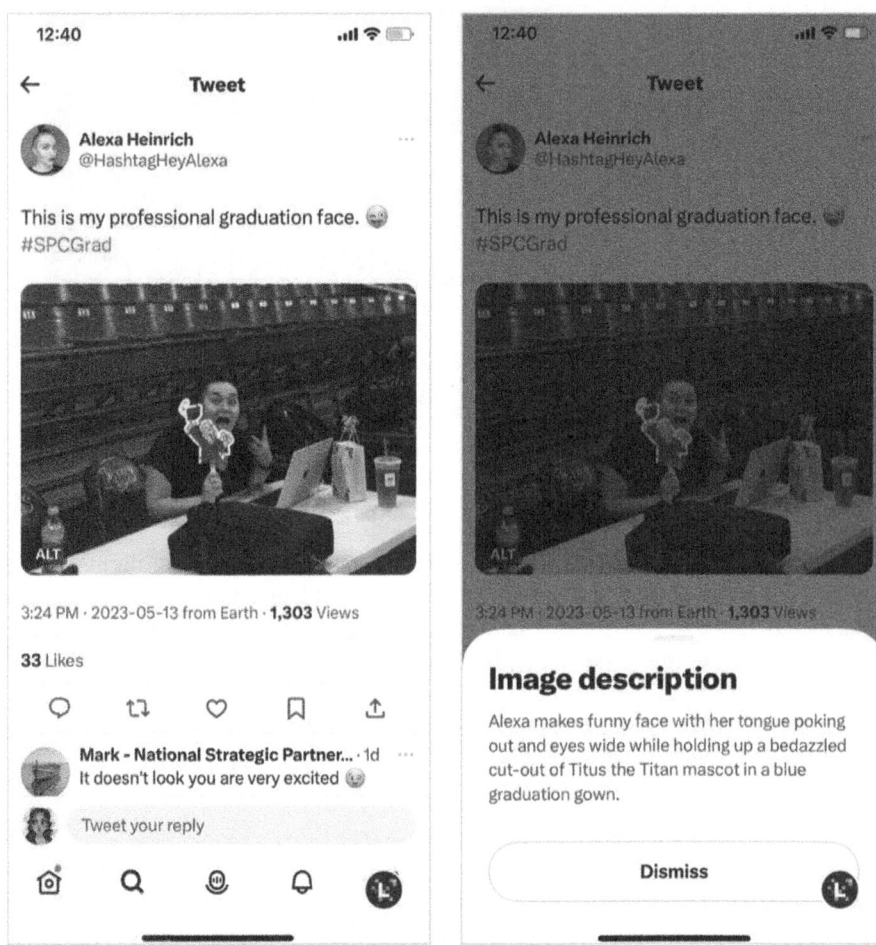

Fig. 2. Example of alt text on Twitter. Credits: [11].

Examine the page source to locate the alt text

```
▼<div class="_aagv"> == $0
    <img alt="Neolaureati lanciano il tocco in cielo" crossorigin="an
    onymous" src="https://scontent.cdninstagram.com/v/t51.29350-15/43
    7349152 1901899680... AfC-IoNSZrom1AJM3IMPmxiT8aNnJmDEaCQz3Ckck969H
    g&oe=661CC9FD&_nc_sid=10d13b" class="x5yr21d xu96u03 x1016tqk x13
    vifvy x87ps6o xh8yej3" style="object-fit: cover;">
```

Fig. 3. Alt-text location

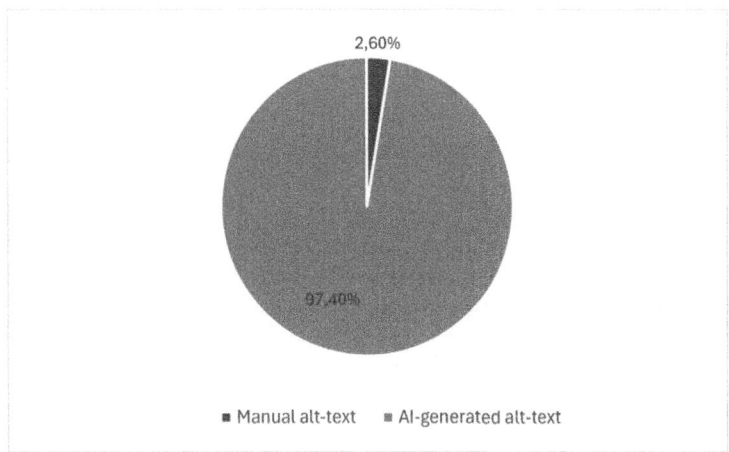

Fig. 4. Percentage of use of AI-generated alt-text or manual alt-text on Instagram profiles among Italian Universities.

Table 1. Results related to the Universities' statement (public, private and telematic)

	N	Manual alt-text presence
Public Universities	58	1
Private Universities	16	1
Telematic Universities	2	0

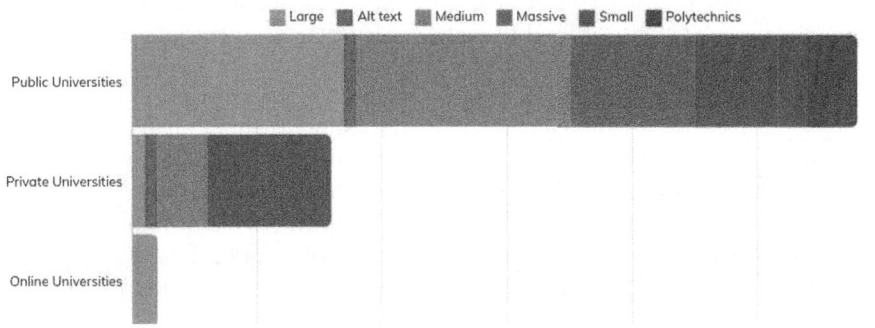

Fig. 5. Results in summary

English-language alt-text can exacerbate language disparities, further marginalizing non-native English speakers.

To address these challenges, Italian Universities must adopt a more inclusive approach to digital communication. This point involves implementing technical solutions, such as mandating the use of manual alt-text and fostering a cultural shift that prioritizes accessibility. While automated tools for generating alt-text have become increasingly advanced, manually crafted alt-text remains the most accurate and contextually relevant approach.

Universities should invest in training staff and faculty on digital accessibility principles, emphasizing the importance of alt-text and the potential negative consequences of neglecting it. Additionally, institutions should establish clear guidelines and policies that mandate the inclusion of accurate and informative alt-text for all visual content.

Moreover, Universities should actively seek feedback from visually impaired students and staff to identify and address barriers to accessibility. By involving these individuals in the process, institutions can ensure that their efforts are genuinely inclusive and responsive to the needs of their diverse student body.

4.1   AI Image Recognition Inaccuracy

Artificial Intelligence (AI) has made significant strides in recent years, revolutionizing various fields, including image recognition. However, AI image recognition systems are not infallible despite their impressive capabilities. They are prone to various errors that can have serious consequences, particularly in applications where accuracy is critical. This essay will delve into the challenges AI image recognition systems face, exploring the factors contributing to their inaccuracies and discussing the potential implications of these errors.

Automated methods, while fast and cheap, do not result in high quality alt text [5]. Fostering inclusion and accessibility is critical in many areas of our society, and every action should be promoted to reduce or preferably remove barriers. Social media represents a tool to reduce the experience gap for people with visual impairments. Recent innovations in artificial intelligence have resulted in the ability to generate image descriptions automatically (e.g., Twitter A11y13). That being said, it should be noted that "automatic" alt-text should not be relied upon as an alternative, as it will likely misidentify objects or not provide an appropriate level of detail in descriptions, especially for scientific purposes [4].

One of the primary challenges facing AI image recognition is the complexity of the human visual system. The human brain is incredibly adept at interpreting visual information and effortlessly recognizing objects, scenes, and even emotions in images. While powerful, AI systems need help to replicate this level of sophistication. They often rely on statistical models and machine learning algorithms that are trained on large datasets of labeled images. However, these models may only capture some of the nuances and subtleties of the human visual system, leading to errors in recognition.

Another challenge is the diversity and variability of the real world. AI systems are trained on specific datasets, which may need to be revised to adequately represent the full range of objects and scenes that they will encounter in real-world applications. For example, an AI system trained on images of cars may struggle to recognize a car obscured by foliage or parked in an unusual location. Additionally, variations in lighting, perspective, and other factors can also impact the accuracy of AI image recognition.

In a 2022 study [6] analyzing various image recognition tools and comparing their results to descriptions provided by Wikipedia contributors for the same images, the authors concluded that manual alt text input is necessary. The research indicates that current automated tools can only sometimes generate descriptions that are as accurate and effective as those written by humans.

While advanced technology can produce high-quality image descriptions, web content producers are encouraged to experiment with different tools to find the best fit for their specific needs. The quality of automated descriptions can vary based on the image type [6].

4.2 Alt Text as Poetry

In the "Alt text as poetry" project, the authors argue that alt text can be used to create evocative and meaningful descriptions of images. This can be a valuable tool for visually impaired users and sighted users who want to appreciate images more deeply. The paper provides several examples of alt-text written in a poetic style. These examples demonstrate how alt-text can be used to create vivid and evocative descriptions of images and convey emotions and ideas.

The paper also discusses the challenges of using alt-text as poetry. These challenges include the need to be concise and informative and the need to avoid using jargon or technical terms. Overall, the paper "Alt Text as Poetry" is a thought-provoking and informative piece that explores the potential for using alt-text as a form of poetic expression [7].

Building on this research, we propose treating alt-text writing as a small creative writing or storytelling exercise. However, we must immediately acknowledge that this idea conflicts with the need for quick, concise, and compelling image descriptions. Nevertheless, we could consider allowing users to choose the type of alt-text they prefer. In any case, a deeper discussion of these topics goes beyond the scope of this paper. Our intent was to introduce a small idea.

4.3 AI Video Recognition

Video accessibility is crucial for blind and low vision users for equitable engagements in education, employment, and entertainment. Despite the availability of professional description services and tools for amateur description, most human-generated descriptions are expensive and time consuming, and the rate of human-generated descriptions simply cannot match the speed of video production. [3] For videos on Instagram, the alt text is automatically replaced by the caption the user provides. The rapid pace of technological advancement, particularly in the realm of artificial intelligence, presents both opportunities and challenges. While it offers the potential to overcome barriers to accessibility, it is crucial to consider the ethical implications of such technologies and to ensure that they are used in a manner that benefits all users. Nevertheless, technological developments, like digitalization, big data, and artificial intelligence, potentially enable us to consider overcoming some types of exclusion in a university environment, even if simultaneously creating ethical issues and schisms among students and staff [8].

4.4 Alt-Text Quality

Alt-text quality is important for visually impaired people who are dealing with the increasing pervasiveness of image-based content. [9] While manually imputed alt-text provides a factual representation of the image, it often lacks the emotional nuance and contextual depth that can be conveyed through human description.

Adhering to a more objective and concise style aligns with Instagram's guidelines for alt-text, but it may limit the ability to fully capture the image's intended message.

Harvard University [10] best practices on writing an effective alt-text:

- Keep it short, usually 1–2 sentences. Do not overthink it.
- Consider critical elements of why you chose this image for your document, instead of describing every detail.
- There is no need to say "image of "or "picture of."
- However, say if it is a logo, illustration, painting, or cartoon.
- Do not duplicate text that's adjacent to the document or website
- End the alt text sentence with a period.

For another example of creating an effective alt-text, please follow the decision tree provided by W3C: the decision tree [11].

For a more inclusive education to include students with disabilities, universities must adapt everything transmitted digitally, in addition to providing accessible infrastructure, starting with the entrance exam, which is currently inaccessible, continuing with the teaching material, and ending with social communication. The sense of belonging to one's university for a visually impaired student develops through a meticulous effort not only of the dedicated service but of all the actors who, trained and sensitized, primarily work towards the common goal, which is that of general scientific research, to improve the quality of life of society and to break down barriers.

5   Conclusions

Alt-text is a cornerstone of inclusive design, bridging the gap for users with disabilities and enhancing the overall user experience. By adhering to best practices and leveraging available tools, developers and designers can ensure that their content is accessible to all users. The commitment to accessible design is not only a legal obligation but a reflection of the broader societal imperative to create a more inclusive digital world. Although the prevailing trend in scientific research is to develop increasingly sophisticated AI-powered image recognition models, this paper advocates for a different approach. To improve overall effectiveness, we should prioritize training and encouraging social media professionals to create manual alt-text descriptions. The neglect of alt-text in Italian higher education represents a missed opportunity to create a more inclusive and equitable learning environment. By prioritizing accessibility and adopting best practices, universities can ensure that their digital communication efforts are accessible to all students, regardless of their visual abilities. The mission of universities in fostering a more inclusive world is pivotal. They catalyze social change by implementing policies that promote diversity, equity, and inclusion (DEI). By prioritizing accessibility, such as through effective use of alt-text, institutions can ensure all students, including those with disabilities, have equal opportunities to thrive academically and socially.

Universities can lead by example, creating environments that embrace diverse perspectives and backgrounds, ultimately enriching the educational experience for everyone involved [9]. This commitment enhances learning and prepares students to engage effectively in a globalized society.

Future research could extend the study to other nations to gain a comprehensive global perspective.

Acknowledgment. We would like to express our gratitude to Dr. Marmo for bringing to our attention the precise placement of the alt text within the page source.

All authors declare that they have no conflicts of interest.

References

1. Gleason, C., Carrington, P., Cassidy, C., Ringel Morris M., Kitani, K.M., Bigham J.P.: It's almost like they're trying to hide it: how user-provided image descriptions have failed to make Twitter accessible. In: The World Wide Web Conference (WWW 2019), pp. 549–559. Association for Computing Machinery, New York, NY, USA (2019). https://doi.org/10.1145/3308558.3313605
2. Web Content Accessibility Guidelines (WCAG). https://www.w3.org/WAI/standards-guidelines/wcag/
3. Bodi, A., et al.: Automated video description for blind and low vision users. In: Extended Abstracts of the 2021 CHI Conference on Human Factors in Computing Systems, pp. 1–7. Association for Computing Machinery, New York, NY, USA (2021). https://doi.org/10.1145/3411763.3451810
4. Chiarella, D., Yarbrough, J., Jackson, C.A.L.: Using alt text to make science Twitter more accessible for people with visual impairments. Nat. Commun. **11**, 5803 (2020). https://doi.org/10.1038/s41467-020-19640-w
5. Bellscheidt, S., Metcalf, H., Elglaly D.P., Elglaly, Y.: Building the habit of authoring alt text: design for making a change. In: Proceedings of the 25th International ACM SIGACCESS Conference on Computers and Accessibility (ASSETS 2023), pp. 1–5. Association for Computing Machinery, New York, NY, USA (2023). https://doi.org/10.1145/3597638.3614495
6. Leotta, M., Mori, F., Ribaudo, M.: Evaluating the effectiveness of automatic image captioning for web accessibility. Univ. Access Inf. Soc. **22**, 1–21 (2022). https://doi.org/10.1007/s10209-022-00906-7
7. Cachia, A. (ed.): Curating Access: Disability Art Activism and Creative Accommodation. Routledge, London (2022). https://doi.org/10.4324/9781003171935
8. Rubel, A., Jones, K.M.L.: Student privacy in learning analytics: an information ethics perspective. Inf. Soc. **32**(2), 143–159 (2016). https://doi.org/10.1080/01972243.2016.1130502
9. Ringel Morris, M., Zolyomi, A., Yao, C., Bahram, S., Bigham, J.P., Kane, S.K.: "With most of it being pictures now, I rarely use it" understanding Twitter's evolving accessibility to blind users. In: Proceedings of the 2016 CHI Conference on Human Factors in Computing Systems (CHI 2016), pp. 5506–5516. Association for Computing Machinery, New York, NY, USA (2016). https://doi.org/10.1145/2858036.2858116
10. https://accessibility.huit.harvard.edu/describe-content-images
11. https://www.w3.org/WAI/tutorials/images/decision-tree/
12. https://later.com/blog/alt-text/

The Use of Artificial Intelligence in Political Campaign: Study Case of Prabowo and Gibran Presidential Campaign on Instagram

Satria Ardhikaputra Yudistio and Indra Prawira[✉] [iD]

Mass Communication, Binus University, West Jakarta, Indonesia
iprawira@binus.edu

Abstract. This research investigates the use of Artificial Intelligence (AI) in contemporary political communication through a case study of the 2024 Indonesian presidential candidates, Prabowo and Gibran's campaign on Instagram. This research focuses on how political candidates are represented through AI. By analyzing Instagram content, this research aims to reveal how AI contributes to the formulation of tailored political messages and the cultivation of candidates' images on social media platforms. This research collects Prabowo and Gibran's campaign images on Instagram and analyzes them using semiotic analysis methods to explore the meaning of messages based on Roland Barthes' model which includes denotation emphasizes unity, happiness, and positive leadership. Connotations of gentleness, joy and seriousness of the leader enrich the message conveyed. Each image carries a myth message of political unity and concern for the future. This research examines Prabowo and Gibran's campaigns to reveal the complex ways AI is integrated into political communication. This research provides valuable insights for political strategists, technologists, and scholars, and offers a perspective on the symbiotic relationship between AI technology, social media, and the complex dynamics of political campaigns on Instagram.

Keywords: Artificial Intelligence · Indonesian politics · Political campaign · social media

1 Introduction

The general election of the 2024 presidential and vice-presidential candidates in Indonesia has recently become the center of attention of Instagram users. One of the candidate pairs took advantage of this campaign moment by using Artificial Intelligence (AI) images, namely Prabowo Gibran. In this campaign, Instagram became one of the best communication venues to convey political messages, build images, and interact directly with voters. Digital technology has now brought humans to a fantasy of their own making, to the extent that cyberspace can now manipulate visual images of the real world. By looking at the social media Instagram, recognition from others of the image formed by a person can be seen from the acquisition of likes, the number of followers, and the number of positive comments on uploaded photos. Social media allows various forces

G. A. Toto (Ed.): ICS exchange 2024, CCIS 2521, pp. 244–256, 2025.
https://doi.org/10.1007/978-3-032-03021-4_17

to convey information to the public beyond traditional sources of information [1]. Given the amount of information, they get through social media platforms such as Instagram, this is expected to influence how they learn about politics, how their opinions and attitudes are formed, and whether and how they will engage in the political process [2]. Artificial intelligence (AI) is defined by Kaplan and Haenlein as a computer system that can perform physical tasks, cognitive functions, or solve various problems [3].

The development of Artificial Intelligence (AI) has opened new opportunities in the realm of political campaigns. With machine learning algorithms, AI is used to analyze data and predict voter behavior. Then using generative AI, just by writing a command text can generate text, images, or all kinds of data based on the internet 1993, AI has achieved some important results and has provided some significant results. AI is a subdiscipline of computer science that focuses on exploring the essence of intelligence through a series of algorithmic procedures to produce intelligent products that approximate human intelligence. The development of Artificial Intelligence (AI) has opened new opportunities in the realm of political campaigns. With machine learning algorithms, AI is used to analyze data and predict voter behavior. Then using generative AI, just by writing a command text can generate text, images, or all kinds of data based on the internet [6].

In an era that continues to develop technologically, the presence of AI has penetrated various sectors of human life, including politics. The development of AI is not only a technological innovation but has also become a strategic tool used in political campaigns. This phenomenon marks a profound transformation in the way politicians interact with voters, strategize campaigns, and utilize data to achieve their political goals. In interacting with voters, the Prabowo Gibran pair uses AI-made images using Instagram social media. Where the image creation uses Generative AI which facilitates the creation process. Only by giving a command sentence does it not take long to produce an image based on the command. They explain most adaptively through the generated content so that the content of the message can be easily understood by the generation above and the generation below. The choice of the word "Gemoy" is a popular diction among young people today, although it has not been officially recorded in the Indonesian Dictionary. However, the circulating meaning of the word can be understood equally by social media users across generations.

Using Barthes' semiological approach, this research aims to dissect the signs contained in political campaign content shared via the Instagram platform. We can see how AI is used to effectively design and package political messages, as well as how these signals are received and interpreted by voters. This research responds to a phenomenon that can be beneficial in modern politics, where artificial intelligence (AI) technology is becoming a tool in political campaigns, especially on social media platforms such as Instagram. Through analysis of related literature, it was found that the dominance of technology in politics, as found in the Journal of Political Marketing and Political Communication, marks a shift towards more technological and authoritarian political practices. Studies in the journal's New Media & Society and social media + Society also show that social media has become a battleground for the manipulation and control of public opinion. In addition, research in the journals Information, Communication & Society and the Journal of Information Technology & Politics highlights the increasing power of technology in shaping voting behavior. By using Roland Barthes' approach, this research is expected to provide a deeper understanding of the use of artificial intelligence in political campaigns, especially in the context of the influence of AI image representation through social media for politics. Thus, this research can make a significant contribution to the study of politics and media, as well as open space for further discussion about the relationship between technology, politic campaign, and ideology in modern politics.

2 Literature Review

2.1 Political Campaigns and Political Communication

Note A political campaign is the process of transforming information into various forms of political messages to audiences with certain communication channels and media to influence and create public opinion. A political campaign is an organized effort aimed at influencing the decision-making process of voters and political campaigns always refer to general election campaigns [7]. Election campaigns are usually to persuade people to support a particular candidate. Social media platforms have replaced traditional media today. For example, Barack Obama made history in 2008 by becoming the first African American to win the US presidency. The Obama campaign's effective use of social media to mobilize voters was largely due to this strategy [8].

Political campaigns often use three different types of frameworks: personal, policy, and strategy. Strategizing is event-driven, emphasizing winning or losing elections, candidate performance, and campaign tactics. Candidates' ideas about policies and solutions to social problems are reflected in the policy framework. Finally, the personal frame draws attention to the lives, identities, ways of life, and personalities of individuals. An additional type is "off-topic", which denotes unimportant posts or announcements that do not align with a particular strategy, policy, or personal frame [9]. Political campaigns and political communication are closely intertwined in the context of the democratic process. Political campaigns are candidates' efforts to win support, and political communication acts as the main tool to convey messages and influence public perception. Communication strategies, such as speeches, advertisements, and social media presence, are key elements in reaching voters. In turn, political campaigns require effective communication skills to respond to issues and shape a positive image in the eyes of voters.

Information and communication between political actors, the public, and the media is called political communication. Each of the three players helps shape the political public sphere [10]. It is said that we are entering the "fourth era of political communication," a significant change in the way politics and media interact. The Internet and related technologies have had a profound impact on business, culture, social interaction, movements, politics, and media, defining this new era. This has led to the creation of the notion of a political communication ecosystem, which is derived from biology and more accurately captures the increasing levels of adaptation, flexibility, and interrelated complexity [10].

In addition, by considering a cross-media perspective, the model distinguishes the various roles of important channels, each of which is controlled by a unique logic. Politicians have total influence over several channels (such as TV ads, emails, and direct messages), but journalists run news media institutions. On the other hand, social media platforms concentrate on sharing content from various sources, such as individuals, journalists, and politicians. Therefore, this model recognizes that content appearing on one channel can be picked up, magnified, or challenged by other channels from the point of view of the flow of communication. In essence, there are many facets to the complex interactions that occur between social media, news media, and political communication. These interactions include various dimensions such as time, space, media specificity, communication style, and influence.

2.2 Content Analysis and Semiotic Theory

By concentrating on the content as well as the underlying themes and meanings that emerge in a text, qualitative content analysis methods aim to identify and investigate patterns of meaning-making and meaning production in communicative aspects of language [9]. Researchers from other disciplines have developed various analytical techniques to move away from theories and methods that assume that language is an autonomous system in which the meanings of words and sentences can always be objectively constructed and internally fixed. These techniques are based on the implications of the "linguistic turn", which was introduced in the humanities by French linguist Ferdinand de Saussure (1974).

The overall aim of qualitative content analysis methods is to create different forms of 'meaning' that emerge from different methods of analysis. Interpretive and qualitative content analysis methods investigate and consider the various meanings that may be attached to an existing event or phenomenon, its relationship to a particular place, and the values that a particular practice or object holds for them. Social media is an example of a space where people use interpretive and qualitative content analysis methods. On social media, people are free to interpret everything from their point of view. Instagram is one of the platforms where this phenomenon occurs. Instagram is a popular photo and video-sharing app that is growing in importance. Instagram gives users the ability to share photos and videos as well as features for interaction such as comments, hashtags, stories, live messages, question and answer boxes, polls, and more.

Semiotics is a form of communication content analysis. Semiotic analysis is closely related to content analysis and concerns how language gives meaning to symbols and signs [11]. The combination of these two approaches allows researchers to uncover patterns and meanings hidden in content and understand how signs work together to form deeper meanings.

Semiotics comes from the Greek word "Semeion" which means sign. In English, semiotics refers to the sign system of all forms of communication involving signs, such as language, meaning, movies, gestures, facial expressions, and literary works in the form of music or human culture itself. According to Barthes, semiology wants to study how humanity interprets things [12]. Barthes considers social life, whatever form it takes, to be a system of signs. Roland Barthes' semiotic theory is almost literally derived from de Saussure's theory of language [12].

Barthes builds on the Saussurean concept of the sign, which consists of two components, the Signifier; the physical form of the sign, such as a word, image, or sound, and the Signified; the concept or meaning associated with the signifier [13]. To illustrate this concept, Barthes notes that many semiological systems are commonplace objects: food is used for sustenance, and clothing is used for protection despite being a symbol, he says: "We intend to call these semiological signs, whose origin is utilitarian and functional; sign functions".

Media undoubtedly plays an important role in our lives, as evidenced by the many academic and empirical studies conducted globally. There is an infinite array of communication, especially when that communication is in the form of visual images, which is a learned language. Therefore, semi-logical analysis is important to understand and decipher the important visual signals used by the media, as well as to generate meanings that refer to socio-cultural and individual relationships at the second level of significance or connotation. Barthes considered the study of concrete sign means, such as texts and images, as vehicles of culture, ideology, or myth in his semiological method. Barthes identifies myth as a type of speech but certainly not any type of speech because 'language requires special conditions to become a myth' (Roland Barthes 1972). The analysis of media phenomena as a system uses the expressed signals, both verbal and nonverbal, which can be analyzed using the two levels of significance - denotation and connotation - proposed by Barthes in his methodology.

Denotation is the first conventionally agreed system of meaning [14]. According to Roland Barthes, in the process of signification, the symbolized message is essential to the connotation and has an analogical quality. Roland Barthes developed the term "connotation" to describe how signs function. In his opinion, "signification, the process that links signifier and signified in a system, is what constitutes connotation." (Roland Barthes 1968) [15]. From here we can say that connotation is built on denotation. Thus, connotation for Barthes is the reproduction of messages both linguistically and visually.

3 Methodology

This research uses a qualitative approach, using descriptive analysis methods. According to Bryman, quantitative research seeks to explain, generalize, and predict patterns through variable analysis, while qualitative research questions are more interested in understanding and interpreting the socially constructed world around us [16]. This means that data is collected through documents, observations, and interviews. Data is often recorded to be analyzed as documents. This analysis uses Roland Barthes' semiotic analysis in the form of exploring the meaning of Denotation, connotation, and myth.

The research focuses on several AI-generated images on Instagram on Prabowo and Gibran's campaigns that contain denotation, connotation, and mythical meanings according to Roland Barthes' semiotic analysis theory. The data was obtained by searching Instagram hashtags #Prabowo, #Gibran, and #prabowogibran in 3 months, namely from October 2023 to December 2023 which obtained 427 Instagram posts. From the data, researchers obtained five main images in visual format and screenshots uploaded through Instagram accounts @gerakanmilenialindonesia, @mediaprabowo, @jktgo, and @koalisi.indonesia.maju.

4 Research Result

This study collected 427 Instagram posts featuring AI-generated images of Indonesia's 2024 presidential candidate Prabowo-Gibran. From the data, there are five main images analyzed in this study. The data was obtained by searching Instagram hashtags #Prabowo, #Gibran, and #prabowogibran. Then the data were analyzed using Roland Barthes' three-stage significance system, namely denotation, connotation, and myth. In Roland Barthes' semiology, denotation is the basic meaning of a sign or symbol, while connotation is a deeper level of meaning, related to interpretation, values, or feelings associated with a sign or symbol. And myth is a form of cultural representation attached to a particular object or sign, creating a more complex symbolic meaning (Tables 1, 2, 3, 4 and 5).

Fig. 1. @mediaprabowo, 30–10-2023, 28.373 Likes and 379 Comment

Table 1. Analysis on Prabowo and His Cat

Object	Denotation	Connotation	Myth
Hug a cat	Fat little boy, black cap, hugging a white cat, bookshelf background	Unlimited happiness, emotional connection with Animals, intellectual and religious	A message about the happiness and wisdom inherent in childhood

5 Research Discussion

The above research has denotations, connotations, and myths in each image analyzed by researchers in the AI images of Prabowo and Gibran's campaign. This research uses Roland Barthes' semiotic analysis theory regarding the meaning of denotation,

Fig. 2. @koalisi.indonesia.maju, 23–11-2023, 27.239 Likes and 683 Comment.

Table 2. Analysis on Prabowo and Gibran Picture

Object	Denotation	Connotation	Myth
In the village	Prabowo holding a cat and Gibran beside him, in a village, clear sky	the gentleness and closeness of leaders, intergenerational cooperation, hope and kindness in the world of politics	past experience and knowledge are united with the present, traditional values of society

connotation, and myth. The analysis used in this research, as explained earlier, is Roland Barthes' semiotic analysis. In a systematic study, semiotic analysis reporting includes Denotation, Connotation, and myth. Semiology examines how humanity gives meaning to a sign or symbol.

5.1 Denotation: Literal Messages in Political Campaigns

Denotation is a sign whose signifier has a high level of agreement and then produces the real meaning. In the denotation analysis in the first picture, a chubby little boy wearing a black cap is seen intimately hugging a white cat in front of a bookshelf. The atmosphere of intimacy emanates from Fig. 2 of Prabowo holding the cat, Gibran is beside him, and they are smiling. The background consisting of a wooden house, a garden, and a clear sky adds a warm feeling. In Fig. 3, there is a scene of a small child walking with a smile in front of a brown background, decorated with the words "GEMOY". The term Gemoy has the equivalent meaning of adorable, while several other sources mention that

Fig. 3. @mediaprabowo, 31–10-2023, 23.032 Likes and 535 Comment

Table 3. Analysis on Prabowo the Gemoy

Object	Denotation	Connotation	Myth
Walking	little boy walking smiling, brown background, "GEMOY"	innocence and happiness, nuanced comfort and warmth on a brown background. "GEMOY" joy and excitement	a positive and cheerful image, conveying a message about children's happiness in a warm and comfortable atmosphere

Gemoy has a denotative meaning of fat and adorable [17]. This scene creates an image of happiness and joy blended with warm colors.

In Fig. 4, a fat man is riding a black horse, while another man leads a white horse beside him. They are followed by a group of people carrying red and white flags. This scene gives an impression of strength and solidarity, creating an image of vigor. And the last image, Mr. Prabowo and Gibran in the form of a young child wearing formal clothes, highlights the image of leadership and responsible family values. With the harmony of these elements, the image is not only a visual representation but also a narrative depicting the familiarity, happiness, solidarity, and leadership that Prabowo and Gibran promote.

There are some similarities in the images, four of the five AI images depict the figure of Prabowo or Gibran in the form of a child and carrying an animal such as a cat or horse. Two of the five AI images also use a black cap and are also seen wearing formal clothing. Also seen in Figs. 1, 3, and 5 which use a brown background. While Fig. 2 has a bright blue-sky background, and Fig. 4 has a background of a group of people carrying a red and white flag.

Fig. 4. @gerakanmilenialindonesia, 1–11-2023, 18.978 Likes and 401 Comment

Table 4. Analysis on "Prabowo and Gibran Horse Riding"

Object	Denotation	Connotation	Myth
Horse riding	Riding black horses and leading white horses, many people carried red and white flags	Physical strength and leadership, wisdom in guidance, spirit of unity and solidarity in a common ideology	Journey together, the success of the nation is a balance between power, wisdom and enthusiasm

Fig. 5. @jktgo (source: @faisalmn), 11–11-2023, 78.704 Likes and 2.021 Comment

Table 5. Analysis on "Prabowo and Gibran Close up"

Object	Denotation	Connotation	Myth
Close up photo	the form of a small child wearing formal clothes	leadership of the younger generation, Formal wear seriousness and professionalism	Political figures convey a message of concern for the future of the next generation, formal clothing is a sign of status and authority

5.2 Connotation: Hidden Implications in Political Messages

Connotation is a subjective meaning that varies. It is a sign whose sign has an open meaning or implicit meaning and is open to new interpretations. The connotation presented in Fig. 1, the little boy gently hugging the cat creates an image of gentleness. The use of a black cap gives the impression of a religious identity or state official, while the bookshelf background gives a connotative touch of intelligence and intellectuality. In Fig. 2, the act of holding the cat expresses concern for the animal, while the smiles of Prabowo and Gibran bring positivity and happiness. The background of the wooden house, the garden, and the clear sky bring connotations of peace and prosperity. In both images there is a cat, Cats are often regarded as animals that can provide a sense of calmness and relaxation. In most cases, cats seem to be a source of additional emotional support [18].

Furthermore, Image 3 highlights the child's smiling expression with a sense of happiness and innocence. The brown background adds a sense of calmness and warmth, while the word "GEMOY" includes connotations of cute and sweet, describing an adorable expression. There is the word "Gemoy" in image number 3. Some time ago on social media, many people threw the word gemoy, this word is a pun on the word gemas which is used to refer to something cute or adorable [19]. The attachment of Gemoy to Prabowo occurred because he was seen dancing in several events displayed by the media, and the emergence of illustrations of Prabowo images in the form of Artificial Intelligence on social media is also considered Gemoy.

In Fig. 4, the figure riding a black horse can be interpreted as a symbol of power and authority. The white horse being led reflects purity, cleanliness, and conservative leadership. The red and white flag carried by the group of people is the national symbol of Indonesia. Therefore, it carries connotations of nationality and patriotism. Seeing this flag can express love for the country and the spirit of nationalism.

Finally, Fig. 5 shows Prabowo and Gibran in the form of young children, wearing formal clothes that carry strong connotations of youth leadership. Formal clothing creates an impression of seriousness and professionalism. The childlike AI images of Prabowo and Gibran convey the meaning of youthful, gentle, and harmless leadership. The entire set of AI images encapsulates a variety of connotative meanings, conveying messages of gentleness, happiness, caring, peace, nationality, and leadership with deep nuances.

5.3   Myth: Collective Narrative and Political Representation

In Barthes' view, myth refers to the interpretation of symbols and images by Society. Figure 1 illustrates the journey of a chubby little boy in a black cap, inspired by his innocence and spiritual connection with a white cat. The black cap symbolizes responsibility, while the bookshelf represents knowledge. The black cap itself has meaning for Indonesian culture, the pioneer who wore a cap was Soekarno. He was determined to wear a cap as a symbol of the nationalist movement [20]. It was pioneered because of the existence of regional tribes that had their characteristics for their head coverings after independence, it made Soekarno make Peci a unifier of each regional tribe and increased nationalism. Peci is used in every activity and until now peci has been used by all circles, regardless of race, ethnicity, or religion even in national events peci is always used as a complementary accessory in official events for State Officials [20].

Figure 2 displays the unity and harmony between two political figures. The smiles of both represent a joint effort to create peace and cooperation in the world of politics. The background carries a myth about the closeness and understanding of political figures in people's daily lives. There is quite an inverse relationship between the lives of people who tend to be poor and that of politician Prabowo, who has lived in wealth since birth. Prabowo's grandfather was the founder of Bank Negara Indonesia and came from a noble family. Meanwhile, Prabowo's father is a former Minister of Finance and Minister of Trade. Since childhood, Prabowo studied abroad and returned to Indonesia to start a military career. After retiring from the military, Prabowo continues his career in Indonesian political life to this day. Likewise, in Gibran's life, becoming Mayor of Surakarta was not difficult. Having a father who once served as Mayor of Surakarta, and served as president for 2 terms, so there is no need to doubt his father's electability. Thus, the life history of Prabowo and Gibran illustrated in Fig. 2 adds a diverse and complex side to the narrative. Even though both do not come from poor families, this picture wants to show their closeness to the people.

Figure 3 depicts small children bringing natural happiness, with a brown background reflecting peace in everyday life. The "GEMOY" myth forms a narrative about the inherent happiness and innocence of young children. In Fig. 4, the myth of the common journey shows that the success of a community or nation requires a balance between power, wisdom, and collective spirit to achieve common goals. The red and white flag of Indonesia carries a deep myth of struggle and independence, reflected in the red color which symbolizes the spirit and blood of heroes. The symbol of unity in Indonesia's cultural and ethnic diversity is manifested in the united colors of red and white.

Finally, Fig. 5 contains a message about the warm side of humanity and concern for the future of the next generation. Their formal attire became a sign of status and authority, adding a mythological dimension to the image. This entire series of images creates a complex myth, combining elements of everyday life with symbols that have deep meaning. The mythical meanings in the images that researchers analyze are always tied to Indonesian culture and traditions. Some of the AI images are seen in the form of small children, which have mythical meanings such as bringing happiness, helplessness, and humanity. That this myth could be beneficial to Prabowo's position because his cases involve human rights violations such as the Trisakti case and East Timor and Aceh. These issues are often directed at Prabowo Subianto, who is known as a soldier or military officer [21].

6 Conclusion

Based on research results regarding the meaning of denotation, connotation, and myth from the campaign images of the 2024 Indonesian Presidential candidates Prabowo and Gibran produced by AI, the researchers draw conclusions that can be conveyed through the meaning of denotation, connotation, and myth. The denotational meanings found are the relationship between humans and animals, harmony between political figures, children's happiness, strength, and solidarity, as well as positive leadership and family values. Connotative meanings include the tenderness and spiritual relationship between humans and animals, happiness and harmony in politics, the joy and innocence of children, the strength and courage of horse riders, the spirit of patriotism of the red and white flag, and the seriousness and professionalism of the images of Prabowo and Gibran in children's form. These connotations help enrich and deepen understanding of the meaning and message to be conveyed. The myth of each image conveys a message of political unity, happiness and peace, and concern for future generations. Apart from that, it reflects the complexity of the lives and political history of Prabowo and Gibran. This myth creates a narrative about Indonesian values, beliefs, and cultural identity. Thus, semiotic analysis provides an in-depth understanding of how visual elements in a campaign can shape certain meanings and perceptions, thus having an important impact in influencing voters' views.

References

1. Katz, Y.: The links between political campaigning and post-truth. Randwick Int. Soc. Sci. J. 4(3), 560–573 (2023). https://doi.org/10.47175/rissj.v4i3.726
2. Errenst, E., Van Remoortere, A., Vermeer, S., Kruikemeier, S.: Instaworthy? Examining the effects of (targeted) civic education ads on Instagram. Media Commun. 11(3), 238–249, 2023. https://doi.org/10.17645/MAC.V11I3.6614
3. Tang, R., et al.: A literature review of artificial intelligence applications in railway systems. Transp. Res. Part C Emerg. Technol. 140 (2022). https://doi.org/10.1016/j.trc.2022.103679
4. Zhang, T., Lu, X., Zhu, X., Zhang, J.: The contributions of AI in the development of ideological and political perspectives in education. Heliyon 9(3) (2023). https://doi.org/10.1016/j.heliyon.2023.e13403
5. Zhang, C., Lu, Y.: Study on artificial intelligence: the state of the art and future prospects. J. Ind. Inf. Integr. 23 (2021). https://doi.org/10.1016/j.jii.2021.100224
6. Sætra, H.S.: Generative AI: here to stay, but for good? Technol. Soc. 75 (2023). https://doi.org/10.1016/j.techsoc.2023.102372
7. Battista, D.: Winning against all odds: Elly Schlein's successful election campaign and Instagram communication strategies. Soc. Sci. 12(6) (2023). https://doi.org/10.3390/socsci12060313
8. Lam, S.Y.B., Cheung, M.F.M., Lo, W.H.: What matters most in the responses to political campaign posts on social media: the candidate, message frame, or message format? Comput. Hum. Behav. 121 (2021). https://doi.org/10.1016/j.chb.2021.106800

9. Biggs, R., de Vos, A., Preiser, R., Clements, H., Maciejewski, K., Schlüter, M.: The Routledge Handbook of Research Methods for Social-Ecological Systems. Routledge, New York (2022)
10. Esser, F., Pfetsch, B.: Comparing political communication: a 2020 update. Polit. Commun. **5**, 1–39 (2020)
11. Vespestad, M.K., Clancy, A.: Exploring the use of content analysis methodology in consumer research. J. Retail. Consum. Serv. **59** (2021). https://doi.org/10.1016/j.jretconser.2020.102427
12. Sadono, T.P., Amina, N.W.R.: The fight for the 2024 presidential election within the PDIP within the framework of tempo (Roland Barthes' semiotics study on the cover of the May 2021 edition of tempo magazine). J. Law Sustain. Dev. **11**(9), e1172 (2023). https://doi.org/10.55908/sdgs.v11i9.1172
13. Uslu, F.: International Conference on Social Sciences and Humanities Abstracts & Proceedings: Istanbul, Turkey, 8–10 September 2014. International Organization Center of Academic Research (2014)
14. Jafar, A., Aso, L., Amstrong, N.: The meaning of denotation, connotation, and myth used in Ariana grande's god is a woman song lyrics **6**(1) (2021)
15. Barthes, R.: Roland-Barthes-Mythologies. Farrar, Straus and Giroux, New York (1991)
16. McMullin, C.: Transcription and qualitative methods: implications for third sector research. Voluntas **34**(1), 140–153 (2023). https://doi.org/10.1007/s11266-021-00400-3
17. Rozi, R.F.: Presidential candidate slogans in the 2024 Indonesian general election; strategic communication with multi-generational characteristics (2023). www.eximiajournal.com
18. Jezierski, T., Camerlink, I., Peden, R.S.E., Chou, J.Y., Sztandarski, P., Marchewka, J.: Cat owners' perception on having a pet cat during the COVID-19 pandemic. PLoS One 16(10) (2021). https://doi.org/10.1371/journal.pone.0257671
19. Maulana Rizik Sihabudin, M., Nur Alfa Laila, H., Kharis, K., Siti Fatimah, R., Sains Komunikasi, J.: Strategi Positioning 'Gemoy' Prabowo Subianto melalui Media Digital 'GEMOY' PRABOWO SUBIANTO MELALUI MEDIA DIGITAL. Jurnal Sosiohumaniora Nusantara 146–154 (2023)
20. Jurnal, H., et al.: JURNAL PENGABDIAN MASYARAKAT INDONESIA OPTIMALISASI DIGITAL MARKETING PADA UMKM PECI ASSAGOFAH DI DESA BANJARWANGI KABUPATEN BOGOR 2(1) (2023)
21. Sriwedari, N.R., Simanjuntak, V.A.: FRAMING PEMBERITAAN CAPRES-CAWAPRES JOKOWI-MA'RUF AMIN DAN PRABOWO SUBIANTO-SANDIAGO UNO DI HARIAN KOMPAS PADA MASA KAMPANYE PEMILIHAN PRESIDEN 2019 **8**(1) (2020). Author, F.: Article title. Journal **2**(5), 99–110 (2016)

Commodification of Digital Activism: Implications of Performance Excellence in @Pandawaragroup

Prabowo Noersetyo Arief and Indra Prawira$^{(\boxtimes)}$

Faculty of Digital Communication and Tourism, Bina Nusantara University Alam Sutera Campus, Jl. Jalur Sutera Bar. No.Kav. 21, RT.001/RW.004, Panunggangan, Kec. Pinang, Kota Tangerang, Banten 15143, Indonesia
iprawira@binus.edu

Abstract. This research study examines the commodification of content within the context of digital activism using Vincent Mosco's commodification of communication theory focusing on the commodification of content and Malcolm Baldridge's framework of performance excellence in digital activism within Pandawara group's Instagram @pandawaragroup and their environmental cleaning activities content while also focusing on how it plays a part in educational contexts that leads to a wider audience engagement. Through the use of qualitative content analysis and thematic analysis, we explore the Instagram account of Pandawara, to investigate the ways in which content is transformed into a commodity by applying the media aesthetics theory and conducting thematic analysis to search for themes and any indications of how as well as finding out how to use this for educational purposes. The results show that media aesthetics play a part in creating a major dynamic for content creation by making it visually stunning in different ways of camerawork and special effects while also boosting the image of the group which also leads to amazing performance excellence by the group. Nevertheless, recommendations are made for future research.

Keywords: Commodification · Digital Activism · Media Aesthetics · Performance Excellence · Social Media

1 Introduction

The rise in social media has helped access towards more sharing on opinions and such, in which there is also an appearance of digital activism a term defined as political participation and activities that are not connected towards any political institute and are conducted in computer mediated environments [1]. To reach more people, the promotion of digital activism is also done through social media with more users joining the platforms due to the trend of having smartphones to ease communication, with social media continuously developing because the freedom of creating content and control provided to users [2]. In addition, students and teachers also gain more knowledge for material from social media for studying material while also having social media become

© The Author(s), under exclusive license to Springer Nature Switzerland AG 2025
G. A. Toto (Ed.): ICS exchange 2024, CCIS 2521, pp. 257–269, 2025.
https://doi.org/10.1007/978-3-032-03021-4_18

a better bridge of communication for students to drive critical discussions, empowering student movements as well [3, 4].

Another significant aspect of digital activism is that it is also commodified to gain more attention from the public. Commodification according to Vincent Mosco, is the transformation of goods to marketable products which will then be sold. Commodification in social media is common by modifying the content to gain more attention, an example would be Widiastuti's (2021) research, they stated that commodification and suiting the content to what the audience wants to see will lead to an increase in traffic or visitors, gaining more attention [5]. Another prior research stated how students leverage social media to educate locals by interesting storytelling for digital activism as it can be leveraged in this digital age to be persuasive [6].

Using media aesthetics is one of the ways that users leverage social media to garner more attention and enhance their content with Smith et al. (2005) defining it as structured moving pictures to have an effective communication for the audience [7].

Pandawara group is a known group of content creators who upload environmental cleaning content and have become viral on their Instagram @pandawaragroup with the content uploaded on their Instagram showcasing their activities in cleaning rivers and such, which lead them to becoming viral and garnering massive attention from the public [8]. After a series of posts using multiple effects, Pandawara's content was seen to have also gained sponsorships from well-known brands such as Nestle and ViCee (Figs. 1 and 2).

Fig. 1. Pandawara sponsored by Nestle Purelife

This research aims to find out how does Pandawara group utilize their content to commodification by analysing through the commodification of communication theory and media aesthetics theory as well as the performance excellence theory by identifying what kind media aesthetics are used to modify their content.

Fig. 2. Pandawara sponsored by Vicee

2 Literature Review

2.1 Commodification of Digital Activism

Originating from the Political Communication, Vincent Mosco stated the term commodification as the transformation of objects to market value, how goods, people, and services can adjust to earn a place in the market and create profit with the goal to suit the needs and standards of their consumers and earning money from it [9]. Mosco (2009) defines commodification of communication into three types, the commodification of content, audience, and labour. This research will focus on the commodification of content, it is defined content is processed in the media to suit the interests of the audience, influenced by the profit value to be then sold to the market and bring profit towards the creator [5].

Previous studies have also highlighted how digital activism has transformed towards a commodification in its practices and how social media has played a part in this. As stated in a previous study by Juliansyahzen (2023) where they researched regarding how the religious studies of hijrah on social media are not only part of a religious text but also a part of religious commodification, they stated that religious discourses and values are positioned as commodity goods with social media as the main platform in sharing these goods and promoting the messages in their activism [10]. Furthermore, social media communication helps users educate and drive critical discussions to others, empowering student movements as well [4]. Teachers and students leverage social media to gain more knowledge and material for studying [3].

2.2 Media Aesthetics

Zettl (2005) defines media aesthetics as how moving screen images are structured and formed for the most effective communication for the audience, which differs from traditional media that focuses only on what is beautiful and what is not. Furthermore, media aesthetics can also be applied towards analysis easily and focuses on the images inside the content [7].

A previous research done by Simakova (2020) states that the use of media aesthetics is also to give feelings and visualisation towards the audience. In their research of infographics, they concluded that the use of media aesthetics is important to give a pleasing feeling, further stating that the structuring of information on the infographic also requires a balance in media aesthetics for maximum effect [11].

2.3 Content Analysis

Content analysis is a method to identify and give interpretation towards communication forms by isolating data and designing a framework to help organize and describe a phenomenon, the methods are varied with the purpose of being able to uncover themes that are recurring and patterns that occur in the field of research [12]. In addition, content analysis helps with a large amount of unanalyzed textual data [13]. In a previous study, content analysis was used as a social listening method to be able to assess the public opinion regarding the use of AI in social media, using the method to analyze the content [14]. In addition, another study conducted used social listening as well to assess situations regarding COVID – 19 information in the media, stating that social media posts hold meaning toward perception and messages within while filtering information that is relevant towards the research that is done [15].

Furthermore, the variety of content analysis also differs on the focus of the analysis in which is done by the research, with types such as conventional content analysis which focuses on a study that starts through observing the data presented which are then coded according to the data, directed content analysis which focuses on theory and coded before and after the analysis takes place, and finally summative content analysis which encompasses keywords identified before the analysis is done [16].

2.4 Pandawara Group's Instagram

The Instagram Pandawara Group has attained a mass amount of attention with one million followers and 105 posts, providing an interesting case study to explore the intersection of political economy commodification theory and performance excellence theory. A previous study mentions how the participants that were researched stated that social media has helped them in reaching a wider audience, managing volunteers and giving them roles according to their duties and sharing information amongst communities, because social media allows communities to learn from others [17].

Pandawara Group's social media garnered attention that led towards a mass amount of collaboration and attention after sharing their content of environmental cleaning, the content is usually documentations of their cleaning activities both in the form of videos and images, as well as infographs regardings matters of the environment to educate users.

2.5 Performance Excellence

Malcolm Baldridge's framework of performance excellence explains how performance excellence is obtained, with 7 criteria provided to obtain performance excellence. The first is leadership, composed of a senior leader, has a vision of the mission, and social responsibility of the team. Second, strategic planning, how they develop strategies. Third is customer focus, where they suit the products to customers' needs. Fourth is measurement, how the organization analyses and manages data and analytics. Fifth is workforce focus, how the organization develops the workers' skills. The sixth is operations focus, how the strategies and operations are designed. Seventh is results, how the performance of the company is in conclusion [18]. Performance excellence is defined as a way organizations maintain their position above competitors [19].

In a previous research done by Rahayu et al. (2021), they used the performance excellence framework to measure the success rate of criteria by analysing the performances of the rural school that they were researching in which they found excellent results from the rural school with an excellent score of 662.75 [18] Furthermore, Ramzan and Khan (2020) explained in a performance excellence perspective regarding their topic, stating how the overall quality changed the ways and performances of TQM to achieve better results [20]

Another study by Baksh et al. (2022) used the performance excellence theory to aid them in their research, in which after conducting multiple qualitative interviews, the results of their analysis showed how the organization staffs' perception on performances decreased after the first cycle of subsequent surveys [21].

3   Methodology

This study employed a qualitative content analysis approach, a method that offers opportunities for analysing, manifesting, and descriptive content, which will result in categories [22, 23]. Afterwards, the data is then analyzed using thematic analysis, which is defined as a method to view and identify recurring themes that are present [24]. This research aims to examine and analyse the commodification of the Instagram account @pandawaragroup, in which the data was collected from the Instagram account @pandawaragroup. The data collection was conducted on April 20th, 2023 until May 20th, 2023.

A total of 105 posts were obtained, however due to some posts having multiple images, a total of 252 images (n = 252) was obtained. A codebook scheme was made to help dissect the posts. The first set of codes comes from R Cohen's codebook for imagery [25], and a codebook from Bernard (2008) for analyzing the content [26]. In addition, an additional code was added from Rokhim (2021) [27].

4   Results

Cohen et al. (2021) provides the first set of codes, with the categories being Video, Visual Image Only (human figure/s, cartoon figure/s of humans, or non-human image of nature, food, animals present), Text Only, (posts that contain only text, such as motivational or educational posts). Finally, Image and Text Combined, (a combination of both image and text together, overlayed upon another) [25].

In addition, the research implemented another codebook by Bernard (2009) to further analyze the data that was gathered [26]. To ensure that the codebook suited the research objectives, the researcher selected specific categories that closely involved the research question through a thorough examination of the categories and the data. The initial code was a valuable starting point for the analysis, however adjustments were made to align with the data establishing a coding scheme that helps the analysis from previous literature.

The first code is the dominant camera angle used in post, what angle was mostly used in the post? The three angles used are High (camera looking down on figure), Straight – On (Camera is level with figure), Low (Camera is looking up at figure, or combination of the three other categories. The next code is the dominant type of camera shot used in post, this code is only applicable if there is a figure in the post, with variables such as tight (head and shoulders), medium (waist up), long (full body shot), or a combination of shots were used.

The dress code highlights the clothes worn by the people in the posts, casual (shirts, sweaters, or jeans), formal, (suits, ties, and coats), and varied (a combination of both). The next code is special effects/ production technique used, focusing on the additional effects used in the post and production techniques to enhance the post, such as montages (a rapid succession of images combined with a common theme), use of stills (still photographs were present in the content), slow motion (speed of post is slower than usual), fast motion (speed of post is faster than usual), computer graphics (letters or words growing or shrinking, pictures grow or shrink), super impositions (images overlaying one another), and split screen (two or more screens present in one post showing separate screens)

The production technique code focuses on how the content is produced, with variables such as cinéma vérité (filmed as if to look live), slides or video clips with print and voice-over or slides or video clips with movement, print, and voice-over (edited snapshots or photos that put into slides to be presented), animation and/or special production (cartoon figures were present and/or special techniques or cameras were used), and candidate head – on (speakers talk directly to the camera as if addressing the viewers). The setting code encompasses the background of the post, giving a backstage feel, with variables such as formal outdoors (the creator is in the outdoors in their formal role), informal outdoors (the creator is in the outdoors but not in a formal role), informal indoors (the creator is indoors but not in a formal role), and formal indoors (the creator is indoors in their formal role).

The staging code highlights if the acts done in the post are natural or not, with variables such as natural staging (everything is naturally done without acting), all obviously staged (the acts are staged), combination of the two, or cannot be determined. The music code finds if music is present or not in the post, which then the type of music is analyzed (modern (rock, jazz, pop), folk, instrumental, or another type (other)). After the analysis, there is an additional code that was added that enriches the coding scheme by addressing a distinct aspect, this code is labeled as the camera movement, with variables such as zoom (changes the focus of the camera on the target), dolly (camera moves closer or further away from the target), tilt (camera moves up and down without changing position), panning (camera looks left and right without moving position), crab (camera movement that is sideways), follow pan (this movement follows the target to maintain the visual), and pedestal (camera movement that moves upwards and downwards and the camera follows the movements rather than staying in one position like tilting) [27].

Table 1. Results of Findings

Code	Variable	Range	Percentage
Dominant camera angle used in ad. (Code only for the candidate)	High	48	19%
	Straight-on	105	42%
	Low	4%	2%
	Movement combination (specify)	63	25%
	Not Applicable	32	13%
Dominant type of camera shot used in ad (Code only for the candidate)	Tight	5	2%
	Medium	26	10%
	Long	110	44%
	Movement combination	54	22%
	Not Applicable	56	22%
Dresscode	Casual	185	73%
	Formal	5	2%
	Varied	4	2%
	Not Applicable	58	23%
Special effects/ production technique used	No Effects	178	71%
	Montage	47	19%
	Use of Stills	1	0%
	Slow Motion	7	3%
	Computer Graphics	19	8%
	Super Impositions	8	3%
	Fast Motion	2	1%
	Split Screen	2	1%
Music	Music	43	17%
Type of Music Used	Other	5	2%
	Modern	33	13%
	Folk	3	1%
	Instrumental	3	1%
Production Technique	Cinema Verite	164	65%
	Slides or video clips with print and voice-over or slides or video clips with movement, print, and voice-over	46	18%
	Animation and/or special production	1	0%

(continued)

Table 1. (*continued*)

	Candidate head-on	4	2%
	Not Applicable	37	15%
Dominant Setting	Not Applicable	51	20%
	Formal Outdoors	159	63%
	Informal Outdoors	35	14%
	Informal Indoors	1	0%
	Formal Indoors	6	2%
Staging	Natural appearing	171	68%
	All obviously staged	10	4%
	Cannot be Determined	4	2%
	Combination	40	16%
	Not Applicable	27	**11%**
Camera Movement	Zoom	49	19%
	Dolly	76	30%
	Tilt	36	14%
	Panning	50	20%
	Crab	8	3%
	Follow Pan	40	16%

Table 1 shows the results of the analysis. It is important to mention that some data may fit into two or more categories in the codebook since some of the posts may have two or more effects within them. The results give us an overall explanation of how the content in Pandawara's Instagram is done. Starting with the most dominant camera angle, the most used camera angle is the "straight – on" angle or eye – level angle with 42% (n = 105). This angle gives the viewers a neutral sense of view or parity when watching the scene, in contrast to low level angles showing dominance and high level which shows vulnerability. Baranowski and Hecht (2018) state in their research that the eye – level angle gives the viewers a sense of trust (Baranowski & Hecht, 2018). In addition, the analysis shows that the most used camera shot is the long camera shot with 44% (n = 110) showing the full length of the body when recording or taking pictures.

Furthermore, the dominant dresscode for Pandawara is casual attire with 73% (n = 185) of their posts are wearing casual attire. Despite most of the posts do not have special effects since a lot of them were pictures, the second most used effect is the use of montages on their videos with 19% (n = 47), the montages were used on most of their videos, this is to move forward the activities quickly and show an overall view rather than making the video long [29]. Along with the montages, are also the presence of music in most of the montages, with 17% (n = 43). The most used music genre for their videos is modern music (rock, pop, jazz) in which in a research done by Mikhaylik (2021), they state that the use of music helps advertisements and media to create an emotional correlation between the viewer and the video, creating a dynamic that will help the viewer be interested in the advertisement, which is the same situation with Pandawara, adding music will help entertain the viewers to view more of their content [30].

On the question of setting, the dominant setting for their content was cinema verite, this setting is also an effective way to give a more physical and emotional effect to the audience since it suggests to the viewers that they are in front of the river that Pandawara is going to clean [31] Having discussed the setting, it is also important to mention that the staging also matters in this, with the dominant staging being natural appearing, this appeal creates an interesting view towards the audience as way to gain social respect and to be approved of good thoughts. Turning now to camera movements, it is important to mention that multiple camera movements could be used in one video, which creates more effect. The most used camera movement is the dolly movement, where the camera moves closer or further from the target. This movement is not just about getting closer or further from the target, but rather gives an inviting vibe towards viewers with smoothness and stability, and can initiate excitement [32]. Pandawara uses this movement mostly in their videos where they would get closer towards the member while he is cleaning the river, giving excitement and also a bigger view of the background.

5 Discussion

After the analysis was done, several themes were seen to have appeared in the data, with the most common theme being the showcase of before and after results of the activities. Pandawara would usually start their content by showing how much trash and how dirty the area is around them, they then proceed to begin showing their cleaning activities, ending with the results of their cleaning (Figs. 3 and 4).

Fig. 3. An example of a moment before Pandawara cleans

Fig. 4. An example of a moment after Pandawara cleans

In a previous study done by Lobodally (2019), they researched regarding how disaster is being commodified by the media, they state that the idea of disaster is being used as a product for the media to attract viewers because disasters are relatable to the viewers as they feel the emotions within the content and also becomes heroic nuances for the audience [33]. In a similar situation, Pandawara showcases the area they are going to clean, which is filled with trash, and then proceed to do a heroic act by cleaning the area while also implementing the right camera movements and special effects to keep the audience entertained. Showcasing the state of the environment gives the audience a sentimental feeling as they see a disaster in front of them, in which it will then be saved in a heroic moment by Pandawara, using this chance as a way to promote their activities through content [33]. They have also used multiple effects, camerawork, and settings to help the audience stay focused on their content. Furthermore, the commodification done can also cause a shift in the views of norms as the algorithm of popular social media content will prioritize only the popular section of it and will only focus on views that are popular rather than ones that focus on cultural significance or the quality of it [34].

The role of media aesthetics can also be implemented in classrooms for students and teachers to use for learning. As students find social media a way to develop critical thinking and problem-solving skills as well as learning new values by viewing positive role models in the media [35], classrooms can also implement ways to teach students how to think critically and garner media literacy to develop critical thinking and information selection skills [36]. With this, students can gain analytical skills for analysis and negotiate their social media use [37]. Pandawara's content of using multiple camera angles, effects, and aesthetics can be used as material to be taught for the students on how to critique the media as it may hold emotional and persuasive impacts for them.

In addition, by teaching on the use media aesthetics and effects, students may also engage them for activism and digital campaigns on social media while also understanding the effects of commodification that happens. Educators can also use the understanding of media aesthetics to help impact student engagement and learning since aesthetic techniques can aid in making students engaging and memorable for viewers using Pandawara's content as an example of how creative aesthetic techniques are used on social media for both educational and visual pleasing purposes.

Furthermore, from a performance excellence perspective, Pandawara showcases a high performance in their content making. Their content is shown in a variety of posts, with engaging inforgraphics, videos showcased in an aesthetic way by applying effects and special camera techniques, and also environmental narratives to inspire their target audience which are the youth of Indonesia [8]. In addition, they have also collaborated with other companies to advertise products and events, reaching a larger audience. In a previous interview done with Pandawara by Cretivox, they stated that the ones in control of all the production and editing of their content are themselves and no additional media teams are present as well as planning their activities [38].

6 Conclusion

This study focuses on how media aesthetics plays a part in content commodification and how students can learn from this to create proper impactful digital media. Despite sometimes not being aware of the act and not having the intention of doing so, the acts of commodification are still unavoidable [39]. Pandawara demonstrated their commodification of content by using multiple media aesthetics and leveraging social media to gain a wider audience, thus creating commodification and giving them partnerships and sponsorship opportunities with multiple brands. By using the media aesthetics, they narrate their content in a way of storytelling to educate and attract their audience about the environment.

There is also the matter of their performance excellence in which they demonstrated a positive outcome, with more collaborations with other companies to advertise products and also gain a wider audience, leveraging social media to its fullest by implementing multiple effects and camerawork to gain more attention.

Pandawara's content commodification can be used as a way to educate others in school and educational institutions regarding the potential social media has for campaigns and activism. A book by Alderfer (2020) stated how the teachers in their research used social media for activism as they find it easier to reach other people in comparison to an offline environment [40]. With this, teachers can leverage social media commodification to teach students on how commodification works on social media, the usage of media aesthetics for fostering media literacy among students, and can help analyze social media campaigns, using Pandawara as an example.

From the research done, suggestions for further research can apply other methods and theories to analyse the commodification from a political perspective and use Vincent Mosco's other two commodification of communication aspects. In addition, the demographic of the audiences can also be gathered to see what types of people are interested in Pandawara's content by interviewing Pandawara and focus also on the authenticity and integrity of activism. In addition, conductions of other techniques can analyse the performance. Finally, this research only focuses on one case study of a single content group and may not be a general form of digital activism.

References

1. Karatzogianni, A.: Firebrand Waves of Digital Activism 1994–2014: The Rise and Spread of Hacktivism and Cyberconflict. Springer (2015)
2. Prajarini, D.: Media Sosial Periklanan Instagram. Deepublish (2020)
3. Ansari, J.A.N., Khan, N.A.: Exploring the role of social media in collaborative learning the new domain of learning. Smart Learn. Environ. **7** (2020)
4. Dey, S.: Let there be clamor: exploring the emergence of a new public sphere in India and use of social media as an instrument of activism. J. Commun. Inq. **44**, 48–68 (2020)
5. Widiastuti, T.: The commodification of virtual community content in increasing media traffic. Media Commun. **9**, 98–109 (2021)
6. Hetrick, C., Wilson, C.M., Reece, E., Hanna, M.O.: Organizing for urban education in the new public square: using social media to advance critical literacy and activism. Urban Rev. **52**, 26–46 (2020)
7. Smith, K., Moriarty, S., Barbatsis, G., Kenney, K.: Handbook of Visual Communication Theory, Methods, and Media (2005)
8. Bagaskara, B.: Pandawara Group, Lima Sahabat Menerjang Sungai demi Pungut Sampah. Detik https://www.detik.com/jabar/jabar-gaskeun/d-6496221/pandawara-group-lima-sahabat-menerjang-sungai-demi-pungut-sampah#:~:text=Tujuan%20Utama%20Pandawa ra,membersihkan%20sam-pah%20di%20depan%20mata. (2023)
9. Mosco, V.: The Political Economy of Communication. SAGE Publications Ltd., London (2009)
10. Juliansyahzen, M.I.: Ideologization of Hijrah in social media: digital activism, religious commodification, and conservative domination. Millah 155–180 (2023) https://doi.org/10.20885/millah.vol22.iss1.art6
11. Simakova, S.: Media aesthetic component of communication and its manifestation in infographic content. Lumina **14**, 84–96 (2020)
12. Reliability, R., Kolbe, R.H., Burnett, M.S.: Content-analysis research: an examination of applications with directives for improving content-analysis research: an examination of applications with directives for improving research reliability and objectivity. J. Consum. Res. **18** (1991)
13. Kleinheksel, A.J., Rockich-Winston, N., Tawfik, H., Wyatt, T.R.: Qualitative research in pharmacy education. Demystifying Content Analysis (2020). https://doi.org/10.5688/ajpe84 17113, http://www.ajpe.org
14. Gao, S., He, L., Chen, Y., Li, D., Lai, K.: Public perception of artificial intelligence in medical care: Content analysis of social media. J. Med. Internet Res. **22**, (2020)
15. El-Awaisi, A., O'Carroll, V., Koraysh, S., Koummich, S., Huber, M.: Perceptions of who is in the healthcare team? A content analysis of social media posts during COVID-19 pandemic. J. Interprofessional Care **34**, 622– 632 (2020). https://doi.org/10.1080/13561820.2020.181 9779
16. Hsieh, H.F., Shannon, S.E.: Three approaches to qualitative content analysis. Qual. Health Res. **15**, 1277–1288 (2005)
17. Sharp, E.N., Carter, H.: Examination of how social media can inform the management of volunteers during a flood disaster. J. Flood Risk Manag. **13**, (2020)
18. Rahayu, N.I., Adawiyah, W.R., Anggraeni, A.I.: Malcolm Baldrige education criteria for performance excellent of vocational school in rural area (2019)
19. Saoudi, I., Dehane, M. & Mehri Constantine, A. A New Perspective on How to Achieve Performance Excellence: A Comparative Analysis of the American and European 2020 Model1 رؤية حديثة ل تحقيق كيفية الأداء ال م: تميز تحليلية نة مقار بين ... A new perspective on how to achieve 2020 والأوروبي يكي الأمر لنموذج لسنة, Imene Saoudi, Mohammad Dehane. Number 02 Journal of Financial Accounting and Managerial Studies 07, 7–07 (2020).

20. Ramzan, A., Khan, A.M., Khan, R.: Conceptual content analysis: policy documentation for the quality of higher education in Pakistan. Pak. J. Educ. **37** (2020)
21. Baksh, M.M., et al.: Striving for performance excellence: ten years' experience & impact of accreditation on quality, safety, and overall performance in King Saud University Medical City (KSUMC)-A Mixed-Methods Study (2022). https://doi.org/10.21203/rs.3.rs-1207353/v1
22. Graneheim, U.H., Lindgren, B.-M., Lundman, B.: Methodological challenges in qualitative content analysis: a discussion paper. Nurse Educ. Today **56**, 29–34 (2017)
23. Graneheim, U.H., Lundman, B.: Qualitative content analysis in nursing research: concepts, procedures and measures to achieve trustworthiness. Nurse Educ. Today **24**, 105–112 (2004)
24. Lochmiller, C.R.: Conducting thematic analysis with qualitative data. Qual. Rep. **26**, 2029–2044 (2021)
25. Cohen, R., Newton-John, T., Slater, A.: The case for body positivity on social media: perspectives on current advances and future directions (2021)
26. Bernard, N.: A. abstract appealing to the Youtube voter: an analysis of barack obama"s 2008 presidential campaign advertisements on Youtube (2009)
27. Rokhim, A.: Metode Tutor Sebaya Sebagai Upaya Peningkatan Prestasi Belajar Komposisi Foto Dan Video (Type Of Shot) Siswa Kelas Xi Pspt (Broadcast) Smk Negeri 1 Bangil Kabupaten Pasuruan. Jurnal Ilmiah Edukasi & Sosial **12**, 1–10 (2021)
28. Baranowski, A.M., Hecht, H.: Effect of camera angle on perception of trust and attractiveness. Empir. Stud. Arts **36**, 90–100 (2018)
29. MasterClass. MasterClass. https://www.masterclass.com/
30. Mikhaylik, E.: The influence of music on consumption (2021)
31. Merdhi, A., Imanjaya, E.: Documentary cinema, plastic waste problem, and environmental sustainability: the case of pulau plastik. In: IOP Conference Series: Earth and Environmental Science, vol. 998. IOP Publishing Ltd. (2022)
32. Yilmaz, M.B., Lotman, E., Karjus, A., Tikka, P.: An embodiment of the cinematographer: emotional and perceptual responses to different camera movement techniques. Front. Neurosci. **17** (2023)
33. Lobodally, A. The Commodification of Disaster in Telkomsel TVC 'Menjadi Relawan Yang Terbaik' Version (2019)
34. P Putri, E.K., Abror, D., F S Maella, N.: A. Content commodification in the digital age: implications and challenges. J. Sci. Appl. Eng. (JSAE) **7** (2024)
35. Guru, K., Raja, S.: A study on impact of social media on student education system. Int. J. Early Childhood Special Education (INT-JECS) **14**, 25–2 (2022)
36. Voronova, A.: Student's media literacy training as a factor of personality development in the inclusive education. Eur. Proc. Soc. Behav. Sci. 153–160 (2021). https://doi.org/10.15405/epsbs.2021.06.04.18
37. Higdon, N.: The critical effect: exploring the influence of critical media literacy pedagogy on college students' social media behaviors and attitudes. J. Media Literacy Educ. **14**, 1–13 (2022)
38. Cretivox. PANDAWARA GROUP PAHLAWAN MASA KINI?! I #SIAPA S1 E13 (2023). https://www.youtube.com/watch?v=2aMdLunK1Go
39. Akmalia, N., Ardiani, S.: Commodification of children on social media endorsement (case study on @zaskiaadyamecca's Instagram account). Jurnal Kajian dan Terapan Media, Bahasa, Komunikasi **2**, 108–123 (2021)
40. Alderfer, K.: Teachers #Resist. Drexel University, Philadelphia, Pennsylvania, United States (2020). https://doi.org/10.17918/t05m-3d61

New Developments in Mental Healthcare: Investigation on the Impact of Telepsychiatry and Cutting-Edge Technologies

Lorenzo Sanesi[1]([✉]) and Domenico Lorusso[2]

[1] Department of Clinical and Experimental Medicine, University of Foggia, 71122 Foggia, Viale Luigi Pinto, Italy
lorenzo.sanesi@unifg.it
[2] Department of Humanities, Letters, Cultural Heritage, Educational Sciences, University of Foggia, Via Arpi, 71121 Foggia, Italy

Abstract. In recent years, telemedicine is increasingly used in psychiatry. This approach has facilitated e.g. diagnoses, remote support and remote treatment. The purpose of this investigation is to evaluate technologies applied to telemedicine in psychiatry, focusing on their applications and their impact. Video conferencing platforms are widely used during psychoanalysis and allow for secure virtual consultations between the patient and mental health professionals in real time. The specialist can monitor the patients and evaluate their progress, provide therapies, and conduct comprehensive assessments remotely. Another technology used are mobile applications and wearable devices. These new technologies like SuperBetter app, MoodHacker app, and SPARX and sensors have improved the management of depression. These devices allow patients to actively engage in their own care and mental health, as they allow for self-monitoring of symptoms, mood and medication adherence. These technologies have led to improved treatment outcomes. Artificial intelligence and machine learning algorithms can be exploited to improve psychiatric diagnosis and treatment planning. These new technologies can be used to find patterns and predict responses to treatments supporting psychiatrists providing more accurate clinical decisions and personalized therapies for patients. Augmented reality and virtual reality are emerging as innovative tools to be applied in psychiatry. These technology with the patient's conventional therapy provide a new approach to manage psychiatric symptoms. In conclusion, telepsychiatry and cutting-edge technology in synergy with conventional patient management can overcome barriers, improve accessibility to care and ameliorate therapeutic responses in patients.

Keywords: Telemedicine · psychiatry · telepsychiatry technology

1 Introduction

The enormous advances in the medical field have led to a significant increase in life expectancy [1]. We therefore see an increase in the elderly population who is more vulnerable to diseases, including psychiatric disease, as demonstrated by the Global

G. A. Toto (Ed.): ICS exchange 2024, CCIS 2521, pp. 270–280, 2025.
https://doi.org/10.1007/978-3-032-03021-4_19

Burden of Disease [2], consequently this leads to an increase in healthcare spending, moreover people with depression are steadily increasing from 1990 to the present day. In the United States, 1 in 5 adults will suffer from a symptom of depression at least once in their lifetime [3]. The management of psychiatric patients could become problematic in the future and for this reason the use of cutting-edge technologies and telemedicine can help in the management of these patients.

Although recently there is an increase of telemedicine application, as a support for distant health care this is not a new concept. Since 1878, the use of the telephone was hypothesized to reduce visits to clinics [4]. Thus, the application of the technology to medicine is a concept that goes hand in hand with early technological inventions.

The 2019 coronavirus pandemic (COVID-19), due to the need for physical distance and because of the shortage of health care providers, has encouraged the rapid and global adoption of telemedicine solutions, facilitating the spread of virtual medical care [5]. Prior to the COVID-19 pandemic, the use of cutting-edge technologies had been applied to rural and remote areas. Many medical doctors have shown concerns about the impact of telepsychiatry on physician workload e.g. administrative, logistical, and clinical [6].These issues may explain, at least in part, the limited adoption of telepsychiatry in urban psychiatric settings prior to the COVID-19 pandemic. In recent years, digital health technology is rapidly changing mental health care and support services, to improve access to and quality of mental health care, thereby improving the clinical management of depression [7].

Several studies have noted that the application of telemedicine, the reliability, effectiveness, and outcomes of telemedicine applied to psychiatry, are overall comparable to conventional care [8–10]. Furthermore, telemedicine leads to a reduction in patient management costs [11]. Currently, the main advanced technologies and e-health solutions are web-based health portals, telehealth services, electronic health records (EHRs), online appointment scheduling, and wearable fitness devices [1]. These new technologies that can be applied to psychiatry concern: Video conferencing platform, AI and Machine Learning, Wearable Devices, Virtual Reality (VR), Mobile Health Apps [12]. The purpose of this investigation is to evaluate technologies applied to telemedicine in psychiatry, focusing on their applications and their impact.

2 Video Conferencing Platform

The use of video conferencing platforms allows secure virtual consultations in real time; thus, the specialist can monitor patients remotely and perform comprehensive assessments [13]. This approach is cost-effective because it offers flexibility to patients and caregivers, reducing need to travel for medical care, thus decreasing health commuting. Moreover, it enhances the continuity of care, facilitating ongoing psychiatric support, particularly for people with mobility problems or in crisis situations [14–17]. This type of approach also provides greater privacy, allowing patients to receive care in their own homes. Several studies have reported that clinical effectiveness, treatment adherence, and patient satisfaction were comparable to conventional methods, as reported by Link et al. in 2023 [18] and by Toreles et al. in 2023 [19].

Link et al. in 2023 [18] observed a group of remotely treated mental health patients during the period of the COVID-19 pandemic in Germany. To ensure continuity of care during their treatment, authors applied the implementation of telemedical assistance via telephone or videoconferencing, and this option was used as much as possible. In this study, both patients and therapists felt that telemedicine during lockdown was an alternative to conventional therapy and that the telemedicine option should continue throughout the duration of the coronavirus pandemic, moreover the results showed a clear trend toward satisfaction with and acceptance of telemedicine care in a heterogeneous group of psychiatric patients. Toreales et al. in 2023 [19] evaluated the satisfaction of patients using the Telepsychiatry service offered by the Department of Psychiatry of the Hospital de Clínicas (National University of Asunción, Paraguay). In this study, 9 out of 10 psychiatric patients felt satisfied with the telepsychiatry service.

One of the principal problems of application of video visits in patients is "digital divide" [20]. The digital divide is due to the different possibility of access to the internet. This is due to the existing structural inequalities that do not allow access and use of information technology due to social problems in the areas and geographical characteristics [20]. Especially, are affected patients who belong to groups that are already disadvantaged, such as racial or ethnic minorities, poor, and the elderly [21, 22]. Recent evidence has pointed out that there was disparity in receiving health care during the COVID 19 pandemic for individuals from these groups [22]. A priority goal for ensuring healthcare through digital platforms is to diminish these inequalities, through solutions that address broadband availability, guaranteed affordable devices, an adequate privacy, and assistance for patients with no digital literacy. Moreover, health care providers/organizations should use user-friendly digital solutions for patients with different cognitive and physical abilities.

2.1 Holographic Video Communication System

A new technology that can be applied to telepsychiatry is an oleographic system calling. This system was released by Google in May 2021 and allows users to see a 3D hologram of the person they are talking to [1]. Google describes this technology as being able to allow users to interact with a person in life-size and three dimensions, thus making the call more natural [1]. Google points out that they have been tested this new technology with health care companies [1]. Its impact on telepsychiatry could be tremendous. This type of approach could enhance telemedicine because the metal health professional, could better interpret nonverbal messages by patients. These types of signals play a key role in message interpretation, for example when a verbal message is ambiguous and is crucial in the diagnosis of psychiatric disorders [23, 24]. In addition, this kind of approach could also promote the clinician's communication toward the patient, thus improving the patient's satisfaction during therapy.

3   Use of App in Mental Healthcare

The use of apps applied to psychiatry represents an interesting recent field of application. This is possible through smartphones and tablets. Recent studies have shown that these can be useful tools for effective and cost-efficient healthcare interventions, especially in the field of tele cognitive rehabilitation [25]. Smartphones and tablets have many functionalities such as geolocation, internet access, sensors, and notifications [26]. These can be used like tools comparable to specific medical device in supporting doctor through application of specific app without apply other instruments that can be burden and generating embarrassment for the patients. Although in the last years there is an increase of applications of app, their use in clinical practice is still low [27, 28]. More than 200 health applications (apps) for smartphones and tablets are uploaded to Apple's App Store and Google Play every day [1]. Of the 300,000 health apps available in the various markets, 20,000 are mental health apps [29]. Some mental health apps are designed to be used standalone, while others are developed to be used in conjunction with conventional therapy [17]. Studies have observed how the use of apps in elderly patients and patients with neurodegenerative diseases was well accepted by users, and was able to stimulate cognitive abilities such as processing speed, prospective and episodic memory, and executive functions, making smartphones and tablets valuable tools for improving cognitive performance [25]. App use has shown particular efficacy in symptom management of depression and generalized anxiety and they showed an efficacy on social anxiety [30], but not shown effects on post-traumatic stress or panic symptoms [30]. However, the use of the apps is not intended to exclude the doctor-patient relationship, but it can be an aid for both the doctor and the patient in the management of psychiatric symptoms. Examples of apps that are used in the management of mental symptoms include: Superbetter, Moodhaker and Sparx. Studies analyzed the effectiveness of these applications by comparing the strengths and weaknesses in their use. The application of Superbetter showed efficacy in reducing psychiatric symptoms in patients who used the app compared with the control population during a 6-week follow-up. In addition, no difference was found in the use of the version of Superbetter using a CBT and positive psychotherapy (PPT) strategies and a general version of the app focused on self-esteem and acceptance. A weakness of the study is the high dropout rate during the study and the sample selection which was done via website and may have taken a particular group of well-motivated or hopeful patients [31]. The use of Moodhaker showed positive results in the management of patients with mild and moderate depression. Patients at 6 and 10 weeks of use reported significant improvement in depressive symptoms compared with the no-treatment group. A limitation of this study is in the convenience of the selected sample, reliance on surveys alone, moreover patients received a compensation to complete the study [32]. SPARX is a "serious" game developed especially for young patients between 12-19 years old with depression symptoms. This application is based on computerized cognitive behavioral therapy consisting of seven modules delivered over a period of four to seven weeks. At 3 months of using this application, the results were not inferior to conventional therapy, and therefore it could be used as an alternative strategy to treat young patients, especially when conventional therapy does not give results [33].

    Use of apps for psychological care of patients today shows various problems such as: lack of evidence and methodological challenges, safety concerns, privacy, and data security, need for regulation and standards and poor user-friendliness.

    Lack of evidence and methodological challenges, as many applications currently used for mental health management have not shown scientifically solid evidence of their effectiveness. Studies conducted on app-based treatments have often shown lower quality in design compared to traditional studies based on the doctor-patient relationship and therefore makes it difficult to evaluate the real effectiveness of the use of these apps [34]. Additionally, some apps have shown security issues, as they may contain potentially harmful content. For example, apps that are used for suicide prevention include inappropriate suggestions such as lists of means of instant death, although such means have been presented as suggestions to eliminate access to such means, or there are incorrect numbers of emergency telephone lines [35, 36]. These data highlight how there may a risk for users to receive advice from these apps. The use of apps available in various markets have shown issues in privacy and data security. The apps have shown issues in managing privacy and processing personal data. These issues are due to the lack of transparency on the sharing of this data, the complexity of privacy policies and the potential for re-identification of anonymized data pose risks to users. This can dissuade individuals from using such apps for fear of misuse or data breaches [37–39]. Furthermore, currently, there is need for regulations and standards development. Although there are various regulations and app evaluation frameworks, their proliferation can confuse both clinicians and patients, making it difficult to choose the appropriate evaluation framework and app, for this reason there is a need to develop clear guidelines and standards for the use of mental health apps [17, 40]. Finally, apps have shown poor user-friendliness of use which may represent another barrier to their adoption for mental health management [41, 42]. In a 2020 survey, consumers interviewed declared themselves dissatisfied with the digital experience due to the difficulty of using the apps [1].

For this reason, in the future, it will be necessary to involve the main stakeholders in the development of mental health apps, such as patients, clinicians, designers, engineers to make the use of apps better in the future.

3.1 Wearables Device

Wearable sensors can be used in the management of mental illness [43]. This approach offers many advantages over traditional methods of mental health assessment as they allow real-time assessment of a patient's emotional state, moreover they are practical and cost-effective. Heart frequency, sleep, and respiratory patterns can be potentially applied to identify and monitor emotional state of the patients in real time [44–46]. Several wearable devices are currently available that have sufficient quality to provide meaningful data targeted to machine learning algorithms. Current results indicate that mental health monitoring is feasible. These technologies may be used in conjunction with telemedicine to provide more comprehensive support for people with panic attacks [47], furthermore, this technology may be used with virtual reality therapy to assess the patient's emotional state in real time.

4   Artificial Intelligence and Machine Learning

Artificial intelligence (AI) can mimic human cognitive functions, such as learning and problem solving. It is therefore capable of simulating human intelligence in machines such as computers and robots. Machine learning (ML) develops algorithms that allow computers to evolve their behavior based on empirical data [48, 49]. Currently, we have increasing access to big data from multiple sources (e.g., EHR, genomics, wearable devices). This data in combination with increasing computing power enables the development of deep learning models. In this way the computer is able to develop increasingly accurate and complex models that are not comparable to the traditional approach, and this allows models to be created directly from raw data [50]. These tools can be applied to psychiatry and can offer various benefits such as improving psychiatric diagnosis and treatment planning and allows to do personalized therapies for each patient. AI allows predict responses to treatment and can also support the clinician in making accurate clinical decisions. Artificial intelligence (AI) can be applied to chatbots and these tools have gained more and more importance since 2022. The development of machine learning and the use of big data in chatbots has enabled the development of a natural language. Chatbots can help mental health management, facilitating access and reducing patient stigma, as well as reducing the cost of expenses. Although they have developed greatly in recent years, their use is still debated and further research is needed to evaluate their real effectiveness [51].

4.1   Chat-GPT

Generative Pre-Trained Transformer (GPT) is an AI language model that is developed by OpenAI and designed for natural language processing (NLP) tasks. Chat-GPT, on the other hand, is a derivative of GPT and is trained to generate human-like text responses from provided prompts [52]. GPT can give two primary NLP tasks such as understanding the meaning of written sentences and providing new sentences based on the prompts given. Thus, GPT can understand the questions asked and generate coherent answers [52]. These features make it a valuable tool applicable to psychiatry [53]. The great development of chatbots in recent years has brought a lot of attention to the application of Chat-GPT in psychiatry, but its use is currently limited. The initial data that have given a major boost to the application of GPT to psychiatry are based on previous data obtained using deep learning, which has already shown promise in classifying psychiatric disorders using neuroimaging and other clinical data [53]. Currently Chat-GPT in psychiatry can carry out routine tasks, while psychotherapy care or patient evaluation is still performed by human therapists [54]. Furthermore, Chat-GPT is currently ready for current applications to reduce the burden of clinical documentation, communications, and research tasks [53, 55]. In the future GPT technology will be able to incorporate empathy, will be able to recognize emotions, evaluate personality and will be able to detect mental health warning signs and will be essential in psychiatric care [55]. Chat-GPT has the potential to help psychiatrists, for example, by processing clinical dictations to generate summaries from medical dialogues, these can be inserted into the patient's medical record, furthermore can also complete the medical record documentation, helping therefore doctors in bureaucratic tasks [56]. Moreover chat-GPT can facilitate communication between doctors with patients [56]. Currently, current technology cannot yet replace the opinion of an expert doctor, the complexity of mental pathologies still makes it impossible to use GPT technology in the clinic, because psychiatry requires empathy in human interaction, which is fundamental for clinical results [57]. So, in the future when GPT technology is equipped with the ability to empathize, recognize emotions, evaluate personality, and detect warnings about mental health signs, it can be applied to clinical psychiatric. GPT will in the future be able to detect mental health warning signs through daily conversations or message exchanges and through telemedicine it will be able to facilitate early and effective intervention when necessary [58]. Creating a fully automated psychotherapy system still requires further technological research and requires the development of clinically trained algorithms, moreover, the system's training data will need to be processed in a way that protects privacy and complies with regulations all professional, ethical and legal standards [58]. So, it is necessary to establish and refine professional ethical and practical standards for the correct implementation of revolutionary GPT technologies in mental health care.

5 Virtual Realty

Virtual reality (VR) is a tool that is used to create a digital environment like the real world [1] and is an innovative tool used in psychiatry and can be used together with conventional therapy. It is useful for managing situations that induce psychiatric symptoms. Through this type of therapy, the patient is exposed to a situation that induces stress and for this reason is useful to menage specific phobias like flight phobia, acrophobia, arachnophobia, or social anxiety disorder such as social scenarios like presentations and meetings [59–61]. Furthermore, VR can be used for the management of post-traumatic symptoms, through the re-exposure of the patient to specific situations that induced the trauma. It is especially useful for soldiers, survivors of terrorist attacks or car accidents. VR can be applied in psychosis, through this psychiatric can performed analysis of symptoms, neurocognitive assessment, evaluation of activities of daily living. The application of VR led to a reduction in paranoia, and an improvement in social interaction in patients [62]. A limitation of the studies on this field are analyzed small-scale of patients, and thus further research are needed. VR can be used in child and adolescent psychiatry [63]. It can be used for the management of ADHD, autism spectrum disorder (ASD) through attention training, social skills training, for cognitive rehabilitation [63]. In addition, virtual classroom programs can be set up, through the simulation of school environments attention span and social adaptability can be improved. This approach has resulted in improved attention span, adaptability, and social skills in young patients.

6 Future Directions

Telepsychiatry is currently widely used, and it is necessary to combine it with new technologies to have a better effect on the patient. The combination of telepsychiatry with AI, VR, and wearable devices has led to more comprehensive care and examples of integrated approaches improving patient outcomes. In the future the use of telemedicine must be widespread not only for normal treatments but can also be used for the management of emergencies. To do this you will need to increase confidence in using these tools. To do this it will be necessary to carry out ethical considerations to understand what the best way of application is and how to protect patient privacy. We must also continue research and innovation on these techniques as the results obtained so far are very promising. Finally, it will be necessary to improve the education and training not only of the patients who will be able to use these technologies independently but also of the healthcare personnel who will have to advise and apply these technologies in the most appropriate way.

7 Conclusions

In conclusion, the use of telemedicine allows access to health services even in remote or unserved areas, also in the management of patients with mental illnesses, thus serving a greater number of patients. This type of approach has made it possible to reduce access to hospitals for emergencies because in this way we can intervene before the disease worsens and access to hospitals is required. It also reduces the time needed to obtain second opinions, thus reducing treatment times. Furthermore, the use of artificial intelligence has made it possible to provide personalized therapies for each patient.

Acknowledgments. We thank the *ICS Exchange Conference 2025* for the opportunity to present this work and for fostering an inspiring academic environment.

Disclosure of Interests. The authors declare no conflict of interest.

References

1. Roth, C.B., et al.: Psychiatry in the digital age: a blessing or a curse? Int. J. Environ. Res. Public Health **18**(16) (2021)
2. Global burden of 369 diseases and injuries in 204 countries and territories, 1990–2019: a systematic analysis for the global burden of disease study 2019. Lancet **396**(10258), 1204–1222 (2020)
3. Hasin, D.S., et al.: Epidemiology of adult DSM-5 major depressive disorder and its specifiers in the United States. JAMA Psychiat. **75**(4), 336–346 (2018)
4. Guinart, D., et al.: Mental health care providers' attitudes toward telepsychiatry: a systemwide, multisite survey during the COVID-19 pandemic. Psychiatr. Serv. **72**(6), 704–707 (2021)
5. Bokolo Anthony, J.: Use of telemedicine and virtual care for remote treatment in response to COVID-19 pandemic. J. Med. Syst. **44**(7), 132 (2020)
6. Lal, S., Abdel-Baki, A., Peredo, R.: Clinician perspectives on providing telepsychiatry services to young adults with first-episode psychosis during COVID-19. Early Interv. Psychiatry **17**(12), 1189–1198 (2023)
7. Naslund, J.A., et al.: Digital technology for treating and preventing mental disorders in low-income and middle-income countries: a narrative review of the literature. Lancet Psychiatry **4**(6), 486–500 (2017)
8. Aparecida Delben, J., et al.: Effect of atmospheric-pressure cold plasma on pathogenic oral biofilms and in vitro reconstituted oral epithelium **11**(5) (2016)
9. Bulkes, N.Z., et al.: Comparing efficacy of telehealth to in-person mental health care in intensive-treatment-seeking adults. J. Psychiatr. Res. **145**, 347–352 (2022)
10. Shaker, A.A., et al.: Psychiatric treatment conducted via telemedicine versus in-person modality in posttraumatic stress disorder, mood disorders, and anxiety disorders: systematic review and meta-analysis. JMIR Ment. Health **10**, e44790 (2023)

11. Hubley, S., et al.: Review of key telepsychiatry outcomes. World J. Psychiatry 6(2), 269–282 (2016)
12. McIntyre, R.S., et al.: Digital health technologies and major depressive disorder. CNS Spectr. 28(6), 662–673 (2023)
13. Cubo, E., et al.: Videoconferencing software options for telemedicine: a review for movement disorder neurologists. Front. Neurol. 12, 745917 (2021)
14. Flowers, D., Goodspeed, E., Daly, M.: Telehealth as an effective care delivery method during the COVID-19 pandemic for the rhode island behavioral health population. Community Ment. Health J. 60(1), 108–114 (2024)
15. Bee, P.E., et al.: Psychotherapy mediated by remote communication technologies: a meta-analytic review. BMC Psychiatry 8, 60 (2008)
16. Hilty, D.M., et al.: The effectiveness of telemental health: a 2013 review. Telemed. J. E Health 19(6), 444–454 (2013)
17. Wilhelm, S., et al.: Cognitive-behavioral therapy in the digital age: presidential address. Behav. Ther. 51(1), 1–14 (2020)
18. Link, K., et al.: Telemedicine treatment of patients with mental disorders during and after the first COVID-19 pandemic lockdown in Germany - an observational study on feasibility and patient satisfaction. BMC Psychiatry 23(1), 654 (2023)
19. Torales, J., et al.: Satisfaction with telepsychiatry during the COVID-19 pandemic: patients' and psychiatrists' report from a University Hospital. Int. J. Soc. Psychiatry 69(1), 156–160 (2023)
20. Choxi, H., et al.: Telehealth and the digital divide: identifying potential care gaps in video visit use. J. Med. Syst. 46(9), 58 (2022)
21. Saeed, S.A., Masters, R.M.: Disparities in health care and the digital divide. Curr. Psychiatry Rep. 23(9), 61 (2021)
22. Busch, A.B., et al.: Telemedicine for treating mental health and substance use disorders: reflections since the pandemic. Neuropsychopharmacology 46(6), 1068–1070 (2021)
23. Mast, M.S.: On the importance of nonverbal communication in the physician-patient interaction. Patient Educ. Couns. 67(3), 315–318 (2007)
24. Almeida, M.S.C., et al.: International classification of diseases - 11th revision: from design to implementation. Rev. Saude Publica 54, 104 (2020)
25. Maggio, M.G., et al.: Can mobile health apps with smartphones and tablets be the new frontier of cognitive rehabilitation in older individuals? A narrative review of a growing field. Neurol. Sci. 45(1), 37–45 (2024)
26. Putzer, G.J., Park, Y.: Are physicians likely to adopt emerging mobile technologies? Attitudes and innovation factors affecting smartphone use in the Southeastern United States. Perspect. Health Inf. Manag. 9(Spring), 1b (2012)
27. de Joode, E., et al.: Efficacy and usability of assistive technology for patients with cognitive deficits: a systematic review. Clin. Rehabil. 24(8), 701–714 (2010)
28. Kim, B.Y., Lee, J.: Smart devices for older adults managing chronic disease: a scoping review. JMIR Mhealth Uhealth 5(5), e69 (2017)
29. Lagan, S., Sandler, L., Torous, J.: Evaluating evaluation frameworks: a scoping review of frameworks for assessing health apps. BMJ Open 11(3), e047001 (2021)
30. Linardon, J., et al.: The efficacy of app-supported smartphone interventions for mental health problems: a meta-analysis of randomized controlled trials. World Psychiatry 18(3), 325–336 (2019)
31. Roepke, A.M., et al.: Randomized controlled trial of superbetter, a smartphone- based/internet-based self-help tool to reduce depressive symptoms. Games Health J. 4(3), 235–246 (2015)
32. Birney, A.J., et al.: MoodHacker Mobile web app with email for adults to self-manage mild-to-moderate depression: randomized controlled trial. JMIR Mhealth Uhealth 4(1), e8 (2016)

33. Merry, S.N., et al.: The effectiveness of SPARX, a computerised self help intervention for adolescents seeking help for depression: randomised controlled non-inferiority trial. BMJ **344**, e2598 (2012)
34. Kretzschmar, K., et al.: Can your phone be your therapist? Young people's ethical perspectives on the use of fully automated conversational agents (Chatbots) in mental health support. Biomed. Inform. Insights **11**, 1178222619829083 (2019)
35. Larsen, M.E., Nicholas, J., Christensen, H.: A systematic assessment of smartphone tools for suicide prevention. PLoS ONE **11**(4), e0152285 (2016)
36. Torous, J., et al.: Digital mental health and COVID-19: using technology today to accelerate the curve on access and quality tomorrow. JMIR Ment Health **7**(3), e18848 (2020)
37. Chan, S.R., et al.: Mobile tele-mental health: increasing applications and a move to hybrid models of care. Healthcare (Basel) **2**(2), 220–233 (2014)
38. Powell, A.C., Singh, P., Torous, J.: The complexity of mental health app privacy policies: a potential barrier to privacy. JMIR Mhealth Uhealth **6**(7), e158 (2018)
39. Grundy, Q., et al.: Data sharing practices of medicines related apps and the mobile ecosystem: traffic, content, and network analysis. BMJ **364**, l920 (2019)
40. Kola, L., et al.: COVID-19 mental health impact and responses in low-income and middle-income countries: reimagining global mental health. Lancet Psychiatry **8**(6), 535–550 (2021)
41. Nicholas, J., et al.: The reviews are in: a qualitative content analysis of consumer perspectives on apps for bipolar disorder. J. Med. Internet Res. **19**(4), e105 (2017)
42. Torous, J., et al.: Clinical review of user engagement with mental health smartphone apps: evidence, theory and improvements. Evid. Based Ment. Health **21**(3), 116–119 (2018)
43. Kang, M., Chai, K.: Wearable sensing systems for monitoring mental health. Sensors **22**(3), 994 (2022)
44. Dikecligil, G.N., Mujica-Parodi, L.R.: Ambulatory and challenge-associated heart rate variability measures predict cardiac responses to real-world acute emotional stress. Biol. Psychiatry **67**(12), 1185–1190 (2010)
45. Tipton, M.J., et al.: The human ventilatory response to stress: rate or depth? J. Physiol. **595**(17), 5729–5752 (2017)
46. Barnes, K.: Sleep monitoring in mental health goes digital. Commun. Med. **1**(1), 50 (2021)
47. Gomes, N., et al.: A survey on wearable sensors for mental health monitoring. Sensors (Basel) **23**(3) (2023)
48. Lee, D., Yoon, S.N.: Application of artificial intelligence-based technologies in the healthcare industry: opportunities and challenges. Int. J. Environ. Res. Public Health **18**(1) (2021)
49. Maddox, T.M., Rumsfeld, J.S., Payne, P.R.O.: Questions for artificial intelligence in health care. JAMA **321**(1), 31–32 (2019)
50. Beam, A.L., Kohane, I.S.: Big data and machine learning in health care. JAMA **319**(13), 1317–1318 (2018)
51. Balcombe, L.: AI Chatbots in digital mental health. Informatics **10**(4), 82 (2023)
52. Raile, P.: The usefulness of ChatGPT for psychotherapists and patients. Humanit. Soc. Sci. Commun. **11**(1), 47 (2024)
53. Kumar, S.: Burnout in psychiatrists. World Psychiatry **6**(3), 186–189 (2007)
54. Ali, S.R., et al.: Using ChatGPT to write patient clinic letters. Lancet Digit Health **5**(4), e179–e181 (2023)
55. Bykov, K.V., et al.: Prevalence of burnout among psychiatrists: a systematic review and meta-analysis. J. Affect. Disord. **308**, 47–64 (2022)
56. Patel, S.B., Lam, K.: ChatGPT: the future of discharge summaries? Lancet Digit Health **5**(3), e107–e108 (2023)
57. Elliott, R., et al.: Therapist empathy and client outcome: an updated meta-analysis. Psychotherapy (Chic.) **55**(4), 399–410 (2018)

58. Cheng, S.W., et al.: The now and future of ChatGPT and GPT in psychiatry. Psychiatry Clin. Neurosci. **77**(11), 592–596 (2023)
59. Botella, C., et al.: Recent progress in virtual reality exposure therapy for phobias: a systematic review. Curr. Psychiatry Rep. **19**(7), 42 (2017)
60. Dellazizzo, L., et al.: Evidence on virtual reality-based therapies for psychiatric disorders: meta-review of meta-analyses. J. Med. Internet Res. **22**(8), e20889 (2020)
61. Bentz, D., et al.: Effectiveness of a stand-alone, smartphone-based virtual reality exposure app to reduce fear of heights in real-life: a randomized trial. NPJ Digit. Med. **4**(1), 16 (2021)
62. Rus-Calafell, M., et al.: Virtual reality in the assessment and treatment of psychosis: a systematic review of its utility, acceptability and effectiveness. Psychol. Med. **48**(3), 362–391 (2018)
63. Pollak, Y., et al.: The utility of a continuous performance test embedded in virtual reality in measuring ADHD-related deficits. J. Dev. Behav. Pediatr. **30**(1), 2–6 (2009)

Standardization Protocol for Education in Emotional Competences Through CASEL Model: Inclusion for Children Project

Alessandro De Santis[(✉)] [iD] and Francesco Antonio Santangelo [iD]

University of Foggia, Puglia, 71121 Foggia, Italy
alessandro.desantis2@unifg.it

Abstract. **(Background)** The development of emotional and social skills is increasingly recognized as fundamental in preventing antisocial behavior and gender-based violence. Early interventions focused on metacognitive development, particularly self-reflection and emotional recognition are essential for reducing violence fenomena and improve socio-emotional competence. **(Objective)** This study, part of the I4C initiative, aims to validate and standardize a research protocol that enhances school inclusion through innovative strategies, advancing emotional literacy and socio-relational skills. In this article we show preliminary data from pre-test phase to confirm revised structural components of DANVA-2-RV (Diagnostic Analysis of Nonverbal Accuracy 2 - Revised Version) instrument. **(Methodologies)** Individual administration of DANVA-2 was performed in First year Primary schools of Foggia Territory. **(Results)** The revised model of the DANVA-2 demonstrates a robust fit across various constructs analyzed. Trait Loading (CFI = 0.938, TLI = 0.915, RMSEA = 0.043, SRMR = 0.083), Correlation Among Traits (CFI = 1.000, TLI = 1.830, RMSEA = 0.000, SRMR = 0.036), Intensity (CFI = 0.545, TLI = 0.647, RMSEA = 0.081), Methods (CFI = 1.000, TLI = 1.000, RMSEA = 0.000, SRMR = 0.000): these results display a strong fit across traits, intensity, and methods, supporting the model's capacity to measure the ability to recognize emotions effectively. **(Conclusion)** The findings suggest that the DANVA-2-RV model is a valid and reliable tool for assessing the ability to recognize emotions, offering a promising opportunity to be integrated into the I4C project as a standardized method to evaluate progress through students' emotional abilities development. Further research is required to confirm these results across larger samples.

Keywords: ERA · Emotional Recognition Ability · socio-emotional competence · school inclusion

1 Introduction

Emotion recognition ability (ERA) plays a crucial role in emotional intelligence (Matthews, Zeidner, & Roberts, 2002; Mayer & Salovey, 1997), social competence (Halberstadt et al., 2001), and emotional competence (Saarni, 2001). It is integral to interpersonal sensitivity, or accurately perceiving one's social environment (Rosip & Hall,

© The Author(s), under exclusive license to Springer Nature Switzerland AG 2025
G. A. Toto (Ed.): ICS exchange 2024, CCIS 2521, pp. 281–299, 2025.
https://doi.org/10.1007/978-3-032-03021-4_20

2004). The ability to identify emotions from nonverbal cues is fundamental for affective development (Herba & Phillips, 2004) and contributes significantly to interpersonal judgments and social adjustments throughout life (Denham et al., 2011).

Research indicates that ERA improves across childhood and adolescence, essential stages for forming social relationships (Durand et al., 2007; Nowicki & Duke, 1994). Tools like the DANVA2 have been effective in measuring emotion recognition across different ages and intensities (Nowicki & Duke, 1994). Despite greater focus on infant and early childhood emotion recognition, the development of ERA during middle childhood and adolescence remains less explored, though it is vital for social adjustment (Thomas et al., 2007).

Emotion recognition relies on discrete neural mechanisms, as suggested by neurodevelopmental research (Adolphs et al., 2001; Herba & Phillips, 2004). Happiness is typically recognized first, while emotions like fear and disgust are less accurately identified, possibly due to cultural specificity (Elfenbein & Ambady, 2002). Emotion recognition involves processing not only facial expressions but also postures, which convey emotional intensity (Piterman & Nowicki, 2004; Ekman, 1965).

The DANVA2, a frequently used tool for assessing ERA, has strong construct validity and measures perceptual accuracy across various ages and emotion types (Baum & Nowicki, 1998; Mayer et al., 2008). Studies have linked lower ERA with social issues, including learning disabilities and behavioral problems (Collins & Nowicki, 2001; McClure & Nowicki, 2001). This study, part of the I4C initiative, aims to validate and standardize the DANVA-2-RV to enhance emotional literacy and social inclusion in schools. Preliminary findings from this research expand on the instrument's construct validity and effectiveness in assessing emotional competence in educational contexts. (Matthews, Zeidner, & Roberts, 2002; Mayer & Salovey, 1997; Nowicki & Duke, 1994).

2   Method

2.1   Participants

Participants were recruited from 5 elementary schools across 4 geographical areas in Foggia (Italy). Informed parental consent was obtained, and participation was voluntary. Exclusion criteria included serious mental impairment, psychiatric diagnosis, learning disability, serious visual impairment, absence from school during test administration, and lack of parental permission.

In total, 12 students did not participate in data collection, either because they did not have consent to participate or due to serious issues that prevented them from taking part in the study.

The final sample size consists of 81 children (50 boys, 31 girls), aged 6 to 7 years old (mean age (SD) = 6.8 (0.3)) who participated. The racial and gender composition of the sample was representative of the Capitanata school populatio. Children from immigrant families and other cultures made up 15% of the sample, but those who participated were born or had been living in Italy for at least two years and were proficient in Italian.

All participants were individually administered the DANVA-2-RV.

2.2 Procedure

Two female and one male gragraduate psychology students and PhD student, previously trained in children's assessment techniques, collected the data. Collaborators from the Learning Science Institute at the University of Foggia individually administered the DANVA-2-RV as part of the study. Their involvement ensured standardized administration procedures and contributed to the accuracy of the data collection process. Administration was performed in quiet private rooms located in the children's schools. Participants completed questionnaires in one sessions on different days to minimize fatigue. Each complete testing session lasted approximately 10-15 minutes per child. The sessions began with an introduction to the project, emphasizing the confidentiality of the study.

2.3 Instrument: DANVA-2-RV

The Diagnostic Analysis of Nonverbal Accuracy Test original version (DANVA2) assesses the ability to accurately decode four emotions (happiness, sadness, anger, and fear) through three nonverbal channels: adult and child facial expressions (DANVA2-AF and DANVA2-CF) and the posture subtest (DANVA2-POS) (Nowicki, 2011; Nowicki & Duke, 1994; Nowicki & Carton, 1993; Baum & Nowicki, 1998; Piterman & Nowicki, 2004). The DANVA2-AF and DANVA2-CF subtests each consist of 24 photographs of adult and child facial expressions, featuring an equal number of high and low intensity images showing happiness, sadness, anger, and fear. The DANVA2-POS subtest contains 24 photographs of individuals in different standing and seated postures, depicting high and low intensities of happiness, sadness, anger, and fear (Piterman & Nowicki, 2004).

The DANVA-2-RV (Diagnostic Analysis of Nonverbal Accuracy 2 - Revised Version) introduces significant improvements while preserving the core elements of the original test. One of the most notable changes is the transition to a computerized system for projecting stimuli, which ensures standardized administration and consistent timing across participants. Additionally, instead of relying on verbal responses, children now use a touchscreen to select emoticons representing happiness, sadness, anger, and fear, providing a more intuitive and accessible way for them to respond. The posture subtest has also been revised, reducing the number of items from 24 to 16 based on a new dataset. This refinement was driven by statistical analyses that examined correct response rates and the naturalness of the postures, ensuring that only the most effective and realistic stimuli were included. Despite these updates, key elements of the original test remain unchanged, such as the use of both adult and child facial expressions (DANVA2-AF and DANVA2-CF) and the inclusion of high and low intensity emotions. The administration process also retains its technical precision, with the automatic disappearance of stimuli after 2 seconds, ensuring consistency in the participants' exposure time.

The Posture Subtest Revision was guided by statistical analyses, including corrected answer rates and evaluations of the naturalness of postures. In dataset, postures that achieved correct recognition rates of less than 0.6 were replaced, and new stimuli were selected based on their realistic representation of emotions, with over 0.8 agreement on naturalness. This revision ensures that the DANVA-2-RV maintains high reliability while using the most accurate and representative stimuli.

2.4 Statistical Analysis

Following the procedure suggested by Bagozzi (1993), previous studies tested two linear models sequentially: a general confirmatory factor analysis (CFA) model and a or- related uniqueness confirmatory factor analysis (CU) model. However, while the CU model had already been explored in previous research, this study specifically focuses on the CFA model alone. The objective is to assess whether the original factor structure can explain the data adequately without the need to account for correlated uniqueness, providing a distinct and focused analysis on the CFA approach.

In previous studies, the Correlated Uniqueness (CU) model was employed to address certain limitations inherent in the Confirmatory Factor Analysis (CFA) model, such as improper parameter estimation and issues with model identification and interpretation (Bagozzi, 1993). The CU model was favored as it allowed for the inclusion of correlated residuals, thus providing a more nuanced representation of shared method effects. In contrast, the current study focuses exclusively on the CFA model to assess whether the factor structure of the data can adequately explain the relationships between observed variables without the need for correlated uniqueness (CU). While earlier research highlighted the CU model as yielding more acceptable solutions, this study aims to determine if the original CFA model can provide an accurate fit, thus offering a more parsimonious explanation. This approach allows for a direct evaluation of the data's underlying structure without introducing additional complexities from correlated residuals. R software-v4.4.1 was used to perform the analyses.

3   Result

3.1   The General Confirmatory Factor Analysis Model (CFA)

The revised model of the DANVA-2 demonstrates a robust fit across various constructs analyzed. Methods (CFI = 1.000, TLI= 1.000, RMSEA = 0.000, SRMR = 0.000), Emotion-Methods (CFI = 0.938, TLI = 0.915, RMSEA = 0.043, SRMR = 0.083) Correlation Among Emotions (CFI = 1.000, TLI = 1.830, RMSEA = 0.000, SRMR = 0.036), Intensity (CFI = 0.545, TLI = 0.647, RMSEA = 0.081) display a moderate-suboptimal fit across traits, intensity, and methods, supporting the model's capacity to measure the ability to recognize emotions effectively.

3.1.1   DANVA-2-RV: CFA for Methods

As previously mentioned, the DANVA-2 is characterized by three fundamental subsets of items: Adult Facial Expressions (DANVA2-AF), Child Facial Expressions (DANVA2-CF), and the Posture Subtest (DANVA2-POS). The fundamental structure of the Revised Version (DANVA-2-RV) remains consistent with the original. The methods model (see Table 1) adopted for the DANVA-2-RV can be considered a perfect fit, as indicated by the following fit indices: CFI = 1.000, TLI = 1.000, RMSEA = 0.000, and SRMR = 0.000. Notably, the Child Faces subtest (DANVA2-CF) contributes significantly to the general factor (Methods of Evaluation) with a loading of 0.82.

Table 1. .

Latent	Estimate	Std.Err	z-value	P(>|z|)	Std.lv	Std.all
Child_F	2,358	0,43	5,488	0	2,358	0,817
Adult_F	2,009	0,415	4,838	0	2,009	0,664
Posture	0,952	0,251	3,787	0	0,952	0,474

Variance	Estimate	Std.Err	z-value	P(>|z|)	Std.lv	Std.all
Child_F	2,778	1,665	1,669	0,095	2,778	0,333
Adult_F	5,129	1,417	3,619	0	5,129	0,56
Posture	3,137	0,558	5,62	0	3,137	0,776
F1*	1				1	1

R²	R-Value	Lambda	F1	Theta	1	2	3
Child_F	0,667	Child_F	0,817	Child_F	0,33	-	-
Adult_F	0,44	Adult_F	0,664	Adult_F	-	0,56	-
Posture	0,224	Posture	0,474	Posture	-	-	0,776

*F1: Methods Factor: table presents estimates of the latent variables Child_F, Adult_F, and Posture in relation to the Methods Factor (F1), including their standardized factor loadings, variances, and R-squared values. All estimates are statistically significant ($p < 0.001$), except for the variance of Child_F ($p = 0.095$). The Child Faces subtest contributes the most to the general factor ($\lambda = 0.817$), followed by the Adult Faces subtest ($\lambda = 0.664$) and the Posture subtest ($\lambda = 0.474$).

3.1.2   DANVA-2-RV: CFA for Correlation Between Emotions and Methods of Evaluation

The other structure analyzed is the fundamental model adopted by both the original and revised versions of DANVA-2. This implies that for the methods, DANVA-Adult Faces, DANVA-Posture, and DANVA-Child Faces, four types of emotions are evaluated: happiness, anger, fear, and sadness (see Table 2). The model shows an overall good fit (Chi-square: 55.297, DF: 48, p-value: 0.218; CFI: 0.938; TLI: 0.915; RMSEA: 0.043; SRMR: 0.083), with several variables making significant contributions to their respective latent factors. Notable factor loadings include Anger Child Faces ($\lambda = 0.935$), Fearful Child Faces ($\lambda = 1.216$), Sadness Child Faces ($\lambda = 0.661$), Sadness Adult Faces ($\lambda =$

0.953), Happiness Child Faces ($\lambda = 0.477$), and Happiness Adult Faces ($\lambda = 0.592$), indicating strong relationships with the latent constructs.

Table 2. .

Latent* Variable	Indicator	Esti-mate	Std.Err	z-value	P(>|z|)	Std.lv	Std.all
Happiness Factor	Happi-ness_CF	0,396	0,115	3,439	0,001	0,396	0,477
Happiness Factor	Happi-ness_AF	0,56	0,14	3,995	0	0,56	0,592
Happiness Factor	Happi-ness_Pos	0,156	0,089	1,747	0,081	0,156	0,242
Saddness Factor	Sad-dness_CF	0,849	0,178	4,766	0	0,849	0,661
Saddness Factor	Sad-dness_AF	0,953	0,208	4,588	0	0,953	0,628
Saddness Factor	Sad-dness_Pos	0,404	0,107	3,776	0	0,404	0,501
Anger Factor	Anger_CF	1,32	0,255	5,174	0	1,32	0,935
Anger Factor	Anger_AF	0,712	0,208	3,417	0,001	0,712	0,45
Anger Factor	Anger_Pos	0,47	0,145	3,248	0,001	0,47	0,422
Fearfull Factor	Fear_CF	1,955	0,465	4,208	0	1,955	1,216
Fearfull Factor	Fear_AF	0,84	0,27	3,11	0,002	0,84	0,465
Fearfull Factor	Fear_Pos	0,297	0,131	2,261	0,024	0,297	0,268

*The Table 2 presents an analysis of several latent variables, specifically examining four emotional factors: Happiness, Sadness, Anger, and Fear. Each of these factors is associated with methods indicators (e.g. Child faces, Adult faces, Posture).

3.1.3   DANVA-2-RV: CFA for Correlation Across Emotions

The Confirmation Factor Analysis (CFA) demonstrated an overall good fit, as indicated by strong fit indices: $\chi2(2) = 1.109$, $p = 0.574$, Comparative Fit Index (CFI) = 1.000, Tucker-Lewis Index (TLI) = 1.830, and Root Mean Square Error of Approximation (RMSEA) = 0.000 with a 90% confidence interval of [0.000, 0.185]. These results indicate that the model is an appropriate representation of the data. Furthermore, the standardized root mean square residual (SRMR) of 0.036 also confirms the satisfactory fit of the model. However, despite the overall good model fit, significant limitations arise in the explanatory power for specific variables (see Table 3). While happiness (factor loading = 0.696, R2 = 0.485) and sadness (factor loading = 0.426, R2 = 0.182) are reasonably well explained by the latent factor Emotions, the same cannot be said for Anger (Rabbia, Anger) and Fear (Paura, Fear). Both R1 and P1 exhibit very low factor loadings (-0.070 and 0.100, respectively) and near-zero R-squares (0.005 and 0.010), indicating that these variables are poorly captured by the latent construct. This observation aligns with findings in the literature, which suggest that Fear is often an outlier with lower loadings compared to other emotions, and Anger similarly exhibits a higher portion of unexplained variance (Ciucci et al., 2011). This suggests that these emotions may require additional latent constructs or a different theoretical framework for better explanation.

Table 3. .

Latent Variable	Estimate	Std.Err	z-value	P(>|z|)	Std.lv	Std.all
Happiness	1,163	1,261	0,922	0,356	1,163	0,696
Saddness	1,183	1,306	0,906	0,365	1,183	0,426
Anger	-0,22	0,499	-0,441	0,659	-0,22	-0,07
Fearfull	0,355	0,585	0,606	0,544	0,355	0,1

Variance	Estimate	Std.Err	z-value	P(>|z|)	Std.lv	Std.all
Happiness	1,438	2,917	0,493	0,622	1,438	0,515
Saddness	6,305	3,168	1,99	0,047	6,305	0,818
Anger	9,952	1,572	6,333	0	9,952	0,995
Fearfull	12,452	1,981	6,287	0	12,452	0,99
F1*	1				1	1

R^2	R-Value	Lambda	F1	Theta	1	2	3	4
Happines	0,485	Happy	0,696	Happy	0,515	-	-	-
Sad	0,182	Sad	0,426	Sad	-	0,818	-	-
Anger	0,005	Anger	-0,07	Anger		-	0,995	-
Fear	0,01	Fear	0,1	Fear	-	-	-	0,99

*F1: Emotion Factor

As shown in Table ---, the lack of significant factor loadings likely reflects the different nature of these four emotions. Since they are heterogeneous, it is not surprising that a single latent factor does not capture their variability well. This insight suggests the possibility of restructuring the model to include multiple latent factors that represent more specific emotional constructs.

3.1.4   DANVA-2-RV: CFA for Emotional Intensity

The results of second order confirmatory factor analysis (CFA) for Emotional Intensity indicate that the current model demonstrates suboptimal fit, as evidenced by key indices such as a Comparative Fit Index (CFI) of 0.545 and a Tucker-Lewis Index (TLI) of 0.647, both of which fall significantly below acceptable thresholds for good model fit. Additionally, the Root Mean Square Error of Approximation (RMSEA) of 0.081, while marginally acceptable, suggests the model still has room for improvement. These indicators imply that the model, in its current configuration, does not adequately capture the relationships among the variables. Notably, the model has not previously been tested in this form. In the next section, the same model is developed by isolating emotional variables and considering them independently, which could potentially improve the fit and provide a more precise understanding of the relationships within the data.

3.1.4.1 Happiness

Results of the Confirmatory Factor Analysis (CFA) on intensity happiness (Table 4) indicate a strong model fit with several positive aspects. The Chi-square test yielded a p-value of 0.107, suggesting no significant difference between the model and observed data, and the fit indices are excellent, with a Comparative Fit Index (CFI) of 0.933 and a Tucker-Lewis Index (TLI) of 0.911, both exceeding the threshold of 0.9. Additionally, the Root Mean Square Error of Approximation (RMSEA) is 0.062, which, along with the p-value for RMSEA ≤ 0.05 at 0.331, suggests an acceptable error margin. The Standardized Root Mean Square Residual (SRMR) of 0.074 further supports the good fit by indicating minimal differences between the observed and predicted correlations. High factor loadings for both factors, such as Item_A23 (0.741), Item_A24 (0.656), Item_P9 (0.685) for Factor 1 (High Intensity) and Item_C12 (0.700), Item_C23 (0.459) for Factor 2 (Low Intensity), demonstrate that the items are strong indicators of their respective

Table 4. .

Latent Variables	Observed Variables	Estimate	Std.Err	z-value	P(>|z|)	Std.lv	Std.all
F1	Item_C16	0,119	0,035	3,399	0,001	0,119	0,398
F1	Item_A23	0,082	0,012	7,081	0	0,082	0,741
F1	Item_A4	0,142	0,023	6,062	0	0,142	0,656
F1	Item_P1	0,145	0,027	5,467	0	0,145	0,603
F1	Item_P9	0,148	0,023	6,398	0	0,148	0,685
F2	Item_C12	0,168	0,028	5,994	0	0,168	0,7
F2	Item_C23	0,11	0,029	3,828	0	0,11	0,459
F2	Item_A4	0,164	0,051	3,176	0,001	0,164	0,386
F2	Item_A7	0,116	0,059	1,956	0,05	0,116	0,243
F2	Item_A10	0,13	0,04	3,254	0,001	0,13	0,395

Covariance (F1 ~ F2)	Estimate	Std.Err	z-value	P(>|z|)	Std.lv	Std.all
0,912	0,912	0,091	10,022	0	0,912	0,912

Observed Variables	Estimate	Std.Err	z-value	P(>|z|)	Std.lv	Std.all
Item_C16	0,075	0,012	6,106	0	0,075	0,841
Item_A23	0,006	0,001	4,663	0	0,006	0,452
Item_A24	0,027	0,005	5,314	0	0,027	0,57

(continued)

Table 4. (*continued*)

Item_P1	0,037	0,007	5,573	0	0,037	0,636
Item_P9	0,025	0,005	5,135	0	0,025	0,531
Item_C12	0,03	0,007	4,19	0	0,03	0,511
Item_C23	0,046	0,008	5,856	0	0,046	0,79
Item_A4	0,153	0,025	6,036	0	0,153	0,851
Item_A7	0,213	0,034	6,249	0	0,213	0,941
Item_A10	0,091	0,015	6,018	0	0,091	0,844

Items	I_C16	I_A23	I_A24	I_P1	I_P9	I_C12	I_C23	I_A4	I_A7	I_A10
I_C16	0,841	-	-	-	-	-	-	-	-	-
I_A23	-	0,452	-	-	-	-	-	-	-	-
I_A24	-	-	0,57	-	-	-	-	-	-	-
I_P1	-	-	-	0,636	-	-	-	-	-	-
I_P9	-	-	-	-	0,531	-	-	-	-	-
I_C12	-	-	-	-	-	0,511	-	-	-	-
I_C23	-	-	-	-	-	-	0,79	-	-	-
I_A4	-	-	-	-	-	-	-	0,85	-	-
I_A7	-	-	-	-	-	-	-	-	0,94	-
I_A10	-	-	-	-	-	-	-	-	-	0,844

*The CFA model shows strong factor loadings for most variables, with significant relationships between latent factors F1 (high-intensity emotion) and F2 (low-intensity emotion). The covariance between F1 and F2 is high (0.912), indicating a strong association between the two factors. Most variables have low error variances, except for Items_A7, which has a lower factor loading and higher unexplained variance. Some variables may need further investigation, like Items_A7, due to its weaker contribution to the latent factor.

latent variables. The covariance between the two factors is notably high (0.912), highlighting a strong relationship between them. Overall, the parameter estimates are highly significant, providing further confidence in the reliability of the model, making this CFA a successful validation of the hypothesized two-factor structure.

3.1.4.2 Sadness
The sadness model (Table 5) demonstrates excellent fit indices for sadness emotion, with a CFI of 1.000 and a TLI of 1.008, which are both above the typical threshold of 0.9, indicating a very strong fit between the model and the observed data. Additionally, the RMSEA of 0.000 further supports this, suggesting that the model has minimal error. Most variables have significant factor loadings, especially for Items_A11 (0.511) and Items_C21 (0.652), indicating that these variables strongly represent their respective latent factors (F1 and F2). A few variables like Items_P11 and Items_A18 have weaker loadings, suggesting they may contribute less to Factor 1 (F1). The covariance between

Table 5. CFA for sadness

Latent Variables	Observed Variables	Estimate	Std.Err	z-value	P(>|z|)	Std.lv	Std.all
F1	Item_C13	0,07	0,051	1,371	0,171	0,07	0,163
F1	Item_A6	0,152	0,062	2,462	0,014	0,152	0,31
F1	Item_A11	0,243	0,068	3,55	0	0,243	0,511
F1	Item_A18	0,101	0,06	1,686	0,092	0,101	0,203
F1	Item_P11	0,063	0,042	1,485	0,138	0,063	0,177
F2	Item_C10	0,18	0,047	3,82	0	0,18	0,464
F2	Item_C17	0,175	0,059	2,975	0,003	0,175	0,368
F2	Item_C21	0,305	0,054	5,619	0	0,305	0,652
F2	Item_A13	0,188	0,061	3,08	0,002	0,188	0,38
F2	Item_A14	0,261	0,047	5,508	0	0,261	0,641
F2	Item_P5	0,123	0,051	2,418	0,016	0,123	0,302

Covariance (F1 ~~ F2)	Estimate	Std.Err	z-value	P(>|z|)	Std.lv	Std.all
1,157	1,157	0,229	5,055	0	1,157	1,157

Observed Variables	Estimate	Std.Err	z-value	P(>|z|)	Std.lv	Std.all
Item_C13	0,181	0,029	6,337	0	0,181	0,974
Item_A6	0,218	0,036	6,131	0	0,218	0,904
Item_A11	0,167	0,035	4,784	0	0,167	0,739
Item_A18	0,24	0,038	6,31	0	0,24	0,959
Item_P11	0,122	0,019	6,329	0	0,122	0,969
Item_C10	0,118	0,02	5,787	0	0,118	0,785
Item_C17	0,196	0,032	6,036	0	0,196	0,865
Item_C21	0,125	0,026	4,763	0	0,125	0,574
Item_A13	0,21	0,035	6,01	0	0,21	0,855
Item_A14	0,098	0,02	4,86	0	0,098	0,589
Item_P5	0,151	0,024	6,154	0	0,151	0,908

Items	I_C13	I_A6	I_A11	I_A18	I_P11	I_C10	I_C17	I_C21	I_A13	QA14	QP5

(*continued*)

Table 5. (*continued*)

I_C1 3	0,974	-	-	-	-	-	-	-	-	-	-
I_A6	-	0,904	-	-	-	-	-	-	-	-	-
I_A1 1	-	-	0,739	-	-	-	-	-	-	-	-
I_A1 8	-	-	-	0,959	-	-	-	-	-	-	-
I_P1 1	-	-	-	-	0,969	-	-	-	-	-	-
I_C1 0	-	-	-	-	-	0,785	-	-	-	-	-
I_C1 7	-	-	-	-	-	-	0,865	-	-	-	-
I_C2 1	-	-	-	-	-	-	-	0,574	-	-	-
I_A1 3	-	-	-	-	-	-	-	-	0,855	-	-
I_A1 4	-	-	-	-	-	-	-	-	-	0,58	-
I_P5	-	-	-	-	-	-	-	-	-	-	0,90

F1 and F2 is 1.157, which is significant and quite high, indicating a strong relationship between the two latent factors. The observed variables have generally low error variances, meaning that the latent factors explain most of the variability. For instance, Items_C13 has a very high error variance (0.974), meaning it is not well explained by the model.

The theta matrix shows the residual error variances for each observed variable, while the lambda values reveal how strongly each observed variable loads on its respective latent factor. These metrics suggest that the model does a good job capturing the relationships, but further investigation of variables with lower loadings or higher residuals (e.g., Items_P11) could enhance model precision.

3.1.4.3 Anger

The model's fit for anger (Table 6) indices indicate a moderate fit, with a Comparative Fit Index (CFI) of 0.817 and a Root Mean Square Error of Approximation (RMSEA) of 0.094. While these values fall short of the commonly accepted thresholds for a good fit (CFI > 0.90, RMSEA < 0.08), they still suggest that the model reasonably fits the data, though improvements could be made. The factor loadings for both latent factors (F1 and F2) are significant, with variables like Items_C20 (0.644) and Items_C9 (0.567) showing strong loadings. However, some variables, such as Items_A15 (0.304), exhibit lower loadings, which might indicate a weaker relationship with the latent construct they are meant to measure. The strong covariance between F1 and F2 (1.168) suggests that the two latent factors are highly correlated, which could indicate shared variance or overlap in the constructs being measured by these factors. Observed variables like Items_A3 (0.871) and Items_A15 (0.908) have relatively high error variances, meaning that a large portion of the variance in these items is not explained by the latent factors. This suggests that these items might not be the best indicators of their respective factors and may benefit from refinement.

Table 6. CFA for anger expression.

Factor	Latent Variables	Std.Err	z-value	P(>|z|)	Std.lv	Std.all
F1	Items_C20	0,058	5,32	0	0,311	0,644
F1	Items_A3	0,056	2,885	0,004	0,162	0,324
F1	Items_A15	0,059	4,202	0	0,248	0,484
F1	Items_P6	0,061	3,421	0,001	0,208	0,422
F1	Items_P15	0,058	3,378	0,001	0,194	0,398
F2	Items_C9	0,065	4,38	0	0,283	0,567
F2	Items_A12	0,056	2,988	0,003	0,166	0,369
F2	Items_A20	0,056	2,988	0,003	0,166	0,369

Cova-riances	Estimate	Std.Err	z-value	P(>|z|)	Std.lv	Std.all
F1 ~~ F2	1,168	0,177	6,603	0	1,168	1,168

Variances	Estimate	Std.Err	P(>|z|)	Std.lv	Std.all
Items_C20	0,136	0,03	4,544	0,136	0,136
Items_A3	0,871	0,029	4,639	0,871	0,871
Items_A15	0,908	0,031	5,846	0,908	0,908
Items_P6	0,822	0,035	5,964	0,822	0,822
Items_P15	0,827	0,031	5,922	0,827	0,827
Items_C9	0,678	0,038	4,621	0,678	0,678
Items_A12	0,826	0,029	6,639	0,826	0,826
Items_A20	0,864	0,029	6,603	0,864	0,864

Items	I_C20	I_A3	I_A15	I_P6	I_P15	I_C9	I_A12	I_A20
I_C20	0,585	-	-	-	-	-	-	-
I_A3	-	0,871	-	-	-	-	-	-
I_A15	-	-	0,908	-	-	-	-	-
I_P6	-	-	-	0,822	-	-	-	-
I_P15	-	-	-	-	0,827	-	-	-
I_C9	-	-	-	-	-	0,678	-	-
I_A12	-	-	-	-	-	-	0,826	-
I_A20	-	-	-	-	-	-	-	0.684

3.1.4.4 Fear

Finally the fear model fit (Table 7) is assessed through various indices such as the Comparative Fit Index (CFI = 0.843) and Root Mean Square Error of Approximation (RMSEA = 0.070). These values indicate a reasonably acceptable fit but suggest room for improvement. The latent variable F1 is strongly associated with variables like Items_C18

Table 7. Sum of model fit for fear emotion.

Latent Variables*	Observed Variables	Estimate	Std.Err	z-value	P(>|z|)	Std.lv	Std.all
F1	I_C18	0.28	0.042	6.742	0.000	0.280	0.704
F1	I_C19	0.178	0.042	4.266	0.000	0.178	0.484
F1	I_C22	0.199	0.032	6.283	0.000	0.199	0.667
F1	I_A9	0.267	0.048	5.601	0.000	0.267	0.609
F1	I_A19	0.248	0.037	6.649	0.000	0.248	0.697
F1	I_A21	0.280	0.046	6.066	0.000	0.280	0.649
F1	I_P8	0.15	0.052	2.864	0.004	0.150	0.336
F1	I_P13	0.101	0.059	1.729	0.084	0.101	0.207
F2	I_C4	0.262	0.049	5.324	0.000	0.262	0.607
F2	I_C11	0.174	0.054	3.239	0.001	0.174	0.391
F2	I_C15	0.290	0.055	5.305	0.000	0.290	0.605
F2	I_A2	0.233	0.059	3.922	0.000	0.233	0.466
F2	I_A8	0.303	0.057	5.323	0.000	0.303	0.607
F2	I_A16	0.215	0.056	3.832	0.000	0.215	0.456
F2	I_P4	0.091	0.062	1.465	0.143	0.091	0.183
F2	I_P10	0.091	0.057	1.598	0.110	0.091	0.199

Covariance (F1 ~~ F2)	Estimate	Std.Err	z-value	P(>|z|)	Std.lv	Std.all
F1 ~~ F2	0.788	0.082	9.642	0.000	0.788	0.788

Observed Variables	Estimate	Std.Err	z-value	P(>|z|)	Std.lv	Std.all
I_C18	0.080	0.015	5.170	0.000	0.080	0.504
I_C19	0.103	0.017	5.997	0.000	0.103	0.766
I_C22	0.049	0.009	5.393	0.000	0.049	0.555
I_A9	0.121	0.021	5.653	0.000	0.121	0.629
I_A19	0.065	0.012	5.220	0.000	0.065	0.514
I_A21	0.108	0.020	5.484	0.000	0.108	0.579
I_P8	0.175	0.028	6.211	0.000	0.175	0.887
I_P13	0.229	0.036	6.310	0.000	0.229	0.957
I_C4	0.117	0.022	5.302	0.000	0.117	0.631
I_C11	0.168	0.028	6.041	0.000	0.168	0.847

(continued)

Table 7. (*continued*)

I_C15	0.146	0.027	5.312	0.000	0.146	0.633
I_A2	0.196	0.033	5.866	0.000	0.196	0.783
I_A8	0.157	0.030	5.302	0.000	0.157	0.631
I_A16	0.176	0.030	5.892	0.000	0.176	0.792
I_P4	0.241	0.038	6.303	0.000	0.241	0.967
I_P10	0.200	0.032	6.291	0.000	0.200	0.960

(loading $= 0.704$) and Items_A19 (loading $= 0.697$), while F2 is linked with variables such as Items_A8 (loading $= 0.607$) and Items_C4 (loading $= 0.607$). There is a significant positive covariance (0.788) between the two latent factors, indicating that high and low-intensity emotions are related. The observed variables display varying levels of unexplained variance, with Items_P13 and Items_P4 having high residuals, indicating less reliable measurement for these variables. The overall analysis highlights the structure of high and low-intensity emotional factors and suggests that while the model has reasonable validity, some observed variables are less robust in their association with the latent constructs.

3.1.5   Discussion and Overall Conclusion on CFA Model

The results of this study provide significant insights into the effectiveness and reliability of the revised DANVA-2-RV (Diagnostic Analysis of Nonverbal Accuracy 2 - Revised Version) in assessing emotional recognition abilities among primary school children. This section will explore the key findings, their implications, and areas for further research.

The Confirmatory Factor Analysis (CFA) demonstrated that the revised DANVA-2-RV model exhibits a strong overall fit, especially in its ability to measure methods of emotional recognition across child and adult faces, as well as postures. Key indicators for Posture, Methods and Correlation across emotion (CFI: 1.000; and RMSEA: 0.000) suggest that the instrument accurately captures the ability of children to recognize nonverbal emotional cues. The excellent fit of the methods factor reinforces the validity of this instrument as a comprehensive tool for assessing nonverbal emotion recognition in school-aged children. However CFA for correlation across emotions, results showed a lack of significant factor loadings, which indicates that the model struggled to capture the variability across the four emotions (happiness, sadness, anger, fear). This finding likely reflects the inherent differences in the nature of these emotions. Since emotions such as happiness and sadness are often easier to identify and interpret than emotions like anger and fear, they exhibit varied recognition patterns. For this reason, we propose a new interpretation of the latent factor by incorporating Intensity factors across emotions. By differentiating between high and low intensity levels for each emotion, the model could more accurately reflect the complexities in emotional recognition. This approach would allow the model to better capture the nuances in how children recognize emotions with varying levels of emotional intensity, offering a more refined and comprehensive understanding of emotional processing.

While the methods construct was robust, the second-order model fit for emotional intensity (CFI = 0.545; RMSEA: 0.081) was suboptimal. This indicates that the model may not fully capture the nuances of emotional intensity in children's responses. The complexity of emotions conveyed through body language may require further refinement in the assessment tool to enhance accuracy in this domain.

Using a first-order CFA, where emotions are treated as separate factors, the model demonstrated strong fits for happiness and sadness, but performed less optimally for anger and fear. For happiness, the fit indices were strong, with a CFI of 0.933 and a TLI of 0.911, both exceeding the acceptable thresholds of 0.9. Similarly, sadness showed an even stronger model fit with a CFI of 1.000 and a TLI of 1.008, suggesting minimal error in capturing the intensity of this emotion.

On the other hand, the model showed moderate fits for anger and fear. For anger, the CFI was 0.817 and the RMSEA was 0.094, indicating some room for improvement. Similarly, fear also exhibited a reasonably acceptable fit with a CFI of 0.843 and an RMSEA of 0.070, but these indices suggest that fear is not captured as well as happiness or sadness.

This issue of anger and fear being more challenging to capture accurately is already well-documented in the literature. Studies have consistently shown that anger and fear are often harder for children and even adults to recognize compared to more universally recognizable emotions like happiness and sadness. This difficulty is attributed to the subtler nonverbal cues associated with these emotions, as well as potential cultural influences on emotional interpretation. This suggests that further refinement is needed when assessing more complex emotions, particularly through better representation of emotional intensity or by incorporating additional latent factors specific to these emotions, in line with existing research findings (Ciucci et al., 2011).

For Happiness, specific items such as Item_C8 and Item_A1 showed a perfect positive correlation (1.00), meaning these two items essentially measure happiness identically, offering no additional unique information. This redundancy suggests that one of these items could be removed to streamline the assessment tool without losing valuable data. Additionally, items such as Item_A23 and Item_A24 demonstrated 0.000 variance, indicating that these items do not differentiate between individuals, as responses to these items were uniform across the sample. A lack of variance implies that these items are ineffective in measuring differences in emotional recognition, particularly for happiness..

Interestingly, the literature supports the notion that happiness is a universally recognized emotion. According to Ekman (1950), happiness is the only emotion consistently recognized by people across all cultures, making it unique among the basic emotions. This may explain why some happiness-related items in this study showed perfect correlations or little variance—happiness is more easily and universally identified than other emotions like anger or fear.

This pattern of perfect correlations and zero/negative variance is not limited to happiness but is also observed in some items across the other emotions (e.g., anger, sadness, and fear). To improve the model's accuracy and efficiency, several items across the four emotions have been removed or revised, ensuring that the remaining items offer unique and meaningful contributions to the measurement of emotional recognition. This refinement aims to enhance the reliability and validity of the instrument by reducing redundancy and including only the most informative items.

The model's pathways (Fig. 1) indicate how well the observed variables represent the latent constructs and provide a visual representation of the overall fit. For happiness and sadness, the paths appear strong and well-defined, reflecting the excellent fit indices previously reported (CFI of 0.933 for happiness, 1.000 for sadness). In contrast, the paths for anger and fear might appear less strong or more complex, reflecting their moderate fit in the earlier analysis (CFI of 0.817 and 0.843, respectively). The final model suggests that certain items have been removed or revised based on their performance across the four emotions. The items retained in the model are those that provide the most distinct and informative contributions to measuring emotional recognition. This aligns with the goal of improving the tool's overall reliability and validity by eliminating redundancy and focusing on items that enhance the precision of emotional assessments.

Overall data showed that happiness and sadness were the most easily recognized emotions, with strong factor loadings for both child and adult facial expressions. The ability to correctly identify these emotions aligns with developmental expectations, as previous research suggests that happiness is typically recognized first by children, followed by sadness. This is particularly evident in the child faces subtest, where recognition scores were higher than for adult faces or postures, highlighting the developmental relevance of peer-related emotional cues.

In contrast, the results for anger and fear revealed lower factor loadings and explanatory power. This finding reflects broader trends in the emotional development literature, which consistently points out that these emotions are more challenging for children to identify. The lower recognition rates of fear and anger may also be culturally influenced, as suggested by studies showing variability in how different emotions are interpreted across cultural contexts. This presents an opportunity for further refinement of the DANVA-2-RV, possibly by integrating more culturally diverse emotional stimuli. The study underscores the importance of accurately measuring emotional recognition abilities in children, as these skills are fundamental to socio-emotional development and peer interactions. The strong performance in recognizing happiness and sadness suggests that interventions targeting these emotions may be effective in promoting emotional literacy. However, the difficulty in recognizing anger and fear points to the need for focused educational strategies aimed at helping children better understand and process these more complex emotions.

The significant role of child faces in the recognition process also highlights the importance of peer relationships at this developmental stage. As children begin to form friendships and navigate social settings outside the family, their ability to decode emotions from peers becomes critical. This finding supports the inclusion of child-specific emotional cues in educational tools designed to foster emotional competence.

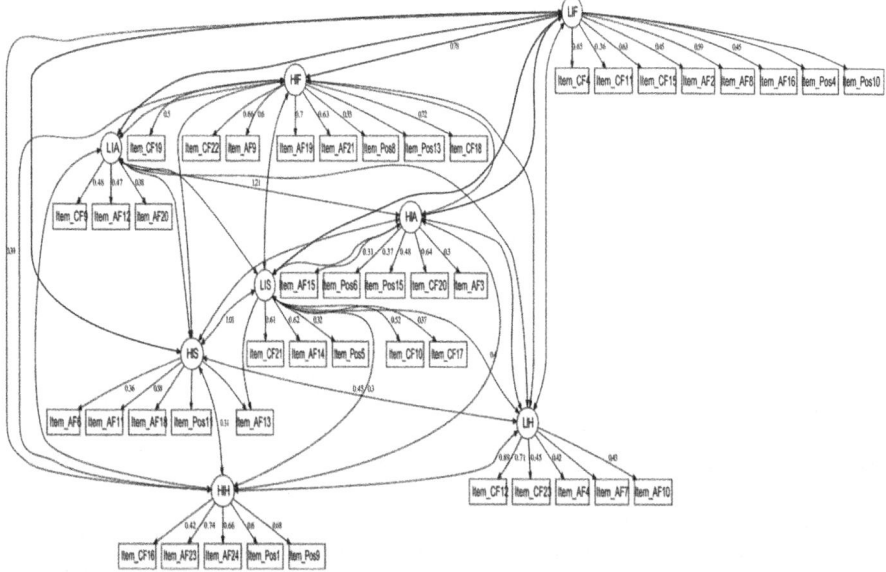

Fig. 1. CFA model for high vs. low emotion intensity and Correlation among DANVA-2-RV Items. Factors. HIH (High Intensity Happiness); LIH (Low Intensity Happiness); HIS (High Intensity Sadness); LIS (Low intensity Sadness); HIA(High Intensity Anger); LIA (Low Intensity Anger); HIF (High Intensity Fear); LIF (Low Intensity Fear). Only significant Values (p < .05) have been considered.

4 Limitation

While the results are promising, there are some limitations that need to be addressed. The suboptimal fit for emotional intensity and the challenges in recognizing certain emotions like anger and fear suggest that further refinement of the DANVA-2-RV is necessary. In particular, more work is needed to explore the role of postural cues, as the lower performance in this area may reflect either a developmental limitation in children's ability to interpret body language or an inadequacy in the stimuli used.

Additionally, while the study sample was representative of the local population, expanding the research to a larger and more diverse population could enhance the generalizability of the findings. More research is also needed to investigate how other factors such as gender, socio-economic background, and cultural influences may affect emotion recognition abilities in children.

5 Conclusion

The results of this study confirm the DANVA-2-RV as a valuable and reliable tool for assessing emotional recognition abilities in young children. The instrument's strong fit across several constructs, particularly in recognizing happiness and sadness, offers a solid foundation for its use in educational settings aimed at promoting emotional literacy and inclusion.

However, future iterations of the instrument should address the challenges associated with emotional intensity and the recognition of complex emotions such as anger and fear. Further research is also needed to investigate how these findings can inform targeted interventions that support children in developing more nuanced emotional competence, particularly in peer-related social contexts.

This discussion highlights the potential of the DANVA-2-RV to be integrated into broader educational initiatives like the I4C project, promoting emotional development and social adjustment in children.

References

Adolphs, R., Baron-Cohen, S., Tranel, D.: The recognition of complex mental states: the development of children's facial recognition abilities. Nat. Rev. Neurosci. **2**(3), 165–170 (2001). https://doi.org/10.1038/35058576

Baum, K., Nowicki, S.: Development of the Diagnostic Analysis of Nonverbal Accuracy 2 (DANVA2). Emory University (1998)

Ciucci, E., Nocentini, A., Calussi, P., Menesini, E., Nowicki, S.: Construct validity of a test to identify emotion in adult and child faces and adult postures, the diagnostic analysis of nonverbal accuracy 2 (DANVA2), in Italian elementary school age children. ETA'EVOLUTIVA **100**, 56–68 (2011)

Collins, L., Nowicki, S.: Receptive nonverbal communication skill and psychosocial adjustment in preschool children. J. Genet. Psychol. **162**(2), 189–201 (2001). https://doi.org/10.1080/002 21320109597958

Denham, S.A., Zinsser, K., Bailey, C.S.: Emotional intelligence in the first five years of life. In: Tremblay, R.E., Boivin, M., Peters, R.D. (eds.) Encyclopedia on Early Childhood Development. Centre of Excellence for Early Childhood Development (2011)

Durand, K., Gallay, M., Seigneuric, A., Robichon, F., Baudouin, J.Y.: The development of facial emotion recognition: the role of configural information. J. Exp. Child Psychol. **97**(1), 14–27 (2007). https://doi.org/10.1016/j.jecp.2006.12.001

Ekman, P.: Differential communication of affect by head and body cues. J. Pers. Soc. Psychol. **2**(5), 726–735 (1965). https://doi.org/10.1037/h0022736

Elfenbein, H.A., Ambady, N.: On the universality and cultural specificity of emotion recognition: a meta-analysis. Psychol. Bull. **128**(2), 203–235 (2002). https://doi.org/10.1037/0033-2909. 128.2.203

Halberstadt, A.G., Denham, S.A., Dunsmore, J.C.: Affective social competence. Soc. Dev. **10**(1), 79–119 (2001). https://doi.org/10.1111/1467-9507.00150

Herba, C., Phillips, M.: Development of facial expression recognition from childhood to adolescence: behavioural and neurological perspectives. J. Child Psychol. Psychiatry **45**(7), 1185–1198 (2004). https://doi.org/10.1111/j.1469-7610.2004.00316.x

Matthews, G., Zeidner, M., Roberts, R.D.: Emotional Intelligence: Science and Myth. MIT Press (2002)

Mayer, J.D., Salovey, P.: What is emotional intelligence? In: Salovey, P., Sluyter, D. (eds.) Emotional Development and Emotional Intelligence: Educational Implications, pp. 3–31. Basic Books (1997)

Mayer, J.D., Roberts, R.D., Barsade, S.G.: Human abilities: emotional intelligence. Annu. Rev. Psychol. **59**, 507–536 (2008). https://doi.org/10.1146/annurev.psych.59.103006.093646

McClure, E.B., Nowicki, S.: Association of social anxiety and depression in children with emotion recognition skills. J. Nonverbal Behav. **25**(1), 3–19 (2001). https://doi.org/10.1023/A:100678 3929723

Nowicki, S., Duke, M.P.: Individual differences in the nonverbal communication of affect: the diagnostic analysis of nonverbal accuracy scale. J. Nonverbal Behav. **18**(1), 9–35 (1994). https://doi.org/10.1007/BF02169077

Piterman, S., Nowicki, S.: The ability to identify emotion in adult and child faces: impact on social functioning. J. Genet. Psychol. **165**(2), 223–240 (2004). https://doi.org/10.3200/GNTP.165.2. 223-240

Rosip, J.C., Hall, J.A.: Knowledge of nonverbal cues, gender, and nonverbal decoding accuracy. J. Nonverbal Behav. **28**(4), 267–286 (2004). https://doi.org/10.1007/s10919-004-4156-7

Saarni, C.: Emotion Competence in Childhood. Cambridge University Press (2001)

Thomas, L.A., De Bellis, M.D., Graham, R., LaBar, K.S.: Development of emotional facial recognition in late childhood and adolescence. Dev. Sci. **10**(5), 547–558 (2007). https://doi.org/10. 1111/j.1467-7687.2007.00614.x

Computational Psychology: Opportunity and Technological Usage for Psychologists

Alessandro De Santis(✉) (iD)

University of Foggia, Puglia, 71121 Foggia, Italy
alessandro.desantis2@unifg.it

Abstract. The integration of digital technologies, including computer vision and advanced data analytics, presents new opportunities for psychologists, particularly those in training. This paper reviews the current applications of digital technologies in psychological assessments and interventions, emphasizing the use of computer vision to analyze non-verbal cues like facial expressions and body language. Machine learning algorithms are explored for their ability to process large datasets, identify patterns, and predict mental health outcomes, offering a data-driven approach to mental health care. These technologies allow for the development of personalized interventions through the analysis of stress indicators collected from digital tools such as mobile applications and wearable devices. The findings suggest that leveraging computer vision and machine learning in psychological settings can significantly enhance both the quality of care provided and the well-being of healthcare professionals. Future research should focus on further developing these tools to ensure their applicability across a broader range of populations and contexts.

Keywords: Computer Vision · Computational Psychology · Machine Learning · Psychological Assessment · Personalized Interventions

1 Introduction

The integration of digital technologies into the healthcare sector has paved the way for innovative intervention methods, particularly in addressing the psychological well-being of healthcare professionals, including psychologists (Bhavnani et al., 2016).

Computer vision technologies can be utilized to analyze facial expressions, body language, and other non-verbal cues to assess psychological states accurately. The implementation of machine learning algorithms enables the processing of large datasets, identifying patterns, and predicting mental health outcomes based on various stress indicators, which aligns with the increasing demand for tailored and data-driven approaches in healthcare (Dang et al., 2017).

Face detection has been a fundamental and well-researched topic in the field of computer vision for many years and remains an active area of study. Its main purpose is to identify whether any faces are present in an image and, if so, to determine their location. While recent methods have significantly enhanced the accuracy of face detection, making

G. A. Toto (Ed.): ICS exchange 2024, CCIS 2521, pp. 300–311, 2025.
https://doi.org/10.1007/978-3-032-03021-4_21

it a reliable solution for many real-world applications, there are still challenges when it comes to detecting faces that are partially obscured or poorly lit.

Many of the most advanced techniques for face detection have been thoroughly reviewed in (Leo et al., 2020).

Face detection acts as the foundational step for most algorithmic pipelines that aim to analyze facial features. However, the subsequent stages of face-related analysis are still being actively researched. Several excellent survey papers have reviewed the latest developments from a technological perspective. These papers address algorithmic methods for biometric identification, even when factors like plastic surgery, occlusions, distortions, low resolution, or noise are present. Additionally, areas like facial muscle movement analysis and emotion recognition are also under continued investigation (Leo et al., 2020).

The integration of computer vision and advanced data analytics into psychological applications represents a significant advancement in the support of healthcare professionals' mental health. As these technologies continue to evolve, they offer promising avenues for reducing work-related stress and improving the overall quality of life for those in the healthcare sector. Future research should focus on refining these tools and expanding their application to broader populations, ensuring that all healthcare professionals have access to the resources they need to maintain their psychological well-being (Norcross, 2000).

This paper provides a comprehensive review of the current state-of-theart in leveraging digital technologies, including computer vision and dataset analysis, for psychological applications. Furthermore, the paper explores the potential of these technologies in creating personalized interventions. By analyzing data from digital tools, such as mobile applications and wearable devices, healthcare providers can gain deeper insights into the stress levels and well-being of psychologists. This data-driven approach facilitates the development of tailored support strategies, enhancing the effectiveness of interventions and ensuring the long-term mental health of professionals in the field.

In the next section, we will delve into the applications of computer vision in healthcare, particularly focusing on its role in psychological settings. We will explore how computer vision technologies can be used for emotion recognition, providing new methods to assess and understand nonverbal cues such as facial expressions and body language. This capability has immense potential to enhance psychological evaluations and interventions. Additionally, we will discuss the critical need for robust datasets to train these computer vision systems effectively, ensuring reliable outcomes. Finally, we will highlight the benefits for psychologists, especially those in training, of utilizing machine learning techniques. These methods empower them to gain deeper insights into patient behaviors and develop personalized, data-driven intervention strategies, ultimately advancing the field of psychological care.

2   What is Computer Vision and How does it Work

A substantial body of psychophysical research supports the "closed-loop" model of human visual perception, particularly in its reliance on feedback mechanisms to interpret visual stimuli. One key aspect of this model is pre-attentive vision phenomena, where salient features of an image seem to "pop out" automatically, capturing attention without conscious effort. This has been widely discussed in the literature (e.g., Treisman & Gelade, 1980; Wolfe, 1994). Another critical element is perceptual constancies, where the perceived properties of familiar objects, such as their size or shape, remain stable despite changes in the viewing conditions—an effect typically attributed to external factors (Rock et al., 1992). These phenomena illustrate the complex processes the human visual system uses to maintain a coherent perception of the environment. However, achieving similar robust behavior in generic computer vision algorithms remains an ongoing challenge. For instance, current preattentive vision models in computer vision tend to focus on region-of-interest delineation before extracting salient features, but they do not yet fully replicate the dynamic, context- sensitive processing found in biological systems (Itti & Koch, 2001).

To address the problem of robustness in computer vision, it is useful to begin with a basic yet profound example from human perception: shape constancy. Imagine observing a door as it opens. The visual image of the door changes from a rectangle to a trapezoid due to the perspective shift, but the observer still perceives it as a door undergoing a simple motion, not a transformation into a different shape. This is possible because the visual system incorporates additional information—specifically, the observer's prior knowledge that doors are rigid structures—into the perceptual process. Hence, the perceived shape remains stable despite the distortions in the retinal image (Gibson, 1950).

In contrast, many computer vision systems lack this ability to integrate external knowledge or contextual cues with visual input, making them susceptible to errors when confronted with variations in object appearance. Perceptual constancies, such as shape, size, and color constancy, are not yet fully modeled in artificial systems, largely because these constancies rely on implicit rules embedded in the human visual system, which allow for adjustments based on real-world knowledge (Palmer, 1999). A classic example of how easily these rules can be deceived is the Ames room illusion, where the violation of perspective-based foreshortening compensation causes objects to appear drastically distorted in size and shape (Ames, 1951). These discrepancies highlight the challenges faced in replicating human-like perceptual stability in computer vision systems.

The previous example does not provide a complete solution. Any current computer vision algorithm for rigid motion recovery tends to follow a similar rigid approach. However, this example highlights that the rigid motion model utilized is tied solely to the available data, rather than being an intrinsic characteristic of the objects in the scene. For instance, if we attempted to model a nonrigid object—such as a flexible door—the current algorithms would likely fail to provide satisfactory results. This demonstrates that robustness in computer vision is inherently linked to the quality and suitability of the employed model for the task at hand (Bar-Shalom & Fortmann, 1988). In modern computer vision systems, information typically flows in a bottom-up manner. Feature extraction occurs first, followed by a grouping process that organizes features into semantic primitives, which are then interpreted based on task-specific criteria. This reliance on bottom-up processing is one of the key reasons why contemporary vision algorithms struggle to autonomously manage visual data under varying conditions. In contrast, human perception integrates both top-down and bottom-up information, using prior knowledge to interpret ambiguous or noisy sensory input. The absence of a top-down flow in machine vision systems significantly limits their adaptability and robustness across a wide range of tasks (Palmer, 1999).

One promising approach to address this limitation is the increasingly popular Bayesian paradigm. In this framework, probabilistic models are used to represent various possible interpretations of the visual data. By integrating multiple hypotheses, the system can update and refine its predictions based on incoming information. This method allows for greater flexibility and adaptability, as it does not rely strictly on one fixed interpretation. Bayesian techniques, including particle filtering and other nonparametric methods, have been successfully applied to problems like motion estimation (Doucet et al., 2001). Incorporating machine learning components into these probabilistic frameworks (e.g., Poggio & Edelman, 1990; Ghahramani, 2001) introduces a top-down influence, enabling the system to make use of higher-level information during the processing phase (Rao, 2005).

Despite these advances, drawing direct comparisons between computer vision systems and the human visual system poses practical difficulties when defining "robustness". Human perception is deeply abstract, allowing us to recognize a chair regardless of its design, size, or even the era in which it was created. However, when object recognition systems are tasked with similar challenges—such as determining whether an image represents a chair—the results are often inconsistent and incomplete (Doucet et al., 2001). Thus, although Bayesian and machine learning approaches provide a pathway toward more robust systems, there is still much work to be done to achieve a level of generalization comparable to that of human perception (Gibson, 1950).

In this discussion, we will not delve into high-level cognitive processes nor the role of top-down information flow in computer vision. For the purposes of this analysis, a computer vision algorithm will be considered robust if it can tolerate outliers—data that does not conform to the assumed model. This definition is consistent with the one commonly used in statistics to describe robustness (Huber, 1981, p.6).

Broadly speaking, robust statistics is a field that addresses the impact of deviations from idealized assumptions in statistical models. Over time, parts of this body of knowledge have been formalized into a coherent theoretical framework. The concept of robustness in computer vision has been around for at least thirty years, with many of the techniques popular today having roots in older methods developed to solve specific image understanding and pattern recognition problems. Some of these techniques have only recently been rediscovered and integrated into modern computer vision approaches.

One of the most famous examples of a robust technique is the Hough Transform, which extracts multiple instances of a low-dimensional manifold from a noisy background. The Hough Transform was patented in 1962 (Hough, 1962) for the detection of linear trajectories of subatomic particles in a bubble chamber. While this patent is often cited when referring to the Hough Transform, an earlier publication (Hough, 1959) also exists, offering a comprehensive discussion of the method. Another widely-used robust technique in computer vision is RANSAC (Random Sample Consensus), proposed in 1980 to solve the perspective-n-point problem (Fischler & Bolles, 1981). The most commonly referenced paper for this method is (Fischler & Bolles, 1981).

Similarly, mean shift, an old pattern recognition technique for density gradient estimation proposed in 1975 [Fukunaga & Hostetler, 1975], has been rediscovered and widely applied in feature space analysis. This method has gained significant popularity in the computer vision community in recent years (Comaniciu & Meer, 2002). For more on this, see (Duda, Hart, & Stork, 2001, p. 535).

In theoretical statistics, the study of robustness began in the early 1960s, and the first robust estimator, the M-estimator, was introduced by Huber in 1964 (Huber, 1964). Another family of robust estimators, including the Least Median of Squares (LMedS), was introduced by Rousseeuw in 1984 (Rousseeuw, 1984). By the late 1980s, these robust statistical techniques began to gain attention in the computer vision field.

Initially, the application of robust methods to computer vision was limited to replacing non-robust parameter estimation modules with their robust counterparts (e.g., Black & Rangarajan, 1996; Meer, 2004; Stewart, 1999; Torr & Zisserman, 2000). A comprehensive review of this early work can be found in (Meer, 2004). While these methods were successful in many instances, some failures were also reported [Matas & Chum, 2005]. We now understand that these failures arose from the limitations of most robust estimators in handling data containing multiple structures, a scenario that occurs frequently in computer vision but is almost absent in classical statistical applications. For example, a sliding window operator might cover an image patch containing two homogeneous regions of roughly equal size, or a scene might include several independently moving objects (Torr & Zisserman, 2000; Kanatani, 1996).

A large portion of today's robust computer vision toolbox has been developed specifically for vision-related tasks. This is because techniques imported from statistics were often designed for data with very different characteristics than those encountered in computer vision. When the assumptions underlying these methods do not align with the nature of the visual data, the resulting performance may fall short of expectations. A large portion of today's robust computer vision toolbox has been developed specifically for vision-related tasks. This is largely because techniques imported from statistics were often designed for data with different characteristics than those typically encountered in computer vision. For instance, statistical methods are usually applied to well-controlled datasets, but in computer vision, the data is often much noisier, containing significant proportions of outliers—data points that do not conform to the assumed model. When the assumptions behind these methods do not align with the nature of the visual data, the performance can degrade. This is where algorithms like Random Sample Consensus (RANSAC) come into play.

RANSAC has emerged as one of the most robust methods for dealing with noisy, real- world data in vision applications. Its core strength lies in its ability to fit models to datasets even when a significant portion of the data consists of outliers. Unlike traditional algorithms such as least-squares fitting, which can be heavily influenced by outliers, RANSAC focuses on finding subsets of the data—those that conform to the desired model—and rejects the outliers.

At its core, the RANSAC algorithm operates by iteratively fitting a model to small, randomly selected subsets of the data. Let's represent the dataset by $D = \{x1, x2, ..., xn\}$ where xi represents an individual data point. The goal is to fit a model $M\theta$, parameterized by θ, that best describes the data. The challenge, however, is that not all data points in D follow the model $M\theta$; many are outliers that will distort any naive model-fitting process.

The first step involves randomly selecting a small subset $S \subset D$, consisting of k points, where k is the minimum number of points required to estimate the model parameters θ. For instance, if we are fitting a line to a set of 2D points, we need at least two points ($k = 2$) to define the line.

Using the points in SI, we estimate the parameters θ of the model $M\theta$. This is done by minimizing an error function over the selected points:

$$\hat{\theta} = \arg \min_{\theta} \sum_{x_i \in S} \text{Error}(x_i, M(\theta)),$$

where $Error\ [(xi, M(\theta)]$ quantifies the difference between the data point xi and the model prediction. For example, in line fitting, this error could be the perpendicular distance from the point xi to the line defined by $M\theta$.

After fitting the model to the subset Si, we check how well the model fits the entire dataset $\mathbf{D}$. To do this, we define a consensus set $C \subset \mathbf{D}$, which includes all points that fit the model within a certain error threshold ϵ. Mathematically, this is expressed as:

$$C = \left\{ x_i \in \mathbf{D} \middle| \text{Error}\left(x_i, M\left(\hat{\theta}\right)\right) < \varepsilon \right\}.$$

The size of the consensus set $|C|$ represents the number of inliers-data points that agree with the model.

This process of random sampling, model fitting, and consensus set evaluation is repeated for a predefined number of iterations $Niter$ and, in each iteration, we compare the size of the consensus set $|C|$ to the largest consensus set found so far. If the current iteration produces a larger consensus set, we update the best model parameters θ^* as follows:

$$\theta^* = \arg \max_{\theta} |C|.$$

The algorithm stops when $Niter$ iterations have been completed, or when a sufficiently large consensus set is found.

One of the key considerations in RANSAC is determining how many iterations $Niter$ are required to ensure a high probability of success (i.e., finding a model that correctly fits all inliers). Let w represent the probability that a randomly selected point is an inlier, and k the number of points needed to estimate the model parameters. In each iteration, the algorithm randomly selects k points, and the probability that all k points are inliers is w^k.

The probability that at least one of the iterations will find a correct solution (i.e., all k points in the sample are inliers) after $Niter$ iterations is:

$$P_{\text{success}} = 1 - \left(1 - w^k\right)^{N_{\text{iter}}}.$$

Thus, the number of iterations required increases as the proportion of inliers decreases or as the model becomes more complex (requiring a larger k).

RANSAC model has become an indispensable tool in computer vision for problems where robustness to outliers is essential. One common application is homography estimation, where the goal is to find a transformation between two images despite mismatched point correspondences. Another prominent use is in epipolar geometry estimation for stereo vision, where the algorithm helps to compute the fundamental matrix that describes the geometric relationship between two views of the same scene. In both cases, RANSAC ensures that the model is fitted to the correct inliers, discarding erroneous matches or noisy points.

While RANSAC is highly effective in rejecting outliers, its performance depends on several factors, such as the threshold ϵ for defining inliers and the number of iterations *Niter*. In scenarios with multiple independent structures in the data—such as scenes containing several moving objects—RANSAC may need to be extended to handle multiple models simultaneously. Despite these challenges, RANSAC remains one of the most widely used techniques for robust model fitting in vision-related tasks.

3 Harnessing Computer Vision in Healthcare: A New Frontier in Patient Care

An example of computer vision applied to a practical use case is its implementation in supporting dementia diagnosis. The rapid growth of the older adult population globally is expected to have a significant impact on healthcare systems, as the increasing number of elderly individuals often face challenges in maintaining self-care capabilities. In response, healthcare and nursing robots have garnered considerable attention in recent years to help support these populations. Somatosensory technology has been introduced to facilitate activity recognition and healthcare interactions for older adults; however, traditional detection methods generally rely on single-modal approaches, limiting their effectiveness in complex care environment (Dang et al., 2017).

To address these limitations, Dang et al. (2017) proposed an innovative approach in their study, "An Interactive Care System Based on a Depth Image and EEG for Aged Patients with Dementia." The authors introduced two novel multimodal sparse autoencoder frameworks, utilizing both motion and mental features to enhance interaction between nurses and dementia patients. The system involves extracting motion data from depth images and recording electroencephalogram (EEG) signals to capture mental features. These inputs are processed using multimodal deep neural networks to recognize the care requirements of patients with dementia. Specifically, the network processes (1) motion features from depth image sensors and (2) mental features derived from EEG signals, allowing it to determine the type of assistance a patient requires. Experimental results demonstrated that the proposed algorithm achieved high accuracy (96.5%) and recall rates (96.4%) for shuffled datasets, and performed well with continuous datasets (90.9% accuracy and 92.6% recall), making it an effective solution compared to traditional single-modal approaches. This multimodal approach not only simplifies data acquisition and processing but also significantly improves action recognition accuracy (Dang et al., 2017).

Deep learning has recently gained widespread popularity in artificial intelligence, particularly for medical applications. For instance, Song et al. (2017) employed several deep learning techniques, including convolutional neural networks (CNN), deep neural networks (DNN), and stacked autoencoders (SAE), to assist in the early diagnosis of lung cancer using computed tomography (CT) images. Their findings showed that CNNs outperformed DNNs and SAEs, demonstrating superior performance in classifying lung nodules and providing doctors with critical diagnostic information (Song et al., 2017).

Furthermore, Kamarudin et al. (2017) proposed a computer-assisted tongue color diagnosis tool in their study, "A Fast SVM-Based Tongue's Colour Classification Aided by k-Means Clustering Identifiers and Colour Attributes." This novel two-stage classification system utilizes clustering identifiers and optimized color attributes to classify three tongue colors: red, light red, and deep red. The tool was found to be highly effective for the early detection of imbalances in the body, significantly reducing computational time by 20% and improving classification accuracy by 15% compared to conventional SVM-based methods (Kamarudin et al., 2017). These advanced diagnostic approaches exemplify the transformative potential of machine learning in enhancing the speed, accuracy, and quality of healthcare solutions.

4 Emotion Recognition Through Computer Vision: Transforming Psychological Assessment

In human communication, facial expressions contain critical nonverbal information that can provide additional clues and meaning to verbal communication (Ekman & Friesen, 1969). Some studies have suggested that 60–80% of communication is nonverbal (Mehrabian, 1971). This nonverbal information includes facial expressions, eye contact, tones of voice, hand gestures, and physical distancing. Facial expression analysis, in particular, has become a popular research topic (Zeng et al., 2009). Facial emotion recognition (FER) has been applied in the field of human–computer interaction (HCI) in areas such as autopilot (Kaur et al., 2020), education, medical treatment, psychological treatment (Martinez et al., 2017), surveillance, and psychological analysis in computer vision (Pantic & Rothkrantz, 2000; Sariyanidi et al., 2015).

The benefits of computer vision extend beyond the neurological field; they can also play a significant role in psychology, particularly in exploring qualitative concepts such as ego psychology and dynamic psychology. In these areas, computer vision technologies can assist in analyzing nonverbal behaviors, facial micro-expressions, and other subtle indicators of psychological states that are critical for understanding a patient's internal dynamics (Pantic & Rothkrantz, 2000). For instance, by leveraging facial expression analysis, computer vision can provide insights into an individual's emotional state, which is a key component in ego psychology for understanding self-perception and defense mechanisms. Similarly, in dynamic psychology, which focuses on unconscious processes and interpersonal relationships, computer vision can facilitate the observation of behavioral cues during therapy, offering deeper insights into the dynamics between therapists and patients, thereby enhancing the therapeutic process. These technologies can augment qualitative assessments by providing objective, data-driven observations that enrich the understanding of complex psychological concepts (Pantic & Rothkrantz, 2000).

In psychology and computer vision, emotions are typically classified into two models: categorical and dimensional (Russell, 1980; Lang, 1995; Ekman, 1992). In the categorical model, Ekman (1992) identified basic human emotions, which include happiness, anger, disgust, fear, sadness, and surprise. In the dimensional model, emotions are evaluated along continuous numerical scales, specifically determining dimensions such as valence (positive or negative emotional value) and arousal (level of emotional activation) (Russell, 1980; Lang, 1995). Facial emotion recognition (FER) is a critical task in computer vision that has numerous practical applications, from human- computer interaction to mental health assessments, and the number of studies on FER has increased significantly in recent years (Zeng et al., 2009; Martinez et al., 2017; Li & Deng, 2020; Sariyanidi et al., 2015), largely driven by advancements in deep neural networks. In particular, convolutional neural networks (CNNs) have demonstrated impressive performance in feature extraction for FER tasks. For instance, He et al. (2016) proposed the residual neural network (ResNet) architecture, which introduced residual learning to a CNN, effectively addressing the issues of vanishing gradients and decreasing accuracy in deep networks.

In the study by Huang et al. (2023), the authors explored how a neural network model identifies facial emotions using convolutional neural networks (CNNs) for feature extraction. They performed a cross-database validation between AffectNet and RAF-DB datasets, demonstrating that models trained on more diverse datasets like AffectNet achieved better accuracy, with transfer learning enhancing performance by 26.95%. The visualizations indicated that areas around the mouth and nose contained the most significant emotional information, which aligns with how humans typically read emotions. The study also observed that the network consistently focused on similar features, regardless of whether classifications were correct or incorrect, highlighting the need for a broader spatial focus for improved recognition accuracy.

The interest in facial emotion recognition (FER) is steadily increasing, leading to the development of new algorithms and innovative approaches. The recent surge in machine learning applications has driven significant advancements in the field, especially with the adoption of deep learning techniques. The progression of FER research is clearly on the right trajectory, integrating knowledge from critical disciplines such as psychology, sociology, and physiology, which has contributed to the emergence of increasingly accurate FER systems.

Despite the substantial progress, challenges remain—particularly with recognizing pose-variant faces in natural, uncontrolled environments. However, the annual emotion recognition challenges continue to drive improvements in robustness, particularly in addressing these pose variations. A key breakthrough was achieved by AlexNet, a convolutional neural network (CNN), which demonstrated the immense potential of deep learning for computer vision by achieving a significant reduction in top-5 error (15.31%) in the ImageNet 2012 competition, far surpassing previous benchmarks. This success spurred interest in CNNs for solving complex computer vision problems, and the subsequent adoption of CNNs in FER has correlated with notable performance gains.

One notable limitation observed across the reviewed studies is the lack of consideration for the environmental context. While many works have made significant strides towards developing multimodal systems, the broader situational context has often been overlooked. For example, in an image depicting a birthday party, the celebratory atmosphere significantly influences the mood of participants, and such contextual factors cannot be ignored, even if a specific individual's facial expression may not fully align with the expected emotional cues. Nevertheless, the continuous focus on annual challenges and the growing interdisciplinary interest have fostered an environment where FER systems are achieving improved results year after year.

5 Conclusion

The use of computer vision, machine learning, and other advanced data analytics in healthcare settings provides deeper insights into stress indicators and emotional well-being, offering tailored and effective interventions. Despite current challenges, such as the need for better handling of pose-variant conditions and contextual influences, the ongoing advances in machine learning and computer vision are creating more robust and reliable solutions. The adoption of these technologies is not only enhancing the accuracy of emotional assessments but also helping psychologists gain a deeper understanding of their patients' needs, ultimately enriching psychological care. This progression is particularly beneficial for psychologists, who can leverage these tools to support their own wellbeing as well as the effective treatment of their clients, signaling a bright future for the integration of technology in psychological practice.

References

Ames, A.: Visual perception and the rotating trapezoidal window. Am. J. Psychol. **64**(2), 289–293 (1951)

Bar-Shalom, Y., Fortmann, T.E.: Tracking and data association. Math. Sci. Eng. **87**, 918–919 (1988)

Barnett, J.E., Baker, E.K., Elman, N.S., Schoener, G.R.: In pursuit of wellness: the self-care imperative. Prof. Psychol. Res. Pract. **38**, 603–612 (2007). https://doi.org/10.1037/0735-7028.38.6.603

Bhavnani, A., Narula, J., Sengupta, P.P.: Mobile technology and the digitization of healthcare. Eur. Heart J. **37**(18), 1428–1438 (2016)

Black, M.J., Rangarajan, A.: Robust anisotropic diffusion. IEEE Trans. Image Process. **7**(3), 421–432 (1996)

Brooke, J.: Sus: a quick and dirty usability. Usab. Eval. Ind. **189**(3), 189–194 (1996)

Huang, Z.Y., et al.: A study on computer vision for facial emotion recognition. Sci. Rep. **13**(1), 8425 (2023). https://doi.org/10.1038/s41598-023-34384-7

Casale, S., Primi, C., Fioravanti, G.: Generalized problematic internet use scale 2: update on the psychometric properties among Italian young adults. In: The Psychology of Social Networking. Identity and Relationships in Online Communities, vol. 2, pp. 202–216 (2016)

Comaniciu, D., Meer, P.: Mean shift: a robust approach toward feature space analysis. IEEE Trans. Pattern Anal. Mach. Intell. **24**(5), 603–619 (2002)

Coster, J.S., Schwebel, M.: Well-functioning in professional psychologists. Prof. Psychol. Res. Pract. **28**(1), 5–13 (1997). https://doi.org/10.1037/0735-7028.28.1.5

Dang, X., Kang, B., Liu, X., Cui, G.: An interactive care system based on a depth image and EEG for aged patients with dementia. J. Healthcare Eng. **2017**(1), 4128183 (2017)

Doucet, A., De Freitas, N., Gordon, N.: An introduction to sequential Monte Carlo methods. Sequential Monte Carlo methods in practice, pp. 3–14 (2001)

Ekman, P.: An argument for basic emotions. Cogn. Emotion **6**(3–4), 169 (1992)

Ekman, P., Friesen, W.V.: The repertoire of nonverbal behavior: categories, origins, usage, and coding. Semiotica 1(1), 49–98 (1969). https://doi.org/10.1515/semi.1969.1.1.49

Fiol-DeRoque, M.A., Ricci-Cabello, I.: A mobile phone–based intervention to reduce mental health problems in health care workers during the COVID-19 pandemic (PsyCovidApp): randomized controlled trial. JMIR Mhealth Uhealth 9(5), e27039 (2021)

Fischler, M.A., Bolles, R.C.: Random sample consensus: a paradigm for model fitting with applications to image analysis and automated cartography. Commun. ACM 24(6), 381–395 (1981)

Fukunaga, K., Hostetler, L.: The estimation of the gradient of a density function, with applications in pattern recognition. IEEE Trans. Inf. Theory 21(1), 32–40 (1975)

Garrido Macías, M., et al.: Assessing self-care in psychologists: a Spanish adaptation of the SCAP scale. Psicothema (2022)

Ghahramani, Z.: An introduction to hidden Markov models and Bayesian networks. Int. J. Pattern Recognit Artif Intell. 15(1), 9–42 (2001)

Gibson, J.J.: The Perception of the Visual World. Houghton Mifflin, Boston. APA PsycInfo (1950). https://psycnet.apa.org/record/1951-04286-000

He, K., Zhang, X., Ren, S., Sun, J.: Deep residual learning for image recognition. In: Proceedings of the IEEE Conference on Computer Vision and Pattern Recognition (CVPR), pp. 770–778 (2016). https://doi.org/10.1109/CVPR.2016.90

Hough, P.V.C.: Machine analysis of bubble chamber pictures. In: Proceedings of the International Conference on High-Energy Accelerators and Instrumentation, CERN 1959, pp. 554–556 (1959)

Hough, P.V.C.: Method and means for recognizing complex patterns. US Patent (3- 69), 654 (1962). https://doi.org/10.1109/TPAMI.2014.2366127

Huang, Z.Y., et al.: A study on computer vision for facial emotion recognition. Sci. Rep. (2023)

Huber, P.J., Ronchetti, E.M.: Robust statistics, ser. Wiley Ser. Probab. Math. Stat. New York, NY, USA Wiley-IEEE 52, 54 (1981)

Itti, L., Koch, C.: Computational modelling of visual attention. Nat. Rev. Neurosci. 2(3), 194–203 (2001)

Kamarudin, N.D., Ooi, C.Y., Kawanabe, T., Odaguchi, H., Kobayashi, F.: A fast SVM-based tongue's colour classification aided by k-means clustering identifiers and colour attributes as computer-assisted tool for tongue diagnosis. J. Healthcare Eng. 2017(1), 7460168 (2017)

Kanatani, K.: Statistical Optimization for Geometric Computation: Theory and Practice. Elsevier (1996)

Kaur, H., Sharma, P., Kumar, V.: A systematic survey on facial expression recognition for autonomous vehicles. J. Adv. Transp. (2020). https://doi.org/10.1155/2020/1234567

Kumpikaitė-Valiūnienė, V., Aslan, I., Duobienė, J., Glińska, E., Anandkumar, V.: Influence of digital competence on perceived stress, burnout and well-being among students studying online during the COVID-19 lockdown: a 4-country perspective. Psychol. Res. Behav. Manag. 1483–1498 (2021)

Lang, P.J.: The emotion probe: studies of motivation and attention. Am. Psychol. 50(5), 372–385 (1995). https://doi.org/10.1037/0003-066X.50.5.372

Leo, M., Carcagnì, P., Mazzeo, P.L., Spagnolo, P., Cazzato, D., Distante, C.: Analysis of facial information for healthcare applications: a survey on computer vision-based approaches. Information 11(3), 128 (2020)

Li, S., Deng, W.: Deep facial expression recognition: a survey. IEEE Trans. Affect. Comput. (2020). https://doi.org/10.1109/TAFFC.2020.2981446

Martinez, A.M., Du, S., Valstar, M.: Advances, challenges, and opportunities in automatic facial expression recognition. Emot. Rev. 9(3), 270–278 (2017). https://doi.org/10.1177/175407391 6670028

Maslach, C., Jackson, S.E., Leiter, M.P.: Maslach burnout inventory. Scarecrow Education (1997)

Matas, J., Chum, O.: Randomized RANSAC with T(d,d) test. In: Proceedings of the British Machine Vision Conference, vol. 2, pp. 448–457 (2005)

Meer, P. (2004). Robust techniques for computer vision. In *Emerging Topics in Computer Vision* (pp. 107–194). Prentice Hall

Mehrabian, A.: Silent Messages. Wadsworth (1971)

Norcross, J.C.: Psychotherapist self-care: practitioner-tested, research-informed strategies. Prof. Psychol. Res. Pract. **31**, 710–713 (2000). https://doi.org/10.1037/0735-7028.31.6.710

Palmer, S.E.: Vision Science: Photons to Phenomenology. MIT Press (1999)

Pantic, M., Rothkrantz, L.J.M.: Automatic analysis of facial expressions: the state of the art. IEEE Trans. Pattern Anal. Mach. Intell. **22**(12), 1424–1445 (2000). https://doi.org/10.1109/34.895976

Poggio, T., Edelman, S.: A network that learns to recognize three-dimensional objects. Nature **343**(6255), 263–266 (1990)

Rao, R.P.N.: Bayesian inference and attentional modulation in the visual cortex. NeuroReport **16**(16), 1843–1848 (2005)

Rock, I., Linnett, C.M., Grant, P., Mack, A.: Perception without attention: results of a new method. Cogn. Psychol. **24**(4), 502–534 (1992)

Rousseeuw, P.J.: Least median of squares regression. J. Am. Stat. Assoc. **79**(388), 871–880 (1984)

Rupert, P.A., Dorociak, K.E.: Self-care, stress, and well-being among practicing psychologists. Prof. Psychol. Res. Pract. **50**(5), 343 (2019)

Russell, J.A.: A circumplex model of affect. J. Pers. Soc. Psychol. **39**(6), 1161–1178 (1980). https://doi.org/10.1037/h0077714

Sariyanidi, E., Gunes, H., Cavallaro, A.: Automatic analysis of facial affect: a survey of registration, representation, and recognition. IEEE Trans. Pattern Anal. Mach. Intell. **37**(6), 1113–1133 (2015)

Sariyanidi, E., Gunes, H., Cavallaro, A.: Automatic analysis of facial affect: a survey of registration, representation, and recognition. IEEE Trans. Pattern Anal. Mach. Intell. **37**(6), 1113–1133 (2015). https://doi.org/10.1109/TPAMI.2014.2366127

Song, Q., Zhao, L., Luo, X., Dou, X.: Using deep learning for classification of lung nodules on computed tomography images. J. Healthcare Eng. **2017**(1), 8314740 (2017)

Torr, P.H.S., Zisserman, A.: MLESAC: a new robust estimator with application to estimating image geometry. Comput. Vis. Image Underst. **78**(1), 138–156 (2000)

Treisman, A., Gelade, G.: A feature-integration theory of attention. Cogn. Psychol. **12**(1), 97–136 (1980)

Wolfe, J.M.: Guided search 2.0: a revised model of visual search. Psychon. Bull. Rev. **1**(2), 202–238 (1994)

Zeng, Z., Pantic, M., Roisman, G.I., Huang, T.S.: A survey of affect recognition methods: audio, visual, and spontaneous expressions. IEEE Trans. Pattern Anal. Mach. Intell. **31**(1), 39–58 (2009). https://doi.org/10.1109/TPAMI.2008.52

Assessing Digital Divide for Tourism Village Development; A Study Case of Kampung Tajur, Desa Pasanggrahan, West Java, Indonesia

Indra Prawira(✉) ⓘ, Medo Maulianza, and Rahmat Edi Irawan

Mass Communication, Binus University, Jakarta, Indonesia
iprawira@binus.edu

Abstract. This research aims to determine the digital divide in Tajur village, Purwakarta, West Java, Indonesia in developing tourism village. The research uses a digital divide theoretical framework with pragmatic research methods. Quantitative data collection techniques were obtained through surveys (n = 100) and qualitative data were obtained through semi-structured interviews with ten village residents. The research results show that the Pasanggrahan village community has gained access to ICT. However, there is a gap in accessing ICT especially in the older age group. Residents have considered ICT (mobile phones and the Internet) as a primary need, but they have not utilized ICT to develop tourist villages, such as a homestay promotion tool, or as a tool for managing their business. The Pasanggrahan villagers have the skills to use mobile phones for communication purposes, and they have the willingness to learn and develop their skills in utilizing ICT for the development of tourist villages.

Keywords: Digital divide · ICT adoption · Indonesian tourism · tourism village

1 Introduction

The Indonesian government has launched various programs to encourage the development of tourist villages throughout the country. The Ministry of Tourism and Creative Economy held the Tourism Village Award (ADWI) to recognise efforts in developing tourist villages. The development of tourist villages is a strategic effort that has various advantages. Firstly, the development of tourist villages fosters a sustainable economy for rural communities [1, 2]. Secondly, the development of tourist villages opens opportunities for equal distribution of rural and urban development [3]. Third, the development of tourist villages is also an effort to maintain regional cultural heritage [4–7].

The Indonesian government and the community work together in developing tourist villages and heritage conservation. Government policies are needed to overcome obstacles to the development of tourist villages [4]. Meanwhile, the local community factor is the most important in developing a tourist village [2]. Other researchers see opportunities for digital technology in developing tourist villages [8–11]. The use of digital technology has helped village development such as the use of the internet and mobile applications

G. A. Toto (Ed.): ICS exchange 2024, CCIS 2521, pp. 312–323, 2025.
https://doi.org/10.1007/978-3-032-03021-4_22

[12], the use of social media [13–15] or opportunities digital village development [16]. However, the use of digital technology cannot be applied in all tourist areas. The problem of digital infrastructure to support village development is challenging [1] which is one of the factors causing the digital divide in village communities regarding access to technology [17]. The digital divide theory could help to understand the conditions of society in making rural development policies.

The digital divide theory developed along with the popular use of information and communication technology (ICT) in regional development. The digital divide theory is used to examine digital village development opportunities [17]. The third level of the digital divide to see the potential of rural youth in Cianjur Regency, West Java, Indonesia. Other researchers examine the digital divide in rural communities and provide solutions to overcome it [9, 10, 18, 19].

This research was conducted in the village of Kampung Tajur which has been named a national tourist village in the 2021 Indonesian Tourism Village Award (ADWI). Kampung Tajur is a village that offers rural tourism by conserving traditional community buildings combined with the conservation of the surrounding nature [4]. The development and conservation of Tajur Village started in 2004, but the number of tourists visiting this village is still low [20]. Therefore, comprehensive efforts are needed to increase the attractiveness of Tajur Village to increase tourist visits. Research is needed to understand the current conditions of Tajur village and provide suggestions for solving problems. As far as researchers have observed, attention has not been paid to the use of ICT and digital divide to support tourist village in the Kampung Tajur. Therefore, the question of this research is what are the key factors of digital divide contributing to the undeveloped the Kampung Tajur Tourist village?

2   Literature Review

2.1   Development of Digital Divide Theory

The digital divide is a theory of the imbalance in the growth of information and communication technology in society. There are different opinions in understanding the phrase "digital divide", but in general, the digital divide is defined as the gap between people who have and do not have access to forms of information and communication technology [21, 22].

The digital divide emerged in the era of Industrial Revolution 4.0 where there was an explosion of information [23]. This rapid development made information technology products diverse [24]. However, not all groups can adapt to developments in information technology, so several groups experience a digital divide [25].

In the 1990s, since the Clinton – Al Gore government in the United States introduced the term digital divide, this issue caught the attention of politicians and researchers. In 1996, the digital divide quickly became a global issue, to the point that it became a phenomenon that occurred globally. According to the ITU (International Telecommunication Union), the digital divide is a term used to address the disturbing gap in terms of access to information technology. The digital divide was initially understood in connection with computer access, internet access, broadband access, and then access to various kinds of information and communication technology. The gap is due to limited access to technology due to equipment costs and expensive operations [26], while the digital gap is the inability of individuals to experience the benefits of information technology due to lack of access and ability to use information technology [27]. OEDC (2001) defined the digital divide as "The gap between individuals, households, businesses, and geographic areas at different socioeconomic levels concerning their opportunities to access information and communication technologies (ICT) and the use of these ICTs in various activities". Gaps occur between individuals, households, businesses, and geographic areas whose socio-economic levels differ based on their opportunities to access information and communication technology [28]. Digital divide researchers pay attention to people's access to ICT [29] while other researchers focus on people's understanding and ability to use ICT.

Van Dijk explained that several mechanisms are quite relevant to ICT access which can encompass mental, material, social, cultural, and temporal contexts [30]. The main mechanisms that cause digital divide are resources, motivation, and skills. The digital divide theory can reveal significant inequities regarding who accesses and benefits from the digital landscape. Digital divide studies are useful for uncovering practices that facilitate digital literacy and participation and recommending policies to reduce the digital divide.

Researchers then attempted to measure the level of the digital divide. Researchers generally use quantitative measurements, but understanding the digital divide is also carried out using a qualitative and pragmatic approach [31]. There are various methods of measurement, such as using surveys [32], website-based surveys [33], or interviews [34]. Meanwhile, research objects generally focus on marginalized groups based on age [31], rural communities [16, 35], or ethnic minorities [21]. Therefore, researchers research to fight for equality, develop rural areas, and develop businesses [36, 37].

In developing rural areas that develop tourism, digital capital theory is used to understand access and use of ICT. The digital divide approach can explain factors such as technical, social, and motivational factors that influence the ability of tourist destinations to fulfil the global tourism ecosystem [37, 38].

2.2 Understanding the Digital Divide in the Indonesian Context

Digital divide research has been known in the Indonesian context in general to highlight differences in ICT adoption [25], regional development [16, 35, 39], and tourism [36]. ICT has great potential to support the development of SMEs, but according to her the use of ICT is still minimal [25]. Meanwhile, other researchers stated that ICT adoption is hampered by geographical factors in Indonesia which consists of 17,000 islands. Indonesia needs ICT infrastructure to support interconnectivity between islands, regions, communities, and agencies. However, many regions in Indonesia are still untouched by ICT infrastructure. At the same time, the development of ICT in urban areas or on the island of Java is taking place rapidly. This condition creates a digital divide in Indonesian society, especially those in urban-rural areas [40].

The Indonesian Ministry of Communication and Information has implemented infrastructure investments to improve community welfare regarding access to Information and Communication Technology. In 2017, the use of digital technology in Indonesia was dominated by men, representing 54.68% of the 143.26 million people of Indonesia's total population. Meanwhile, in the 2016 survey, 48.57% were women and 51.43% men. According to the results of this data, in Indonesia, there is a digital gap between men and women, because there are still many women in Indonesia who do not know how to use digital technology effectively [41].

The digital divide in the eastern part of Indonesia is caused by a lack of internet service infrastructure, which causes a lack of educational services [42]. This problem means that only two large companies provide telecommunications services, namely Telkomsel and Indosat, where the lack of bandwidth is the reason for the problem of the digital divide. At the same time, the need for ICT is not considered to be a major need for society, this is due to a lack of knowledge and motivation to meet information needs or it could be said that it is not considered important.

The development of ICT and all its supports is a strategic thing carried out by the Indonesian government, but attention to the conservation of cultural heritage buildings must be maintained [43]. Historical relics can build historical awareness and connect people's collective memories [44]. The development of rural tourism is a profitable and long-term investment for the government because Indonesia has sufficient human and natural resources,

Infrastructure development while maintaining local wisdom is something that must be fought for. The development of tourist villages, for example, has the main aim of economic development but is also an effort to conserve culture. One of Indonesia's national economic development priorities is tourism development, and one of the programs is the development of tourist villages. To develop a tourist village, an appropriate strategy is needed based on the potential resources of the area. Supporting indicators for tourist villages include physical, social, spatial, building, cultural, craft, and ritual aspects. In Indonesia, the development of tourist villages based on culture and natural potential is growing rapidly, and this provides large income for development [45]. Attention to tourism development has made Indonesian tourism grow rapidly [46] However, this development will not occur if there is no community participation. For example, community participation supports the development of the Pentingsari Tourism Village. They participate in planning and decision making regarding the establishment of a tourist village [47].

Another factor that supports the development of tourist villages is the role of local government. For example, the Bali Province Regional Regulation (Perda) stipulates the preservation of the cultural heritage of the Kaba-Kaba Tourism Village. As a leading cycling tourism destination, Kaba-Kaba Village utilizes cultural heritage as a characteristic of village development in addition to offering the beauty of rice fields [48]. The development of tourist villages can also be in harmony with the development of heritage potential and National history [49] or maintaining local wisdom [50]. Local wisdom, which comes from a culture that has been preserved as a tourism attraction, requires methods to attract tourists to see it, such as a marketing mix, advertising, products, and development of tourist attractions and activities, accommodation, access to tourist destinations, and supporting media for marketing tourism [50].

The village government chose community empowerment to deal with problems in the village, be they economic, social, or cultural. Community empowerment is a way to find a solution to this problem in the capacity of the village government as an implementer of policies, regulations, and supervisors [51]. The number of tourist villages developing each year has increased significantly. So far, the development of natural, artificial, and culinary tourism villages is still the main focus. However, the current phenomenon shows that several villages still fail to manage tourist villages well, causing the existence of tourist villages to be unsustainable.

Not much has been done to see the potential of villages by considering local culture [52]. If there is cultural heritage in an area, local communities must be involved in utilizing it. Conservation and utilization activities involve communities located around cultural heritage sites. According to Republic of Indonesia Law Number 11/2010 concerning Cultural Heritage, the community is responsible for the preservation, security, protection, and maintenance of cultural preservation. The empowerment program involves many stakeholders, such as tourism development, creative economy, arts and culture, and entrepreneurship [53].

3   The Methodology

This research uses a pragmatic approach with the convergence parallel mix method. Quantitative data was obtained through a survey of 100 residents of Pasanggrahan Village, while qualitative data was obtained through face-to-face semi-structured interviews with ten village residents. Distribution of questionnaires for quantitative data was carried out via Google Form, which was distributed via the RT/RW WhatsApp group and village officials. Meanwhile, residents were selected using purposive sampling for qualitative interviews. Survey and interview questions based on the digital divide theory focus on first-order effects, namely on ownership, availability, and affordability of ICT, as well as digital divide problems, which generally focus on second-order effects (benefits), namely related to the use of ICT in everyday life [54].

4   Result and Discussion

4.1   Result

The quantitative demographic data in pic.1 regarding the age of respondents shows the percentage of ICT users in Pasanggrahan Village. Data created by clusters following age clusters [55] shows that the largest number of ICT users are of productive age, namely 25–54 years old. Meanwhile, the group that uses ICT the least is the older group.

This is by researchers' concerns that the digital divide occurs in the elderly [31, 34] said that the older group was the one who was the slowest to adapt to ICT. According to them, there have been many efforts to accommodate the older group. However, these efforts will not be meaningful because the older group has a low willingness to learn ICT. Similarly, the low willingness to learn factor of older people creates a digital divide [56]. This condition even results in poor health services received by older people (Fig. 1).

Other quantitative data is the use of social media by the residents of Pasanggrahan Village as seen in Table 1. This data shows that the WhatsApp application is the most used application by residents of Pasanggrahan Village. Meanwhile, social media application users are men. This confirms research by Marini et al. (2020), which stated that there is a

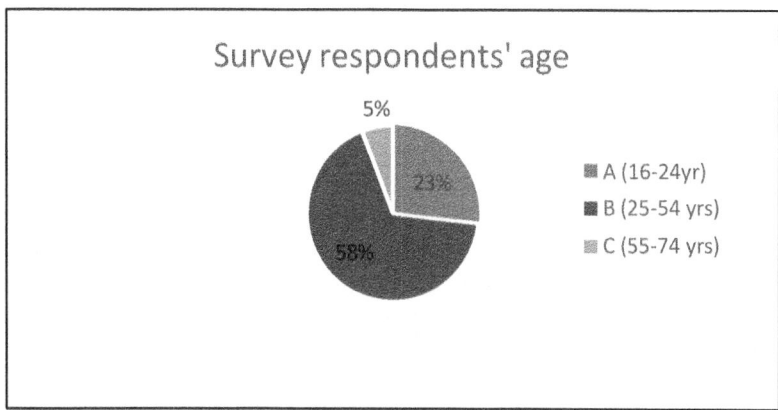

Fig. 1. Survey respondents' age.

digital gap between men and women in Indonesia [41]. This gap is bigger when women live in rural areas [57].

Survey data as shown in Table 2 shows the factors that support the digital divide in Pasanggrahan Village. Almost all respondents do not have problems with ICT ownership, especially mobile phones. However, residents of Pasanggrahan Village are experiencing problems with cellular signals and Internet connections.

Table 1. The Number of Social Media users

		Social Media				Total
		WhatsApp	Facebook	Instagram	TikTok	
Gender	Men	55	4	3	3	65
	Women	27	2	1	6	36
Total		82	6	4	9	101

Qualitative Data

Qualitative data was obtained through interviews with ten villagers selected purposively. The selection of sources is based on demographics and geography or where the interviewee lives. Research questions are based on ownership, availability, usefulness, and skills. The interviews lasted an average of 50 min and then the interview results were transcribed for analysis through open coding, axial, and selective coding.

Ownership of ICT for Tourism Business Use

The information and communication technology referred to in this research is hardware such as cellphones, computers or laptops, internet technology, and social media. Qualitative data shows that most informants in this study have access to ICT ownership. The interviewee said that all family members, except small children, have mobile phone devices. However, each age group's knowledge about ICT is different. The older age group only uses mobile phones for communication purposes using the WhatsApp application to call, send messages, and join RT/RW and village groups. One interviewee said he was not worried about using mobile phone technology because his children would help him to understand.

"Thank God, If you don't know how to access it, I'll ask my children. Children will know (ICT) faster" (Asep Saipudin, 2023).

The results of this study confirm previous research that attention to the digital divide in older age deserves attention as done by [31, 34] The digital technology literacy gap is also related to the lack of vocational experience in using ICT. Analysis of interview data shows that the majority cannot use ICT (mobile phones) other than calling and texting via WhatsApp. Some other elders recognize other social media but rarely use them and are only limited users.

All residents interviewed had no problems accessing mobile phone hardware or accessing internet service subscriptions. However, the use of other ICTs such as personal computers, laptops, or Android televisions is rarely done. All residents interviewed considered owning a mobile phone to be a must. Mobile phones and internet access have become primary needs, so their ownership is a priority for every citizen and family member. However, some residents are still concerned about unstable internet access. Currently, only the XL, Telkomsel, and Axis networks can be accessed by the residents of Pasanggrahan village. However, the internet service network or cell phone service cannot be accessed in several places. There is also a subscription internet access service that uses cable. However, this service is also very limited because procurement depends on the number of applications from residents.

"As for cellphones, sometimes the lights go out, sometimes they don't, depending on the weather. If the weather is bad, it rains or what, it usually depends on the location, if sometimes when you enter the house there is no signal, it depends. So, the signal is still bad if the lights go out" (Much Hamdan, 2023).

"Apart from geographical barriers, cellular and internet connections are also hampered by weather. Several sources complained that if the weather is bad, the connection will be disrupted and even disconnected. There is only a certain time if the internet goes out here, the lights immediately paralyze and completely shut down. There is no signal at all" (Tuti, 2023).

Tajur Village is geographically located on the island of Java, less than 100 km from Jakarta. However, the close distance from the Indonesian capital, Jakarta, does not guarantee a good internet network connection. These findings add to Tabor and Yoon (2015) which stated that Indonesia has interconnectivity problems related to archipelagic geography. Geographical locations on the same island as the capital can also have connectivity problems.

Most residents said that using mobile phones and the WhatsApp application was very helpful in communicating. The ICT has become a primary need for the residents of Pasanggrahan Village. However, most residents do not have the desire to learn about other ICTs that have the potential to help the tourism village businesses they run. Most of the residents don't know how to use online booking applications such as the Traveloka application, Airbnb, and others. For them, the use of ICT is not related to their work. Social media is an emerging media in tourism as a promotional medium to attract tourists to visit tourist villages [13–15]. However, in general, the residents of Pasanggrahan Village, Tajur Village, are farmers, and the accommodation and homestay business they run is a side job. They think that social media or other ICT is not related to their work.

"The thing is, it's a cultural village, maybe it still prioritizes its culture. So, there are still many people there who don't know about the internet, mostly their parents. If school children already know the internet. They focus more on their work, 90% of them are farmers. So yes, for them it's not important, because the network and tools don't exist either" (Igin, 2023).

The results of the interview show that ICT is needed by the people of the Tajur village. However, the use of ICT is only used for personal communication with family. Most people, for example, do not know the potential of using social media to attract tourists for their homestay accommodation business. Others already understand the use of social media but don't know how to use it.

"WhatsApp, and IG, are only limited to the use, and cannot be used for anything else. For information, for example, communication, it's like that" (Iin, 2023).

"I want to, like when we open TikTok we also see what other people's activities are like. There are those selling, there are advertisements from the area, I also want to go there" (Yoseph, 2023).

The interview results show that ICT is for interpersonal communication needs, even though ICT provides opportunities to help residents develop the homestay business they manage. Literacy is needed regarding the importance of marketing communications to bring tourists to Tajur Village, especially homestay tourists. At the same time, infrastructure conditions to overcome communication barriers, and poor signal in Tajur village, need to be addressed. Another alternative is the use of ICT such as websites in centralized homestay management.

5 Discussion

Quantitative data and qualitative data show that the community has extensive access to ICT in Pasanggrahan Village. There are problems with cellular and internet signal reception in certain places, however, this does not affect their daily lives. The level of literacy regarding the benefits of ICT is still low so they do not complain about the lack of ICT services in their area. The most widely used ICT device is the cell phone, but mobile phone applications that support the homestay business have not been utilized. The majority of the people of Pasanggrahan Village use mobile phones only for communication. There are gaps in access based on age groups. Some members of the older group who generally work as farmers do not have access to ICT. The older group gets ICT access from their children or other family members.

This research data shows that the availability of ICT in Pasanggrahan Village has increased rapidly in recent years. The people of Pasanggrahan village in general can access ICT services such as cell phones, computers, and internet services. However, internet service in Padanggrahan village is uneven due to geographic and business factors. For example, the people of Tajur Village often have problems with cellular connections because they are geographically located in remote villages. Meanwhile, Depok Village does not get cable internet subscription services because it does not meet the quota for the number of users.

Quantitative and qualitative data show that there is a gap in citizens' skills in utilizing ICT. The first skills gap can be seen from the differences in age groups. The older age group does not consider mastering the ability to use ICT to be relevant to their lives as farmers. The older group are homeowners who are involved in the homestay business, but the majority of homestay owners are passive. They generally do not use ICT to market the homestays they manage.

Qualitative research data complements the quantitative data that was obtained beforehand. Qualitative data can explain in more depth the problem of digital inequality among the residents of Pasanggrahan Village. Qualitative data was obtained through direct face-to-face meetings, thus providing a better understanding of the digital gap. Apart from that, qualitative data complements quantitative data collected through distributing Google Form questionnaires via WhatsApp group. This means that the quantitative data does not include residents who do not have access to mobile phones.

6   Conclusion

This research aims to explore the digital divide factors in Tajur Pasanggrahan Village, Purwakarta, West Java in understanding contemporary ICT adoption in the context of a tourist village. Tajur Village is a tourist village that offers homestays and conserves cultural heritage such as traditional houses, and local community customs. The research results show that the Pasanggrahan village community has gained access to ICT. However, there is a digital divide, especially in the older age group. For older people, efforts to maintain culture are contradictory to the innovations offered by ICT developments. Residents have considered ICT (mobile phones and the Internet) as a primary need, but residents have not utilized ICT to develop tourist villages, such as a homestay promotion tool, or as a tool for managing their business. The people of Pasanggrahan village have the skills to use mobile phones for communication purposes. However, they have the willingness to learn and develop their skills in utilizing ICT for the development of tourist villages.

Acknowledgments. This research is funded by Penelitian Terapan Binus (PTB) Binus University No: 028/VRRTT/III/2023.

References

1. Purnomo, S., Rahayu, E.S., Riani, A.L., Suminah, S., Udin, U.: Empowerment model for sustainable tourism village in an emerging country. J. Asian Finan. Econ. Bus. **7**(2) (2020). https://doi.org/10.13106/jafeb.2020.vol7.no2.261
2. Purwaningtyas: Implementasi community based tourism dalam evaluasi desa wisata di kabupaten banyuwangi. Jurnal Javanica **2**(1) (2023). https://doi.org/10.57203/javanica.v2i1.2023. 40-50
3. Nabal, R.J., Djaja, K.: Dampak kepariwisataan terhadap perubahan pola urbanisasi di Indonesia Region. Jurnal Pembangunan Wilayah dan Perencanaan Partisipatif **17**(1) (2022). https://doi.org/10.20961/region.v17i1.41465

4. Altassan: Sustainability of heritage villages through eco-tourism investment (case study: Al-Khabra village, Saudi Arabia. Sustainability (Switzerland) **15**(9) (2023). https://doi.org/10.3390/su15097172

5. Anwar, M.A., Syahrani, G., Maulana, A.Z., Putryanda, Y., Wajidi: Strategi pengembangan wisata berbasis kearifan lokal di kalimantan selatan. Jurnal Kebijakan Pembangunan **13**(2) (2018)

6. Arintoko, A.A. Ahmad, D.S. Gunawan, Supadi, S.: Community-based tourism village development strategies: a case of Borobudur tourism village area, Indonesia. Geojournal of Tourism and Geosites **29**(2) (2020). https://doi.org/10.30892/gtg.29202-477

7. Insani, N., Ariani, Y., Ningrum, E.V.K., A'rachman, F.R.: Developing a tourism strategy for heritage villages in the Kayutangan area. KnE Soc. Sci. (2022). https://doi.org/10.18502/kss.v7i16.12166

8. Fauziah, N.R.: Hubungan antara partisipasi masyarakat dengan pemanfaatan digital pada desa wisata. Jurnal Sains Komunikasi dan Pengembangan Masyarakat [JSKPM] **5**(1) (2021). https://doi.org/10.29244/jskpm.v5i1.806

9. Hermawan, H., Anwari, H., Nugroho, D.S.: Pengembangan Produk dan Pemasaran Desa Wisata Digital: Program Insentif Pengabdian Masyarakat Terintegrasi dengan Merdeka Belajar Kampus Merdeka. Abdimas Pariwisata (2023)

10. Sangari, M.T., Tulenan, V., Rumbayan, M.: Implementasi teknologi realitas tertambah desa lalumpe untuk mewujudkan desa wisata digital. Jurnal Teknik Elektro dan Komputer **11**(2) (2022). https://doi.org/10.35793/jtek.11.2.2022.41058

11. Wibowo, K.A., Sevilla, J.: Tantangan mewujudkan desa wisata digital di Kelurahan Kenep, Kabupaten Sukoharjo. In: Prosiding Seminar Pesona Pariwisata (SEMESTA) 2022Seri2 (2022)

12. Putra, G.B., Atmaja, E.J.J.: Pedampingan penggunaan sistem informasi profil desa banyuasin berbasis internet dan aplikasi mobile. Jurdimas (Jurnal Pengabdian Kepada Masyarakat) Royal **4**(1) (2021). https://doi.org/10.33330/jurdimas.v4i1.897

13. Asriandhini, B., Thosien, M.A.K.: Pelatihan komunikasi naratif untuk mendukung digital village branding. Artinara **1**(01) (2021). https://doi.org/10.36080/an.v1i01.4

14. Hendro, F., Setiawan, T., Setiawati, D.: Mempertahankan Eksistensi Tradisi Tungguk Tembakau melalui Media Sosial. Jurnal Ilmu Komunikasi **19**(1) (2021). https://doi.org/10.31315/jik.v19i1.3918

15. Ningsih, F.W., Dyatmika, T.: Pengembangan potensi sumber daya manusia melalui teknologi komunikasi media sosial di era milenial desa kampil. JPKMI Jurnal Pengabdian Kepada Masyarakat Indonesia **2**(4) (2021). https://doi.org/10.36596/jpkmi.v2i4.225

16. Izharsyah, J.R., Saputra, A., Mahardika, A., Ulayya, A.: Formulasi administrasi desa melalui pengembangan kampung digital di desa pematang johar kabupaten deli serdang. JMM Jurnal Masyarakat Mandiri **6**(5) (2022). https://doi.org/10.31764/jmm.v6i5.10351

17. Fajar, "Kesenjangan Digital Tingkat Ketiga pada Pemuda Pedesaan di Kabupaten Cianjur, Indonesia," Jurnal Komunika: Jurnal Komunikasi, Media dan Informatika, vol. 10, no. 1, 2021, https://doi.org/10.31504/komunika.v10i1.4260

18. Alvaro, R., Octavia, E.: Desa digital: potensi dan tantangannya peningkatan kredit UMKM melalui rasio intermediasi makroprudensial tantangan revolusi industri 4.0 di sektor pertanian. Buletin DPR **4**(8) (2019)

19. Sari, V.P.: Pendirian pojok digital dalam upaya mengatasi tantangan kesenjangan digital di desa jatihurip. Dharmakarya **11**(4) (2023). https://doi.org/10.24198/dharmakarya.v11i4.37335

20. Maulana, I., Aprianto, M.C.: Strategi pengembangan ekowisata berbasis ekonomi kearifan lokal: sebuah kasus di kampung tajur, purwakarta. Eqien: J. Ekonomi dan Bisnis **5**(2) (2018). https://doi.org/10.34308/eqien.v5i2.60

21. Choudrie, J., Zamani, E., Obuekwe, C.: Bridging the digital divide in ethnic minority older adults: an organisational qualitative study. Inf. Syst. Front. **24**(4) (2022). https://doi.org/10. 1007/s10796-021-10126-8
22. Van Dijk, J.A.G.M.: Digital divide: impact of access. Int. Encycl. Media Effects (2017). https://doi.org/10.1002/9781118783764.wbieme0043
23. Fadilla, N., Konsentrasi, M., Perpustakaan, I., Informasi, D.: Kesenjangan Digital di Era Revolusi Industri 4.0 dan Hubungannya dengan Perpustakaan sebagai Penyedia Informasi. Libria **12**(1) (2020)
24. Zulham, M.: Kesenjangan Digital di Kalangan Guru SMP (Studi Deskriptif mengenai Kesenjangan Aksesibilitas dan Kapabilitas Teknologi Informasi di kalangan Guru SMP Kecamatan Krian). Universitas Airlangga J. **3**(3) (2014)
25. Azizah A.A.: Kesenjangan Digital di Kalangan Pengelola Usaha Mikro Kecil Menengah (UMKM) Surabaya Surabaya (2019)
26. Kadiman: Penelitian, Pengembangan dan Penerapan Ilmu Pengetahuan dan Teknologi Bidang Teknologi Informasi dan Komunikasi Tahun 2005–2025 (2006)
27. Riggins, F., Dewan, S.: The digital divide: current and future research directions. J. Assoc. Inf. Syst. **6**(12), 298–337 (2005). https://doi.org/10.17705/1jais.00074
28. OECD: Understanding the digital divide (2001)
29. Nasution, Z.: Perkembangan Teknologi Komunikasi. Universitas Terbuka, Jakarta (2014)
30. Van Dijk, J.A.G.M.: Acknowledgements 2 research into and theory of the digital divide 8 social and digital inequality. The Digital Divide (2019)
31. Fang, M.L., Canham, S.L., Battersby, L., Sixsmith, J., Wada, M., Sixsmith, A.: Exploring privilege in the digital divide: implications for theory, policy, and practice. Gerontologist **59**(1) (2019). https://doi.org/10.1093/geront/gny037
32. Morris, J., Morris, W., Bowen, R.: Implications of the digital divide on rural SME resilience. J. Rural. Stud. **89** (2022). https://doi.org/10.1016/j.jrurstud.2022.01.005
33. Purnia, D.S., Adiwisastra, M.F., Muhajir, H., Supriadi, D.: Pengukuran kesenjangan digital menggunakan metode deskriptif berbasis website. EVOLUSI : Jurnal Sains dan Manajemen **8**(2) (2020). https://doi.org/10.31294/evolusi.v8i2.8942
34. Qureshi, M.A., Khaskheli, A., Qureshi, J.A., Raza, S.A., Yousufi, S.Q.: Factors affecting students' learning performance through collaborative learning and engagement. Interact. Learn. Environ. **31**(4), 2371–2391 (2023). https://doi.org/10.1080/10494820.2021.1884886
35. Tyas, D.L., Djoko Budiyanto, A., Santoso, A.J.: Pengukuran Kesenjangan Digital Masyarakat Di Kota Pekalongan. Seminar Nasional Teknologi Informasi dan Komunikasi **2016**(Sentika) (2016)
36. Dhakal, S.P., Tjokro, S.P.: Tourism enterprises in Indonesia and the fourth industrial revolution–are they ready? Tour. Recreat. Res. (2021). https://doi.org/10.1080/02508281.2021.199 6687
37. Minghetti, V.: Digital divide in tourism. Encyclopedia Tourism Manage. Mark. (2022). https:// doi.org/10.4337/9781800377486.digital.divide.in
38. Minghetti, V., Buhalis, D.: Digital divide in tourism. J. Travel Res. **49**(3) (2010). https://doi. org/10.1177/0047287509346843
39. Insyiroh, I.M., Hariani, E.P., Mubaroq, S.: Pendidikan berbasis kearifan lokal sebagai solusi menghadapi kesenjangan digital dalam kebijakan pembelajaran jarak jauh pada masa pandemi di Indonesia. Indonesian J. Soc. Dev. **1**(1), 2020
40. Onitsuka, K., Hidayat, A.R.R.T., Huang, W.: Challenges for the next level of digital divide in rural Indonesian communities. Electron. J. Inf. Syst. Dev. Countries **84**(2) (2018). https:// doi.org/10.1002/isd2.12021
41. Marini, S., Hanum, F., Sulistiyo, A.: Digital literacy: empowering Indonesian women in overcoming digital divide (2020). https://doi.org/10.2991/assehr.k.200130.029

42. Ariansyah, K., Anandhita, V.H., Sari, D.: Investigating the next level digital divide in Indonesia. In: TIMES-iCON 2019 2019 4th Technology Innovation Management and Engineering Science International Conference (2019). https://doi.org/10.1109/TIMESiCON47539.2019.9024668

43. Istiqomah, R., Yasmin, P.A., Wikananto, D.: Melihat eksistensi dan geliat bangunan peninggalan cagar budaya : kontestasi pasar beringharjo dengan pertokoan modern di kawasan malioboro. J. Analisa Sosiologi **11**(2) (2022). https://doi.org/10.20961/jas.v11i2.57688

44. Rahman, A.: Cagar Budaya Dan Memori Kolektif: Membangun Kesadaran Sejarah Masyarakat Lokal Berbasis Peninggalan Cagar Budaya Di Aceh Bagian Timur. Mozaik Humaniora **20**(1) (2020). https://doi.org/10.20473/mozaik.v20i1.15346

45. Rahmatillah, T.P., Insyan, O., Nurafifah, N., Hirsan, F.P.: Strategi Pengembangan Desa Wisata Berbasis Wisata Alam dan Budaya Sebagai Media Promosi Desa Sangiang. Jurnal Planoearth **4**(2) (2019). https://doi.org/10.31764/jpe.v4i2.970

46. Suprobowati, D., Sugiharto, M., Miskan, M.: Strategi pengembangan desa wisata kreatif berbasis masyarakat kearifan lokal hendrosari gresik. Jurnal ilmiah Manajemen Publik dan Kebijakan Sosial **6**(1) (2022). https://doi.org/10.25139/jmnegara.v6i1.4551

47. Wahyuni, D.: Pengembangan Desa Wisata Pentingsari, Kabupaten Sleman dalam Perspektif Partisipasi Masyarakat, Aspirasi: Jurnal Masalah-masalah Sosial **10**(2) (2019). https://doi.org/10.46807/aspirasi.v10i2.1386

48. Darma Oka, I.M., Sudiarta, M., Widya Darmayanti, P.: Warisan cagar budaya sebagai ikon desa wisata kaba-kaba, kabupaten tabanan, Bali. Mudra Jurnal Seni Budaya **36**(2) (2021). https://doi.org/10.31091/mudra.v36i2.1459

49. Fitria, F., et al.: Pengembangan Potensi Peninggalan Sejarah di Desa Bendoasri dan Tritik Nganjuk Sebagai Desa Wisata Edukasi Sejarah. Archive: Jurnal Pengabdian Kepada Masyarakat **1**(2) (2022). https://doi.org/10.55506/arch.v1i2.35

50. Hasanah, R.: Kearifan lokal sebagai daya tarik wisata budaya di desa sade kabupaten lombok tengah. DESKOVI: Art Des. J. **2**(1) (2019). https://doi.org/10.51804/deskovi.v2i1.409

51. Syaifudin, M.Y., Ma'ruf, M.F.: Peran pemerintah desa dalam pengembangan dan pemberdayaan masyarakat melalui desa wisata (studi di desa jurug kabupaten ponorogo), Publika (2022). https://doi.org/10.26740/publika.v10n2.p365-380

52. Eprilianto, D.F., Pradana, G.W., Megawati, S., Febriyanti, E., Shobirin, D.R. and Sajida, R.H.: Pendampingan pengembangan desawisata budaya lokal di desa tlemang kecamatan ngimbang kabupaten lamongan. Communnity Dev. J. **4**(3), 6295–6302 (2023)

53. Raharjana, D.T., Kutanegara, P.M.: Pemberdayaan Masyarakat di Kawasan Cagar Budaya. Jurnal Tata Kelola Seni **5**(1) (2019). https://doi.org/10.24821/jtks.v5i1.3145

54. Gündüz, H.B.: Digital divide in Turkish primary schools: Sakarya sample. Turkish Online J. Educ. Technol. **9**(1), 43–53 (2010)

55. van Dijk, J.A.G.M.: One Europe, Digitally Divided. In: Routledge Handbook of Internet Politics (2008).https://doi.org/10.4324/9780203962541-24

56. Alkureishi, M.A., et al.: Digitally disconnected: qualitative study of patient perspectives on the digital divide and potential solutions. JMIR Hum Factors **8**(4) (2021). https://doi.org/10.2196/33364

57. Nahumury, A.P., Antony, R.: Semi-online learning as a solution to the digital divide in education in frontier, outermost, and disadvantaged regions. Jurnal Kependidikan: Jurnal Hasil Penelitian dan Kajian Kepustakaan di Bidang Pendidikan, Pengajaran dan Pembelajaran **8**(2) (2022). https://doi.org/10.33394/jk.v8i2.4960

Can Digital Literacy Counter Cyberbullying?
A Scoping Review

Francesco Pio Savino(✉) ⓘ, Francesco Antonio Santangelo ⓘ,
and Francesca Cangelli ⓘ

Università di Foggia, Foggia, Italy
francesco.savino@unifg.it

Abstract. The article examines the dynamic interplay between digital literacy and chatbots in the fight against cyberbullying. Digital literacy, defined as the competence to use digital technologies mindfully in order to access, comprehend, create, and share information, emerges as a crucial deterrent against cyberbullying. This proficiency involves understanding online dynamics, promoting responsible online behaviour, and equipping individuals with the tools to manage their online presence and digital identity effectively. It encourages awareness of digital interactions, fosters responsible conduct, and provides individuals with the skills needed to navigate the online environment securely. Research by Hinduja and Patchin (2015) [9] highlights the importance of digital literacy in reducing the risk of aggressive online behaviour, while Marrazzo's study (2018) [6] underscores its role in fostering a safe digital space and addressing the issue of cyberbullying. In this context, the article aims to explore the current state of the scientific literature on the use of chatbots in combatting cyberbullying, identifying the ideal and functional characteristics that chatbots should possess [11]. The purpose of this scoping review is to develop a chatbot capable of identifying instances of cyberbullying in real time, detecting offensive language, and offering immediate, personalised responses to provide users with instant support, thereby enhancing their online safety and well-being.

Keywords: digital literacy · cyberbulling · chatbots

1 Introduction

Bullying and cyberbullying are presented as serious and widespread global issues, having a profoundly negative impact on students and leading to detrimental consequences for their well-being and academic progress. In this context, the academic literature has converged on providing consistent definitions of these phenomena. According to a UNESCO report, there are various forms of school violence and types of bullying. Bullying, in this regard, is characterised by aggressive behaviour involving unwanted, negative actions that are repeated over time, with an imbalance of power or strength between the perpetrator(s) and the victim. This includes physical bullying, psychological bullying, sexual bullying, and cyberbullying [12].

© The Author(s), under exclusive license to Springer Nature Switzerland AG 2025
G. A. Toto (Ed.): ICS exchange 2024, CCIS 2521, pp. 324–333, 2025.
https://doi.org/10.1007/978-3-032-03021-4_23

In recent years, the widespread access to technological devices and tools, coupled with the rise of online communities such as social networks, has contributed to a concerning increase in cyberbullying. According to the United Nations Children's Fund (UNICEF) [13], the recent pandemic and periods of lockdown have made it even clearer that for children, being online is essential for key aspects of childhood, such as learning, socialisation, and developing an awareness of both the threats posed by the internet and the fact that online behaviour has real-world consequences.

In this framework, one of the most effective solutions is to promote digital literacy. There is no single, universally accepted definition of "digital literacy", which is why the authors have adopted the definition provided by UNESCO in its report *A Global Framework of Reference on Digital Literacy Skills for Indicator 4.4.2* (2018) [5]. According to UNESCO, digital literacy involves the skills required to access, handle, comprehend, combine, share, assess, and generate information securely and effectively using digital tools. These skills support career opportunities, decent work, and entrepreneurship. It also encompasses related competencies such as computer literacy, ICT skills, information literacy, and media literacy. This definition of digital literacy is aligned with *The Digital Competence Framework for Citizens* (DigComp 2.2), which includes six dimensions of competence (see Fig. 1) that can help improve children's safety online [14].

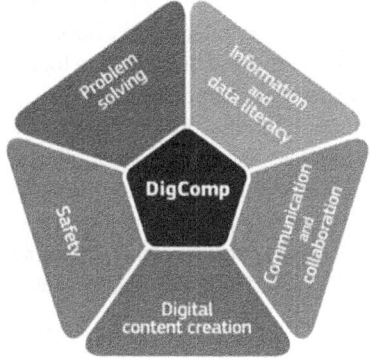

Fig. 1. The five dimensions of digital competences included in DigComp 2.2: The Digital Competence Framework for Citizens

In this perspective, and according to UNICEF, keeping children informed, engaged, and empowered to use the internet safely is critical to mitigating risks while ensuring their rights to equal access to technologies. Other research has shown that, while educating children about the risks and strategies to mitigate them, as well as providing counselling and reporting services, can help counteract cyberbullying, victims of online abuse often refrain from speaking out due to feelings of shame or guilt, uncertainty about whom to approach, or simply not realising they are being abused.

In this context, platforms such as social media, gaming sites, and messaging services are key players in this issue, but they are still struggling to find effective ways to moderate cyberbullying. Emerging technologies, such as Artificial Intelligence (AI), could prove valuable in supporting victims of online abuse. According to Piccolo and colleagues (2021) [10], victims of online abuse have expressed a desire to be listened to without being judged. Additionally, the study by Mendoza-Pinto [7] demonstrated that chatbots are able to provide an elementary level of emotional support to users, offering messages of encouragement and guidance in dealing with bullying situations. Furthermore, integrating advanced models such as ChatGPT into chatbots has shown to significantly improve their responsiveness. Given these findings, the purpose of this scoping review is to explore how a chatbot can be designed to be an effective tool in both combating and preventing cyberbullying. The author (F.A.S.) has developed a basic chatbot, which will be tested in subsequent studies. In this scoping review, we present the initial results from our interactions with the chatbot, which we have named "Vito".

2   Methods

To investigate the above, the authors conducted a scoping review on the correlation between digital literacy, digital skills, and cyberbullying. The scoping review was conducted using three different databases: Scopus, EBSCO, and Web of Science. The authors employed the following search strategy: ("digital literacy") AND ("Student*") AND ("Bullying*"). Using this strategy, we found 12 records in Scopus, 13 in EBSCO, and 18 in Web of Science, for a total of 43 records.

In the research process, we used an online open-source software called Rayyan to manage the records. Using the "research duplicates" tool in this software, we identified 12 duplicate records. After removing these duplicates, a total of 31 records were retained and moved forward to the abstract screening phase.

During this stage, the authors applied a set of exclusion criteria to ensure the relevance and quality of the selected studies. Papers were excluded if they were not written in English, not Open Access, focused on an irrelevant population, were not academic in nature, relied on an unsuitable theoretical framework, or were published outside the timeframe of 2019 to 2024. Following this rigorous screening process, 9 records met all the criteria and were ultimately included in the final review.

3   Study Selection

All study designs were considered, including qualitative and quantitative methods, such as methodology reports. The authors included in this review only those studies that met the inclusion criteria. The inclusion criteria for this review were carefully defined to ensure relevance and quality. First, only academic papers were considered, as these provide a reliable and scholarly foundation for analysis.

The papers had to be written in English to ensure consistency in language and accessibility. Additionally, only studies published within the last five years were included, ensuring that the findings and discussions reflect the most recent advancements in the field. Open Access articles were prioritised, allowing unrestricted access to the content.

The selected papers specifically needed to address the development of chatbots, ensuring that the research aligned with the technological focus of this study. Finally, the articles had to discuss topics related to cyberbullying, providing insights into how chatbots can be leveraged to tackle this critical issue.

4 Discussion

In recent years, many studies have shown that the use of chatbots in the learning process can produce positive effects, such as increasing students' digital literacy and stimulating prosocial behaviour. Consequently, chatbots can be used as a deterrent againstcyberbullying[1–7]. According to Gabrielli and colleagues [3], the use of the internet and digital solutions by young people is increasing worldwide and proves to be an effective way to reach this population with self-help programmes. In fact, chatbot intervention programmes could easily be integrated into existing school programmes and initiatives for bullying and cyberbullying prevention.

Furthermore, the results of the study by Mendoza-Pinto [7] showed that chatbots demonstrated their ability to provide an elementary level of emotional support to users interacting with them. They also offered messages of encouragement and guidance in dealing with bullying situations. The integration of the ChatGPT model into the chatbots had a significant impact on their responsiveness. According to Zhong and colleagues [15], the level of digital literacy among students is positively correlated with the level of cyberbullying. In fact, the proportion of positive and responsible learning/work time online shows a significant negative relationship with the likelihood of being cyberbullied.

In the context of social behaviour, various forms of online interaction are significantly correlated with involvement in cyberbullying, either as perpetrators or victims. Specifically, students who engage in self-expression and actively participate in online discussions tend to exhibit higher average scores for cyberbullying behaviour. Students who engage in these two behaviours typically belong to more active social network types and are prone to voicing their views and following suit in debates. When questioned, refuted, or when engaging in discussions with others, these students are more likely to have conflicts and may even engage in cyber-stalking or invade others' privacy, thereby cyberbullying others. In terms of average scores for being cyberbullied, students who exhibit self-expressive behaviour scored significantly higher than those with other behavioural traits. This suggests that individuals who frequently voice their opinions and ideas online are more likely to be targeted by cyberbullying, particularly when their views or perspectives are not accepted by others. Finally, according to Zhong and colleagues [15], increasing the digital literacy of young users can have a positive effect on reducing the level of cyberbullying and is positively correlated with a decreased risk of becoming cyberbullies.

From another perspective, Herbert and colleagues [4] argue that the early and extensive use of new technologies has been linked to many health risks among children and adolescents over the years. There is substantial evidence that violent media (movies, television, video games) is a risk factor for aggressive behaviour in young people around the world. From this standpoint, cyberbullying is closely connected to the messages conveyed by new media.

In conclusion, while increasing digital literacy among young users can play a pivotal role in mitigating cyberbullying, it is equally important to recognise the broader health risks posed by the early and excessive use of new technologies. As highlighted, violent media contributes to aggressive behaviour, creating a complex relationship between media content and cyberbullying. Addressing these challenges requires a multifaceted approach that promotes digital literacy, responsible media consumption, and greater awareness of the potential health risks associated with technology use.

5 Main Results and Future Research

The data included in this review show that the scientific literature on the effect of digital literacy in the fight against bullying is still limited. In this scoping review, we aim to demonstrate how the literature on the effect of digital literacy in combatting bullying and cyberbullying is lacking. We also focus on papers that discuss the development of new tools that can be effective in addressing bullying. According to the authors included in this study, the goal has been to create a tool that uses digital technology.

To provide a practical example of the literature analysed, we built a simple chatbot based on the OpenRouter environment, an open and unified interface that aggregates APIs from different artificial intelligence models. The chatbot is configured to use "OpenChat 3.5," a free artificial intelligence model. As a result, its level of responsiveness is relatively limited compared to more advanced models. Specifically, OpenChat 3.5 does not use a crawler to collect data from the internet in real time, and its training database is limited to knowledge acquired up until 2022. This results in some obsolescence in its responses, particularly in areas that are subject to rapid change or continuous updates.

Another limitation is language localization. The quality of responses in Italian is often inferior because the model relies on machine translations from English, which are not always accurate or fluent. This can negatively impact user interaction, especially in contexts where clarity and linguistic precision are critical, such as education or professional counselling.

However, integrating more advanced and specific technologies could solve many of these issues. To improve the chatbot's performance, it would be beneficial to transition to paid artificial intelligence models that offer enhanced language comprehension and generation capabilities, as well as constant updates to their knowledge bases. These models could provide more effective support for Italian, ensuring more accurate and consistent responses over time.

Another development perspective involves creating a custom model, trained on a specific corpus related to the chatbot's knowledge domain. This solution would allow the chatbot to better respond to user needs by offering more targeted and in-depth responses on sector-specific topics. Integrating a custom model via the OpenRouter interface would enable the full potential of AI to be harnessed, creating a highly personalised user experience optimised for the specific needs of the project.

In conclusion, this scoping review highlights the significant gap in the scientific literature regarding the impact of digital literacy in combating bullying and cyberbullying. While there are promising efforts to develop digital tools, including chatbots, to address these challenges, the field remains underexplored and in need of further innovation. Our practical example, which involved building a basic chatbot using the OpenRouter environment, illustrates both the potential and the current limitations of such tools. Despite constraints in responsiveness, language localization, and up-to-date knowledge, this prototype serves as a stepping stone toward more sophisticated solutions.

To advance this field, future research and development should focus on leveraging more advanced AI models with enhanced capabilities, ensuring up-to-date and contextually accurate knowledge bases. Additionally, creating custom models trained on domain-specific data could lead to highly personalised and effective tools for addressing bullying. By investing in these directions, researchers can better harness digital technologies to foster safer online and offline environments, ultimately making strides in the fight against bullying and cyberbullying (Table 1).

Table 1. Study included in scoping review.

n	Authors	Years of publication	Study design	aim	Intervention	Results
1	Gabrielli, S., Rizzi, S., Carbone, S., Donisi, V	2020	Pilot Study	Co-designed a life skill coaching through the use of AI tools	Use of chatbot for to raise awareness of the issue of cyberbullying and to train middle or high school children on the issue of cyberbullying	All 21 participants who took part in the feasibility test successfully completed the eight coaching sessions and filled in the relevant questionnaires. Across all eight sessions, using a scale from 1 (very little) to 5 (very much), the majority of participants (16 out of 21, or 76%) rated the usefulness of the sessions as either 4 or 5. The sessions were also rated 4 or 5 by most participants for ease of use (19 out of 21, or 90%) and for their innovativeness (17 out of 21, or 81%)
2	Mendoza-Pinto, R	2023	Multidisciplinary study	Explore the feasibility of the AI in the search for relief by victim of cyberbullying	Developed a chatbot using the Telegram platform and the GPTChat model as a platform for complaints and emotional assistance for student victims of bullying	The chatbot demonstrated its ability to provide an elementary level of emotional support to users interacting with the victims

(continued)

Table 1. (*continued*)

n	Authors	Years of publication	Study design	aim	Intervention	Results
3	Ferri, F., D'Andrea, A., D'Ulizia	2020	Experimental	Demostrate that using a co-creation approach to design a MOOCs	The study involved teachers and students from a primary school in Rome. The study provided a technology enhanced intervention based on a co-creation strategy that integrated two technological approaches such as digital storytelling and MOOCs	The results obtained by the authors from the implemented case study confirm the author's hypothesis that the use of a co-creation approach to design the MOOCs allows amplification of the learning experience as well as the children's knowledge and awareness of digital health literacy issues
4	Herbert, P.C., Rhodes, D., Tiberi-Ramos, J., Cichon, T., Bear, H., Cox, C		Longitudinal study	The article aims to explore how media and community influences affect youth behaviours related to bullying and substance abuse and to evaluate whether a media literacy curriculum can change these perceptions	The authors have structured a six-week intervention. Intervention involved a curriculum designed to increase awareness of the negative effects of substance abuse and bullying and to reduce the perceived influence of media on these behaviors The program focused on teaching young people about media influence, improving decision making skills, and promoting safe practices on social media	The pre-post results showed that, after the intervention, the peers have a least influence on the decisions of the participants on the engage in cyberbullying (SD = 0.92). The same results were also shown with regard to the influence of the community, on the same item

(*continued*)

Table 1. (*continued*)

n	Authors	Years of publication	Study design	aim	Intervention	Results
5	Zhong, J., Zheng, Y., Huang, X., Mo, D Gong, J., Li, M. Huang, J	2021	Qualitative study	understand how to effectively combat cyber-bullying, identifying the factors that influence it. This study focused on the individual-level factors of university students and divided these influences into five categories: personal characteristics, internet usage patterns and social network habits, personality traits, emotional aspects and skills related to digital citizenship	Questions regarding students' personal back- ground and student's routine on internet, The Big Five personality test, Emotional questionnaire, a digital citizenship and a cyber -bullying questionnaire	The study finds that cyberbullying among Chinese college students is generally low. Key factors influencing it include gender, with significant effects on both perpetration and victimization. While daily online time isn't strongly linked to cyberbullying, more time spent on non-educational online activities is positively associated with it. Personality traits and life satisfaction also play roles, with lower life satisfaction linked to increased victimization. Empathy, especially in terms of stress and concern, correlates with higher rates of cyberbullying among female students. Understanding and following internet etiquette helps reduce cyberbullying
6	Chen, C.W	2017	Qualitative	Examine whether Project-Based Learning (PBL) was conducive to student's learning of language and the issue of cyberbullying	A series of questionnaire was administered to 947 Chinese university students. In particular the authors have administered The project spanned over 9 weeks in a university in Taiwan, and it involved 30 English majors. The cyberbullying project followed Alan and Stoller's criteria for PBL i.e. a	The results indicated that the 9week project work heightened students' awareness of cyberbullying and other social issues and enhanced their language skills. Students also held an overall positive attitude toward the project work

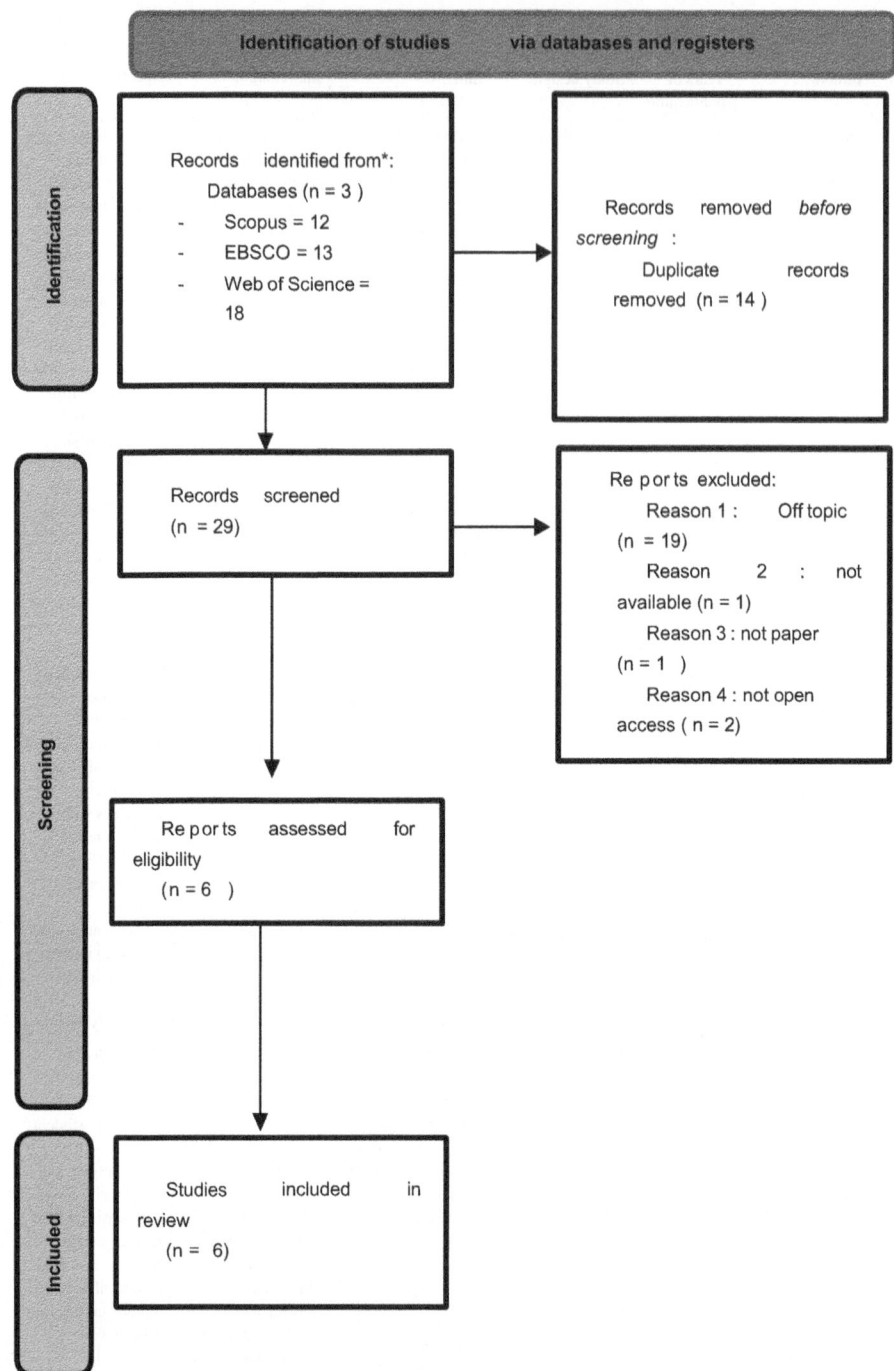

References

1. Chen, C.W.Y.: Think before you type: the effectiveness of implementing an anti-cyberbullying project in an EFL classroom. Pedagogies Int. J. **13**(1), 1–18 (2018)
2. Ferri, F., D'Andrea, A., D'Ulizia, A., Grifoni, P.: Co-creation of eLearning content: the case study of a MOOC on health and cyber-bullying. J. Univers. Comput. Sci. **26**(2), 200–219 (2020)
3. Gabrielli, S., Rizzi, S., Carbone, S., Donisi, V.: A Chatbot-based coaching intervention for adolescents to promote life skills: pilot study. JMIR Hum. Factors **7**(1), e16762 (2020)
4. Herbert, P.C., Rhodes, D., Cichon, T., Baer, H., Cox, C.: Perceived media influence on youth bullying and substance abuse behaviors. Am. J. Health Stud. **33**(4) (2018)
5. Law, N.W.Y., Woo, D.J., De la Torre, J., Wong, K.W.G.: A global framework of reference on digital literacy skills for indicator 4.4. 2 (2018)
6. Marrazzo, F.: La complessità del cyberbullismo. Un approccio di digital literacy. Fuori Luogo. Rivista di Sociologia del Territorio, Turismo, Tecnologia, **4**(2), 73–90 (2018)
7. Mendoza-Pinto, R.: Artificial intelligence in the fight against bullying: integration of ChatGPT in an emotional support Chatbot. In: CEUR Workshop Proceedings, vol. 1613, pp. 0073 (2023). http://ceurws.org
8. Milosevic, T., Van Royen, K., Davis, B.: Artificial Intelligence to address cyberbullying, harassment and abuse: new directions in the midst of complexity. Int. J. Bullying Prevent. **4** (2022).https://doi.org/10.1007/s42380-022-00117-x
9. Patchin, J.W., Hinduja, S.: Measuring cyberbullying: implications for research. Aggress. Violent. Beh. **23**, 69–74 (2015)
10. Piccolo, L.S.G., Troullinou, P., Alani, H.: Chatbots to support children in coping with online threats: Socio-technical requirements. In: Proceedings of the 2021 ACM Designing Interactive Systems Conference, pp. 1504–1517 (2021)
11. Pollock, D., et al.: Methodological quality, guidance, and tools in scoping reviews: a scoping review protocol. JBI Evidence Synthesis **20**(4), 1098–1105 (2022)
12. UNESCO: Behind the Numbers: Ending School Violence and Bullying. UNESCO, Paris (2019)
13. Unicef: COVID-19 and its implications for protecting children online. Retrieved July, 2020-04 (2020)
14. Vuorikari, R., Kluzer, S., Punie, Y., DigComp 2.2: The digital competence framework for citizens - With new examples of knowledge, skills and attitudes, EUR 31006 EN, Publications Office of the European Union, Luxembourg, 2022, ISBN 978-92-76-48883-5, https://doi.org/10.2760/490274, JRC128415
15. Zhong, J., et al.: Study of the influencing factors of cyberbullying among Chinese college students incorporated with digital citizenship: from the perspective of individual students. Front. Psychol. **12**, 621418 (2021)

Evolving Education: The Triple Helix for Innovation and Collaboration

Maria Carmina Sgambato[1]([⊠]) and Elvira Martini[2]

[1] University of Foggia, Foggia, Italy
m.sgambato@unifortunato.eu
[2] Giustino Fortunato University, Benevento, Italy

Abstract. The concept of the Triple Helix, based on collaboration among government, industry, and academic institutions, has proven crucial in promoting socio-economic-educational development through innovation. The main idea underlying this work concerns the role of academia as a socio-economic catalyst: indeed, through its traditional research work, it embraces an innovative study approach, defined as the "third mission." The role of academia has undergone a revolution based on a process that places it at the center not only of knowledge creation but also of knowledge transfer and practical application, implying close interconnection with governmental institutions. This study aims to promote an interdisciplinary and collaborative approach to education by applying the concept of the triple helix to innovative teaching. The goal is to prepare students for a rapidly evolving world, where solutions to problems often require a multidisciplinary approach. This may include practical learning projects, internships in companies, collaborations with government entities, and the development of innovative solutions to local and global challenges. A crucial role in the educational process is played by ICT: by promoting universal access to connectivity and stimulating technological innovation, students are prepared for the challenges offered by the world of digital innovations. Through case studies we will illustrate the ways in which educational institutions can integrate the principles of the Triple Helix into their pedagogical approach.

Keywords: Triple Helix · future education · Entrepreneurial Education

1 Knowledge as a Strategic Resource

In today's economic and social context, knowledge has become a fundamental resource, more powerful than traditional production factors such as land, labor, and capital. This paradigm shift reflects the emergence of a knowledge economy that has radically transformed pre-existing economic and production models. The growing centrality of knowledge as a cognitive, social, and technological resource has influenced innovation dynamics, transforming not only the economy but also social and organizational structures. As Bacon (1597) emphasized, knowledge is "power" and it has indeed demonstrated its power in the broadest possible sense. In an era of globalization and digitalization, knowledge becomes the primary driver of growth and innovation, capable of propelling economies toward new models of development (Stehr, 2001; Martini, 2011).

G. A. Toto (Ed.): ICS exchange 2024, CCIS 2521, pp. 334–345, 2025.
https://doi.org/10.1007/978-3-032-03021-4_24

The knowledge society, as defined by Martini (2011), is characterized by a transition from the production and accumulation of material goods to the creation and transfer of ideas and skills. Knowledge is no longer merely an intellectual product confined to academia but a continuous flow of information that interacts, influences, and guides the evolution of industries, markets, and organizations. Martini (2011) underscores that knowledge, by its nature, is dynamic and constantly evolving, and its value-generation capacity depends on its distribution, accessibility, and interaction with other productive sectors. The spread of digital technologies and globalization has indeed enabled a connected society where knowledge is shared through networks and collaborative platforms, overcoming traditional barriers of space and time (Martini, 2011).

2   The Triple Helix Model: An Evolved and Interactive Approach

The Triple Helix model, developed by Etzkowitz and Leydesdorff in the 1990s, presented an innovative response to the increasing complexity of the global socio-economic system. Traditionally, relationships among universities, businesses, and governments were seen as bilateral, with each of these actors operating relatively independently. However, with the advent of an economy increasingly based on knowledge, a new model of interaction became necessary, one in which these three actors interact dynamically and collaboratively. Etzkowitz and Leydesdorff (1998) identified the Triple Helix as a model in which universities, businesses, and governments are seen not only as distinct actors but as partners that collaborate interdependently to create and disseminate innovation and knowledge.

In the Triple Helix model, universities are no longer regarded merely as centers of research and teaching but also as hubs for innovation and technology transfer. The idea that universities should actively contribute to economic and social growth underpins this approach. Consequently, universities are seen not just as places of learning and research but as actors that create new business and development opportunities. Similarly, businesses are no longer passive consumers of university research but become active participants in the innovation process. Governments, for their part, must provide the regulatory framework and policies needed to encourage cooperation among these actors and foster innovation. This approach has given rise to a new strategic alliance that promotes technological progress and entrepreneurship.

Over time, the Triple Helix model has evolved from an initial conception of interactions among three independent actors (universities, businesses, and governments) to a more complex and dynamic vision that emphasizes interaction among these institutions through well-defined but highly interconnected boundaries. In a more advanced version of the Triple Helix (II), the three circles maintain a degree of institutional autonomy but are connected by solid lines representing intermediary organizations such as technology transfer offices or legal offices. These intermediary entities play a crucial role in facilitating the flow of knowledge and resources among the three spheres, strengthening relationships, and creating new opportunities for innovation (Martini, 2023).

Martini (2023) explains that in the evolved Triple Helix (III), the three institutional spheres not only continue to perform their traditional roles but also take on the perspectives and functions of the other actors. For example, universities no longer limit themselves to producing research but can also play a quasi-governmental role as local organizers of innovation, facilitating the translation of ideas into practical applications and policies. This approach reflects a paradigm shift in understanding the role of universities, which are no longer seen merely as educational and research entities but as dynamic players in the process of economic and social development.

Specifically, Triple Helix IIIa appears as three overlapping circles, where a small central circle, symbolizing the internal communication core, becomes the connection point among the different spheres. Here, interactions among universities, businesses, and governments are no longer limited by traditional functional boundaries but intertwine in ways that foster new models of governance and innovation. However, as Leydesdorff (2006) notes, in some cases, this overlap may lead to a "void" at the center of the system, representing negative entropy. In such circumstances, continuous and differentiated communication among the spheres is necessary to prevent integration from becoming ineffective. If properly managed, this overlap can give rise to a hypercycle that integrates systems in a differentiated manner, promoting innovation and continuous adaptation to emerging challenges.

This interaction process occurs not only at a macro level but also at a micro level, where knowledge circulation within each sphere is equally crucial. Macro circulation, referring to exchanges among the spheres, is fundamental for creating policies, projects, and collaborative networks (Martini, 2023). Micro circulation, developed within individual spheres, enables the generation of more radical innovations, stimulated by horizontal social mobility and the introduction of experts from other social sectors. As Etzkowitz (2008) emphasizes, this form of horizontal mobility tends to radicalize innovation compared to vertical circulation, which is more tied to the conservatism of existing structures.

Moreover, Martini (2023) stresses the importance of a deeper reading of the model, where micro-actors—such as university researchers who become entrepreneurs of their own technologies or entrepreneurs collaborating with universities in technology transfer processes—are essential to revealing the system's evolutionary characteristics.

These actors not only develop innovative technologies and solutions but also participate in managing regional technology transfer agencies, creating hybrid knowledge systems that contribute to a multidimensional approach to innovation (Viale & Ghiglione, 1998; Martini & De Luca Picione, 2022).

The Triple Helix model, therefore, operates on three levels:

Micro Level: Where actors such as researchers, entrepreneurs, and policymakers play a crucial role in transferring knowledge among spheres and developing new ideas.

Meso Level: Represented by institutions that organize and facilitate innovation through innovation agencies, technology spin-offs, and venture capital.

Macro Level: Concerned with regulation, public policies, and fiscal incentives that guide actors' behavior within the system, directing resources toward strategic areas of innovation (Martini, 2023).

The key to this model's success lies in the ability to manage the interfaces among systems, fostering the creation of new social and organizational forms that synergistically combine inputs from the three institutional spheres. As Martini (2023) emphasizes, the diversity of cultures and expertise among universities, businesses, and governments is not an obstacle but rather a fundamental resource for stimulating innovation hybridization and the emergence of new social formats.

In summary, the Triple Helix model evolves from a static and separate model to a more fluid and dynamic one that responds to the challenges of an increasingly interconnected and global world. Martini (2023) invites us to reflect on how these interactions, if well managed, can lead to a virtuous cycle of innovation and sustainable growth, creating an ecosystem where knowledge and collaboration among universities, businesses, and governments underpin socio-economic progress.

2.1 The Dynamics of the Triple Helix: An Open and Interactive Innovation System

In the Triple Helix model, collaboration among universities, businesses, and governments is not static but takes the form of a dynamic and continuous process. The actors involved interact constantly, contributing to the system's evolution and the emergence of new ideas and solutions. As Luhmann (1995) points out, the growing complexity of the global system requires the ability to handle uncertainty and manage interactions flexibly. In this sense, the Triple Helix model represents a response to the challenges posed by globalization and digitalization, promoting open collaboration that stimulates innovation through the integration of knowledge and expertise from various sectors and disciplines.

This dynamic approach is strongly oriented toward interdisciplinarity, which has become a fundamental feature of the contemporary innovation system. As Martini (2011) observes, the creation of economic and social value today occurs through the interaction of different fields of knowledge, ranging from science and technology to economics and social sciences. Interdisciplinarity is no longer an optional condition but a necessity, as global challenges and complex problems require approaches that transcend traditional boundaries of individual disciplines. In this perspective, the Triple Helix model not only fosters technological innovation but also promotes knowledge transfer among universities, businesses, and governments, creating a fertile environment for co-learning and co-creation.

2.2 The Quintuple Helix: A Model of Sustainable Innovation

While the Triple Helix model focuses on the interaction between universities, businesses, and governments, the concept of the Quintuple Helix further expands this vision by including civil society as a key player in the innovation ecosystem. According to Martini and Vespasiano (2015), knowledge is the fundamental resource for achieving success in sustainable development, improving economic competitiveness, and fostering a higher and more sustainable quality of life. Countries focusing on societal progress, economic competitiveness, and a better and more sustainable life must integrate knowledge as a central strategic resource (Lundvall, 1992). In other words, knowledge is not just a means to fuel innovation but becomes a "core foundation" of resources that drive long-term development and prosperity (Carayannis & Formica, 2006).

The Quintuple Helix model, as an evolution of the Triple Helix, goes beyond the triad of universities, businesses, and governments by also including civil society and the natural environment. This expansion acknowledges that sustainability and innovation can no longer be treated as isolated phenomena and that collaboration across all societal sectors is essential for addressing global challenges. The concept of knowledge as a resource, as highlighted by Martini (2023), lies at the heart of this model, as knowledge drives innovative creations with the potential to transform economic and social systems toward greater sustainability. Creativity in knowledge creation, as emphasized by Carayannis and Campbell (2010), plays a central role in this context, where innovation is not seen as a linear activity but as a dynamic, collective process involving all social spheres.

In the Quintuple Helix, the interaction among the five spheres—universities, businesses, governments, civil society, and the natural environment—creates a holistic innovation model that not only promotes economic growth but also seeks to integrate sustainability at every stage of the innovation process. This holistic approach, as noted by Martini (2023), aims to foster the horizontal circulation of knowledge, stimulating the invention of new social formats and economic models, and creating synergies between institutions and citizens. Unlike traditional innovation models, which tend to focus on specific inputs such as investments in R&D, scientific institutions, and human resources, the Quintuple Helix model seeks to overcome the linear view of innovation by recognizing the importance of factors such as civil society participation and environmental respect (Yawson, 2009).

According to Martini (2023), the Quintuple Helix does not solely focus on generating innovation but also aims to build inclusive public policies that engage all social groups and promote growth that is sustainable not only economically but also socially and ecologically. Interaction among the different spheres encourages the circulation of knowledge, fostering collective creativity by uniting diverse skills to address global challenges such as climate change, social inequalities, and digital transformation. In this context, civil society plays a fundamental role in ensuring that innovation addresses real-world problems, while governments and businesses provide the infrastructure and resources necessary to turn these ideas into concrete actions.

In summary, the Quintuple Helix model represents an evolved and complex vision of innovation, recognizing the centrality of knowledge as a resource for sustainable development and social inclusion. Integrating civil society and the natural environment into the innovation process creates a more robust and resilient system capable of addressing future economic, social, and ecological challenges. As highlighted by Martini (2023), only through cooperation across all sectors of society can an innovation ecosystem be built that promotes not only economic progress but also a better and more sustainable life for everyone.

2.3 Contamination Labs: An Example of the Triple Helix Application

In Italy, a concrete example of the Triple Helix model in action can be represented by the Contamination Labs (CLabs), spaces dedicated to innovation and entrepreneurship arising from the cooperation between universities, businesses, and governments. CLabs are environments designed to foster the creation of new entrepreneurial ideas through collaboration among students, researchers, entrepreneurs, and professionals. These contamination laboratories allow students to acquire entrepreneurial skills, test their ideas through concrete projects, and interact directly with the business and research world (Secundo, Rippa, Meoli, 2020).

As highlighted by Secundo, Rippa, and Meoli (2020), Italian CLabs have adopted an innovative approach by integrating digital technologies to enhance learning and innovation. Technologies such as blockchain, augmented reality, 3D printing, and digital platforms have improved participants' ability to collaborate and experiment, making the entrepreneurial process more fluid and interactive. These digital tools not only support the development of entrepreneurial ideas but also increase the effectiveness of entrepreneurial education, allowing students to apply theories and models in a practical context. Thus, CLabs represent a tangible example of how the Triple Helix model can be applied to create innovation ecosystems that foster the generation of new knowledge and entrepreneurial skills.

Digital Technologies in CLabs: Impacts and Opportunities

Secundo, Rippa, and Meoli (2020) analyzed the adoption of digital technologies within Italian CLabs. Their research revealed that CLabs primarily use social media and digital platforms for promotional activities but are increasingly adopting MOOCs, distance learning, and other digital technologies to enrich the educational offerings and stimulate student participation. Although the use of digital technologies in CLabs is still limited, a clear intention has emerged to expand the use of these resources in the coming years to enhance entrepreneurial education processes and support the creation of innovative startups.

The growing digitalization of educational and entrepreneurial processes offers numerous opportunities for CLabs, enabling them to reach a wider audience and expand access to entrepreneurial education and training. Additionally, the integration of emerging technologies such as blockchain and augmented reality allows students to test new business models and simulate entrepreneurial scenarios in real-time, enhancing the learning experience and making it more interactive.

Entrepreneurial Education and Innovation: The Future of CLabs

In the long term, CLabs could play a crucial role in shaping the future of entrepreneurial education in Italy and globally. The increasing adoption of digital technologies, collaboration among universities, businesses, and governments, and an interdisciplinary orientation are key factors that could ensure the success of these innovation spaces. However, as noted by Martini (2011), entrepreneurial education must be continuously updated and adapted to economic, social, and technological transformations. Only through a dynamic and flexible approach will it be possible to support the creation of new entrepreneurial solutions that can respond to future global challenges.

In this context, Contamination Labs represent a tangible example of how the Triple Helix model can materialize in an innovation and training environment. By fostering collaboration among various stakeholders and using advanced technologies, CLabs support the growth of new ideas, startups, and innovative businesses. Their evolution will depend on their ability to adapt to the needs of a constantly changing world, leveraging the potential offered by new technologies and creating fertile ground for sustainable growth and development in global economies.

Entrepreneurial Education in the Digital Era

Alongside the adoption of digital technologies, entrepreneurial education is undergoing a profound transformation through the integration of emerging technologies. Universities and Contamination Labs (CLabs) are leveraging digital platforms, augmented reality, 3D printing, and other innovative tools to create interactive and practical learning experiences. These tools enable students to acquire advanced entrepreneurial skills, such as identifying market opportunities, creating innovative solutions, and managing complex business projects (Martini, 2011). In this context, entrepreneurial education becomes a fundamental component within the triple helix model of development between universities, businesses, and government.

3   Conclusions

Despite the successes of the Triple Helix model and the growing adoption of digital technologies, several challenges remain. These include the need to strengthen digital infrastructure, improve collaborative platforms, and promote greater inclusivity in access to educational and entrepreneurial resources. At the same time, the opportunities offered by the Triple Helix model are vast, with the potential to create more resilient and sustainable innovation ecosystems capable of addressing global challenges through cooperation among universities, businesses, and governments.

The Triple Helix model, integrating knowledge, innovation, and collaboration, offers a comprehensive framework for addressing the challenges and opportunities of a rapidly evolving global landscape. This model's dynamic interplay among universities, industries, and governments fosters environments conducive to collective learning, the generation of new knowledge, and the creation of resilient and sustainable ecosystems of innovation.

The European Commission has emphasized the importance of cultivating an entrepreneurial mindset in young people as a crucial driver for societal and economic progress, as highlighted in pivotal frameworks like the "Oslo Agenda for Entrepreneurship Education" (European Commission 2006)) and the "Entrepreneurship 2020 Action Plan" (2013). This mindset encompasses creativity, confidence, and the ability to navigate uncertainty and complexity, which are vital in today's fast-changing markets (European Commission, 2008; Gibb, 2005). Entrepreneurship Education (EE) has evolved into a critical research area, expanding beyond traditional business schools to include fields like engineering and the sciences, where fostering entrepreneurial thinking is increasingly recognized as strategically essential (Lynch et al., 2019; Ndou et al., 2018).

The Contamination Labs (CLabs) in Italy exemplify the Triple Helix model's practical application, combining education on, for, and through entrepreneurship. These labs offer students a mix of theoretical learning, practical business modeling, and direct interaction with industry stakeholders, including investors and venture capitalists. CLabs promote interdisciplinary collaboration, enabling students to transform ideas into successful ventures while developing essential skills like business planning, risk analysis, and market navigation (Secundo et al., 2020b; Honig & Karlsson, 2004). By integrating diverse learning approaches—from traditional classroom settings to action-based initiatives—these labs serve as hubs of knowledge exchange, experiential learning, and mutual growth for students, universities, and industries (Guerrero & Urbano, 2012).

Looking ahead, the Triple Helix calls for considering alternative futures, fostering creative thinking, and embracing multidisciplinary perspectives. This proactive and innovative approach involves adopting participatory and interactive methods to enable collective learning and the creation of shared visions (Barré & Keenan, 2008). Anticipatory intelligence, developed through scenario planning, aligns diverse stakeholder motivations, and facilitates coordinated actions. Beyond envisioning possible futures, foresight must drive the formulation of strategies to seize emerging opportunities or mitigate imminent threats, enhancing the capacity for adaptive learning and policy refinement.

The integration of entrepreneurship education within this model reinforces its role in shaping entrepreneurial cultures and equipping students to meet the demands of a digitized economy. Italian universities have recognized this priority, with the Ministry of Universities and Research (MIUR) supporting the creation of CLabs to bridge education and practical entrepreneurship. These initiatives underscore the necessity of fostering interdisciplinary partnerships, enabling economic and technological cross-pollination to enrich the learning process (Geissinger et al., 2019).

Yet, the future of the Triple Helix presents challenges, such as balancing expert and non-expert knowledge, managing diverse and sometimes conflicting viewpoints, and ensuring inclusivity in decision-making processes. Addressing these challenges demands new tools, conceptual models, and a paradigm shift in mindset and competencies. Crafting anticipatory strategies and developing the skills to navigate complex scenarios are crucial not only for enterprises and public administrations but for society as a whole.

In this context, the Triple Helix becomes more than a theoretical model; it is a call to action for cultivating spaces of innovation, foresight, and collaboration that ensure digital transitions are sustainable and inclusive. Through its emphasis on collaboration, adaptability, and shared vision, the Triple Helix offers a robust foundation for navigating the complexities of the 21st century and fostering equitable growth and innovation.

Generating knowledge using multidisciplinary foundations and evidence-based approaches to promote participatory and collective interactions.

Encouraging participation to bring more perspectives into the decision-making process, shaping behaviors and actions toward a shared vision of the future.

These aspects present significant challenges, such as balancing "expert" and "non-expert" knowledge and managing divergent opinions in participatory contexts. It is crucial to create not only spaces for knowledge and innovation, such as the Triple, Quintuple, or N-Helix models (Martini, 2011; De Luca Picione, 2022), but also for technological foresight, which is indispensable in a globalized society for anticipating the ethical and social consequences of future technological developments.

Addressing these challenges requires a new mindset and the development of innovative skills: the ability to craft scenarios and design anticipatory strategies must permeate businesses, public administration, the third sector, and society as a whole. Only in this way can a truly sustainable digital transition be achieved, enhancing resilience, and fostering equitable and shared growth.

References

Ardolino, M., Rapaccini, M., Saccani, N., Gaiardelli, P., Crespi, G., Ruggeri, C.: The role of digital technologies for the service transformation of industrial companies. Int. J. Prod. Res. **56**(6), 2116–2132 (2018)

Atchison, M., Gotlieb, P.: Innovation and the future of cooperative education. In: Coll, R., Eames, C. (eds.) International Handbook for Cooperative Education: An International Perspective of the Theory, Research, and Practice of Work-Integrated Learning, pp. 261–269. World Association for Cooperative Education, Boston, MA (2004)

awson, M. R.: The ecological system of innovation: a new architectural framework for a functional evidence-based platform for science and innovation policy. In: Huizingh, K.R.E., Conn, S., Torkkeli, M., Bitran, I. (eds.) The Future of Innovation. Proceedings of XX ISPIM 2009 Conference, Wien (2009)

Bacow, L.S., Bowen, W.G., Guthrie, K.M., Long, M.P., Lack, K.A.: Barriers to Adoption of Online Learning Systems in US Higher Education. Ithaka, New York, NY (2012)

Bae, T.J., Qian, S., Miao, C., Fiet, J.O.: The relationship between entrepreneurship education and entrepreneurial intentions: a meta-analytic review. Entrepreneurship: Theory Pract. **38**(2), 217–254 (2014)

Barré, R., Keenan, M.: Revisiting Foresight Rationales: What Lessons from the Social Sciences and Humanities? In: Cagnin, C., Keenan, M., Johnston, R., Scapolo, F., Barré, R. (eds.) Future-Oriented Technology Analysis: Strategic Intelligence for an Innovative Economy, pp. 151–166. Springer, Berlin (2008). https://doi.org/10.1007/978-3-540-68811-2_4

Bharadwaj, A., El Sawy, O.A., Pavlou, P.A., Venkatraman, N.: Digital business strategy: toward a next generation of insights. MIS Q. **37**(2), 471–482 (2013)

Birtchnell, T., Böhme, T., Gorkin, R.: 3D printing and the third mission: the university in the materialization of intellectual capital. Technol. Forecast. Soc. Chang. **123**, 240–249 (2017)

Boffo, V., Adebakin, A.B., Terzaroli, C.: Supporting entrepreneurship in higher education for young adults' employability: a cross-border comparative study. In: Adult Education and Work Contexts: International Perspectives and Challenges, pp. 123–142 (2017)

Boffo, V., Federighi, P., Torlone, F.: Educational Jobs: Youth and Employability in the Social Economy: Investigations in Italy, Malta, Portugal, Romania, Spain, United Kingdom, vol. 2. Firenze University Press, Firenze (2015)

Carayannis, E.G., Campbell, D.F.J.: Triple helix, quadruple helix and quintuple helix and how do knowledge, innovation, and environment relate to each other? Int. J. Soc. Ecol. Sustain. Dev. **1**, 41–69 (2010). https://doi.org/10.4018/jsesd.2010010105

Carayannis, E.G., Formica, P.: Intellectual venture capitalists: an emerging breed of knowledge entrepreneurs. Ind. High. Educ. **20**, 151–156 (2006). https://doi.org/10.5367/000000006777691034

Cassia, L., De Massis, A., Meoli, M., Minola, T.: Entrepreneurship research centers around the world: research orientation, knowledge transfer and performance. J. Technol. Transfer. **39**(3), 376–392 (2014)

Cohen, B., Amorós, J.E., Lundy, L.: The generative potential of emerging technology to support startups and new ecosystems. Bus. Horiz. **60**(6), 741–745 (2017)

Curci, N., Micozzi, A.: Entrepreneurial activity and education in Italy. L'industria **38**(3), 385–410 (2017)

Del-Palacio, I., Sole, F., Batista-Foguet, J.M.: University entrepreneurship centres as service businesses. Serv. Ind. J. **28**(7), 939–951 (2008)

Der Foo, M., Wong, P.K., Ong, A.: Do others think you have a viable business idea? Team diversity and judges' evaluation of ideas in a business plan competition. J. Bus. Ventur. **20**(3), 385–402 (2005)

DeTienne, D.R., Chandler, G.N.: Opportunity identification and its role in the entrepreneurial classroom: a pedagogical approach and empirical test. Acad. Manag. Learn. Educ. **3**(3), 242–257 (2004)

Eisenhardt, K.M., Graebner, M.E.: Theory building from cases: opportunities and challenges. Acad. Manag. J. **50**(1), 25–32 (2007)

Ekbia, H.R.: Digital artifacts as quasi-objects: qualification, mediation, and materiality. J. Am. Soc. Inform. Sci. Technol. **60**(12), 2554–2566 (2009)

Etzkowitz, H., Leydesdoff, L.: The triple helix university-industry-government relations: a laboratory for knowledge-based economic development. EASST Review **14**, 14–19 (1995)

Etzkowitz, H., Leydesdoff, L.: The triple helix as a model for innovation studies. Sci. Public Policy **25**, 195–203 (1998)

European Commission: Entrepreneurship education in Europe: Fostering entrepreneurial mindsets through education and learning conference. The Oslo agenda for entrepreneurship education in Europe (2006)

Commission, E.: Entrepreneurship. Belgium, Brussels (2013)

European Commission: Entrepreneurship 2020: Action Plan Reigniting the Entrepreneurial Spirit in Europe. Communication from the Commission to the European Parliament, the Council, the European Economic and Social Committee and the Committee of the Regions, COM. European Commission (2013). https://goo.gl/WCmgGo

Fayolle, A., Gailly, B., Lassas-Clerc, N.: Assessing the impact of entrepreneurship education programmes: a new methodology. J. Eur. Ind. Train. **30**(9), 701–720 (2006)

Finkle, T.A., Kuratko, D.F., Goldsby, M.G.: An examination of entrepreneurship centers in the United States: a national survey. J. Small Bus. Manage. **44**(2), 184–206 (2006)

Finkle, T.A., Menzies, T.V., Kuratko, D.F., Goldsby, M.G.: An examination of the financial challenges of entrepreneurship centers throughout the world. J. Small Bus. Entrep. **26**(1), 67–85 (2013)

Fischer, E., Reuber, A.R.: Social interaction via new social media: (how) can interactions on Twitter affect effectual thinking and behavior? J. Bus. Venture **26**(1), 1–18 (2011)

Geissinger, A., et al.: How sustainable is the sharing economy? On the sustainability connotations of sharing economy platforms. J. Clean. Prod. **212**, 277–286 (2019). https://doi.org/10.1016/j.jclepro.2018.11.201

Gibb, A.: Towards the Entrepreneurial University: Entrepreneurship Education as a Lever for Change. National Council for Graduate Entrepreneurship Policy Paper (2005)

Giones, F., Brem, A.: Digital technology entrepreneurship: a definition and research agenda. Technol. Innov. Manag. Rev. **7**(5), 44–51 (2017)

Guerra Guerra, A., De Gómez, L.S.: From a FabLab towards a social entrepreneurship and business lab. J. Cases Inf. Technol. **18**(4), 1–21 (2016)

Guerrero, M., Urbano, D.: The development of an entrepreneurial university. J. Technol. Transfer. **37**(1), 43–74 (2012)

Gupta, N., Bharadwaj, S.S.: Agility in business school education through richness and reach: a conceptual model. Educ. Train. **55**(4), 370–384 (2013)

Hahn, D., Minola, T., Van Gils, A., Huybrechts, J.: Entrepreneurial education and learning at universities: exploring multilevel contingencies. Entrep. Reg. Dev. **29**(9–10), 945–974 (2017)

Honig, B., Karlsson, T.: Institutional forces and written business plan. J. Manag. **30**(1), 29–48 (2004)

Honig, B.: Entrepreneurship education: toward a model of contingency-based business planning. Acad. Manag. Learn. Educ. **3**(3), 258–273 (2004)

Huffman, D., Quigley, J.M.: The role of university in attracting high tech entrepreneurship: a silicon valley tale. Ann. Reg. Sci. **36**(3), 403–419 (2002)

Iacobucci, D., Micozzi, A.: Entrepreneurship education in Italian universities: trend, situation, and opportunities. Educ.+Train. **54**(8/9), 673–696 (2012)

Kallinikos, J., Aaltonen, A., Marton, A.: The ambivalent ontology of digital artifacts. MIS Q., **37**, 357–370 (2013)

Lenka, S., Parida, V., Wincent, J.: Digitalization capabilities as enablers of value co-creation in servitizing firms. Psychol. Mark. **34**(1), 92–100 (2017)

Leydesdorff, L.: The Knowledge-Based Economy. Modeled, Measured, Simulated. Universal-Publishers, Irvine (2006)

Luhmann, N.: Social Systems. Stanford University Press, Standford (1995)

Lundvall, B.Å.: National Systems of Innovation: Towards a Theory of Innovation and Interactive Learning. Pinter Publishers, London (1992)

Lynch, M., Kamovich, U., Longva, K.K., Steinert, M.: Combining Technology and Entrepreneurial Education through Design Thinking: Students' Reflections on the Learning Process. Technol. Forecast. Soc. Change **164**, 119689 (2019)

Martini, E., De Luca Picione, R.: Triple helix model: a device for social construction of knowledge and innovation. In: Marchisio, E. (ed.) Handbook of Research on Applying Emerging Technologies Across Multiple Disciplines, pp. 433–452. Igi Global, Pensylvania (2022)

Martini, E., Vespasiano, F.: Scienza con coscienza: la riflessività sociale, per un'etica del futuro. Stud. Sociol. **1**, 65–79 (2017)

Martini, E., Vespasiano, F.: Territorial dynamics: the rules of innovation helices. In: Vrontis, D., Sakka, G., Amirkhanpour, M. (eds.) Management Innovation, Entrepreneurship and Human Resource Management Practices: a Global Perspective, pp. 75–91. Cambridge Scholars Publishing, Newcastle upon Tyne (2015)

Martini, E., Vespasiano, F.: The paradigm of the social construction of knowledge: the triple helix model. In: Papanikos, G.T. (ed.) Essays on Social Themes, pp. 175–190. Athens Institute for Education and Research, Athens (2011)

Martini, E.: A quintuple helix model for foresight: Analyzing the developments of digital technologies in order to outline possible future scenarios. Front. Sociol. **7**, 1102815 (2023). https://doi.org/10.3389/fsoc.2022.1102815

Martini, E.: Socializzare per Innovare. Il Modello Della Tripla Elica. Loffredo, Napoli (2011)

Ndou, V., Secundo, G., Schiuma, G., Passiante, G.: Insights for shaping entrepreneurship education: evidence from the European entrepreneurship centers. Sustainability **10**(11), 4323 (2018)

Paparella, N.: A proposito di terza missione: una nuova versione del modello di tripla elica. In: Formica, C. (ed.) Terza Missione. Parametro di Qualità del Sistema Universitario, pp. 11–38. Giapeto Editore, Napoli (2014)

Ulmer, M.W.: Anticipation. In: Approximate Dynamic Programming for Dynamic Vehicle Routing. ORSIS, vol. 61, pp. 63–69. Springer, Cham (2017). https://doi.org/10.1007/978-3-319-55511-9_5

Poli, R.: Forecasting. In: Glaveanu, V. (ed.) The Palgrave Encyclopaedia of the Possible, pp. 1–6. Springer, Switzerland (2020)

Poli, R.: Lavorare con il Futuro. Idee e Strumenti per Governare l'Incertezza. Egea, Milano (2019)

Poli, R.: Le basi teoriche della previsione sociale. In: Arnaldi, S., Poli, R. (eds.) La Previsione Sociale. Introduzione Allo Studio dei Futuri, pp. 23–36. Carocci, Roma (2012)

Secundo, G., Rippa, P., Meoli, M.: Digital transformation in entrepreneurship education centres: preliminary evidence from the Italian contamination labs network. Int. J. Entrep. Behav. Res. **26**(7), 1589–1605 (2020). https://doi.org/10.1108/IJEBR-11-2019-0618

Stehr, N.: A world made of knowledge. Society **39**, 89–92 (2001). https://doi.org/10.1007/BF0 2712625

Viale, R., Ghiglione, B.: The triple helix model: a tool for the study of European regional. Eur. Comm. PTS Rep. **29**, 1–8 (1998) von Schomberg, R.: From the Ethics of Technology towards an Ethics of Knowledge Policy and Knowledge Assessment. European Commission, Directorate-General for Research and Innovation: Publications Office (2007)

Yawson, M.R.: The ecological system of innovation: a new architectural framework for a functional evidence-based platform for science and innovation policy. In: Huizingh, K.R.E., Conn, S., Torkkeli, M., Wien, I.B. (eds.) The Future of Innovation. Proceedings of XX ISPIM 2009 Conference (2009)

Assessments Redesigned to Be Inclusive and Concept-Based

Nidhi Oswal(✉)

Faculty of Business Liwa College, Abu Dhabi, UAE
nidhi.oswal@lc.ac.ae

Abstract. Students' underperformance in assessments is often attributed to their background characteristics or perceived diversity. Such underperformance may also be due to unfair assessment designs that exclude certain students. This article aims to introduce inclusive assessment practices so that diverse students can benefit from them and are not disadvantaged by assessment practices. In this article, we discuss three central concerns related to traditional assessment design, achievement of learning outcomes, and academic integrity and critique the assumptions underlying assessment design. This article describes connecting the classroom to real-world experiences, progressive assessment, and assessment for distinctiveness to recognize unique and complex student achievements as contemporary approaches to assessment for inclusion. As a result, assessment for inclusion combines the best practices of inclusive practice and good assessment design that better prepares students to succeed beyond the classroom.

Keywords: Diversity · education · Inclusion · assessment design · disability · social Inclusion · concept application · Learning Outcomes · Academic Integrity

1 Introduction

Assessments in higher education should not discriminate against students based on characteristics or abilities unrelated to measuring desired learning outcomes. Providing equal opportunities for all students to develop and showcase their talents is important. Support and guidance must be fair and unbiased, and every individual must be able to access the resources and assistance they need. In the shift to mass higher education, student diversity has increased. Non-traditional students and students of determination (SOD) are encouraged to pursue higher education (Marginson, 2016). In the past, when students from equity groups performed poorly in assessments, it was often assumed that the problem lay with the students themselves (Boud et al., 2022). To address this, accommodations and additional support were provided to improve. The problem with this approach was that it failed to consider the possibility that the assessment could be flawed or unsuitable for its intended purpose. The more significant issue of the assessment's suitability was overlooked by focusing solely on the student's perceived deficiencies. This prevented the student from demonstrating his full potential. A lack of motivation and engagement resulted in discouragement and frustration. It is important to consider

G. A. Toto (Ed.): ICS exchange 2024, CCIS 2521, pp. 346–358, 2025.
https://doi.org/10.1007/978-3-032-03021-4_25

both students' needs and assessments' suitability. Assessment plays a vital role in evaluating learning. A well-designed assessment should be able to distinguish between the learners' levels of achievement. Furthermore, assessment should encourage students to step out of their comfort zone and challenge themselves for their development, which is called "assessment for learning" (Boud & Molloy, 2013). A student's performance on an assessment may also be discriminated against or excluded if the assessment requirements are irrelevant to the outcomes being evaluated (Tai et al., 2022). It will lead to poor validity of the assessment.

Consequently, assessment design must be reevaluated from an inclusive perspective. Disability and social inclusion have been equally emphasized in higher education as inclusion (Douglas et al., 2015). Social inclusion and disability encompass a wide range of groups.

Individuals with disabilities include those with learning disabilities, physical disabilities, and mental health conditions. Additionally, they facilitate social inclusion, such as access for students returning to education after a 15-year gap and women from non-traditional backgrounds. Although these groups represent heterogeneous groups of individuals, there are many possible sub-groups (Turner et al., 2012). It is important to focus on the common problems associated with conventional assessments. Several studies have shown that activities performed by the specific institution, including assessments, affect student success more than characteristics of students themselves, such as age, gender, type of attendance, mode of attendance, and socioeconomic status (Cook-Sather & Luz, 2014).

It is crucial to prioritize inclusion during assessment design by looking closely at assessment tasks. Without explicit attention from the people responsible for assessments, it is unlikely that they will readily identify opportunities for inclusive assessments. Their perspective is likely shaped by the experiences they have had with dominant assessment approaches, as well as similar values and definitions of success (Archer & Leatherwood, 2003)

It may not always be possible to achieve greater inclusion merely by doing more of the same. A clear assessment instruction alone will not promote inclusion because clarifying instructions in enough detail does not ensure that everyone understands what is required (Bearman et al., 2016). This article aims to discuss how to design inclusive assessments that recognize student diversity and eliminate discrimination in the assessment process based on factors other than their ability to meet standards. This paper examines how practitioners and researchers can develop inclusive assessments. The first step is to define what inclusion assessment entails. Here, we examine common design flaws that prevent students from achieving their assessment potential. Afterwards, we will discuss how to promote inclusion through modern assessment techniques. As we discuss disability and social inclusion, we will look beyond the mere accommodation of designated equity groups to identify general guidelines for assessment design.

2   Assessment for Inclusion and Concept Application

The higher education assessment system has made significant efforts to improve student equity for some time (Elton, 2004). By introducing the concept of 'inclusive assessment', Messick (2013) argues that all student capabilities should be considered. In contrast, this approach stands in place of 'contingent assessment' (adapting existing assessments with modifications) and 'alternative assessment' (offering a different assessment). Inclusive assessment is creating and implementing impartial and efficient assessment methods and practices that allow all students to exhibit their full potential in demonstrating their knowledge, understanding, and skills (Tsolou et al., 2021). This definition was provided in her report on inclusive learning and teaching. In her research, she identified substantial evidence that assessments disadvantaged and benefited specific groups of students, and she suggested that alternative assessment methods may mitigate the effects of assessment. The study, however, found that many of the current assessment methods introduced barriers to a wide range of students in terms of learning (Lawrie et al., 2017), so it is unlikely that these recommendations have translated into widespread improved practice in higher education (Bearman et al., 2016).

Beets & van Louw (2011) introduced assessment for social justice to achieve fair and just outcomes in higher education. The concept emphasizes the role of assessment in nurturing learning that contributes to a more equitable society. McArthur (2015) challenged that treating students fairly in assessment processes always results in just outcomes. Fairness in assessment can be viewed in terms of procedural and outcomes fairness. While procedural fairness is necessary, focusing solely on it can limit inclusion by promoting narrow definitions of success. Thus, a comprehensive approach to fairness in assessment that considers complexity should be employed to promote equitable and just student outcomes (Ajjawi et al., 2022).

We propose 'assessment for inclusion' as an approach to assessment based on the philosophy of social justice and the significance of outcomes. This approach aims to ensure that assessment for learning considers the unique strengths and abilities of a wide range of students. The goal is to promote societal diversity by accounting for and supporting all students' diverse needs. We hope to facilitate a better balance between theory and practice by introducing this term. We also hope to use assessment as a tool for social justice. The key is to focus on assessment design, which must consider the immediate task and the broader course and institutional context (Bennett et al., 2011).

Diverse identities exist across many spectrums in assessment for inclusion. Intersectionality (Crenshaw, 1991) is commonly used to describe how these spectrums overlap when assessing individuals. The evaluation of learners should be based on how well they perform on the task at hand, not on irrelevant characteristics or abilities. Furthermore, it is crucial to continuously question whether features are permanently associated with task capability and whether the task itself may be discriminatory. Contextual factors also play a part in demonstrating capability since they occur in a particular context. All assessments are, therefore, limited in their generalizability. Additionally, new insights into social issues lead us to recognize new ways we are still not inclusive. As a result, designing an inclusion assessment should be considered an ongoing, forward-looking process, not a fixed viewpoint on what has been excluded in the past.

3   Drawbacks of Current Assessments

In the assessment of inclusion, a common challenge is the difference between how we imagine work should be done and how it is done (Hollnagel, 2017). While it may be easy to develop ideal assessment practices, it is far more difficult to implement them in real-world situations involving budgets, time constraints, and departmental politics (Bearman et al., 2016). Since assessments are created at specific times and places, inclusive practices must consider this. This section will explore how assessment operates in practice, focusing on academic traditions' assumptions.

Assessment design and implementation are vital components of any academic discipline or institution. However, modern assessment methods prioritize individual performance and often overlook teamwork and collaboration (Jessop & Tomas, 2016). Furthermore, these methods deprive students of normal resources, such as internet access and peer advice, readily available in everyday practice. These limitations are frequently unquestioned and can significantly impact the performance of those who would benefit from a more inclusive approach to assessment.

Table 1 presents several limitations that are not necessarily inherent requirements for a particular task. These limitations could potentially exclude some students and, as such, should be scrutinized. By examining these assumptions, educators can gain useful insights into approaching assessment practices differently in their contexts. Additionally, promoting more inclusive assessment practices can be achieved by incrementally improving assessment or course design. The table lists five basic assessment assumptions identified, analyses these assumptions from both assessment design and inclusion perspectives and highlights the potential disadvantages that result from these assumptions. This interrelationship between effective assessment design and inclusivity is illustrated in Table 1.

When assessment practices are exclusionary, they are typically addressed by providing adjustments for students who need them. However, it is important to note that adjustments do not cure everything and can become even more challenging for those requiring them. Although it is unlikely that any assessment will fully account for every student's needs and abilities, adjustments for some students will always be necessary. Academicians must go beyond minor adjustments, such as additional breaks or ten extra minutes. They must address the central aspects of the assessment, including the task's format and content. Challenging commonly employed adjustments and their relationship to assessment assumptions is crucial to ensure inclusion for all students.

It is imperative to note that solely focusing on adjustments in the assessment process implies that the fundamental requirements should not be questioned or changed. However, due to the COVID-19 pandemic, many things considered unchangeable in assessment and higher education have been altered when necessary (Cao et al., 2020); (Hu, 2019). It has been suggested that different processes could be designed to support assessment for inclusion. Despite the extensive literature on comprehensive education that provides conceptual articles on assessment, there is less empirical research. Research on assessment focuses on students' perceptions of it. Inclusive assessment practices are typically directed at students with disabilities, particularly those with dyslexia. Additionally, it is essential to implement interventions in situations where the instruction language is not the student's first language. This is true for international students or those in countries where multiple languages are recognized. There is a shortage of empirical research on inclusive assessment. Most studies have focused on minor adjustments to assessment methods instead of questioning assessment principles. Only one study, conducted by O'Neill in 2017, explored the impact of inclusive assessment on student performance

Table 1. Analyses of basic assessment assumptions.

	Basic Assessment Assumptions	Assessment design implication	Inclusion Perspective
1	Closed-book midterm and final exams	Implies that memorization is the desired outcome, which may not foster true learning	Recalling information quickly under pressure may not be relevant to evaluating specific skills
2	Assignments require a specific mode of completion, typically in writing	Direct student focus toward the mastery of specific assessment methods rather than the actual learning outcomes being evaluated. Additionally, these formats may be chosen for convenience or familiarity rather than being the most effective choice for the given task	Some modes are unnecessary for the task and exclude certain students. For instance, writing by hand during an exam can be mentally or physically exhausting; essays favour a style of writing that may not be relevant to a specific subject; oral presentations can cause severe anxiety but may not be essential
3	No replacement assessments with alternatives that ensure learning outcomes	reduces opportunities for distinctiveness and creativity	Alternative tasks allow for broader ways of knowing and communicating
4	The linguistic standards	In several instances, the assessment does not aim to ensure language proficiency as the fundamental capability	Emphasizing high linguistic standards when they are not needed can disadvantage those with processing disabilities
5	Deadlines for submissions of assessments	Time rigidity prioritises convenience and not task complexity	Students with work and carer commitments and health conditions suffer from the system's inflexibility

through grade comparison. There is a noticeable lack of focused discussion on implementing inclusive assessment on a broader scale within higher education and how it could be integrated with common assessment dilemmas. It is crucial to address these dilemmas, and therefore, the following section identifies three major concerns about assessment design.

4 Concerns Designing Inclusive Assessment and Concept Application

Policies, procedures, and accreditation requirements sometimes impede educators' efforts to change assessment practices. It is important to note that these obstacles are often beliefs rather than actual barriers, and they perpetuate ineffective assessment practices. We address the three most common arguments against changing assessment practices: "We do things this way," "Learning outcomes must be assessed," and "Students will cheat if we do not assess in this way." We propose potential solutions to overcome each argument.

4.1 Perspective and Practices are Ingrained in the System

Academics from different disciplines and professions have unique worldviews and philosophical approaches to conducting assessments, as Hanafin et al. (2006) mentioned. Moreover, educational institutions may have assessment traditions, and students' prior experiences and assumptions can influence assessments. Various perspectives influence the validity and success of assessments. Socially constructed norms or stereotypes, such as gender, age, race, or class assumptions, can affect how students perceive competency and motivation (Ryan & Deci, 2000). How assessments, including examinations or oral presentations, are designed and conducted can send messages to students about who belongs in higher education. Common solutions to address student deficits, such as writing workshops, English support classes, or suggesting a different course of study, often promote conformity. The benefit of engaging staff members in discussions that promote reflection and consideration is to encourage them to identify the effects of the assumptions they take for granted.

This approach may create change opportunities. Additionally, low-stakes early assessments could help build student confidence by providing opportunities to practice and develop capabilities.

4.2 Learning Outcomes Achievement

Assessing work involves comparing it to a quality concept or standard. A group of professionals may explicitly define or understand these standards. Identifying learning outcomes and ensuring students achieve them is crucial to modern quality frameworks. In this context, however, examining the learning outcomes the assessment aims to assess is imperative. This is not just the assessment itself. There is a risk that learning outcomes become inflexible, limiting assessment practices, when the learning outcomes themselves need to be challenged. A narrow interpretation of outcomes and assessment methods can lead to unintended exclusion. Students might meet these requirements if defined in other equally legitimate ways. Furthermore, assessments involve balancing competing interests and ideals to meet stakeholders' needs in the real world. Instead of assuming that a particular stakeholder only accepts one assessment configuration, discussions should be held with those stakeholders (such as accreditation bodies and industry representatives) to consider how outcomes and assessments are defined and what different assessment designs might be acceptable.

4.3 Academic Integrity

Academic dishonesty negatively impacts assessments. The most common way to conduct exams is with closed books to prevent cheating. This method is often preferred due to concerns about cheating when there is no invigilation. However, this approach may compromise the assessor's judgment. While this method ensures equality, it does not guarantee equity, as it creates the same conditions for all students. This approach also challenges those who cannot attend the scheduled exam due to responsibilities such as caring for someone. Exam effects can be so profound that test anxiety is now a research topic associated with poor exam performance. Remotely proctored exams have also been criticized for being ableist, as features like eye tracking require unobstructed neurotypical eye movement.

It is imperative to address cheating while promoting inclusivity. Academic integrity aims to develop students' ability to work ethically in university and beyond, which aligns with inclusion values. Integrity education and honour codes alone cannot address cheating problems. Institutions have implemented assessment security measures such as invigilated exams or text- matching software to enforce anti-cheating rules. However, such measures do not guarantee integrity and can reinforce exclusion by enforcing a limited set of normative behaviours in assessment. It is essential to uphold integrity in ways that embrace inclusion. Therefore, any proposed integrity or security practice must consider its impact on the most diverse students.

5 Redesigning for Inclusive Assessments and Concept Application

Assessing for learning and assessing for inclusion often overlap in good assessment design practices. Even though authentic or programmatic assessments were not initially designed for inclusion purposes, they can easily be adapted to serve inclusion and concept application across a wide range of students' backgrounds, present capabilities, and future goals. This section will demonstrate how three assessment design approaches can serve an inclusion and concept application concern.

6 Linking Classroom Learning to Real-World Learning-Concept Application

Authentic assessments are considered highly valuable in engaging students in learning and preparing them for real-world challenges (Birenbaum, 2006). These assessments involve the entire person by integrating what students know, how they act, and who they are (Ketonen et al., 2023). Won et al. (2017) contend that application-based assessments enhance conceptual achievement by involving students in intellectually stimulating and meaningful activities that create a product, such as an act performance, e-portfolio, or exhibition.

Concept-based learning assessments aim to reproduce a discipline or profession's tasks and performance standards (Ajjawi et al., 2022). To prepare students for success in their professional careers, they should be exposed to real-world situations and problems. It has been shown that using applied assessments in real-life situations increases motivation, increases students' agency in learning, and increases their employability by providing skills and knowledge (Colthorpe et al., 2020; Wiewiora & Kowalkiewicz, 2018; Villarroel et al., 2017; Janse van Rensburg et al., 2021; Schmulian & Coetzee, 2018). In addition, providing students with multiple opportunities to improve their work helps them grow intellectually and as professionals. Learning should be an interactive process where all learners can put in their best efforts and always have their voices heard. This is directly connected to equity.

Students' learning journeys, regardless of their background, origin, socioeconomic status, or learning abilities, can be supported through creative assessment design to apply classroom concepts to real-world scenarios. By offering support structures and guidance, this goal can be accomplished. Authentic learning experiences connected to real-world and disciplinary practices are insufficient to create inclusive and practical learning. However, with the help of experts, mentoring, and thoughtful feedback throughout learning experiences, students can develop their skills and find their learning path. Students should be given the choice of how they will be assessed so they can pursue their interests and passions. By analyzing real-life scenarios or working on real-life projects, they will be able to select the assessment method that is most appropriate for them.

7 Progressive Assessment

Assessment is meant to evaluate the student's achievement in terms of the program's learning objectives. However, the assessment can adversely affect the program's intended learning outcomes. Even though the program necessitates assessment, it is ultimately the assessment that drives the program. The creation and execution of an assessment system consumes a significant amount of staff time, yet it has minimal or even negative effects on desirable learning outcomes. (Bok et al., 2013). Assessments focusing on program outcomes significantly impact student success, especially in the inclusion context. Although individual unit assessments can be modified with a modest impact on the overall program, it is crucial to consider program assessment activities. This is to maintain the course's accreditation and credibility. Recognizing that assessments involve compromises to meet diverse stakeholder needs, exploring how individual assessments can be combined may be beneficial. This will provide a more comprehensive understanding of student capabilities. It is also helpful to consider learning and demonstrating capabilities over time and space (Dagavarian & Walters, 2004). This could account for a constellation of approaches, which, when taken separately, may be imperfect but serve some student groups better than others. However, they may provide equitable opportunities to demonstrate capability when taken together.

While students and educators are equally concerned about preparing for the world beyond university, not all skills must be assessed simultaneously. This is as long as they are evaluated throughout the study programme. It is imperative to consider which combinations of skills should be assessed together. It is important to consider why certain assessment formats are used and what content is included across the programme. By explicitly focusing on students' development and progress over time, it is possible to support student learning more holistically. With the help of mentors and faculty members, students are encouraged and assisted to improve themselves through the progressive assessment process.

8   Recognizing Unique and Complex Student Achievements

To succeed as graduates, students should aim to showcase their unique achievements rather than blend in with their peers. Employers' preferences and requirements are highly variable. Graduates with the same qualifications occupy vastly distinct roles, each valuing different skills and personal attributes. As the number of students graduating with indistinguishable qualifications from increasingly larger cohorts rises, it has become increasingly clear that students require opportunities to differentiate themselves. Therefore, assessments should highlight commonalities and portray individual differences (Coetzee, 2014); (Hill & Walkington, 2016).

It is unrealistic to assume that giving the same assessment to all students will ensure equal achievement opportunities. The conditions under which assessments occur are never the same due to each student's unique personal history and lived realities. A student's distinctive perspectives, skills, personal attributes, and experiences cannot be recognized when he or she is required to perform the same tasks and be evaluated against the same standards. This also limits opportunities for students to build upon their prior learning and pursue growth relevant to their aspirations. Instead, assessments should be designed in more open-ended ways that support students in developing and demonstrating their unique capabilities. This aligns with the Universal Design for Learning guidelines, which suggest that various means of engagement in and expression of learning should be offered (Almeqdad et al., 2023). Criteria would then need to be developed to consider this range of possibilities.

The curriculum can be enriched with distinctive learning opportunities that allow students to leverage their unique achievements. For instance, internships and placements offer students the chance to gain valuable work experience by performing tasks relevant to their career ambitions. This is done in diverse workplace settings. Applied projects allow students to create valuable outputs for organizations, communities, or disciplines. Despite this, it may not be possible for all students to participate in such projects. Such projects often require partnerships with external stakeholders and necessitate individual mentoring or supervision.

Providing personalized learning opportunities can be challenging but assessing them need not be more difficult than assessing equivalent learning. Personalized learning can be scalable by implementing certain methods. For example, group projects or placements require less individual supervision and provide students with personalized evidence of achievement. This is as long as they are evaluated on their contribution to the group, not just the outcome. Students can personalize their assessment, where they must demonstrate learning outcomes by integrating theory and practice from their degree with other experiences or achievements. Contemporary students have and benefit from diverse life experiences, from working in career roles to volunteering and involvement in clubs and societies. All these experiences are relevant to developing skills and enhancing employability. Assessments can indicate an individual's skills and personal qualities relevant to potential employers. Such assessments need not burden students or teachers. They can be in various artefacts, from written reflections to curated portfolios or short video pitches. These assessments can improve students' ability to showcase their professional identities and enhance their employability confidence (Steen-Utheim & Hopfenbeck, 2018; Goodwin et al., 2019; Jorre et al. et al., 2019). Students could be given a choice in how they demonstrate learning outcomes, resulting in more personalized evidence of their unique abilities.

9 Conclusion

The process of inclusion is an ongoing process that demands thorough discussion. Assessment design is never impartial, as it either supports or hinders inclusion and impacts different individuals in various ways. The article illustrates that although assessment issues are easily recognized, no one-size-fits-all solution works in every situation, so global solutions cannot be expected to be accurate. Reimagining and redeveloping assessments will not be easy for educators, especially when students resist change due to their familiarity with past assessment methods. Additionally, historically advantaged students may object to changes that challenge or reduce their privileges.

Certain approaches may challenge traditional teaching, learning, and assessment methods in the quest for inclusive assessment. It is, therefore, crucial to reevaluate the role of students and academics in higher education. This is necessary to ensure that diverse student populations receive adequate support in the future. It is imperative to acknowledge that this article has both strengths and limitations. Firstly, we approached this work solely from an assessment perspective. Our focus on assessment and feedback limits our understanding of other perspectives. Secondly, we did not include outside perspectives. In future work, it would be valuable to collaborate with a more diverse audience, including stakeholders with diverse perspectives. It would also be valuable to host discussions at various venues across universities. Nevertheless, this article is a significant starting point for challenging assumptions about assessment and exploring creative and inclusive approaches. It is crucial to maintain the current momentum. Inclusive practice and effective assessment design aim to eliminate irrelevant factors in determining student capabilities. This is achieved by questioning our assumptions and understanding how they affect different individuals. Implementing concept applications, progressive assessment design, and recognition of Unique and Complex Student Achievements can foster inclusive environments. Designing an assessment for inclusion changes assessment practices and fundamentally reconsiders what discriminations are and are inappropriate within the assessment. It is highly critical to ensure that diverse students have equitable opportunities to learn from assessment and be equitably judged within assessment.

References

Ajjawi, R., Tai, J., Boud, D., De St Jorre, T. J.: Assessment for Inclusion in Higher Education. Taylor & Francis (2022)

Almeqdad, Q.I., Alodat, A.M., Alquraan, M.F., Mohaidat, M.A., Al-Makhzoomy, A.K.: The effectiveness of universal design for learning: A systematic review of the literatureandmeta-analysis.Cogent Educ.**10**(1) (2023). https://doi.org/10.1080/2331186x.2023.2218191

Archer, L., Leathwood, C.: New times-old inequalities: diverse working-class femininities in education. Editorial. Gender Educ. **15**(3), 227–235 (2003).https://doi.org/10.1080/095402503 03861

Bearman, M., et al.: How university teachers design assessments: a cross-disciplinary study. Higher Education; Springer Science+Business Media (2016). https://doi.org/10.1007/s10734-016-0027-7

Bearman, M., et al.: How university teachers design assessments: a cross-disciplinary study. High. Educ. **74**(1), 49–64 (2016). https://doi.org/10.1007/s10734-016-0027-7

Bearman, M., Dawson, P., Boud, D., Bennett, S., Hall, M., Molloy, E.: Support for assessment practice: developing the assessment design decisions framework. TeachinginHigh. Educ. **21**(5), 545–556 (2016). https://doi.org/10.1080/13562517.2016.1160217

Beets, P., van Louw, T.: Social justice implications of South African school assessment practices. Africa Educ. Rev. **8**(2), 302–317 (2011). https://doi.org/10.1080/18146627.2011.602844

Bennett, S., Thomas, L., Agostinho, S., Lockyer, L., Jones, J., Harper, B.: Understanding the design context for Australian university teachers: implications for the future of learning design. Learn. Media Technol. **36**(2), 151–167 (2011). https://doi.org/10.1080/17439884.2011.553622

Birenbaum, M.: New Insights Into Learning and Teaching and Their Implications for Assessment. Kluwer Academic Publishers eBooks (2006). https://doi.org/10.1007/0-306-48125-1_2

Bok, H. G. J., et al.: Programmatic assessment of competency-based workplace learning: when theory meets practice. BMC Med. Educ. BioMed Central (2013). https://doi.org/10.1186/1472-6920-13- 123

Boud, D., Molloy, E.: Rethinking models of feedback for learning: the challenge of design. Assessm. Eval. High. Educ. **38**(6), 698–712 (2013). https://doi.org/10.1080/02602938.2012.691462

Boud, D., Costley, C., Cranfield, S., Desai, J., Nikolou-Walker, E., Nottingham, P., Wilson, D.: The pivotal role of student assessment in work-integrated learning. High. Educ. Res. Dev. **42**(6), 1323–1337 (2022). https://doi.org/10.1080/07294360.2022.2152981

Cao, W., et al.: The psychological impact of the COVID-19 epidemic on college students in China. Psychiatry Res. **287**, 112934 (2020). https://doi.org/10.1016/j.psychres.2020.112934

Coetzee, M.: Measuring student graduateness: reliability and construct validity of the graduate skills and attributes scale. High. Educ. Res. Dev. **33**(5), 887–902 (2014). https://doi.org/10.1080/07294360.2014.890572

Colthorpe, K., Gray, H., Ainscough, L., Ernst, H.: Drivers for authenticity: student approaches and responses to an authentic assessment task. Assess. Eval. High. Educ. **46**(7),995–1007 (2020). https://doi.org/10.1080/02602938.2020.1845298

Cook-Sather, A., Luz, A.: Greater engagement in and responsibility for learning: what happens when students cross the threshold of student–faculty partnership. High. Educ. Res. Dev. **34**(6), 1097–1109 (2014). https://doi.org/10.1080/07294360.2014.911263

Crenshaw, K.W.: Mapping the Margins: Intersectionality, Identity Politics, and Violence against Women of Color. Stanford Law Review. Stanford Law School (1991). https://doi.org/10.2307/1229039

Dagavarian, D.A., Walters, W.M.: Prior learning assessment: outcomes assessment of prior learning assessment programs. J. Continuing High. Educ. **52**(1), 54–57 (2004). https://doi.org/10.1080/07377366.2004.10400278

Douglas, G., McLinden, M., Robertson, C., Travers, J., Smith, E.: Including pupils with special educational needs and disability in national assessment: comparison of three country case studies through an inclusive assessment framework. Int. J. Disabil. Dev. Educ. **63**(1), 98–121 (2015). https://doi.org/10.1080/1034912x.2015.1111306

Elton, L.: A challenge to established assessment practice. High. Educ. Q. **58**(1), 43–62 (2004). https://doi.org/10.1111/j.1468-2273.2004.00259.x

Goodwin, J.T., Goh, J., Verkoeyen, S., Lithgow, K.: Can students be taught to articulate employability skills? J. Educ. Train. (2019). https://doi.org/10.1108/et-08-2018-0186

Hanafin, J., Shevlin, M., Kenny, M., Neela, E.M.: Including young people with disabilities: assessment challenges in higher education. High. Educ. Springer Science+Business Media. https://doi.org/10.1007/s10734-006-9005-9

Hill, J., Walkington, H.: Developing graduate attributes through participation in undergraduate research conferences. J. Geography High. Educ. **40**(2), 222–237 (2016). https://doi.org/10.1080/03098265.2016.1140128

Hollnagel, E.: Why is Work-as-Imagined Different from Work-as- Done? CRC Press eBooks (2017). https://doi.org/10.1201/9781315605739-24

Hu, W.: Joseph E. Aoun: Robot-proof: higher education in the age of artificial intelligence. High. Educ. **78**(6), 1143–1145 (2019). https://doi.org/10.1007/s10734-019-00387-3

Janse van Rensburg, C., Coetzee, S.A., Schmulian, A.: Developing digital creativity through authentic assessment. Assess. Eval. High. Educ. **47**(6), 857–877 (2021). https://doi.org/10.1080/02602938.2021.1968791

Jessop, T., Tomas, C.: The implications of programme assessment patterns for student learning. Assess. Eval. High. Educ. **42**(6), 990–999 (2016). https://doi.org/10.1080/02602938.2016.1217501

Ketonen, L., Körkkö, M., Pöysä, S.: Authentic assessment as a support for student teachers' reflection. Eur. J. Teach. Educ., 1–22 (2023). https://doi.org/10.1080/02619768.2023.2229004

Lawrie, G., et al.: Moving towards inclusive learning and teaching: A synthesis of recent literature. Teaching & Learning Inquiry: The ISSOTL Journal. University of Calgary (2017). https://doi.org/10.20343/teachlearninqu.5.1.3

McArthur, J.: Assessment for social justice: the role of assessment in achieving social justice. Assess. Eval. High. Educ. **41**(7), 967–981 (2015). https://doi.org/10.1080/02602938.2015.1053429

Marginson, S.: The worldwide trend to high participation higher education: dynamics of social stratification in inclusive systems. Higher Educ. **72**(4), 413–434 (2016). https://doi.org/10.1007/s10734-016-0016-x

Messick, S.J. (ed.). (2013). Assessment in Higher Education. https://doi.org/10.4324/9781315045009

O'Neill, G.: It's not fair! Students and staff views on the equity of the procedures and outcomes of students' choice of assessment methods. Irish Educ. Stud. **36**(2), 221–236 (2017). https://doi.org/10.1080/03323315.2017.1324805

Ryan, R.M., Deci, E.L.: Self-determination theory and the facilitation of intrinsic motivation, social development, and well-being. Am. Psychol. **55**(1), 68–78 (2000). https://doi.org/10.1037/0003-066x.55.1.68

Schmulian, A., Coetzee, S.A.: Students' experience of team assessment with immediate feedback in a large accounting class. Assess. Eval. High Educ. **44**(4), 516–532 (2018). https://doi.org/10.1080/02602938.2018.1522295

Steen-Utheim, A., Hopfenbeck, T.N.: To do or not to do with feedback. A study of undergraduate students' engagement and use of feedback within a portfolio assessment design. Assess. Eval. High. Educ. **44**(1), 80–96 (2018). https://doi.org/10.1080/02602938.2018.1476669

Tai, J., Ajjawi, R., Bearman, M., Boud, D., Dawson, P., Jorre de St Jorre, T.: Assessment for inclusion: rethinking contemporary strategies in assessment design. High. Educ. Res. Dev. **42**(2), 483–497 (2022). https://doi.org/10.1080/07294360.2022.2057451

Technology-enabled assessment and improvement of inclusive learning and quality of life in higher education. Quantifying Qual. Life, 319–353 (2022).https://doi.org/10.1007/978-3-030-94212-0_13

Tsolou, O., Babalis, T., Tsoli, K.: The impact of COVID-19 pandemic on education: social exclusion and dropping out of school. Creat. Educ.. Educ. **12**(03), 529–544 (2021). https://doi.org/10.4236/ce.2021.123036

Turner, R., Shulruf, B., Li, M., Yuan, J.: University admission models that address quality and equity. Asia Pacific J. Educ. **32**(2), 225–239 (2012). https://doi.org/10.1080/02188791.2012.684955

Villarroel, V., Bloxham, S., Bruna, D., Bruna, C., Herrera-Seda, C.: Authentic assessment: creating a blueprint for course design. Assess. Eval. High. Educ. **43**(5), 840–854 (2017). https://doi.org/10.1080/02602938.2017.1412396

Wiewiora, A., Kowalkiewicz, A.: The role of authentic assessment in developing authentic leadership identity and competencies. Assess. Eval. High. Educ. **44**(3), 415–430 (2018). https://doi.org/10.1080/02602938.2018.1516730

Won, S., Wolters, C.A., Mueller, S.A.: Sense of belonging and self- regulated learning: testing achievement goals as mediators. J. Exp. Educ. **86**(3), 402–418 (2017). https://doi.org/10.1080/00220973.2016.1277337

Technology-Based Interventions for Gender Equality Education and Fostering Well-Being

Harshith B. Nair[⊠] [ID]

Department of Education (DE), Regional Institute of Education (NCERT), Mysuru, India
hbnair184@gmail.com

Abstract. The rise of technology presents a unique opportunity to address social inequalities and promote mental well-being among youngsters. This paper delves into the potential of technology-based interventions, specifically focusing on their role in fostering gender equality education and promoting positive mental health in young people.

Through an extensive review of existing research, the paper explores various digital learning platforms, serious games, and gamification practices. It examines their effectiveness in promoting gender-equitable attitudes, challenging stereotypes, and fostering inclusive learning environments. This review will highlight successful strategies utilized in existing interventions, analyse the impact on students' well-being, and identify potential limitations and areas for further development.

The paper explores the practical application of these interventions. It provides concrete examples of how educators can integrate technology-based tools into their classrooms to promote gender equality education. This section will offer practical guidance for teachers, teacher educators, and curriculum developers, empowering them to leverage the power of technology to create inclusive learning spaces.

By bridging the gap between theory and practice, this paper aims to contribute to a growing body of knowledge surrounding technology-based interventions for social change. It seeks to empower educators and promote the development of innovative, evidence-based digital tools that can foster positive mental health and advance gender equality education for young people.

1 Introduction

The pursuit of gender equality remains a critical challenge in the 21st century. Gender stereotypes and biases continue to limit opportunities and well-being for individuals across the globe. Education has long been recognized as a cornerstone in achieving gender equality by empowering individuals with knowledge, skills, and the confidence to challenge the status quo.

Gender equality education and fostering well-being are crucial components of societal progress and development. However, traditional educational methods often face limitations in reach, scalability, and engagement.

Measuring progress in gender equality in education is essential for tracking trends and identifying areas for improvement. Studies analysing gender equality in educational

G. A. Toto (Ed.): ICS exchange 2024, CCIS 2521, pp. 359–372, 2025.
https://doi.org/10.1007/978-3-032-03021-4_26

settings across different countries provide valuable insights into the effectiveness of interventions and policies (Psaki et al., 2017). Despite efforts to enhance gender equality in academia, challenges persist, particularly in achieving parity at higher university levels and in fields like science and tech- nology (Zippel et al., 2016).

Addressing these challenges requires a comprehensive approach that considers the capabilities and needs of all individuals involved in the educational process. Educating future teachers to promote sustainable gender equality practices is a critical step towards fostering a more inclusive educa- tional environment (Lee, 2021). Gender equality plans in academic institutions play a vital role in addressing systemic inequalities and power dynamics, emphasizing the importance of justice and transformative in- terventions (Clavero & Galligan, 2021). Work-family balance policies and in- stitutional arrange- ments have been shown to influence gender-role attitudes, highlighting the significance of supportive structures in promoting egalitarian values (Lomazzi et al., 2018).

Incorporating gender issues into educational curricula and creating gender-sen- sitive learning environments are essential for nurturing gender equality consciousness among students (Lim et al., 2021). Initiatives such as women-only leadership development pro- grams have been identified as effective strategies for enhancing gender parity in leader- ship positions (Peterson, 2019). Furthermore, promoting gender equality in universities requires a harmonized approach that aligns with national and international initiatives to drive structural change and foster inclusivity (Bencivenga & Drew, 2021).

This is where technology presents itself as a powerful tool for advancing gender equality education. The ubiquitous nature of technology, particularly mobile technolo- gies, offers unprecedented opportunities to deliver educational content to geographically dispersed populations and create engaging learning experi- ences. A growing body of research explores the potential of technology-based interventions (TBIs) in promoting gender equality education (Niiranen, 2017).

The endeavour to promote gender equality through technology-based interventions is a multifaceted and challenging task that requires a deep understanding of historical, social, and cultural dynamics (Htun & Weldon, 2011). Policies aimed at advancing gender equality often confront established norms and power.

Structures, necessitating a re-evaluation of the roles of the state, religion, and cultural entities in shaping citizenship and social interactions (Htun & Weldon, 2011). Moreover, the influence of religion on gender equality perceptions in various societies underscores the complexity of gendered socialization and the potential for individuals to challenge traditional patriarchal interpretations.

This research thematic paper delves deeper into the potential of TBIs for promoting gender equality education and fostering well-being. By critically examining existing research, exploring successful case studies, and addressing the challenges, this paper aims to contribute to a comprehensive understanding of how technology can be harnessed for a more just and equitable world.

2 Methodology

This paper employed a narrative review methodology to summarise and synthesise research findings from a variety of sources and gain an overview of the concept at hand. The components of the methodology are as follows:

2.1 Search Strategy

Databases. A multi-database search was conducted across academic databases specializing in social science, psychology, public health, and education technology. Examples include Scopus, EBSCO, PsycINFO, PubMed, Web of Science, Mendeley and ERIC.

Keywords. A combination of keywords and Boolean operators (AND, OR, NOT) were used to target the specific research question. Examples include "technology-based interventions," "gender equality education," "adolescents," "youth," "mental health," "well-being," "e-learning," "mobile applications," "se- rious games," and "social media."

2.2 Inclusion and Exclusion Criteria

Studies Were Included If They. Focused on the effectiveness of technology-based interventions (e.g., online courses, mobile apps, virtual reality simulations) in promoting gender equality education for young people (ages 10–24).

- Evaluated the impact of these interventions on fostering positive mental health outcomes and addressing gender-related stereotypes.
- Were published in peer-reviewed academic journals within the last 25 years (2000-2024) to capture the evolving field of educational technology.
- Were available in full text and in English language.

Studies Were Excluded If They. Did not focus on technology-based interventions in education.

- Did not address gender equality as a core component of the intervention.
- Focused on outcomes unrelated to mental health or well-being.
- Were not published in peer-reviewed journals or were not available in full text.

2.3 Selection Process

- Initial search results were exported and duplicates were removed.
- Titles and abstracts were screened based on the inclusion and exclusion criteria. Potentially relevant studies were selected for full-text review.
- Full-text articles were thoroughly evaluated for their content, methodology, and relevance to the research question.

2.4 Data Extraction and Analysis

A data extraction form was used to collect key information from each included study. This may include: Author(s) and publication year, Study design and methodology (e.g., quantitative, qualitative, mixed methods), Description of the technology-based intervention, Sample characteristics (age, gender, etc.), Key findings regarding the impact on gender equality education and youth well-being.

Extracted data was analyzed thematically to identify key themes and patterns emerging from the research. This involved coding and categorization of data to identify the most effective types of technology-based interventions for pro- moting gender equality education and fostering positive mental health out- comes.

2.5 Quality Assessment

The quality of the included studies was assessed using established criteria for evaluating research methodology and data analysis. Considerations include the study's design, sample size, instrumentation, and data interpretation.

2.6 Limitations

This review was limited to studies published in English language and may not capture research conducted in other languages. While the search strategy included diverse databases, it's possible that some relevant studies may not have been identified.

This comprehensive methodology ensures a systematic and rigorous approach to the literature review. The identified research will inform the development of the paper on technology-based interventions for promoting gender equality education and fostering positive mental health among young people (Fig. 1).

3 Literature Review

3.1 The Challenge of Gender Inequality and Mental Health in Young People

Gender inequality manifests in various ways, from societal expectations and stereotypes to discrimination and violence. These factors create a complex web of challenges that can negatively impact young people's mental health. Research consistently demonstrates

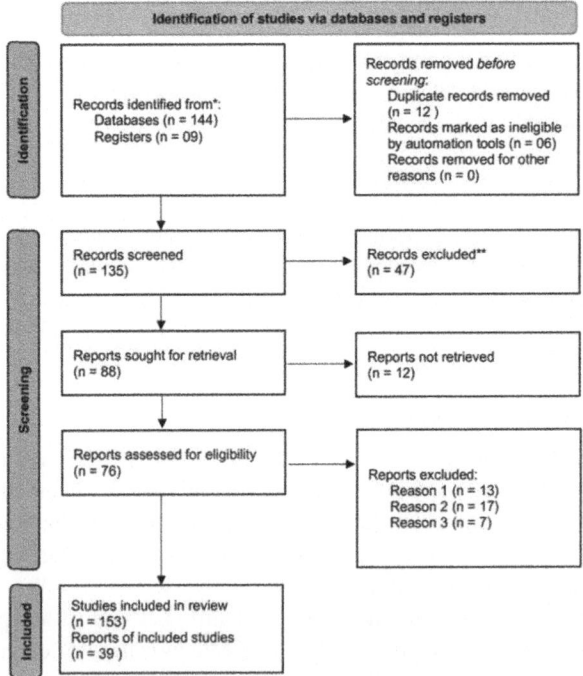

Fig. 1. PRISMA Diagram of Review[27]

a significant gender gap, with girls and young women often experiencing higher rates of depression, anxiety, and eating disorders compared to boys (World Health Organization, 2020; Brucki et al., 2023).

A significant contributor is the process of socialization, where young people learn about expected behaviours, roles, and values associated with their gender. Rigid gender roles and stereotypes can limit young people's sense of self and can lead to feelings of inadequacy and isolation. For example, girls who excel in traditionally masculine domains like math and science may face social ostra- cism, leading to feelings of alienation and potentially impacting self-esteem (Leder, 2019). Similarly, boys pressured to conform to a culture of emo- tional stoicism and restricted expression may struggle with healthy coping.

Mechanisms for emotional distress, increasing vulnerability to substance abuse and risky behaviours (Hearn et al., 2023).

Another key factor is the prevalence of gender-based violence. Young people experiencing violence, harassment, or discrimination based on their gender are at increased risk for anxiety, depression, and post-traumatic stress disorder (PTSD) (Friedberg et al., 2023). This includes experiences like discrimination at school, bullying, sexual harassment, and intimate partner violence. The trauma associated with these experiences can have lasting psychological effects, hindering emotional development and impacting self-worth. LGBTQ + youth, who often face societal stigma and discrimination related to their gender identity or sexual orientation at school, are particularly vulnerable to gender-based violence and its negative mental health consequences (Russell and Fish, 2016).

3.2 Accessibility Bridging the Gender Divide

Education technology is a valuable tool in reducing the gender gap in education by enhancing access to educational resources. By utilizing digital tools and platforms, educational institutions can offer equal learning opportunities to individuals regardless of gender. This approach is crucial for promoting gender equality in education, which is not only a matter of social justice but also a driver of economic growth (Klasen and Lamanna, 2009). Gender equality in education is further underscored by the importance of establishing gender-equal environments in educational settings, advocating for gender equality in society, and providing systematic training for educators on gender equality education (Nowak, 2021).

Integrating gender equality education into digital education can help address gender imbalances in digital disciplines and create enhanced learning opportunities for women (Wang, 2022). Online courses, digital libraries, and educa- tional software can transcend physical limitations, allowing students in under- served areas to connect with educators and curriculum from around the world (UNESCO, 2021). Mobile learning platforms offer flexibility and accessibility, particularly in regions with limited internet connectivity. Mobile apps and downloadable educational content can empower students to learn inde- pendently, at their own pace, and on devices they may already have access to (Keengwe et al., 2014). This is particularly beneficial for adult learners, working professionals, or students facing geographical constraints on attending traditional classroom settings.

Efforts to bridge the gender gap in education through technology also involve tackling the digital gender divide. This includes ensuring equitable access to technology, employment, and training in digital tools. Gender equality plans are essential for increasing the visibility of women in the technology field, promoting equal parenting, reducing the gender wage gap, and fostering inclusivity in digital education (Nath & Barah, 2017).

Gender-responsive pedagogy is crucial for educating teachers about gender- specific learning needs and eliminating discriminatory practices in education (Lee, 2021). Gender equality in education is not only a matter of justice but also a means of empowerment and human development. Providing equal opportunities for all individuals, regardless of gender, is essential for achieving positive social outcomes and upholding human rights (Willie & Kershaw, 2019).

3.3 Personalised Instruction Promoting Gender Equality

Personalized learning technologies have been recognized as a key development trend in higher education, aiming to cater to individual student needs and preferences (Ambele et al., 2022). By tailoring educational content and methods to suit each learner's pace and style, technology can address gender disparities by providing equal opportu- nities for all students to excel (Shemshack & Spector, 2020). Technology can foster inclusive learning environments by catering to diverse learning styles and needs (Nair & Karan, 2024). Adaptive learning platforms can tailor instruction to each student's individual strengths and weaknesses, providing targeted support and differentiated instruction (Meyer et al., 2014).

Studies have shown that gender biases and stereotypes are deeply embedded in educational materials, such as textbooks, which can perpetuate inequality (Blumberg, 2009). By utilizing education technology, educators can create gender-neutral and inclusive learning environments that challenge traditional biases present in educational resources (Blumberg, 2009). This shift towards gender-sensitive education can help break down barriers and promote equality in the classroom.

For students with disabilities, technology can be a powerful tool for overcom- ing barriers to learning. Assistive technologies, such as text-to-speech software and screen readers, can provide equitable access to educational materials for students with visual impairments (Tuttle & Carter, 2022). Similarly, for students with learning difficulties, dyslexia software and other digital tools can offer personalized support and improve reading comprehension.

3.4 Inclusivity Promoting Gender Equality

Education technology has emerged as a powerful tool in reducing the gender divide in inclusive classrooms (Niiranen, 2017). By leveraging technology, educators can create more equitable learning environments that cater to the diverse needs of all students, regardless of gender. Research has shown that exposure to counter stereotypical role models can significantly influence girls' and women's career choices and aspirations (Olsson & Martiny, 2018). This highlights the importance of representation and diversity in educational settings to challenge traditional gender norms.

Inclusive education practices play a crucial role in shaping attitudes and perceptions towards gender inclusivity in the classroom. Studies have indicated that demographic differences can impact pre-service teachers' attitudes and concerns about inclusive education, emphasizing the need for targeted interventions to promote inclusivity (Forlin et al., 2009). Additionally, the use of information and communication technology has been linked to increased female economic participation, showcasing the potential of technology in bridging gender gaps.

Inclusive teaching approaches are essential for fostering gender equity in STEM education. By adopting inclusive practices, instructors can help reduce achievement gaps and promote the success of students from marginalized groups (Daraz et al., 2024). Implementing strategies that support and affirm gender and sexual diversity in educational settings can create a more inclusive learning environment for all students (Araujo Dawson et al., 2022). Moreover, leveraging new technologies and mobile devices can enhance the participation of students with disabilities in mainstream classrooms, promoting inclusivity and equal access to education (Karagianni & Drigas, 2023).

3.5   EdTech Tools and Strategies for Gender Equality

Countering Stereotypes and Biases. *Curated Content and Role Models.* Integrating diverse content and highlighting female role models in STEM fields through educational software and online platforms can help challenge stereotypes and inspire girls to pursue traditionally male-dominated subjects (National Center for Women and Information Technology, 2023). Platforms like "Girls Who Code" provide interactive coding tutorials led by female professionals, fostering confidence and interest in computer science.

Implicit Bias Training Modules. Equipping teachers with access to online training modules on implicit bias can raise awareness of unconscious stereotypes that may inadvertently disadvantage girls in the classroom (Harvard University, Project Implicit).

Personalized Learning and Diverse Learning Styles. *Adaptive Learning Platforms.* These platforms utilize algorithms to assess individual strengths and weaknesses, tailoring instruction and providing differentiated learning experiences. This can cater to diverse learning styles, allowing girls who may be more auditory or kinesthetic learners to thrive alongside their visual-spatial learning counterparts (Pashler et al., 2009). Platforms like Khan Academy and IXL offer personalized learning pathways in various subjects, catering to individual learning paces and needs.

Gamification and Interactive. Learning Educational games can make learning engaging and enjoyable, particularly for girls who may be traditionally less drawn to passive learning methods (Li et al., 2024). Games like Minecraft Education Edition allow students to collaborate and problem-solve in virtual worlds, fostering critical thinking and teamwork skills in a fun and immersive environment.

AR & VR. Augmented reality and Virtual Reality can create or offer immersive and engaging ways to explore STEM fields, providing girls with unique learning experiences and potentially sparking interest in traditionally male dominated areas (Lampropoulos et al., 2022).

Building Confidence and Growth Mindset. *Mastery-Based Learning.* Platforms These platforms focus on achieving mastery of concepts over simply accumulating points. This approach can promote a growth mindset, encouraging girls to persevere through challenges and celebrate their progress, fostering confidence in their abilities (Dweck, 2006). Platforms like DreamBox Learning utilize adaptive learning and mastery-based progression to help students build strong foundations in math.

Project-Based Learning with Technology. Integration Collaborative projects utilizing technology tools like online research databases and presentation software can empower girls to take ownership of their learning and showcase their skills in a public forum. This can cultivate self-confidence and encourage them to actively participate in classroom discussions.

Addressing Access and Equity Issues. *Low-Tech and Offline Solutions.* While technology plays a significant role, it's crucial to acknowledge limitations in access. Initiatives like mobile learning apps with downloadable content can ensure learning continuity even in areas with limited internet connectivity (Keengwe et al., 2014). Providing offline coding tools or downloadable educational resources can offer alternative learning pathways for girls in underserved communities.

Bridging the Digital Divide. Investing in infrastructure to expand internet access and providing affordable devices to low-income communities is vital for ensuring equitable access to EdTech resources. Integrating digital literacy training into the curriculum can empower girls to navigate the online learning landscape with confidence.

Artificial Intelligence and Education. The integration of Artificial Intelligence (AI) into EdTech holds immense potential for further bridging the gender gap and fostering well-being in education. AI-powered tutors can offer personalized learning pathways that cater to individual needs and learning styles, providing targeted support and fostering a sense of accomplishment for all students, regardless of gender. Studies have shown that personalized learning approaches utilizing AI can improve student engagement and academic achievement, potentially narrowing the gender gap in traditionally male-dominated subjects like STEM (Huang et al., 2023).

AI can also be utilized to create more inclusive learning environments. For example, AI-powered chatbots can provide real-time emotional support and address anxieties students may face, particularly those who might hesitate to seek help traditionally. A study by Wu & Yu (2024) exploring the use of AI chatbots for student support found that students reported feeling more comfortable discussing their concerns with a virtual assistant compared to a human counsellor, potentially reducing stigma and promoting help-seeking behaviour. AI can personalize feedback mechanisms to be more encouraging and growth-oriented, promoting a positive learning experience and boosting well-being for all students (Canning et al., 2024).

Technology for Well-being. Technology-based interventions are increasingly important in promoting gender equality education and well-being. Wang (2022) emphasizes the significance of technology in advancing gender equality education in the digital era. This highlights the importance of leveraging technology to address gender dis- parities and promote equality through educational initiatives. Technology- based interventions have been shown to positively impact individual well-being (Cotten, 2008).

4 Case Study: Girls Who Code: Bridging the Gender Gap in Tech Through EdTech

Girls Who Code, founded in 2012 by Reshma Saujani, is a widely recognized non- profit organization dedicated to closing the gender gap in the technology sector. Their mission revolves around empowering girls through computer science education and fostering a future where women are well-represented in the tech workforce.

4.1 EdTech Tools and Strategies

- **Interactive Coding Tutorials.** Girls Who Code utilizes online platforms and mobile apps featuring interactive coding tutorials. These engaging lessons are led by female professionals, providing girls with positive role models and fostering a sense of belonging in the tech field.
- **Project-Based Learning.** The curriculum emphasizes project-based learning, where girls work collaboratively to design, develop, and code their own projects. This approach fosters creativity, problem-solving skills, and teamwork, all essential for success in computer science careers.
- **Community Building.** Girls Who Code places a strong emphasis on building a supportive community for girls interested in technology. Online forums, local chapters, and mentorship programs connect girls with peers and industry professionals, fostering a sense of belonging and encouraging them to persist in their pursuit of tech careers.

4.2 Impact and Achievements

Increased Confidence and Interest. Studies have shown that Girls Who Code programs effectively equip girls with the necessary skills and confidence to pursue computer science. Girls who participate in the program report a significant increase in their interest and self-efficacy in coding and related fields.

Closing the Gender Gap. With over 500,000 alumni globally (as of 2022), Girls Who Code is making significant strides in closing the gender gap in tech. Their success stories showcase the transformative power of EdTech in empowering girls to pursue careers in traditionally male-dominated fields.

Challenges and Considerations:

Accessibility. While Girls Who Code offers various programs, ensuring equitable access for girls from underserved communities remains a challenge. Bridging the digital divide and providing resources for low-income families is crucial for maximizing the program's impact.

Scalability. As Girls Who Code expands its reach globally, maintaining program quality and effectiveness across diverse contexts requires careful planning and adaptation.

5 Discussions

The literature review paints a compelling picture of the challenges and opportunities presented by gender inequality and mental health in young people. It highlights the significant gender gap in mental health, with girls and young women disproportionately affected by issues like depression and anxiety. The root causes are complex, intertwined with social expectations, gender-based violence, and limited access to resources. The review also offers a beacon of hope through educational technology (EdTech). EdTech's potential lies in its ability to personalize learning experiences. By utilizing adaptive learning platforms and catering to diverse learning styles, EdTech can address the unique needs of girls who may be auditory, kinesthetic, or visual learners. This can level the playing field, allowing girls to thrive alongside their peers regardless of their preferred learning method.

The review emphasizes the importance of dismantling gender stereotypes in educational materials. By integrating diverse content and highlighting female role models in STEM fields, EdTech can inspire girls to pursue traditionally male-dominated subjects. Additionally, project-based learning with technology tools can empower girls to take ownership of their learning and showcase their skills, fostering confidence and encouraging active participation.

EdTech can be instrumental in creating inclusive learning environments. Technology offers various tools for students with disabilities, such as text-to- speech software and screen readers. AI-powered chatbots can provide real- time emotional support, particularly for students who may hesitate to seek help traditionally. However, the review acknowledges the digital divide and emphasizes the need for low-tech solutions and initiatives to bridge the gap. This ensures equitable access to EdTech resources for all students, regardless of socioeconomic background.

The potential of AI in promoting gender equality and well-being in education is undeniable. Personalized learning pathways powered by AI can cater to individual needs and learning styles, fostering a sense of accomplishment for all students. The review rightly highlights the crucial role of ethical considerations. Ensuring AI algorithms are free from bias and that human oversight remains paramount is vital to prevent the amplification of existing inequalities.

One inspiring example of EdTech's role in promoting gender equality is the work of Girls Who Code. This non-profit organization utilizes a variety of EdTech tools, including interactive coding tutorials, project-based learning experiences, and online communities. Their programs have demonstrably in- creased girls' confidence and interest in computer science, with many graduates pursuing careers in technology fields. Girls Who Code exemplifies the transformative power of EdTech in empowering girls and dismantling stereo- types, paving the way for a more inclusive future in the tech industry.

While EdTech offers a powerful toolkit, the review underscores the need for a comprehensive approach. It emphasizes the importance of gender- responsive pedagogy, which equips teachers to address gender-specific learning needs. Collaboration between educators, policymakers, technology developers, and students is crucial for sustainable change. Only through a collective effort can we leverage EdTech to dismantle gender stereotypes, create inclusive learning environments, and ultimately, promote well-being for all students.

6 Conclusion

The reviewed literature overwhelmingly supports the proposition that educational technology (EdTech) has the potential to be a transformative force in promoting gender equality and fostering well-being in education. By personalizing learning experiences, dismantling stereotypes, and fostering inclusive environments, EdTech can empower all students, regardless of gender, to thrive and reach their full potential.

The ability to tailor instruction to individual needs and learning styles can be particularly beneficial for girls, who may have been traditionally underserved by a one-size-fits-all approach. EdTech offers tools and resources to challenge gender bias, highlight inspiring role models, and create a safe and supportive learning environment for all students.

For EdTech to reach its full potential, a holistic approach is required. Efforts to bridge the digital divide, ensure ethical considerations in AI implementation, and cultivate gender-responsive pedagogy among educators are all crucial for sustainable change. Collaboration across stakeholders, including educators, policymakers, technology developers, and students themselves, will be key in harnessing the power of EdTech to create a more equitable and inclusive educational landscape for future generations.

7 Future Research Areas

Future research should focus on EdTech's long-term impact on girls' achievement and career choices in STEM. Exploring how EdTech can tackle implicit bias and cater to diverse learners across gender, race, and socioeconomic backgrounds is crucial to truly understand how technology-based instruction can nullify gender inequality and foster well-being.

Acknowledgments. The Author acknowledges the organizing team at ICS Exchange who were crucial for the successful completion of this study and the support of RIEM Library in aiding access of multiple databases, which was crucial for this study.

Disclosure of Interests. The author has no conflict of interests to disclose at this juncture.

References

Ambele, R.M., Kaijage, S.F. Dida, M.A., Trojer, L., Kyando, N.M.: A review of the development trend of personalized learning technologies and its applications. Int. J. Adv. Sci. Res. Eng. (IJASRE) (2022). https://doi.org/10.31695/IJASRE.2022.8.11.9

Araujo Dawson, B., Kilgore, W., Rawcliffe, R.M.: Strategies for creating inclusive learning environments through a social justice lens. J. Educ. Res. Pract. **12**, 3–27 (2022). https://doi.org/10.5590/JERAP.2022.12.0.02

Bencivenga, R., Drew, E.: Promoting gender equality and structural change in academia through gender equality plans: Harmonising EU and national initiatives. GENDER – Zeitschrift für Geschlecht, Kultur und Gesellschaft **13**(1), 27–42 (2021). https://doi.org/10.3224/gender.v13 i1.03

Blumberg, R.L.: The invisible obstacle to educational equality: gender bias in textbooks. Prospects **38**, 345–361 (2009). https://doi.org/10.1007/s11125-009-9086-1

Brucki, B.M., Bagade, T., Majeed, T.: A health impact assessment of gender inequities associated with psychological distress during COVID-19 in Australia's most lockeddownstate—Victoria. BMCPublicHealth **23**, 233 (2023). https://doi.org/10.1186/s12889-022-14356-6

Canning, E. A., White, M., Davis, W. B.: Growth mindset messages from instructors improve academic performance among first-generation college students. *CBE Life Sci. Educ.* **23**(2), ar14 (2024). https://doi.org/10.1187/cbe.23-07-0131

Clavero, S., Galligan, Y.: Delivering gender justice in academia through gender equality plans? Normative and practical challenges. Gend. Work Organ. **28**(3), 1115–1132 (2021). https://doi.org/10.1111/gwao.12658

Cotten, S.R.: Students' technology use and the impacts on well-being. New Dir. Stud. Serv. **2008**(124), 55–70 (2008). https://doi.org/10.1002/ss.295

Daraz, U., Khan, Y., Azeem Ashraf, M., Maekele Tsegay, S.: Bridging the gap: progressive teaching strategies for gender equity in STEM education. IntechOpen (2024). https://doi.org/10.5772/intechopen.114860

Dweck, C. S.: Mindset: the new psychology of success. Random House (2006)

Efobi, U. R., Tanankem, B. V., Asongu, S. A.: Female economic participation with information and communication technology advancement: Evidence from Sub- Saharan Africa. South African J. Econ. **86**(2), 231–246 (2018). https://doi.org/10.1111/saje.12194

Forlin, C., Loreman, T., Sharma, U., Earle, C.: Demographic differences in changing pre-service teachers' attitudes, sentiments and concerns about inclusive education. Int. J. Incl. Educ. **13**, 195–209 (2009). https://doi.org/10.1080/13603110701365356

Friedberg, R., Baiocchi, M., Rosenman, E., Amuyunzu-Nyamongo, M., Nyairo, G., Sarnquist, C.: Mental health and gender-based violence: an exploration of depression, PTSD, and anxiety among adolescents in Kenyan informal settlements participating in an empowerment intervention. PLoS ONE **18**(3), e0281800 (2023). https://doi.org/10.1371/journal.pone.0281800

Girls Who Code (2012). Retrieved from: https://girlswhocode.com/

Harvard University, Project Implicit. https://implicit.harvard.edu/implicit/takea- touchtestv2.html

Hearn, J., de Boise, S., Goedecke, K.: Men and masculinities: structures, practices, and identities. In: Zurbriggen, E.L., Capdevila, R. (eds) The Palgrave Handbook of Power, Gender, and Psychology . Palgrave Macmillan, Cham (2023). https://doi.org/10.1007/978-3-031- 41531-9_12.

Htun, M., Weldon, L.: Sex equality in family law: Historical legacies, feminist activism, and religious power in 70 countries (Background Paper, World Development Report 2012). World Bank (2011). https://openknowledge.worldbank.org/server/api/core/bitstreams/11663daf-e479-59cd-9e5f-d45acb1e36d8/content

Huang, A.Y.Q., Lu, O.H.T., Yang, S.J.H.: Effects of artificial intelligence–enabled personalized recommendations on learners' learning engagement, motivation, and outcomes in a flipped classroom. Comput. Educ. **194**, 104684 (2023). https://doi.org/10.1016/j.compedu.2022.104684

Karagianni, E., Drigas, A.: Using new technologies and mobiles for students with disabilities to build a sustainable inclusive learning and development ecosystem. Int. J. Interact. Mobile Technol. (iJIM) **17**(01), 57–73 (2023). https://doi.org/10.3991/ijim.v17i01.36359

Keengwe, J., Schnellert, G., Jonas, D.: Mobile phones in education: challenges and opportunities for learning. Educ. Info. Technol. **19**, 441 (2314). https://doi.org/10.1007/s10639-012-9235-7

Klasen, S., Lamanna, F.: The impact of gender inequality in education and employment on economic growth: New evidence for a panel of countries. Feminist Econ. **15**(3), 91–132 (2009). https://doi.org/10.1080/13545700902893106

Lampropoulos, G., Keramopoulos, E., Diamantaras, K., Evangelidis, G.: Augmented reality and gamification in education: a systematic literature review of research, applications, and empirical studies. Appl. Sci. **12**(13), 6809 (2022). https://doi.org/10.3390/app12136809

Leder, G. C.: Gender and mathematics education: an overview. In: Kaiser, G., Presmeg, N., (Eds.), *Compendium for early career researchers in mathematics education,* (pp. 289–308). Springer (2019). https://doi.org/10.1007/978-3-030-15636-7_13

Lee, S. M.: Exploring gender-responsive pedagogy for STEM education. IISRR- MANUU Workshop Issue **7**(2) (2021). ISSN 2394–885X

Li, Y., Chen, D., Deng, X.: The impact of digital educational games on student's motivation for learning: The mediating effect of learning engagement and the moderating effect of the digital environment. PLoS ONE **19**(1), e0294350 (2024). https://doi.org/10.1371/journal.pone.029 4350

Lim, W.H., Wong, C., Jain, S.R., Ng, C.H., Tai, C.H., Devi, M.K., et al.: The unspoken reality of gender bias in surgery: A qualitative systematic review. PLoS ONE **16**(2), e0246420 (2021). https://doi.org/10.1371/journal.pone.0246420

Lomazzi, V., Israel, S., Crespi, I.: Gender equality in Europe and the effect of work-family balance policies on gender-role attitudes. Soc. Sci. **8**, Article No. 5 (2018). https://doi.org/10.3390/soc sci8010005

Meyer, A., Rose, D.H., Gordon, D.: Universal design for learning: Theory and practice. CAST Professional Publishing, Wakefield (2014)

Nair, Harshith, B, Karan, S P.: Knowledge, Attitude and usage of information and com- munication technology (ICT) and digital resources in pre-service teachers.TheNewEdu. Rev. **75**(1),228–243 (2024). https://doi.org/10.15804/tner.2024.75.1.18, Available at SSRN: https://ssrn.com/ab- stract=4798180

Nath, M., Barah, P.: Digital India and women: Bridging the digital gender divide. In *Proceedings of the 10th International Conference on Theory and Practice of Electronic Governance,* (pp. 302–310) (2017). ACM. https://doi.org/10.1145/3047273.3047319

NCWITv (2023). Retrieved from: https://ncwit.org

Niiranen, S.: Gender and Technology Education. In: de Vries, M. (eds) Handbook of Technology Education. Springer International Handbooks of Education. Springer, Cham (2017). https://doi.org/10.1007/978-3-319-38889-2_61-1

Nowak, J. K.: Gender inequality in education. In Human, Technologies and Quality of Education, 2021 (pp. 384–396) (2021). https://doi.org/10.22364/htqe.2021.31

Olsson, M., Martiny, S.E.: Does Exposure to counterstereotypical role models influence girls' and women's gender stereotypes and career choices? A review of social psychological research. Front. Psychol. **9**, 2264 (2018). https://doi.org/10.3389/fpsyg.2018.02264

Page, M.J., McKenzie, J.E., Bossuyt, P.M., Boutron, I., Hoffmann, T.C., Mulrow, C.D., et al.: The PRISMA 2020 statement: an updated guideline for reporting systematic reviews. BMJ **372**, n71 (2021). https://doi.org/10.1136/bmj.n71

Pashler, H.E., McDaniel, M.A., Rohrer, D., Bjork, R.A.: Learning styles: Con- cepts and evidence. Psychol. Sci. Pub. Inter. **10**(3), 105–166 (2009). https://doi.org/10.1111/j.1539-6053.2009.010 38.x

Psaki, S.R., Mensch, B.S., Soler-Hampejsek, E.: Associations between violence in school and at home and education outcomes in rural Malawi: A longitudinal analysis. Comp. Educ. Rev. **61**(2), 354–390 (2017). https://doi.org/10.1086/691117

Peterson, D.A.M., Biederman, L.A., Andersen, D., Ditonto, T.M., Roe, K.: Mitigating gender bias in student evaluations of teaching. PLoS ONE **14**(5), e0216241 (2019). https://doi.org/10. 1371/journal.pone.0216241

Russell, S.T., Fish, J.N.: Mental health in lesbian, gay, bisexual, and transgender (LGBT) youth. Annu. Rev. Clin. Psychol. **12**, 465–487 (2016). https://doi.org/10.1146/annurev-clinpsy-021 815-093153

Shemshack, A., Spector, J.M.: A systematic literature review of personalized learning terms. Smart Learn. Environ. **7**, 33 (2020). https://doi.org/10.1186/s40561-020-00140-9

Tuttle, M., Carter, E.W.: Examining high-tech assistive technology use of students with visual impairments. J. Vis. Imp. Blind. **116**(4), 473–484 (2022). https://doi.org/10.1177/0145482X221120265

UNESCO. Education in a changing world: The global education monitoring report 2021/2022 inclusion and education: All means all. UNESCO Publishing (2021). https://www.unesco.org/gem-report/en

Wang, W.: New concept and new practice of gender equality education in the background of a digital society. SHS Web Conf. **148**, 01017 (2022). https://doi.org/10.1051/shsconf/202214801017

Willie, T.C., Kershaw, T.S.: An ecological analysis of gender inequality and intimate partner violence in the United States. Prev. Med. **118**, 257–263 (2019). https://doi.org/10.1016/j.ypmed.2018.10.019

World Health Organization. Adolescent mental health (2020). https://www.who.int/news-room/fact-sheets/detail/adolescent-mental-health

Wu, R., Yu, Z.: Do AI Chatbots improve students' learning outcomes? Evidence from a meta-analysis. Br. J. Edu. Technol. **55**(1), 10–33 (2024). https://doi.org/10.1111/bjet.13334

Zippel, K., Ferree, M.M., Zimmermann, K.: Gender equality in German universities: vernacularising the battle for the best brains. Gend. Educ. **28**(7), 867–885 (2016). https://doi.org/10.1080/09540253.2015.1123229

The Use of Educational Robotics in Autism

Domenico Lorusso[(✉)] , Lucia Melchiorre , and Giusi Antonia Toto

Department of Humanities, Letters, Cultural Heritage, Educational Sciences, University of
Foggia, Via Arpi 176, 71121 Foggia, Italy
{domenico.lorusso,luci.melchiorre,giusi.toto}@unifg.it

Abstract. Over the last decade, numerous studies have been conducted on the
application of robotics to stimulate deficit social and communication skills in children with Autism Spectrum Disorder (ASD). The contribution aims to understand
if and how social robots can be used to support autistic children's communication
and improve their attention and involvement. It is interesting to investigate which
technologies could work in order to derive usable reflections in the preparation
of future intervention protocols. The paper pursues an exploratory investigation
through a Scoping Review aimed at understanding if and how social robots can
be used to support the autistic child's communication, encouraging attention, imitation and the implementation of new social behaviours (Abu Amara et al. 2021).
Studies have shown that robots improve the social skills of autistic children, for
whom interaction with other people can be disorienting, due to the varied expressiveness of the human face and social signals that are difficult to interpret. The
educational robot, programmable according to the child's needs, facilitates communication by allowing cognitive relief and predictability of action. Attention is
also focused more on the robot, maintaining greater eye contact. The support of
social robots has proven to be more effective than other 'technological' therapies,
such as video games or apps: the robot encourages interaction. Unlike other tools
such as software, which completely capture children's attention, humanoid robots
facilitate natural face-to-face interactions.

Keywords: Educational robotics · autism · social skills · prosocial behaviour ·
shared attention · communicative interaction

1 Introduction

The field of Artificial Intelligence (AI), since its formalization in 1956, has gone through
phases of intense theoretical and practical development, interspersed with periods of
stalemate due to the computational limitations of the time. The evolution of AI has led
to the proliferation of several subdisciplines, including Machine Learning, Deep Learning, Natural Language Processing and Computer Vision. In this context, social robots
represent an advanced application of AI, in which autonomous agents equipped with
physical embodiment interact in a proactive and socially competent way with humans.
This paradigm, known as embodied artificial intelligence, aims to simulate not only

G. A. Toto (Ed.): ICS exchange 2024, CCIS 2521, pp. 373–386, 2025.
https://doi.org/10.1007/978-3-032-03021-4_27

higher cognitive functions, but also the affective and social aspects of human intelligence, thus overcoming the limits of traditional cognitive architectures. Social robots, thanks to their ability to simulate human behaviors and adapt to individual needs, offer new perspectives for the design of innovative and personalized learning environments. In particular, in the field of early childhood education, social robots are presented as potential mediators for the development of cognitive, socioemotional and linguistic skills. Scientific literature, however, highlights the need to deepen empirical research in this area, in order to better understand the psychological mechanisms underlying the interaction between children and robots, as well as to define the optimal conditions for the use of these tools in formal educational contexts. In particular, it is crucial to investigate the impact of social robots on the development of interpersonal relationships, on motivation to learn and on the construction of mental representations of the world (Brignone, Grimaldi, & Palmieri, 2021).

The development of social robots requires the design of complex cognitive architectures capable of integrating different functionalities, including sensory perception, movement planning, natural language processing and emotion management. The creation of robots capable of interacting naturally with humans involves the resolution of numerous technical problems, such as the design of intuitive user interfaces, the development of effective machine learning algorithms and the creation of realistic simulation environments. Furthermore, it is necessary to address the challenges related to the realization of expressive robotic bodies capable of performing fluid and coordinated movements. Despite technological progress, the realization of social robots capable of meeting users' expectations is still an ambitious challenge.

Social interactions between humans and robots are influenced by a variety of factors, including the physical characteristics of the robot, its ability to perform tasks and the quality of communication. The physical presence of the robot in a shared space creates a social context that can facilitate or inhibit the emergence of meaningful relationships. The anthropomorphic appearance of the robot can influence users' expectations and the quality of their interaction. Furthermore, the ability of the robot to communicate effectively, both verbally and non-verbally, is essential to convey social and emotional meanings, and to establish a relationship of trust and collaboration.

In particular, numerous studies have been conducted in recent years on the use of robotics in the disability sector. A significant portion of this research has focused on the use of robotic technologies to stimulate impaired skills in Autism Spectrum Disorder (ASD).

The autism triad, also known as the "triad of impairments," is a concept that refers to three main areas of difficulty that often occur in people with Autism Spectrum Disorder (ASD). These three areas are:

- Social communication difficulties: People with ASD may have difficulty understanding nonverbal social rules, such as eye contact, facial expressions, and gestures. They may find it difficult to initiate or maintain a conversation, and may have difficulty understanding the emotions of others.
- Verbal and nonverbal communication difficulties: People with ASD may have difficulty understanding the meaning of words, following conversations, asking questions, and responding appropriately. They may also have difficulty interpreting the

body language and facial expressions of others. Repetitive behaviors and restricted interests.

• Understanding these areas of difficulty can help provide targeted support and interventions to people with ASD to improve their quality of life and well-being.

Robots can play many roles in enhancing emotional, intellectual and social skills in people with autism spectrum disorder (ASD).

Robotic technologies, in particular socially interactive robots (SARs), offer new perspectives for the education of children with autism. Due to their ability to adapt behaviour to individual needs, SARs can be used to promote the development of social, cognitive and communication skills. One of the most promising areas of assistive technologies based on Social Robotics is precisely its effectiveness for the development of adaptive and prosocial behaviour (Scassellati et al., 2018). In this context, robots become educational mediators, facilitating the construction of knowledge and active participation in learning activities.

2 Aims of the Analysis Conducted

Studies have confirmed that social robots can facilitate the opening of a communication channel with children with autism, encouraging eye contact and promoting the adoption of new social behaviours. Experimental data have shown that it is easier for a child with autism to approach and interact with a companion robot than with a human interlocutor, as the robot is predictable, facilitates communication by allowing cognitive relief and can be programmed to respond to the specific needs of the child (Pennazio, 2019). Consequently, this creates predictable and emotionally reassuring relational situations, reducing the anxiety associated with uncertainty.

Robots, in fact, provide simplified social signals capable of reducing over- stimulation in children; they offer more predictable and reliable responses than the signals of a human partner with changing social demands.

Closely linked to the growth of social skills in ASD is the development of imitation skills, which are a typical deficiency of the disorder. Imitation skills are crucial for the progress of a child's social understanding and are drastically impaired in all cases of ASD, especially those with low functionality. Therefore, the best approaches for educational intervention involve teaching even basic imitation skills through the encouragement of behaviours that imitate simple postures or gestures of a human model.

Positive results have been obtained with the use of robots for the maintenance of shared attention, i.e. the ability to maintain eye contact on the same object observed by several people.

The robot's role is not to replace human interaction, but to act as a social conduit between the child and an adult or peer. The aim is to reduce the distance between the autistic child's desired environment, which requires stability, predictability and security, and the complex and unpredictable world of human interactions. In other words, the robot acts as a bridge between the autistic child's need for routine and safety and the variety and complexity of human interactions, thus facilitating its inclusion in wider social contexts. This perspective suggests that the robot is conceived as a support tool to foster social interaction and communication, rather than as a replacement for human relationships.

Starting from the above observations, the contribution aims at outlining the current state of the art of studies conducted in the field of autism with the use of robotics in order to derive reflections that can be used in the preparation of future intervention protocols.

Robots are believed to be able to open communication channels with autistic subjects and activate processes of shared attention and imitation: their relative predictability, also given the ability of autistic persons to analyse and understand the rules governing closed systems, as well as their poverty of emotional expression, combined however with human features, would make them, according to some authors, less 'intimidating' than human interaction companions and therefore more suitable to act as mediators for therapeutic, rehabilitation and learning purposes.

3   The First Robots Used in Autism Therapy

The first social robot used in autism therapy was called Kaspar and was designed by British researchers at the University of Hertfordshire; it was a child-like robot with simple technology: it smiled, waved and hugged. Being repetitive and not very expressive, it was reassuring for autistic children. Kaspar was succeeded by other robots, such as NAO and Pepper, capable of learning from data acquired directly on each child through videos of their expressions and gestures and physiological records such as heart rate. Both are able to recognise the age and gender of those in front of them but also to grasp their emotions and thus regulate and plan responses to certain situations and stimuli. They also see the outside world by means of video cameras that capture a continuous stream of images, and through programming work it is possible to create a shared memory so that they can recognise objects and faces within an environment when they appear in front of them (Brignone, Grimaldi, & Palmieri, 2021). Another robot was designed by the RobotiCSS Lab (Laboratory of Robotics for Cognitive and Social Sciences) of the Department of Human Sciences for Education at the University of Milan-Bicocca. The innovative element of their research is in the choice of using robots not only as therapy and rehabilitation tools, but also and above all as a cognitive tool, to learn more about how autistic patients' minds work. The use of robots in autism therapy is based on the hypothesis that the unambiguous nature of interactions with these devices can facilitate the learning of social and communicative skills.

3.1   Educational Robotics

The integration of social robotics principles and techniques within educational contexts has given rise to a new paradigm of intervention, characterised by a highly customised and structured approach, capable of promoting the development of cognitive, perceptual and motor skills in children with DSA.

Indeed, educational robotics is an innovative teaching paradigm that transcends the limits of traditional teaching methodologies. Through interaction with technological artefacts, it offers children a unique opportunity to develop numerous skills, ranging from the cognitive to the socio-emotional and social sphere.

In the preschool context, robotics is harmoniously integrated with play activities, stimulating active and participative learning. Robots, understood not only as simple objects, but as real educational mediators, become tools through which children can explore the world around them, experiment, make mistakes and learn from their successes and failures.

Robotic tools thus become elements to reflect on and interact with. Integrated into traditional didactics, they offer the possibility, on the one hand, to improve attention, develop the first abstractions on sequential events, test the validity of reasoning, stimulate the ability to narrate and formulate hypotheses, and explore the created space; on the other hand, they allow for social action, living different emotional experiences. Through didactics based on play, educational robotics stimulates the learning of that computational thinking that is nowadays an essential tool for surviving and living, but above all, living well and in a balanced way in the digital world. Wanting to take on a definition, we could say, in short, that (educational) robotics is a game, progressively more and more difficult, functional first and foremost to learning a method of reasoning and experimentation, promoting the creative aptitudes of children and young people and their communication and cooperation skills (Bozzi, Zecca, Datteri, 2021).

In addition to computational thinking, robotics fosters the development of other key skills, such as creativity, problem solving, collaboration and communication. Indeed, designing and building a robot requires children to work in groups, share ideas, negotiate and find common solutions. Moreover, robotics stimulates curiosity and the desire to explore, promoting an approach to knowledge based on discovery and experimentation.

The use of robots in pre-school for children with autism is not limited to the development of cognitive skills. It also has a significant impact on the children's socialemotional sphere, fostering the development of empathy, self-esteem and selfawareness. Through interaction with robots, children learn to recognise and manage their emotions, develop meaningful relationships with others and cooperate to achieve common goals.

The offer of educational robots is wide and varied, ranging from pre-constructed models, such as Bee-Bots, ideal for introducing children to basic sequencing and programming concepts, to more complex robotic kits, such as Lego WeDo, which offer more flexibility and allow children to build and programme their own robots.

Educational robotics is not a separate discipline, but integrates seamlessly with other areas of the curriculum. Through robotics, it is possible to address topics related to mathematics, science, technology, Italian language and foreign languages, fostering cross-curricular and meaningful learning.

Education set up in this way, then, represents a powerful resource for schools, as it offers a unique opportunity to develop in children the skills needed to face the challenges of the contemporary world. Through interaction with robots, children become active players in their own learning, building meaningful knowledge and developing a positive attitude towards technology.

Educational robotics is a constantly evolving field, and it is expected that in the coming years we will see a further development of new technologies and educational applications. In particular, social robots, capable of interacting with children in a more natural and personalised way, and collaborative robots, which will allow children to work together to solve complex problems, are expected to grow in use.

3.2   The Characteristics of Robots

The choice of social robot is a crucial factor in determining the effectiveness of rehabilitation interventions for children with autism spectrum disorder (ASD). The complexity of social interactions and the need to customise interventions require a careful evaluation of the characteristics of the robotic device. It is not enough, in fact, to introduce a simple robot in an educational or rehabilitation context; it is fundamental that the robot possesses specific characteristics capable of facilitating the emergence of appropriate and flexible social behaviour.

The design of collaborative activities between a child with autism and a robot must be carefully planned, taking into account individualised therapeutic objectives and available resources. The therapist plays a crucial role in facilitating the interaction, modelling appropriate social behaviours and providing feedback to the child.

The elements to be considered when selecting a social robot are:

- Anthropomorphism: The degree to which the robot resembles a human affects the child's social perception and propensity to interact. Too high a level of anthropomorphism may be overloading for some children, while too low a level may not arouse interest. What is known for sure is that the robot should in no way arouse anxiety and fear and create sensory overstimulation (Pennazio, 2019).
- Expressiveness: The robot's ability to express emotions and moods through visual, auditory and tactile signals is crucial to foster empathy and understanding of social interactions.
- Customisation: The possibility of customising the robot's physical appearance, voice and behaviour allows it to be adapted to the child's individual preferences, increasing motivation and engagement.
- Interactivity: The robot's ability to respond contingently to the child's actions is essential to create a dynamic and engaging interaction.
- Functionality: The robot should be equipped with sensors and actuators that allow it to interact with the environment and the child safely and effectively.
- Autonomy - Autonomous robots or robots that can take advantage of remote control are preferable. Increasing the robot's autonomy can make the experience smoother, improve child-robot interaction and ease the therapist/educator/researcher's control and supervision burden. In increasing the robot's autonomy, it is necessary to conduct a careful analysis of sensory information (gaze estimation, facial expression recognition, eye-tracking detection) and to take into account that increased robot autonomy corresponds to an increased possibility of generalisation of learned skills into human interactions.

Emerging evidence suggests that the preferences of children with autism towards social robots are not solely determined by the physical characteristics of the robot, but depend to a large extent on its behavioural capabilities and the nature of the interaction. Although some studies have shown a preference for robots with less pronounced human features, others have shown that the simplicity of robotic behaviour and the minimisation of superfluous physical details can facilitate interaction, regardless of the robot's outward appearance.

What degree of customisation must the robot have in order to be effective in promoting the sociality of the child with autism? The scientific literature (Pennazio, 2017) has highlighted the need to develop robots made up of modules (distinct body parts) that can be programmed to create motor sequences linked to the emission of a congruent emotional response with variable intensity. Such flexibility is crucial to avoid sensory overload in children with autism and to adapt to their specific needs. Furthermore, the importance of providing operators with intuitive tools to programme and personalise robot-child interactions was emphasised.

In this direction, Tennyson and collaborators proposed an interesting implementation of a fourth-generation robotic agent using inexpensive platforms such as Lego NXT and customised social scripts. Their results demonstrated the effectiveness of this solution in reducing stereotypies, improving attention and facilitating eye contact in children with autism. The authors also emphasised the importance of a modular and configurable design in terms of both hardware and software, in order to facilitate maintenance, reliability and customisation of the robot.

Huijnen et al. (2017) conducted an in-depth meta-analysis to identify the essential requirements a social robot must possess to be effective in educational and therapeutic interventions for autism. The authors highlighted a gap between the current characteristics of available robots and long-term therapeutic goals, using a mapping of goals to be achieved on an ICF-CY basis, such as self-care, independent living, preschool skills, emotional well-being and functioning in everyday reality.

3.3 Integration with Other Technologies. Combining Social Robotics with Other Assistive Technologies, Such as Virtual Reality and Augmented Reality

The interest of the scientific community has focused not only on the development of educational robotics, but also on the application of virtual reality in clinical rehabilitation for autism.

Virtual reality (VR) is a technology that, through the computer processing of images and sounds, generates simulated environments capable of deeply engaging the user, offering a sensory experience that mimics the perception of the real world or, conversely, fantastic worlds that cannot be experienced in conventional physical reality (Smutny, Babluch, &Foltynek, 2019). Despite the growing contemporary interest in virtual reality (VR), its roots lie in the past: the first prototypes of digital VR systems date back as far as 1966, with the aim of developing flight simulators for training military pilots.

As a therapeutic tool for autism, VR offers significant potential to improve patients' quality of life by fostering the development of fundamental skills for social interaction and, as Abu-Amara, Bensefia, Mohammad, & Tamimi (2021) argue, numerous benefits, including:

1. providing a controlled and safe environment;
2. providing an immersive environment, easily adaptable to the abilities of the individual with ASD;
3. providing the opportunity to emulate various everyday life skills in order to achieve autonomy;
4. provide training in a realistic environment; 5. Provide immediate and continuous feedback.

The application of virtual reality (VR) in autism treatments, like educational robotics, is the subject of an increasing amount of research and scientific publications. The study conducted by Halabi and collaborators (2017) at Qatar University developed a sophisticated interactive virtual reality (VR) system, consisting of a series of virtual scenarios, with the aim of stimulating and improving communication skills in children with autism spectrum disorder (ASD). According to the authors, the design of effective immersive environments requires the ability to elicit specific and predictable responses from users.

To facilitate social interaction, a virtual scenario simulating a typical classroom greeting was designed. The virtual character and surroundings were carefully crafted to resemble real situations as closely as possible and familiar to the users. The results of the study showed a significant improvement in the participants' communication skills, demonstrating that immersion in virtual reality facilitated more effective learning than using a simple screen.

Virtual reality (VR) is not limited to improving communication skills, but also finds application in enhancing more general social skills. Rosenfield et al. (2019) developed an immersive Serious Game, set in a fish market, that uses a VR visor and microphone to simulate everyday life experiences and improve the autonomy of individuals with autism. Following a similar approach, Adjorlu and colleagues (2017) employed VR systems to teach activities of daily living such as shopping or driving.

This modality allows individuals with ASD to acquire or reinforce skills in virtual contexts that simulate reality, offering a safe and controlled environment in which to experiment and learn through the trial-and-error method, without the potential negative consequences associated with real-life situations. (Rossi, Ciletti, Scarinci, & Toto, 2023).

4   Research Methodology

The contribution is declined through an exploratory investigation by means of a scoping review aimed at understanding whether and how social robots can be used to support communication with the autistic child, fostering attention, imitation and the implementation of new social behaviours.

The main questions that guided the literature search presented here were:

1. Can the use of robots improve attention and engagement of children with ASD, increase imitation and promote social and communicative interaction?
2. Can insights be gained from these technologies that can be used in the preparation of future intervention protocols?
3. Are robots more effective than other 'technological' therapies, such as video games or apps?

The literature search started in January 2024 and ended in March of the same year. A time span of 10 years (from 2014 to 2024) was considered and a number of keywords were identified (e.g. 'educational robotics', 'autism', 'social skills', 'prosocial behaviour', 'shared attention' 'communicative interaction') in order to ensure a broad exploration of the available databases.

A scoping review was conducted via the main academic databases (such as Scopus, Web of Science, and Google Scholar), including relevant articles, reports and conference proceedings.

The collected contributions were critically examined in order to outline an up-to-date overview of the use of robotics in the context of autism interventions. In particular, research investigating the use of robots to improve attention, imitation, and social and communication skills in children with Autism Spectrum Disorder (ASD) was reviewed in order to identify new therapeutic strategies in the design of future intervention protocols.

4.1 Literature Analysis

The search was conducted by directing the focus on children and young people with ASD of various ages and levels of severity and produced a total of 47 articles that were analysed in total.

It was decided to eliminate the contributions that did not meet the criteria sought: age of the participants, specific intervention on social skills, focus on autism, arriving at the selection of 24 contributions between articles, chapters, conference proceedings, subsequently subdivided, according to the topics covered, into 4 categories (social skills; physical characteristics of the interaction robot; triadic interaction; communication skills). The following table (Table 1) shows the list of selected studies, subdivided by year, author, journal and focus investigated.

Table 1. Summary table of results.

Author	Text	Magazine/Book/Proceedings	Year	Focus
Abu Amara et al	Robot and virtual reality- based intervention in autism: A comprehensive review	International Journal of Information Techmangy	2021	Social, communicative, emotional skill
Adjoriu et al	Daily living skills training in virtual reality to help children with autism spectrum disorder in a real shopping scenario	16th IEEE International Symposium on Mixed and Augmented Reality	2017	Everyday life skills
Barbato	Theory of mind and Autismo: intervention strategies to enhance quality of life in adults. Development of a theory of mind and its impairment	Phenomena Journal - Giornale Internazionale di Psicopatologia, Neuroscienze e Psicoterapia	2021	Theory of Mind for Understanding and Treating Autism

(continued)

Table 1. (*continued*)

Author	Text	Magazine/Book/Proceedings	Year	Focus
Belpaeme et al	Social robots for education: A review	Science robotics	2018	Students' cognitive and emotional learn
Bozzi et al	Interazione bambini-robot: riflessioni teoriche, risultati sperimentali, esperienze	Franco Angeli	2021	Creativity, communication and cooperation
Brignone et al	Intelligenza Artificiale e social robot: applicazioni nel sistema di riproduzione biopsichico	ENDOXA	2021	Development of interpersonal relationships, learning motivation and the construction of mental representations of the world
Campitiello et al	Emorobot: an opensource robot to promote the development of social skills in children with autism	Giornale Italiano di Educazione alla Salute, Sport e Didattica Inclusiva	2022	Social interaction
Cerdá et al	Augmented reality in intervention with people with autism spectrum disorder, protocol activities	International Conference on Education and New Developments	2020	Social interaction
Conti et al	Uso della robotica per stimolare l'imitazione nell'Autismo. Uno studio pilota	NEA-SCIENCE - Giornale Italiano di neuroscienze, psicologia e riabilitazione	2015	Body awareness and creativity
Grimaldi et al	I social robot, cosa sono, come utilizzarli nel settore dell'educazione	AGENDA DIGITALE EU	2020	Disciplinary and transversal competences
Halabi et al	Design of immersive virtual reality system to improve communication skills in individuals with autism	International Journal of Emerging Technologies in Learning	2017	Communication skills

(*continued*)

Table 1. (*continued*)

Author	Text	Magazine/Book/Proc eedings	Year	Focus
Hashim et al	Augmented reality mobile application for children with autism: stakeholders' acceptance and I thoughts	Arab World World English Journal	2021	Language skills
Huijnen et al	How to Implement Robots in Interventions for Children with Autism? A Co-Creation Study Involving People with Autism, Parents and Professionals	Journal of Autism and Developmental Disorders	2017	Interventions for Children with Autism
Ismail et al	Leveraging robotics research for children with autism: a review	International Journal of Social Robotics	2019	Robotic research
Pennazio	Social Robotic to Help Children with Autism in the Interaction Through Imitation	Research on Education and Media	2017	Social interactions
Pennazio	Robotica e sviluppo delle abilità sociali nell'autismo. Una review critica	Mondo digitale, rivista di cultura informatica	2019	Social interactions
Richardson et al	Robot enhanced therapy for children with autism (DREAM): A social model of autism	IEEE Technology and society magazine	2018	Social skills
Rosenfield	A virtual reality system for practicing convers skills for children with autism	Multimodal Technologies Interact	2019	Social interactions
Rossi et al	Apprendere attraverso il metaverso e la realtà immersiva: nuove prospettive inclusive	IUL Research	2023	Educational opportunities

(*continued*)

Table 1. (*continued*)

Author	Text	Magazine/Book/Proc eedings	Year	Focus
Scassellati et al	Improving social skills in children with ASD using a long-term, inhomesocial robot	Science Robotics	2018	Social skills
Smutny et al	A review of the virtual reality applications in education and training	20th International Carpathian Control Conference	2019	Educational opportunities
Tennyson et al	Accessible Robots for Improving Social Skills of Individuals with Autism	Journal of Artificial Intelligence and Soft Computing Research	2016	Social Skills
Toto et al	Per una cultura dell'inclusione	Progedit	2023	Social Skills
Wood et al	Developing kaspar: a humanoid robot for children with autism	International Journal of Social Robotics	2021	Robotic research

5 Conclusions

Meta-analyses conducted on the topic indicate a general trend of decreasing maladaptive behaviors and the development of prosocial behaviors, attributable to the development of imitative and joint attention skills (on interactive experiences mediated by social robotics devices indicate a trend of increasing prosocial behaviors, likely attributable to improved communication and attention sharing skills (Thill et al., 2012; Pennisi et al., 2016; Belpaeme et al., 2018).

It should be noted that the robotic device, in this perspective, is considered an assistive element that can facilitate both the sharing of attention with the educator and the generation of interactive experiences with the educator, in which the common object of attention is represented by the device (Scassellati et al., 2018). The relationship with the device, in other words, should be presented in the form of structured and prolonged training, always conducted under the supervision of the educator. In addition, the use of the robot also stimulates motivation, which further incentivizes the little ones to active participation and involvement.

The possibility of leading the child with autism toward the development of appropriate and, as far as possible, empathetic and flexible social behaviors depends primarily on the characteristics of the robot to be used. It is important to weigh the choice well, since the introduction of a robotic support in rehabilitation and/or educational settings is not alone sufficient to achieve the desired goal. In addition to detailed planning of activities (including preparation of appropriate scripts and observation protocols), it is essential that the robot have specific characteristics.

The natural tendency of autistic children to interact with humanoid robots raises a fundamental question: can these technologies offer new perspectives for the development of intervention protocols? The answer is positive. Interaction with another human being may, in fact, provide too many stimuli that are difficult for individuals diagnosed with autism to interpret. Designing collaborative activities between child and robot allows the therapist to explore new immersive and engaging intervention techniques through which the child can experience firsthand and with less tension. Importantly, compared with other technological therapies such as video games or apps, robots offer numerous advantages in autism therapy. Robots can provide more physical and tangible interaction than video games or apps and, therefore, can be more engaging for children with ASD. In addition, robots can be customized to fit the specific needs of the child, providing a high therapeutic experience.

Several variables, both personal and context-related, can influence how the person and caregiver interact during a treatment session with the robot and, consequently, the effectiveness of the treatment itself. It is crucial to initially assess the attitude and predisposition of the user and caregivers toward these tools, as well as to adequately inform them about the advantages and limitations of using these new tools.

Despite the advantages that Socially Intelligent Robots seem to offer and the existence of numerous scientific studies that have tested and verified their applicability in the field of inclusive education, they are still not widely used and have a high cost. Most of the research reviewed has focused mainly on therapy and rehabilitation situations. However, it would be advantageous to extend these interventions to the educational field as well, such as in schools, in order to facilitate the process of transfer and generalization.

In the future, a multidisciplinary approach will be needed in which computer scientists, psychologists, teachers and educators can collaborate in the development, through robots, of new therapeutic expedients to be applied to the cognitive abilities of autistic individuals for effective rehabilitation.

References

Abu Amara, F., Bensefia, A., Mohammad, H., Tamimi, H.: Robot and virtual reality- based intervention in autism: a comprehensive review. Int. J. Inf. Tech. 13(5), 1879–1891 (2021)

Adjoriu, A., Hoeg, E., Mangano, L., Serafin, S.: Daily living skills training in virtual reality to help children with autism spectrum disorder in a real shopping scenario. 16th IEEE International Symposium on Mixed and Augmented Reality (ISMAR-A- djunct), pp. 294–302 (2017)

Barbato, L.: Teoria della mente e Autismo: strategie di intervento per migliorare la qualità di vita nell'età adulta. Sviluppo della teoria della mente ed arresto evolutivo. Phenomena Journal - Giornale Internazionale di Psicopatologia, Neuroscienze e Psicoterapia 3(2), 68–80 (2021)

Belpaeme, T., Kennedy, J., Ramachandran, A., Scassellati, B., Tanaka, F.: Social robots for education: a review, Sci. Robot. 3(21), eaat5954 (2018)

Bozzi, G., Zecca, L., Datteri, E.: Interazione bambini-robot: riflessioni teoriche, risultati sperimentali, esperienze. Franco Angeli, Milano (2021)

Brignone, S., Grimaldi, R., Palmieri, S.: Intelligenza Artificiale e social robot: applicazioni nel sistema di riproduzione biopsichico. ENDOXA 34, 35–40 (2021)

Campitiello, L., Todino, M. D., Di Tore, P.A., Di Tore, S.: Emorobot: an opensource robot to promote the development of social skills in children with autism. Giornale Italiano di Educazione alla Salute, Sport e Didattica Inclusiva, 6(1) (2022)

Cerdá, A.G., Albaladejo, E.G., Vázquez, E.P., Lledó, G., Carreres, A., Lledó, A.L.: Augmented reality in intervention with people with autism spectrum disorder, protocol activities. In International Conference on Education and New Developments (2020)

Conti, D., Di Nuovo, S., Buono, S., Trubia, G., Di Nuovo, A.: Uso della robotica per stimolare l'imitazione nell'Autismo. Uno studio pilota. NEA-SCIENCE - Giornale Italiano di neuroscienze, psicologia e riabilitazione 1(5), 91–98) (2015)

Grimaldi, R., Palmieri, S.: I social robot, cosa sono, come utilizzarli nel settore dell'educazione. AGENDA DIGITALE EU, pp. 1–6 (2020)

Halabi, O., El-Seoud, S.A., Alja'am, J., Alpona, H., Al-Hemadi, M., Al-Hassan, D.: Design of immersive virtual reality system to improve communication skills in individuals with autism. Int. J. Emerg. Technol. Learn. (IJET) 12(5), 5064 (2017)

Hashim, H.U., Yunus, M.M., Norman, H.: Augmented reality mobile application for children with autism: stakeholders' acceptance and I thoughts. Arab World World English J. 12(4), 132–141 (2021)

Huijnen, C.A.G.J., Lexis, M.A.S., Jansens, R., De Witte, L.P.: How to implement robots in interventions for children with autism? A co-creation study involving people with autism, parents and professionals. J. Autism Dev. Disord. 47(10), 3079–3096 (2017)

Hodges, H., Fealko, C., Soares, N.: Autism spectrum disorder: definition, epidemiology, causes, and clinical evaluation. Transl. Pediatr. 9(Suppl. 1), S55 (2020)

Ismail, L.I., Verhoeven, T., Dambre, J., Wyffels, F.: Leveraging robotics research for children with autism: a review. Int. J. Soc. Robot. 11, 389–410 (2019)

Pennazio, V.: Social robotic to help children with autism in the interaction through imitation. REM 9, 10–16 (2017)

Pennazio, V.: Robotica e sviluppo delle abilità sociali nell'autismo. Una review critica. Mondo digitale, rivista di cultura informatica (2019)

Richardson, K., et al.: Robot enhanced therapy for children with autism (DREAM): a social model of autism. IEEE Technol. Soc. Mag. 37(1), 30–39 (2018)

Rosenfield, N.S., Lamkin, K., Re, J., Day, K., Boyd, L., Linstead, E.: A virtual reality system for practicing convers skills for children with autism. Multimodal Technol. Interact 3, 28 (2019)

Rossi, M., Ciletti, M., Scarinci, A., Toto, G.A.: Apprendere attraverso il metaverso e la realtà immersiva: nuove prospettive inclusive. IUL Research 4(7), 176 (2023)

Scassellati, B., et al.: Improving social skills in children with ASD using a long-term, inhomesocial robot. Sci. Robot. 3, eaat7544 (2018)

Smutny, P., Babiuch, M., Foltynek, P.: A review of the virtual reality applications in education and training. In: 2019 20th International Carpathian Control Conference (ICCC), pp. 1–4. IEEE (2019)

Tennyson, M., Kuester, D.A., Casteel, J., Nikolopoulos, C.: Accessible robots for improving social skills of individuals with autism. J. Artif. Intell. Soft Comput. Res. 6(4), 21–47 (2016)

Toto, G. A., Traetta, L.: Per una cultura dell'inclusione. Progedit Bari (2023)

Wood, L.J., Zaraki, A., Robins, B., Dautenhahn, K.: Developing kaspar: a humanoid robot for children with autism. Int. J. Soc. Robot. 13, 491–508 (2021)

The Critical Role of AI in Teachers' Training

Alessandro Monchietto[1]([⊠]) and Luca Ballestra Caffaratti[2]

[1] University of Turin, Via Sant'Ottavio 20, 10124 Turin, Italy
alessandro.monchietto@unito.it
[2] University of Valencia, Plaça de Cisneros, 446003 Valencia, Spain
lubacaf@alumni.uv.es

Abstract. The integration of Artificial Intelligence (AI) into education systems marks shift in learning and teaching methods, fostering a paradigm shift towards more personalized and inclusive learning environments. Our study examines the integration of AI in two teacher training (TT) initiatives: the "Expert in the Processes of Inclusive Education" programme, designed for the training of trainers for new teachers, and the "Specialisation Course in Special Educational Needs", aimed at preparing new support teachers. The curricula of both courses include a section on new learning technologies in which training on AI was offered.

The article illustrates the potential of AI to personalise learning pathways, enhance language assessments and modify texts to improve comprehension and accessibility for students with different abilities. Despite the opportunities, the integration of AI in education also brings challenges. The authors take a critical look at potential risks, such as AI-induced distortions of reality perception, and emphasise the need to integrate AI into educational practise in a pedagogically meaningful way and to promote a critical and responsible approach to AI among educators.

Finally, the authors propose a framework for the effective integration of AI into educational practise and highlights the central role of TT in maximising the benefits of AI and minimising its drawbacks. This framework is intended to contribute to the ongoing discourse on AIED and emphasise the need for a comprehensive understanding of the impact of AI on the educational ecosystem.

Keywords: Artificial Intelligence · School Inclusion · Teacher Training

1 Introduction

The rapid technological advances of recent years have profoundly influenced educational practices, with Artificial Intelligence (AI) emerging as a pivotal tool in the transformation of learning environments. The integration of AI into education systems is not just an enhancement of traditional methods, but rather a paradigm shift towards more personalized, accessible and inclusive learning pathways. As AI-driven tools are increasingly used, they have the potential to reshape teacher-student interactions and promote individualised learning experiences that meet the diverse needs of students (Holmes et al., 2019). This shift is particularly important in the context of inclusive education, where

G. A. Toto (Ed.): ICS exchange 2024, CCIS 2521, pp. 387–398, 2025.
https://doi.org/10.1007/978-3-032-03021-4_28

AI can act as a mediator to bridge gaps in accessibility and learning support for students with disabilities or special educational needs (SEN) (Reiss, 2021). In the context of teacher training, it is of paramount importance to equip teachers with the knowledge and skills they need to use AI effectively as a pedagogical tool. The increasing complexity of educational environments, driven by diversity in classrooms, requires a sophisticated understanding of how AI can be integrated to support both teaching and learning. This paper examines two specific teacher training (TT) initiatives that focus on preparing trainers and new educators to use AI in inclusive education. These initiatives, the "Expert in the Processes of Inclusive Education" Programme (EPIE) and the "Specialisation Course in Special Educational Needs" (CSA), provide valuable insights into the practical application of AI in educational contexts. By exploring these programmes, we aim to highlight the role of AI in personalising educational experiences, enhancing language assessments and modifying teaching materials to improve comprehension for students with different abilities.

However, the integration of AI into education is not without its challenges. While AI offers opportunities for more inclusive education, it also presents risks that need to be critically examined. These include concerns about algorithmic bias, the potential distortion of reality by AI-generated content and the ethical implications of relying on machine-driven systems in human-centred learning environments (Ninaus & Sailer, 2022). This paper proposes a framework for the effective integration of AI into classroom practise, focusing on the central role of teacher education in maximising the benefits of AI and mitigating its drawbacks.

In the following sections, we will explore how AI can be used as a facilitator for inclusive education. We discuss its practical applications, the challenges involved and the pedagogical strategies required for ethical and effective use. Ultimately, we aim to contribute to the ongoing discourse on Artificial Intelligence in Education (AIED) and emphasise the need for comprehensive teacher training programmes that prepare educators to navigate this rapidly evolving environment.

2 Theoretical Framework

From a pedagogical standpoint, the ability of AI to personalise teaching is one of its most important contributions. As highlighted in recent UNESCO reports (2019, 2021, 2024), AI technologies offer significant opportunities to promote inclusive and equitable education: AI's capacity to personalise learning experiences can help ensure that students from different backgrounds – whether due to socio-economic status, cultural differences or learning abilities – receive the support they need to succeed.

AI systems can help provide customised learning pathways that adapt to the individual student's abilities and provide differentiated instruction based on real-time data analysis. This capability is particularly important for students with disabilities or learning difficulties, where AI can act as an assistive technology adapting content and offering scaffolding to support autonomous learning. Recent studies have highlighted the effectiveness of AI-driven interventions in improving students' self-regulation, enhancing their ability to manage their learning processes independently (Pogorskiy & Beckmann,

2023). AI tools integrated into Learning Management Systems (LMS) can provide continuous feedback on student performance, allowing teachers to monitor progress and adjust teaching strategies accordingly (Chih-Yuan Sun et al., 2023).

AI technologies can help adapt teaching materials to the specific needs of students with learning difficulties, such as dyslexia, by providing real-time feedback on writing tasks or simplifying texts to improve comprehension (Zhai *et al.*, 2023). Similarly, AI applications can support students from different cultural backgrounds by creating personalised learning paths tailored to their linguistic and cultural contexts (Salas-Pilco et al., 2022). In addition, AI-driven platforms can provide real-time feedback, allowing students to self-regulate their learning and progress based on individualised feedback loops (Pogorskiy & Beckmann, 2023). In this sense, AI serves as an educational mediator, enabling more responsive and accessible learning experiences.

For students with autism spectrum disorder (ASD), AI technologies offer additional benefits by helping to monitor classroom interactions and provide individualised support based on each student's behaviour and communication patterns (Smith et al., 2023). AI can help create structured learning environments that are often beneficial for students with autism by providing clear routines and predictable interactions that reduce anxiety and improve concentration.

The potential of AI for personalised learning also extends to its use in adaptive learning systems that adjust content and learning pace based on a student's real-time performance. These systems are already helping students improve their self-regulation skills by providing scaffolding to help them manage their learning independently (Pogorskiy & Beckmann, 2023). While these technologies can significantly increase motivation and engagement, they also raise the question of how to maintain students' agency. Bandura's (2006) concept of agency, which refers to a person's ability to act independently, plays a central role in this discussion. While AI systems can provide essential support, they must not undermine the development of students' decision-making and problem-solving skills. Brod et al. (2023) have identified four levels of control in educational environments where AI is used: full control by the student, shared control between the student and the AI, full control by the teacher, and shared control between the teacher and the AI. These distinctions emphasise the need to strike a balance between the role of AI as a facilitator and the need to maintain human supervision and control over the learning process.

Although AI is promising, it also poses a major challenge, particularly in terms of ethics, pedagogical integration and the necessary training for teachers. As recognised in the Artificial Intelligence Act (European Parliament, 2023), careful regulation is needed to prevent the misuse of AI and avoid the risk of exacerbating existing inequalities in education (Flores-Vivar & García-Peñalvo, 2023). A growing body of literature emphasises that while AI systems are powerful, they are not inherently neutral. They reflect the data on which they have been trained, and if these data sets reflect societal biases, AI systems may unintentionally perpetuate inequalities (Islam, 2024). Further-more, the statistical and probabilistic nature of algorithmic processing that relies on data available online can create errors and cause students to develop a distorted view of reality (Watanabe, 2023). The lack of transparency of these algorithms can make decision-making processes opaque and increase the risk of biases that may reinforce pre-existing inequalities and promote false perceptions of the world. The introduction of AI systems into classrooms brings with it concerns about algorithmic bias, privilege and the digital divide. AI models are only as objective as the data on which they are trained. Therefore, teachers need to be trained not only in the technical application of AI, but also in the critical evaluation of its outcomes to ensure that AI applications are used in education in a fair, transparent and inclusive way.

3   Generative AI: A Technological and Social Revolution

At this point, it is crucial to distinguish between "Strong AI" and "Weak AI" as understanding this difference informs our approach to integrating AI into education. "Strong AI", or Artificial General Intelligence (AGI), refers to AI systems that possess the full range of human cognitive abilities, including consciousness and self-awareness (Searle, 1990). Despite significant technological advances, achieving true AGI remains a distant goal. The potential of the human mind in terms of flexibility and complexity – as emphasised in the psycho-pedagogical tradition of the latter part of the 20th century (Gardner, 1983; Sternberg, 1988; Goleman, 1996) – is still unmatched by AI devices.

In contrast, "Weak AI" refers to systems that use algorithms and statistical models to simulate human outcomes in specific tasks such as object recognition, automatic text completion and data sorting. Most of the AI devices recently launched on the market are based on Weak AI systems: so-called "Generative AI" is distinguished by its ability to produce content based on user input. This distinction is crucial when integrating AI into educational practise, as it underscores the need for educators to critically engage with AI tools and ensure that these technologies serve as supporting tools rather than substitutes for human intelligence and interaction.

The development and use of Generative AI systems has seen exponential growth, particularly with the release of publicly available tools such as ChatGPT, which use Large Language Models (LLMs) to make natural language processing (NLP) accessible to a mass audience. The introduction of these systems has sparked widespread public debate and prompted several technology companies to launch their own AI-powered tools, such as Microsoft's Copilot and Google's Gemini (Kamalov et al., 2023). The proliferation of these technologies has accelerated human-computer interaction in various areas of life— from education to healthcare, and from personal assistance to professional tasks (Weber-Guskar, 2021). As more users interact with these AI systems, the feedback generated helps refine and improve the underlying models, ensuring continuous enhancement of their performance.

The rapid progress of AI technologies must be viewed within the broader context of technological development over the last three decades. From the emergence of the World Wide Web in the early 1990s to the widespread adoption of smartphones and social networks in the 2000s, these innovations have gradually redefined the digital landscape. The release of AI tools as ChatGPT, Gemini etc. represents the most recent phase of this transformation, characterised by significant changes in the way individuals and institutions interact with technology. A key milestone in this journey was the introduction of algorithms in 2009 that enabled personalised profiling and indexing of search results, contributing to the commercialisation and data extraction of modern digital services (Zuboff, 2019; Casilli, 2019). These algorithms, now embedded in AI tools such as Google Gemini, drive user engagement through targeted notifications and adaptive systems, further solidifying the use of AI in everyday life.

Legal concerns regarding privacy and data governance have increasingly come to the fore as these systems collect large amounts of personal information, often without clear safeguards (Radanliev *et al.*, 2023). The socio-economic impact of AI is also far-reaching: while new employment opportunities are being created in areas related to AI development and management, there are legitimate concerns that automation could render certain human tasks redundant (Capraro et al., 2024). From an ethical perspective, the opaque nature of AI decision-making processes raises questions about the accountability and transparency of algorithms, especially as biases in AI outcomes can perpetuate and even exacerbate existing inequalities (Islam, 2024). This emphasises the importance of a critical and responsible approach to the integration of AI into education and other areas.

Furthermore, from a psychological perspective, the increasing reliance on AI-based systems such as virtual assistants may influence human decision-making and affect relationship dynamics. Research has pointed to potential changes in human behaviour due to regular interaction with AI, including changes in decision-making autonomy and the emergence of new behavioural patterns (Ojha, 2024). These changes require a cautious and balanced approach to the integration of AI, ensuring that while the technology advances, it is in line with ethical principles and values.

4 The Importance of Teacher Training in AI Integration

One of the biggest challenges in introducing AI in education is the limited knowledge and skills of educators regarding how to use these technologies effectively. The adoption of AI in Educational Technology (EdTech) has largely been driven by a technical approach that focuses on the development of predictive models, often without sufficient consideration of psycho-pedagogical theories (Zawacki-Richter et al., 2019). The emphasis on technical functionality rather than student-centred learning has raised concerns about the long-term impact of AI on education.

As Hrastinski et al. (2019) note, most teachers lack the necessary expertise to use AI systems in a pedagogically meaningful way. They often struggle with the technical complexity of AI and are unsure how to integrate it into their teaching practise in a meaningful way. This gap is particularly evident in teacher education, where AI-related training is still scarce, especially in initial teacher training. The importance of equipping teachers with the necessary skills to use AI effectively cannot be overstated, as teachers' attitudes towards AI are a crucial factor in its pedagogical impact (Tzu-Chi Yang & Jian-Hua Chen, 2023). Without proper training, there is a risk that AI tools will be underutilised or misapplied, leading to superficial benefits rather than real improvement in student learning.

To address these challenges, UNESCO has developed the AI Competency Framework for Teachers (AI CFT), which provides a structured approach to building teacher capacity for the use of AI in education (UNESCO, 2024). The framework is divided into three sequential phases – acquisition, consolidation and building – each focusing on different stages of AI competency development. It includes five key aspects: a human-centred mindset, AI ethics, the foundations and applications of AI, AI pedagogy and

AI for professional development. At the "creation" level, the framework encourages teachers to actively contribute to the development of ethical guidelines and principles for the use of AI in education. This includes promoting critical discussions about the social and ethical implications of AI in the classroom and ensuring that AI tools are used to enhance, rather than detract from, educational equity. Emphasising a reflective and ethical approach will not only prepare educators to use AI, but also to take a leadership role in its responsible implementation. With the right training, teachers can transform AI from a mere tool into a means of promoting educational equity and deeper learning.

5   Teacher Training Initiatives: EPIE and CSA Programs

The increasing use of AI in education requires a comprehensive rethink of how teachers are trained to effectively incorporate these tools into their classrooms. In this context, the two initiatives studied – the "Expert in the Processes of Inclusive Education" Programme (EPIE) and the "Specialisation Course in Special Educational Needs" (CSA) – provide valuable models for how AI can be integrated into teacher training (TT) with the aim of promoting inclusive educational practises. This section looks at the specific structure, aims and content of these programmes and offers insights into how AI has been integrated into the curricula and the impact it has had on participants.

The CSA is a key initiative aimed at equipping future support teachers with the knowledge and skills required to work with students with disabilities and learning difficulties. At the heart of the programme's philosophy is the idea that inclusive education is not just about providing additional support to students with disabilities, but about transforming the entire learning environment to meet the diverse needs of all students. One of the most important components of this training programme is the emphasis on teaching and communication technologies (ICT) labs. A key component of the labs is the integration of new learning technologies, that are introduced as mediators to support inclusive education. In addition, participants in the CSA programme are required to put the knowledge and skills acquired in the ICT labs into practise in a 150-h internship in schools. This practical component is essential for the development of an integrative approach to educational activities involving information and communication technologies (ICT). Guided by the principles of Universal Design for Learning (UDL; CAST, 2018) within the conceptual framework of inclusive pedagogy, participants design, implement, experiment and share multimedia projects tailored to the needs and characteristics of their professional environment during the internship. This hands-on experience ensures that the integration of AI and new technologies is not only theoretical, but also applied in real educational environments to enhance future teachers' ability to promote inclusive practises through technology.

The second programme, EPIE, focuses on the training of trainers and was developed in response to the need to promote the development of the competences of teachers with a higher education qualification in special educational needs by improving the competences of their trainers, especially those responsible for the laboratory activities of the specialisation courses (Di Masi et al., 2023). The didactical structure of the courses is founded on a Competency-based education and training approach (Burke, 2005). The EPIE pathway consists of a total of 100 h of blended training, divided into general and workshop parts, where trainees work together to develop a shared culture and exchange good practices. This initiative, led by the Department of Philosophy and Education with the support of the Piedmont Region, is part of a broader effort to promote an inclusive educational culture throughout the region. The course was designed not only to provide technical training, but also to train educators to become true "ambassadors" of inclusive values and able to spread these principles throughout the education system.

One of the most important aspects of these training programmes is the focus on teacher agency in the use of AI. Teachers are not expected to passively rely on AI tools, but to use them as assistive technologies that enhance their ability to provide individualised support to students. This approach is in line with recent research findings that show different levels of action in the interaction between students, teachers and AI systems (Brod et al., 2023). Teachers are trained to manage these different levels of control – from full control by the teacher to shared control by the teacher and AI – to ensure that the AI tools support, rather than replace, human decision-making. This dynamic interaction between human action and AI is particularly important when working with students with special needs, as individualised and flexible teaching strategies are essential for overcoming the particular challenges of these students.

The success of these training programs relies on the development of practical guidelines to support teachers in their professional practices. These guidelines are essential for helping educators navigate complex classroom environments and apply instructional strategies that are tailored to the specific needs of their students.

6 Collaborative Workshops and the Development of the Decalogue

To address the specific challenges of AI integration in education, the University of Turin organised a series of workshops in the summer of 2023 as part of the third edition of the EPIE programme. These workshops aimed to promote joint reflections on the use of AI in teacher training, especially in the context of inclusive education. The discussions were characterized by a horizontal, collaborative approach, with both trainers and participants actively contributing to the exchange of ideas and practices.

One of the most notable outcomes of the EPIE programme was the development of a Decalogue of principles for the intentional integration of AI in inclusive education (Atzei et al., 2023). This framework, developed in collaboration between educators and participants, is intended to guide future teachers in the responsible use of AI to promote equitable, accessible and personalised learning experiences for all students.

The 10 principles that emerged from the workshops, which were conducted in collaboration with lecturers from the University of Turin's ICT Lab, emphasise several key elements. These include the need for teachers to explore a wide range of AI applications beyond mainstream tools such as ChatGPT and to ensure that the AI tools selected align with the specific educational objectives of the classroom. The Decalogue also highlights the importance of teachers retaining control of the teaching process while using AI to automate routine tasks so that they can focus on more complex, cognitive and creative activities. Other principles address the importance of reviewing AI outcomes, managing the entire process of AI integration and ensuring that AI-generated content meets pedagogical objectives. The principles also emphasise the importance of critically evaluating AI outcomes and ensuring that teachers have the expertise to verify, refine and validate AI-generated content to avoid bias or misinterpretation. Teachers are advised to maintain control over the entire process of AI integration, from prompt creation to output validation, to ensure that the technology enhances learning outcomes without jeopardising pedagogical integrity.

In addition, the EPIE Lab has emphasised the dynamic nature of AI outputs and encouraged teachers to be aware that AI-generated materials may change over time as the underlying models evolve. This requires ongoing teacher involvement in validating and refining AI outputs to ensure they remain pedagogically relevant and accurate. Participants also discussed the importance of developing school policies that govern the use of AI and address issues such as choice of device, licencing and costs to ensure that the benefits of AI are evenly distributed across educational institutions.

The EPIE approach to integrating AI culminated in several practical experiments conducted during the 2023–2024 academic year, consolidating the theoretical-practical approach developed at CSA of Turin. For example, AI was used to support the creation of personalised learning materials, including customised texts and interactive images tailored to the individual needs of students. The use of AI for text manipulation, such as controlled writing and storytelling, proved particularly effective in creating content that can be customised for students with different abilities. Similarly, AI-generated images proved useful to visually illustrate learning contexts, supporting interactive teaching strategies. These AI-generated materials were then incorporated into wider educational strategies via platforms such as Padlet and Moodle, further enhancing the overall accessibility of the learning process.

However, these experiments also revealed some limitations of AI tools, particularly in tasks requiring a deep understanding of theoretical knowledge. For example, while AIgenerated graphical representations of knowledge were useful, they often fell short of the precision and conceptual depth that can be achieved using traditional methods. This highlights a key point from the EPIE lab's findings: while AI can support and enhance certain aspects of teaching, it cannot completely replace the expertise and judgement of teachers. The human element remains crucial in ensuring that AI-driven tools are pedagogically effective and align with the overall goals of inclusive education.

7 Conclusion

The integration of AI into inclusive education, as explored in the EPIE initiative and the CSA labs at the University of Turin, represents both a significant opportunity and a complex challenge for modern education systems. The experiences described in this chapter illustrate the transformative potential of AI in supporting personalised, accessible and more equitable learning environments.

One of the key findings is the importance of teacher agency in the use of AI. The practical experience gained in the EPIE programme underlines the importance of human supervision, especially in the validation of AI-generated results. While AI can generate content, such as customised learning materials, these tools often need to be refined and contextualised by teachers to ensure they meet pedagogical standards and learning objectives. The complementary role of AI allows teachers to free up valuable time and resources to focus on more important pedagogical aspects.

The discussions and practical experiments conducted at EPIE also emphasised the dynamic nature of AI technologies. The evolving outputs of AI models require the continuous involvement of teachers, who must constantly evaluate and adapt the content generated by AI to ensure its relevance and accuracy. This emphasises the importance of developing not only technical skills but also critical thinking and evaluation skills in teachers. Teachers must not only be empowered to use AI, but also to question its outcomes, challenge its assumptions and use their expertise to ensure that AI tools support meaningful learning experiences.

One of the most notable outcomes of the CSA programme was the successful implementation of AI-driven tools and technologies in the classroom during the internships that participants completed. For example, participants used chatbots such as Google Gemini and specialised AI tools for text simplification such as Diffit for text manipulation and storytelling. Image creation tools such as DALL-E and Midjourney were also used to support the development of visual aids. These internships provided the future support teachers the opportunity to apply the theoretical knowledge gained in the ICT labs to real-life teaching scenarios.

The projects designed and implemented by the participants – such as adaptive learning materials and multimedia tools customised for students with disabilities – showed significant progress in improving the inclusivity of educational practises. For example, AI tools were used to personalise teaching content to meet the different needs of students with learning difficulties and provide more individualised support. In addition, the projects developed during the internships were not only focused on immediate classroom needs, but also aimed to contribute to long-term inclusive practises. By integrating AI into personalised learning pathways and support systems, participants have shown that AI can play a crucial role in reducing educational barriers for students with disabilities. However, they also emphasised the need for continuous professional development and reflective practise among educators.

As highlighted by Brauner et al. (2023), AI has proven particularly effective in handling mechanical and repetitive tasks, such as formatting standard documents and creating data tables. This capability enables teachers to save time on low-value, time-consuming activities. By automating these processes, teachers can spend more time on the creative, relational and strategic aspects of teaching, such as designing personalised learning experiences, fostering deeper interactions with students and developing innovative teaching materials. This allows teachers to invest more in the emotional and intellectual development of their students, which improves the overall quality of education. However, it is important to remember that AI should be seen as a complementary tool in the educational process and not as a replacement for human thought and judgement. The true value of AI lies in its ability to support teachers in the routine aspects of their work and allow them to focus on tasks that require human creativity, empathy and critical thinking.

As the field of education evolves alongside advances in AI technology, it is crucial to develop comprehensive training programmes for teachers that not only equip them with the technical skills to use AI, but also promote a critical and ethical approach to its integration. The emphasis on inclusive, student-centred learning in both the EPIE and CSA programmes, reinforced by the integration of AI, serves as a model for how

AI can be used effectively to support diverse learners, particularly those with special educational needs. In summary, while AI offers transformative potential for inclusive education, its success is clearly dependent on the skills and expertise of educators. The frameworks of the EPIE and CSA programmes provide a valuable roadmap for navigating the complexities of AI in education and ensuring that the technology promotes, rather than undermines, core values of equity and accessibility. As AI evolves, the pedagogical strategies and ethical frameworks that guide its use must also be adapted to ensure that its application remains focused on improving educational outcomes and supporting the diverse needs of students.

Acknowledgments. This study was supported by the Region of Piedmont in collaboration with the Department of Philosophy and Education at the University of Turin. The authors wish to thank all participants of the EPIE and CSA programs for their valuable contributions. The authors would also like to extend a special thanks to Senior Professor Marco Guastavigna for his decade-long dedication to the specialization courses on educational support for students with disabilities at the University of Turin. His invaluable contributions and commitment have significantly enriched the training and development of educators in the field of inclusive education.

The article was jointly designed by the two authors who edited the following paragraphs: Luca Ballestra Caffaratti paragraphs 1, 2 and 3, Alessandro Monchietto paragraphs 4, 5 and 6; the conclusions are the result of a collaborative effort.

Disclosure of Interests. The authors have no competing interests to declare that are relevant to the content of this article.

References

Atzei, A., et al.: Impostare percorsi di formazione di insegnanti sull'assistenza artificiale alla mediazione didattica. Loescher Editore (2023). https://laricerca.loescher.it/impostare-percorsi-di-formazione-di-insegnanti-sullassist-enza-artificiale-alla-mediazione-didattica/

Bandura, A.: Toward a psychology of human agency. Perspect. Psychol. Sci. 1(2), 164–180 (2006)

Brauner, P., Hick, A., Philipsen, R., Ziefle, M.: What does the public think about artificial intelligence? A criticality map to understand bias in the public perception of AI. Front. Comput. Sci. 5, 1113903 (2023). https://doi.org/10.3389/fcomp.2023.1113903

Brod, G., Kucirkova, N., Shepherd, J., Jolles, D., Molenaar, I.: Agency in educational technology: interdisciplinary perspectives and implications for learning design. Educ. Psychol. Rev. 35(25) (2023). https://doi.org/10.1007/s10648-023-09749-x

Burke, J. (ed.): Competence Based Education and Training. Taylor & Francis, Bristol (2005)

Capraro, V., et al.: The impact of generative artificial intelligence on socioeconomic inequalities and policymaking. PNAS Nexus 3(6), 191 (2024). https://doi.org/10.1093/pnasnexus/pgae191

Casilli, A.: En attendant les robots: Enquête sur le travail du clic. Seuil, Paris (2019)

CAST: Universal design for learning guidelines version 2.2 (2018). http://udlguide-lines.cast.org

Chih-Yuan Sun, J., Tsai, H.-E., Cheng, W.K.R.: Effects of integrating an open learner model with AI-enabled visualization on students' self-regulation strategies usage and behavioural patterns in an online research ethics course. Comput. Educ. Artif. Intell. 4, 100120 (2023). https://doi.org/10.1016/j.caeai.2022.100120

Di Masi, D., Seira Ozino, M., Monchietto, A., Berretta, C.: Dal filo al tessuto: Trame e orditi del tirocinio nella formazione del docente inclusivo. In: Coggi, C., Bellacicco, R. (eds.) Per l'inclusione, pp. 198–212. FrancoAngeli, Milan (2023)

European parliament: Artificial Intelligence Act: Deal on comprehensive rules for trustworthy AI (2023). https://www.euro-parl.europa.eu/news/en/press-room/20231206IPR15699/art ificial-intelligence-act-deal-on-comprehensive-rules-for-trustworthy-ai

Flores-Vivar, J.-M., García-Peñalvo, F.-J.: Reflections on the ethics, potential, and challenges of artificial intelligence in the framework of quality education (SDG4). Comunicar **30**(74), 35–44 (2023). https://doi.org/10.3916/C74-2023-03

Gardner, H.: Frames of Mind: The Theory of Multiple Intelligences. Basic Books, New York (1983)

Goleman, D.: Emotional Intelligence: Why It Can Matter More Than IQ. Bantam Books, New York (1995)

Holmes, W., Bialik, M., Fadel, C.: Artificial Intelligence in Education: Promises and Implications for Teaching and Learning. Center for Curriculum Redesign, Boston (2019)

Hrastinski, S., Olofsson, A.D., Arkenback, C.: Critical imaginaries and reflections on artificial intelligence and robots in Postdigital K-12 education. Postdigital Sci. Educ. **1**, 427–445 (2019). https://doi.org/10.1007/s42438-019-00046-x

Islam, M.: Ethical considerations in AI: navigating the complexities of bias and accountability. J. Artif. Intell. General Sci. **3**(1), 2–30 (2024). https://doi.org/10.60087/jaigs.v3i1.62

Kamalov, F., Santandreu Calonge, D., Gurrib, I.: New era of artificial intelligence in education: towards a sustainable multifaceted revolution. Sustainability **15**, 12451 (2023). https://doi.org/10.3390/su151612451

Ninaus, M., Sailer, M.: Closing the loop: the human role in artificial intelligence for education. Front. Psychol. **13**, 956798 (2022). https://doi.org/10.3389/fpsyg.2022.956798

Ojha, A.K.: Psychological impact of AI: Understanding human responses and adaptations. J. Artif. Intell. Mach. Learn. Neural Netw. **4**(2), 48–54 (2024). https://doi.org/10.55529/jaimlnn. 42.48.54

Pogorskiy, E., Beckmann, J.F.: From procrastination to engagement? An experimental exploration of the effects of an adaptive virtual assistant on self-regulation in online learning. Comput. Educ. Artif. Intell. **4**, 100111 (2023). https://doi.org/10.1016/j.caeai.2022.100111

Radanliev, P., De Roure, D., Novitzky, P., Sluganovic, I.: Accessibility and inclusiveness of new information and communication technologies for disabled users and content creators in the metaverse. Disabil. Rehabil. Assist. Technol. (2023). https://doi.org/10.48550/arXiv.2308. 01925

Reiss, M. J.: The use of AI in education: practicalities and ethical considerations. London Rev. Educ. **19**(1), 5 (2021). https://doi.org/10.14324/LRE.19.1.05

Salas-Pilco, S. Z., Xiao, K., Oshima, J.: Artificial intelligence and new technologies in inclusive education for minority students: a systematic review. Sustainability **14**(13572) (2022). https://doi.org/10.3390/su142013572

Searle, J.R.: Is the brain's mind a computer program? Sci. Am. **262**(1), 25–31 (1990)

Smith, E.M., Graham, D., Morgan, C., MacLachlan, M.: Artificial intelligence and assistive technology: risks, rewards, challenges, and opportunities. Assist. Technol. **35**(5), 375–377 (2023). https://doi.org/10.1080/10400435.2023.2259247

Sternberg, R.J.: Beyond IQ: A Triarchic Theory of Human Intelligence. Cambridge University Press, New York (1985)

Sun, J.C.-Y., Tsai, H.-E., Cheng, W.K.R.: Effects of integrating an open learner model with AI-enabled visualization on students' self-regulation strategies usage and behavioural patterns in an online research ethics course. Comput. Educ. Artif. Intell. **4**, 100120 (2023). https://doi.org/ 10.1016/j.caeai.2022.100120

Yang, T.-C., Chen, J.-H.: Pre-service teachers' perceptions and intentions regarding the use of Chatbots through statistical and lag sequential analysis. Comput. Educ. Artif. Intell. **4**, 100119 (2023). https://doi.org/10.1016/j.caeai.2022.100119

Ullrich, A., Vladova, G., Eigelshoven, F., Renz, A. (2022). Data mining of scientific research on artificial intelligence in teaching and administration in higher education institutions: a bibliometrics analysis and recommendation for future research. Discover Artif. Intell. **2**(16). https://doi.org/10.1007/s44163-022-00031-7

UNESCO (Ed.): Artificial intelligence in education: challenges and opportunities for sustainable development. UNESCO Working Papers on Education Policy. UNESCO, Paris (2019). https://bit.ly/3z6BQvN

UNESCO (Ed.): International forum on AI and the futures of education: developing competencies for the AI Era. UNESCO, Paris (2021). https://bit.ly/3zoB6AS

UNESCO (Ed.): Recommendation on the ethics of artificial intelligence. UNESCO, Paris (2021). https://unesdoc.unesco.org/ark:/48223/pf0000380455

UNESCO: AI Competency Framework for Teachers: United nations educational, scientific and cultural organization, Paris (2024). https://doi.org/10.54675/ZJTE2084

Watanabe, A.: Exploring totalitarian elements of artificial intelligence in higher education with Hannah Arendt. Int. J. Technoethics **14**(1), 1–15 (2023). https://doi.org/10.4018/IJT.329239

Weber-Guskar, E.: How to feel about emotionalized artificial intelligence? When robot pets, holograms, and Chatbots become affective partners. Ethics Inf. Technol. **23**, 601–610 (2021). https://doi.org/10.1007/s10676-021-09598-8

Zawacki-Richter, O., Marín, V.I., Bond, M., Gouverneur, F.: Systematic review of research on artificial intelligence applications in higher education—Where are the educators? Int. J. Educ. Technol. High. Educ. **16**(1), 39 (2019). https://doi.org/10.1186/s41239-019-0171-0

Zhai, X., Panjwani-Charania, S.: AI for students with learning disabilities: a systematic review. In: Zhai, X., Krajcik, J. (eds.) Uses of Artificial Intelligence in STEM Education. Oxford University Press, Oxford (2023). https://ssrn.com/abstract=4617715

Zuboff, S.: The Age of Surveillance Capitalism: The Fight for a Human Future at the New Frontier of Power. PublicAffairs, New York (2019)

Dyslexic Reliance on Statistical Knowledge and Lexical Processing Under Time-Pressure Conditions

Giuliana Nardacchione[1]([✉]) [ID], Pierluigi Zoccolotti[2,3] [ID], Paola Angelelli[4] [ID], and Chiara Valeria Marinelli[1] [ID]

[1] Cognitive and Affective Neuroscience Lab, Department of Humanities, Letters, Cultural Heritage and Educational Studies, Foggia University, Foggia, Italy
giuliana.nardacchione@unifg.it
[2] Department of Psychology, Sapienza University of Rome, Rome, Italy
[3] Tuscany Rehabilitation Clinic, Montevarchi, Arezzo, Italy
[4] Department of Experimental Medicine, Lab of Applied Psychology and Intervention, University of Salento, Lecce, Italy

Abstract. The prevalent reliance on sublexical processing leads to slower reading times in adults with dyslexia. This study examined the lexical processing and use of distributional knowledge by adults with dyslexia under time-pressure conditions. Forty-four adults with dyslexia (mean age: 21.4 years) and 51 typical readers (mean age: 20.9 years) performed an orthographic judgement task involving high- and low-frequency irregular words (with either typical or atypical transcription) and regular words. Stimuli were presented in pure lists. Fakes were homophonic only to irregular words. Accuracy scores within the time limit were analyzed using an ANOVA, with group (dyslexic vs controls) as a between-subjects factor and stimulus type (regular, typical irregular, atypical irregular) and word frequency (high vs low) as within-subjects factors. The analysis included correct words and derived fakes, focusing on the frequency effect of the original words. A second ANOVA incorporated the version factor (correct words vs fakes). Variations in the number and order of words and fakes across pages, along with incomplete judgments due to time constraints, mean the version effect findings are suggestive. Participants performed worse when judging low-frequency irregular stimuli, especially those with atypical transcription. Controls showed a transcription typicality effect (better performance on typically transcribed words than atypical ones) and a very large regularity effect (better performance on regular words than irregular ones); this latter effect was maximized by using a pure (blocked) list. Adults with dyslexia showed a smaller regularity effect, significant only when atypical irregular stimuli and regular stimuli were compared. Statistical knowledge allowed them to process irregular words with typical transcription more accurately, achieving an accuracy like regular stimuli. Furthermore, adults with dyslexia showed a larger version effect (with greater difficulty in detecting homophonic fakes) and smaller pure list facilitation compared to typically developing readers. The results indicate that adults with dyslexia have a limited orthographic lexicon. However, they partially compensate for their lexical difficulty by the reliance on statistical-distributional knowledge. Time pressure further compromises dyslexic performance due to their reliance on sublexical reading

G. A. Toto (Ed.): ICS exchange 2024, CCIS 2521, pp. 399–414, 2025.
https://doi.org/10.1007/978-3-032-03021-4_29

strategy but does not undermine their use of statistical-distributional knowledge as a compensatory strategy.

Keywords: dyslexia · lexical processing · distributional properties · reading · spelling · statistical learning

1   Introduction

Orthographies with consistent grapheme-phoneme correspondences, like Italian (the language examined in this study), exhibit few orthographic ambiguities [1]. Apart from stress assignment, the main exception and source of ambiguity in Italian concerns some phonemes that have more than one possible orthographic solution, all homophonic, but only one orthographically correct [2]. For example, the group of phonemes [kw] within the word can be transcribed with the orthographic sequences QU or CU or CQU (e.g. ['akkwa'], "acqua", can be spelled as AQUA, ACUA and AQUA, of which only the first is correct), while at the beginning of the word, it can be transcribed as either QU or CU (e.g. [kwore], "heart", "can be spelled as CUORE and QUORE, with only the first being correct). As for consistent orthographies, which typically lack irregular words in reading, the orthographic judgment task is useful for identifying lexical reading deficits [3]. Since the sublexical procedure cannot distinguish between two or three homophonic spelling options, only lexical knowledge enables participants to correctly judge or spell irregular words (for further examples, see [4, 5]).

Children with dyslexia in consistent orthographies typically show sequential processing, which indicates a prevalent reliance on sublexical procedures [6, 7] and limited efficiency in lexical processing for both reading and spelling [3, 4]. They show a marked lexical deficit [8, 9], with the prevalent use of the sublexical procedure leading to slow and impaired reading [7, 10, 11]. This is reflected in their difficulty recognizing homophonic fakes in the orthographic judgment task [3–5], as well as phonologically plausible errors when spelling irregular words [2–6]. Children with dyslexia also have slower vocal reaction times (RT) than typical readers during word and non-word reading. Additionally, they also exhibit a stronger effect word length effect, where longer words lead to longer RTs an index of reliance on sequential decoding and serial analysis of written stimuli [6, 7, 11, 12]. Not only do vocal RTs support this pattern, but also eye movement recordings [13, 14] and psycholinguistic error analysis [10, 15] provide converging evidence of a predominant reliance on sub-lexical processes. These findings reveal poor efficiency in the lexical reading strategy of readers with dyslexia dealing with orthographically consistent languages. Furthermore, they show a more pronounced frequency effect [16, 17], indicating that their lexicon expansion is limited to higher-frequency words [4].

However, most of these studies focus on children, with only a few examining adults with dyslexia. Cross-linguistic studies suggest that the high level of accuracy achieved in reading some consistent orthographies makes accuracy an unsuitable indicator of reading deficit in adults. Instead, slow reading is a more reliable marker of dyslexia in these languages (e.g., [18, 19]). Speed enhancements can still be observed after 15 years of reading experience [20, 21], making fluency deficit a discriminating factor between dyslexic and control readers, regardless of age and type of orthography. In a recent study, Vizzi et al. [19] investigated the reading abilities of Italian university students with dyslexia, examining vocal RTs in single-word reading. The results indicated a general slowing compared to control readers: despite prolonged school attendance, college students with dyslexia still exhibited marked RT slowing across various word stimuli. The dyslexic deficit in reading time has remained quite stable over the years despite prolonged exposure to print and reading experience. Fluency continues to be a relevant issue for adults with dyslexia across all orthographies [22]. Vizzi et al.'s [19] findings highlight difficulties in forming a pre-lexical representation of the orthographic string, as well as a lexical deficit, particularly evident in the difficulty of reading irregularly stressed words, which represent a source of irregularity in Italian orthography among Italian college students with developmental dyslexia.

A deficit in lexical expansion among Italian adults with dyslexia has also been demonstrated by a recent study [23], which examined both reading (through an orthographic judgment task) and spelling. Compared to control readers, adults with dyslexia showed a greater frequency effect and more difficulty in judging irregular stimuli than regular ones. However, despite their lexical difficulties, they were sensitive to spelling regularities, demonstrating statistical learning. This form of implicit learning allows for the extraction of language regularities [24], which can improve reading [25], writing (e.g., [26]), and learning orthographic representations (e.g., [27]). In the Italian language, statistical-distributional knowledge may also aid in spelling and judging the orthography of ambiguous words with more than one homophonic transcription. Often, there is an asymmetry in the frequency of occurrences of the two orthographic solutions, where one is more frequent (typical) and the other is less frequent (atypical). For example, the phoneme [kw] is rarely transcribed as CQU, more frequently with CU and in most cases with QU. In this regard, Marinelli et al. [5, 28] found that children with dyslexia also used distributional properties to increase their accuracy in spelling and reading irregular words with typical (more frequent) mappings. Using distributional properties allows an accuracy comparable to regular words when reading and spelling irregular words with typical segments. Even when orthographic representations are absent (as in pseudowords), children with dyslexia rely on distributional properties and use the ambiguous segment with the most frequent transcription in 75% of cases [28]. The frequency of phoneme-grapheme mapping modulates the performance of children with dyslexia to a greater extent than that of children with typical development, likely because the reduced orthographic lexicon in children with dyslexia compels them to rely heavily on the distributional properties of orthography [5, 28]. In a recent study [23], we found that adults with dyslexia also relied on distributional knowledge, partially compensating for their lexical deficit in reading and spelling. They improved their accuracy and speed in judging typical irregular words compared to atypical ones due to their reliance on statistical-distributional knowledge. However, we do not know what strategy by introducing time pressure in the test conditions. Nardacchione et al. [23] found that when the compensatory strategy was hindered by a dual task of articulatory suppression during writing, the performance of typical adult readers was also worsened. Notably, this detrimental effect was more pronounced among adults with dyslexia. Also, in dual-task conditions, adults with dyslexia continued to rely on a compensatory strategy based on distributional knowledge: in fact, segment typicality influenced the performance of adults with dyslexia even more than controls. Similar evidence for reading is lacking.

In the present study, we explore lexical processing and distributional properties in adults with dyslexia compared to controls in conditions of time pressure. This approach aims to disrupt the compensatory overreliance on sublexical reading strategies and statistical-distributional knowledge among dyslexic individuals. We employed a judgement task involving irregular words with atypical transcription, regular words with typical transcription, and regular words under time pressure to compare the performance of adults with dyslexia with peers with typical literacy skills. The stimuli were the same as Nardacchione et al. [23]. They consisted of two types: half were high-frequency stimuli, which have more stable orthographic representation in participants' lexicons, and half were low-frequency ones, which are more difficult to process using the lexical procedure. All six experimental conditions were presented in separate pure blocks (different from Nardacchione et al.'s [23] study, in which the same stimuli were presented in mixed lists). It is well established that exception and regular words are read faster in pure than in mixed list conditions [29, 30]. The expectation of encountering exception words in a pure list slows the sub-lexical process and results in faster RTs than in mixed lists (see [31]). Therefore, in the present study, using pure lists combined with time pressure is expected to enhance the reliance on the lexical procedure among both typical readers and adults with dyslexia, potentially amplifying the differences between the groups.

The general expectation is that adults with dyslexia will perform worse than controls. In particular, they are expected to exhibit a greater regularity effect (*i.e.*, a more pronounced difficulty than controls in processing irregular words compared to regular words) due to their lexical deficit, consistently with dyslexic children's findings [3–5]. They are also expected to show a greater frequency effect stemming from their reduced lexicon, which makes lexical processing challenging for low-frequency words (consistent with developmental age studies, e.g. [5, 16, 17]). Coherently with Nardacchione et al. [23], we also expect to observe a compensatory use of statistical distributional knowledge to offset lexical deficits, particularly in reading low-frequency stimuli, with better performance in judging typical than atypical irregular words. In this experiment, the use of pure lists in a time-pressure task (as opposed to the mixed list conditions used in Nardacchione et al.'s. study [23]) should lead to a greater reliance on the lexical procedure, thereby highlighting both more pronounced regularity effects in typical and dyslexic adults and a more significant deficit in adults with dyslexia.

As it regards consistent orthographies, the efficiency of sublexical reading may improve with years of reading practice, partially compensating for the lexical reading deficit [32, 33]. Adequate sublexical skills can ensure near-complete reading accuracy (except for sounding-out behaviors and difficulties in recognizing homophonic fakes) in a consistent orthography like Italian [10, 34], although this process is time-consuming. In this study, time pressure may worsen the performance of adults with dyslexia due to their reliance on the sublexical procedure, which is slower than the lexical one. Under time pressure, dyslexic individuals may not have enough time to rely on distributional knowledge to compensate for their difficulties, and the sublexical procedure may not be fast enough to ensure good performance in the orthographic judgment task.

2   Materials and Methods

2.1   Participants

Participants included 44 university students with dyslexia (F: 34; M:10; mean age = 21.4, SD = 3.7) and 51 typically developing peers (F: 42; M: 9; mean age = 20.9, SD = 2.4). Dyslexic participants were selected based on i) impaired performance (at least 1.65 standard deviations below the normative sample mean) in reading speed and/or accuracy on a text passage, as well as on at least a subset of words and pseudowords test (LCS-SUA; [35], see paragraph 2.1.a), ii) performance within the norm on Raven's (2000) Standard Progressive Matrices (SPM [36]). Inclusion in the control sample required performance within the normal range for reading speed and/or accuracy on the text passage, word and pseudoword reading tests (LCS-SUA [35]), as well on Raven's SPMs [36], and the absence of dyscalculia and dysgraphia (LCS-SUA [35]).

Participants also completed the One Minute Reading Test [37] (see paragraph 2.1.b) and two experimental reading tests (see paragraph 2.1.c). Results are presented in Table 1. As reported in Table 1, the groups did not differ in terms of gender ($X2 < 1$), age ($F < 1$), or Raven CPM performance ($F < 1$). Adults with dyslexia showed impaired performance in all reading measures: they are more inaccurate and slower than normal readers in text, pseudoword and word reading (irrespective of frequency and length).

Each participant provided informed consent for participation in the study and the processing of personal data. Data were collected following the principles of the Helsinki Declaration. The research was approved by the ethics committee (Prot. 011/CEpsi). Participants were examined in a quiet and peaceful laboratory of the University of Foggia.

LCS-SUA

The following tests of the LCS-SUA battery [35] were administered:

a. Reading text: the subject reads a passage aloud as accurately and fluently as possible while the experimenter records both speed (syllables per second) and the total number of errors made. Errors are penalized with 1 point for (a) inaccurate word reading due to elision, substitution, insertion and/or syllable inversion; (b) omission of syllables, words, or phrases; (c) addition of syllable or word, and rereading of the same phrases; (d) pause longer more than 5 s. The following errors are penalized with 0.5 points: (a) accent shift; (b) self-correction on a 1-point error (self-corrections for 0.5-point errors are not considered); (c) significant hesitation (e.g., sounding out behaviors); (d) 1-point errors that do not alter the meaning of the sentence. Errors repeated several times on the same word are counted only once.

b. Word reading: the subject read aloud as quickly and accurately as possible: (a) short (2 or 3 syllables) high-frequency words; (b) short (2 or 3 syllables) low-frequency words; (c) long (4 syllable) high-frequency words; (d) long (4 syllable) low-frequency words. Speed (syllables/seconds) and errors are recorded (1 point for each word omitted or misread; self-corrections and hesitations are not counted as errors).

c. Pseudoword reading: the subject read aloud short (2 or 3 syllables) and long (4 syllables) pseudowords. Speed (syllables/seconds) and errors are measured (1 point for each word omitted or misread; self-corrections and hesitations are not counted as errors).

Table 1. Demographic and clinical variables of the sample.

	Typically developing adults		Adults with dyslexia			
Gender	9M	42F	10M	34F	X2 = 0.38	p = 0.54
	mean	ds	mean	ds	t(94)	p
Age (years)	21.37	3.69	20.94	2.40	0.66	0.511
Raven SPM (accuracy)	40.57	11.08	43.75	13.37	1.24	0.215
ONE MINUTE TEST (accuracy)	90.84	23.54	114.20	26.06	4.33	0.000
Word reading (accuracy)	63.68	23.72	83.57	20.44	4.18	0.000
Pseudoword reading (accuracy)	22.61	10.87	43.73	14.04	7.07	0.000
LCS SUA: Short high frequency words (seconds)	17.43	7.33	12.61	2.57	4.19	0.000
LCS SUA: Short high frequency words (errors)	0.59	0.90	0.10	0.30	3.56	0.000
LCS SUA: Short low frequency words (seconds)	25.30	9.91	16.33	3.16	5.62	0.000
LCS SUA: Short low frequency words (errors)	2.18	2.22	0.73	0.85	4.13	0.000
LCS SUA: Long high frequency words (seconds)	27.00	11.97	17.10	3.02	5.29	0.000
LCS SUA: Long high frequency words (errors)	0.70	0.90	0.06	0.31	4.53	0.000
LCS SUA: Long low frequency words (seconds)	46.34	15.94	28.90	7.10	6.33	0.000
LCS SUA: Long low frequency words (errors)	3.95	2.56	1.31	1.33	5.86	0.000
LCS SUA: Short pseudowords (seconds)	30.73	13.01	19.29	4.81	5.39	0.000
LCS SUA: Short pseudowords (errors)	2.16	1.79	0.25	0.48	6.51	0.000
LCS SUA: Long pseudowords (seconds)	64.16	20.77	43.20	10.93	5.74	0.000
LCS SUA: Long pseudowords (errors)	7.02	3.79	3.27	2.32	5.44	0.000
LCS SUA: text reading (sill/sec)	4.44	1.10	5.82	0.80	6.31	0.000
LCS SUA: text reading (errors)	9.82	5.21	2.83	1.55	7.75	0.000

One-Minute Reading Test

The subject must read aloud as many words as possible correctly, within a 1-min time limit, from a list of words arranged on a page [37]. The list contains 158 lowfrequency, 5-letter disyllabic words (mean frequency = 15.42, SD = 21.78; Colfis database [38]) with a high number of orthographic neighbors (mean 8.45, SD = 4.12; Colfis database [20]). The total score is determined by the words read correctly within the time limit.

Word and Pseudoword Reading Test

The subject must read aloud seconds as many words as possible correctly, within a maximum time of 45 s from a page of words and a page of pseudowords. The words are 100 long words (average number of letters = 8.00, SD = 1.13) with mediumlow frequency (mean frequency = 27.03, SD = 20.03; Colfis database [38]). The pseudowords are derived by changing about three letters in each word (average number of letters = 8.01, SD = 0.76). The words and pseudowords did not differ in letter number or ortho-syllabic difficulties (e.g., presence of double consonants or consonant clusters, contextual rules, etc.; Ts < 1). The number of words and pseudowords correctly read within the time limit were the total scores.

2.2 Orthographic Judgment Test with Time Pressure

The Orthographic Judgment Test under pressure time requires participants to judge the spelling correctness of a list containing high and low-frequency regular stimuli, irregular stimuli with typical segments, and irregular stimuli with atypical segments (for a total of 6 conditions). The task evaluates both the presence of a) lexical deficit (indicated by greater difficulty in recognizing phonologically plausible errors in irregular words compared to phonologically implausible errors embedded in regular words) and b) sensitivity to distributional properties (since irregular words may contain ambiguous segments transcribed in a typical or atypical way).

The stimuli were the same as [23] but presented in a pure list, with each experimental condition on a separate page. Fakes were created by changing, adding, or deleting one letter. For irregular words, fakes are phonologically plausible and homophonic to the original word (and thus detectable only through lexical reading), while for regular words, the fakes are not homophonic (and, as such, detectable also through sublexical decoding). Each experimental condition appeared on a separate page, with both words and their corresponding fakes randomized on the same page. Participants had a 30 s time limit to judge the orthographic correctness of each page, crossing either the YES or NO option for each stimulus.

All the 110 stimuli were printed on a sheet of paper in Times New Roman font (size 14) and arranged in two columns. YES/NO answer boxes were placed on the right side of each item.

The total of correctly judged items per page within the time limit was recorded and converted into a percentage of the total number of stimuli on each page (independently from the overall number of stimuli judged by each participant within the time limit). Additionally, for each page, the number of correctly judged words and fakes was computed and converted into percentages.

2.3 Data Analysis

The statistical analyses were conducted using JAMOVI software [40–42]. Accuracy scores, obtained within the time limit, were analyzed through an ANOVA, with the group (dyslexic vs controls) as a between-subjects factor, and stimulus type (regular stimuli vs typical irregular stimuli vs atypical irregular stimuli), word frequency (high vs low) as within-subjects factors. Note that in this analysis, the accuracy obtained in judging each page (i.e., experimental condition) has been analyzed and that on each page, there are both correct words and derived fakes. The frequency effect refers to the frequency of the correct word and of the original word from which the fakes derived. Significant interactions were explored with the Tukey post-hoc test.

The ANOVA was also replicated on the accuracy scores for judging words and fakes, with version (correct word vs fake version) included as a within-subjects factor. Note that the order of appearance of fakes and words varied across pages; for example, in the first column of each page/experimental condition, the number of fakes could differ, affecting the a priori probability of making an error in judging these stimuli. Due to time pressure, participants did not always finish judging the stimuli on each page, so it is not possible to be certain that each subject judged the same number of words and fakes per page. Therefore, these analyses should be considered suggestive of the version effect. For brevity, only the version effect and significant interactions involving the version effect are discussed in the analysis. All other effects or interactions are explored in the first ANOVA. Also, in this case, significant interactions were explored using the Tukey post-hoc test.

3   Results

The ANOVA showed the significance of the main effects of group ($F(1,93) = 15.6$, $p < .001$), type of stimulus ($F(2,186) = 43.21$ $p < .001$), and frequency ($F(1,93) = 15.24$ $p < .001$), indicating lower accuracy for adults with dyslexia (49.1%) compared to controls (61.9%); for low-frequency stimuli (53%) compared to high-frequency stimuli (58%); and irregular atypical stimuli (47.9%) compared to irregular typical stimuli (56.5%) and regular stimuli (62.1%; all differences were significant at least at $p < .001$).

The stimulus x group interaction was significant ($F(2,186) = 7.73$, $p < .001$, see Fig. 1) and highlighted that adults with dyslexia were generally less accurate than controls, but the size of the group differences varied as a function of the stimulus type. The difference was small for irregular atypical stimuli (43.9% vs 51.9% for adults with dyslexia and controls, respectively; mean difference $\Delta = 8.0\%$, $p < .05$), larger for irregular typical stimuli (51.1% vs 62%; $\Delta = 10.9\%$, $p < .01$) and maximal in the case of regular stimuli (52.3% vs 71.9%; $\Delta = 19.6\%$, $p < .001$). A typicality effect (i.e., higher accuracy in judging typical irregular stimuli compared to atypical ones) was present and similar in both groups (at least $p < .001$). The regularity effect was observed for typical readers (with an advantage in judging regular stimuli compared to irregular typical ones, and especially irregular atypical ones, at least $p < .001$) and for adults with dyslexia (in this case, the only significant difference was between regular stimuli and irregular atypical ones, $p < .001$, while the difference between regular and irregular typical transcription stimuli was not significant).

The type of stimulus x frequency interaction ($F(2,186) = 6.38$, $p < .001$, see Fig. 2) was significant: the difference between high- and low-frequency stimuli was substantial for irregular atypical stimuli ($\Delta = 8.6\%$, $p < .001$) and irregular typical stimuli ($\Delta =$

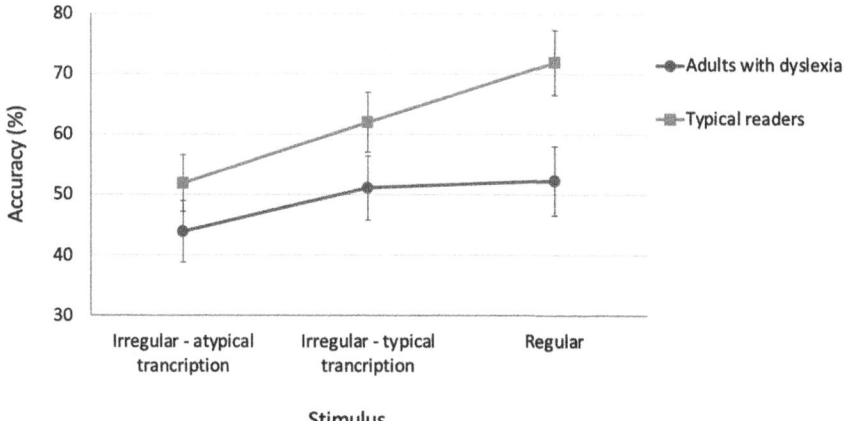

Fig. 1. Performance at the orthographic judgment test with the time pressure of adults with dyslexia and typical readers as a function of the type of stimulus. Error bars indicate 95% confidence limits.

6.6%, p < .001), but absent for regular stimuli (Δ = -0.4%). For low-frequency stimuli, accuracy was progressively higher for regular stimuli, typical irregular stimuli, and atypical irregular stimuli (all differences were significant at least p < .001), showing significant typicality and regularity effects. For high-frequency stimuli, the typicality effect was significant (p < .001), with better accuracy in judging typical than atypical irregular stimuli, while the regularity effect was significant only when comparing regular stimuli to atypical irregular ones (p < .001) but not when comparing regular high-frequency stimuli to typical irregular stimuli. All other interactions were not significant.

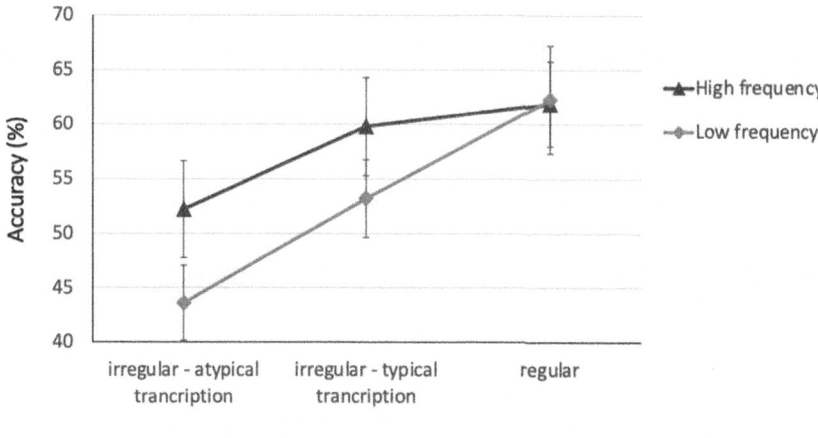

Fig. 2. Performance at the orthographic judgment test with the time pressure as a function of word frequency. Error bars indicate 95% confidence limits.

When the analysis was replicated with version as within-subject factor, all previous results were confirmed: group effect (F (1,93) = 15.2, p < .001), type of stimulus effect (F (2,186) = 49.01 p < .001), frequency effect (F (1,93) = 14.21, p < .001), type of stimulus x frequency interaction (F (2,186) = 7.32, p < .001) and type of stimulus x group interaction (F (2,186) = 6.22, p < .01). The effect of version was significant (F (1,93) = 87.05, p < .001), indicating better performance for words (59.6%) than fakes (51.6%). The effect of version interacted with group (F (1,93) = 4.02, p < .05), indicating larger group differences in judging fakes (Δ between dyslexics and controls = 11.44%, p < .001) compared to correct versions (Δ = 11.03%, p < .01). There was a larger version effect among dyslexic participants (Δ between correct versions and fakes = 9.64%, p < .001) than among typically developing adults (Δ = 6.23%, p < .001).

The frequency x version (F (2,186) = 58.25, p < .001) and the frequency x version x type of stimulus (F (2,186) = 57.39, p < .001, see Fig. 3) interactions were significant. The latter interaction highlights that accuracy in judging words was not modulated by frequency but only by stimulus typicality (at least p < .05) and regularity (at least p < .05), with lower accuracy for irregular atypical words. In judging fakes, accuracy was moderate with high-frequency fakes and lower for irregular low-frequency fakes. In particular, the accuracy decreases dramatically in judging atypical irregular low-frequency fakes (31.3%). The frequency effect was absent for regular fakes (Δ between high and low-frequency fakes = 3.34%, ns), larger for typical irregular fakes (Δ = 10.99%, p < .001), and enormous for atypical irregular fakes (Δ = 22.22%, p < .001). In the case of fakes, the typicality effect was very large for low-frequency stimuli (Δ = 27.40%, p < .01) and smaller for high-frequency ones (Δ = 5.19%, p < .01). The regularity effect was always significant and large for low-frequency fakes (at least p < .001); while for high-frequency stimuli, the regularity effect was significant only when comparing regular and atypical irregular fakes (p < .001), but not when comparing regular and typical irregular fakes. This pattern did not interact with the group effect. All other interactions were not significant.

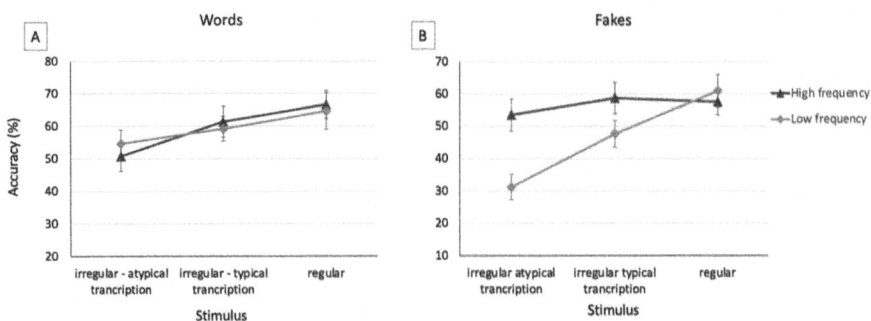

Fig. 3. Performance at the orthographic judgment test with the time pressure as a function of word frequency. A. Words. B. Fakes. Error bars indicate 95% confidence limits.

4 Discussion

Individuals with dyslexia experience reading difficulties that persist into adulthood [43, 44]. The manifestations of dyslexia in adulthood are not well understood, partly due to their overreliance on compensatory strategies, which obscure and isolate the specific deficits. Understanding the strengths and weaknesses of this population is critical, given the growing number of students with dyslexia in higher education institutions [45]. In this study, we explore lexical processing in adults with dyslexia and their reliance on a compensatory probabilistic strategy based on the frequency of occurrence (typicality) of the transcription type for irregular words in Italian, a largely consistent orthography. We use an orthographic judgment task with time pressure to perturb compensatory mechanisms based on the over-reliance on the sublexical procedure (which is slower) or on a probabilistic strategy based on statistical distributional knowledge.

The task under time pressure was difficult for both dyslexic and typically developing adults: even typical readers showed significantly lower performance in the most challenging conditions, i.e., with atypical irregular stimuli. In fact, in this latter condition, the group difference was attenuated. Thus, time pressure affects the decision-making component of the judgement task, which is more involved in the case of atypical irregular words. In fact, for irregular fakes with atypical transcription, the joint processing of all the procedures and information available to the reader produces discordant outcomes: 1. Only the lexical procedure allows for fake detection (as the target is absent in the orthographic lexicon), while 2. The sublexical procedure is erroneously induced to not recognize the target due to its homophony with the correct version of the word, and 3. Statistical distributional knowledge erroneously leads the subject to believe that the fake is correct because it is (erroneously) written with the most frequent (i.e., typical) type of transcription. This conflicting information results in slower decision-making times and lower accuracy in judging atypical fakes for both groups, but especially for adults with dyslexia. Furthermore, in both groups, these difficulties are considerably greater for low-frequency stimuli, for which the output from the lexical pathway is neither strong nor rapid due to poorly established representations in the lexicon. In the case of correct versions of atypical irregular words, however, both the lexical and sublexical procedures allow for accurate judgments, while the statistical distributional knowledge may lead readers to doubt and produce a slowdown as the transcription is atypical.

The present study shows that adults with dyslexia, consistent with studies in school-age individuals [4, 9, 46], have a limited expansion of their orthographic lexicon, as highlighted by the larger version effect (with great difficulty in detecting homophonic fakes) compared to typically developing readers, as well as the presence of a regularity effect. However, the regularity effect was smaller than the one in Nardacchione et al.'s study [23]. The time pressure not only makes the task more difficult (as highlighted by the generally low accuracy) but also obscures the advantage of processing regular over irregular words. Without a time limit, through the sublexical procedure, participants might achieve a very high level of accuracy in judging regular stimuli; however, this procedure is insufficient for judging irregular words due to the homophony of fakes. Thus, without a time limit, the regularity effect is substantial for all participants, including adults with dyslexia. When a time limit is imposed, the reliance of dyslexic participants on the sublexical procedure produces significant delays that impact the processing of all stimuli (both regular and irregular). Adults with dyslexia are slower because they use sublexical reading to judge any type of stimulus. Consequently, they can judge a limited number of regular stimuli within the time limit, making the regularity effect less pronounced and detectable only when regular and atypical stimuli are compared. The excessive dependence on the sublexical procedure and the poor lexical reading skills of Italian adults with dyslexia confirm the results of previous studies on Italian dyslexic children [2–5, 28, 47] and adults [19, 23], as well as adults with dyslexia in other consistent orthography such as German/Austrian (e.g., [9]).

However, it is noteworthy that dyslexic adults used their knowledge of distributional properties of orthography to try to compensate for their difficulty in judging irregular stimuli, achieving accuracy in judging typical irregular stimuli similar to that obtained with regular stimuli. Adults with dyslexia showed greater accuracy with irregular stimuli featuring typical transcription than with those featuring irregular stimuli. Thus, like adults with typical reading acquisition, they acquire the distributional properties of their orthography and use this knowledge to compensate for their difficulties when lexical processing is not available. These findings are consistent with recent findings on dyslexic children [5, 28, 47] and adults [23]. Italian adults with dyslexia use statistical knowledge to facilitate their misspelling recognition, indicating a strong statistical learning ability [23]. The present results indicate that the presence of time pressure did not compromise the use of this compensatory strategy based on distributional knowledge.

Note that in this experiment, we used a pure blocked lists experimental design. Based on the dual-route interpretation, this is expected to favor the lexical procedure over sublexical decoding, thus producing larger regularity effects [29]. In this study, we found this effect only for typically developing readers and not for dyslexic adults. Compared to Nardacchione et al.'s study [23], typical readers in this study generally showed a larger regularity effect, consistent with the prediction for pure lists. The absence of an advantage for pure lists in participants with dyslexia may be due to their predominant reliance on sublexical procedures to solve the task across all experimental conditions and independent of the facilitation provided by the pure list effect. Thus, the lack of pure list facilitation further evidences the lexical deficit in adults with dyslexia. Both groups performed poorly with low-frequency stimuli, especially in recognizing low-frequency fakes, indicating difficulty in relying on lexical representations to solve the task involving low-frequency stimuli. No interaction of the frequency effect with the group is detectable. In both groups, the absence of a frequency effect for regular stimuli highlights that when both lexical and sublexical procedures converge in determining the subject's response (as for regular stimuli), the lack of conflictual information makes the judgment fast and accurate, regardless of frequency. For irregular fakes, the conflicting information provided by the two reading procedures results in a slowdown and lower accuracy in orthographic judgment. This difficulty with irregular stimuli is less pronounced for high-frequency stimuli, for which the lexical representations are more consolidated; therefore, the lexical procedure influences the subject's response more strongly than the phonological one. This phenomenon results in worse performance with low-frequency irregular stimuli than with high-frequency stimuli. This occurs for both types of irregular stimuli, but especially for irregular stimuli with atypical transcription compared to typical ones. In the first case, not only does the sub-lexical procedure but also the use of statistical-distributional knowledge produces information that contradicts the output of the lexical procedure. Therefore, the lexical retrieval is limited for the low-frequency stimuli and does not prevail over the outcomes of the other two processing mechanisms (sublexical and statistical-probabilistic strategies) in determining the subject's response. As a result, accuracy is lower than in the other conditions.

As reported above, the frequency effect never interacts with the group, neither alone nor in interaction with other variables, but is always comparable between the two groups. This is an expected result. Both studies with vocal RTs [16, 17] and those using the orthographic judgment task [3, 5] showed larger frequency effects among Italian dyslexic children compared to typically developing children. Additionally, findings on adults with dyslexia reported larger frequency effects in this population, both in vocal reaction times [19] and in the orthographic judgment task [23]. Note that in Nardacchione et al.'s study [23], the stimuli used in the orthographic judgment task were the same as those used in this study but were presented in mixed list conditions. In this study, the use of blocked pure lists should have maximized the lexical effects and, therefore, the frequency effects as well. The expectation of having all high-frequency irregular stimuli should have enhanced the use of the lexical procedure. Therefore, the absence of a greater frequency effect in adults with dyslexia is probably attributable to the use of an experimental paradigm with time pressure. Further studies will be needed to better understand this finding.

5 Limitations

Some limitations of the present research should be highlighted. To foster lexical processing in line with the dual-route tradition [29, 48], we used pure list conditions. They are removed from the typical real-life reading conditions as well as those of standard clinical testing. Therefore, in future research, it would be important to confirm the present findings and extend them to more ecological conditions, e.g., including mixed list manipulations.

6 Conclusions

This study highlights a reduced lexical processing capacity and an excessive reliance on the sublexical procedure in Italian adults with dyslexia compared to typical readers. However, adults with dyslexia also rely on distributional properties to partially compensate for their difficulties, allowing them to gain an advantage in the processing of irregular words with typical transcription (achieving an accuracy like regular stimuli). The use of time pressure poses a challenge for them, given their slowness due to sublexical reliance, but does not hinder the use of the compensatory probabilistic strategies based on statistical distributional knowledge. Thus, readers with dyslexia use both sublexical processing and distributional knowledge to partially compensate for their lexical deficit.

This study provides heuristic information for rehabilitation programs and teaching, emphasizing the importance of effective compensation strategies. The statistical learning capacity spared in adults with dyslexia should be considered a valuable resource for planning rehabilitation and enhancing reading and spelling performance. Targeted and specific training aimed at fostering the explicit acquisition of distributional knowledge could further strengthen this capacity, enabling individuals with dyslexia to compensate for their poor lexical processing (see, for example, [47]) and improve accuracy in spelling and reading. Raising awareness that, between two homophonic orthographic solutions of irregular segments, a more frequent one (occurring in 75%-80% of cases) could increase the likelihood of using the more frequent orthographic solution and, therefore, achieving accuracy (despite their lexical deficit). For learning disorders manifested in adults, it seems important to encourage the use of compensation strategies. In addition to this metacognitive teaching, there is a need to increase exposure to low-frequency atypical irregular words through prolonged and repeated learning opportunities to foster the acquisition of orthographic representations in the lexicon of these words as well.

Acknowledgements. This study was funded by Next Generation EU - PNRR M4C2 1.1 PRIN 2022 (grant number 20229PSYEP - CUP D53D23009500006) to CVM.

Disclosure of Interests. The authors have no competing interests to declare that are relevant to the content of this article.

References

1. Burani, C., Thornton, A., Zoccolotti, P.: Learning to read Italian. In: Verhoeven, L., Perfetti, C. (eds.), Learning to Read across Languages and Writing Systems, pp. 211–242. Cambridge: Cambridge University Press (2017). https://doi.org/10.1017/9781316155752.009
2. Angelelli, P., Judica, A., Spinelli, D., Zoccolotti, P., Luzzatti, C.: Characteristics of writing disorders in Italian dyslexic children. Cogn. Behav. Neurol. **17**, 18–31 (2004)
3. Marinelli, C.V., Angelelli, P., Notarnicola, A., Luzzatti, C.: Do Italian dyslexic children use efficiently the lexical route of reading? An orthographic judgement task. Read. Writ. **22**, 333–351 (2009)
4. Angelelli, P., Marinelli, C.V., Zoccolotti, P.: Single or dual orthographic representations for reading and spelling? A study on Italian dyslexic and dysgraphic children. Cogn. Neuropsychol. **27**, 305–333 (2010)
5. Marinelli, C.V., Cellini, P., Zoccolotti, P., Angelelli, P.: Lexical processing and distributional knowledge in sound-spelling mapping in a consistent orthography: a longitudinal study of reading and spelling on dyslexic and typically developing children. Cogn. Neuropsychol. **34**, 163–186 (2017)
6. Zoccolotti, P., De Luca, M., Di Pace, E., Judica, A., Orlandi, M., Spinelli, D.: Markers of developmental surface dyslexia in a language (Italian) with high grapheme-phoneme correspondence. Appl. Psycholinguist. **20**, 191–216 (1999)

7. Martens, V.E., de Jong, P.F.: The effect of word length on lexical decision in dyslexic and normal reading children. Brain Lang. **98**(2), 140–149 (2006)
8. Zoccolotti, P., De Luca, M., Marinelli, C.V.: Interpreting developmental surface dyslexia within a co-morbidity perspective. Brain Sci. **11**, 1568 (2021)
9. Bergmann, J., Wimmer, H.: A dual-route perspective on poor reading in a regular orthography: evidence from phonological and orthographic lexical decisions. Cogn. Neuropsychol. **25**(5), 653–676 (2008)
10. Trenta, M., Benassi, M., Di Filippo, G., Pontillo, M., Zoccolotti, P.: Analysis of error profile in a regular orthography: role of reading deficit and strategic control. Cogn. Neuropsychol. **30**, 147–171 (2013)
11. Spinelli, D., De Luca, M., Di Filippo, G., Mancini, M. Martelli M., Zoccolotti, P.: Length effect in word naming latencies: role of reading experience and reading deficit. Dev. Neuropsychol. **27**, 217–235 (2005)
12. Zoccolotti, P., De Luca, M., Gasperini, F., Judica, A., Spinelli, D.: Word length effect in early reading and in developmental dyslexia. Brain Lang. **93**, 369–373 (2005)
13. De Luca, M., Borrelli, M., Judica, A., Spinelli, D., Zoccolotti, P.: Reading words and pseudo-words: an eye movement study of developmental dyslexia. Brain Lang. **80**, 617–626 (2002)
14. Hawelka, S., Gagl, B., Wimmer, H.: A dual-route perspective on eye movements of dyslexic readers. Cognition **115**(3), 367–379 (2010)
15. Hendriks, A.W., Kolk, H.H.: Strategic control in developmental dyslexia. Cogn. Neuropsychol. **14**(3), 321–366 (1997)
16. Barca, L., Burani, C., Di Filippo, G., Zoccolotti, P.: Italian developmental dyslexic and proficient readers: where are the differences? Brain Lang. **98**, 347–351 (2006)
17. Marinelli, C.V., Traficante, D., Zoccolotti, P., Burani, C.: Orthographic neighborhood-size effects on the reading aloud of Italian children with and without dyslexia. Sci. Stud. Read. **17**, 333–349 (2013)
18. Goulandris, N.E.: Dyslexia in Different Languages: Cross-Linguistic Comparisons. Whurr Publishers, London (2003)
19. Vizzi, F., Marinelli, C.V., Iaia, M., Turi, M., Zoccolotti, P., Angelelli, P.: Dyslexia in higher education: specific and global components of the reading profile (submitted)
20. Carver, R.P.: Reading rate: theory, research, and practical implications. J. Read. **36**(2), 84–95 (1992)
21. Brysbaert, M.: How many words do we read per minute? A review and meta-analysis of reading rate. J. Mem. Lang. **109**, 104047 (2019)
22. Reis, A., Araújo, S., Morais, I.S., Faísca, L.: Reading and reading-related skills in adults with dyslexia from different orthographic systems: a review and meta-analysis. Ann. Dyslexia **70**(3), 339–368 (2020)
23. Nardacchione, G., Angelelli, P., Zoccolotti, P., Marinelli, C.V.: Lexical processing and sensitivity to statistical distributional properties in adults with developmental dyslexia (submitted)
24. Perruchet, P., Pacton, S.: Implicit learning and statistical learning: one phenomenon, two approaches. Trends Cogn. Sci. **10**, 233–238 (2006)
25. Pacton, S., Fayol, M., Perruchet, P.: The acquisition of untaught orthographic regularities in French. In: L. Verhoeven, P. Reitsma, C., Elbro (eds.) Precursors of Functional Literacy, pp. 121–137. John Benjamins B.V., Amsterdam, The Netherlands (2002)
26. Treiman, R.: Statistical learning and spelling. Lang. Speech Hear. Serv. Sch. **49**, 644–652 (2018)
27. Pacton, S., Sobaco, A., Fayol, M., Treiman, R.: How does graphotactic knowledge influence children's learning of new spellings? Front. Psychol. **4**, 701 (2013)

28. Marinelli, C.V., Iaia, M., Burani, C., Angelelli, P.: Sensitivity to distributional properties of the orthography in the spelling of Italian children with dyslexia. Q. J. Exp. Psychol. **74**(6), 1007–1020 (2021)
29. Monsell, S., Patterson, K.E., Graham, A., Hughes, C.H., Milroy, R.: Lexical and sublexical translation of spelling to sound: strategic anticipation of lexical status. J. Exp. Psychol. Learn. Mem. Cogn. **18**(3), 452–467 (1992)
30. Lupker, S.J., Brown, P., Colombo, L.: Strategic control in a naming task: changing routes or changing deadlines? J. Exp. Psychol. Learn. Mem. Cogn. **23**(3), 570–590 (1997)
31. Traficante, D., Burani, C.: List context effects in languages with opaque and transparent orthographies: a challenge for models of reading. Front. Psychol. **5**, 1023 (2014)
32. Kemp, N., Parrila, R.K., Kirby, J.R.: Phonological and orthographic spelling in high-functioning adult dyslexics. Dyslexia **15**(2), 105–128 (2009)
33. Afonso, O., Suárez-Coalla, P., Cuetos, F.: Spelling impairments in Spanish dyslexic adults. Front. Psychol. **6**, 466 (2015)
34. Marinelli, C.V., Romani, C., McGowan, V.A., Giustizieri, S., Zoccolotti, P.: Characterization of reading errors in languages with different orthographic regularity: an Italian-English comparison. J. Cult. Cognit. Sci. **7**, 95–120 (2023)
35. Montesano, L., Valenti, A., Cornoldi, C.: LCS-SUA. Prove di lettura, comprensione del testo, scrittura e calcolo. Batteria per la valutazione dei DSA e altri disturbi in studenti universitari e adulti. Erickson, Trento (2020)
36. Raven, J.: The Raven's progressive Matrices: change and stability over culture and time. Cogn. Psychol. **41**, 1–48 (2000)
37. Conforti, S., Marinelli, C.V., Zoccolotti, P., Martelli, M.: The metrics of reading speed: understanding developmental dyslexia. Sci. Rep. **14**, 4109 (2024)
38. Bertinetto, P.M., et al: Corpus e Lessico di Frequenza Dell'italiano Scritto (CoLFIS) (2005)
39. Zoccolotti, P., De Luca, M., Marinelli, C.V., Spinelli, D.: Predicting individual differences in reading, spelling and maths in a sample of typically developing children: a study in the perspective of comorbidity. PlosOne **15**(4), e0231937 (2020)
40. Lenth, R.: Emmeans: Estimated marginal means, aka least-squares means. [R package]. (2020). https://cran.rproject.org/package=emmeans
41. Singmann, H.: Afex: Analysis of factorial experiments. [R package] (2018). https://cran.r-project.org/package=afex
42. R Core Team: R: A language and environment for statistical computing. (Version 4.0) [Computer software]. https://cran.r-project.org. (R packages retrieved from MRAN snapshot 2021-04-01) (2021)
43. Hatcher, J., Snowling, M.J., Griffiths, Y.M.: Cognitive assessment of dyslexic students in higher education. Br. J. Educ. Psychol. **72**(1), 119–133 (2002)
44. Pammer, K.: Temporal sampling in vision and the implications for dyslexia. Front. Hum. Neurosci. **7**, 933 (2014)
45. Pino, M., Mortari, L.: The inclusion of students with dyslexia in higher education: a systematic review using narrative synthesis. Dyslexia **20**(4), 346–369 (2014)
46. Hanley, J.R., Hastie, K., Kay, J.: Developmental surface dyslexia and dysgraphia: an orthographic processing impairment. Q. J. Exp. Psychol. **44**(2), 285–319 (1992)
47. Arfè, B., Cona, E., Merella, A.: Training implicit learning of spelling in Italian children with developmental dyslexia. Top. Lang. Disord. **38**, 299–315 (2018)
48. Coltheart, M., Rastle, K., Perry, C., Langdon, R., Ziegler, J.: DRC: a dual route cascaded model of visual word recognition and reading aloud. Psychol. Rev. **108**(1), 204–256 (2001)

Values, Messages, and Representations in the Film Barbie: An Exploratory Inquiry and Intersectional Pedagogical Analysis

Barbara Centrone[(✉)] [ID]

Roma Tre University, Rome, Italy
barbara.centrone@uniroma3.it

Abstract. In a world made of images (Thoman, 1999), pedagogy has often devoted its attention to media education (Centrone et al., 2023; Rivoltella, 2019) and to the analysis of the relationship between the messages conveyed by mainstream media products enjoyed by children and adults, and the dominant values within a cultural-historical context (Bocci et al., 2022). This paper will intersectionally analyze the film "Barbie" (Greta Gerwig, 2023) from a pedagogical perspective, using the lens of Disability Studies, Gender studies, and Feminist studies to analyze the themes addressed by the blockbuster film. Lastly, the paper will report on the results of an exploratory survey conducted with teachers from several primary and secondary schools in Italy who were asked to express opinions about the film and to reflect on the possible use of the film to address certain issues with their students.

Keywords: Barbie · Intersectional Pedagogical Analysis · Media Education

1 Introduction. Media Education and Film Analysis Skills: What is Media Literacy and Why is it Important?

In a world made of images (Thoman, 1999), pedagogy has often devoted its attention to media education (Centrone et al., 2023; Rivoltella, 2019) and the analysis of the relationship between the messages conveyed by mainstream media products enjoyed by children and adults, and the dominant values within a cultural-historical context (Bocci et al., 2022).

The field of media education encompasses the critical analysis and understanding of media, which has become increasingly relevant in the digital age where media permeates every aspect of daily life. Media literacy, a fundamental component of media education, provides individuals with the skills necessary to interpret, analyse and create media content in a critical and conscious manner.

The theoretical foundations of media education are numerous and complex. One of the most significant is Marshall McLuhan's concept of "the medium is the message" (McLuhan, 1964), which emphasises how the medium of communication influences

G. A. Toto (Ed.): ICS exchange 2024, CCIS 2521, pp. 415–448, 2025.
https://doi.org/10.1007/978-3-032-03021-4_30

the perception and interpretation of content. McLuhan emphasised the importance of understanding not only the content of media but also their structural and cultural impact. This approach facilitated a more profound comprehension of how media shape our experience of the world.

Another notable contribution to the field of media education is that of David Buckingham, who developed a critical approach to the subject. Buckingham (2003) emphasises the importance of education that does not merely protect young people from the influence of the media, but rather prepares them to engage with it in a critical and creative manner. He argues that media education should promote an understanding of the media as social and cultural constructions, encouraging students to reflect on how media represent the world. This critical approach is essential for developing an active and informed citizenship capable of navigating the complex media landscape of today.

Media literacy is crucial in a context where digital media are ubiquitous. According to Renee Hobbs, a leading expert in the field, media literacy involves not only the ability to decode media messages but also to understand the role of media in society and to participate actively as informed citizens (Hobbs, 2011). Hobbs identifies five key competencies of media literacy: access, analysis, evaluation, creation, and action. These competencies are vital for avoiding misinformation and promoting active and informed citizenship.

In relation to media analysis, Thoman makes a compelling case for considering that all messages conveyed by the media are *built* by a select group of individuals for an external audience through a creative language that adheres to specific rules. Furthermore, he asserts that different individuals may perceive the same message in varying ways and that media disseminate values and perspectives shaped by a particular sociocultural context. It is crucial to recognize that these tools are shaped by the logic of capitalism. This understanding aligns with the broader goals of media education, which seeks to equip individuals with the skills to critically engage with media content.

The implementation of media education in educational institutions provides students with the capacity to decipher implicit messages, cultivate a discerning and informed approach to media consumption, comprehend the linguistic nuances of film, and recognize the manner in which diverse elements converge to convey meanings and evoke sentiments and values. Furthermore, it provides an avenue for reflection and discourse on social, cultural, and political matters through the lens of film (Buckingham, 2006; Maragliano & Pireddu, 2014). This educational approach is essential for developing critical thinking and reflective capacity in students, as highlighted by Hobbs (2011).

The practice of media education requires that educators have the requisite skills and tools to analyse the relationship between the messages conveyed by mainstream media products consumed by children and adults and the dominant values within a cultural-historical context (Centrone et al., 2023). This presents an avenue for further research and study in the field of teacher training, which must also incorporate proficiency in film analysis.

As Jenkins et al. (2009) suggest, teachers must provide students with the tools to critically analyse media content and understand the dynamics underlying it. This pedagogical approach is essential for developing an active and informed citizenship capable of navigating the complex media landscape of today.

Furthermore, knowledge of the mainstream films that students watch is essential for teachers, as these films often reflect and influence students' cultural and social perceptions. Buckingham (2003) argues that understanding these films allows teachers to better connect with students, using relevant examples to stimulate critical discussions and promote deeper learning. By using films as pedagogical tools, teachers can facilitate a learning environment that values diverse opinions and promotes intercultural understanding (Burn & Durran, 2007). These pedagogical strategies not only enrich the educational experience but also prepare students to become informed and responsible citizens in a world increasingly dominated by media. As Masterman (2003) points out, media education must be integrated into the school curriculum to develop a critical and conscious understanding of the media themselves.

In light of the discussion above, there is a substantial body of research investigating whether teachers possess the necessary skills in film media analysis. This paper does not claim to provide definitive answers to this question. Instead, it aims to analyse the characters and plot of the film "Barbie" (Gerwig, 2023) through an intersectional lens to discern its educational values and messages. Additionally, it presents the outcomes of an exploratory study conducted with 209 Italian teachers, who were asked to express their personal and pedagogical opinions regarding the film.

2   Barbie (2023) the Movie: An Intersectional Analysis

Directed by Greta Gerwig, Barbie (2023) became the 14th highest-grossing film in cinema history, with a first-day gross of $155 million, making it the highest-grossing female-directed film. It is also the first female-directed live-action film to reach one billion worldwide and the highest-grossing female-directed film in the United States.

The billboards proclaim, "She's everything. He's just Ken." The following is a concise overview of the film, which elucidates the analysis of pertinent characters and scenes.

The principal character, Stereotype Barbie, resides in Barbieland, a utopia where everything is ideal, everyone is joyful, and Barbies occupy prominent roles while Ken dolls serve as mere accessories.

One day, Stereotype Barbie begins to contemplate the finitude of life due to the emergence of a portal between the real world and Barbieland. As a result, Stereotype Barbie's body undergoes a transformation, acquiring a human form with normal-sized feet, the presence of bad breath upon waking, the development of cellulite, and the emergence of hair that is no longer perfectly coiffed.

Weird Barbie, ostracised by Barbieland due to her physical appearance and behavioural characteristics, discloses to Stereotype Barbie that in order to ascertain solutions and reestablish equilibrium, she must depart from Barbieland and embark on a journey to the Real World to address the concerns of the young girl who plays with her in that world, who is visibly distressed and preoccupied with thoughts of mortality.

Ken subsequently follows her. The transition into the Real World proved to be a profound experience for Stereotype Barbie and Ken. Stereotype Barbie, who had previously held the belief that gender and women's issues had been effectively addressed through Mattel's diverse production of Barbies, was left grappling with the stark reality of persistent challenges. In contrast, the real world is characterised by patriarchy, with women facing barriers to employment and experiencing harassment and catcalling. Ken, on the other hand, discovers that as a man he has the potential to pursue a life beyond the role of a mere Barbie accessory and to exert power. Stereotype Barbie discovers that the individual playing with her is not a young girl, but an adult woman named Gloria, who is employed at Mattel. Gloria is experiencing a challenging period, characterised by feelings of frustration, a decline in creativity and a sense of estrangement from her teenage daughter, Sasha.

As Stereotype Barbie confronts the truth -that Barbie dolls have not advanced the status of women globally-, and as she realizes that the Mattel company is exclusively male-dominated, Ken initiates a patriarchal takeover of Barbieland.

Upon returning to Barbieland with Gloria and Sasha, Stereotype Barbie discovers that the situation has reversed. Barbieland is now Kendom Land, a place where Kens objectify and sexualise Barbies and are served by them. The other Barbies appear to have fallen prey to a spell that makes them submissive to men and devoid of personality and interests.

Having resolved an identity crisis, Stereotype Barbie, encouraged by a motivational speech and critique of patriarchy made by Gloria, constructs a plan with Sasha and Weird Barbie. The plan entails rousing the Barbies from this sort of social spell, dismantling the new Ken-centred system, and returning Barbieland to its former state. The plan involves the use of patriarchal structures to neutralise the Ken characters, pitting them against each other to distract them. This will create an opportunity to establish a new social system that allows individuals to choose their identity without external pressure or the influence of power hierarchies. This system will also accommodate the Ken characters, even in positions where they may previously have been marginalised.

The film Barbie was met both with acclaim and criticism in the Western world, with public opinion divided almost down the middle. Those who praised the film highlighted its effective portrayal of feminist, gender, and patriarchy-related themes, which they felt resonated with mainstream audiences. Conversely, those who offered criticism often described the film as trivial or exaggerated.

In the midst of the controversy and criticism that emerged from the outset of the marketing campaign and persisted following the film's theatrical release, a pivotal question lingered: "Is Barbie a feminist film?" (La Porte & Cavusoglu, 2023). It is not a straightforward matter to answer this question, primarily because the term 'feminist' is a highly polysemous adjective. Feminisms are claim movements that, in different historical and geographical contexts, have assumed a variety of forms.

The aim of this study is to analyse the main characters and a series of salient moments of the film in order to identify its educational messages, employing an intersectional feminist lens.

The film opens with the narrator elucidating the interconnection between Barbieland and the tangible world: "Barbie can be whoever she wants, women can be whoever they want and this is reflected in the girls. [...] Thanks to Barbie the problems of feminism have been solved, or at least that's what Barbies think".

It is notable that the term *feminism* is referenced in the opening moments of the film, which is a relatively uncommon occurrence, particularly in a film aimed at a mainstream audience.

The initial scenes introduce a variety of Barbies, showcasing a range of physical attributes, identities, and professions. There are: President Barbie, Nobel Prize Barbie, and so forth. On initial observation, this appears to be a diverse and nuanced representation. However, upon closer examination, it becomes evident that, with the exception of ethnic diversity, there is a tendency towards tokenism (Kianpour, 2023). For instance, while there is a Barbie who is fat and white, her body is consistently depicted in a less revealing manner than that of other characters -even at the beach she is the only one whose arms and legs are covered by leggings. Additionally, there is only one Barbie with a motor impairment who uses a wheelchair and who is not even given a line: she makes an appearance during the choreography for a few seconds and then disappears.

Some Barbies are given lines that could be considered quasi-educational slogans: "Barbie is not ashamed," "I have no difficulty holding emotion and logic at the same time, and this does not diminish my power." These statements could be regarded as thought-provoking with regard to gender stereotypes.

2.1 Stereotype Barbie

The character of Stereotype Barbie, played by Margot Robbie, represents a trenchant critique of Western beauty ideals and traditional gender roles. Surrounded by other Barbies embodying successful roles and professions, such as Nobel Prize Barbie or Medical Barbie, Stereotype Barbie stands out for her lack of specific talents or merits. Instead, she embodies the conventional –and archetypal-Western female beauty standards associated with the Barbie doll: white, tall, with a narrow waist, symmetrical breasts, tapered fingers, walks on tiptoes, impeccable blonde hair, blue eyes, full pink lips and blemish-free skin - "I am the Barbie you think of when you say think of a Barbie".

She resides in Barbie's Dream House where she socialises with friends who epitomise the stereotypes of success, beauty, and happiness. Her ostensibly idyllic existence reflects the assumption that women can attain any goal by adhering to the dictates of patriarchy. This notion has been extensively examined in feminist and transfeminist literature, including works by Beauvoir (1949), Bordo (1993), and Ahmed (2010).

However, Stereotype Barbie's life is characterized by a lack of depth and authenticity, a central theme in feminist critiques of the representation of women in the media (Gill, 2007). When she begins to think about death, the veil that covers her alienating and contrived pink world is torn: the reaction of the other Barbies is the same as that of Western society, which has made death a taboo, something to be pushed away and avoided through the illusion that she can control it, even by purchasing products to rejuvenate or slow aging.

This rupture leads to a transformation of the Stereotype Barbie's body, which becomes less and less perfect: her feet no longer keep their toes, the much-demonized cellulite appears, her morning breath stinks... And so on. This process of humanization represents a critique of the unattainable ideals of beauty and unrealistic expectations imposed on women (Bordo, 1993). This triggering event makes it clear that this film is a coming-of-age novel: reflecting on the finiteness of life and coping with bodily changes challenge Barbie's constitutive principle of perfection and initiate her journey of self-discovery.

The other Barbies tell her that the only one who can help her return to her perfect appearance is Weird Barbie, who presents her with a forced choice: stay imperfect, "With cellulite, and you'll start to be sad, melancholy, complicated" and risk becoming "as crazy" as she is, or venture out into the real world to solve the sadness that plagues the little girl who plays with her in the Real World. This scene hints at a narrative trope that represents a crucial moment of personal growth: standing still is never a good thing, growing up means taking risks, facing one's fears, and embracing change. This moment can be compared to the onset of sexual development. The process of menarche marks the transition to adulthood, which is characterised by a number of challenges, including social pressures to conform and the onset of more complex emotions. This marks the end of the idyllic, pink, perfect, worry-free phase that childhood is often perceived to be.

In the real world, Stereotype Barbie has the opportunity to explore her identity in a more complex and authentic context. However, she is also confronted with the facts, which indicate that the existence of Barbies has not resulted in the universal happiness and empowerment of women. Furthermore, she is subjected to repeated catcalling and sexual harassment by both male strangers and law enforcement officials. This treatment appears to be a form of sanction for her actual status as a woman in the real world, where harassment is a pervasive and daily reality for women.

The dialogue between Barbie and Ken who are skating at Venice Beach allows the discourse of harassment, consent, and power relations to be addressed:

Stereotype Barbie: "I feel kind of ill at ease, like I don't know the word for it but I'm...conscious, but it's...myself that I'm conscious of."

Ken: "I'm not getting any of that. I feel what can only be described as admired but not ogled. And there's no undertone of violence."

Stereotype Barbie: "Mine very much has an undertone of violence."

Her attempts to interact with Sasha, the young girl she assumes to be her companion, are ultimately unsuccessful. The adolescent rejects her and asserts that she is the catalyst for the resurgence of feminist discourse, which has led to a pervasive sense of inadequacy among women globally.

In a state of emotional distress, Stereotype Barbie, upon concluding the interaction with Sasha, who had accused her of being "A fascist", experienced a deeply moving and profound moment. As the camera focuses on an elderly woman at a bus stop, the image shifts to details of her body, allowing the viewer to discern the direction of Barbie Stereotype's gaze: the wrinkles, the modest attire, the swollen ankles. Barbie is touched and the viewer too, aided by Billie Eilish's background music. "You're beautiful" she says, "I know" answers the old woman. This moment of emotional complexity is described as "Painful but beautiful": Stereotype Barbie is thus confronted with the fragility and imperfection of life, discovering that true beauty is not limited to a superficial ideal. This journey of personal discovery is emblematic of transfeminist theories that promote acceptance of the diversity and complexity of gender identity (Stryker, 2008).

Stereotype Barbie is kidnapped by Mattel agents who take her to the general office building - a phallic-shaped building- where she discovers that the Mattel executives are all men. They suggest that Stereotype Barbie return to her own box and forget everything. But she has experienced too much of *the truth* and decides to *stay awake* and escape.

While escaping, she discovers that it was not a child who played with her in the Real World, but an adult: Gloria, the woman who saved her from the Mattel agents. Together with her and her daughter Sasha, they return to Barbieland, which has now become a patriarchy.

At this stage of her journey, Stereotype Barbie feels confused and vulnerable, but she also begins to recognize the power of her experiences and to question her role as a symbol of femininity. Her evolution reflects a movement toward authenticity and self-acceptance, issues that are central to contemporary discussions about gender representation in the media (Ahmed, 2010).

Fear plays an important role in this evolution: although the word never appears in the film, it is possible to recognize it as a product of the objectifying reality of the structure of the real world, both triggered by uncertainty about the bodily and non-bodily changes she is undergoing. When Barbieland has become Kendom Land, she is paralyzed by fear: she blames it all on Gloria, who opened the portal with her "complicated human thoughts and feelings".

It is noteworthy that anxiety plays a significant role in this context. Essentialist philosophers posit that anxiety is a defining characteristic of human beings. As she had already informed Weird Barbie, she reiterates "I never wanted anything to change". Gloria at this point, like a fairy godmother, reveals to her, "Oh, honey, that's life. It's all change." Stereotype Barbie is terrified, "That's…that's terrifying. I don't want that. Not my life! No thank you! Just no. I'm just gonna sit here and wait and hope that one of the more leadership-oriented Barbies just snaps out of it and does something about this whole mess". When she learns not to shy away from it but to welcome it and walk through it, that is when Stereotype Barbie no longer feels like a perfect doll; she feels more human. This is similar to what happens to Pinocchio when he becomes a *real child.*

Stereotype Barbie's evolution reaches a pivotal point where she gains a profound understanding of the social structures that shape femininity and success, and the essence of what it means to be human. Throughout her transformative journey, the film illuminates the conflict between conformity to patriarchal norms and the pursuit of an authentic identity, a theme that aligns with de Lauretis' (1987) theories on the social construction of gender and the significance of personal narrative in redefining identities.

2.2   Ken

The character of Ken, portrayed by Ryan Gosling, represents as a pivotal figure through which complex themes of identity, masculinity, and the quest for meaning are explored. Ken's narrative transcends mere parody of toxic masculinity, offering a profound reflection on how men, too, are shaped and constrained by gender expectations (Armengol, 2022).

An intersectional and cinematic analysis of his character reveals both the satirical elements and the deeper messages about how patriarchy affects even those who benefit from it (Armengol, 2019;2024).

Initially, Ken is defined solely by his emotional and identity-based dependence on Barbie; his existence is meaningful only in relation to her proximity and approval. In Barbieland, Ken is relegated to an accessory role, lacking autonomous purpose. This asymmetrical relationship between Stereotype Barbie and Ken satirizes inverted gender dynamics, highlighting what occurs when an individual is deprived of the opportunity to develop an independent identity. This dependency reflects a psychological dynamic that can be interpreted as a need for external validation and a lack of self-autonomy, a condition prevalent in the construction of contemporary male identities, particularly in patriarchal societies (Connell, 2005; Kimmel, 2008).

The character of Ken enables the filmmaker to explore various manifestations of masculinity that exist within the collective consciousness and social fabric.

The narrative voice at the beginning of the film states: "Barbie has a great day every day, but Ken only has a great day if Barbie looks at him". Indeed, at the outset, Ken personifies masculinity, which, in a society that does not instruct males to cultivate an authentic identity devoid of conditioning and gender stereotypes, is founded upon inadequacy and the relentless pursuit of recognition through the establishment of romantic and especially sexual relationships. Many men who fail to achieve this status become so-called "incels" who perpetrate violence, both online and in other ways (Costello et al., 2022; Glace et al., 2021).

The continuous search for approval from the Barbie gaze results in a continuous competition among the Kens. This phenomenon occurs in a patriarchal society, where women are socialized to compete because they are taught that their own worth depends on the male gaze and approval (Snow, 1989). Campbell (2004) notes that in patriarchal societies, where opportunities for women are limited, sisterhood is often opposed. This is evidenced by actions against witches aimed at dissolving social rituals of female solidarity, which were perceived as dangerous and anarchic (Federici, 2020).

In the second phase of the narrative, Ken encounters the Real World, which is characterised by a culture of male success and dominance -"Man rule the world!". He observes a diverse array of individuals, including men in suits and men in furs, law enforcement personnel, and men greeting each other by showcasing their musculature and exclaiming "male, male, male!". He observes men shushing a woman by placing an open hand in front of her face; he discovers that there are only men's faces on the bills. "Why didn't Barbie tell me about patriarchy, which, to my understanding, is where men and horses run everything?" -convinced that he can get what he wants with the sole requirement of being a man, Ken asks a businessman for a well-paid job that allows him to make decisions and is told that he must have specific qualifications: Ken: "Isn't being a man enough?".

Businessman: "Actually, right now, it's kind of the opposite" Ken: "You guys are clearly not doing Patriarchy very well".

Businessman: "Nah...no .. we're doing it well. Yeah. We just hide it better now".

In the throes of euphoria he starts to consider Barbieland the perfect place to establish a patriarchal system from its fundamental principles. This realization presents an opportunity for him to resolve his identity crisis, leading him to transform Barbieland into Kendom Land, The Land of the Free and the Men. The Barbie Dream Houses are transformed into the Mojo Dojo Casa Houses, which feature small beer fridges, posters of cars, and pictures of horses that are regarded as an extension of men. As it is explained to all the Kens: "Everything exists to expand and elevate the presence of men". Seduced by the power he enjoys in the "pure and flawless system of patriarchy," Ken masks his interest in Stereotype Barbie, whom he now calls "baby" and "little girl" with an attitude of condescension: "you can stay as my uncommitted girl wife". At this point in the film, Ken represents a caricature of toxic masculinity (Harrington, 2021). The effort he expends on performing a certain way and the dissatisfaction that persists within him illustrate how rigid, binary gender roles constrain men as well as women. He doesn't feel K-enough, however, and this causes him frustration: a reminder of the social pressures men face to conform to standards of success and performativity-the verses of his song "I'm always number two" and "Anywhere else I'd be a ten" are references to the need to be evaluated according to a system that quantifies one's worth in this capitalist society that pursues a meritocratic ideology on a performative basis (Zappino, 2019).

Ken's transformation is a powerful commentary on the true freedom that lies in self-acceptance and the construction of an autonomous identity beyond societal expectations: that personal worth depends on performativity, power, and external recognition is an illusion.

The film uses Ken's character to critique traditional masculinity and the patriarchal system, demonstrating how men are also ensnared by unrealistic expectations and oppressive roles (Brittan, 1989; MacInnes, 1998). The themes of inadequacy and lack of recognition embodied by Ken reflect the social pressure many men face to conform to standards of success and external approval.

From an intersectional perspective, Ken's character is intriguing because it underscores that men, too, are shaped and limited by gender roles: the film emphasizes that patriarchy does not liberate even those who appear to benefit from it, as it imposes unrealistic standards and roles that can be oppressive (hooks, 2004; Messner, 1997; Gasparrini, 2020).

Ken's pursuit of power and status recognition ultimately proves inadequate in addressing his underlying feelings of loneliness and insecurity. The pursuit of domination and control, while seemingly effective in achieving external validation, ultimately prove ineffective in fostering a sense of identity and worth.

In the film's ending he has not resolved his identity crisis but no longer fears that he does not exist except "in the warmth of Barbie's gaze": he understands that being Ken is K-enough.

2.3 Weird Barbie

The character of Weird Barbie, as portrayed by Kate McKinnon, is a Barbie with an outwardly exuberant temperament. In terms of her physical appearance, she is no longer considered to be aesthetically perfect. This is due to her having been subjected to violent physical manipulation in the Real World, including the bending of her limbs, the cutting and burning of her hair, and the scrawling of graffiti on her face. Consequently, her fate is sealed: she is destined to spend eternity making other Barbies perfect.

Moreover, she is portrayed as a nonconforming body that is marginalised and perceived as monstrous due to its inability to conform to the established standards of aesthetics and performativity (Centrone, 2024). Indeed, Weird Barbie occupies a distinctive residence, designated as *Weird House*, which is distinguished by its eccentricity, vibrant hues, and unconventional architectural style. The house is located at a considerable distance from the centre of Barbieland, which serves to underscore the isolation and marginalisation experienced by the character.

The fact that she is no longer aesthetically perfect renders her almost *less Barbie*. She is foul-mouthed and makes objectifying comments about Ken in a manner that would be expected of a man. This is reminiscent of Monique Wittig's (1997) argument that lesbians cannot be considered women because the cultural construct of womanhood is intrinsically tied to heterosexuality and certain canons related to aesthetics and behaviour.

Her status as an outsider affords her a unique perspective on the inner workings of Barbieland. With her insight, resilience, and guidance, she challenges Stereotype Barbie to confront the underlying issues of the young girl who plays with her. She warns that if these issues remain unresolved, the world will become increasingly distorted, and Stereotype Barbie will risk becoming [*weird*] as Weird Barbie.

The reference to The Matrix (Wachowski L., Wachowski L., 1999) is an allusion to the film's premise that the reality of the simulation is not the actuality. This is evidenced in the scene where Weird Barbie inquires about the type of footwear Stereotype Barbie desires. In terms of footwear, there is a dichotomy between the pink heels, which are representative of the ideal of beauty and commodification of the female body, and the brown sandals, which are more practical and suitable for everyday life. *Red pill or blue one?* That is: do you prefer the image of you or the authentic you?

Weird Barbie represents a subversive character who challenges the aesthetic ideals of beauty and perfection that Mattel has historically proposed and standardized. She is not constrained by the conventional norms of beauty and does not aspire to fit these standards. This allows her the freedom to be authentically herself. In drawing on studies of stigma and deviance (Goffman, 1963; Becker, 1963), Weird Barbie can be seen as a representation of positive deviance. This concept suggests that the rejection of social norms can give rise to novel forms of expression and identity that challenge social norms.

The character of Weird Barbie encourages reflection on the significance of embracing one's eccentricities and authentic characteristics, which the system often defines as *imperfections* solely because they do not conform to established norms. The dialogues between the two characters reveal not only a critique of the patriarchal ideals that are imposed upon them, but also a lesson that solidarity and cooperation are essential for the empowerment of women. "Genuine empowerment entails utilizing one's influence to facilitate the advancement of other women, who are often constrained by sexist impediments that impede their recognition and valuation. "If it serves only you, it is not feminism[1] (Murgia, 2021).

The irreverence, aesthetic appeal and distinctive character of Weird Barbie evoke the image of an individual who has engaged in the process of exploring and defining their own identity, including their gender identity. This exploration is evident in her creative use of scissors and colours, as well as her experimentation with concepts of

---

[1] Author's translation

"disorder" and "irregularities". Indeed, Weird Barbie is the sole individual who has learned to reside on the margins, both geographically and far from the rigid confines of conventional beauty and perfection. Her existence serves to illustrate that these concepts are, in fact, an illusion perpetuated by patriarchal systems to appease the malevolent gaze (Lorde, 2012). It can be argued that the eccentricity of the character reflects aspects of queerness and neuroqueerness, without undue emphasis (Centrone, 2023; Marocchini, 2024; Bocci & Domenici, 2019). Weird Barbie encourages Stereotype Barbie to abandon the pursuit of an idealised form of perfection and instead embrace authenticity in self-discovery, free from the constraints of social conditioning and expectations. The director seeks to ascribe a stigmatised identity to Weird Barbie, situating her on the margins of society.

This representation aims to illustrate the transformative potential of individuals who challenge the status quo and dominant structures through their mere existence.

2.4 Gloria

The character of Gloria, as portrayed by America Ferrera, represents a multifaceted interplay between identity and social pressures, whereby the character's identity is shaped by the social pressures she encounters. Gloria is employed by Mattel, the company responsible for the production of the iconic Barbie dolls. Consequently, she is subjected to dual stressors, originating from both her occupational and familial contexts. On the one hand, the professional environment provides implicit negative feedback, emphasising her lack of conformity to the ideals of glamour and her physical dissimilarity to Barbie. Conversely, Gloria encounters mounting difficulties in her attempts to forge an emotional bond with her teenage daughter, Sasha.

This incongruence between her professional and personal circumstances serves to reinforce her nostalgic connection to the Barbie figure, which is perceived as a symbol of possibilities and unrealised dreams in the real world. She begins to create drawings of models, including "Barbie Irrepressible Thoughts of Death," "Barbie Crippling Thoughts," and "Barbie Cellulite Full Body." In doing so, she establishes a connection with the Stereotype Barbie by creating a portal that links the Barbieland with the real world. She makes the following statement:, "While playing, I became sad and, because I couldn't be like you, I made you like me."

Gloria is revealed to be a disruptive presence within the cinematic narrative, as she does not embody the conventional Barbie-like perfection or represent the archetypal young rebel defying gender norms. The director appears to be attempting to draw attention to the oppression, invisibility, and systematic misrepresentation of the social category to which Gloria belongs: a Latina woman, a mother, and a worker, who attempts to assert her identity in a world that does not recognise her either in the most prevalent models of beauty and female empowerment or in those of more radical resistance to the system, which have only recently begun to find space in mainstream cinema. (Bocci & Straniero, 2020; Butler, 2002; Crenshaw, 1989; Centrone, 2023a, b.

Gloria represents the demographic of women who exist on the margins of society, striving to fulfil the expectations of numerous roles without ever feeling that they are able to do so adequately. The character's arc in the film does not result in a transformation towards perfection or a simplistic solution. Instead, it culminates in an acknowledgement of the intrinsic beauty in imperfections and vulnerability. Her monologue is not merely an act of catharsis; rather, it is an appeal for solidarity. This appeal is for individuals to liberate themselves from unattainable standards and to embrace authenticity, even when it manifests in disordered and incomplete forms (Gill, 2007; hooks, 2000).

In conclusion, Gloria's narrative not only assists Barbie in her journey of self-discovery but also facilitates her own and her daughter's understanding that value does not solely reside in the pursuit of perfection. Her narrative implies that the genuine revolution is the acceptance and celebration of the multifaceted dimensions of identity, without the constant pressure to conform to an unattainable ideal.

2.5 Allan

There is only one Allan, played by Michael Cera. As he himself notes, "There are no copies of Allan, there is only Allan.".

He does not correspond with the conventional dichotomy between Barbie and Ken. In 1964, Mattel marketed Allan as Ken's best friend, conceptualising him as a character with no specific status or job and no particular symbolic attributes. However, in the film, Allan is depicted as interacting more frequently with the Barbies.

The fact that Allan is "just Allan," that he does not belong to Barbie's perfection nor to Ken's patriarchal masculinity, that he exists in an autonomous, independent, authentic, non-stereotypical space, suggests interesting reflections on identity, belonging, and liminality from a queercrip perspective (Centrone, in press; McRuer, 2008).

Allan can be considered a liminal body, existing on the margins of socially established categories. In the context of the Barbie universe, where power relations between groups are shaped by predefined and hyper-defined gender models, Barbie represents the extreme of the stereotype of white femininity, as represented by Ken. Masculinity, initially submissive and then dominant, is positioned in opposition to femininity. However, Allan does not occupy a position of compromise; rather, he exists outside of these dynamics. He is not compelled to conform to the expectations of performativity.

His singularity can be understood as a form of emancipation, enabling him to transcend social expectations and situate himself as an external, perceptive observer, cognizant of the inherent deficiencies of both power structures. His non-conforming body and his otherness can be understood as acts of resistance to the socio-culturally established patterns of the patriarchal system (Cohen, 1996; Centrone, 2024). In this way, the character of Allan, who has been socialised as masculine but does not conform to the standards of masculinity that are prevalent among the Kens, can be seen as an example of an alternative, non-machismo masculinity. This form of masculinity is not contingent on demonstrating masculinity, competition, and success with women.

Furthermore, Allan can be regarded as an allegorical representation of gender non-conformity. Allan exists independently of any external relationship, rejects the notion of having to perform a specific role, and thus exemplifies a central theme in queer studies and gender studies (Butler, 2004; Stryker, 2008).

In contrast to Weird Barbie, who was a conventional Barbie and has since undergone changes, and who lives on the fringes of Barbieland and is subjected to teasing "behind her back and also to her face," the singularity and difference embodied by Allan do not result in his social exclusion. Allan has been able to identify spaces, methods, and interpersonal dynamics that enable him to thrive in a world that does not inherently accommodate his needs.

2.6 Sasha

At the outset of the film, Sasha, portrayed by Ariana Greenblatt, is depicted as a cynical and sarcastic adolescent female with a markedly disenchanted perspective on Barbie. Her aesthetic evinces a resemblance to that of the Bratz dolls, which were introduced to the market in the 2000s and, for an extended period, constituted Barbie's principal competitors.

In her initial encounter with the Barbie doll, which is perceived as a symbol of female progress, Sasha does not hesitate to label it as "a patriarchal doll" and openly challenges the notion that the doll can be viewed as a positive representation of women:

"You've been making women feel bad about themselves since you were invented. You represent everything wrong with our culture. Sexualized capitalism, unrealistic physical ideals You set the feminist movement back 50 years. You destroy girls' innate sense of worth and you are killing the planet with your glorification of rampant consumerism".

Sasha views Barbie as an anachronistic and problematic icon, an embodiment of superficiality and consumerism, and a toxic symbol of unattainable perfection and an ideal of femininity imposed from above. She asserts that Barbie has perpetuated a culture of female inadequacy and self-loathing since its inception, stating, "You've been making women feel wrong ever since you were invented [] You've destroyed the self-esteem of every little girl."

Sasha's statements and arguments are consistent with the ongoing discourse surrounding the representation of women in contemporary society. This discourse is frequently spearheaded by individuals who identify as women, non-binary, or members of marginalised groups who feel alienated from the conventional ideals associated with femininity. These individuals promote the use of more diverse, less stereotypical, and more authentic portrayals that challenge the narrow definition of perfection and success often associated with traditional representations of women.

As the film progresses, Sasha's perspective undergoes a gradual shift. Upon joining Barbie in her mission to liberate Barbieland from patriarchal oppression, Sasha gains a broader understanding of the world, humanity, and the roles we play within it through her engagement with Barbie as a multifaceted and nuanced character. While maintaining her critical perspective, which is not necessarily cynical, Sasha becomes open to the possibility of change and discovers that what appears to be superficial, due to its association with pink, may in fact have transformative potential. The filmmaker thus appears to seek to emphasise the significance of conflict and multiplicity. The act of critiquing the system encompasses a range of positions and visions that can evolve and occasionally collide. Opening up to dialogue does not entail simplifying ambiguities and assimilating; rather, it entails harnessing conflict as a means of growth and enrichment (Yuval-Davis, 2006).

Sasha represents those who reject the myths imposed on them by mainstream narratives and education. Instead, they seek to coexist and appreciate the complexity of people and the transformative value of stories. Sasha thus stands as a bridge between the past and the future, helping both Gloria and Stereotype Barbie to reevaluate their relationship with themselves and the world.

Additionally, Sasha plays a pivotal role at the conclusion of the film, wherein she imparts the lesson of discerning beyond mere appearances, thus assisting Stereotype Barbie in comprehending that transformation is an inherent aspect of life and that the pursuit of perfection is not a prerequisite for becoming an icon capable of instilling hope in young girls and women for a brighter future.

2.7   The Relationship Between Gloria and Sasha

The relationship between Sasha and her mother Gloria represents a pivotal emotional aspect of the film, reflecting a prevalent familial dynamic: the generational discrepancy between parents and children with regard to social values and expectations. Gloria, who had a strong affinity for Barbie during her own childhood, is disheartened to observe that her daughter does not evince the same level of enthusiasm. Sasha's perspective is that the world does not require Barbie; rather, it requires tangible actions and representations that are not idealised.

This represents a conflict between two distinct waves of feminism. Gloria represents a more traditional concept of emancipation, whereby the portrayal of the strong and idealised woman, exemplified by Barbie, is perceived as a form of progress. This reflects the "Second Wave" of feminism, which focused on issues such as labour equality and the right to choose for oneself, as well as the promotion of strong, independent, and successful female role models (Friedan, 1963; Beauvoir, 1949). For a considerable number of young girls, Barbie represents the aspiration of a life without limitations and an inspiration to achieve significant achievements. However, Gloria is also aware of the limitations that women still face despite progress, and the pressures they face from society (hooks, 1984; MacKinnon, 1989).

In contrast, Sasha's perspective aligns with the fourth-wave feminism, which emphasises the examination of cultural symbols and their underlying contradictions and hypocrisies, as well as a critical stance towards the dominant forms of mainstream feminism in previous generations (Butler, 1990; Crenshaw, 1989; Lorde, 1984; Ahmed, 2010).

In response to Stereotype Barbie's assertion that she loves women, Sasha counters with the observation that "everyone hates women, both women and men."

An analysis of this tension reveals the necessity of an intergenerational dialogue in the film and an ideological one in real life. Such a dialogue can facilitate an understanding of two equally valid points of view, thereby enabling a more nuanced and multifaceted perspective to emerge. On the one hand, positive representation has the effect of enriching the imaginations of girls with positive hopes and inspiring them to identify with role models who exemplify the kind of woman they would like to become. The slogan "if you want, you can" provides an illustrative example of a positive representation that serves to enrich girls' imaginations with positive hopes and inspire them to emulate positive role models. However, it is also important to recognise the necessity of developing more varied, complex and less stereotypical representations that are less subservient to performative logics. This is because the message conveyed by the slogan "if you want, you can" is not entirely accurate. The assertion that success is the sole determining factor in one's life is, in fact, a fallacy.

In the concluding section of the film, the significance of interpersonal connections and compassion is illustrated. Gloria and Sasha reaffirm the value of mutual support and collaborative effort in navigating challenges, thereby exemplifying the importance of such values in achieving successful outcomes. This is also an important pedagogical message, namely that change is not a solitary endeavour, but rather requires dialogue, alliance and mutual care (Gilligan, 1982; Noddings, 1995). The journey of Gloria and Sasha serves to illustrate the potential for intergenerational learning. As Gloria reacquaints herself with the capacity for hope and imagination, Sasha learns to recognise the potential of imperfect symbols to inspire.

2.8   The Turning Point: Gloria's Monologue

Gloria's monologue represents a pivotal moment in the film, marking a key turning point in both the plot and the emotional and psychological journey of the characters. In the narrative, this speech occurs when the plot reaches a critical point, with Barbieland now known as Kendom. Here, patriarchy is firmly established, and Barbie dolls are subjugated to Ken dolls. Stereotype Barbie, overwhelmed by these circumstances, appears to be experiencing an identity crisis.

At this juncture, Gloria advances and articulates her exasperation, not merely to encourage Stereotype Barbie in the spirit of feminist collaboration, understood as a joint effort among those who aspire to transcend the imaginaries of male domination (Lippi and Maniglier, 2024), but also to assert her own experience as a woman.

Her monologue reflects on personal challenges and becomes a structural critique of the patriarchal system that imposes unattainable standards of beauty, personality, and behavior on women, effectively confining them within narrow gender roles.

"It is literally impossible to be a woman.[.]. Like, we have to always be extraordinary, but somehow we're always doing it wrong. You have to be thin, but not too thin. And you can never say you want to be thin. You have to say you want to be healthy, but also you have to be thin. You have to have money, but you can't ask for money, because that's crass. You have to be a boss, but you can't be mean. You have to lead, but you can't squash other people's ideas. You're supposed to love being a mother, but don't talk about your kids all the damn time. You have to be a career woman, but also always be looking out for other people. You have to answer for men's bad behavior, which is insane, but if you point that out, you're accused of complaining. You're supposed to stay pretty for men, but not so pretty that you tempt them too much or that you threaten other women, because you're supposed to be part of the sisterhood. But always stand out. And always be grateful. But never forget that the system is rigged. So find a way to acknowledge that but also always be grateful. You have to never get old, never be rude, never show off, never be selfish, never fall down, never fail, never show fear, never get out of line. It's too hard! It's too contradictory! And nobody gives you a medal or says thank you! And it turns out in fact that not only are you doing everything wrong, but also everything is your fault."

The monologue reaches its conclusion with a cathartic release of emotions and an acknowledgement of the social and emotional constraints imposed by patriarchal, capitalist, and individualistic norms. It provides a penetrating examination of the unattainable standards to which women are perpetually subjected, necessitating the expenditure of considerable energy, time, and cognitive resources to navigate the contradictory expectations placed upon them. In conclusion, the system ultimately deems them to be inadequate.

The monologue can be interpreted in accordance with a variety of different theoretical perspectives. One possible approach to analysing the monologue is to consider the intersection of Gloria's multiple axes of identity. These include her status as a Latina mother over the age of 40, a middle-class working woman, and the ways in which these identities are positioned in mainstream film narratives. As a middle-class woman, Gloria represents a type of femininity that is often absent from mainstream representations. She does not exemplify the characteristics of a charismatic leader nor does she exhibit exceptional or rebellious traits. She is an ordinary woman attempting to reconcile the competing demands of family care and the workplace. It is this banality of her experience that renders her so powerful a figure. The film draws attention to the systematic devaluation and invisibility of the emotional and domestic work performed by women, even when it serves as the foundation for their lives. As a Latina woman, she is subjected to the particular pressures that non-white women are compelled to endure. The dominant culture requires women like Gloria to demonstrate gratitude and submission, even when the system is manifestly unjust. The imperative to express gratitude is an implicit critique of the tendency to reduce ethnic minority women to supporting and caring roles, both within the family and in the workplace.

The second reading lens allows for an examination of the text in its universal significance, addressing all individuals socialised within the context of femininity. The monologue thus allows for an examination of the imposed standards of female beauty and performativity that are rooted in the hegemonic values of a Western, patriarchal, heterosexist, misogynistic, allomononormative, fatphobic, and racist culture. This culture exerts pressure on individuals to adhere to unattainable ideals, which in turn fosters a sense of inadequacy and a pervasive sense of guilt for never being enough (Vassallo, 2022; Farrel, 2011). The capitalist system engenders a sense of inadequacy among women, encouraging them to strive for excellence without detracting from the achievements of men. This frequently manifests as a pressure to produce results that are on a par with those of men, to conform to certain standards, and to differentiate themselves from other women. However, should they align too closely with traditional masculine norms, they risk losing their attractiveness. Consequently, women are often positioned as commodities serving the male gaze and power, and as a labour force with the capacity to consume. This encompasses elements such as dietary habits, fashion trends, and other forms of consumption. (Zappino, 2016). Furthermore, women are responsible for the physical and mental burden of unpaid care work, which is often considered a natural role for them (de Beauvoir, 1949). The message is unambiguously pedagogical in nature, asserting that there is no singular, definitive manner in which a woman should conduct herself.

Additionally, the monologue may be evaluated with regard to its potential to facilitate collective awareness among the other Barbies depicted in the film, as well as among the viewers, who are situated within an environment shaped by patriarchal norms. By denouncing the status quo, Gloria encourages other women to recognise and accept their own vulnerabilities, and to dismantle the sexist dynamics that encourage competition between women (Romeo, 2012). She posits that the attainment of freedom and the dismantling of patriarchy are achievable objectives through the formation of sister-hood and through the enactment of quotidian acts of defiance and rejection of socio-culturally imposed oppressive norms (Lonzi, 1970).

More generally, the monologue conveys what Menapace (2008) refers to as an intersectional feminist message, emphasising the value of sisterhood and collective care, self-awareness, and Freire's (1970) concept of conscientization. These concepts serve as vital tools for establishing a society founded upon the freedom to be authentically oneself and to embrace and respect the multifaceted aspects of identity.

2.9 Is Being *just Ken* K-enough? the Identity Crisis of the Male and the Critique of Toxic Masculinity

In light of the recognition that the prevailing structure in the Real World is reversed, Ken introduces a system of patriarchy to Barbieland. The patriarchy that forms the foundation of Kendom Land is a parody of traditional machismo and hegemonic masculinity. However, this system fails to provide Ken with the sense of stability and self-recognition that he has been seeking. The sense of empowerment that Ken experiences is ultimately ephemeral and illusory, as it fails to adequately address the underlying emotional and psychological needs that remain unmet. At this point in the film, Ken, in another dimension, performs a song and dance routine with other Kens, proclaiming, "I'm Just Ken."

This ballad, which has become one of the most iconic moments in the film, represents the culmination of frustration resulting from being "just Ken," an entity perceived as ancillary and insignificant. Furthermore, it reflects the inner conflict he experiences and serves as a means of becoming aware of his own identity crisis.

The lyrics of the song reflect Ken's feelings of desperation and vulnerability, as well as his sense of being trapped in a situation in which he is unable to achieve a sense of adequacy. Irrespective of his actions, he is aware that they are inconsequential, given that he is consistently positioned in a subordinate role. In the Barbie universe, Ken is presented as an accessory, lacking an autonomous identity of his own. The verses that highlight his frustration at never being considered "enough" serve as a reference point and critique of the social pressure that many men face to conform to standards of success and external approval.

The rationale behind Barbie's ostensible acquiescence to this dynamic remains opaque. The lyrics "All my life, been so polite/ But I'll sleep alone tonight" indicate that the singer anticipates some form of reciprocation for her amiability, which could be perceived as an absence of consent. This verse provides an opportunity to discuss the nuances of consent and the complexities inherent in interpersonal relationships.

The idea that "anywhere else I'd be a 10" is both ironic and tragic. This represents Ken's need to be valued and appreciated, yet within a system that quantifies the value of individuals as if they were commodities or based on their performance (Edwards, 2006; Whitehead, 2002).

Ken thus raises the question of whether his destiny is to "live and die a life of blonde fragility." Patriarchy establishes standards of normative masculinity, disdains vulnerability, and dictates that those who do not meet expectations of power and control are devalued and excluded. The set design and choreography fail to reflect the profound despondency conveyed in the lyrics of the song. This can be interpreted as an allegorical representation of the illusory nature of patriarchal masculinity. The concept of toxic masculinity, which is characterised by a set of behaviours and attitudes that are detrimental to both men and society, can be observed in various forms. These include a tendency to equate masculinity with dominance and strength, a glorification of the male body, and a focus on competition and the commodification of women. These behaviours serve to disguise vulnerability behind a facade of power and prevarication.

The song serves to illustrate Ken's growing realisation that the patriarchal system offers no viable path to liberation; rather, it provides a different form of constraint, necessitating the repression of emotional expression. This is exemplified by the line, "Am I not hot when I'm in my feelings?" This realisation prompts him to reflect on his "Kenergy" and the notion that he does not need to be exceptional or powerful to possess value. He ultimately reaches the conclusion that he is sufficient in himself as Ken.

The song does not immediately resolve the protagonist's crisis; however, it marks the beginning of her realisation that she cannot define her own worth through the character of Barbie or patriarchal values. This moment establishes the context for his ultimate transformation, in which he acknowledges that he is "Kenough" – enough in his current state, without the necessity to adhere to unattainable ideals. Ken's transformation reflects a social change advocated by intersectional transfeminist movements, which aims to revalue vulnerability, claim the right to be authentically oneself outside the logics of performative capitalism, promote horizontal interpersonal relationships without hierarchies of power and control, and create spaces for self-experimentation where binary gender roles can be dismantled.

"I'm Just Ken" encourages a critical examination of the notion that patriarchy is beneficial to no one. Those in positions of privilege and power are not exempt from the constant pressure to adhere to roles that are, in fact, artificial and performative. Moreover, it allows for the parody of the ideals of toxic masculinity, which are based on notions of strength, masculinity, absolute independence, emotional repression, and competition. Furthermore, it prompts reflection on how to identify and dismantle the structures that constrain our ability to authentically express ourselves, even in the face of uncertainty and failure. Furthermore, it enables the formation of alternative masculinities that are authentic, liberating, and do not perpetuate limiting beliefs.

2.10   The Film's Conclusion

The characters of Weird Barbie, Stereotype Barbie, Gloria, and Sasha devise a plan to emancipate the Barbies from the patriarchal constraints that have held them in bondage.

Gloria and Sasha reiterate the importance of mutual support and collaborative effort in overcoming challenges. This highlights a crucial pedagogical message: transformation is not an individual pursuit, but rather requires dialogue, coalition, and shared concern.

The strategy for dismantling patriarchy and reclaiming Barbieland is consistent with that proposed by second-wave feminists, namely that of education and awareness through mutual aid. The process of self-education and sisterhood is initiated through the sharing of personal experiences, which enables the comprehension of the influence of patriarchy on each individual. Gloria's speech thus serves as a feminist manifesto, recited each time one of the Barbies is captured. The objective is to apprehend Barbies who have been attired in diminutive garments and are currently engaged in the delivery of beverages to the Kens and the performance of cheerleading activities. The method is straightforward: it involves the utilisation of the very tools that have been employed by those in positions of power to dismantle the existing power structures. This implies that the Barbies, already stimulated by the spell, feign distress or ignorance of computing, prompting one Ken to engage in a phenomenon known as "mansplaining." Some individuals feign insecurity about their appearance in order to elicit approval from males, while others instigate conflict between the Kens. Such tactics enable the Barbies to divert the attention of the Kens, thereby facilitating the kidnapping of one Barbie at a time.

Having established their collective worth, the Barbies reclaim Barbieland without. the necessity of a coup. The Kens, driven by an exaggerated sense of masculine pride, engage in conflict with one another to establish who is the most authentic Ken and therefore possesses greater authority. At this point, the phrase previously uttered by a Mattel employee, "I'm a man with no power, does that make me a woman?", assumes even greater significance.

Following the recovery of Barbieland, Ken finds himself in a state of crisis. As anticipated, Ken has removed the initial layer of social conditioning and has come to recognise his intrinsic adequacy. The shift from seeking power to attain value to recognizing that one's worth is not contingent on the logic of domination and control represents a profound transformation with far-reaching implications for identity construction, gender expectations, and emancipation from oppressive social roles. Subsequently, Ken must remove the second mask, which comprises the beliefs that we internalise over time and with which we identify.

Ken must ascertain his identity in the absence of Barbie, irrespective of his occupation or Barbie's gaze. He must also determine his worth independently of competition with other Kens, embracing his vulnerability and insecurities:

S. Barbie: "Okay, Ken, you have to figure out who you are without me."

Ken: "Why?".

S.B: "You're not your girlfriend. You're not your house. You're not your mink."

K: "Beach…?".

S.B: "Nope, you're not even beach. Maybe all the things you thought made you, you, aren't…really…you. Maybe it's Barbie and…*it's Ken.*"

The message of being "Kenough" offers a transformative pedagogy, which suggests the necessity to rewrite the norms of masculinity in a way that they are not grounded in power, performance, or competition. The pedagogy of "Kenough" can be interpreted as an invitation to create and embrace an infinite plurality of alternative masculine identities in opposition to the toxic one. This is accomplished through the understanding

that one can attain a sense of wholeness without the constant need for external validation. Furthermore, it entails acknowledging that emotional vulnerability and the human
capacity for it are not deficiencies, but rather intrinsic aspects of the human condition. In
conclusion, it involves the dismantling of the logics of performativity and domination.
The realisation that human beings possess intrinsic value, irrespective of their adherence
to standards of success and performance, encourages reflection on social expectations,
the avoidance of competition, and the deconstruction of power hierarchies.

Another of the Kens states, "We were only fighting because we didn't know who we
were".. Meanwhile, another individual ponders who was truly engaged in the conflict, if
not them. The director's brief interjection serves to illustrate that conflicts are inherently
ego-driven and that it is not the external forces with which we engage in conflict, but
rather the masks we wear when we lack self-knowledge and are afraid.

"Ken is me!" shouts Gosling's Ken, in an act of awareness and taking a stand. For
Stereotype Barbie, it's not so simple: "I'm not really sure where I belong anymore.
I don't think I have an ending.

At this point of uncertainty, Stereotype Barbie turns to Ruth the creator of the Barbie
doll, whom she also met in the real world in the Mattel office building - and confides,
"Maybe I'm not Barbie anymore". Ruth's wisdom leads her down a path of awareness
and reflection:

R: "You understand that humans only have one ending. *Ideas live forever*. Humans,
not so much. You know that, right?".

S. B: "I do."

R: "Being a human can be pretty uncomfortable."

S. B: "I know."

R: "Humans make things up, like patriarchy and Barbie just to deal with how
uncomfortable it is."

S. B: "I understand that."

R: "And then you die!".

S. B: [laughing] "...yeah. Yeah. I wanna be part of the people that *make meaning*,
not the thing that's made. I want to do the imagining. I don't want to be the idea.
Does that make sense?".

The conventional notion of Barbie as a mere stereotype is no longer sufficient to
capture her essence. She has transcended the limitations of an idea, an object, or a
commodified representation of an idealized body. She aspires to embody sentiments,
intricacy, and mortality. Thus, she is no longer a mere Stereotype Barbie; she is no
longer even a Barbie at all. She is simply identified as "Barbie."

Ruth, clothed in azure garments reminiscent of those worn by the Blue Fairy in
Pinocchio, extends her hands and exhorts her to experience the true essence of humanity:
"Now, feel".

Subsequently, a video montage of scenes depicting individuals experiencing a range
of emotional states is initiated, accompanied by Billie Elish's performance of "What

Was I Made For?," a song characterised by a pervasive sense of melancholy. The video demonstrates that life, in contrast to the idealised version portrayed in Barbieland, is characterised by uncertainty, challenges and the potential for both joy and pain. The video depicts the transition from a carefree, childlike existence to a more complex and nuanced understanding of life as a human being. It illustrates that the knowledge that there are no guarantees is an inherent part of this experience. Barbie makes a conscious decision to leave Barbieland and pursue a life in the tangible world.

The final scene portrays Gloria and Sasha accompanying Barbie in a vehicle in front of a building. The atmosphere is characterised by a sense of anticipation, as though an imminent and significant event is about to take place. The mother and daughter bestow their blessings upon her, after which Barbie exits the vehicle. She then proceeds to the examination room, where it becomes evident that she is undergoing her inaugural gynaecological examination. Having previously existed as a Barbie without genitalia, she is now Barbara, a woman who exercises autonomy over her body and makes decisions about her reproductive health with agency. This transition signifies her emergence as a fully realised individual.

3   An Exploratory Inquiry with Italian Teachers on the film Barbie (2023)

Since Barbie (2023) is a blockbuster movie at the box office that is seen and commented on by people of all ages and backgrounds, I wondered what the opinion of Italian teachers was about this movie.

To this end, an ad hoc semi-structured interview was created and administered through the free Google Forms platform. The survey comprised five questions pertaining to socio-anagraphical data and seven questions about the film. It was disseminated online via Facebook groups comprising teachers, a process known as snowball sampling, which enabled the participation of 209 teachers. The sample had an average age of 40, with 189 individuals identifying as female, 14 as male, four as non-binary, and one as questioning (Fig. 1).

In regard to their profession (Fig. 2), 44.76% (n = 94) are employed in primary education, where they instruct children between the ages of 6 and 10. 26.19% (n = 54) are engaged in secondary education at the first grade level, where they instruct teenagers between the ages of 11 and 13. 29.05% (n = 61) are employed in secondary education at the second grade level, where they instruct teenagers between the ages of 14 and 19.

Regarding educational qualification: 81% (n = 171) has a master's degree; 4% (n = 9) have a bachelor's degree; 5 people have a PhD; 17 hold only a secondary school diploma and of these 4 are students in the Primary Education degree program; 8 hold a postgraduate master's degree.

The first question inherent to the movie was formulated as follows, "Why did you decide to watch the movie 'Barbie'?" The analysis of the answers (Table 1) showed that the main motivation was curiosity, but also a nostalgic connection with the doll that was part of one's childhood: "I have so many wonderful memories related to this doll"; "I have always loved Barbie: she was an innovative doll who gave a lot to women's

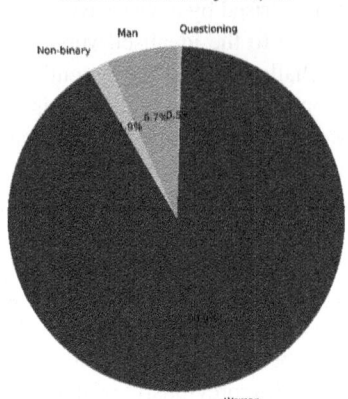

Fig. 1. Gender Distribution among partecipants

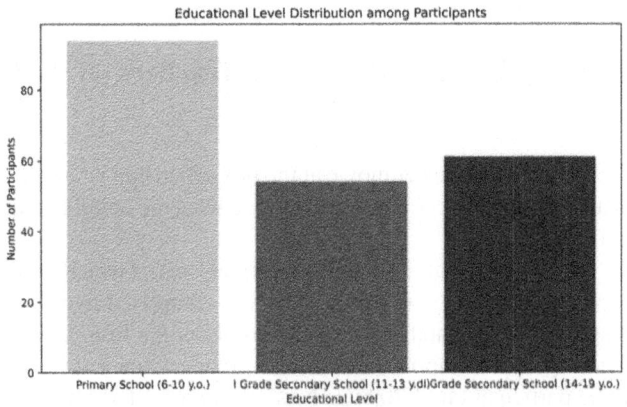

Fig. 2. Educational Level Distribution

emancipation. She took care of herself. She had professions, she was not a mother, she loved to have fun."

Some people wrote that they watched the film because they had "high expectations of the twisting of the classic role of Barbies," or because they expected a film "about women's empowerment," a film that was "important," "funny," and "liberating" that "makes people laugh but also reflect." Someone went to the cinema "to see if they wanted to change the stereotype of the perfect woman always attributed to this doll" because of the "positive reviews from feminist activists I respect," attracted by the "feminist themes that the film promised to deal with"-such as "the denunciation of patriarchy"-and thus by the fact that the film could be "an opportunity to reflect on important issues in an original way."

Someone decided to see it "to turn off the brain," someone else "to understand what lay beyond the apparent trashiness," one person because he was surprised to read a positive review published in a Catholic association magazine. One specified that she saw it because her pupils had watched it: "How can I talk to my pupils if I don't know what animates their debates?" (Table 1).

Table 1. Reasons for watching the film

Why did you decide to watch the film?	n. answers
out of curiosity	129
connection with Barbie dolls from childhood	32
to accompany someone	27
for the reviews/opinions of other people	14
I like the director	9
entertainment	8
for the plot/themes addressed	8
I was influenced by the marketing operation	7
for the cast	6
it was recommended to me	5
attracted by the trailer	5
I watch all the films	4
for the music and atmosphere	2
desire to be controversial	1

To investigate the degree of appreciation of the movie, I used a 5-point Lickert scale, asking the question "How much did you like the movie?" and providing 5 response alternatives: "not at all," "a little," "quite a lot," and "very much." No one selected "very much," 34.45% (n = 72) liked it "a lot," 38.76% (n = 81) "quite a lot," 21.05% (n = 44) "a little," 5.74% (n = 12) "not at all."

Only 5 people said that the expectations they had were disregarded in the negative, 2% that the film exceeded their expectations-"I thought it was a film that commodified women's bodies [...] it was unexpected. It is actually a denunciation of the condition of women, but it shows that the supremacy of someone (the man in our reality and the Barbies in Barbie Land), generate frustration in the one who feels sidelined."

By virtue of the trend of the online debate about the film, I found it interesting to cross-reference the data on levels of appreciation with gender (Fig. 3), age (Fig. 4) and the order of school in which the sample of teachers work (Fig. 5).

From the categorical analysis of the responses given to explain the level of appreciation, the following emerged (Fig. 6, Fig. 7): 52 people appreciated the "funny," "ironic," "at times irreverent," "light," and "profound" way in which the messages are conveyed; others found it "trivial" (n = 20), "exaggerated/cloying (n = 5) ("too exasperating all that pink"); 5 found it 'stupid' ("a demented, stupid, girly movie"). Regarding the theme of stereotypes: 34 people saw the staging of gender stereotypes as a criticism of them; 12 people felt instead that the film reinforced them.

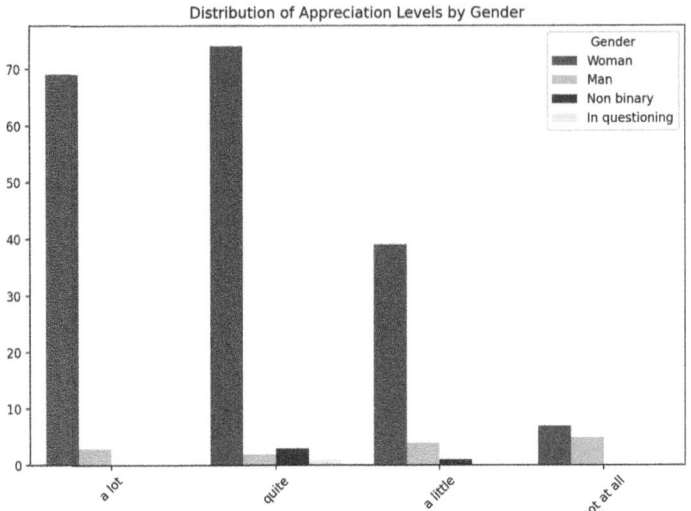

Fig. 3. Distribution of Appreciation Levels by Gender

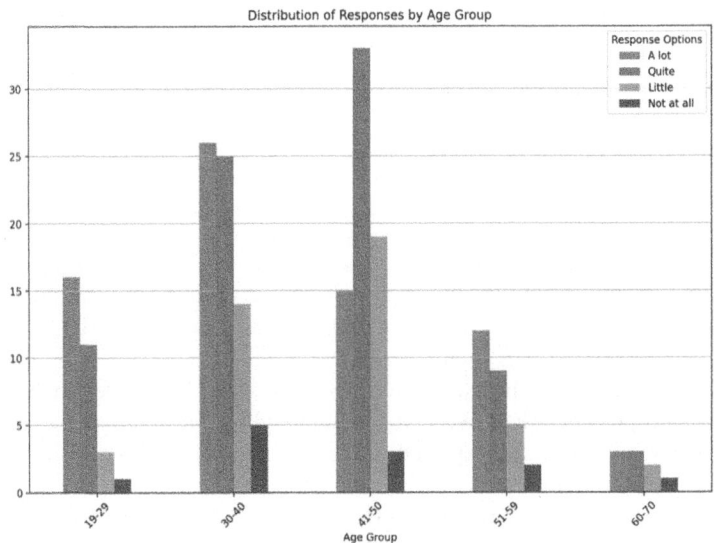

Fig. 4. Distribution of Appreciation Levels by Age Group

Cross-referencing the levels of appreciation and motivations with gender, it becomes evident that men, who represent a small part of the sample, showed lower levels of appreciation, calling the film "a demented movie for little girls" "full of boring rhetoric," "useless" because it "lacks content," and "a sensationalist Americanism, a marketing operation for a movie that is not a movie but is entertainment." Some also explicitly referred to not liking the way the male gender is portrayed in the film: "Ken is unbearable

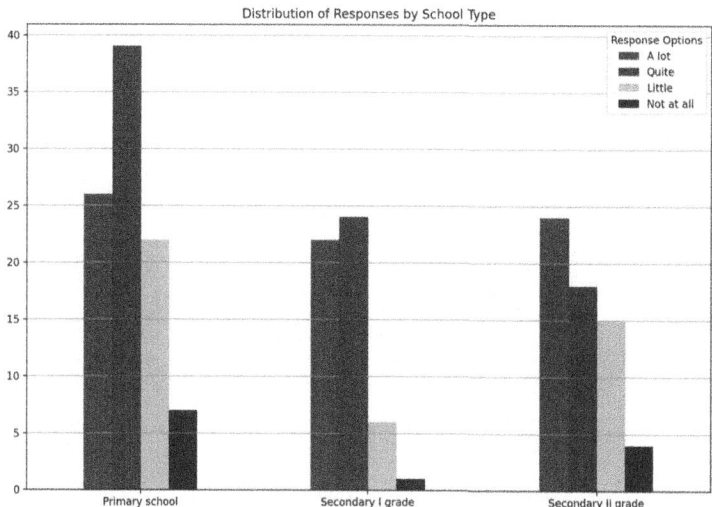

Fig. 5. Distribution of Appreciation Levels by School Type

because the director is a feminist," "it's one thing to fight patriarchy but here they want to propagate matriarchy and that's not right." Others, referring to the messages conveyed called it a "dangerous" film (n = 3) because "it makes one believe that with aesthetics one becomes popular"; 5 stated that there is no educational message: "It doesn't teach anything because the film is a series of ideological and objectively boring catchphrases," "It is a meaningless film made only to make people angry," "If someone will let children see it, I hope they will at least laugh at the nonsense that is put forward as if it were grand ideals," "It is only suitable for little girls").

With the next question, it was asked, "Would you let your students see the movie?"; and they were given a choice of three response options, "Yes, all of it," "Yes, some scenes/parts," and "No," asking them to give reasons for their chosen option. 56 people stated that they would not show it to their pupils, 85 that they would show it all of it, 68 that they would show only some parts/scenes of it. The results were then cross-referenced with levels of appreciation and the type of school in which they work (Fig. 8).

Through the responses provided by survey participants, several key themes emerge that deserve careful consideration. One of the most relevant aspects that emerged from the responses is the different ability to understand the film according to the age of the audience.

None of the participants reported any reflection on the representation of BIPOC, disabled and fat people in the film (Laffier & Westley; 2024; Centrone, 2023), nor on the multiple allegories embodied by the character of Allan -who is neither Barbie nor Ken, but authentically and uniquely Allan as discussed in the previous paragraph.

Many participants emphasize how the film can be more thoroughly appreciated and understood by adolescents and adults than by younger children. This is due to the complexity of the themes covered, such as patriarchy, feminism, and gender stereotypes, which require greater maturity and awareness to be fully assimilated. It was then asked

	Banal	6	plasticky	1
	Stupid	2	useless	1
not at all	insignificant/uninterest ing	2	Nosey	1
	masculinist/ patriarchal	2	disappointed my expectations	1
	Too many stereotypes	1	cloying	1
	I consider it not well done	1	is a series of ideological and objectively boring catchphrases that even overwhelmed the plot.	1

	Banal	14	frivolous/at times demented	2
	disappointed my expectations	11	Not my film genre	2
little	Nosey	4	Because I heard the terms too much: sadness, anxiety, die and I don't find them suitable for the public of the very young	1
	Too many stereotypes	4	It seemed confused and contradictory	1
	Exaggerated	3	cloying	1
	Stupid	3	sad morality	1

Fig.6. Categorical analysis of the answers given to the question "How much did you like the film? And why?"

"do you think the movie Barbie is suitable for an audience of" and it was possible to tick more than one option from the following: "children (6–12)," "young adults (13- 18)," "adults > 18."

29.19% (n = 61) considered it a suitable film for children (6–12); 81.34% (n = 170) considered it suitable for young adults (13–18); 57.89% (n = 121) considered it suitable for adults. A central theme of the film is the deconstruction of gender stereotypes and the promotion of equality between men and women. Many participants highlight how the film ironically and provocatively addresses these issues, questioning the roles traditionally associated with male and female. There also emerges an awareness that gender stereotypes are harmful not only to women, but also to men, limiting their freedom of expression and personal fulfillment. Despite the complexity of some of the themes, many participants believe that the film can be suitable for different age groups, as long as it is accompanied by appropriate adult mediation and explanation. While younger children might grasp mainly the playful and narrative aspects, adolescents and adults would be able to understand more deeply the educational messages and reflections on gender roles.

quite	The way the film was made/developed the story/treated the themes	23	disappointed my expectations	5
	Because it deals with and brings us closer to the issues of feminism	21	Because it breaks down stereotypes	4
	For the messages conveyed/themes	19	offers insights for discussion	3
	For the direction / cast / setting.	12	Not my film genre	2
	it makes one think	8	because of the way Barbie was portrayed	2
	nostalgia/connection with childhood	6	exceeded my expectations	2

a lot	The way the film was made/developed the story/treated the themes	29	For the direction / cast / setting.	7
	For the messages conveyed/themes	29	exceeded my expectations	7
	Because it deals with and brings us closer to the issues of feminism	23	nostalgia/connection with childhood	4
	it makes one think	8	Not my film genre	2
	Because it breaks down stereotypes	8	offers insights for discussion	1

Fig. 7. Categorical analysis of the answers given to the question "How much did you like the film? And why?"

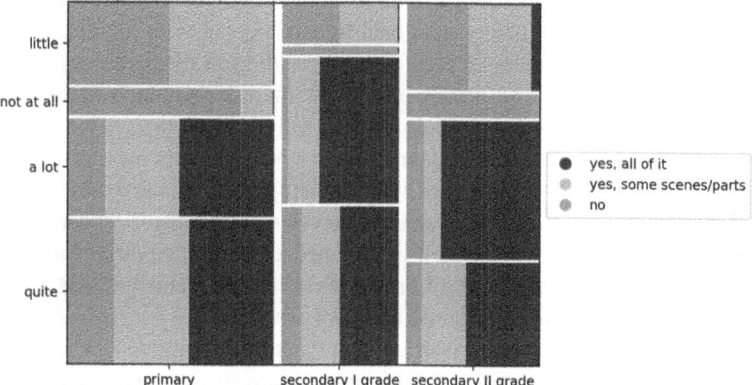

Fig. 8. Mosaic of the distribution of appreciation levels by order of school in which the sample works and the response to the question "would you show the film to your students?"

Data were cross-referenced with the type of school in which teachers work (Fig. 9).

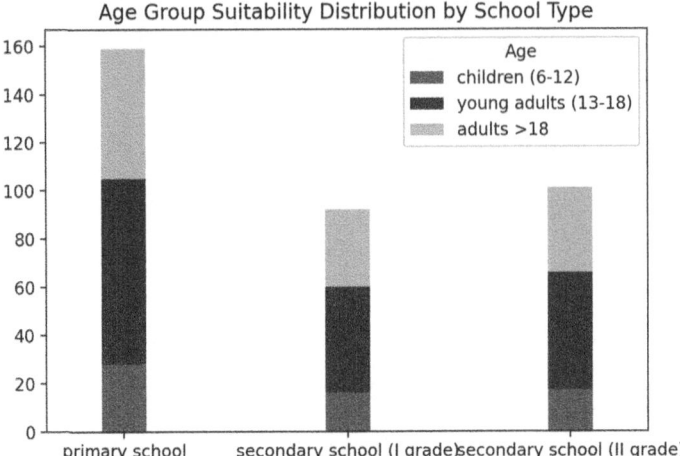

Fig. 9. Distribution of Age Group Suitability by Teacher's School Type Categorical analysis of the responses given to motivate the choice of age group considered most suitable reveals that 43.5% of participants discussed the suitability of the film for different age groups, highlighting the importance of adult mediation to ensure proper understanding of the film's messages. 12.9% addressed issues of understanding and interpretation, while 3.3% focused on gender stereotypes. The film's complexity and educational messages were mentioned by 2.9% of participants, respectively.

The semi-structured interview concluded with the question, "What values and educational messages do you think the film can convey?" 15 people explicitly stated that the film contained "no educational message," and among them one wrote "I think the intent was feminist so no educational message," and one specified that he was confused "by the contradictory and therefore non-educational messages." Confusion about what the adjective feminist means and what feminism is emerges from other responses. It is interesting to juxtapose two responses given by two people with identical socio-anagraphic characteristics (female, 42 years of age, residing in the same city, having the same educational qualification): one asserted that "there is too much feminism in this film" while the other that "it is a masculinist film with little depth."

Through an analysis of audience perceptions, several key themes have been identified, reflecting the film's engagement with contemporary social issues. Participants attributed the messages conveyed by the film to seven macro-categories: gender equality and empowerment, authenticity and self-acceptance, challenging patriarchal structures, the importance of relationships and solidarity, diversity and inclusion, personal growth and determination, and facing ambiguity and contradictions.

Gender equality and empowerment were frequently highlighted, with 12.44% of responses mentioning this theme: respondents noted how the film challenges traditional gender stereotypes and promotes equal rights for women. As one viewer observed, the film "promotes the idea of gender equality and challenges the patriarchal structures that have historically oppressed women." This sentiment underscores the film's role in advocating for a more equitable society.

Authenticity and self-acceptance emerged as another critical theme, appearing in 0.96% of responses. The film encourages viewers to embrace their unique identities and resist societal pressures to conform. This message resonates with contemporary movements advocating for authenticity and diversity. A respondent expressed this by stating, "The film encourages self-acceptance and the importance of being true to oneself, rather than conforming to societal expectations."

The film also critiques patriarchal structures and power dynamics, a theme present in 5.74% of responses, raising awareness about the need to dismantle these systems. This theme aligns with broader societal efforts to address systemic inequalities and promote social justice. One viewer remarked: "The film addresses and critiques the patriarchal structures, encouraging viewers to question and challenge these power dynamics." The importance of relationships and solidarity is another theme, highlighted in 1.44% of responses, emphasizing the value of connection and support among individuals. The film underscores the power of relationships in fostering understanding and collaboration, which is crucial in today's interconnected world.

26% say that educational messages include looking beyond appearances, rethinking women as subjects with intelligence and agency, and female independence and power- "Women can aspire to power roles. Women can do any profession." 1 argued that the film conveys the message that women are stupid.

Diversity and inclusion are central to the film's message, mentioned in 6.7% of responses, promoting a more inclusive understanding of identity and encouraging viewers to look beyond physical appearance. This theme is particularly relevant in the context of ongoing debates about body positivity and the need to redefine beauty standards.

Personal growth and determination are emphasized, with 6.22% of responses reflecting this theme, conveying the message of overcoming limitations and pursuing one's dreams. This theme inspires viewers to break free from societal constraints and strive for personal and professional aspirations.

Finally, the theme of facing ambiguity and contradictions was not explicitly mentioned in the responses, indicating a potential area for further exploration in understanding the film's impact.

The film Barbie has emerged as a significant cultural artefact, prompting debate about its educational messages and societal impact. An analysis of the participants' responses reveals the richness and complexity of the film, which is capable of stimulating critical reflection on issues of great social and cultural relevance. Despite its apparent light-heartedness, the film proves to be an efficacious instrument for the elevation of awareness and the advancement of gender equality. It is adaptable to different age groups and offers a multiplicity of insights and discussion points.

Awareness of the film's complexity, which extends beyond a mere critique of gender stereotypes to encompass a multitude of interpretative possibilities, was evident in a significant proportion of the sample. Indeed, some participants highlighted that the film can be viewed as a metaphor for society, encompassing its mechanisms of power and exclusion, and as an invitation for broader reflection on the human condition and the values of equality, respect and acceptance of differences.

The diversity of opinions underscores the importance of discussing gender stereo-types from an early age, suggesting that the film can serve as a starting point for educational conversations on these issues (Belotti, 1991).

4 Conclusions

The analysis of the readability levels of a mainstream film such as Barbie (2023) is a challenging undertaking, particularly when employing an intersectional lens to assess the extent to which it incorporates feminist themes in a manner that is both accessible and reflective of current educational practices. This analysis may also inform the potential use of the film in an educational setting, such as in the classroom, with the objective of fostering critical engagement with cinematic content among students.

The analysis of the film's educational messages and the exploratory survey conducted with 209 Italian teachers did not provide sufficient evidence to answer the question of whether Barbie can be considered a feminist movie. This analysis does not seek to determine whether a mainstream film, which opens with the Mattel sign, can be considered a feminist manifesto. It is therefore important to consider why films created by women for women are often entrusted with the responsibility of representing the demands of feminism, despite the fact that Barbie can also be enjoyed and discussed by non-female audiences. It is possible that there is a dearth of films directed by women that are aimed at a socially-defined female audience.

The film Barbie serves as an effective vehicle for exposing the hypocrisies and flaws inherent to patriarchy. This is achieved in two ways: firstly, through the actions and dialogue of certain characters; secondly, through the film's plot and performances. The film denounces the status of women and offers a critique of toxic masculinity and power structures that impede the establishment of a society based on personal freedom and mutual respect. It is unclear whether this is sufficient to qualify the film as a "feminist film", but it is undoubtedly a film that can be utilised in an educational setting as a tool for reflection on a multitude of issues.

The findings of the exploratory survey, which was conducted among 209 Italian teachers, indicate that more than half of the participants lacked the necessary film analy-sis tools to fully comprehend the educational messages and values conveyed by the film. The claim that the film's objective was to convey a feminist message, yet it lacks an educational component, or that it is excessively feminist, indicates a lack of understand-ing of the tenets of feminism and the demands of feminist movements. The comments regarding appreciation and educational messages are diverse and reflect the polarisation of the online debate that commenced even before the film's theatrical release. The film Barbie is perceived by its audience to convey a number of important educational mes-sages, including those related to gender equality, self-acceptance, respect for diversity, the importance of seeking one's authentic self, and the challenge to patriarchal norms. These themes are significant in the context of contemporary social issues and indicate the film's potential to influence societal perceptions and discourse. By addressing these piv-otal issues, the film makes a contribution to the ongoing discourse surrounding equality, empowerment and the celebration of diversity.

The following topics may be considered: representations, the ideal of perfection, standards of bodily conformity, social pressures, gender stereotypes, generational confrontation, waves of feminism, the intergenerational clash, machismo and toxic masculinity, performativity, gender stereotypes and gender roles, the absence of women in top positions, competitiveness, self-seeking, power dynamics, friendship and love relationships, anxiety, the meaning of life, self-determination and agency. These are among the messages and values that can be discussed from viewing this film, which illustrates that the dismantling of patriarchy must involve all subjectivities, as no individual can truly be free within this structure. It would appear that not all of the teachers who participated in the survey were able to fully comprehend the full complexity of the messages.

The film Barbie should prompt reflection on the education imparted to males, who must be encouraged and placed in a position to manifest, reason and express their emotions in freedom and without fear of judgement. Furthermore, it should prompt reflection on how to deconstruct the ideals of beauty and performativity in the classroom through continuous cross-disciplinary work that highlights the constraints and contradictions of an individualistic and capitalist system. Ultimately, it should prompt reflection on how gender expectations influence one's growth and freedom to discover one's authentic self.

Moreover, the online debate and the findings of this preliminary investigation prompt us to consider the nature of the training provided to teachers. What knowledge and skills should those tasked with the education and training of young adults in our society possess? It is therefore imperative to consider how we can instill in our students the capacity for critical thinking and analysis, given that those responsible for their education lack even the most basic understanding of the history of feminist liberation movements. It is these movements that have enabled our students to enjoy fundamental rights and freedoms, including the capacity to respond to a written questionnaire independently.

It is evident that the sample used in this study is not representative; however, the findings are not unexpected, as they corroborate the existing literature on the limited literacy and competence in matters pertaining to gender equality, education for differences, and the prevention of homosexual-, biphobic, ableist and fatphobic bullying (Batini & Santoni, 2009; Cajola & Ciraci, 2018; Centrone, 2024; Fiorucci, 2018; Elamè, 2013; Menesini et al., 2017). Moreover, the online debate and the findings of this preliminary investigation prompt us to consider the nature of the training provided to teachers. What knowledge and skills should those tasked with the education and training of young adults in our society possess? It is therefore imperative to consider how we can instill in our students the capacity for critical thinking and analysis, given that those responsible for their education lack even the most basic understanding of the history of feminist liberation movements. It is these movements that have enabled our students to enjoy fundamental rights and freedoms, including the capacity to respond to a written questionnaire independently.

It is evident that the sample used in this study is not representative; however, the findings are not unexpected, as they corroborate the existing literature on the limited literacy and competence in matters pertaining to gender equality, education for differences, and the prevention of homosexual-, biphobic, ableist and fatphobic bullying (Batini & Santoni, 2009; Cajola & Ciraci, 2018; Centrone, 2024; Fiorucci, 2018; Elamè, 2013; Menesini et al., 2017).

It can be concluded that, although the survey question pertained to the teachers' opinions and appreciation of the film, the data analysis outcomes and the subsequent paper suggest that the viewing and discussion of the film Barbie should be included in the teacher training courses that are currently delivered at the University of Roma Tre (It- aly). A subsequent contribution will address the aforementioned outcomes in greater detail.

Disclosure of Interests. The author have no competing interests to declare that are relevant to the content of this article.

References

Ahmed, S.: The promise of happiness. Duke University Press (2020)
Anderson, E.K., Long, C.: Film Review: Tiny Shoulders: Rethinking Barbie. *Teaching Sociology* **52**(1), 100–102 (2024)
Armengol, J. M.: Masculinities and literary studies: Past, present, and future directions. In: Routledge International Handbook of Masculinity Studies, pp. 425–433. Routledge (2019)
Armengol, J. M.: Reescrituras de la masculinidad: hombres y feminismo. Alianza Editorial (2022)
Armengol, J. M.: Rewriting White Masculinities in Contemporary Fiction and Film. Springer International Publishing AG (2024)
Batini, F., Santoni, B. (eds.): L'identità sessuale a scuola. Educare alla diversità e prevenire l'omofobia. Liguori (2009)
Becker, H.S.: Outsiders. Studies in the Sociology of Deviance, 1 (1963)
Belotti, E.G.: Dalla parte delle bambine: l'influenza dei condizionamenti sociali nella for- mazione del ruolo femminile nei primi anni di vita, vol. 45. Feltrinelli Editore (1991)
Bocci, F., Domenici, V.: La diversità nelle narrazioni seriali contemporanee. Un'analisi critica dei processi di incorporazione e immunizzazione. *Italian Journal of special education for inclusion* **7**(2), 416–429 (2019)
Bocci, F., Straniero, A.M.: Altri corpi. Visioni e rappresentazioni della (e incursioni sulla) disabilità e diversità, vol. 10. Roma TrE-Press (2020)
Bocci, F., Gaggioli, C., Giannoumis, A.,& Ranieri, M.: Editoriale. Un numero speciale per riflettere su Media Education e Inclusione. Media Educ. **13**(1), 3–5 (2022)
Bordo, S.: Unbearable weight: Feminism, Western culture, and the body. Univ of California Press (2023)
Brittan, A.: Masculinity and Power. Basil Blackwell (1989)
Buckingham, D.: Media education and the end of the critical consumer. Harvard educational review **73**(3), 309–327 (2003)
Buckingham, D.: Media education. Alfabetizzazione, apprendimento e cultura contemporanea. Edizioni Erickson (2006)
Buenavista, T.L., et al.: A praxis of critical race love: Toward the abolition of cishet- eropatriarchy and toxic masculinity in educational justice formations. Educ. Stud. **57**(3), 238–249 (2021)
Burn, A.: Media literacy in schools: Practice, production and progression. Paul Chapman (2007)
Butler, J.: Gender Trouble: Feminism and the Subversion of Identity. Routledge (1990)
Butler, J.: Gender trouble. Routledge (2002)
Butler, J.: Undoing Gender. Routledge (2004)
Cajola, L. C., & Ciraci, A. M.: Il docente inclusivo tra bisogni formativi e pratiche didat- tiche. Un'indagine empirica sulla efficacia dei corsi di formazione. *MeTis-Mondi educativi. Temi indagini suggestioni* **8**(2), 292–329 (2018)

Campbell, A.: Female competition: Causes, constraints, content, and contexts. J. Sex Res. **41**(1), 16–26 (2004)

Carabí, À., Armengol, J.M. (eds.): Alternative masculinities for a changing world, p. 1. Palgrave Macmillan, New York (2014)

Centrone, B.: Corpi dissidenti, menti divergenti, esistenze irriverenti: i Crip Studies. In: Valtellina, E. (ed.) Introduzione ai Disability Studies. UTET (in press)

Centrone, B.: Intersezione spettro autistico e queerness. In: Corbisiero, F., Monaco, S. (eds.) Manuale di studi LGBTQIA+. UTET Università, Torino (2023)

Centrone, B.: La mostrificazione come processo di discriminazione. Una rilettura secondo la prospettiva dei Disability Studies. In: Bocci, F. and Valtellina, E. (eds.) Freakery. La costruzione del «mostro» (I), *Minority Reports. Cultural Disability Studies*, vol. 17, n. 2 (2024)

Centrone, B., Travaglini, A., Guerini, I.: Disabilità e narrazioni animate. Luci e ombre su cui riflettere. Q-TIMES WEBMAGAZINE, 361–375 (2023)

Centrone, B.: Anche una parola cambia tutto. Un'indagine esplorativa su pregiudizi, linguaggio e rappresentazioni di e con un gruppo di futuri/e insegnanti. In: Pinelli, S., Fiorucci, A., Giaconi, C. (eds.) I linguaggi della Pedagogia Speciale. Pensamultimedia (2024)

Cohen, J.J.: Monster Theory: Reading Culture. University of Minnesota, Minneap- olis (1996)

Collodi, C.: Le avventure di Pinocchio. Libreria Editrice Felice Paggi (1881)

Connell, R.W.: Masculinities. University of California Press, Berkeley, Los Angeles (2005)

Costello, W., Rolon, V., Thomas, A.G., Schmitt, D.: Levels of well-being among men who are incel (involuntarily celibate). Evol. Psychol. Sci. **8**(4), 375–390 (2022)

Crenshaw, K.: Demarginalizing the Intersection of Race and Sex: A Black Feminist Cri- tique of Antidiscrimination Doctrine, Feminist Theory and Antiracist Politics. *University of Chicago Legal Forum* (1989)

de Beauvoir, S.: The Second Sex. Gallimard (1949)

de Beauvoir, S.: The second sex (1st Vintage Books ed.). (C. Borde, S. Malovany-Chevallier, & J. Thurman, Trans.) (1949)

De Lauretis, T.: Technologies of Gender: Essays on Theory, Film, and Fiction. Indiana University Press (1987)

Edwards, T.: Cultures of Masculinity. Routledge (2006)

Elamé, E.: Bullismo discriminante e pedagogia interculturale. Franco Angeli (2013)

Farrell, A.E.: Fat shame: Stigma and the fat body in American culture. NYU Press (2011)

Federici, S.: Calibano e la strega: le donne, il corpo e l'accumulazione originaria. Mimesis (2020)

Fiorucci, A.: Omofobia, bullismo e scuola. Atteggiamenti degli insegnanti e sviluppo di pratiche inclusive a sostegno della differenza. Erickson (2018)

Fiorucci, A.: Omofobia, bullismo e scuola: Atteggiamenti degli insegnanti e sviluppo di pratiche inclusive a sostegno della differenza. Edizioni Centro Studi Erickson (2023)

Freire, P.: Pedagogy of the Oppressed. Herder and Herder (1970)

Gancitano, M.: Specchio delle mie brame. Einaudi, Torino (2022)

Gasparrini, L.: Perché il femminismo serve anche agli uomini. Eris (2020)

Gerwig, G. (Director): Barbie [Film]. Warner Bros. Pictures (2023)

Gill, R.: Postfeminist Media Culture: Elements of a Sensibility. Europ. J. Cultural Stud. **10**(2), 147–166 (2007)

Gilligan, C.: New maps of development: new visions of maturity. *American Journal of Orthopsychiatry* 52(2), 199 (1982)

Glace, A.M., Dover, T.L., Zatkin, J.G.: Taking the black pill: An empirical analysis of the "Incel". Psychol. Men Masculinities **22**(2), 288 (2021)

Goffman, E.: Stigma: Notes on the management of spoiled identity. Simon and schuster (2009)

Harrington, C.: What is "toxic masculinity" and why does it matter? Men masculinities **24**(2), 345–352 (2021)

Hobbs, R.: Digital and media literacy: Connecting culture and classroom. Corwin Press (2011)

Hooks, B.: Feminism is for Everybody: Passionate Politics. South End Press (2000)

Hooks, B.: The Will to Change: Men, Masculinity, and Love. Washington Square Press (2004)

Jenkins, H.: Confronting the challenges of participatory culture: Media education for the 21st century, p. 145. The MIT press (2009)

Kianpour, C.K.: The political speech rights of the tokenized. Critical Rev. Int. Soc. Political Philosophy, 1–21 (2023)

Kellner, D., Share, J.: Critical media literacy: Crucial policy choices for a twenty-first- century democracy. Policy Futures Educ. 5(1), 59–69 (2007)

Kimmel, M.S.: Guyland: The Perilous World Where Boys Become Men. HarperCollins (2008)

La Porte, A., Cavusoglu, L.: Faux Feminism in a Capitalistic Fever Dream: A Review of Greta Gerwig's Barbie (2023). Markets, Globalization & Development Review 8(2) (2023)

Laffier, J., Westley, M.: Exploring classroom media, trauma, and impacts on marginalized youth. In: EDULEARN24 Proceedings, pp. 7877–7886. IATED (2024)

Lippi, S., Maniglier, P.: Sorellanze. Per una psicoanalisi femminista. Deriveapprodi, Bologna (2024)

Lonzi, C.: Sputiamo su Hegel. Scritti di Rivolta Femminile (1970)

Lorde, A.: Sister outsider: Essays and speeches. Crossing Press (2012)

MacInnes, J.: The End of Masculinity: The Confusion of Sexual Genesis and Sexual Difference in Modern Society. Open University Press (1998)

Maragliano, R., Pireddu, M.: Storia e pedagogia nei media. Narcissus.me (2014)

Marocchini, E.: Neurodivergente. Edizioni Tlon (2024)

Masterman, L.: Teaching the media. Routledge (2003)

McLuhan, M.: Understanding media: The extensions of man. MIT press (1994)

McRuer, R.: Crip theory. Cultural signs of queerness and disability (2008)

Menapace, L.: Il futurismo della parola. Edizioni Gruppo Abele (2008)

Menesini, E., Nocentini, A. e Palladino, B.E.: Prevenire e contrastare il bullismo e il cyberbullismo. Il Mulino (2017)

Messner, M. A.: Politics of masculinities: Men in movements, vol. 3. Rowman & Littlefield (1997)

Murgia, M.: Stai zitta. Einaudi (2021)

Naylor, R.L.: Why Barbie and not Oppenheimer: A Film Review of Barbie, directed by Greta Gerwig. Warner Bros. Pictures, 2023. Endeavour 47(3), 100873 (2023)

Noddings, N.: An ethic of caring. In: Justice and care: Essential readings in feminist ethics, pp. 699–712 (1995)

Romeo, C. S.: Femminismo postcoloniale. In: Femministe a parole. Grovigli da districare, pp. 101–105. Ediesse (2012)

Rivoltella, P.C.: Media education. Idea, metodo, ricerca. Scholé (2019)

Snow, E.: Theorizing the male gaze: Some problems. Representations (25), 30–41 (1989)

Stoll, L. C., Meadows, A., von Liebenstein, S., Carlsen, C.E.: Fatphobia. In: Global Agenda for Social Justice 2, pp. 37–44. Policy Press (2022)

Stryker, S.: Transgender History. Seal Press, Berkeley, CA (2008)

Thoman, E.: Skills and strategies for media education. Educ. Leadership 56, 50–54 (1999)

Vassallo, B.: Per una rivoluzione degli affetti: Pensiero monogamo e terrore poliamoroso. effequ (2022)

Whitehead, S.M.: Men and Masculinities: Key Themes and New Directions. Polity Press (2002)

Wittig, M.: One is not born a woman. Taylor & Francis (1997)

Yuval-Davis, N.: Intersectionality and feminist politics. Europ. J. Women's Stud. 13(3), 193–209 (2006)

Zappino, F.: Il genere tra neoliberismo e neofondamentalismo. ombre corte, Verona (2016)

Zappino, F.: Comunismo queer: Note per una sovversione dell'eterosessualità. Mimesis (2019)

Webtvs as Channels for Scientific Communication: A Case Study from the University of Foggia

Alice Rizzi(✉) ⒾⒹ, Marco di Furia ⒾⒹ, and Giusi Antonia Toto ⒾⒹ

Università degli Studi di Foggia, 71121 Foggia, FG, Italy
{alice.rizzi,marco.difuria,giusi.toto}@unifg.it

Abstract. In the digital age, universities, as centers of research and innovation, are embracing new modes of communication by integrating digital tools to disseminate educational content, engage diverse audiences, and enhance learning experiences. University Web TV stands as a prime example of this evolution, serving as a versatile multimedia platform for delivering academic lectures, seminars, and other educational resources to a global audience. By breaking down geographic barriers, it democratizes access to knowledge. Moreover, it enables universities to showcase their research initiatives, cultural events, and community outreach programs. This article aims to delve deeper into the significance of university Web TV and analyze its potential as a tool for research, data collection, and scientific dissemination. Finally, adopting a multidisciplinary approach, this paper will scrutinize the successful case of University Web TV at the University of Foggia ("WeUnifg" project). As an innovative and multifaceted tool, university Web TV has the potential to become the university channel of the future. Its myriad uses, from facilitating access to education to innovating teaching methods and promoting student involvement in academic research activities (and vice versa), are yet to be fully explored. Moreover, it holds significance in shaping public perception of science and attracting new talent to research.

Keywords: WebTV · University · Digital Media

1 Introduction

In the digital age, universities, as centers of research and innovation, are embracing new modes of communication, integrating digital tools to enhance the dissemination of educational content, engage diverse audiences, and improve learning experiences. University Web TV stands out as a prime example of this transformation, offering a versatile multimedia platform for delivering academic lectures, seminars, and educational resources to a global audience [1]. By breaking down geographic barriers, it democratizes access to knowledge [2], while allowing universities and other educational agencies to showcase research initiatives, cultural events, and community outreach programs [3, 4]. This article examines the significance of university Web TV and proposes it as a tool for observation and research in the context of innovative scientific dissemination

G. A. Toto (Ed.): ICS exchange 2024, CCIS 2521, pp. 449–460, 2025.
https://doi.org/10.1007/978-3-032-03021-4_31

through digital platforms. Moreover, it explores its role in fostering the participation of both temporary and permanent members of the academic community.

As a multifaceted and innovative tool, university Web TV holds potential to become the communication channel of the future, offering benefits such as facilitating access to education, promoting student involvement in academic research, and innovating teaching methods. Furthermore, it plays a key role in shaping public perceptions of science and attracting new talent to research. Our study provides an overview of Web TV initiatives in universities, particularly focusing on the local context, and outlines research pathways that, based on best practices, could lead to its further development in the near future.

A notable case study is the University of Foggia's Web TV, launched in 2022 as an extension of its Web RADIO ("WeUnifg"), which originated as part of the University's internal Contamination Lab (C-Lab) project. The "WeUnifg" project captures the mission of providing a platform for the entire academic community, giving voice to students, faculty, researchers, and administrative staff. Since its inception, the Web TV has produced 46 video podcasts on topics such as teacher education, scientific research, teaching innovation, and cultural initiatives, expanding on the success of the 51 podcasts previously created by the radio project.

The University of Foggia's Web TV offers various services that illustrate its potential. These include the recording and distribution of lectures and seminars as open educational resources (OERs), providing the advantage of being accessible anytime without spatio-temporal limitations [5]. It also enhances the distribution and preservation of research outputs, thereby increasing their social impact [6]. Additionally, the Web TV plays a significant role in cultural events organized by the University, in alignment with the "Third Mission," which evaluates the University's societal impact [7].

Ultimately, the University of Foggia's Web TV serves as an exemplary model for how this tool can be utilized in academia. By studying its application at the local level, we can draw insights that contribute to the ongoing development and expansion of Web TV in universities, allowing it to become a key instrument in scientific dissemination and academic engagement in the near future.

2   Digital Integrations in the University Context: A Contemporary Challenge

2.1   The Impact of Contemporary Media in Educational and Institutional Settings

During the 20th and 21st centuries, the development of digital culture and new technologies has enabled not only the integration but also the enhancement of education through a wide range of resources accessible remotely. The term ICT – Information and Communications Technology – refers to the set of technological processes and tools employed to develop and improve knowledge and learning methods [8]. Currently, the use of ICT in supporting educational paths and processes is rapidly expanding, with the aim of promoting continuous and lifelong learning, overcoming the traditional spatial and temporal constraints of conventional educational systems [9, 10].

Another crucial aspect to consider is that the introduction of new technologies has radically transformed the environment in which the educational process takes place, also facilitating work processes, particularly in terms of organization and decision-making. Moreover, the ability to offer diverse learning spaces and environments broadens the opportunities to meet individual needs [11]. This shift, facilitated by technological evolution, represents a transition from a linear model of knowledge acquisition, limited by the temporal constraint of the "here and now", to a networked model. In this context, formal, informal, and social learning processes, once considered separate, are progressively integrating and harmonizing, further enhancing the effectiveness of both educational and work processes [12].

In this changing perspective, it is essential to emphasize how the advent of new technologies has transformed not only the environment in which the educational process takes place but also the learning needs and requirements of students. Emerging technologies have redefined both the educational context and learning methods, necessitating a more dynamic and flexible approach [5].

The challenge facing public communication within universities today lies in the ability to create spaces, activities, and professional roles aimed at fostering dialogue, exchanges, and relationships between universities, the academic community, and citizens. The spread of mass media and new media has generated enormous potential for innovation in institutional communication spaces [13], which have become polyphonic environments where diverse actors interact and contribute to shaping the image of the university and the content of its institutional communication activities.

Universities are prepared to make a fundamental contribution to the innovation of the core values underpinning their mission (research, teaching, culture, and services) through an innovative network in which university radio and television become central tools in this process [14]. In this sense, the knowledge cultivated within academic institutions reclaims a new centrality, asserting the capacity to lead - and in some cases, accelerate - progressive societal change.

University media, in fact, allow institutions to secure a space of visibility within society, contributing to the reproduction of a shared governance model that engages both students and citizens within the university space to collaboratively address specific problems [15]. At the same time, university media play a decisive role in preparing students for their future entry into the workforce.

This type of student experience, particularly in recent years, highlights and confirms the high potential for integration between tradition and innovation within alternative communication projects of great relevance. A directive issued by the italian Prime Minister on January 27, 1994, outlines the core principles that should characterize innovation in public administration services, particularly in communication, which include:

1. Transparency – visibility
2. Listening – feedback
3. Simplification
4. Participation
5. Evaluation – correction

These principles can be applied to the function of university media (primarily web radio and web TV), which are increasingly becoming public communication tools for academic administrations. They generate a significant impact in terms of information, knowledge, communication, and creativity, engaging an audience that is increasingly involved in content creation and in shaping the identity of their university, especially through social networks.

From this perspective, digital skills are a particularly significant challenge for any educational system, as they are a necessary condition for living in today's world and closely linked to the labor market. Digital competence is, in fact, one of the key competencies that the European Union identified as early as 2006. The European Digital Competence Framework (EQF) has been DigComp since 2013, the first framework for transversal digital competencies, serving as a fundamental reference point for Member States seeking to support the development of their citizens' digital skills.

The model identifies five characteristics that define digital competence:

- **Multidimensional** (requiring the activation of resources from diversedisciplinary-fields,notlimited to information and communication technologies, but also involving various conceptual dimensions, including cognitive, social, and ethical aspects)
- **Transversal** (integrating with other competencies such as problem-solving and metacognition)
- **Historically contextualized** (acquiring meanings that have evolved over time, both due to technological advancements and in relation to the contexts in which it developed)
- **Independent of specific products** (conceived with lifelong learning in mind, it is not tied to a single tool but adapts to changes in commercial products)
- **Adaptable to different usage contexts** (since it is modulated based on the socio-cultural context in which it is applied, it adapts to various situations of use).

In this paper, our aim is to present the experience of the University of Foggia's Web TV as a good practice of this new way of understanding institutional communication, combining the latter with the most interesting aspects of learning through new technologies and new media, as part of a broad discourse around digital skills and media literacy.

2.2 University Web TVs

In both common and academic language, the term "television" often conflates a series of distinct elements:

- The distribution platform
- The technological devices used for access
- The various types of content produced
- The business model that enables its distribution
- The medium itself, understood as the set of cultural, political, social, and economic practices that have made television possible and continue to sustain it today

According to some scholars, the medium is shifting from a producer-controlled flow to one that is increasingly user-generated [16]. The process of digitalization and the first decade of widespread internet use did not significantly impact the evolution of television. It was only from 2005 onward, with the advent of Web 2.0, the proliferation of broadband connectivity, the integration of mobile devices with the internet, and the growing centrality of social networks, that traditional broadcasters began to perceive a real threat. New forms of television, experimented with in the web environment—sometimes with broadcasters themselves leading the innovation—aimed to adapt and reach broader audiences via IP-based platforms.

In the past decade, numerous universities have established well-structured television centers, often initiated by student groups and occasionally with the support of faculty members. Although their creation was sometimes fragmented and overly ambitious, these centers have gradually evolved into technically advanced operations with established content, crucial for both educational and documentary purposes. These university television centers have reached such a level of complexity that they now require dedicated spaces and technological and editorial infrastructures comparable to those of commercial broadcasters.

A university web TV should not limit itself to documenting local events; it should instead evolve into a full-fledged television production that redefines and enriches the events it covers, becoming an additional and distinctive element. The expertise in television production must adapt existing formats, tailoring them to the context of the broadcast while considering an audience that is diverse in both age and skill level. In this process, the use of innovative technologies, from recording equipment to editing and post-production platforms, is crucial in ensuring the effectiveness and strength of the medium as an information tool.

The technologies used for filming and production, as well as the dissemination methodologies, are essential components in which students can be involved, even in the long term. Within universities, this television model has developed its own identity and is constantly evolving, demonstrating significant productive and educational potential.

The development of a university web TV offers multiple learning opportunities on different levels, allowing students to gain a deep understanding of this medium. In terms of content, maintaining an active university web TV requires managing an editorial team and organizing and curating materials. The news production cycle, from editorial management to quality control of the content, involves groups of students in various stages of the process.

A central aspect in all universities is the promotion of student creativity, with students participating in television production by designing original and specific formats that reflect and represent the reality of their university environment [17].

The mission: to move the university beyond self-referentiality by developing innovative communication strategies that interact with the local community, making the university as transparent and visible as possible in everyday social processes; intra- and extra-university service communication; and fostering youth inventiveness and student creativity.

These considerations are fundamental to understanding the target audience of university public communication and the social categories it can address:

- **Students**: an interesting but challenging audience, as they tend to engage less with specialized information.

- **Faculty and staff**: this group requires significant attention. Professors often approach their work in isolation, but communication can help them see that the university's mission is not about individualistic teaching (the belief that their subject is more important than others) but about fostering synergy among faculty to provide a comprehensive education.
- **External audiences**: primarily the families of students, who increasingly want to be involved in their children's educational journey.
- **Businesses and local institutions**: who frequently collaborate with the university to support innovative ideas and talented individuals, creating strategic and innovative human resources for the development of youth entrepreneurship.

One of the most significant topics in describing the functioning of university media is the intersection between the professional television production world and university web TV. These are two realms that, at first glance, seem to have little in common; it is unusual to see the television production world—with its imperative to combine creative ability with the demands of the market—within university classrooms.

Bringing together television producers with faculty and students was an unprecedented insight and represents a pivotal moment in the entire process of creating and sustaining a web TV that is both educational and cultural. It is clear, however, that these two worlds are different: a web TV cannot be reduced to a purely mechanistic production process like a commercial broadcaster. It is essential to respect the educational and formative values inherent in the academic environment, channeling and organizing them into a "pseudo-web-television" perspective.

The interaction between television professionals and students represents an exchange that is sometimes crucial for transforming youthful passion into creative professionalism within an alternative television structure like that of a university web TV.

Students gain experience working on a common project, personally verifying the utility of various tasks: archiving, filming, editing, creating proper editions, planning the shooting schedule, and managing all production phases. This means learning everything that goes into "making television": a thematic TV channel with the same commitment and seriousness required in any similar structure, but with a constant connection to both academic functioning and educational purposes [18].

3   Web TV Experience at the University of Foggia: Project, Workshop, Student Training

3.1   We Unifg

The University of Foggia's Web TV was born by budding off from the Web Radio named "We Unifg," a name that encapsulates the mission and essential meaning of the University of Foggia's internal Contamination Lab (C-Lab) project. The digital broadcaster was born in 2022 as a communication and scientific dissemination channel that could represent the entire academic community, giving voice to students, faculty, researchers, PhD students and technical-administrative and library staff.

Over time, 51 podcasts with cultural and scientific themes have been produced within the "We Unifg" project and, after the birth of Web TV 46 video-podcasts on the topics of teacher education, scientific research, teaching innovation and cultural projects active in the area. The University of Foggia's Web TV represents an interesting case study since it can be taken as a model for understanding how effectively this type of medium can be used in the academic context. Among the services offered by the University of Foggia's Web TV are:

- lectures and seminars recorded and available as open educational resources (OERs), with the advantage of being usable at any time, without spatio-temporal limitations [5];
- presentations of content and research products, enhancing and improving their distribution and preservation and thus their impact on the social fabric [6];
- cultural events organized by and in collaboration with the University in compliance with the so-called Third Mission, a piece that is now considered fundamental for assessing the impact of the academic body's action on the territory [7];

3.2 Web TV Unifg

The Web TV of the University of Foggia is managed by a team of four people (a host and writer, a writer, and two audio and video technicians). Since the official launch and inauguration of the channel in September 2023, two main formats have been produced:

- **We Live**, a weekly live broadcast featuring a guest in the studio, who could be a professor, researcher, or administrative staff member, discussing a new degree program, a specific course, ongoing research, or a particular initiative in which the University of Foggia is involved as a partner.
- **ReCup**, a weekly show dedicated to students, where they engage with professors or experts on topics related to their university life.

In one year, the channel has garnered thousands of views and around a hundred subscribers on YouTube (Fig. 1).

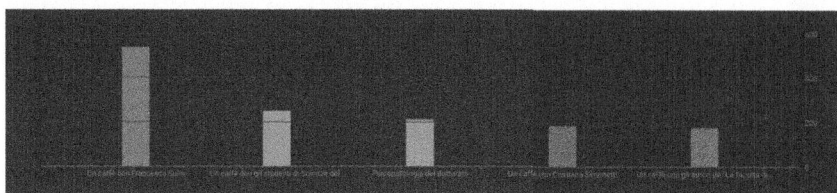

Fig. 1. Data extracted from the YouTube channel – 5 episodes with the most views and impressions.

The most viewed episode, according to this data, features a professor of evolutionary psychology in conversation with a group of students about exam anxiety and how to manage it.

Four out of the five most-watched episodes belong to the **ReCup** series (the one involving students and focusing on topics related to university life) and cover themes such as mental health, failure and fear of failure, and guidance on choosing a university.

Fig. 2. Episodes following the initial five

Below the top five, we find episodes addressing topics like gender-based violence, healthy sex education, and the use of artificial intelligence (Fig. 2).

Based on this initial review, it became clear that the most engaging episodes were those that combined three key factors:

1. The direct involvement of students
2. Addressing topics of interest to the audience, primarily the mental health of those pursuing a university education
3. Covering topics of public interest and social relevance

3.3 Students' Experience

Based on the experience gained during the first seven months of the University of Foggia's Web TV, students enrolled in the Modern Literature degree program, attending the Digital Culture course, were assigned a graded exercise consisting of the production of a Web TV episode. The project was organized into five phases (Table 1).

Table 1. Working steps

Phase	Description
1. Content choice survey	Through a survey, the top-rated topics were chosen
2. Division into working groups	The class group was divided into working groups based on each person's abilities
3. Authoring phase of content writing	Working out the questions to be asked of the guests and the topics to be covered
4. Research and invitation of guests	Identification of guests based on topics to be covered, sending invitation to participate
5. Realization of the episode	Recording of the episode in the studio

Each phase aimed to develop specific skills in participants and ensure the creation of quality content.

The first phase was devoted to gathering students' preferences on the topics to be covered. A survey was conducted to identify the topics of greatest interest. This made it possible to select the top-rated topics, which would then be developed during the workshop (Fig. 3).

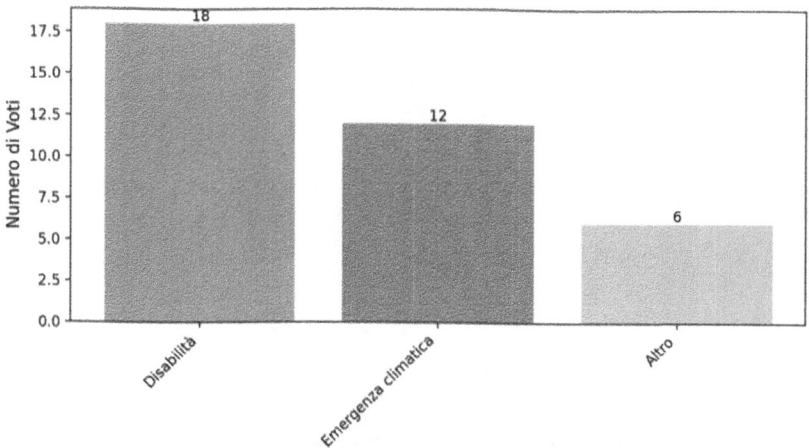

Fig. 3. Survey to identify the topics

Next, the class group was divided into teams, based on the skills and competencies of each participant. Each group had specific tasks, so as to make the best use of students' technical, organizational and creative skills.

In the writing phase, the groups focused on preparing the content. They drafted the questions to be asked of the guests and defined the key topics to be covered. This required research and planning to ensure that each episode was informative and interesting to the audience.

Once the topics and questions were defined, the groups identified potential guests to invite to the podcast, based on their experience and expertise on the chosen topics. Official invitations were sent out to participate in the recordings. The guests chosen were Barbara Centrone, an activist on disability and neurodivergence issues, and Antonio Stasi, professor of Food Business Economics and Management at the Department of Agricultural Sciences, University of Foggia.

The last stage involved the actual production. Episodes were recorded in the studio, with participants engaged in various technical and organizational activities, from managing equipment to conducting interviews (Figs. 4 and 5).

This structure enabled students to develop practical skills in the world of video podcasting, combining research, planning, and multimedia production.

4   Limitations

This analysis presents some limitations, mainly due to the lack of direct empirical research. The data considered come exclusively from the YouTube channels of the University of Foggia's web TV, without any field investigation or interviews with the

Fig. 4. Students after recording with Barbara Centrone

Fig. 5. Students during the recording with Antonio Stasi

station managers. This approach may have impacted the full understanding of the internal dynamics of such platforms, a topic of great interest for future research. A more comprehensive analysis should also cover a broader range of university web TV stations, differentiated across various geographical and institutional contexts in which they operate. Furthermore, a representative sample of the entire national university web TV landscape should not be limited solely to those active on YouTube. In addition, there is currently no extensive and systematic literature on the topic, and this work aims to contribute to the development of a future research perspective in this regard. In the future, it would be interesting to replicate the study by expanding data collection to other distribution platforms or conducting more direct investigations with individual web TV operators, including comparisons between universities in different regions or focusing on specific aspects, such as content differentiation based on audience type or academic context.

5   Conclusions

In conclusion, this study has examined the potential of university Web TVs as innovative tools for research and science dissemination, focusing on the WeUnifg project at the University of Foggia. In the ever-evolving landscape of higher education, the emergence of web-based platforms has revolutionized the way institutions engage with their students, faculty, and the broader community. The University of Foggia's Web TV stands as a prime example of this transformative shift, offering a unique medium for content delivery, knowledge sharing, and community building.

The findings underscore the versatility of university Web TVs as multimedia platforms that democratize knowledge access by transcending geographic boundaries and highlighting research initiatives, cultural events, and community outreach programs. The WeUnifg project exemplifies how Web TV can effectively engage the entire academic community, providing a voice to students, faculty, researchers, and administrative staff. Our analysis indicates that the most engaging content combines direct student involvement, topics related to student mental health and wellbeing, and issues of broader social relevance.

The analysis of usage patterns within the University of Foggia's Web TV platform provides valuable insights into the changing dynamics of educational content consumption. The exponential growth in the adoption of video-based learning further underscores the significance of the University of Foggia's Web TV initiative.

The implementation of the University of Foggia's Web TV aligns with the blended learning model described in research on educational video services in universities. This model empowers students to balance in-class participation with remote access to video-recorded content, expanding the reach and accessibility of educational resources. By offering a versatile platform that combines live broadcasts, recorded lectures, and student-produced content, the Web TV initiative not only enhances the learning experience but also fosters a sense of community and engagement within the university ecosystem.

The integration of Web TV projects into the curriculum, as demonstrated by the Digital Culture course exercise, equips students with valuable practical skills in media production, content creation, and project management. Furthermore, university Web TVs have shown potential to bridge the gap between academic institutions and the wider public, fostering transparency and enhancing the university's societal role.

Looking ahead, these platforms hold significant promise for evolving into comprehensive communication channels that can enhance education, promote research, and strengthen community engagement. Future research could delve into the long-term impact of these initiatives on student learning outcomes, research dissemination metrics, and public perceptions of academic institutions. As universities continue to adapt to the digital age, Web TV and similar tools will likely play an increasingly crucial role in shaping the future of academic communication and outreach. By embracing these technologies, universities can create more dynamic, inclusive, and far-reaching platforms for knowledge sharing and community building. The WeUnifg experience serves as a compelling example of how university Web TVs can be leveraged to create innovative spaces for learning, research dissemination, and public engagement in higher education.

The success of this initiative demonstrates the potential of web-based video platforms to bridge the gap between traditional classroom instruction and the digital learning preferences of modern students, ultimately contributing to a more inclusive and flexible educational environment. As the adoption of video-based learning continues to grow exponentially, initiatives like the University of Foggia's Web TV are positioned at the forefront of innovation in higher education communication and engagement strategies, paving the way for a more connected and accessible academic landscape.

References

1. Tsipas, N., Zapartas, P., Vrysis, L., Dimoulas, C.: Augmenting social multimedia semantic interaction through audio-enhanced web-TV services. In: Proceedings of the audio mostly 2015 on interaction with sound, pp. 1–7, Association for Computing Machinery, New York (2015)
2. Mazzoleni, G.: Comunicazione e media. L'informazione bibliografica **28**(2), 153–167 (2002)
3. Silva, A.B., de Amorim, A.C.: A Brazilian educational experiment: teleradiology on web TV. J. Telemed. Telecare **15**(7), 373–376 (2009)
4. Mohamad, M., Ismail, I.S., Wahab, N., Mamat, S.: Medical students'challenges and strategies in producing web TV programs on YouTube. Creat. Educ. **7**(4), 604–618 (2016)
5. Toto, G. A.: Didattica digitale e drop-out: osservazioni da un corso diformazione iniziale degli insegnanti durante la pandemia da Covid-19. J. Inclusive Methodol. Technol. Learn. Teach. **1**(1), 1–9 (2021)
6. Giglia, E.: La comunicazione scientifica nell'era digitale. In: Fare open access: la libera diffusione del sapere scientifico nell'era digitale, pp. 29–52. Ledizioni, Milano (2017)
7. Sobrero, M., Spigarelli, F.: La valutazione e gli indicatori di terza missione. In: GRUPPO DI LAVORO, vol. 4, pp. 1–15. Osservatorio Fondazione CRUI Università–Impresa, Roma (2015)
8. Limone, P., Toto, G.A.: ICT Handbook for Inclusive Education. McGraw-Hill, Milano (2023)
9. Haldorai, A., Murugan, S., Ramu, A.: Evolution, challenges, and application of intelligent ICT education: an overview. Comput. Appl. Eng. Educ. **29**(3), 562–571 (2021)
10. Tas, E.M.: ICT education for development—A case study. Procedia Comput. Sci. **3**, 507–512 (2011)
11. Tang, H.: Implementing open educational resources in digital education. Educ. Tech. Res. Dev. **69**(1), 389–392 (2021)
12. Limone, P.: Ambienti di apprendimento e progettazione didattica proposte per un sistema educativo transmediale. 2nd edn. Carocci Editore, Roma (2021)
13. Becker, L.B., Hollifield, C.A., Vlad, T.: Predictors of technical and administrative innovation in professional communication education at institutions of higher education. Journalism Research and Education Section of the International Association for Media and Communication Research, Hyderabad, India (2014)
14. Morcellini M.: Posfazione. In: Extracampus. La televisione uni-versitaria. Case-history di un'esperienza vincente, pp. 220–224. CARTMAN, Torino (2008)
15. Arena, G.: La comunicazione di interesse generale. Il Mulino, Bologna (1995)
16. Uricchio, W.: The future of a Medium once known as television. In: The YouTube Reader, pp. 24–39. Wall Flower, London (2009)
17. Boldrini, M., Morcellini, M.: Un'idea di Università. Comunicazione universitaria e logica dei Media. Franco Angeli, Milano (2005)
18. Menduni E.: I linguaggi della radio e della televisione. Teorie, tecniche, formati. Laterza, Roma-Bari (2008)

Online Instructional Planning Platforms for Scaffolding Self-Regulated Learning: An Overview

Piergiorgio Guarini(✉) (iD) and Giusi Antonia Toto (iD)

Learning Science Institute, University of Foggia, 71121 Foggia, Italy
piergiorgio.guarini@unifg.it

Abstract. In recent years, learning and teaching paradigms have undergone significant transformation, particularly through the integration of digital tools. Online and hybrid courses exemplify this shift, altering the student-teacher relationship by placing greater emphasis on student autonomy and self-efficacy. Digital instructional design tools, such as online lesson planning platforms like Google Classroom, facilitate self-regulated learning by providing scaffolding from teachers or trainers. These platforms enable the establishment of comprehensive teaching pathways in synchronous and asynchronous formats, allowing educators to offer various resources—both original and sourced externally—to support student learning. This paper presents a scenario analysis of these platforms, synthesizing existing literature and records to highlight their role in enhancing educational experiences. The findings emphasize the capacity for realtime feedback and task participation, which fosters a clear understanding of student progress. Widely adopted during the COVID-19 lockdowns, these platforms have since evolved to support adult education and broaden training offerings in higher education, facilitating self-learning opportunities across diverse age groups with ongoing teacher support.

Keywords: Online Teaching Platforms · Scaffolding · Self-Regulated Learning

1 The Transformation of the Paradigms of Learning and Teaching

In recent years, the paradigms of learning and teaching have been transformed in many ways. On the one hand, modes have opened up to new means and channels, exploiting the potential of digital. Online or hybrid courses and the use of digital learning materials are undoubtedly the most adequate and immediate examples of this transformation [1]. On the other hand, the very relationship between student and teacher has changed, toward an increasing centrality of the former. The learning experience is now conceived as a path that can be adapted to the learner's needs, providing not only knowledge but also opportunities to develop a sense of autonomy and self-efficacy [2].

© The Author(s), under exclusive license to Springer Nature Switzerland AG 2025
G. A. Toto (Ed.): ICS exchange 2024, CCIS 2521, pp. 461–475, 2025.
https://doi.org/10.1007/978-3-032-03021-4_32

1.1 Defining Online Learning

Online learning refers to a mode of education where teaching and learning activities are conducted primarily over the internet. This model eliminates the need for physical presence in a classroom, allowing students to access course materials, participate in discussions, submit assignments, and communicate with instructors—all from any location with an internet connection. The flexibility of online learning is one of its most significant advantages, as it allows students to balance their studies with work, family, or other commitments [2].

Some of the key characteristics of online learning include the use of Learning Management Systems (LMS), multimedia content (such as video lectures, interactive simulations, and reading materials), and asynchronous or synchronous communication between students and instructors [3]. Platforms such as Moodle, Blackboard, and Canvas are commonly used to host online courses, providing a centralized space where all course-related activities can take place. This is particularly beneficial for learners who may be geographically dispersed or those with mobility issues, providing them with access to education that might otherwise be unavailable [4].

However, while the flexibility of online learning is a major benefit, it also comes with its own set of challenges. For instance, students may experience a sense of isolation, lack of motivation, or difficulty staying engaged due to the absence of face-to-face interactions. Instructors, likewise, face challenges in maintaining student engagement, providing personalized feedback, and ensuring that students are meeting learning outcomes.

1.2 Hybrid Learning: Blended Online and Face-to-Face Learning

Hybrid learning, also known as blended learning, represents a model that combines traditional in-person teaching with online instruction. In this model, students attend some classes on campus while completing other components of the course online. This hybrid structure aims to take advantage of the benefits of both face-to-face instruction (such as immediate interaction with the instructor and peers) and the flexibility of online learning (such as self-paced activities and access to digital resources) [1].

There are several different models of hybrid learning, each with varying degrees of online and in-person components. One common approach is the "flipped classroom," where students are required to review course content online before attending in-person sessions, which are then used for discussions, collaborative work, and hands-on activities. Other models may involve rotating between online and in-person learning days, or integrating online assignments with classroom activities [5].

Hybrid learning is particularly effective in addressing the needs of diverse student populations, as it allows for differentiated instruction, greater flexibility, and the possibility for more personalized learning experiences. Students who are unable to attend every class in person due to work or family commitments can still engage with the content online and participate in the learning process at their own pace [1]. For instructors, hybrid learning provides an opportunity to enrich their teaching with multimedia resources, foster peer collaboration through online discussions, and tailor their instruction to meet individual student needs [6].

1.3   The Evolution of Online and Hybrid Learning Before the Covid-19 Pandemic

Before 2019, online learning was already gaining traction, especially in higher education, in the form of blended learning [7, 8]. However, their widespread adoption had been slow compared to traditional face-to-face models. Institutions with established online programs, such as those offering distance education for non-traditional or adult learners, were the early adopters of online learning technologies [9].

The growth of hybrid learning during this period was driven by a desire to balance the benefits of face-to-face interaction with the flexibility of online learning. Many institutions began experimenting with blended models to reach a broader audience and accommodate the needs of working professionals or students with family responsibilities. Research conducted during this time, such as the work by Garrison and Kanuka [10], highlighted the positive outcomes of hybrid learning, including greater student satisfaction and improved learning outcomes when online components were carefully integrated with traditional teaching.

While the pre-2019 adoption of online and hybrid learning was still somewhat limited, it was clear that these models held significant potential for transforming the educational experience. As technology continued to improve and access to the internet expanded globally, educators and institutions began to see the promise of a more flexible, accessible, and personalized approach to teaching and learning.

1.4   The Role of Technology in Shaping Learning Models

The evolution of online and hybrid learning is closely tied to advancements in digital technology. Early online courses, for example, were often static, text-based, and relatively simple in terms of content delivery. Over time, however, the integration of multimedia elements such as video lectures, interactive simulations, and podcasts has enriched the learning experience, making it more engaging and dynamic. Furthermore, the advent of more sophisticated Learning Management Systems (LMS) has allowed for more effective course design, communication, and assessment [11].

The increasing use of cloud-based tools and mobile technologies also facilitated the widespread adoption of hybrid and online learning, allowing students to access learning materials from anywhere and at any time. In fact, many online courses and programs prior to 2019 were already designed to be fully mobile-compatible, ensuring that students could learn on the go, whether on their smartphones, tablets, or laptops. This growing emphasis on technology-enabled learning [12] was gradually reshaping the educational landscape, pointing toward a future where traditional, face-to-face learning was just one part of a much more flexible, diverse learning ecosystem.

2   Impact of the Covid-19 Pandemic on Online and Hybrid Learning

The COVID-19 pandemic, which began in early 2020, brought about unprecedented disruptions to global education systems. Schools, colleges, and universities around the world were forced to transition to remote learning almost overnight, creating a unique set of challenges and opportunities for both educators and learners. The pandemic not only accelerated the adoption of online learning but also fundamentally reshaped the way education is delivered and experienced [13].

2.1 The Sudden Shift to Online Learning

In the months following the global outbreak of the COVID-19 virus, educational institutions were faced with the sudden necessity of shifting their instructional models to online formats. What had previously been an option for some institutions and a supplementary mode of learning for others became the default for the majority of schools, universities, and training centers. This rapid shift was an emergency response to the widespread closure of physical campuses, with many institutions scrambling to implement online teaching tools and digital resources in a matter of weeks [14].

For many teachers, the transition to online teaching was daunting. Prior to the pandemic, only a fraction of educators had experience in designing and delivering courses entirely online. Those with limited technical skills or experience with online pedagogy had to quickly adapt to new technologies, such as video conferencing software (e.g., Zoom), virtual classrooms, and online assessment tools. Meanwhile, students also had to adjust to new forms of learning, often without the preparation or resources needed for effective engagement in a fully online environment [14].

While some students were able to transition smoothly into online learning, others struggled with issues related to technology access, inadequate digital literacy, and the lack of face-to-face interaction. The digital divide—where students in rural or under-privileged areas had limited access to reliable internet connections or devices—became a significant issue in many regions [15]. This led to concerns over equity and access to education during the pandemic, as students from disadvantaged backgrounds were disproportionately affected by the shift to online learning.

2.2 Consequences on Educational Organization and Instructional Delivery

The pandemic's abrupt transition to online learning forced educational institutions to rethink how they structured and delivered instruction. Traditional in-person classroom activities, such as lectures, seminars, and practical sessions, were replaced with virtual classes and asynchronous learning materials. Teachers who were accustomed to in-person interactions had to learn to engage students through digital platforms, often facing challenges such as the difficulty of reading non-verbal cues, maintaining student motivation, and managing online discussions [14].

Many institutions adopted video conferencing tools like Zoom, Microsoft Teams, and Google Meet for synchronous classes, while also using Learning Management Systems (LMS) to host asynchronous content, such as pre-recorded lectures, assignments, and quizzes. In some cases, this hybrid approach—where synchronous sessions were complemented by asynchronous learning activities—mirrored the hybrid learning models that had been gaining traction in the years before the pandemic [11].

In terms of instructional delivery, the pandemic also saw an explosion in the use of digital instructional materials, including interactive media, video-based learning, and collaborative tools such as Google Docs or Microsoft Office 365. These technologies allowed for more dynamic, engaging, and interactive learning experiences, enabling students to engage with content in a variety of formats [16]. In many ways, the rapid implementation of online learning during the pandemic mirrored trends that had been slowly emerging in education prior to 2020 but had now become a necessity rather than an option.

2.3 Impact on Learning Outcomes and Students' Engagement

The transition to online learning during the pandemic resulted in a wide range of outcomes for students. On one hand, many students benefited from the flexibility offered by online education. They could work at their own pace, access resources at any time, and engage in independent learning, which aligned well with self-regulated learning (SRL) principles. The pandemic, in this sense, created an opportunity for students to develop greater autonomy in their learning process, an essential skill for lifelong learning [17].

On the other hand, the shift to online learning highlighted several significant chalenges related to engagement, motivation, and the quality of learning. Research conducted during the pandemic [18–20] indicated that many students experienced feelings of isolation, anxiety, and disengagement due to the lack of in-person interactions and the challenges of navigating online platforms. The absence of structured, face-to-face learning environments made it harder for some students to stay focused and motivated. Additionally, without the direct oversight of a teacher in a classroom, students struggled with time management and prioritizing tasks, a key component of self-regulated learning.

There were also concerns about the effectiveness of online assessments [21] because traditional in-person exams, with their emphasis on controlled environments, could no longer be relied upon during the pandemic. As a result, many institutions turned to online assessments, including open-book exams, take-home assignments, and projects. While these assessments offered some flexibility, they also presented challenges in terms of maintaining academic integrity and ensuring that students were truly demonstrating their learning.

2.4 Students' Perception of Learning During the Pandemic

Student perceptions of online learning during the pandemic were mixed. Some students appreciated the flexibility and autonomy that online learning offered, especially in terms of balancing personal and academic responsibilities. For example, adult learners, working professionals, and students with caregiving responsibilities found online learning to be a welcome change that allowed them to continue their education without the constraints of a fixed schedule or commuting to a physical campus.

However, for many students, the experience of learning online was less than ideal [17, 20]: the lack of in-person interactions, which are crucial for social learning, collaboration, and building a sense of community, was a major drawback for many. Additionally, some students reported that they found it difficult to concentrate on online classes or that they struggled with the amount of screen time required for remote learning.

Interestingly, the pandemic also brought attention to the importance of digital literacy [22]. Students who were already proficient in using technology were generally able to adapt more quickly to online learning, while those with limited digital skills faced a steeper learning curve. This highlighted the need for improved digital literacy training, both for students and instructors, as a prerequisite for successful online and hybrid learning experiences.

2.5   The Long-Term Implications for Education

While the COVID-19 pandemic was an unprecedented event, it underscored the necessity for educational systems to be adaptable and resilient in the face of unexpected challenges. The widespread adoption of online learning during the pandemic was a transformative experience for both students and educators, one that will have lasting implications for the future of education.

In the post-pandemic world, it is expected that many educational institutions will continue to offer online and hybrid learning opportunities, not just as a response to emergencies, but as a strategic choice. The flexibility of online learning, coupled with the accessibility it offers to diverse student populations, suggests that hybrid models will become a permanent feature of the educational landscape.

Moreover, the pandemic highlighted the importance of investing in digital infrastructure, as well as the need for effective pedagogical strategies that can engage students and support their learning in virtual environments. Moving forward, educational institutions will need to consider how to incorporate the lessons learned during the pandemic into their long-term strategies for digital transformation [23].

3   Digital Instructional Design Tools: Empowering Educators and Facilitating Self-Regulated Learning (SRL)

The rise of digital instructional design tools has been one of the most significant developments in education over the past two decades. These tools have revolutionized the way teachers design, deliver, and assess learning experiences, providing them with powerful resources to create more engaging, personalized, and flexible learning environments. Digital instructional design tools not only streamline the process of course creation but also enhance the effectiveness of teaching by enabling more interactive, dynamic, and responsive learning experiences.

3.1   What Are Digital Instructional Design Tools?

Digital instructional design tools are software applications or platforms that assist educators in creating, organizing, and delivering educational content in digital formats. These tools typically allow educators to develop interactive and multimedia-rich courses that can be accessed online. They provide a range of functionalities, including the ability to upload course materials (text, videos, quizzes, etc.), track student progress, facilitate communication, and design assessments. Some of the most widely used digital instructional design tools include:

- **Learning Management Systems (LMS):** platforms such as Moodle, Canvas, and Blackboard provide a central hub for organizing course materials, assessments, and student interactions. These systems allow for seamless integration of content delivery, student tracking, and communication tools;
- **Collaborative Tools:** tools like Google Workspace, Microsoft Teams, and Slack enable real-time collaboration among students and between students and instructors. They allow for group work, discussion forums, and shared document editing, which fosters a sense of community and collaboration in an otherwise virtual environment;
- **Content Creation Tools:** applications such as Adobe Captivate, Articulate Storyline, and Canva are commonly used to create interactive learning modules, e-learning courses, and multimedia content. These tools allow instructors to design engaging materials such as quizzes, simulations, and infographics that enhance the learning experience;
- **Assessment Tools:** platform like Turnitin, Google Forms, and Quizlet provide educators with the tools to create and grade assignments, quizzes, and exams. These tools also allow for instant feedback, which is crucial in supporting self-regulated learning.

The overarching goal of these tools is to enhance the educational experience by creating interactive, engaging, and personalized learning environments. They enable instructors to move away from traditional lecture-based teaching and towards more active learning methods that promote deeper student engagement and better learning outcomes [24].

3.2 Digital Instructional Tools and Self-Regulated Learning (SRL)

SRL refers to the process by which students take control of their own learning through goal setting, self-monitoring, and self-reflection. SRL is a student-centered approach that places learners in charge of their own educational journey, empowering them to set learning goals, monitor their progress, and make adjustments as needed. Digital instructional design tools are ideally suited to support SRL, as they provide students with the resources and scaffolding needed to manage their learning independently.

The connection between digital tools and SRL lies in the ability of these tools to offer personalized learning experiences, track progress in real time, and provide immediate feedback. For example, platforms like Google Classroom or Moodle allow students to monitor their assignments, deadlines, and grades, which supports their ability to set goals, track progress, and reflect on their learning. Furthermore, digital instructional tools enable teachers to provide scaffolding in the form of supplementary materials (videos, articles, additional readings), real-time feedback, and guided assessments that help students improve their learning strategies.

Some of the key ways in which digital instructional tools facilitate SRL include [25]:

- **Goal Setting and Planning:** digital tools allow students to set clear, measurable goals and track their progress toward achieving them. For instance, many LMS platforms offer built-in progress tracking features, allowing students to see how much of the course content they have completed and what tasks remain. These features support goal setting and time management, two essential components of SRL;

- **Access to Resources:** digital tools provide students with easy access to a wealth of learning materials, such as videos, articles, and interactive simulations. These resources can be accessed at any time, which supports self-paced learning. Students are able to revisit materials they find challenging, reinforcing their understanding and facilitating self-directed learning;
- **Immediate Feedback:** feedback is an integral part of SRL, as it helps students assess their progress and adjust their learning strategies. Digital tools like Google Forms or Quizlet allow students to receive immediate feedback on quizzes or assignments, helping them identify areas where they need to improve. This feedback loop supports continuous improvement and encourages a growth mindset
- **Reflection and Self-Assessment:** many digital platforms offer opportunities for students to reflect on their learning. For example, they might be asked to complete self-assessment questionnaires or engage in reflective journals. These activities promote metacognition, which is crucial for SRL as it enables students to evaluate their own learning strategies and outcomes.

The integration of digital tools into the learning process also helps to create an environment where students feel more accountable for their learning. They can track their own progress, adjust their approach when necessary, and seek out additional resources to improve their understanding. This autonomy is central to self-regulated learning, as it empowers students to become active participants in their educational journey.

3.3 Why Digital Instructional Design Tools are Still Relevant Post-pandemic

While the COVID-19 pandemic forced an urgent shift to online learning, the adoption of digital instructional tools is expected to continue even after the crisis has passed. Many educators and students have come to appreciate the flexibility, accessibility, and personalization that digital tools offer. As institutions move toward hybrid learning models and increasingly rely on online components, the role of digital instructional tools will remain vital in shaping the future of education.

Post-pandemic, digital tools continue to support personalized learning and provide opportunities for both students and instructors to engage in more meaningful ways. For example, hybrid classrooms, which combine face-to-face and online elements, require tools that can seamlessly integrate both modes of delivery. These tools not only enhance the learning experience but also enable instructors to manage and deliver content more efficiently, regardless of the learning environment [26].

Furthermore, the increasing demand for lifelong learning, especially among adult learners and professionals seeking to upskill or reskill, will drive continued reliance on digital instructional tools [27]. Many professional development courses, certifications, and continuing education programs are now delivered online, with learners using digital tools to engage with course content, track their progress, and interact with instructors. The ongoing use of these tools ensures that education remains accessible and adaptable, meeting the diverse needs of learners in a rapidly changing world.

In conclusion, digital instructional design tools play a crucial role in the modern educational ecosystem. They not only facilitate the delivery of online and hybrid learning but also support the development of self-regulated learners. By providing students with the resources, feedback, and flexibility they need to manage their own learning, these tools help foster greater autonomy, motivation, and achievement. As we move beyond the pandemic, these tools will continue to shape the future of education, providing teachers and learners with the means to create more dynamic, engaging, and personalized learning experiences [26].

4 Google Classroom: A Tool for Self-Regulated Learning in Online Environments

Among the numerous digital instructional design tools available to educators today, Google Classroom stands out as one of the most widely adopted platforms for organizing and delivering online education. Initially developed to streamline the management of classroom assignments and communication, Google Classroom has evolved into a comprehensive learning management tool that supports both synchronous and asynchronous learning. Its ability to integrate with other Google tools, such as Google Drive, Google Docs, and Google Meet, makes it particularly useful in facilitating a cohesive learning environment.

In this section, we will explore how Google Classroom functions, its key features and functionalities, and why it is particularly suited to support SRL in online teaching environments.

4.1 How Google Classroom Works: An Overview of Its Features

Google Classroom functions as a hub for teachers and students to interact and engage with educational content. Teachers can create classes, post assignments, distribute learning materials, and track student progress—all in one place. The platform is designed to be user-friendly and accessible, both for educators who may not be tech-savvy and for students who are accustomed to using Google's ecosystem of tools.

The main features of Google Classroom include:

- **Class Creation and Organization** Teachers can easily set up classes within Google Classroom, organizing them by subject, grade, or course type. Once a class is created, teachers can invite students to join via an enrollment code or email invitation. The class dashboard provides a clear and simple interface for both teachers and students to see class announcements, assignments, and upcoming deadlines;
- **Assignment Distribution and Management** Teachers can upload assignments and materials directly onto the platform, allowing students to access them at any time. These assignments can take various forms, including quizzes, essays, multimedia projects, and collaborative tasks. Google Classroom integrates seamlessly with Google Docs, Sheets, Slides, and other Google tools, making it easy for students to complete their work within the platform itself. Teachers can also assign due dates, set reminders, and track student progress, offering a transparent view of each student's work;
- **Grading and Feedback** Google Classroom provides built-in grading functionality, where teachers can grade assignments directly within the platform. Instructors can

leave feedback for students in real time, either in the form of text comments, voice notes, or video recordings. This feedback loop is crucial in supporting self-regulated learning, as it provides immediate, constructive feedback on students' performance and progress, helping them understand their strengths and areas for improvement;

- **Communication Tools** Communication between students and teachers is facilitated through announcements, email notifications, and the class stream. Students can ask questions, engage in discussions, or seek clarification on assignments. This level of interaction fosters a sense of community, even in an online or hybrid learning environment. Teachers can also provide additional learning resources, post reminders, and offer supplementary materials to support students in their self-directed learning journeys;

- **Integration with Google Suite and Other Tools** One of the standout features of Google Classroom is its integration with other Google applications, such as Google Drive, Google Meet, Google Calendar, and Google Forms. These integrations allow teachers to organize materials in shared Google Drive folders, schedule virtual meetings via Google Meet, and collect student responses through Google Forms. This holistic integration of tools enables a seamless teaching and learning experience, all within the Google ecosystem [28–30].

4.2 Why Google Classroom is Suited for SRL

SRL is characterized by the ability to plan, monitor, and evaluate one's learning progress independently. Google Classroom supports SRL in several important ways, facilitating a learning environment where students can take ownership of their educational experience.

- **Autonomy and Flexibility** One of the primary advantages of Google Classroom is the flexibility it offers both teachers and students. Students can access course materials, assignments, and feedback at their own pace, allowing them to manage their time and workload according to their personal preferences. The ability to set deadlines and plan ahead also encourages students to take responsibility for their learning process, a fundamental aspect of self-regulation;

- **Progress tracking and Reflection** Google Classroom enables students to track their progress through a simple, visually clear system that shows completed assignments, upcoming tasks, and grades. Students can quickly see how much work remains to be done, which helps them set goals and prioritize tasks. This type of self-monitoring is crucial for SRL, as it encourages students to reflect on their progress and make adjustments if necessary;

- **Instant Feedback for Continuous Improvement** Feedback is a core component of SRL, as it allows students to assess their learning strategies and outcomes. In Google Classroom, teachers can provide instant feedback on assignments, which students can use to make revisions or improve their understanding of the material. This feedback loop fosters continuous learning and self-assessment, helping students become more aware of their strengths and weaknesses;

- **Collaboration and Peer Learning** Google Classroom facilitates collaboration through its integration with tools like Google Docs and Google Drive, which enable students to work together on group projects, share resources, and provide mutual feedback. Collaborative learning is an essential part of SRL, as it allows students to learn from each other, exchange ideas, and develop new strategies for understanding the content. Additionally, peer interactions help create a supportive learning community that encourages engagement and motivation;

- **Personalized Learning Pathways** Teachers can use Google Classroom to offer differentiated learning experiences tailored to individual students' needs. For example, teachers can assign different tasks or resources based on students' previous performance, learning styles, or specific challenges. By offering personalized learning opportunities, Google Classroom supports students in taking control of their learning process and helps them navigate challenges on their own;
- **Encouraging Goal Setting and Time Management** Google Classroom helps students plan and manage their time effectively by displaying a clear list of assignments and deadlines. The ability to break tasks down into smaller, manageable chunks enables students to set specific goals and monitor their progress. This organizational aspect of the platform supports SRL by promoting effective time management and goal setting, two key components of self-regulation [25, 28–30].

4.3 Google Classroom in Hybrid and Blended Learning Environments

Google Classroom is not only suited for fully online courses but is also highly effective in hybrid or blended learning environments. In these settings, students attend in-person classes while also engaging with online materials and assignments. Google Classroom allows teachers to bridge the gap between in-person and online learning by providing a central space where students can access both types of resources, track their progress, and engage with their instructors.

In a blended learning environment, teachers can use Google Classroom to:

- Post digital materials (videos, readings, slides) before or after face-to-face classes, enabling students to learn at their own pace;
- Assign collaborative group tasks that require both in-person and online components;
- Host live sessions via Google Meet to supplement face-to-face instruction and maintain interaction among students;
- Track student progress through formative assessments and provide ongoing feedback. [28–30].

This flexibility allows for a seamless blend of online and offline learning experiences, offering students the best of both worlds while supporting their ability to regulate their learning independently.

In addition to its use in K-12 and higher education contexts, Google Classroom has also become an important tool for adult learners and lifelong education. As more adults return to education for professional development, career advancement, or personal enrichment, the need for flexible and self-paced learning opportunities has increased. Google Classroom is well-suited to meet the demands of adult learners, providing them with the tools they need to manage their education independently, track their progress, and receive personalized feedback.

Adult learners, often balancing education with work and family responsibilities, benefit from the ability to access course materials and assignments at any time. Furthermore, Google Classroom's organizational features help adult learners set clear goals, manage deadlines, and reflect on their learning—all crucial aspects of self-regulated learning [31].

5 Conclusion: The Future of Online Instruction and the Role of Google Classroom in Facilitating SRL

As we move beyond the challenges of the COVID-19 pandemic, the landscape of education has undergone a profound transformation. The rapid shift to online and hybrid learning models, accelerated by the global health crisis, has not only reshaped how education is delivered but also how students engage with their learning [14]. The widespread adoption of digital instructional tools, such as Google Classroom, has played a pivotal role in supporting both educators and learners in this new era of education. These tools have proven to be indispensable in providing flexible, personalized, and interactive learning experiences [28].

5.1 The Evolution of Online and Hybrid Learning Post-pandemic

The COVID-19 pandemic catalyzed a rapid, global transition to online learning, forcing educational institutions to quickly adapt to remote teaching and learning. While this was initially a response to an unprecedented situation, the long-term impact of this shift has led to the normalization of hybrid and blended learning models. Today, many institutions have embraced hybrid learning as a permanent feature of their teaching strategies, offering a combination of in-person and online elements to meet the diverse needs of students [17].

Post-pandemic, the integration of digital platforms like Google Classroom into traditional educational settings is no longer a temporary solution but rather a fundamental component of modern education. These platforms enable institutions to deliver a wide range of learning experiences, from synchronous classes with real-time interaction to asynchronous content that students can access at their own pace. Google Classroom, in particular, stands out as an accessible and versatile tool that supports these hybrid and blended learning environments, allowing teachers to seamlessly combine in-person and online teaching strategies [23].

One of the most significant benefits of online and hybrid learning models is the flexibility they offer. Students can engage with course materials at their own pace, collaborate with peers in virtual settings, and receive timely feedback from their instructors— all of which contribute to a more personalized and adaptable learning experience. For many students, particularly those balancing work or family commitments, this flexibility is a game-changer, making education more accessible and inclusive [20].

The future of education will likely see an increasing reliance on hybrid and online learning models, with a greater emphasis on personalized, student-centered approaches. In this evolving landscape, tools like Google Classroom will continue to play a central role in facilitating self-regulated learning and fostering lifelong learning skills [23].

5.2   The Role of Digital Tools in Supporting SRL

SRL is a critical skill that empowers students to take charge of their own learning process, set personal goals, monitor their progress, and adjust their strategies based on feedback and reflection. As education becomes increasingly digital and self-paced, the importance of fostering self-regulation among students has never been greater [25]. Digital tools like Google Classroom are ideally suited to support this type of learning, as they provide students with the autonomy, flexibility, and resources they need to manage their learning independently [27].

By enabling students to track their progress, access materials on demand, receive timely feedback, and collaborate with peers, platforms like Google Classroom offer an environment that nurtures self-regulation. These tools allow students to set goals, evaluate their performance, and make adjustments to their learning strategies in real time. Whether working independently on assignments or engaging in group discussions, students can take responsibility for their learning, which is essential for developing lifelong learning skills [26].

Furthermore, digital tools foster metacognition, a key component of SRL. With Google Classroom's built-in tools for tracking assignments, grades, and deadlines, students are constantly prompted to reflect on their own learning. This reflection process encourages students to assess their strengths, identify areas for improvement, and refine their learning strategies. Over time, this promotes greater self-awareness and enhances students' ability to regulate their learning in a way that is meaningful and effective. By providing students with the means to track, monitor, and reflect on their learning, Google Classroom helps to create a learning environment where self-regulation is not only supported but actively encouraged. This approach aligns with the broader educational goal of preparing students to become autonomous, lifelong learners who can continue to adapt and grow in an ever-changing world [29, 30].

5.3   Lifelong Learning and the Continued Relevance of Digital Tools

The increasing importance of lifelong learning is another reason why the continued use of digital tools like Google Classroom is essential [30]. As the workforce and society at large undergo rapid technological and economic changes, individuals must continually develop new skills to stay relevant and competitive. Digital platforms offer the flexibility and scalability necessary to support lifelong learning, enabling learners of all ages to engage with educational content at their own pace, from anywhere, at any time. Adult learners, in particular, benefit from the accessibility and flexibility of platforms like Google Classroom. Whether pursuing professional development, certification programs, or personal enrichment, adult learners often require a learning environment that fits around their busy lives. Google Classroom's ability to support asynchronous learning, deliver instant feedback, and allow for personalized learning pathways makes it an ideal tool for these learners. Moreover, as adults are typically more self-motivated and goal-driven, Google Classroom's emphasis on self-regulation and autonomy aligns perfectly with the needs of adult education [31].

By supporting lifelong learning, Google Classroom plays a vital role in helping individuals continue their education throughout their lives. As more people embrace the need for continuous learning, the role of digital tools in facilitating this process will become even more pronounced [30].

5.4 Final Thoughts

As educational technology continues to evolve, it is important to recognize the potential of platforms like Google Classroom not just for enhancing traditional learning but also for transforming the future of education. Moving forward, we can expect further innovations in digital learning tools that will further personalize and optimize the learning experience. These tools will increasingly support learners in developing critical skills such as self-regulation, problem-solving, and collaboration—skills that will be essential for success in the 21st century.

References

1. Caulfield, J.: How to Design and Teach a Hybrid Course: Achieving Student-Centered Learning Through Blended Classroom, Online and Experiential Activities. Taylor and Francis (2023)
2. Baeten, M., Kyndt, E., Struyven, K., Dochy, F.: Using student-centred learning environments to stimulate deep approaches to learning: factors encouraging or discouraging their effectiveness. Educ. Res. Rev. **5**(3), 243–260 (2010)
3. Turnbull, D., Chugh, R., Luck, J.: Learning management systems, an overview. In: Encyclopedia of education and information technologies, pp. 1052–1058. (2020)
4. Bradley, V.M.: Learning Management System (LMS) use with online instruction. Int. J. Technol. Educ. **4**(1), 68–92 (2021)
5. Nurhayati, N., Ampera, D., Chalid, S., Farihah, F., Baharuddin, B.: Development of blended learning type and flipped classroom-based cultural arts subjects. Int. J. Educ. Math. Sci. Technol. (IJEMST) **9**(4), 655–667 (2021). https://doi.org/10.46328/ijemst.1975
6. Syafril, S., Latifah, S., Engkizar, E., Damri, D., Asril, Z., Yaumas, N. E.: Hybrid learning on problem-solving abiities in physics learning: a literature review. In: Journal of Physics: Conference Series, vol. 1796, no. 1, p. 012021. IOP Publishing (2021)
7. Bliuc, A.M., Goodyear, P., Ellis, R.A.: Research focus and methodological choices in studies into students' experiences of blended learning in higher education. Internet High. Educ. **10**(4), 231–244 (2007)
8. Dziuban, C., Graham, C.R., Moskal, P.D., Norberg, A., Sicilia, N.: Blended learning: the new normal and emerging technologies. Int. J. Educ. Technol. High. Educ. **15**, 1–16 (2018)
9. Sarno, E.: Emergenza sanitaria e chiusura di scuole e università. Il divario culturale come ulteriore effetto del Covid-19. Documenti geografici 1, 219–229 (2020)
10. Garrison, D.R., Kanuka, H.: Blended learning: uncovering its transformative potential in higher education. Internet High. Educ. **7**(2), 95–105 (2004)
11. Riyantika, F., Nisa, K., Kadaryanto, B.: University students' perception of online learning: a case study of Virtual Class learning management system in the University of Lampung. (2021)
12. Ewing, L.A., Cooper, H.B.: Technology-enabled remote learning during COVID-19: perspectives of Australian teachers, students and parents. Technol. Pedagog. Educ. **30**(1), 41–57 (2021)
13. Süt, H.M., Öznaçar, B.: Effects of COVID-19 period on educational systems and institutions: effects of COVID-19 period. Int. J. Curriculum Instruct. **13**(1), 537–551 (2021)

14. Maqsood, A., Abbas, J., Rehman, G., Mubeen, R.: The paradigm shift for educational system continuance in the advent of COVID-19 pandemic: mental health challenges and reflections. Curr. Res. Behav. Sci. **2**, 100011 (2021)
15. Litchfield, I., Shukla, D., Greenfield, S.: Impact of COVID-19 on the digital divide: a rapid review. BMJ Open **11**(10), e053440 (2021)
16. Rice, M.F., Ortiz, K.R.: Evaluating digital instructional materials for K-12 online and blended learning. TechTrends **65**(6), 977–992 (2021)
17. Baber, H.: Determinants of students' perceived learning outcome and satisfaction in online learning during the pandemic of COVID-19. J. Educ. e-learn. Res. **7**(3), 285–292 (2020)
18. Raza, S.A., Qazi, W., Umer, B.: Examining the impact of case-based learning on student engagement, learning motivation and learning performance among university students. J. Appl. Res. High. Educ. **12**(3), 517–533 (2020)
19. Capone, R., Lepore, M.: From distance learning to integrated digital learning: a fuzzy cognitive analysis focused on engagement, motivation, and participation during COVID-19 pandemic. Technol. Knowl. Learn. **27**(4), 1259–1289 (2022)
20. Zapata-Cuervo, N., Montes-Guerra, M.I., Shin, H.H., Jeong, M., Cho, M.H.: Students' psychological perceptions toward online learning engagement and outcomes during the COVID-19 pandemic: a comparative analysis of students in three different countries. J. Hosp. Tour. Educ. **35**(2), 108–122 (2023)
21. Tartavulea, C.V., Albu, C.N., Albu, N., Dieaconescu, R.I., Petre, S.: Online teaching practices and the effectiveness of the educational process in the wake of the COVID-19 pandemic. Amfiteatru Econ. **22**(55), 920–936 (2020)
22. Yu, Z.: Sustaining student roles, digital literacy, learning achievements, and motivation in online learning environments during the COVID-19 pandemic. Sustainability **14**(8), 4388 (2022)
23. Kaffenberger, M.: Modelling the long-run learning impact of the Covid-19 learning shock: actions to (more than) mitigate loss. Int. J. Educ. Dev. **81**, 102326 (2021)
24. Aithal, P.S., Aithal, S.: Stakeholders' analysis of the effect of ubiquitous education technologies on higher education. Int. J. Appl. Eng. Manage. Lett. (IJAEML) **7**(2), 102–133 (2023)
25. Hadwin, A.F., Järvelä, S., Miller, M.: Self-regulated, co-regulated, and socially shared regulation of learning. Handb. Self-regulation Learn. Perform. **30**, 65–84 (2011)
26. Petherbridge, D., Bartlett, M., White, J., Chapman, D.: Instructional designers' perceptions of the practice of instructional design in a post-pandemic workplace. In: International Journal on E-Learning, pp. 259–281. Association for the Advancement of Computing in Education (AACE). (2023)
27. Lyndgaard, S.F., Storey, R., Kanfer, R.: Technological support for lifelong learning: the application of a multilevel, person-centric framework. J. Vocat. Behav. **153**, 104027 (2024)
28. Iftakhar, S.: Google classroom: what works and how. J. Educ. Soc. Sci. **3**(1), 12–18 (2016)
29. Fitriningtiyas, D. A., Umamah, N., Sumardi, S.: Google classroom: as a media of learning history. In: IOP Conference Series: Earth and Environmental Science, vol. 243 (2019)
30. Al-Maroof, R.A.S., Al-Emran, M.: Students acceptance of google classroom: an exploratory study using PLS-SEM approach. Int. J. Emerg. Technol. Learn. (Online) **13**(6), 112 (2018)
31. Azhar, K.A., Iqbal, N.: Effectiveness of Google classroom: teachers' perceptions. Prizren Soc. Sci. J. **2**(2), 52 (2018)

Successful Distance Learning: Pedagogical Strategies for Teachers to Enhance Self-Regulated Learning

Azusa Nakata(✉) (iD), Sara Ahola(iD), and Hanna Järvenoja(iD)

University of Oulu, Pentti Kaiteran Katu 1, 90570 Oulu, Finland
azusa.nakata@oulu.fi

Abstract. Research on self-regulated learning (SRL) has shown that students who are capable of taking an agentic role in their learning process can use more appropriate learning strategies and preserve their motivation for learning, resulting in better academic performance. The importance of SRL is particularly emphasised in distance learning settings where a teacher's timely support, namely scaffolding, can be limited. Because students with good SRL skills can manage tasks, plan work, and keep their motivation, they can better maintain their wellbeing in remote schooling. Hence, it has been argued that fostering distance learning requires educators to provide a supportive environment that facilitates students' engagement in regulating their own learning.

Teachers can facilitate students' self-regulation by enhancing students' awareness of their learning processes and supporting them in monitoring and controlling their cognition, motivation, emotions, and behaviour. The critical element here is the teachers' own understanding about the mechanisms of SRL. Prior research suggest that teachers become capable of designing learning tasks and implementing prompts to promote students' SRL into their teaching after acquiring the adequate information and training. In this paper, we introduce a set of evidenced-based strategies, accompanied by a designated pedagogical framework, that have been developed to address the increased need for supporting teachers in developing students' SRL skills in distance learning.

First, we have reviewed literature of SRL and motivation, deciding on our definition and theoretical model to develop a scientifically grounded pedagogical framework. We start by determining the different areas of learning that benefit from SRL support, then draw attention to different phases of SRL. Then, we suggest how educators can provide support for their students in these phases, particularly in distance learning settings. While acknowledging that it is challenging to teach in a distance environment, we shed light on the advantage of this unique setting that keeps students' traces of actions. We conclude, by going back to the agentic role of the learner in distance learning settings, that scaffolding processes eventually help develop students' SRL skills though gradually shifting pedagogical decision making from a teacher to the students themselves.

Keywords: Self-regulated learning (SRL) · Distance learning · Teacher support · Scaffolding

G. A. Toto (Ed.): ICS exchange 2024, CCIS 2521, pp. 476–487, 2025.
https://doi.org/10.1007/978-3-032-03021-4_33

1 Introduction

Self-regulated learning (SRL) is a crucial skill for students in academic settings and the modern working world [1]. SRL skills are the backbone of continuous learning because SRL involves learners in actively planning learning goals and strategies and monitoring, controlling, and reflecting on their cognition, motivation, emotions, and behaviour [1].

As a result, SRL skills enhance not only content acquisition but also engage learners in the learning and interaction processes, fostering deeper learning through active, purposeful, and goal-oriented participation, which leads to enhance learners' life-long learning competences.

Another important factor in the 21st century is the development of digital competencies. European Commission states, "EU has identified digital competence as one of eight key competencies for lifelong learning, highlighting its importance for all stages of education, both formal and informal, and across all segments of the EU population" [2]. As we all know, the COVID-19 pandemic has accelerated shifting learning environments into more online and blended modes all over the world. Since then, distance teaching has permanently multiplied in higher education contexts and the importance of SRL skills in digital learning environments has also been amplified.

Skills that response to digital society have remained crucial since the pandemic. Adaptive and personalized approaches to acquiring knowledge and skills are highly valued in the modern world, and online and blended learning environments maximize the flexibility of learning. In such learning settings, students' autonomy and SRL skills are a key for successful learning [3, 4]. Hence, there is a need for teachers to guide their students to proactively regulate their learning in online environments by applying various pedagogical approaches and technological support tools. To address the increased need for supporting teachers in developing students' SRL skills in distance learning, we introduce a set of evidenced-based strategies, accompanied by a designated pedagogical framework, that have been developed in the context of the Erasmus+funded TUNED project [5].

2 Theoretical Framework

2.1 Self-Regulated Learning: Phases and Targets

Self-regulated learning (SRL) is a continuous process where learners actively monitor, guide, and adjust their actions based on their goals and the environmental context [6]. SRL is a dynamic, iterative process involving different phases where learners set goals, create strategic plans, track their progress, adjust their approaches, and reflect on their learning process and outcomes [6, 7]. Several models for SRL exist [6–11], one of the most cited ones being Zimmerman's cyclical model of SRL [7, 12]. According to Zimmerman, SRL is a dynamic and cyclical process consisting of different phases: the forethought phase, performance phase, and self-reflection phase [7]. Through these phases learners set goals for their learning and engage in strategic planning, monitor their progress, and adapt their strategies if needed, and finally reflect on their own learning process and outcomes [6, 7] (see Fig. 1).

Fig. 1. Cyclical process of SRL and different target areas. Referring to Hadwin et al. (2018), Pintritch (2000), Winne and Hadwin (1998) and Zimmerman (2002). Copyright 2023 by TUNED.

The self-regulatory processes in these phases can facilitate cognitive functions. Cognitive processes involve the mental mechanisms individuals use to process information, including activities such as rehearsing or transforming information into a different format [13]. Good self-regulated learners know the best methods for performing cognitive tasks, such as memorizing vocabulary. They are skilled at choosing and using suitable strategies while recognizing gaps in their knowledge and identifying what they still need to learn.

Besides, the self-regulatory process also target one's motivation and emotional aspects of learning. For instance, learner's decision about how to approach the learning task is directed by their goal and expected outcome as well as one's own judgement about their capability of doing it, namely self-efficacy [13, 14]. Self-regulated learners can maintain their motivation by addressing factors such as self-efficacy, interest, and personal values [6, 14]. Emotional reaction to the task such as positive (e.g., excitement, joy) or negative (e.g., anxiety, fear) has significant impact on one's motivational factors [6, 8]. Personal motivational state or characteristics of learning task or context influence their emotional experiences and perception of the situation, and these experienced emotions impact on regulation of learning [6, 15]. Hence, paying attention to cognitive processes and motivational and emotional processes are equally important in successful SRL [13].

Distinguishing between these targets in practice can be challenging, as they are interconnected and in a state of constant change. Nonetheless, it is essential for learners to be able to skilfully direct their regulatory efforts toward the root causes of challenging situations [9]. Good self-regulated learners excel at accurate self-monitoring across various target areas of regulation and can apply effective strategies based on their knowledge of themselves, the task at hand, and their prior experiences (see metacognitive knowledge from [16]). They demonstrate the ability to control their cognitive, motivational, and emotional states when faced with challenges during learning.

2.2 Teacher Intervention to Enhance Students' Self-Regulated Learning in Distance Settings

Students need modelling and support to become self-regulated learners. Self-regulatory processes can be taught and practised with more capable persons, such as teachers, parents or even peers. Students can influence each other's regulatory processes (coregulation) and a group's collective processes (socially shared regulation) through social interactions [17]. Teachers can facilitate students' self-regulation by enhancing students' awareness of their learning processes and supporting them in monitoring and controlling their cognition, motivation, emotions and behaviour [17].

Enhancing students' SRL skills is particularly vital in online learning scenarios, in which learners may lack physical support from teachers and peers. By developing SRL skills, students get more engaged and motivated during challenging and complicated tasks [8, 12] and have a greater extent of well-being because they experience less stress and fewer burnouts [18]. Some studies indicate that students with high levels of SRL skills demonstrate better performance in online learning compared to traditional teaching methods, possibly due to greater autonomy and control over their learning pace [19, 20]. In other words, learners cannot fully benefit from the flexibility of distance learning without strong SRL skills [21].

The critical element in successfully designing distance learning is the teachers' own understanding about the mechanisms of SRL. However, teachers' knowledge about SRL and beliefs of its benefits are often limited [22]. Luckily, prior research suggests that teachers become capable of designing learning tasks and implementing prompts to promote students' SRL into their teaching after acquiring the adequate information and training [23]. Providing scientifically grounded strategies to teachers can support them in better designing the online learning experience, cultivating their students' skills to maintain and take control of their own learning process and to leverage the flexibility of distance learning.

3 Aim

The present work aims to suggest practical strategies for teachers to enhance their students' SRL skills for a successful distance learning implementation. To develop a scientifically grounded pedagogical framework, we have reviewed literature of SRL and motivation, deciding on our definition and theoretical model. We start by determining the different areas of learning that benefit from SRL support then draw attention to different phases of SRL [7]. This is followed by research-based suggestions on the different methods and tools that educators can implement to provide support for their students, particularly in distance learning settings, based on the recent empirical studies addressing teacher support and students' SRL.

4 Findings

4.1 Supporting Students' Motivation, Emotions and Cognitive Processes in Different Phases

The learning process is encompassed by a range of cognitive, motivational, and socioemotional challenges. In the context of SRL, learners actively monitor, evaluate, and modify their cognitive and emotional states, as well as their motivation [17, 24]. SRL may involve changing and adjusting current cognitive processes; building, sustaining, or restoring motivation; and managing emotional states. Learners can face a need to regulate their cognitive processes [25] in different phases of their learning, for example, when they perceive a lack in their task understanding. In distance learning situations, a learner's motivation is also crucial, especially if the task feels challenging. Regulating motivational processes [26] focuses on initiating and sustaining learning-oriented activities, incorporating factors that significantly guide human behaviour, such as interest, values, self-efficacy beliefs, and goal orientations [27]. Learners can also aim to regulate their emotional processes related to learning to cope with challenging situations, such as negative emotional experiences that hinder performance [28, 29].

Learners need a specific, timely support to regulate these aspects in different phases of SRL cycle. For instance, the forethought phase includes analyzing tasks, setting goals, and planning, and it is fueled by learners' motivational beliefs. In this phase, learners define tasks, assess the difficulty and available resources, and create a plan based on their prior knowledge. They strive to understand the task's purpose and stimulate their motivation towards it. Hence, teachers are encouraged to stimulate students' thinking and feeling about the task at the beginning of the learning journey.

In the performance phase, learners execute tasks while monitoring their progress and using effective learning strategies. They assess if they're on track or facing challenges, adjusting their strategies on the go to control cognition, motivation, emotions and behaviour. Here, help-seeking from peers and/or teachers plays important role in helping learners to understand their state and cope with the challenge at hand. Giving assistance can positively change students' perceptions or feelings towards the task and enable them to apply different learning strategies to adapt to the situation.

During the self-reflection phase, students evaluate and reflect on their task performance, attributing the success or failure of their learning to their behaviour and context. These attributions impact self-reactions and further influence future approaches to similar tasks. This phase includes adapting lessons learned for future goal setting [7]. Hence, supporting learners to properly reflect their learning experience and attribute success or failure is crucial for the future learning experience.

While SRL is fundamentally a cyclical, goal-driven process using a strategically planned approach, it also incorporates context-dependent actions aimed at optimizing learning within the present circumstances [30]. SRL skills, therefore, allow students to align their cognitive, motivational, and emotional processes with these situational factors in the learning environment. Learners take on an active, constructive role, continuously assessing their environment, making decisions, and acting upon them [6, 13]. Learners dynamically monitor, control, and reflect on their learning, adjusting or redirecting their cognitive processes, sustaining or rebuilding motivation, or managing their emotional state [9]. These targets are often interconnected and continuously shifting, making it difficult to distinguish between each other, yet it is essential that learners accurately direct their regulation efforts to address the underlying causes of the challenging situation [9].

4.2 Teachers as Facilitators of Self-Regulated Learning in Distance Learning

In the previous section, we have presented different target areas of regulation and the broad idea of how they can be supported in different cyclical phases. In this section, we will provide more detailed tips for teachers to design their teaching that incorporates targeted, timely SRL support, especially in distance learning environments. Table 1 shows a summary of the recommended design strategies based on the literature.

Before moving on to the tips, we would like to emphasise the role of students' autonomy. Zimmerman and his colleagues state that the pedagogical decision the teachers make, should (gradually) shift the responsibilities of learning to students by changing students' mindsets towards learning; they are not passive takers, but should be encouraged to become active controllers of their own learning [31]. Student autonomy is a key, particularly in distance learning situations, where the active, agentic learner is often a requirement for completing the course or task successfully. Recent studies revealed that one's self-regulated learning skills are associated with competence and autonomy in distance learning settings [3, 4]. Technology-supported learning environments enable educators to prompt, support, monitor, and evaluate learners' cognitive and self-regulatory processes, while also providing opportunities for learners to gradually assume responsibility for their own learning.

Considering that, first and foremost, teachers should encourage students to set goals and make plans for their learning before a lecture, task, or an upcoming project. To facilitate this, teachers can design the learning environment or task in such a way that it explicitly or implicitly guides students to make decisions that support their learning, for example, by emphasising the role of planning and setting goals or prompts to evaluate progress in certain sub-phases [32, 33]. Teachers can also support students' help-seeking and emotional regulation by creating opportunities such as forums or informal meetings to encourage students to cope with the challenges during distance study [29].

To capture the students' temporal changes, we encourage teachers to design a systematic monitoring structure with different evaluation formats in the study course. The notable advantage of digital environments is that students leave traces of their actions (or lack of them), which can indicate teachers on many aspects of their students' learning process [34]. Teachers should also be encouraging and supporting students to self-monitor their learning progress along the task. Research states that self-assessment is an important practice for SRL [10, 35]. Teachers can prompt students to reflect on their learning, identifying areas they need to work on, and strategies to improve. This approach fosters student ownership of their learning and the development of metacognitive skills. For example, the use of learning diaries is particularly effective in promoting student self-reflection [36]. In addition to self-assessment, incorporating peer-reflection moments after an online classroom session or at the end of a short-term course allows students to share their learning outcomes, thoughts, and challenges with their peers.

In order to help students develop their own SRL skills, teachers need to be scaffolding students in the face of challenges by assisting their analysis of the problem and

Table 1. Summary of recommended design strategies for enhancing SRL in distance learning.

SRL phases	Target	Recommended strategies	Reference
Forethought phase	Cognition	Encourage students to set goals and make plans for their learning	Chang et al. (2013) Järvenoja et al. (2020a)
	Motivation Emotion	Support students' help-seeking and emotional regulation to cope with the challenges (e.g., open a digital forum, organize informal meetings etc.)	Järvenoja et al. (2020b)
Performance phase	Cognition	Implement systematic monitoring structure using varied evaluation formats	Perry & Winne (2006)
		Use formative assessments, quizzes, or short assignments to assist with analysing the current state	Perry & Rahim (2011) Gikandi et al. (2011)
	Motivation Emotion	Tracing the students' activity logs (e.g., using LMS) to check progress and engagement	Sáiz-Manzanares et al. (2021)
		Provide regular feedback to increase sense of support	Guethler (2023) Järvenoja et al. (2020a, b)
		Promote awareness of motivational and emotional issues for both individuals and groups (e.g., using GAT)	Moeller et al. (2023) Schnaubert & Bodemer (2019)
Self-reflection phase	Cognition	Prompt self-reflection e.g., by using learning diary to identify areas/strategies to improve	Cenka et al. (2023)
	Motivation Emotion	Encourage self-assessment of their learning	Panadero et al. (2013)

helping new goal setting and strategy selection [37–39]. By following the students' learning path, the teachers can support students' learning process in different SRL phases, increase awareness of the challenge and assist them in addressing the issue. In online learning settings, formative assessments such as quizzes or short assignments are beneficial for gauging students' understanding of the learning material. [40]. In a Massive Open Online Course (MOOC) environment, teachers can set small assignments and tests after each section to track students' progress and comprehension. Breaking down the content into smaller components through step-by-step assessments can help structure the learning path. Similarly, different Learning Management Systems (LMS) have benefits for monitoring students' progress and engagement [41]. LMS platforms, such as Moodle, enable teachers to track when students access course materials, complete assignments, or participate in online discussions. Moodle, for example, visualises student interaction on specific course pages and provides log data on accessing the system. Another key aspect has to do with regular feedback and communication with students [42]. Teachers should schedule regular check-ins using various communication channels, such as email, video conferences, or online discussion boards. This approach not only helps teachers identify any challenges or problems students may be facing but also provides students with a sense of support, even in distant learning environments.

In addition, teachers should find ways for promoting awareness of motivational and emotional issues influencing students' learning decisions [12, 33, 43]. Digital tools have proven their usefulness in collecting data on student engagement and feelings towards the learning task [33, 44]. Especially in collaborative learning settings, group awareness tools (GATs) can aid teachers in visualising students' engagement, feelings towards tasks, and group dynamics in collaborative learning tasks [29, 45]. While GAT is designed to facilitate group learning processes, the information focuses on individual cognitive and social behaviours towards the task [45, 46]. As a result, it can improve awareness of individual SRL, which in turn, can strengthen group-level monitoring and regulation by providing a visual representation of members' situations and potential challenges within the group task [47]. In addition, learners can be supported with adaptive computer based pedagogical tools or pedagogical agents to facilitate self-regulated learning, especially the metacognition involved in those processes [34, 48].

5   Conclusion

In conclusion, it is crucial for teachers to understand the specific characteristics of online learning, particularly in relation to self-regulation of learning, as this mode of instruction presents unique challenges and opportunities for students. A self-regulated learner is an active, constructive agent in their learning process as they engage in constant decision-making and act on it [6, 13, 24]. This means that SRL is a set of skills that depends on learners' metacognitive competencies, such as awareness and monitoring. Online, blended as well as hybrid learning environments which combine face-to-face and remote elements, often vary in structure and flexibility, requiring students to adapt to different learning contexts. These varying settings demand an increased level of SRL, as students must manage their time, set goals, and monitor their progress more independently. For these skills to be implemented in practice, learners must take an active role and responsibility for their own learning process. The process of acquiring these skills requires support from the teacher, a tutor, or peers.

Teachers who are aware of these demands can provide targeted support and help students develop the necessary SRL skills to navigate the complexities of learning in digital environments. Research indicates that there are various strategies for teachers to prompt and capture their students' progress and engagement in distance learning settings in order to facilitate SRL. Particularly in online learning settings, optimising the learning environment to enhance students' SRL and help them maintain their motivation is crucial. Through the affordances of different technological solutions, different types of support can be provided for both individual learning as well as collaborative learning of the student groups. The important thing is to know when to intervene and how to detect the moment when the students are facing challenges. To support the development of SRL skills, we suggest teachers transfer the learning responsibilities gradually to students. This enables shifting students' mindsets towards viewing themselves as active controllers of their learning, rather than passive recipients [31, 49], which in turn leads to a successful distance learning implementation. By fostering these skills, educators not only improve student outcomes in the immediate distance context but also equip students with lifelong learning strategies essential for success in a constantly changing academic and professional landscape.

In summary, understanding the unique characteristics of online learning environments is essential for teachers to effectively support their students' development of self-regulation skills. As education continues to evolve and increasingly contains digital elements, the ability to foster SRL will be key to ensuring student success. By actively guiding students toward greater autonomy and responsibility in their learning processes, educators can help them navigate these varied learning settings. Ultimately, this support empowers students not only to succeed academically but also to succeed in their future personal and professional lives as self-regulated, life-long learners.

Acknowledgments. This work is supported by the Erasmus+ TUNED project (No. 2021-IT02-KA220-HED-000032188).

Disclosure of Interests. The authors have no competing interests to declare that are relevant to the content of this article.

References

1. Zimmerman, B.J.: Becoming a self-regulated learner: an overview. Theory Pract. **41**(2), 64–70 (2002)
2. European commission, education and training monitor (2020). https://op.europa.eu/webpub/eac/education-and-training-monitor-2020/en/chapters/chapter1.html. Accessed 11 Jan 2024
3. Geduld, B.: Exploring differences between self-regulated learning strategies of high and low achievers in open distance learning. Africa Educ. Rev. **13**(1), 164–181 (2016)
4. Vanslambrouck, S., Zhu, C., Pynoo, B., Thomas, V., Lombaerts, K., Tondeur, J.: An indepth analysis of adult students in blended environments: do they regulate their learning in an 'old school' way? Comput. Educ. **128**, 75–87 (2019)

5. TUNED: A Pedagogical Framework on Self-Regulated Learning for Online and Blended Higher Education: A Guidebook for Educators. Zenodo (2023). https://doi.org/10.5281/zenodo.8081590

6. Pintrich, P. R.: The role of goal orientation in self-regulated learning. In: Boekaerts, M., Pintrich, P.R., Zeidner, M. (eds.) Handbook of Self-regulation, pp. 452–502. Elsevier (2000)

7. Zimmerman, B. J.: Attaining self-regulation. In: Boekaerts, M., Pintrich, P. R., Zeidner, M. (eds.) Handbook of Self-regulation, pp. 13–39. Elsevier (2000)

8. Boekaerts, M.: Self-regulated learning: a new concept embraced by researchers, policy makers, educators, teachers, and students. Learn. Instr. **7**(2), 11–186 (1997)

9. Winne, P. H., Hadwin, A. F.: The weave of motivation and self-regulated learning. In: Schunk, D. H., Zimmerman, B. J. (eds.) Motivation and Self-regulated Learning: Theory, Research, and Applications, pp. 297–314. Lawrence Erlbaum Associates (2008)

10. Winne, P.H., Hadwin, A.F.: Studying as self-regulated learning. In: Hacker, D.J., Dunlosky, J., Graesser, A.C. (eds.) Metacognition in Educational Theory and Practice, pp. 277–304. Erlbaum, Mahwah (1998)

11. Zimmerman, B.J.: Development of self-regulated learning: which are the key subprocesses? Contemp. Educ. Psychol. **16**, 307–313 (1986)

12. Zimmerman, B.J.: Investigating self-regulation and motivation: historical background, methodological developments, and future prospects. Am. Educ. Res. J. **45**(1), 166–183 (2008)

13. Winne, P.H.: Self-regulated learning. In: Wright, J.D. (ed.) International Encyclopedia of the Social & Behavioral Sciences, pp. 535–540. Elsevier, Amsterdam (2015)

14. Bandura, A.: Self-efficacy: The Exercise of Control. W. H. Freeman and Company (1997)

15. Järvenoja, H.: Socially shared regulation of motivation and emotions in collaborative learning. University of Oulu (2010)

16. Flavell, J.H.: Metacognition and cognitive monitoring: a new area of cognitive developmental inquiry. Am. Psychol. **34**(10), 906–911 (1979)

17. Hadwin, A. F., Järvelä, S., Miller, M.: Self-regulation, co-regulation, and shared regulation in collaborative learning environments. In: Schunk D. H., Greene, J. A. (eds.) Handbook of Self-regulation of Learning and Performance, pp. 83–106. Routledge (2017)

18. Heikkilä, A., Lonka, K., Nieminen, J., Niemivirta, M.: Relations between teacher students' approaches to learning, cognitive and attributional strategies, well-being, and study success. High. Educ. **64**, 455–471 (2012)

19. Lin, J.W.: Hybrid online learning for a software practice course and how it affects students with different self-regulated learning levels. Australas. J. Educ. Technol. **38**(5), 77–89 (2022)

20. Deci, E.L., Ryan, R.M.: The" what" and" why" of goal pursuits, human needs and the self-determination of behavior. Psychol. Inq. **11**(4), 227–268 (2000)

21. Azevedo, R.: The role of self-regulated learning about science with hypermedia. In: Robinson, D. H., Schraw, G. (eds.), Recent Innovations in Educational Technology that Facilitate Student Learning, pp. 127–156. Information Age Publishing (2008)

22. Dignath-van Ewijk, C., Van der Werf, G.: What teachers think about self-regulated learning: Investigating teacher beliefs and teacher behavior of enhancing students' self-regulation. Educ. Res. Int. **2012**, 741713 (2012)

23. Perry, N.E., Phillips, L., Hutchinson, L.: Mentoring student teachers to support self-regulated learning. Elem. Sch. J. **106**(3), 237–254 (2006)

24. Pintrich, P. R., Zusho, A.: Student motivation and self-regulated learning in the college classroom. In: Smart, J.C., Tierney, W. G. (eds.) Higher Education: Handbook of Theory and Research, Agathon Press, New York (2002)

25. Hadwin, A. F., Winne, P.H.: Promoting learning skills in undergraduate students. In: Kirby, J.R., Lawson, M. J. (eds.) Enhancing the Quality of Learning: Dispositions, Instruction, and Learning Processes, pp. 201–227. Cambridge University Press (2012)

26. Wolters, C.A.: Regulation of motivation: evaluating an underemphasized aspect of self-regulated learning. Educ. Psychol. **38**(4), 189–205 (2003)
27. Zimmerman, B. J., Schunk, D. H.: An essential dimension of self-regulated learning. In: Schunk, D. H., Zimmerman, B. J. (eds.) Motivation and Self-regulated Learning: Theory, Research, and Applications, pp. 1–30. Taylor & Francis Group (2008)
28. Corno, L., Kanfer, R.: The role of volition in learning and performance. In: Darling-Hammond, L. (ed.) Review of Research in Education, pp. 3–43. AERA (1993)
29. Järvenoja, H., Järvelä, S., Malmberg, J.: Supporting groups' emotion and motivation regulation during collaborative learning. Learn. Instr. **70**, 101090 (2020)
30. Järvenoja, H., Järvelä, S., Malmberg, J.: Understanding regulated learning in situative and contextual frameworks. Educ. Psychol. **50**(3), 204–219 (2015)
31. Zimmerman, B. J., Bonner, S., Kovach, R.: Developing Self-regulated Learners: Beyond Achievement to Self-efficacy. American Psychological Association (1996)
32. Chang, C.C., Tseng, K.H., Liang, C., Liao, Y.M.: Constructing and evaluating online goal setting mechanisms in web-based portfolio assessment system for facilitating self-regulated learning. Comput. Educ. **69**, 237–249 (2013)
33. Järvenoja, H., et al.: A collaborative learning design for promoting and analyzing adaptive motivation and emotion regulation in the science classroom. Front. Educ. **5**, 111 (2020)
34. Perry, N.E., Winne, P.H.: Learning from learning kits: gStudy traces of students' self-regulated engagements with computerized content. Educ. Psychol. Rev. **18**(3), 211–228 (2006)
35. Panadero, E., Alonso-Tapia, J., Reche, E.: Rubrics vs. self-assessment scripts effect on self-regulation, performance and self-efficacy in pre-service teachers. Stud. Educ. Eval. **39**(3), 125–132 (2013)
36. Cenka, B.A.N., Santoso, H.B., Junus, K.: The third wave of self-regulated learning's measurement and intervention tools: designing 'diaria' as a new generation of learning diary. Int. J. Emerg. Technol. Learn. **18**(9), 216–242 (2023)
37. Boekaerts, M., Niemivirta, M.: Self-regulated learning: Finding a balance between learning goals and ego-protective goals. In: Boekaerts, M., Pintrich, P. R., Zeidner, M. (eds.) Handbook of Self-regulation, pp. 417–450. Academic Press (2000)
38. Järvenoja, H., Kurki, K., Järvelä, S.: Motivoidutaan yhdessä. In: Salmela-Aro, K. (ed.) Motivaatio ja oppiminen, pp. 141–159. PS-kustannus (2018)
39. Perry, N.E., Rahim, A.: Studying self-regulated learning in classrooms. In: Zimmerman, B. J., Schunk, D. H. (eds.) Handbook of Self-regulation of Learning and Performance, pp. 122–136. Routledge (2011)
40. Gikandi, J.W., Morrow, D., Davis, N.E.: Online formative assessment in higher education: a review of the literature. Comput. Educ. **57**(4), 2333–2351 (2011)
41. Sáiz-Manzanares, M.C., Rodríguez-Díez, J.J., Díez-Pastor, J.F., Rodríguez-Arribas, S., Marticorena-Sánchez, R., Ji, Y.P.: Monitoring of student learning in learning management systems: an application of educational data mining techniques. Appl. Sci. **11**(6), 2677 (2021)
42. Guethler, A.: One intervention, two benefits: a qualitative analysis of students' use of reflective prompting for self-regulated learning in an online course. Educ. Inf. Technol., 1–23 (2023). https://doi.org/10.1007/s10639-023-12016-9
43. Järvenoja, H., Järvelä, S.: Emotion control in collaborative learning situations: do students regulate emotions evoked by social challenges. Br. J. Educ. Psychol. **79**(3), 463–481 (2009)
44. Moeller, J., Dietrich, J., Baars, J.: The Experience Sampling Method in the research on achievement-related emotions and motivation. In: Hagenauer, G., Lazarides, R., Järvenoja, H. (eds.) Motivation and Emotion in Learning and Teaching across Educational Contexts, pp. 178–196. Routledge (2023)
45. Schnaubert, L., Bodemer, D.: Providing different types of group awareness information to guide collaborative learning. Int. J. Comput.-Support. Collab. Learn. **14**, 7–51 (2019)

46. Kirschner, P.A., Strijbos, J.W., Kreijns, K., Beers, P.J.: Designing electronic collaborative learning environments. Educ. Tech. Res. Dev. **52**(3), 47–66 (2004)
47. Järvelä, S., et al.: Enhancing socially shared regulation in collaborative learning groups: designing for CSCL regulation tools. Educ. Technol. Res. Dev. **63**, 125– 142 (2015)
48. Azevedo, R., Hadwin, A.F.: Scaffolding self-regulated learning and metacognition - Implications for the design of computer-based scaffolds. Instr. Sci. **33**, 367–379 (2005)
49. Zimmerman, B.J.: Self-regulated learning: theories measures and outcomes. In: Wright, J.D. (ed.) International Encyclopedia of the Social & Behavioral Sciences, pp. 541–546. Elsevier, Amsterdam (2015)

Author Index

The manufacturer's authorised representative in the EU is Springer

Nature Customer Service Centre GmbH, Europaplatz 3, 69115 Heidelberg,

Germany. If you have any concerns regarding our products, please

contact ProductSafety@springernature.com

Printed and bound by CPI Group (UK) Ltd, Croydon, CR0 4YY

28/04/2026

02098524-0011